Democratization of Africa and Its Impact on the Global Economy

Ndwakhulu Tshishonga
University of KwaZulu-Natal, South Africa

Icarbord Tshabangu
Leeds Trinity University, UK

A volume in the Advances in Finance, Accounting, and Economics (AFAE) Book Series

IGI Global
PUBLISHER of TIMELY KNOWLEDGE

Published in the United States of America by
IGI Global
Information Science Reference (an imprint of IGI Global)
701 E. Chocolate Avenue
Hershey PA, USA 17033
Tel: 717-533-8845
Fax: 717-533-8661
E-mail: cust@igi-global.com
Web site: http://www.igi-global.com

Library of Congress Cataloging-in-Publication Data

Names: Tshishonga, Ndwakhulu, 1964- editor. | Tshabangu, Icarbord, 1968- editor.
Title: Democratization of Africa and its impact on the global economy / edited by Ndwakhulu Tshishonga, Icarbord Tshabangu.
Description: Hershey : Information Science Reference, 2024. | Includes bibliographical references and index. | Summary: "This edited book seeks to reflect on issues and factors that influence democracy, governance and development in Africa. This book equally provides scholars and practitioners with an empirical and practical forum to deliberate on issues, discourses, models, challenges and prospects for Africa's political development and economic growth"-- Provided by publisher.
Identifiers: LCCN 2023038682 | ISBN 9798369304778 (hardcover) | ISBN 9798369304815 (paperback) | ISBN 9798369304785 (ebook)
Subjects: LCSH: Democratization--Africa. | Democratization--Economic aspects--Africa. | Africa--Politics and government--21st century. | Africa--Economic conditions--21st century.
Classification: LCC JQ1879.A15 D4676 2023 | DDC 320.96--dc23/eng/20230822
LC record available at https://lccn.loc.gov/2023038682

This book is published in the IGI Global book series Advances in Finance, Accounting, and Economics (AFAE) (ISSN: 2327-5677; eISSN: 2327-5685)

British Cataloguing in Publication Data
A Cataloguing in Publication record for this book is available from the British Library.

Advances in Finance, Accounting, and Economics (AFAE) Book Series

Ahmed Driouchi
Al Akhawayn University, Morocco

ISSN:2327-5677
EISSN:2327-5685

Mission

In our changing economic and business environment, it is important to consider the financial changes occurring internationally as well as within individual organizations and business environments. Understanding these changes as well as the factors that influence them is crucial in preparing for our financial future and ensuring economic sustainability and growth.

The **Advances in Finance, Accounting, and Economics (AFAE)** book series aims to publish comprehensive and informative titles in all areas of economics and economic theory, finance, and accounting to assist in advancing the available knowledge and providing for further research development in these dynamic fields.

Coverage

- Managerial Accounting
- Banking
- Economics of Natural and Environmental Resources
- Labor Economics
- Corporate Finance
- Health Economics
- Risk Analysis and Management
- Microeconomics
- Investments and Derivatives
- Borrowing and Lending

IGI Global is currently accepting manuscripts for publication within this series. To submit a proposal for a volume in this series, please contact our Acquisition Editors at Acquisitions@igi-global.com or visit: http://www.igi-global.com/publish/.

The Advances in Finance, Accounting, and Economics (AFAE) Book Series (ISSN 2327-5677) is published by IGI Global, 701 E. Chocolate Avenue, Hershey, PA 17033-1240, USA, www.igi-global.com. This series is composed of titles available for purchase individually; each title is edited to be contextually exclusive from any other title within the series. For pricing and ordering information please visit http://www.igi-global.com/book-series/advances-finance-accounting-economics/73685. Postmaster: Send all address changes to above address.

Titles in this Series

For a list of additional titles in this series, please visit: www.igi-global.com/book-series

Econometric Analyses on Global Finance and Economic Development
Yekeen Oku Abdul-Maliq (University of Abuja, Nieria)
Business Science Reference • © 2024 • 300pp • H/C (ISBN: 9798369316108) • US $265.00

Fintech Applications in Islamic Finance AI, Machine Learning, and Blockchain Techniques
Mohammad Irfan (Business School, NSB Academy, Bangalore, India) Seifedine Kadry (Noroff University College, Norway) Muhammad Sharif (Department of CS, COMSATS University Islamabad, Wah Cantt, Pakistan) and Habib Ullah Khan (Qatar University, atar)
Business Science Reference • © 2024 • 334pp • H/C (ISBN: 9798369310380) • US $265.00

Sustainable Investments in Green Finance
Sanjay Taneja (Graphic Era University (Deemed), India) Pawan Kumar (Chandigarh University, India) Simon Grima (Department of Insurance, Faculty of Economics Management and Accountancy, University of Malta, Malta & Faculty of Business, Management and Economics, University of Latvia, Latvia) Ercan Ozen (Usak University, Turkey) and Kiran Sood (Chitkara Business School, Chitkara University, India)
Business Science Reference • © 2024 • 373pp • H/C (ISBN: 9798369313886) • US $275.00

Empowering Women Through Microfinance in Developing Countries
Yahaya Alhassan (University of Sunderland in London, UK) and Uzoechi Nwagbara (University of Sunderland in London, UK)
Business Science Reference • © 2023 • 281pp • H/C (ISBN: 9781668489796) • US $240.00

Management, Technology, and Economic Growth in Smart and Sustainable Cities
Jorge A. Ruiz-Vanoye (Universidad Politécnica de Pachuca, Mexico)
Business Science Reference • © 2023 • 341pp • H/C (ISBN: 9798369303733) • US $240.00

Enhancing Sustainability Through Non-Financial Reporting
Albertina Monteiro (ISCAP, CEOS, Polytechnic of Porto, Portugal) Ana Pinto Borges (ISAG - European Business School, Portugal & CICET-FCVC, Portugal & COMEGI, Portugal) and Elvira Vieira (ISAG - European Business School, Portugal & CICET-FCVC, Portugal & Polytechnic Institute of Viana do Castelo, Portugal & UNIAG, Portugal)
Business Science Reference • © 2023 • 313pp • H/C (ISBN: 9781668490761) • US $225.00

IGI Global
PUBLISHER of TIMELY KNOWLEDGE

701 East Chocolate Avenue, Hershey, PA 17033, USA
Tel: 717-533-8845 x100 • Fax: 717-533-8661
E-Mail: cust@igi-global.com • www.igi-global.com

Table of Contents

Detailed Table of Contents

This chapter examines notions of democracy and citizenship, the democratic models, and how some of these have manifested in practice, particularly within the African context. While there has been a wave of democratisation globally in the last half a century, this has occurred amidst fierce contestations, some militarily. Furthermore, the practice of democracy from a global standpoint, both within liberal and illiberal states, has been saddled with numerous contradictions in so far as democratic values are concerned. Drawing from varied historical literature sources and analysing contemporary practices of democracy, it is noted that despite existing contestations, contradictions, and imperfections of democracy, this political system remains the best alternative in the 21st century, especially for developing nations that still have weaker systems of governance and have a greater need for economic growth and protection of human rights. The role of citizenship education is also posited as a critical structure, necessary for an informed polity to make those who govern more accountable.

This chapter serves as a mechanism of recognizing and acknowledging the illegitimacy of historic and traditional Western approaches to narratives of African feminist epistemology. These approaches have engendered lenses of perspective which are irrefutably skewed by colonialism and whose address is warranted in ensuring both a means of learning about the end of an era and the prospect of a more authentically framed future framed, shaped, and determined from within African culture and context by those. To undertake this, acknowledgement and recognition is one of the first and much belated to framing steps in ensuring that the articulation of truth lies best with those whose lived truths they are, rather than any tokenistic perceptions of them, consequently articulated through Western lenses of perspective. The central tenet of the chapter revolves around the positing of African citizenship, indeed all individual citizenship as fundamentally unique and known authentically only to those who have socially constructed knowledge of it.

Good governance and accountability, amongst others, are hallmarks of a democratic system of government, practiced by most African countries. At the inception of democracy in most African nations, political parties were formed according to constitutional laws, and eligible candidates were voted into political office through elections. African politics is majorly marred with the problem of leadership as argued by most scholars and non-scholars alike. Against this backdrop, the lead questions are: Is democracy in Africa progressive or retrogressive? Is leadership the only major problem of African politics? In what practical ways can one ensure good governance in African politics? Thus, this chapter argues that every problem marring African politics is traceable to attitudinal crises, which must be addressed to guarantee and promote good governance in Africa.

This chapter highlights the role of stakeholder engagement and community participation in sustainable development and growth in Southern Africa. It emphasizes the relevance of inclusive collaboration and traditional knowledge to tackle the socio-economic and environmental challenges in the region. This chapter discusses adopting stakeholder engagement processes with a robust and inclusive community participation approach in projects and initiatives promoting sustainable growth and development in the Southern African region. Additionally, the chapter stresses the value of open communication channels and partnerships for fostering sustainable development. This chapter shares best practices and suggestions for all stakeholders involved in sustainable development initiatives by analyzing empirical evidence and case studies. It accentuates the need for inclusive strategies based on ethical cooperation, transparency, and gender equity that consider the voices of local communities and facilitate innovation to ensure a more equitable and sustainable future.

The role of women in peacebuilding has largely been underrepresented and marginalized. This chapter explores the potential of women's leadership in peacebuilding in Nigeria and how their participation can strengthen the peace-building processes. Using desktop review approach, the chapter investigates the

Foreword

Democracy is a widely contested topic globally and some trace its history to ancient Greece, while Africans claim that they had their form of democracy which preceded that of Greece and was predicated on consensus as opposed to simple majority widely accepted as one of the characteristics of liberal democracy (Mandela, 1994). The Kingdom of Eswatini, for example, uses *Tinkhundla* as a system of governance. The argument espoused by the proponents of *Tinkhundla* is that the system ensures that all the country's regions are represented in government thus ensuring that less represented groups have a voice in the governance of the country. This book addresses critical arguments on democratisation, noting that across the African continent, the demise of colonialism ushered in a new political phase, premised on democracy. From a Western perspective, this marked Africa's first experience with democracy or democratisation processes. Contrary to this view, the Africanist perspective is that Africans did not experience democracy through their erstwhile colonisers. They argue that their governance systems were democratic in the sense that different voices were heard as exemplified by precolonial African kingdoms such as those of Ghana, Mali Songhai, and Buganda (among others) further debunking notions that African kings were autocratic. It is noted that liberal democracy which was adopted by most African countries at independence in the mid-1900s took the shape and form of Western democracies. Most African nationalist leaders accepted this form of democracy unequivocally while others opted for a one-party rule system. Totalitarian regimes were frowned upon by the global community. Even countries that had experimented with multi-party democracy later reverted to either the one-party system or dictatorship. In 1973, King Sobhuza II of Eswatini passed a decree ending multi-party rule. He argued that political parties were tearing his nation apart – including families. Years later, President Yoweri Museveni introduced what he called 'no-party democracy' (ACCORD, 2000).

In other African countries, dictatorship became a common feature. Nigeria is one such example where coups became the order of the day – with some lasting only a few years or even months. However, the year 1999 is seen as the most significant period in the democratization of Africa, marking the beginning of the longest periods of uninterrupted democratic rule. In Kenya, the Constitution was amended in 1999 bringing back into the fray multi-party politics. Although ethnic divisions (especially between the Kikuyu and the Luo) continued unabated, and although the Kalenjin of President Daniel Arap Mooi continued to dominate Kenyan politics, the democratization process seemed to thrive compared to yesteryears. The direct link between democratisation and the economy has been acknowledged by several authors in this book. This does not come as a surprise. Whenever a country faces economic upheavals, democratic institutions are shaken, and political instability prevails. Similarly, in a country where democratization is adversely affected, it is not always possible to have a thriving economy. Furthermore, states tend to use their financial and material resources to contain the volatile political situations, plunging such countries into deep economic chaos and derailing any efforts for democratisation.

The book has effectively dealt with Issues of governance, democracy, and development as these are inextricably interwoven. Both endogenous and exogenous causal factors are responsible for the sustenance or lack of these processes. In the African context, there has been an attempt to understand why Africa is poor (Mills, 2010). In this regard, the analysis has looked at the impact of the role of external factors as well as how African leaders have contributed to the problem through their various policy choices at different political moments – more especially since independence. Issues such as tribalism, ethnicity, nepotism, political avarice, partisanship, civil wars, as well as failure to adopt and embrace meritocracy have been highlighted as some of the causal factors. Against this background, this book is a significant contribution to the body of knowledge on the democratisation processes in Africa and how these have affected the continent economically. Of critical importance in this book is that it casts its eyes on the global economy. By so doing, the book's authors tacitly concede that Africa as a continent is not an island. Instead, the history, politics and economies of the African continent are inextricably intertwined with the global economy. The 2008 global economic recession demonstrated how a problem which starts in one country or continent can quickly spill over to other countries of the world, impacting them differently. Such impact will depend on each country's economic strength political stability and level of democratisation. Therefore, when African countries democratise, they do not only do this for themselves (important as that might be), on the contrary, their actions have global relevance – especially in the realm of the global economy which can make or break nations. Therefore, this volume is long overdue given its relevance both in Africa and in the global contexts. Furthermore, the realisation that economic growth is critical and intertwined with the democratisation project forced the African political leadership to work towards the establishment of the Africa Continental Free Trade Area (Afcfta).

In a nutshell, this book is both timely and relevant. The link between democracy and the economy is clearly articulated as these are two sides of the same coin. A problem in one will result in a problem in the other. As the African continent engages in self-introspection on various issues, democratisation and democratic practice should form part of that process. This book will be a great resource to Africanist scholars as well as government officials, policymakers and students of leadership studies, history, economics, and politics. It also promises to make a good read to various audiences.

Bheki R. Mngomezulu
Nelson Mandela University, South Africa

Bheki R. Mngomezulu *is a Full Professor of Political Science and International Relations. He is the Director of the Centre for the Advancement of Non-Racialism and Democracy (CANRAD) at Nelson Mandela University. Previously, he was the Deputy Dean of Research in the Economic and Management Sciences Faculty at the University of the Western Cape and a Senate Representative to the University Council. He served as the President of the Economic History Society of Southern Africa the Faculty Research Coordinator at Durban University of Technology and an Academic Leader at the University of KwaZulu-Natal.*

Preface

Africa's progress and prosperity are intrinsically linked to its democracy, governance, and development. Since political independence Africa adopted political development systems with the hope of advancing its governance and developmental agenda. Significantly, in line with the African Union (2002) Agenda, Africa aspired to forge sustainable development through the promotion of democratic principles and institutional capacity, popular participation, and good governance. Thus, the interdependence of democracy, democratic governance and development is fundamental for Africa's development (Ndulo & Gazibo, 2016). Africa's problems of insecurity protracted civil wars, weak governance, stagnant development and lack of state capacity cannot be well understood without revisiting the legacies and political economy of colonialism, imperialism and apartheid regimes (Amtaika, 2017; Honwana, 2013; Nugent, 2012). Thus, Africa is the product of protracted years of colonialism, imperialism and apartheid brutal invasions and conquest. The existence and imposition of these socio-economic and political development systems led to Africa's underdevelopment in governance, economics, education, and health sectors.

Africa's socioeconomic and political underdevelopment has been predicated on projects of slavery, colonialism and neo-colonialism which were orchestrated to squander natural resources. The 'scramble for Africa' and what Adekeye (2010) calls the 'Curse of Berlin' produced ambitious leaders as colonial collaborators, proxy wars, military coups and squandering of resources (Landsberg, 2018: 16-17). The legacies of Western democratic, development models and approaches adopted in the 1960s made political scientists describe Africa as a 'hopeless continent' (Welz, 2021: 116) with limited prospects to recover from its socio-economic situation. Nevertheless, there have been several attempts to deal with democratic development impasse across the continent. At the institutional continental front, the formation of the African Unity (OAU) in 1963, revamped as African Union (AU) in 2002; the New Partnership for Africa's Development (NEPAD) in 2001 and African Peer Review Mechanism (APRM) as well as the regional economic communities (Economic Community of Central African States (ECCAS) of Central Africa, Economic Community of African States (ECOWAS) of West Africa, Intergovernmental Authority on Development (ICAD) at the Horn of Africa and South African Development Community (SADC) in Southern Africa) (Kalu, 2017; Signe, 2017; Welz, 2021) are classical examples. These institutions are formed to advance the social, economic and political development of Africa. However, without political will, decolonisation of democratic development and political economy systems as well as institutionalisation of accountable governance based on principles of good governance, human development, and effective state institutional capacity accompanied by civic engagement, Africa will remain in the vicious cycle of socio-economic and political underdevelopment. For Africa to break the democratic and developmental impasse, it is imperative to acknowledge factors and issues underpinning "How Europe Underdeveloped Africa" by Walter Rodney (2018) on How Africa continues to under-develop in the 21st Century. This edited book, therefore, intends to interrogate discourses, issues and conditions conducive to democracy, governance and development in Africa.

Democratization is the shift from a dictatorial government to a democratic one (Márquez, 2016). In the past several decades, democratization has advanced significantly across Africa (Diamond and Plattner, 2010). Nevertheless, the global economy continues to be significantly impacted by Africa's democratic transition (Haggard and Kaufman, 2018). The democratization of societies has further made it possible to articulate the developmental challenges that continue to impact weaker segments of society, women, rural residents, members of minority groups, and the physically handicapped (Olayode, 2016). According to Anyanwu and Yameogo (2015), substantial foreign direct investment which fuels economic growth, is being positioned as an attractive option for African states in their transition to democratic governance. Political stability is another benefit of democratization. Kim (2010) asserts that it is something investors consider when evaluating long-term economic prospects. This notion is supported by Olayode (2016) who attests that the existence of a conducive environment which has opened alternative political programs to be projected is a significant success of democratization in Africa.

According to Carbone, Memoli and Quartapelle (2016), democratic processes indicate that the methods for changing the administration are more open and unambiguous, hence lowering political volatility and unpredictability that would otherwise impede advancements. Ajayi (2001) contends that African countries have been able to undertake integration both at the regional and global levels, which is also a result of their economies' liberalization and globalization. Genyi (2017) maintains that globalization has achieved its pinnacle in the 21st Century, with the industrialization of the world hastening the economic pattern of global economic integration. Pangestu (2023) is of the view that through this integration African states have been able to access international markets, advance commerce and draw in foreign capital. Genyi (2017) notes that the democratization process across Africa as resuscitated by globalization, has expedited the process of developing responsible and responsive governance.

Olayode (2016) notes that while democracy is considered to foreshadow growth, Africa's economic situation remains problematic due to limited capital flows and competition from advanced economies. This assertion is confirmed by Ng'oma (2016) who notes that due to several obstacles, the establishment of democracy in Africa has not made significant inroads to the stage it was anticipated. While democracy aids in growth, it is also afflicted by extreme poverty, which jeopardizes people's ability to survive Olayode (2016). Carbone, Memoli and Quartapelle (2016) highlighted that democracy, which increases welfare programs reduces economic disparity, and makes governmental institutions attentive to the needs of the poor, yet does so at the price of physical capital accumulation.

Democracy is a governance system in which institutions follow democratic processes and standards within and in their interactions with other entities (Sorensen, 2018). According to Christiano (2018), democracy entails the engagement of all citizens in the distribution of power, the resolution of divergent interests and the use of majority rule to make decisions. Keping (2018) maintains that governance is the utilization of authority in politics and administration at all degrees to run an entity's affairs. Popoola (2020) asserts that development is a way of enhancing an individual's economic, social, and political fulfilment. Although some contend that democracy and development are interwoven and dependent upon one another, others assert that the two ideas are distinct from one another and may each be attained independently of one another (ACCORD, 2017).

Those who embrace the relationship between the two claim that democracy and development are inextricably linked and rely on and result in one another (Sikuka, 2017). Khatun (2022) also contends that democracy and development are two distinct conditions that have no bearing on one another. Sikuka (2017) maintains that regardless of being regarded as one of the least democratic countries in the world, China has managed to achieve spectacular economic progress in recent decades, at a considerably quicker rate than other democratic countries. Aryeetey (2022) postulates that governments can function more effectively as vehicles of economic growth in African states where democracy exists. Sikuka (2017) adds that most African countries have had some economic progress since the attainment of democracy, which is, a significant indication that to some degree, democracy is vital for development.

According to Adebisi (2014), democracy is essential for African growth but there are several obstacles due to poor leadership and management. The solidification of democracy and effective governance institutions is critical in eliminating poverty, enabling sustainable economic growth, and attaining development in Africa (Mawere and Mwanaka, 2015). Alence (2009) contends that research shows that governments function better as vehicles of economic growth in African nations where democracy is well-installed. The combination of transparent and capable government agencies with conceptions of democracy and the rule of law is prevalent in governance arguments because they are inextricably linked and mutually reinforcing (Bekkers, Dijkstra and Fenger, 2016). It has been argued elsewhere that the degree of peace and stability as well as the chances for economic growth and development in Africa are influenced and modelled qualities of governance (Crocker, 2019). According to Aryeetey (2022), the desire for economic independence, and higher standards of living, are all part of the African people's democratic aspirations, and these demands necessitate strong governance institutions.

The economic problems facing Africa in the global economy are numerous and intricate (Tchamyou, 2017). According to Legas (2015), lack of access to finance and funding is a problem across several African nations, which makes it challenging for enterprises to develop and thrive. Mafusire, Brixiova, Anyanwu and Meng (2017) state that significant infrastructure deficiencies continue to exist in Africa (inadequate roads and energy suppliers) and this has impeded economic development and provided limited options for African nations to compete globally. This view is supported by Dethier (2015) who suggests that infrastructure is crucial for enhancing productivity and achieving economic progress, hence African countries cannot ignore its significance.

Siddiqui (2019) asserts that many African nations lack strong institutions and governance frameworks, which may breed corruption, lack transparency, and difficult economic conditions for both indigenous and foreign investors. According to Ghura and Basu (2000) numerous economic issues that Africa suffers from in the global economy, include the continent's slow economic development, poverty and its weak financial institutions that continue to exacerbate this position. Similarly, Jeary, Adolph, and Franks (2022) contend that African nations have uneven and fragmented policies that impede economic growth and development which deters investment. Nyangau (2014) asserts that the dearth of access to high-quality education and training opportunities in Africa prevents the formation of a skilled workforce, which is essential for economic growth and development as well as viability in the global economy.

Poncian and Mgaya (2015) assert that underdevelopment is one of the problems the African continent faces. Nkurayija (2011) identifies challenges such as excessive inequalities, restricted access to funds, social isolation, and environmental deterioration. Solimano (2006) claims that there are worrisome trends such as high poverty levels, poor living conditions, and vulnerability, all of which hurt the development of Africa's economies.

According to Zha and Santos-Paulino (2021), the fundamental solution to this impasse rests in sustainable and creative finance approaches to mobilize local resources, attract international investment, and promote novel financial channels to aid Africa's development. Gumede (2016) suggests that African nations need to adapt the developmental state framework to ensure that their societies and economies develop. The United Nations Development Programme (UNDP) initiatives have suggested a host of options such as the provision of youth and women economic opportunities, encouraging their involvement in decision-making, and providing them the tools they need to contribute to Africa's development (UNDP, 2020).

The South-South Cooperation (SCC) has been cited by Asante (2018) as an institutional cooperative mechanism for African countries to work together with other countries in exchange information, resources, and solutions to common problems to advance regional integration, commerce, and investment. This notion is supported by Patel (1990) who attests that SCC is crucial for boosting commerce, exchanging development insights, and fostering unity among developing nations. The growth of Africa depends on effective governance, which is a major tenet of the UNDP's updated strategic offer for the continent (Africa and UNDP, 2017). Nwoko (2013) makes the case for strategic collaboration amongst non-oil industries to broaden the development of economies and expansion.

Democratization of Africa and Its Impact on the Global Economy delves into the intricate relationship between democracy, governance, and development in Africa, shedding light on the continent's progress and its implications for the global economy. From its historical context rooted in colonialism and apartheid regimes to the present-day challenges of weak governance and underdevelopment, this book critically examines the factors that have shaped Africa's political and socioeconomic landscape. This book offers a comprehensive exploration of democracy, governance, and development in Africa. It delves into various topics such as models of democracy, electoral systems, political leadership, state-building, democratic deficits, political violence, corruption, and the challenges of democratic consolidation. Additionally, it examines the significance of democratic governance, good governance principles, civil society engagement, and political accountability in shaping Africa's political landscape.

Further, it examines the concept of development in Africa, highlighting the impact of Western development models and exploring alternative approaches rooted in indigenous knowledge systems and sustainable growth. It addresses the role of institutions, regional integration, globalization, technology, and foreign interference in Africa's socio-economic development. Through a multi-disciplinary lens encompassing political science, development studies, anthropology, sociology, international relations, and public administration, the book offers a platform for scholars, practitioners, policymakers, and researchers to engage in critical dialogue and propose innovative strategies for Africa's renewal. The book covers the following themes: African Colonialism; African Governance; Democracy; Democratization; Development; Economic Growth of institutions; Political Corruption; Political Independence; Political Violence; Socio-economic Development; Sustainable Development; Underdevelopment, etc.

INSIDE THIS BOOK

The book is divided into five parts. Section 1 focuses on 'Understanding Democracy, Participation and Challenges' and Section 2 discusses 'Barriers and the Advancement of Democratic Practice'. Section 3 deals with 'Democracy, Trade and the Economy'. Section 4 discusses 'Some Factors Influencing Democratic Practice in African States' and Section 5 addresses 'Questions and Critique of Some Democratic Practices'.

Chapter 1 examines notions of democracy and citizenship, the democratic models and how some of these have manifested in practice, particularly within the African context. While there has been a wave of democratisation globally, in the last half a century, this has occurred amidst fierce contestations, some militarily. Furthermore, the practice of democracy from a global standpoint, both within liberal and illiberal states has been saddled with numerous contradictions in so far as democratic values are concerned. Drawing from varied historical literature sources and analysing contemporary practices of democracy, it is noted that despite existing contestations, contradictions and imperfections of democracy, this political system remains the best alternative in the 21st century, especially for developing nations that still have weaker systems of governance and have a greater need for economic growth and protection of human rights. The role of citizenship education is also posited as a critical structure, necessary for an informed polity to make those who govern, more accountable.

Chapter 2 provides a mechanism for recognizing and acknowledging the illegitimacy of historic and traditional Western approaches to narratives of African feminist epistemology. These approaches have engendered lenses of perspective which are irrefutably skewed by colonialism and whose address is warranted in ensuring both a means of learning about the end of an era and the prospect of a more authentically framed future framed, shaped, and determined from within African culture and context by those. To undertake this acknowledgement and recognition is one of the first and much-belated framing steps in ensuring that the articulation of truth lies best with those whose lived truths they are, rather than any tokenistic perceptions of them, consequently articulated through Western lenses of perspective.

Chapter 3 discusses good governance and accountability, amongst others, as hallmarks of a democratic system of government, practised by most African countries. At the inception of democracy in most African nations, political parties were formed according to constitutional laws, and eligible candidates were voted into political office through elections. African politics is majorly marred with the problem of leadership as argued by most scholars and non-scholars alike. Against this backdrop, our lead questions are: Is democracy in Africa progressive or retrogressive? Is leadership the only major problem of African politics? In what practical ways, can one ensure good governance in African politics? Thus, this chapter argues that every problem marring African politics is traceable to attitudinal crises, which must be addressed to guarantee and promote good governance in Africa.

Chapter 4 highlights the role of stakeholder engagement and community participation in sustainable development and growth in Southern Africa. It emphasizes the relevance of inclusive collaboration and traditional knowledge to tackle the socio-economic and environmental challenges in the region. This chapter discusses adopting stakeholder engagement processes with a robust and inclusive community participation approach in projects and initiatives promoting sustainable growth and development in the Southern African region. Additionally, the chapter stresses the value of open communication channels and partnerships for fostering sustainable development. This chapter shares best practices and suggestions for all stakeholders involved in sustainable development initiatives by analyzing empirical evidence and case studies. It accentuates the need for inclusive strategies based on ethical cooperation, transparency, and gender equity that consider the voices of local communities and facilitate innovation to ensure a more equitable and sustainable future.

Chapter 5 notes that the role of women in peacebuilding has largely been underrepresented and marginalized. It explores the potential of women's leadership in peacebuilding in Nigeria and how their participation can strengthen the peace-building processes. Using the desktop review approach, the paper investigates the obstacles such as patriarchal attitudes and structural barriers to women's leadership in peacebuilding. It argues that increasing women's participation is critical to strengthening peacebuilding in Nigeria. This necessitates a multifaceted strategy that addresses structural barriers to women's participation. It concludes that women's peace-building leadership is critical for achieving long-term peace and security in Nigeria and by extension, Africa. However, turning rhetoric into reality necessitates a collaborative effort on the part of all stakeholders. It necessitates a commitment to gender equality and women's empowerment, as well as an understanding of the unique perspectives and contributions that women can bring to peace-building efforts.

Chapter 6 asserts that the African continent and the SADC region have embraced the basic principles of democratic governance such as political accountability. Through democratic governance, governments exercise their power in the advancement of social, economic, and political development (UNDP, 2007). To achieve this democratic mandate, bureaucracy should be held politically accountable through formal and informal mechanisms (Heywood, 2019). Despite the monarchs in Lesotho and Eswatini, SADC has a traceable record of upholding democratic governance through the promotion of elections. Elections in any democratic order are regarded as a pillar of democracy. This tendency is juxtaposed with citizens' expectations of their leaders to discharge their responsibilities based on good governance principles of accountability, social justice, impartiality, equality and equity. Ethical and accountable leadership is needed to deal with governance challenges such as corruption and democratic deficit.

Chapter 7 observes that in Zimbabwe, it has long been believed that corruption is the main barrier to economic growth. Corruption has frustrated all chances for socio-economic and political justice in Zimbabwe. The democratic space has also been shrunk as evidenced by judicial failure to effect reasonable punishment on perpetrators of corruption. This chapter examines recorded incidents of corruption in Zimbabwe that have not received the proper attention, resulting in the deterioration of socioeconomic and political justice.

Chapter 8 examines the colonial legacy, neo-colonial influences, and the fight for democratic government as root reasons for Africa's developmental issues. Institutional responses to these problems are examined, including the African Union (AU), the New Partnership for Africa's Development (NEPAD), and the African Peer Review. A decolonized perspective on development and political will are both emphasized. Relying on Walter Rodney's claims, this chapter stresses the significance of accountable governance, human rights, and civic engagement in addressing Africa's self-underdevelopment.

Chapter 9 asserts that the place of political participation in the democratization process in Africa necessitates understanding the motivation for participation as an integral component of democracy. For Nigeria and Africa, this is crucial for the emergence of good governance and the development of democratic processes and governance. This paper explored political participation in Nigeria and the issues of political apathy as a Challenge of the Democratization Process. Using a desktop review technique, the paper explored the causes of political apathy and its possible effect on Nigeria's democratization process as a template for Africa. While the factors and impacts identified in this paper for political apathy in Nigeria are not exhaustive, the implication for the democratization process is significant. Therefore, there is a need for all stakeholders, government, and citizens alike to embrace proactive measures in curtailing political apathy in Nigeria and, by inference, Africa's democratization process.

Chapter 10 asserts that the Arab Spring, the wave of protests that swept over the Middle East and North Africa in 2011, failed to impose democracy there. However, only in Tunisia did the Arab Spring result in a democratic change in 2011. Tunisia has been dealing with several difficulties since the country's democratic transition, including political unrest and terrorist assaults. This study looks at Tunisia's political growth between 2011 and 2022 to determine the chances and challenges for the country to consolidate its democracy. Using a case study approach and Samuel P. Huntington's theory of democratic consolidation, the study has identified two barriers to democratic consolidation: the democratic government's inability to deliver economic reforms and the political elite's unwillingness to work together to find solutions. Since the political elite has used Tunisia's economic woes to gain undemocratically more power, the study also explains the failure of democratic consolidation with the absence of the formation of a democratic political culture in the nation.

Chapter 11 analyses factors that influence the exchange rate in Nigeria during the period of democracy; by using the Generalized Method of Moments (GMM) and Granger causality tests for analyses. The democratic system of governance is associated with a reduction in arbitrariness, policy continuity, protection of property rights, human rights, freedom, free market, community development, consensus and human development. The results of the analysis show that GDP growth and FDI have long-run inverse relationships with foreign exchange while export and consumption have long-run positive relationships with foreign exchange.

Chapter 12 posits that every country in the world requires financial capital for economic growth and development. It lubricates the wheels of the economy for development. The developed countries of the world held on to continuous capital investments in the economy and these resulted in rapid economic growth. The case of most developing countries is different. They do not have sufficient capital to be invested in their economy therefore they need to depend on the external hands of the developed countries. The research question is what is the prospect and bane of foreign direct investment on the economy? The theoretical framework of dependency theory is used to analyse the prospect and bane of foreign direct investment. The methodology adopted utilises data from the World Bank which is analysed using descriptive techniques. The paper concludes that being over-dependent on foreign direct investment will make the recipient countries an extension of the donor countries.

Chapter 13 investigates factors that constrain the development of rural startups in the Ugandan rural entrepreneurial ecosystem in light of the importance of entrepreneurship in reducing poverty worldwide. Based on a review of the literature on entrepreneurial ecosystems, necessity and opportunity entrepreneurship plus a range of theoretical approaches, the study demonstrates that the characteristics of the rural population, the social-cultural context and the lack of physical infrastructure greatly constrain the start and growth of rural startups. Recommendations as to what should be done to promote rural startups are proposed.

Chapter 14 is concerned with the Southern African Development Community (SADC) and its trade potential to increase continental integration in Africa. The chapter argues that SADC has the potential not only to increase continental integration but also as the building block for AfCTA to realise its vision of promoting continental economic integration, equitable human development and advancing African institutions' development. Regional theory was adopted to comprehend the role, shared interests, challenges, and goals among SADC member countries. The chapter found that the SADC region is endowed with natural, cultural, and human resources, but lacks state capacity, cooperation and integration to optimize such resources. The chapter is qualitative and uses a systematic literature review to deliberate on the role and challenges faced by SADC in increasing continental integration and further forging socio-economic development between and intra its members.

Chapter 15 discusses the role of the European Union (EU) in Africa in the establishment of democracy. Many African countries need the help of Western democracy to pave the way for the democratization process on this continent. This study aims to discover the leading role of the EU in Africa in assisting to build strong democratic institutions. Further, the EU as a democratic institution has played an important role in uniting the European countries under its democratic legacy and motivating them to adopt and implement the "Copenhagen Criteria" which are basic principles of the democratization process of the member states in Europe in this sense how the EU has been working on the implementation of the democratic ethos in African countries. On the other hand, the internal situation of African countries differs from that of EU Member States because many countries gained independence in the late 1990s and dozens of countries are in civil war crises in many regions.

Chapter 16 assesses South Africa's quiet diplomacy in Zimbabwe during the tenure of Thabo Mbeki as president. Post the colonial era, hegemonic powers have always been considered critical role-players within their specific continent or regions because of their robust economies, military might, and soft power credentials, abuse, especially from the ruling Zimbabwean African National Union (ZANU – PF) regime. Instead of acting on its neighbour, the Mbeki regime opted for the quiet diplomacy route. With South Africa entering the African political landscape after the apartheid era and becoming a member of the Southern African Development Community (SADC), many considered it the driving force regarding the political landscape in Africa, particularly Southern Africa. While the Mandela administration achieved some of this, many eyebrows were raised throughout Mbeki's era, particularly in his quiet diplomacy towards Zimbabwe.

Chapter 17 asserts that billions of dollars in funding for infrastructure development are managed by multilateral development banks. Due to their function as development financiers, these institutions are vulnerable to fraud and corruption, both internally inside their organizations and externally from political stakeholders given that they are frequently state-owned businesses. Historically, they have relied on national law enforcement agencies to investigate corruption-related activities. However, multilateral development banks (MDBS) have been acting more proactively in recent years to combat corruption. The African Development Bank is one of several global multilateral development banks that have started to play a role in recent years. This chapter discusses its work.

Chapter 18 identifies the important notion regarding Lesotho's persistent political and security instability as revolving around the politicisation of the military, which ultimately poses major threats to Lesotho's fragile democracy. The security sector, especially the military in Lesotho, is vulnerable to political influence to the point where they are to blame for their undue interference in the political arena. They tend to become involved directly and/indirectly in high-level political battles. Hence this reality is referred to as the 'militarisation of politics' and 'politicisation of the military. This phenomenon of exasperating politics-military relations has led to the security sector being actively and openly involved and/or used in high-level political disputes. However, at the heart of Lesotho's culture of violence lies the historical trend of militarisation. This persistent culture of violence can be attributed to the historical relationship between politics and the military, but more significantly and to a large extent, to events following post-colonialization.

Chapter 19 asserts that democracy in many African countries faces serious challenges linked to weak leadership, poor governance, malfunctioning state institutions, and slow or stagnant development. For these countries, the challenges can be attributed to an exploitative system rooted in colonialism, neocolonialism, imperialism, and apartheid. Digital transformation and the global rise of digital technologies have created new opportunities to meet the challenges of democracy concerning citizen engagement, broadening public debate, increasing transparency and accountability, and improving service delivery. This chapter critically examines whether using digital technologies in political settings strengthens or weakens democracy on the continent. It highlights three main scholarly debates about using digital tools to address the declining quality of democracy. Data from various secondary sources was used to address the problem. The author found that digitalisation undoubtedly exposes democracy to new threats, but its benefits far outweigh the concerns.

Chapter 20 observes that the roles played by advocacy groups and the media in engaging governments as long-term partners are both important and problematic. While some governments are progressive and happy to include alternative views, others eschew consultations. This study of civil society and state disaccord in three country contexts of the southern African region interrogates the non-governmental partners' roles at critical junctures. Partnerships between state and non-state actors are buffeted by geo-political dynamics and economic reversals that have rattled the post-liberation project in three countries. This chapter explores how a multi-sectoral oversight of key policy initiatives might avert the possibility of political expediency impinging on the imperatives of good governance and economic stability. The chapter incorporates conversations that ensued during a two-day Inclusive Democracy for Sustainable Development conference in Windhoek, Namibia, attended by government and civil society actors. It also draws on desk research and personal observations.

Chapter 21 presents a novel approach to understanding the Economic Freedom Fighters (EFF) role in South African politics. The party has been called populist, fascist, and a threat to South Africa's democracy. This study was conducted through virtual ethnography research on the role of the EFF in South Africa's politics and presents the research findings here to understand if the EFF is merely populist, a threat to democracy, or encouraging citizens' political participation. The study's findings indicate that the EFF uses populist stances to attract supporters and voters to the party. But unlike the views of some commentators and scholars, the study presents different findings regarding the EFF's populist attitudes in the country's democracy. While some see such populist stances as a threat to democracy, the study views it as the party's advantage, among others, to encourage citizen political participation.

Chapter 22 argues that there is a gap between development and underdevelopment. To cross from one level to the other requires a bridge. This is the developmental gap bridge that will enhance the cross-over from the underdeveloped status to the developed status. This study focuses on Africa as largely on the underdeveloped or developing status and requires to use of the bridge to cross over to the developed level. The research question pertinent to be answered is, when will Africa bridge the development gap? The World Bank data using nine (9) variables are analysed, and the findings revealed that Africa is lagging in most sectors and must cross the bridge of development to the developed status. Political and economic solutions are proffered to correct this skirmish.

CONCLUSION

This preface has highlighted how Africa's progress and prosperity are intrinsically linked to its democracy, governance, and development hence the need to develop political systems that advance human rights-sensitive forms of governance despite complexities and contestations. The last part of the preface outlines the contents of the book by explaining what each chapter focuses on. It is hoped that the issues discussed in this book will aid policymakers and practitioners, especially within the African context, as well as scholars and researchers working in academic institutions. The book chapters have reflected on issues and factors that influence democracy, governance, and development in Africa and shared insights and emerging scholarly debates on the interdependence of democracy, governance and development along Africa's quest to be a democratic developmental state in the 21st Century. This book equally provides scholars and practitioners with an empirical and practical forum to deliberate on issues, discourses, models, challenges and prospects for Africa's political development and economic growth and forges alternative pathways to advance Africa's renewal.

Ndwakhulu Tshishonga
University of KwaZulu Natal, South Africa

Icarbord Tshabangu
Leeds Trinity University, United Kingdom

Acknowledgment

The editors would like to acknowledge the help of all the people involved in this project and, more specifically, the chapter authors who took part in both the review process and chapter contribution respectively. Without their support, this book would not have become a reality.

Our sincere gratitude also goes to the main reviewers who helped assess and/or review most chapters for approval. Their contribution, time and expertise proved invaluable to this book project, particularly in raising the quality of the product.

Ndwakhulu Tshishonga
University of KwaZulu Natal, South Africa

Icarbord Tshabangu
Leeds Trinity University, UK

Section 1
Understanding Democracy: Participation and Challenges

Chapter 1
The Quest for Democratic Citizenship:
Contestations and Geopolitical Contradictions

Icarbord Tshabangu
https://orcid.org/0000-0003-4875-9369
Leeds Trinity University, UK

ABSTRACT

This chapter examines notions of democracy and citizenship, the democratic models, and how some of these have manifested in practice, particularly within the African context. While there has been a wave of democratisation globally in the last half a century, this has occurred amidst fierce contestations, some militarily. Furthermore, the practice of democracy from a global standpoint, both within liberal and illiberal states, has been saddled with numerous contradictions in so far as democratic values are concerned. Drawing from varied historical literature sources and analysing contemporary practices of democracy, it is noted that despite existing contestations, contradictions, and imperfections of democracy, this political system remains the best alternative in the 21st century, especially for developing nations that still have weaker systems of governance and have a greater need for economic growth and protection of human rights. The role of citizenship education is also posited as a critical structure, necessary for an informed polity to make those who govern more accountable.

INTRODUCTION

The wave of democratisation and the rationale behind the claim that liberal democracy remains the best alternative for current civilisations compared to other political systems in history continue to influence the global governance culture. This chapter considered some attributes of liberal democracy as the best political system and examined why it also remains a strong alternative for Africa's development. In their preamble, the United Nations 2030 Agenda for Sustainable Development, states that, *"We are*

DOI: 10.4018/979-8-3693-0477-8.ch001

determined to foster peaceful, just and inclusive societies which are free from fear and violence. There can be no sustainable development without peace and no peace without sustainable development". The quest for democracy and any efforts towards democratisation whether within governments or educational systems are critical for world peace and development (Przeworski, et al., 2012; Rudebeck, 2016). The democratic peace theory or democratic pacifism claims that liberal democracies hardly ever go to war with one another (Robbins, 1976; Ceadel, 1980), arguing that democracies tend to use democratic and diplomatic arbitration and that the accountability demanded of them by citizens often compels leaders to be less likely to use force (Bhuiya & Jahan, 2023). However, some have found this contentious given the so-called 'just wars' that have been waged by some democracies especially in the Middle East, often-times against wider public opinion. Nevertheless, since democracy is perceived as likely to bring peace, its ideology has found favour in many revolutions as seen in the last quarter of the 20th century (Dahl, 1989; Potter et al, 1997; List, 2022), where there has been an upsurge in democratisation.

The world's population living under democracy have steadily increased since the 1900s and has taken root in most countries, however, in most African countries this is yet to manifest, except for a few states such as Mauritius (Oluwole, 2023). The 20th-century expansion of democracy has not taken the form of a slow transition in each country but as successive waves of democracy some associated with wars. In some cases, there was an explicit imposition of democracy, through external military force such as the Japanese case by America in the 1940s. The collapse of the Soviet Union followed by liberalisation and democratisation of the independent republics has undoubtedly added to world democratisation (Ostrovsky, 2015). In the recent past one can also refer to alleged externally induced 'democratisation' efforts in Iraq, Afghanistan, and Libya, despite glaring contradictions and contestations to such claims. To some supporters of democracy, this was liberation, implying that no prior consent was required. The nominally democratic states of Europe were mainly born out of the First World War. In Africa, the revolutionary struggles against colonialism also led to the establishment of partial and liberal democracies in some countries (Potter et al, 1997). Furthermore, it is noted that there has also been a general acceptance of illiberal democratic countries by liberal democracies (Dahl, 1989). This has broadened not only the number of countries subscribing to or appearing to be democratic but also the concept of democracy in citizenship.

From a moral standpoint, humanity is inclined to justice which makes democracy possible, but man's potential for committing injustices makes democracy a necessity (Niebuhr in Crick 2002: 120). In the 21st century, democracy has developed to become the only ethical way to govern and any deviation to the contrary will generally be perceived as lacking legitimacy (Ceadel, 1980; Harber, 1995; Crick, 2002). Nevertheless, democratisation efforts have generally faced opposition. In the Sahel region of Africa and some northern African countries, such as Tunisia democratisation has lagged and several states remain unstable (Cavatorta, 2018; Trisnaningtyas, 2022). At a global level, there exist notable challenges to liberal democracy either due to communist ideologies as notable with China or some theocracies such as Iran and Saudi Arabia (Galston, 2018). There has also been a challenge to liberal democracy through the rise of technological giants who control social media, as self-strengthening monopolies (Gersbach, 2020). Such evidence of their influence and control of narratives was evident during the COVID-19 pandemic, leading many lovers of freedom and liberty to question their 'cancel culture' approach to social media users and the 'iron-fisted' dealings with the flow of information critical for citizens' ability to make informed choices.

Recently Africa has also witnessed military coups like in Gabon, Guinea, Mali, Burkina Faso, Niger etc. (Obangome, 2023), and transitional problems in Sudan, Zimbabwe etc., dealing a huge blow to liberal democratic principles. Despite these challenges, there is promise and hope in other countries like Zambia, Malawi, Sierra Leone, Liberia, and Seychelles etc, whose institutions, such as the judiciary, have shown resilience in ensuring democratic practice (International IDEA (2021). This chapter therefore posits liberal democracy as a viable political system that has undeniably permeated the life fabric of this age and suggests that there seems no better political system compared to democracy, despite its contradictions, contestations, and shortcomings (Harber, 1995; Crick, 2002; Sandel, 2022).

BACKGROUND

The commonly known political systems preceding democracy have been monarchy, feudalism, absolutism, imperialism, democracy, and communism (Okey, 1986). Some of the political systems linked to the above include an oligarchy, a theocracy, and an aristocracy. Since these political systems afforded fewer rights to citizens throughout history, democratic struggles emerged to enable citizens to appropriate more rights in different parts of the world. Most of these struggles were driven by the Enlightenment ideals of freedom, liberty, and justice, which took root and grew stronger in the 18th century (Hyland, Gomez and Greensides, 2003; Israel, 2011). The Enlightenment is relevant to democratic notions of citizenship in this chapter since the articulate governance ideas of freedom and social justice largely emerged from that period. Before the Enlightenment, the political systems were often highly structured and centralised. The citizens, especially those at the lower strands of the socio-political structure had only one duty, that is, to defer and obey. Furthermore, the political systems were largely authoritarian condemning citizens to obscurity and political patronage. After the Enlightenment age, the power to reason freely and the advancement of citizens' rights, coupled with a surge in individualism, took centre stage and became manifest in the practice of democracy. A gradual shift could be seen in the balance of power, globally, where lower-class citizens started to challenge the status quo leading to various revolutions ousting imperialism, and communism and to the subsequent establishment of liberal and partial democracies in the 21st century (Okey, 1986; Potter et al, 1997; List, 2022 Israel, 2011).

DEMOCRACY IN HISTORY

In Europe, the first people to use democracy as a form of governance were the ancient Greeks. The daily governance of the state was put under the charge of male citizens under Pericles (Kagan, 1998; Baird, 2010). Ironically, this kind of democratic rule was exclusive as it discriminated against women, the young and the slaves (Crick, 2002; Lakoff, 1996). In about 150 CE democracy found its way into Europe and by 1215CE King John of England, under compulsion from the English nobility signed a Great Charter which was to be known as the Magna Carta, recognizing their rights as landowners, citizens of England and subjects of the king (Crick, 2002; Jones, 2016). England's Glorious Revolution followed in 1688 and moved the country toward a partial democracy, with a parliamentary system. Most former colonies tend to have inherited the same parliamentary system at their political independence, hence the notion that the British Westminster parliament is the 'mother of parliaments'. 1776 saw American colonies declare their independence from England and modelled their ideals after the Enlightenment thinkers, closely linked to democratic principles. This was followed by the French Revolution in 1789 and by that of Latin America from 1790 to the early 1800s. Since then, democracy has continued to be partially practised in most parts of the globe. Also driven by enlightenment ideologies, the mid-19th century saw most of Asia and Africa raise the stakes in agitating for an end to colonial rule, especially after the Second World War. In Africa, revolutions against colonialism were largely aided by the USSR, and to some extent, China, a communist bloc, which set most African states on socialist, pro-communist statehood, steeped in one one-party statism after their political independence. The communist revolutions in Africa, therefore consisted of people rising against repressive, imperialistic colonial regimes. Both socialism and nationalism became used as a rallying point, leading to the demise of colonialism. The African continent has since then witnessed fluctuating democracies. The section below delves into some key models of democracy to establish a better understanding, and well as draw some useful connections.

MODELS OF DEMOCRACY IN CITIZENSHIP

It is noted that the models of democracy only help in the appreciation of democratic citizenship amidst a culturally dynamic world and constantly changing contexts. Pragmatically subscribing to these seems the best way forward, especially for ethnically and culturally diverse communities such as in Africa. The concept of citizenship can be described as the interdependence of self and society (Twine 1994) as well as the study of institutional arrangements and power structures. There are four core concepts in these models, namely: the ***individual,*** the ***community***, ***political leadership*** and ***'layman-ship'*** (Hoff, 1999).

The institutional arrangements stated above will most likely include the arms of government such as the monarchy, the presidency, the parliament, and the judiciary. Drawing from the above assertion it can be observed that citizenship as described by Twine (1994) has always existed in organised societies, as they struggled to revolutionise or define members' roles and responsibilities in the tribe/nation (Isin and Wood 1999). For example, the tribal wars and assimilation of other tribes in pre-colonial Africa, (Tyrell and Jurgens 1983), the plebeians and patricians in Rome (Isin and Wood, 1999) and the running battles between Greek warriors and peasants remind us that citizenship boundaries have always been contested and it may be narrow to confine citizenship to a particular time and place in history let alone to certain origins as Weber (1927 cited in Turner, 1993) has sought to do. Turner (1993) founded on Weber (1927) alludes to citizenship as a modern and Western phenomenon, a view Isin and Wood (1999: 13) rightly dismiss as problematic if not ethnocentric. The search and struggle for liberty is a human desire that cuts across ethnic divides. Below is a discussion of some models in democracy to help in the appreciation of democratic citizenship within a culturally dynamic world context.

Liberalism is described as a relationship between the individual and the democratic character of leadership. Though liberalism has taken many forms since the time of Locke (1693), the dominant feature has been personal autonomy. Under liberalism, all individuals must have equal opportunities to design and master their destiny irrespective of background (Hoff, 1999; Osler and Starkey, 2005). The state's role should be that of ensuring rights and justice. In the neo-liberal view, possibly due to a rise in statism, the state is even seen as an inhibiting factor towards individual freedom. Participating to influence decisions is not seen as enough and what is advocated is freedom of choice among various political alternatives. While citizens are granted personal rights, political rights, and economic rights, it is expected that they in turn be responsible and accountable for their actions. In this regard, I am persuaded to sum up the liberal ideal as inclined towards multiculturalism and driven by choice. As noted earlier under the

Enlightenment, most constitutions in Africa are largely founded on liberal ideals and the legislature is often bound by such thinking despite varied political climates that are sometimes anathema to the rule of law. This may explain in part why citizenship education should incorporate liberal ideals.

Republicanism is seen as comprising a relationship between community and political leaders. The citizen is groomed towards and expected to participate actively in the political life of the community (Hoff, 1999; Osler and Starkey, 2005). In Republicanism, civil and political rights are more important than individual rights, thus we may conclude that a republican ideal is driven by or centred on voice. In contemporary politics, most states operate as republics where political representatives are elected periodically to represent the majority. Such indirect forms of democracy have been criticised by some as too limiting, with individual citizens exercising their rights maybe once in four years, that is, during elections (Chamberlin, 1989). Republicanism is significant for citizenship in Africa in that most countries' political systems are based on representative democracy. This is important because its proper appreciation may help deal with many of the political problems engulfing some countries, such as accountability, the rule of law and the ability to represent others fairly through effective and socially just processes of decision-making. Republicanism is even more pivotal considering that the focus is on citizens 'voices or their participation in decision-making processes, as expected in a democratic republic.

Communitarianism mainly consists of three principles namely *cooperative enquiry*, *common values* and *mutual responsibility*, and *communitarian power relations* (Tam, 1998). The cooperative thinking principle requires that any claim to truth may be judged to be valid only if informed participants, deliberating together under conditions of cooperative inquiry, would accept that claim (Tam, 1998).

Reliance on individuals and decision-making by a selected few is discouraged (Osler and Starkey, 2005; Ploeg, Knoben & Vermeulen, 2022). It is observed that while for example, a parliamentary caucus modelled under republicanism may be in place in a legislature, caution may need to be taken on any over-reliance on a few selected members as this may be regarded as unfair and not truly democratic.

Contrary to what Fukuyama (1992: 326) sees as 'robbing individuals of their rights and giving back power to communities', communitarianism does not necessarily require going back to the Golden Age (Etzioni, 1996) but its proponents argue that it demands an 'open exchange' which holds key to identifying specific beliefs and values on which to anchor a strong community life. In defence of any allegations that communitarians are pre-modern, they argue that theirs are traditions, which look not backward, but forward to improved conditions of life made possible by the cooperative efforts of citizens (Tam 1998: 18). Politically, Etzioni (1995: 122) asserts that the goal of communitarianism is to 'provide the social bonds that sustain the moral voice but at the same time avoid tight networks that suppress pluralism and dissent.'

On common values and mutual responsibility, communitarians believe that there are values that have stood the test of time and every member of each community should help others toward pursuing those values. In communitarianism, structures of power at any level of governance are negotiated by those directly affected and citizens may be regarded as participating on an almost equal footing. Unlike Republicanism, communitarians argue that theirs is not a mere concern of allocation of power to a few individuals who seek to rule others but as Tam (1998: 17) observes, '*Instead, it would involve citizens learning about, reviewing, and determining how to reform decision-making processes about not only government institutions but also to businesses and community organisations which may affect their lives.*

Communitarianism is therefore seen as a community-centred approach to governance though there is potential for extreme 'right' politics where individual 'outsiders' may not be heard. It is also noted that communitarianism like other models of democracy, may be appropriated differently in different cultures.

However, the positive attributes of communitarianism as noted in the quote above may be helpful as part of consensus building in decision-making, inclusive of marginalised citizens. Furthermore, traditional forms of democracy in Africa existed largely in the communitarian mode and still exist as such in some parts of rural Africa (Tyrell and Jurgens, 1983; Ace Project, 2003). In the villages, there is what they call 'inkundla' or 'dare', a meeting place, where the villagers have an open forum accessible to all sexes and age groups. In these meetings, there are hardly any dictatorial tendencies as people from all levels guided by the love and respect of their immediate community seek to reach a consensus through genuine inter-subjectivity. In these meetings, everything directly affecting the village is discussed and the group makes decisions. However, the introduction of district ward councillors in most countries (elected representatives to the district council) has partly diluted the communitarian flow, because at times, instead of reaching concrete decisions and acting on them, villagers surrender to a bureaucratic republican model of working where the councillor takes up their reasoned recommendations. Communitarianism as a system of politics may readily flourish in most rural parts of Africa but may also diminish in the face of liberal and republican ideals (largely palatable in the urban areas) that are enshrined in civic and national laws coupled with inhibitive bureaucratic systems.

Radical Democratic Theory. This model is in a post-structuralist mould. Though it does subscribe to some aspects of the above models (Hoff, 1999; Volk, 2018) The emphasis on the relationship between 'laymanship' and 'individuals' is strong. Hoff (1999, 2) observes that the individual is '*neither the antecedently individuated individual of liberal theory nor the (pre-)modern 'layman' of communitarianism. Rather this individual is a (post-) modern political amateur bound to his/her (political) community not by 'natural', historical and culturally specific ties, but through the minimum requirement of acknowledging and accepting diversity; something learned and reproduced through the practise of civility.*

Unlike the other models, the post-modernist is not confined to any traditional epistemological standpoint. Such post-structuralist viewpoints on phenomena are sometimes seen as residing in scepticism about most institutional arrangements or forms of order. This largely fluid radical democratic theory may be unpopular with some politicians (or those in authority especially as it makes them clueless as to what the citizens may decide (Crick, 2002; Travers, 2001). In the larger African context, where paternalistic ideologies are obtained, such democratic practices that are heavily tilted towards this model may face resistance across most subcultures.

With the rise of statism where some governments have gradually concentrated power in themselves under republicanism and majority rule, the rights of individuals and small communities often become more threatened which thus negatively affects the communitarian, the liberal democrat and the postmodernist.

DEMOCRATIC CITIZENSHIP AND SOME CONTESTATIONS

It is noted that liberal democracy is against the centralisation of power at any level of governance whether. Statism and centralisation of power often breed suppression of individuals and communities. According to the liberal democracy paradigm, true freedom cannot exist or be realised under such a regime, since 'Freedom and responsibility are two sides of the same coin.' What this means is that if a highly structured and centralised authority exists within a state, the environment is likely to be inhibitive and less free to the inhabitants of that polity. Such lack of freedom may often adversely affect general growth and development as individuals and small communities' levels of innovation and responsibility are forced by statism to diminish. Patriotism in state politics is also one of the debasing tools used to harness the masses in pursuit of selfish political ends (Tolstoy, 1894; Dahl, 1989). Tolstoy (1894) further argued that: '*It would seem that owing to the spread of education, of speedier locomotion, of greater intercourse between different nations, to the widening of literature, and chiefly to the decrease of danger from other nations, the fraud of patriotism ought daily to become more difficult and at length impossible to practise'*. In the distant past, citizens were largely uneducated. Rulers often had a monopoly of information and thus often demanded and enforced obedience without question. In the last half a century the media and technology have revolutionised modern democracy and promoted liberalism, such that authoritarian forms of leadership at every level have diminished and a greater demand for shared leadership has taken root. It is now unthinkable that the role of a citizen can only be limited to mere deference towards the status quo. It is because of such factors that have led to more quest for liberal democracy, precipitated by global and community demands both in the political and in the business world.

Democracy and Development

This section discusses the contested relationship between democracy and development as this has some parallels with democratic citizenship. The major question embedded in this section is whether the establishment of democracy is associated with improved standards of living and economic development. At the governance level, the question would be whether the democratisation of political practices and processes can result in the quality of citizens' lives. The Commonwealth Secretariat (2002: 1) observes that 'The quality of democracy greatly affects the quality of development.' The theory behind this statement is that where democracy is established and its quality is enhanced, development in most spheres of life often readily occurs.

On the contrary, in the 1960s to the 1980s, an elitist view on the relationship between democracy and development emerged which stated that democracy depended on development (Bhagwati, 1966). Bhagwati (1966) argued that underdeveloped countries faced a dilemma and had to choose between democracy and development, democracy being the product. In some way, he asserted that underdeveloped societies could not be fit for democracy. One of the proponents of this argument was the former Singaporean Prime Minister, Lee Kuan Yew, who argued that Singaporean economic growth would not have been possible without inhibitions on political and civil rights (Rivera-Batiz, 1999). Rivera–Batiz (1999) also notes that several authors have cited the existence of interest lobby groups under democracy as a possible cause for policy gridlock. Such authors have cited communist China for example as a good example of a non-democracy but fast-developing economy (Galston, 2018). Such authors go on to conclude that the existence of democratic institutions may or may not be associated with economic development.

After exhausting numerous arguments as to whether democracy inhibits or promotes development and as to what extent these claims can stand scrutiny, The Economist (2005) offers a befitting closure in this matter, stating,

'But the main point is this; democracy is not valuable only or mainly because of the contribution it may make to development. It is a great good in its own right. A proudly democratic India that grows at 6% a year (8% of which is entirely achievable) would be even better and should be congratulated...than a brutal anti-democratic China, which grows at 10% a year. There is more to life than GDP'.

The notion that the quality of democracy affects the quality of development was later developed and strengthened by Sen (1999). He argued that it was not right to ask if a country was fit for democracy, but that a country was fit through democracy. His assertions were based on his study findings that no substantial famine has ever occurred in any independent and democratic country with a relatively free press. He concluded that it is not a lack of food that causes famines but a lack of democracy. In Africa for example, it is noted that despite the severity of droughts, those nations that have survived, have done so partly due to access and presence of the media to cover affected areas which helped initiate some solutions. The drought effects in autocratic states have been made worse by the suppression of the media and the politicisation of the issue by the government (Human Rights Forum, 2005; Detges, 2017). Rivera–Batiz (1999) on the one hand observes that though, *'Authoritarian regimes may randomly provide high quality* (in economic production), *but if they do not, they can only be changed by force, which may take years or decades longer than under democratic institutions'.*

It is noted that the descent into an authoritarian regime incapacitates the state in terms of dealing with what could have been avoidable hunger and deprivation amongst its people, including among other ills the alleged denial of food relief to citizens along partisan lines (Human Rights Forum, 2005; Raftopoulos, 2003; Stiff 2002). Furthermore, the non-availability of democratic means to peacefully oust an allegedly corrupt and illegitimate government in the long run has been extremely detrimental to people's quality of life. In states where dictatorship has presided over economic downfall, Goetzmann (1999 cited in Rivera-Batiz, 1999) observes that *'Tens of millions of people in emerging markets have recently fallen back into poverty. Without a democratic voice, they had no control over the risks their governments assumed. Even more outrageous, without transparent political institutions and a free press they had no way to understand these risks…Some would call it taxation without representation. History is filled with examples of non-democratic governments causing great harm to their citizens.*

After renouncing his earlier theory that development should precede democracy and accepting the new thinking that the quality of democracy affects the quality of development, Bhagwati (1995) further acknowledged that the challenge remains firmly fixed on the improvement of the quality of democracy.

Therefore the improvement of the quality of democracy is synonymous with improved lifestyles, and development agents such as education have a key role in the establishment and sustenance of such a democratic culture from within the micro-politics of institutions and further in the macro-political arena.

DEMOCRATIC CITIZENSHIP AND THE AFRICAN CONTEXT

This section looks at the African context from colonialism through to the present and explores what ideological influences democracy has had or continues to have on the continent in general and Africa in particular, and to what extent democratic citizenship is relevant to the challenges that face institutions and society. It has been highlighted earlier that republican and liberal democratic ideals are legally, socially, and politically embedded in African life, especially in the urban areas amongst the elite. In rural areas, though communitarianism is still strong, and its systems are permissible by law (for example the role of traditional leaders), the whole legal system is far from being favourable to traditionalists. It is noted that those democratic ideals favoured by legislation in most countries are liberal and republican and often aided and still sustain capitalism both during colonialism and in the postcolonial era. Capitalism was and still is a 'colourful' determinant in the state of Africa.

It is most unlikely therefore that one can fully appreciate the ongoing democratic struggles in Africa unless one comes to a deeper understanding of how capitalism through colonialism affected the continent psychologically politically and socio-economically, in ways that served to arrest development (Babu 1984, Rodney, 1981). The literary works of such writers as Ngugi Wa Thiong'o on *Decolonising the Mind*, attest to the fact that capitalist colonialism was not just a socio-economic activity occupying a brief phase in African history but left behind deep-seated psychological scars. Due to capitalism and socialist ambitions, most of Africa and her people still live in abject poverty and squalor side by side with the luxury enjoyed by the corrupt leaders (Mbah and Igariwey, 2001; Moyo, 2010; Burgis, 2016).

The key impediments to Africa can arguably be summed up in two ideological mishaps: imperialistic private capitalism and state socialism. While capitalism was superimposed on the African citizens by the coloniser, state socialism became an imposition by the nationalist liberators from colonialism. These aspects are explored in-depth, linking to liberal democratic citizenship. It is noted that in both periods most citizens of Africa have experienced fluctuating democratic peace and development.

Some Socio-Economic Factors

When the industrial powers of Europe colonised Africa in the 19th century they produced a capitalist economy with similarities to their own countries. Africa was intended to serve two purposes: firstly, to provide a potential market and secondly a source of raw materials (Mbah and Igariwey, 2001). In the process, Africa was turned from a pre-colonial, self-sufficient communal agricultural economy to one embracing interdependence with other economies coming up. Villagers were encouraged (and in some areas forced) to grow cash crops to meet export demands. In numerous contexts most Africans found themselves having to work on farms and mines, and in the factories of European masters to make a living. Gradually the society was stratified and modelled after capitalism. This formation took the nature of a bourgeois class who owned land and capital and lowered down the petit bourgeoisie and still lower down, the working masses (or proletariat). Just as such developments served to establish capitalism in Africa they also served as an embryonic stage to socialism. It should be noted that under colonial rule only the white settlers had the power to vote and participate in government office, even though their population often accounted for less than 3% in most colonised countries. It was a selective/exclusive form of democracy reminiscent of apartheid America in the mid-20th century where rights activists such as Martin Luther King Jr. painfully observed that when the American white folk talked of equal rights, they only meant equal rights amongst themselves.

When class consciousness developed in Africa and manifested itself in agitations against working conditions, and some forms of apartheid discrimination it led to the formation of what were later regarded as aggressive trade unions whose socialist messages found fertile ground in a restive colonised people of Africa. These protesting socialist forces under trade unionism later transformed themselves into a political voice that was to confront and overpower colonialism. At independence, most African countries became socialist states or elected to follow state socialism. But either way, state socialism like state capitalism did not provide respite.

Excessive capitalism is tied up with the maintenance of an exploitative relationship that has continued to suppress the working people of Africa through unfair trade. As a result, western countries have been able to provide their workers with an increased standard of living, thereby maintaining industrial peace at the expense of exploited Africa (Rodney, 1981; Babu, 1984; Moyo, 2010; Burgis, 2016). Though socialism by its nature centres on satisfying human needs as opposed to capitalism's obsession with profit, socialism under statism seems to have failed Africa. As stated earlier under the models of democracy communitarianism is often favourable in rural areas, and most political and economic development programmes ought to take this into account while being mindful of already embellished liberal ideals of individualism in both rural and urban communities. Policies that are founded on nostalgia and a lack of appreciation of contemporary culture and the international laws that govern global relationships are likely to fail.

Some Socio-Political Factors

It was noted earlier how colonialism disintegrated and divided societies in Africa. In most British colonies the policy was that of divide and rule (Mbah and Igariwey, 2001) and the French often used assimilation, which was also consequentially divisive. At the inception of colonialism and during the drawing of boundaries, ethnic groups were regrouped into artificial political boundaries, which often created and still created ethnic tensions and social-political discrimination in the newly independent countries (Lwanga, 2005; Salih, 2001). This animosity and antagonism are often exacerbated when competition over the control of government apparatuses and capitalistic means of production spiral to evoke ethnic sentiments which set one ethnic group against the other. This divisive method has also been used to conceal class divisions to the point where class consciousness, has been undermined in favour of a lingering, stagnant ethnic/state consciousness. A good example is where the workers, instead of mobilising against a repressive status quo to address socio-economic inequalities, sometimes turn against each other along ethnic lines and thus forfeit opportunities to confront the status quo as a united force. In Africa, particularly towards elections, it is not uncommon for the ruling elite to fan ethnic sentiments as a divisive measure and by doing so, shield themselves from popular anger, arising from class consciousness. These issues above have serious negative implications for the development of democratic citizenship in Africa generally and Africa, in particular.

Colonialism also witnessed the creation of cities through industrialisation and the expropriation of prime land for mining and farming by the colonizer (Kibble, 2003). This in turn culminated in the forcible creation of dry dusty rural areas under varied colonial laws. Though most urbanites are still in some way connected to their rural folk, the cultures existing between these two are immense. The urban dweller is often seen as more capitalistic than the communal rural dweller (Ake, 2000). In the drive towards liberal democratisation processes in contemporary Africa, Ake (2000) observes that this phenomenon is a largely urban one. Taking into consideration that the larger population in Africa (about 60% or more) is situated in rural areas this creates a problem for the development of liberal democratic citizenship. The rural people are often at the lower strand of the political structure and are often easily cowed to submission by state terror or manipulation as evidenced in the pattern of election campaigns in some African states and elsewhere. The trend of election results has been that ruling parties often hold sway in rural areas while the opposition often enjoys success in urban areas. Ake (2000) further observes that due to the marginalisation of the rural poor in Africa, democratisation has often only opened political competition to the elite such as the intellectuals, students, and trade unionists. He concludes that in the end most people in Africa become faced with only one right and that is choosing between the two oppressors and not choosing between liberty and oppression.

The existing forms of democratic participation (liberal and republican) often make little sense to the rural folk, probably because they are pro-communitarian. This implies that liberal and republican democratisation efforts remain largely a part of an urbanite preserve. From these two subcultures (besides ethnicity) it can be seen why Africa remains politically complex and how the application of democracy as imposed by the West, continues to be illusory. Any form of sustainable democratisation in Africa may have to incorporate the traditions of Africa especially the communitarian political leadership ethos of the past which is summed up in some old African proverbs such as; *'The power of the fish is in the water',* or 'inkosi yinkosi ngabantu', meaning *leader is only a leader because of his people.'* (Tyrell and Jurgens,1983). These proverbial sayings give testimony and further weight to a view that in rural Africa despotic leaders may not be tolerated for long by the governed under a communitarian governance system. This is not meant to romanticise the past but rather acknowledge that although pre-colonial leadership styles had their imperfections, in the form of pre-colonial communitarianism, they nevertheless served most societies better compared to some models of democracy today. This could be because communitarian principles of governance were appreciated more thoroughly by the citizens than other political models laden with imported ideologies in the postcolonial era. In the pre-colonial era, authoritarian leaders did not rule for long before their subjects could stop them from unaccountable governance. On the other hand, under some imposed forms of republicanism whose ethos and principles most Africans have little or no knowledge of, to hold their leaders accountable, some cruel dictators have continued to govern with an iron fist and manipulation for decades, resulting in the so-called 'failed states.' The next chapter discusses the role that education may play in Africa's democratisation efforts.

THE NEED FOR DEMOCRATISATION THROUGH EDUCATION

If we consider Tonello's (2020) argument that, how can one defend democracy when citizens themselves display an unquestioning deference to political leaders and inability to hold them accountable or fail to perform tasks necessary for strengthening democratic institutions, then the democratic education becomes apparent. In education, we note that sometimes students' rights to participate in decision-making processes or to be consulted are often violated under the guise of upholding and maintaining discipline. Students are sometimes made to follow a 'straight-jacketed' way of doing things at the expense of rationality and personal leadership development, lest they be seen as undisciplined. The U.N. Convention on the Rights of the Child Article 12.1 states that a child shall be entitled to participate once he or she can form his or her opinions. Children's rights to be heard, informed and included should be embedded within all educational processes (Nthontho, 2017). In developing a liberal democratic society, educators should socialize learners into active 'namers of the world' (Freire, 1970) and avoid letting others name the world for them. The failure to train young people in this way only prepares them to be leaders who are subservient to other leaders, even on the world stage when they should be representing their countries' interests.

Since those who will govern tomorrow and those who should make them accountable are in education today, education institutions provide an opportunity for the effective democratisation of nation-states. Education should not just mirror society (Forster, 1997) but ought to provide opportunities to use its influences to promote a democratic culture both through learning e.g., in a Citizenship Education subject and through practice, that is, engendering democratic processes all parties within education.

Citizenship Education

There are two forms of citizenship education, which are often in opposition. There is a platonic, conservative view of citizenship education whose purpose seeks only to nurture a sense of loyalty and obligation to the state, as seen under absolutist monarchies or dictatorships. In this type of citizenship, there is absolute deference towards the social and political elite and a strong sense of pride in the empire (Garratt, 2003; Prauscello, L. (2014). A good example in parts of Africa is where the government has narrowed national patriotism and citizenship to partisan dictates. This is evidenced in the indoctrination of the youth militia by some ruling elites, festering intolerance and promoting violence towards those seen or perceived as opponents (Sibanda, 2015). Such a narrow view of citizenship is distinctly functional and only serves to cement existing institutional arrangements, and produces an engineered passive citizenry, uncritical and with fatalistic attitudes.

Then there is democratic citizenship education that empowers and is laden with democratic values. It is not based on a citizen who merely understands and obeys, but one who is informed, active, responsible, and critical of institutional arrangements (Twine, 1994; Kovalchuk and Rapoport, 2020). Educating towards democratic citizenship engenders a view that learners have a sacred, moral, and legal right to be active citizens in the search for solutions bedevilling their world of existence. The notion that learners are 'citizens to be and not active citizens' as they pass through educational institutions needs revisiting.

Some of the notable pillars of citizenship in a democracy and applicable to the education system would entail the promotion of the following attributes in learners.

- **Rationality:** that is, the ability to master cognitively complex situations, be they social or moral because the surrender to irrationality or blind obedience to others' decisions invites all the brutalities of totalitarian regimes (Bailey, 2000).
- **Empathy** is another important pillar, which implies never judging a person until you have walked in his shoes. Tolerance becomes the keyword.
- **Empowerment and self-esteem** are crucial elements in citizenship education because more than just rationalising and empathizing, they are action-orientated. The citizens should not be paralysed by rationalizing and empathizing but be empowered by it. It is normally those with positive self-esteem, who develop a strong moral voice within a nation and are often helpful to others (Etzioni, 1996) Democratic citizenship education should therefore make students feel sufficiently secure and trusted such that they feel able to be of service to their fellow citizens.
- **Non-authoritarian** approaches where educational leaders model students to be partners and not competitors within the learning process. Teachers not operating as 'the haves' (knowledge) and the students 'the have-nots' but engaging co-creatively and collaboratively to the benefit of all.
- **Giving a voice** is critical. Students' voicelessness within the educational process is counter-productive to democratic citizenship. As children grow so does their capacity to make decisions. Freire (1970: 69) observes that 'human existence cannot be silent, nor can it be nourished by false words ... human beings are not built in silence, but in word, in work in action-reflection.'
- **Participation** in decisions should occur naturally. Half-hearted attempts at student involvement in decision-making are deemed as counterproductive as students can easily see through such (Harber 1995). Most students are likely to notice a patronising staff that keeps them away from significant issues and the consequences could be adverse, e.g., strikes or disruptive tendencies.

- **Being dialogical** is important and thus avoids the banking concept of education (Freire, 1970), seen as mechanistic (as evidenced in the 'examination-centred' curriculum). Such tends to resist dialogue, is static and naturalistic and often promotes a spatial view of consciousness, which transforms students into receiving objects.
- **Problem-posing education** in democratic citizenship empowers teachers and students to become subjects (not objects) and critical thinkers within the educational process thus avoiding being overcome by alienating intellectualism.
- **Patience is a prerequisite.** In the same way, educators may need to revisit some of their values. For example, democratising the educational environment may result in delayed decision-making, mundane processes or 'gridlocks' through consultations, but the long-term benefits may be positive. The largely examination-centred education systems in most countries may find some democratic initiatives inhibitive (Grout, Jenkins and Propper (2000). Patience is therefore critical for effective training of the young towards a democratic polity.
- **Politicisation of knowledge**. to be effective agents of democratisation educational institutions should avoid inculcating partisan values or political knowledge that often breeds intolerance, forcing some to express views only supportive of the status quo.

The democratisation of organisations, institutions and governance systems as a conceptual mediating artefact remains essential for the realisation of fuller liberal democratic practice in a polity and educational institutions provide the most viable agency possible.

DIRECTIONS FOR FUTURE RESEARCH

Though democracy, as a political system, has advanced to a level of universality, its manifestations differ in varied regions and countries of the world. It is imperative therefore for constitutionalist and political leaders in each nation-state to collectively consultatively canvass among their citizens and revisit their national constitutions, most of which are 'Western', to establish which model of democracy could be suitable in line with their traditions and culture. It is not democratically healthy or politically sound, especially for most African countries to have accepted externally imposed forms of democratic governance with only minor modifications. Such borrowed constitutions only tend to serve the interest of former colonial masters, at the expense of the masses. There is also a need to revisit the education systems in some countries to ensure that democratic citizenship education is not only taught but also promoted in educational processes in all educational institutions.

CONCLUSION

This chapter has examined the models of democracy about citizenship, and how some of these are applied in practice, especially within the African context. The global wave of democratisation in the last half of the century was noted and a view advanced that liberal democracy remains the best alternative form of governance despite contestations contradictions and shortcomings, especially for developing nations such as those in Africa, most of whom still contend with weaker systems of governance, authoritarian regimes, and poor social security and safety nets for citizens. It was also noted how illiberal forces have caused fluctuating democracies and negatively impacted economic growth. Democratic education, especially under citizenship education was also posited as a key instrument for the democratisation of any nation's macropolitics, which may result in an informed populace able to hold accountable those who govern.

REFERENCES

Ace Project. (2003). *Democracy: What the hell is that?* http: //www.aceproject.org/main/english/ve/vek05b01.htm

Ake, C. (1996). *Democracy and development in Africa.* Brookings Institution.

Ake, C. (1996). *Theory of human life for citizenship and civil society.* http: //www.istr.org/conferences/toronto/abstracts/Isumonah.pdf

Babu, A. M. (1981). *African socialism or socialist Africa?* Zimbabwe Publishing House.

Bailey, R. (Ed.). (2000). *Teaching Values and Citizenship Across the Curriculum.* Kogan Page.

Baird, F. E. (2010). Philosophic Classics, Volume I: Ancient Philosophy. Routledge.

Bhagwati, J. (1966). *Economics of Underdeveloped Countries.* McGraw-Hill.

Bhagwati, J. (1995). New Thinking on Development. *Journal of Democracy, 6*(4), 59.

Bhuiya, S., & Jahan, M. (2023). The justification of Democracy Peace Theory in the 21st century. *Social Science Review, 39*(1), 211–229. doi:10.3329sr.v39i1.64921

Broch-Due, V. (2005). *Violence and belonging: the quest for identity in post-colonial Africa.* Routledge.

Cavatorta, F. (2018). The Middle East and North Africa. In Democratisation (pp 364-383). Oxford University Press.

Ceadel, M. (1980). *Pacifism in Britain, 1914-1945: the defining of a faith.* Clarendon Press.

Chamberlin, R. (1989). *Free children and democratic schools: a philosophical study of liberty and education.* Falmer.

Cloke, K., & Goldsmith, J. (2002). *The end of management and the rise of organisational democracy.* Jossey-Bass.

Commonwealth Secretariat. (2002). *The quality of democracy in the Pacific.* A Report for the 2002 Roundtable of Heads of Government [Denarau Island, Fiji Islands, 19-20 August 2002].

Crain, W. (1992). *Theories of Development.* Prentice Hall.

Crick, B. (2002). *Democracy: a very short introduction.* Oxford University Press.

Dahl, R. A. (1961). *Who Governs?* Yale University Press.

Dahl, R. A. (1989). *Democracy and its Critics.* Yale University Press.

Detges, A. (2017). Droughts, state-citizen relations and support for political violence in Sub-Saharan Africa: A micro-level analysis. *Political Geography*, *61*, 88–98. doi:10.1016/j.polgeo.2017.07.005

Du Bois, S. G. (1958). Du Bois Speaks to Africa. In *The life of W.E. B. Du Bois: Cheer the Lonesome Traveller*. The Dial Press.

Economist. (2005). *India: Democracy vs. development: A false choice*. http: //www.economist.com

Etzioni, A. (1996). *The New Golden Rule: Community and Morality in a Democratic Society*. Harper Collins.

Fanon, F. (1965). *Wretched of the Earth*. Penguin.

Flekky, M. G. E., & Kaufman, N. H. (1997). *The Participation Rights of the Child: Rights and Responsibilities in Family and Society*. Jessica Kingsley Publishers.

Forster. (1993). *People and Education in the Third World*. Longman.

Freire, A. M. A., & Macedo, D. (Eds.). (1998). The Paulo Freire reader. Continuum.

Freire, P. (1970). *Pedagogy of the Oppressed*. Penguin.

Fukuyama, F. (1992). *The end of history and the last man*. Penguin.

Galston, W. (2018). Populist challenge to liberal democracy. *Journal of Democracy*, *29*(2), 5–19. doi:10.1353/jod.2018.0020

Garratt, D. (2003). Education for Citizenship. In D. Burton & S. Barlet (Eds.), *Education Studies: themes and issues*. Sage.

Gersbach, H. (2020). Democratizing Tech Giants! A roadmap. *Economics of Governance*, *21*(4), 351–361. doi:10.100710101-020-00244-5

Griffith, R. (1998). *Educational Citizenship and Independent Learning*. Jessica Kingsley.

Harber, C. (1995). *Developing Democratic Education*. Education Now Books.

Harber, C. (1999). *Voices for Democracy: a North – South Dialogue on Education for Sustainable Democracy*. Education Now Books.

Hoff, J. (1999). *Towards a Theory of Democracy for the Information Age*. Discussion paper democracy platform UK-Nordic Meeting Copenhagen. http: //virtualsociety.sbs.ox.ac.uk/nordic/democracyplatform.htm

Hyland, P. (2003). The Enlightenment: a sourcebook and reader. London: Routledge.

Indabawa. (1993). *Education, Autonomy and Democratic Citizenship- Philosophy in a changing world*. Routledge.

International IDEA. (2021). *The state of democracy in Africa and the Middle East. Resilient democratic aspirations and opportunities for consolidation*. https://www.idea.in7>files

Israel, J. (2011). *A Revolution of the Mind: Radical Enlightenment and the Intellectual Origins of Modern Democracy*. Princeton University Press.

Jones, D. (2016). *Magna Carta: The Birth of Liberty*. Penguin Books.

Kagan, D. (1998). *Pericles Of Athens and The Birth of Democracy*. Free Press.

Kovalchuk, S., & Rapoport, A. (2020). *Democratic Citizenship Education in Non-Western Contexts: Implications for Theory and Research*. Routledge. doi:10.4324/9780429293313

Kropotkin, P. (1897). *The State*. Freedom Press.

Lakoff, S. (1996). *Democracy: history, theory, practice*. Westview. Press.

List, F. (2022). *The National System of Political Economy*. Imperium Press.

Mbah, S., & Igariwey, I. E. (2001). *African Anarchism: The History of a Movement Tucson*. Sharp Press.

Ngugi, W. A. (1981). Decolonising the Mind: The Politics of Language in African Literature. Heinemann.

Nthontho, A. N. (2017). Children as stakeholders in education: Does their voice matter? *South African Journal of Childhood Education*, *7*(1), 7. doi:10.4102ajce.v7i1.434

Obangome, G. W. (2023). *Gabon officers declare military coup, President Ali Bongo detained*. Reuters. https://www.reuters.com/world/africa/gabonese-military-officers-announce-they-have-seized-power-2023-08-30

Okey, R. (1986). *Eastern Europe 1740-1985: feudalism to communism*. Hutchinson Education.

Oloka-Onyango, J. (Ed.). (2001). *Constitutionalism in Africa: Creating opportunities, facing challenges*. Fountain Publishers.

Oluwole, V. (2023). African countries leading in democracy index rankings. *Business Insider, Africa*.

Osler, A., & Starkey, H. (2005). *Changing Citizenship – Democracy and Inclusion in Education*. Open University Press.

Ostrovsky, A. (2015). *The Invention of Russia: The Journey from Gorbachev's Freedom to Putin's War*. Atlantic Books.

Ploeg, M., Knoben, J., & Vermeulen, P. (2022). We are in it together: Communitarianism and the performance- Innovation relationships. Research Polity, 51(5).

Polyarchy Organisation. (2003). *Polyarchy: A paradigm*. http: //www.polyarchy.org/paradigm/english/democracy.html

Popper, K. R. (1972). *Objective Knowledge: An Evolutionary Approach*. University Press.

Popper. (1945). *Teaching Values and Citizenship*. Sage.

Potter, D., Goldplatt, D., Kiloh, M., & Lewis, P. (1997). *Democracy: From Classical times to the present*. Polity Press.

Prauscello, L. (2014). *Performing Citizenship in Plato's Laws (Cambridge Classical Studies)*. Cambridge University Press. doi:10.1017/CBO9781139680882

Przeworski, A., Alvarez, M. E., Cheibub, J. A., & Limongi, F. (2012). Democracy and Development: Political Institutions and Well-Being in the World, 1950–1990. Cambridge University Press.

Raftopoulos, B. (2003). *Education and the Crisis in Zimbabwe, Cannon Collins Memorial Lecture 2003*. Canon Collins Educational Trust.

Rivera-Batiz, F. L. (1999). *Democracy, governance and economic growth: Theory and evidence*. Columbia University.

Robbins, K. (1976). *The Abolition of War: the Peace Movement in Britain, 1914–1919*. The University of Wales Press.

Rodney, W. (1981). *How Europe Underdeveloped Africa*. Howard University Press.

Rudebeck, L. (2016). Democracy and Development – A Disputed Pair. *Africa Development. Afrique et Developpement*, *41*(1), 1–22. https://www.jstor.org/stable/90001832

Salih, M. M. A. (2001). *African Democracies and African Politics*. Pluto Press.

Sandel, M. J. (2022). *Democracy's Discontent: A New Edition for Our Perilous Times*. Harvard University Press.

Sibanda, P. (2015). Citizenship Education and its relevance to Zimbabwe. *Scientific Journal of Pure and Applied Sciences*, *4*(10), 180–184. doi:10.14196jpas.v4.101908

Tam, H. (1998). Communitarianism. New York University Press.

TolstoyL. N. (1894). *On Patriotism*. http: //www.panarchy.org/tolstoy/189

Tonello, S. (2020). *Resolving the democratic dilemma- Contestation, anti-power and democracy* [Thesis]. University of Wellington.

Trisnaningtyas, J. P. N. (2022). Forecasting Tunisia's future: A lesson learnt from the past. Ijd. *Demos (Mexico City, Mexico)*, *4*(1), 1. Advance online publication. doi:10.37950/iijd.v4:1.208

Turner, B. S. (Eds.). (1993). Citizenship and Social Theory. Sage.

Twine, F. (1994). *Citizenship and Social Rights*. Sage.

Tyrell, P., & Jurgens, B. (1983). *African Heritage*. Macmillan Press.

Volk, C. (2018). On a radical democratic theory of political protest: Potentials and shortcomings. *Critical Review of International Social and Political Philosophy*, *24*(4), 437–459. doi:10.1080/13698230.2018.1555684

Chapter 2
Hermeneutical Injustice via Interpretive Harm:
Epistemologies of Change for Structural Oppression in Africa

Catherine Hayes
https://orcid.org/0000-0003-3870-2668
University of Sunderland, UK

ABSTRACT

This chapter serves as a mechanism of recognizing and acknowledging the illegitimacy of historic and traditional Western approaches to narratives of African feminist epistemology. These approaches have engendered lenses of perspective which are irrefutably skewed by colonialism and whose address is warranted in ensuring both a means of learning about the end of an era and the prospect of a more authentically framed future framed, shaped, and determined from within African culture and context by those. To undertake this, acknowledgement and recognition is one of the first and much belated to framing steps in ensuring that the articulation of truth lies best with those whose lived truths they are, rather than any tokenistic perceptions of them, consequently articulated through Western lenses of perspective. The central tenet of the chapter revolves around the positing of African citizenship, indeed all individual citizenship as fundamentally unique and known authentically only to those who have socially constructed knowledge of it.

INTRODUCTION

In the consciousness of the truth he has perceived man now sees everywhere only the awfulness or the absurdity of existence and loathing seizes him. (Friedrich Nietzsche, 1844-1900)

DOI: 10.4018/979-8-3693-0477-8.ch002

Hermeneutical injustice via interpretive harm has been recognised as a longstanding impact of colonialism and has been directly attributed to structural oppression (Berenstain, 2016). Traditionalist approaches to Social Constructivist methodologies have become a mechanism by which this oppression can be actively perpetuated (Falola, 2022). This results in contention within the context of African feminist epistemology since this too relies on an interpretive lens within which, acknowledgement of the epistemic position of the researcher is made (Adebayo & Njoku, 2023). The outcome is that this acknowledgement of positionality still uses a one-dimensional concept to make meaning of a three-dimensional intersectional lived experience. The impact of this has been that both African men's and women's capacity for knowing in the field of African feminist epistemology has only actually been visible through the lens of white feminist methodology (Mellor, 2022).

The integration of the epistemologies and conceptual bases of domination has the effect of being hidden within traditional white feminist research, which predominantly serves to place the source of challenges and issues within black female populations with little or no regard for the structural inequalities of oppression which actively pervade African lives (Wielanga, 2022). The impact of this is to further entrench perceptions of the West within conceptual foundations now tarnished by ideologies that neither serves to represent or interpret the concept of hermeneutical justice (Akoleowo, 2022). In the context of the paradigmatic sufficiency of social research, epistemology remains an integral component in the relationship between ontology, philosophy, methodology and methods (Jackson et al, 2022). This chapter will provide an overview of how African feminist epistemology in the context of knowledge and knowledge acquisition has largely become the preserve of white feminists whose portrayal of cause and effect within an interpretive lens continues to impact the capacity of African feminists to identify, acknowledge and address the structural inequalities which constrain efforts to engender authentic change. An insight will be gained into the relative differences that can exist between different types of knowledge and how this then influences how knowledge is established, articulated and regarded in the wider context of research.

For this chapter epistemology, is operationally defined as the nature and form of knowledge about how this relationship is articulated in feminist praxis. Underpinning this definition is the assumption that the basis of all human knowledge is subjective and is rooted in the socially constructed meaning-making that underpins human curiosity, inquiry and subsequently assumption (Hester, 2020). The issue of contention is not this assumption but rather the assumption that an interpretive lens as applied to African feminist epistemology can refract a vision which is not in any way authentic and remains void of the truth of experience lived within structural oppression (Ossome, 2023). As a white Western author myself, I seek not to challenge this but rather acknowledge it so that it can be accounted for and acknowledged by my Western and Eurocentric counterparts who seek to wholly interpret and represent the voices of those who live lives still dominated by the structural oppression imposed upon them (Hurlbut, 2021). The context of social science presents an ideal arena from a disciplinary perspective to consider the relationship between what it is possible to know and the knower. What this relationship constitutes is a prevailing dilemma in the study of epistemology that has been continually extended to incorporate the concept of the personal in epistemic cognition. What that dilemma constitutes, is the fundamental difference between truth and verisimilitude and the contention of whether a re-examination of the constructive alignment of methodological approaches to Western social research methodologies concerning what they make possible to interpret is required (Bernecka, 2022). The overall aim of the chapter is to afford readers an alternative perspective lens through which the address of social justice can ever take place, via the voice of a Western academic who is keen to see these injustices acknowledged. The skewed narratives of the West necessitate the prospect of exploring the broad intersectional bases of African feminist epistemology, such as race, gender, culture, and the polemic debates which serve to recognise and acknowledge the tensions that arise by theorizing from the perspective of post-colonial legacies and influences.

CONSIDERING VISUAL EPISTEMOLOGY

The acquisition of knowledge about sensory engagement with specific artefacts, such as art, or media, such as music, presents an alternative insight into what knowledge is, especially in contrast to the study of propositional knowledge or truth in African feminist epistemology, regardless of geographical context (Simba and Davids, 2020). It is here that it can be posited that the relative inseparability of cognitive skill and affective impact is evident and where the concept of aesthetic knowledge is open to question in terms of the internalisation of perceived reality. In turn, this raises questions of what constitutes knowledge or whether knowledge itself can be perceived in the context of sensory engagement, a process of critical reflection which can potentially lead to critical reflexivity in action (Nzegwu, 2019). Academic researchers doubtlessly use reflection to challenge their personally held assumptions and translate this into deliberate action in the real world – as with seminal academic texts, such as the work of Shakespeare, the universality of creative practice has the potential to transcend generations and become an embedded part of historical knowledge, capturing an insight into our cultural heritage and ancestry (Stupples, 2017).

Whilst art does not seek or necessitate propositional truth in the same sense, as evidence-based approaches to health and social care, it can be posited that it provides a metaphorical anchor for the recognition that all interpretation is essentially subjective, when perceived and reported by humankind. Ultimately all ways of knowing, regardless of discipline, can shape how sense is made of the world within which humankind exists (Van Veeren, 2019). As such it can be stated that all epistemological stances are beyond disciplinarity, and it is methodological approaches that define our signature and traditionally adopted methods for the acquisition of knowledge in practice.

Providing an insight into the liminal space between what is the basis of 'knowing' and the knower is essential to deconstructing meaning in the context of perception (Fox, 2017). This insight can then be used to consider how personal epistemology influences the choice of philosophical underpinnings in processes of research design and methodology. By facilitating the consideration of both traditional and contemporary epistemological lenses, using recognised philosophical perspectives it is possible to raise awareness of a wider range of epistemological stances. Making sense is an integral part of being human (Eisner, 2017). It lies at the heart of the fundamental understanding explanation and comprehension (Park, 2017). In terms of human need, control of extraneous environments and the emotions that regulate interaction with them are the pivotal basis of the need to 'make sure'. This has now also become a core characteristic of how tacit knowledge can become 'transferrable knowledge' in the context of gamification (ter Vrugte and de Jong, 2017). It implies the relationship between the human mind and the universe in which it is acknowledged to exist is pivotal to knowledge and subsequent understanding.

CONTEXTUALISING AND FRAMING AFRICAN FEMINIST EPISTEMOLOGY

Epistemology extends beyond the scope of purist philosophy, which is significant in how it effectively reaches beyond the context of individual and collective identities in social research settings. Epistemology is not only an academic endeavour or pursuit but also pivotal in the transgenerational sharing of knowledge from one to the next where knowledge rather than perception ultimately underpins belief (Kaplan, Sanchez and Hoffman, 2017). For any sustainable change in culture for women and their advocates to occur beyond the here and now, the difference between truth and verisimilitude is pivotal to acknowledge and embed in societal structures.

Justifying or providing an evidence base for knowledge is now a fundamental part of any sociological research. It is the basis of rationalism, empiricism and the fundamental structure of knowledge. The concept of perceived versus actual reality is important in differentiating what we perceive knowledge to be from what it is (Inkpin, 2021). The differentiation between what knowledge is and what knowledge constitutes is also paramount since it impacts the capacity humankind has to react to it in practice (Carter, 2017). The lens of perspective that white Western and Eurocentric epistemologies have placed upon African epistemology can be revealed as a deficit model, in the progression of equality, equity and the acknowledgement of the necessity of each in any democratic global society.

It ought to be acknowledged, too, that many individuals embody or espouse an absolutist perspective and that a more evaluative perspective of different domains of knowledge in sociological research is necessary in practice (Markauskaite and Goodyear, 2017). Within this chapter, the contemplation of both theory and practice in applied research design and methodology is considered alongside the contextual significance of African feminist epistemology, as perceived through that Western and Eurocentric lens and then the skewed implications of this to the lives of millions.

BINDING TIES OF IMPOSED ONTOLOGY AND EPISTEMOLOGY

Where theoretical positioning illuminates the whole rationale for social research, the significance of ontology and epistemology in framing and contextualising African feminist epistemology is irrefutable (Cunliffe and Scaratti, 2017). An understanding of both ontology and epistemology and their symbiotic relationship is essential in subsequently understanding the connection between the origins and foundations of post-colonial research. The morphologic design of research is dependent on the ontological and epistemological stance underpinning it and then supporting the adoption of specific methodologies and methods which serve to advocate question-led rather than methods-driven research approaches. Certain ontological and epistemological stances offer the opportunity for African Feminist researchers to acknowledge their embedded stance or philosophical assumptions which can potentially influence their interpretive capacity and ability to disseminate findings in the context of social research methods. Within the context of African feminist epistemology, the resonance of colonialism and post-colonial perspectives still pervades into the 21st Century.

The term ontology can be operationally defined in relation to its relationship with epistemology. Essentially, two distinct ontological positions exist, foundationalism and anti-foundationalism. Both deal with the nature of being, truth and reality. It is the theoretical significance of ontology that embeds it into the very being of an epistemological stance. The longstanding issue is exactly where the origins of imposed epistemologies have stemmed from, indeed raising the question of why African feminist perspectives have not been articulated as such and why a clouded lens of post-colonialism still pervades despite Western allusions to the contrary. Of greater relevance is the notion of Foundationalism. Foundationalism posits that the reality of the world exists in the form of a mosaic, composed of the material substances of a physical world. These materials are extraneous and independent of the human experience. Anti-foundationalism in contrast posits that there can be nothing independent of knowledge since the social construction of the world by human actors is what gives them their meaning, sense-making and ultimately their reality (Spiegel, 2017). It is here that by speaking through a lens of perception unknown and only assumed, Western and Eurocentric approaches to African feminist epistemologies have skewed knowledge in this disciplinary field.

Foundationalism and anti-foundationalism as the two most prominent ontological stances frame and determine epistemological stances or 'ways of knowing'. Most associated with the two distinctions in ontological stance are (a) empirical or positivist epistemology (the notion that world reality exists value-free and independently of man's knowledge of it) and (b) subjective or interpretivist epistemology (which posits that there is a social construction of the work that has engendered meaning and subjectivity).

The illumination of subjective interpretation of African feminist epistemology can therefore be regarded as a double hermeneutic, which negates the need for objectivity in the construction of new theoretical perspectives. The objective entity represented by the world means it is possible to generate specific questions or hypotheses which can be tested by direct observation. In this sense, there is a parallel position with natural science which also uses theoretical perspectives to generate new hypotheses that can also be tested by direct observation. In an ideal world, who undertakes this research ought to be an integral part of stating the researcher's positionality and epistemic stance.

If these suppositions hold, it is possible to state that the world itself represents an objective entity, which can subsequently be subject to verification and further investigation. Differentiating the aim of explaining action rather than the meaning of it is what characterises positivist inquiry. The interpretivist stance stands in contrast to this, positing that without perceived reality, things cannot exist. It is from this stance that interpretivist research seeks the multiple subjective realities of those experiencing specific phenomena i.e.) perspectives on African feminist epistemology from the perspective of men and women of African origin, whose own authentic experiences are most representative of this

METHODOLOGICAL AUTHENTICITY AND TRUSTWORTHINESS

There is an evident and frequently reported constructive alignment between ontology, epistemology, philosophy, methodology and methods (Choi and Richards, 2017). With this alignment, it is possible to see the assumed precedence of each in the context of African feminist research. There is inevitably an assumed resultant methodological stance that results as a direct consequence of differing ontological or epistemological origins. The collective consideration of all is essential in the context of African feminist research if there is to be an authentic degree of systematisation of emergent theoretical perspectives.

Since a dichotomy can exist between ontological and epistemological stances then it is possible to have alternative resultant views of the same phenomena in research. There is a functional dependence rather than a hierarchical sense of precedence between ontology, epistemology, philosophy, methodology and methods and it is this which provides an overarching means of knowing the world and developing a universal understanding of it.

Within a different signature discipline, African feminist epistemology provides an opportunity for new knowledge development and the making of the essential beliefs and values people hold into tangible objects or phenomena that act as central foci for the development of cognition and epistemological understanding. The trustworthiness and authenticity of findings ultimately lie in the transparency of how knowledge is created and by whom, with the epistemic stance of the researcher lying at the crux of their coherence.

In terms of operationally defining philosophical standpoint, it can be posited that this is where Interpretivist stances align with knowledge in the context of praxis. The resultant impact of it is to move epistemology or ways of knowing from a process of transactional gain to one of the facilitation of being able to articulate inherent experience alongside personal and collective belief (Russell and Martin, 2017). The epistemology of perception is such that the psychological or cognitive impact of sociology is permitted visibility and authentic resonance. Linked to this is the evocation of cognitive capacity, the potential for experience to add to epistemic cognition and the foundation of the debate as to whether cognitive and affective capacity are truly inseparable. These affective/emotive standpoints are pivotal to any consideration of applied sociological practice and understanding since they facilitate the theoretical embedding of social constructionism or situate it in broader contexts of contextualised human thought, which hold particular resonance concerning African feminist epistemology (Akoleowu, 2022).

Approaches to epistemological relativism across the interpretive research paradigm illustrate this, they can provide an alternative reflexive lens for examining the subtle difference between the production rather than the discovery of 'truth' in empirical inquiry (Latour, 1986). These approaches have the potential to be a mechanism of recognizing and segregating epistemic cognition since they permit research participants to define the world 'in their terms' (Latour, 1999). Whittle and Spicer's (2008) insight into knowledge acquisition highlights that, whether intentional or not, ethnocentrism within qualitative research methods, as highlighted by Bloomfield and Vurdubakis, (1999), implies that participant explanations are at best naïve or at their worst wrong, which can potentially frame some approaches as simply a series of grand narratives (Lee and Brown 1994). To be truly reflexive, though, necessitates a value-laden approach to all perceived realities having a degree of intrinsic truth. Where Western researchers have regularly fallen short, is in their willingness to acknowledge their role in the establishment of this. The conceptual common denominator in this process is cognition and it is at this point that the question of where human epistemology sits relative to human cognition is significant, certainly in the context of African feminist epistemology. Rand's (1990) response to this was to note that man's cognitive faculty is conceptual, which again stems back to the original nature of truth and knowledge (ontology).

Metaphysics embraces this context and is embedded in metacognition to form what is commonly termed epistemic cognition. From a metaphysical perspective, representation or meaning-making posits or evokes emotion and hence authentically posited African feminist epistemology becomes a means of making tangible metaphysics in the form of specific phenomena (Kitchener, 1983).

INTEGRATING CONCEPTUAL KNOWLEDGE AND PERCEIVED REALITY

History points towards the issues of African feminism being rooted in the raising of social consciousness of the injustice women experience on both a personal and collective level. It is the intersectional divide between their individual lives and the context of economics, sexual politics and identity framing which framed the context of what was commonly termed a feminist revolution in the 1970s Western and

Eurocentric societies. A key driver for this was the visual aesthetics of the era via art, which provided a nexus between politicised issues and the embodiment that women in contemporary society at the time were experiencing. Belying this was the initiation of early ethnographic studies where story-making for storytelling became an initial anchor for the mimetic representation of lived experience. Since works of art became central to this, then interpretation and meaning-making remained the power preserve of Western and Eurocentric influence and development. The notion of progress narratives not only illuminated lived experience; it also further enabled the clouding of authentic meaning by the Western and Eurocentric lenses of perspective placed upon it. As trajectories of time entailed, the global power dimensions inflicted by the Western and Eurocentric world have gradually and rightly started to be more critically regarded in terms of their relevance to contextually positioned political and sociocultural narratives. The whole concept of legitimate peripheral participation has now been framed and identified as a potential barrier to the construction of new, authentic and embodied, subjective knowledge. It is here that not only illuminates a void between truth and verisimilitude but on a more positive note provides a platform for the renegotiation and reworking of what the future of African feminist epistemology may become and what it might one day authentically represent within and between global sociocultural boundaries. On a positive note, this may lead to the future eminence of question-led rather than methods-driven approaches to African feminist research which can ultimately be hinged around the concept of situated cognition and the notion of embodied agentic enquiry. It is here that there is an evident opportunity for the constraints of Westernised and Eurocentric imperialism with historical origins in the extent of power held by major global geopolitical players to become a key consideration in any interrogation of where power lies and, in the identification, and approaches to new knowledge creation. Deconstruction of these inequities can only be made possible by handing back and acknowledging the authentic ownership of epistemology to spatial and temporal domains of embodied knowledge and understanding.

VISUAL REPRESENTATIONS OF AFRICAN FEMINIST EPISTEMOLOGY

The integration of conceptual knowledge with sense data facilitates how visual abstractions can be linked to cognition. This is framed in the conceptual designation or delivery of cognate mechanisms where sensory perception begins and ends, for example via the eyes, touch sensors in the skin, the ears or the nose concerning our ability to smell (Eisner, 2017). It can be posited that every living individual possesses their own perceived reality of the world, which can be regarded as subjective truth (Bruce and Young, 1998). Essentially there are four aspects of human experience which are of significance to epistemic cognition, namely:

1. Corporeality, which alludes to the notion of lived bodily experiences.
2. Spatiality, which considers the concept of lived space.
3. Relationality is directly concerned with lived human relationships.
4. Temporality is an engagement with the concept of lived time.

Because of these four aspects, methodologically speaking, the only credible, valid, and authentic person to disseminate the reality of lived experience is the subject themselves but these aspects can also become a relational element of acknowledged epistemic cognition by the researcher. Considering their interrelationships provides an insight into how Western and Eurocentric researchers, however well-intentioned, add the additional level of complexity of a post-colonial lens, in terms of their epistemic positionality and consequent epistemic bias. Understanding human behaviour and experience requires that the person must interpret the action or experience from the researcher and then the researcher must interpret the explanation provided by the person (Miščević, 2017). It is the most significant emotionally charged aspect of reality concept formation that ought to characterise question-led research, since all inquiry, however empirical still must stem from human inquiry and human curiosity (Jiménez *et al*, 2017). The significance of the phenomena is also important since it entails the selective recreation of objective reality rather than the metaphysical assumptions surrounding it at an epistemic level (Pollner, 1975). It is here that the authenticity of Western and Eurocentric-led research of African feminist epistemology can be contested and challenged within social science research both in terms of ethical responsibility and the morality of Western and Eurocentric research approaches.

Critical reflection and the capacity for reflexivity in the context of decision-making now characterise the majority of social science investigations (Kinsella, 2010). This has entrenched the notion of an ethical stance as an integral part of professional research practice. This lies in stark contrast to romantic epistemology, which advocated that imagination in conjunction and often in preference to rationalising ways of knowing was the greatest stance. It stems from the notion that accountability in terms of 'being' in the world belies the contextual and situational basis of how we might begin to 'know' in practice. From this perspective, it can be posited that epistemic reflexivity differs distinctly in terms of context specificity and that it is this which provides a mechanism of embedding what is epistemically and creatively derived back into processes of institutional approach, polemics, or technicality (Eisner, 2017).

Whilst creative practice offers no mechanism of addressing any empirical basis of truth, about the seeking of propositional knowledge, the opportunity to be at one with a representational object offers a means by which the transience of self-legitimised inner thoughts can be examined. As such it necessitates a re-examination of the pre-suppositions we make about how we 'know' and gain knowledge from anything non-propositional in nature and presentation.

The concept of a visual epistemology has its origins in the notion of a constructed and idealised mental imagery, which in turn is reflective of the cognitive processes involved in its making. African feminist epistemology is characterised by this across the various media by which it is presented. Once translated into a mimetic object, depiction via abstraction is possible, at the heart of which is thinking and creation. As such, the representation of worldviews and life worlds through images remains a contentious debate in the field of visual epistemology and one which can never be confined purely to the discipline of arts and creative practice and which has consequently occupied an intersectional space between them and social sciences. This leads clearly to what has been termed 'the epistemic potential of pictures' via visual thinking and perception which still has direct relevance to African feminist truth today (Klinke, 2014).

INTENTIONALITY AND WAYS OF KNOWING

Capacity for human reasoning and defence lies at the heart of propositional knowledge, the debate remains as to the relative impact of misrepresentation can potentially serve to skew processes and outcomes of knowledge creation. Klinke highlighted how Plato's "Allegory of the Cave" describes a system of epistemology in which there are three stages of understanding—from interpreting mere shadows to understanding that these are shadows only and grasping the ideas behind the apparent world. For Plato, those ideas, not the material world, are the highest forms of reality and constitute 'real knowledge' (Klinke,

2014). When applied to the context of African feminist epistemology, the resonance of needing to represent knowledge through experience rather than Western and Eurocentric perception of that experience is evident. It is here that the notion of Hermeneutical ignorance can be differentiated from many of the intentional Colonial perspectives that preceded it. Whereas current Western and Eurocentric approaches now seek to acknowledge the epistemic injustice that cultures and contexts have been subjected to over centuries of disempowerment, epistemic responsibility is still relatively misunderstood, misrepresented and misplaced in tokenistic attempts to right historical wrongs which still echo in the lives of African populations today (Ndofirepi & Gwaravanda, 2019). Only a clear differentiation between truth, verisimilitude and the doxastic injustice inflicted by Western and Eurocentric researchers, despite how well intentioned can begin to instil a sense of perspective transformation for those committed to authentic African feminism (Tobi, 2020).

Hermeneutical ignorance and doxastic injustice both impact the potential interactions from a moral political and ethical perspective for those whose lives have been historically misrepresented. Not only does misrepresentation of new knowledge impact the authenticity and trustworthiness of research undertaken, but it also has a broader impact in terms of the potential for intersectional epistemic injustice within and between cultural contexts (Jiménez et al, 2017). The perpetuation of colonialist perspectives on the articulation of experience through a Eurocentric lens only contributes further to the epistemic injustice inflicted within the context of African feminist epistemology. Traditionally approaches to hermeneutics have not permitted cognisance of the contextually situated values and beliefs of marginalised communities and this causes further damage to authentic accounts of cultural heritage (Horn, 2020). It can be contested stances adopted to the foundations of cultural heritage by Western and Eurocentric social science researchers and politicians whose focus remains in abstraction from the salient issues that these marginalised communities face daily (ibid, 2020). The resultant epistemic injustice can go on to influence whole cultures and their heritage not simply the individual people for whom African Feminism is an issue of fundamental significance (Agra, 2020).

Counterbalancing debates of doxastic injustice versus hermeneutical injustice concerning African feminist epistemology also warrants consideration of how efforts to decolonise traditionally labelled geographical contexts have failed. Whilst this has been far more apparent in South Africa versus the context of Sub-Saharan Africa, the need for a sense of epistemic decoloniality has long been posited. Harms' research indicated that Western and Eurocentric approaches to philosophy and theorising had engendered a series of professional identities which caused contradictory stances in terms of how the knowledge of those with the greatest authentic experience has often been posited as indigenous and peripheral to central political issues. Whilst the context of Harm's work is social work, the potential for transferability to similar contexts and settings is apparent where, for example in contexts of African feminist epistemology still heavily influenced or overshadowed by Coloniality characterised by power, the creation of new knowledge and existentialism, which frames future projected philosophical perspectives (Harms, 2019). African feminist epistemology ought also to be challenged in terms of its ideology and tradition. Understanding and embracing both provides a means of truly understanding the impact of power dynamics, the legacy of colonisation, despite repeated attempts to decolonise, and the acknowledgement of centuries of white supremacy. If a new template of individual and undiluted expression is to characterise the future of African feminist epistemology, then this rich history will serve to benchmark the socio-political landscape which is now a starting point for progressive change and authenticity (Akinkunmi, 2021).

CONCLUSION

This chapter, in keeping with the overall aim of the book has offered an alternative perspective in terms of the Western lens through which it is posited by the author, a UK academic. The chapter was written in recognition of the gross injustice, which has often characterised the lived experiences of African women and which has ensured their opinions have remained secondary to those dominant narratives of the West. The pivotal impact of these narratives has been discussed and this chapter has explored some of the intersectional bases of African feminist epistemology, such as race, gender, culture, and the polemic debates which serve to recognise and acknowledge the tensions that arise by theorizing from the perspective of post-colonial legacies and influences. Whilst, in theory, Feminism stemmed from the Enlightenment Period's ideologies of emancipation and social justice, the application of African feminist epistemology at best represents a contradiction where tokenistic efforts at co-construction and co-creation of truth are questionable in terms of their trustworthiness and authenticity about the concept of post-colonialism in Western and Eurocentric approaches. What is apparent from the chapter is the progressive development of purist rather than tokenistic approaches to African women's feminism which ought to prevail, if these women are ever to have a voice beyond that of spectator in their life trajectories and articulated journeys. To omit this is to omit the voices of truth from those with the authentic capacity to speak in the 21st Century. Western academia must recognise, acknowledge, and address this if true intellectual progress is ever to be made.

REFERENCES

Adebayo, K. O., & Njoku, E. T. (2023). Local and transnational identity, positionality and knowledge production in Africa and the African diaspora. *Field Methods*, *35*(1), 18–32. doi:10.1177/1525822X211051574

Agra, K. L. R. P. (2020). Epistemic Injustice, Epistemic Paralysis, and Epistemic Resistance: A (Feminist) Liberatory Approach to Epistemology. *Kritike: An Online Journal of Philosophy*, *14*(1).

Akinkunmi, K. (2021). An Analysis of "Encountering Development: The Making and Unmaking of the Third World" by Arturo Escobar. *Sustinere—The University of Toronto's Journal of Sustainable Development, 1*(1), 64-71.

Akoleowo, V. O. O. (2022). African feminism, activism and decolonisation: The case of Alimotu Pelewura. *African Identities*, 1–16. doi:10.1080/14725843.2022.2157246

Berenstain, N. (2016). *Epistemic exploitation.* Academic Press.

Bernecker, S. (2022). Knowledge from Falsehood and Truth-Closeness. *Philosophia*, *50*(4), 1623–1638. doi:10.100711406-022-00479-y

Bloomfield, B. P., & Vurdubakis, T. (1999). The outer limits: Monsters, actor networks and the writing of displacement. *Organization*, *6*(4), 625–647. doi:10.1177/135050849964004

Bruce, V., & Young, A. (1998). *In the eye of the beholder: The science of face perception.* Oxford university press.

Carter, J. A. (2017). Epistemological Implications of Relativism. In J. J. Ichikawa (Ed.), *The Routledge Handbook of Epistemic Contextualism*. Routledge. doi:10.4324/9781315745275-24

Choi, S., & Richards, K. (2017). *Interdisciplinary discourse: Communicating across disciplines*. Springer. doi:10.1057/978-1-137-47040-9

Cunliffe, A. L., & Scaratti, G. (2017). Embedding Impact in Engaged Research: Developing Socially Useful Knowledge through Dialogical Sensemaking. *British Journal of Management, 28*(1), 29–44. doi:10.1111/1467-8551.12204

Eisner, E. W. (2017). *The enlightened eye: Qualitative inquiry and the enhancement of educational practice*. Teachers College Press.

Falola, T. (2022). *Decolonizing African Knowledge: Autoethnography and African Epistemologies*. Cambridge University Press. doi:10.1017/9781009049634

Fox, H. M. (2017). A way of knowing in search of our true identity. *Self and Society, 45*(1), 72–75. do i:10.1080/03060497.2017.1290453

Harms Smith, L. (2019). *Epistemic decoloniality as a pedagogical movement: A turn to anticolonial theorists such as Fanon, Biko and Freire*. Taylor & Francis.

Hester, J. P. (2020). The Subjective Import of Moral Knowledge. *Humanities Bulletin, 3*(2), 140–156.

Horn, J. (2020). Decolonising emotional well-being and mental health in development: African feminist innovations. *Gender and Development, 28*(1), 85–98. doi:10.1080/13552074.2020.1717177

Hurlbut, C. D. (2021). *Crit: A Mixed Methods Examination of Epistemic Cognition During Source Evaluations*. McGill University.

Inkpin, A. (2021). Merleau-Ponty's 'sensible ideas' and embodied-embedded practice. *Phenomenology and the Cognitive Sciences*, 1–24.

Jackson, I., Watson, D. L., White, C. D., & Gallo, M. (2022). Research as (re) vision: Laying claim to oral history as a just-us research methodology. *International Journal of Research & Method in Education, 45*(4), 330–342. doi:10.1080/1743727X.2022.2076827

Jiménez, A. C., Galilei, G., Strathern, M., & Serres, M. (2017). How knowledge grows: an anthropological anamorphosis. *Cosmopolitics*, 227.

Kaplan, M., Sanchez, M., & Hoffman, J. (2017). Intergenerational Strategies for Establishing Sustainable Work Environments. In *Intergenerational Pathways to a Sustainable Society* (pp. 141–162). Springer International Publishing. doi:10.1007/978-3-319-47019-1_7

Kinsella, E. A. (2010). Professional knowledge and the epistemology of reflective practice. *Nursing Philosophy, 11*(1), 3–14. doi:10.1111/j.1466-769X.2009.00428.x PMID:20017878

Kitchner, K. S. (1983). Cognition, metacognition, and epistemic cognition. *Human Development, 26*(4), 222–232. doi:10.1159/000272885

Klinke, H. (Ed.). (2014). *Art theory as visual epistemology*. Cambridge Scholars Publishing.

Latour, B. (1986). Visualization and cognition. *Knowledge in Society*, *6*(6), 1–40.

Latour, B. (1999). *Pandora's hope: Essays on the reality of science studies*. Harvard university press.

Markauskaite, L., & Goodyear, P. (2017). Professional Epistemic Games. In *Epistemic Fluency and Professional Education* (pp. 395–434). Springer Netherlands. doi:10.1007/978-94-007-4369-4_14

Mellor, K. (2022). Developing a decolonial gaze: Articulating research/er positionality and relationship to colonial power. *Access: Critical Explorations of Equity in Higher Education, 10*(1), 26-41.

Miščević, N. (2017). Thought experiments in political philosophy. In *The Routledge companion to thought experiments* (pp. 153–170). Routledge. doi:10.4324/9781315175027-9

Ndofirepi, A. P., & Gwaravanda, E. T. (2019). Epistemic (in) justice in African universities: A perspective of the politics of knowledge. *Educational Review*, *71*(5), 581–594. doi:10.1080/00131911.2018.1459477

Nzegwu, N. (2019). African Art in Deep Time: De-race-ing Aesthetics and De-racializing Visual Art: Nzegwu African Art in Deep Time. *The Journal of Aesthetics and Art Criticism*, *77*(4), 367–378. doi:10.1111/jaac.12674

Ossome, L. (2020). African feminism. In *Routledge Handbook of Pan-Africanism* (pp. 159–170). Routledge. doi:10.4324/9780429020193-11

Park, C. L. (2017). Distinctions to promote an integrated perspective on meaning: Global meaning and meaning-making processes. *Journal of Constructivist Psychology*, *30*(1), 14–19. doi:10.1080/10720537.2015.1119082

Pollner, M. (1975). 'The very coinage of your brain': The anatomy of reality disjunctures. *Philosophy of the Social Sciences*, *5*(3), 411–430. doi:10.1177/004839317500500304

Rand, A. (1990). *Introduction to Objectivist Epistemology: Expanded* (2nd ed.). Penguin.

Russell, T., & Martin, A. K. (2017). Reflective practice: Epistemological perspectives on learning from experience in teacher education. *Reflective theory and practice in teacher education*, 27-47.

Simba, P., & Davids, N. (2020). Cultivating Third Space thinking in ('African') feminism through the works of Nandipha Mntambo. *Agenda (Durban, South Africa)*, *34*(3), 87–99. doi:10.1080/10130950.2020.1790302

Spiegel, T. J. (2017). 2 Naturalism, Quietism. *On What It Is: Perspectives on Metaphilosophy*, 47.

Stupples, P. (2017). Beyond the predicted: Expanding our understanding of creative agency in international development through practice and policy. *International Journal of Cultural Policy*, *23*(1), 52–67. doi:10.1080/10286632.2015.1035264

ter Vrugte, J., & de Jong, T. (2017). Self-Explanations in Game-Based Learning: From Tacit to Transferable Knowledge. In Instructional Techniques to Facilitate Learning and Motivation of Serious Games (pp. 141-159). Springer International Publishing.

Tobi, A. T. (2020). Towards a plausible account of epistemic decolonisation. *Philosophical Papers*, *49*(2), 253–278. doi:10.1080/05568641.2020.1779602

Van Veeren, E. (2019). Layered wanderings: Epistemic justice through the art of Wangechi Mutu and Njideka Akunyili Crosby. *International Feminist Journal of Politics*, *21*(3), 488–498. doi:10.1080/14616742.2019.1619468

Whittle, A., & Spicer, A. (2008). Is actor network theory critique? *Organization Studies*, *29*(4), 611–629. doi:10.1177/0170840607082223

Wielenga, C. (2022). African Feminisms and Justice on the Ground. *African Feminisms and Women in the Context of Justice in Southern Africa*, 19-39.

ADDITIONAL READING

Ahikire, J. (2014). African feminism in context: Reflections on the legitimation battles, victories and reversals. *Feminist Africa*, *19*(7), 7–23.

Bayu, E. K. (2019). A comparative analysis on the perspectives of African Feminism Vs Western Feminism: Philosophical debate with their criticism and its implication for womens rights in Ethiopia context. *International Journal of Sociology and Anthropology*, *11*(4), 54–58.

Dillard, C. B. (2000). The substance of things hoped for, the evidence of things not seen: Examining an endarkened feminist epistemology in educational research and leadership. *International Journal of Qualitative Studies in Education : QSE*, *13*(6), 661–681. doi:10.1080/09518390050211565

du Toit, L., & Coetzee, A. (2017). Gendering African philosophy, or: African feminism as decolonizing force. The Palgrave handbook of African philosophy, 333-347.

Griffiths, D. (2022). Decoloniality and the (im) possibility of an African feminist philosophy. *South African Journal of Philosophy*, *41*(3), 240–252. doi:10.1080/02580136.2022.2087144

Kwachou, M. (2022). In response to Acker: Black and African feminist theories on gender and education. *Comparative Education*, 1–24.

Lenine, E., & Alves, J. A. D. A. (2022). African feminisms and feminist political theory: Conceptual and epistemological encounters. *Revista Brasileira de Ciências Sociais*, 37. doi:10.1590/3711002/2022

Okech, A. (2020). African feminist epistemic communities and decoloniality. *Critical African Studies*, *12*(3), 313–329. doi:10.1080/21681392.2020.1810086

Oyewumi, O. (2000). Family bonds/conceptual binds: African notes on feminist epistemologies. *Signs (Chicago, Ill.)*, *25*(4), 1093–1098. doi:10.1086/495526

Segalo, P., & Fine, M. (2020). Under lying conditions of gender-based violence—Decolonial feminism meets epistemic ignorance: Critical transnational conversations. *Social and Personality Psychology Compass*, *14*(10), 1–10. doi:10.1111pc3.12568

KEY TERMS AND DEFINITIONS

Authenticity: The quality or condition of being authentic, trustworthy, or genuine.

Colonialism: The operational policy or practice of the acquisition of full or partial political control over other countries, occupying them with people who seek to exploit it both economically and socially.

Doxastic Injustice: Doxastic injustice serves to underpin the assumption that what is used to represent others can essentially be damaging to them in terms of what others believe as a consequence.

Epistemic Injustice: Epistemic injustice is pertains to knowledge which is used to misrepresent, exclude or silence authentic meaning. Often this can emanate from inequity in terms of power relations which has the potential to diminish value of the perceptions and opinions of underrepresented or marginalised individuals or communities.

Epistemic Responsibility: Epistemic responsibility is the that despite not having been able, as researchers to directly experience or reason with a specific positional stance that it is still worthy of belief and accurate articulation.

Hermeneutical Ignorance: Hermeneutical ignorance stems from dominantly positioned or situated creators of knowledge who refuse to acknowledge their own sense of epistemic bias in relation to those who are directly experienced in terms of credibility and dependability.

Intersectionality: Pertains to the interconnected nature of identifiable classifications such as gender, class, and race as applied to collective or individual groups, which contribute to a distinct overlap in terms of the emergence of discrimination and active disadvantage.

Perspective Transformation: A key seminal theory of Jack Mezirow (1978), Perspective Transformation pertains to a structural change in terms of self-perception. The process reformulates the process of critical reflexivity, resulting in new and much developed attitudes and behaviour.

Verisimilitude: Is the appearance of truth or reality rather than actual truth or reality.

Chapter 3
Rethinking Democratic Governance in African Politics

Basil Osayin Daudu
https://orcid.org/0009-0000-9162-9426
Kogi State University, Nigeria

Goddy Uwa Osimen
Covenant University, Nigeria

Amodu Salisu Ameh
Kogi State University, Nigeria

ABSTRACT

Good governance and accountability, amongst others, are hallmarks of a democratic system of government, practiced by most African countries. At the inception of democracy in most African nations, political parties were formed according to constitutional laws, and eligible candidates were voted into political office through elections. African politics is majorly marred with the problem of leadership as argued by most scholars and non-scholars alike. Against this backdrop, the lead questions are: Is democracy in Africa progressive or retrogressive? Is leadership the only major problem of African politics? In what practical ways can one ensure good governance in African politics? Thus, this chapter argues that every problem marring African politics is traceable to attitudinal crises, which must be addressed to guarantee and promote good governance in Africa.

INTRODUCTION

Most African nations got their independence in the 1960s and one would have thought that by now, these African nations would have put things in the right perspectives but the reverse is the case. What seems to be the problem? Is it systemic? Is it a lack of patriotism as Chinua Achebe and others have claimed? Or lack of vision as Karl Maier and others would say? What of the issue of dysfunctional institutions as other scholars have laid claim to? Thus, hardly can one find a country without a political structure! The

DOI: 10.4018/979-8-3693-0477-8.ch003

political structure of a nation has an impact on the other structures of the same nation. That is to say, failure in the political life of a nation is tantamount to failure in the other aspects of the same nation.

Presently, African politics is majorly democratic where elected representatives are at the helm of affairs and they are controlled by constitutional laws. But how true is this when some individuals see themselves as untouchable, people above the law as their interests precede the interest of the common good? The Constitution is legitimate, and on no account should it be compromised for selfish reasons by an individual, group of individuals, or political parties. Little wonder, the father of political Science, Aristotle sees the Constitution as the way of life the state has chosen for itself. He identified the constitution with government and argued that the best government is one that has the interest of its citizens (*Politics*, Book III, section 1279b; Barker 1962). The United States of America, for instance, has had several political leaders, presidents, and senators who returned to their private lives upon the completion of their tenure in office. But in Africa, the reverse is the case as political leaders prefer to die while in office. Even after they had reluctantly left office, they still wanted to receive government allowance (funds) for their past services. They have a sit-tight syndrome, which is an aberration of the highest order.

Furthermore, African people see politics as a profession or a career, a self-enriching business, "politics of the belly" (Bayart, 1993). At this point, one cannot but ask, is democracy in Africa genuine or pseudo? How can the interest of the governed be well represented? In response, several works have been done on good governance in African politics. The problems beclouding African politics as well as insightful recommendations in tackling the said problems have also been proffered by several scholars. Thus, lending our voice to the discourse, we spotted attitudinal crises as the root cause of the anomalies in African politics, which are intimately connected to the African person (be it the leader or the leader). And to liberate the African person caught in the web of attitudinal crises, the way out is the right perception, right mentality, and right attitude to politics. This will eventually ensure good governance in Africa.

Attitudinal Crisis Explained

According to (MacGregor, 2010), politics is the "driver of change' and the ultimate cause of people's security and access to justice" but in Africa, politics is marred with numerous setbacks which are traceable to attitudinal crisis, the crux of this chapter. But what exactly does attitudinal crisis mean? Attitudinal crisis refers to the wrong mindset attitude or disposition towards politics. It is prevalent in all African nations but it varies in degree from one African country to another. The attitudinal crisis is found in the leaders and the led, the agents and agencies of the political structure of a nation. Man by Aristotle, is a political animal. It is through politics that people's needs are met, that is, choosing their leaders through elections to meet their needs. But Africans are yet to understand and accept what ideal politics means. They are yet to know the difference between the "who" and the "what". The former refers to a mere or common perspective while the latter refers to the ideal. This is the reason why democracy as practised in Africa is termed pseudo. It is one thing to claim to have democracy and it is another thing to respect democratic principles. Running democracy in an African way will not yield positive results per se. when elected leaders fail to perform, to fulfil the promises they made during campaigns, it is a clear sign of attitudinal crisis on their part. This category of African leaders does not fit into Plato's description of a statesman because of their wrong attitude to politics.

Another area of interest is the coexistence of agents and agencies. By agencies, we mean political institutions manned by government and private workers or agents. These political institutions are legitimate in themselves, institutions such as the executive, judiciary, legislature, political parties, paramilitary outfits, government and private organizations. The legitimacy of these institutions can be threatened by the unchecked power of political parties. For instance, Nigeria as of 2015 is technically running a one-party system, APC (All Peoples Congress) the ruling party. Before 2015, it was PDP (People's Democratic Party). In all this, there is no room for inclusiveness. The ruling party is determined to rule over all the 36 states of Nigeria not minding what it takes to achieve it.

Appointments are made based on loyalty to the party and not to the country. Party members are placed in strategic positions to defend and promote the interest of the party and not the common good. Rules that will serve the interest of the masses or the common good are been bent in favour of the interest of the ruling party. In his social contract theory, John Locke recognizes the rights of the citizens and their power to change their elected leaders if they fail in their responsibilities. But can this be said of the Africans? It is pertinent to say that North Africans tend to be more likely than West Africans to resist bad government. This resistance could be bloody at the expense of lives and property utterly destroyed. In a nutshell, the attitudinal crisis occurs will leaders are after their interest rather than the interest of the people, and when the people or the leaders are comfortable with their pathetic state under an irresponsible and irresponsive government.

BACKGROUND

Africa and its democratic journey thus far

In the 21st Century, the system of government practised in most African countries is democracy. The meaning of democracy is equivocal. Nevertheless, a democratic system of government entrusts power to the people. In this regard, democracy has been remade in Africa (Bates, 2010). Democracy is a political competition (Schumpeter, 1950) recognizing equal rights and freedom of rival political parties (Dahl, 1971). Generally speaking, the underlying principles of democracy are legitimacy (acceptance and recognition of the power to govern), separation of powers (power shared between the executive, legislature, and judiciary arms of government), popular participation (direct or representative leadership), periodic elections (avenues for electing leaders), checks and balances (limited power), rule of law (supremacy of the law) and fundamental human rights (inalienable and immutable) (Edeh, 2020). On democratic performance (based on electoral processes, political culture, participation, government functioning, and civil liberties), Oluwole (2023) reported that "virtually no one in Africa lives under full democracy, aside from Mauritius. Only 12% of countries in Africa are operating at some type of democracy."

According to the Economist Intelligence Unit (EIU), the top 10 African countries leading in the Democracy Index are Mauritius (8.14), Botswana (7.81), Cape Verde (7.67) Namibia (7.20), Ghana (6.95), Senegal (6.88), South Africa (6.83), Tunisia (6.67), Kenya (6.55) and Madagascar (5.70) (cited in Oluwole, 2023). As of 2022, Mauritius' democracy was given 8.14 points. The index is based, according to the source, on the electoral process and pluralism, the government functions, political participation, and culture as well as civil liberties. Many Sub-Saharan and North African political systems are among the least democratic countries in the world. The Democratic Republic of the Congo has the most authoritarian regime in Africa and the fourth worldwide, after North Korea. Further, countries such as Cabo Verde, Botswana, South Africa, Namibia, Ghana, and Lesotho fell within the "hybrid regimes", with a score ranging from 6.3 points to 7.65 points, meaning that they experienced, for example, elections with irregularities, widespread corruption, and harassment of journalists.

Economist Intelligence Unit (2022) reported that In the year 2022, out of 167 countries in the world, 44 countries from Sub-Saharan Africa, 23 are authoritarian, 14 are hybrid regimes, 6 are flawed democracies and 1 is full democracy all with an average score of 4.14 while 20 countries from the Middle East and North Africa of which 17 are authoritarian, 2 are hybrid regimes, 1 is flawed democracy and none is full democracy all with an average score of 3.34. Thus, none of the African countries is recorded under full democracy. Flawed democracy (Botswana, Ghana, Lesotho, Nambia and South Africa), hybrid regime (Morocco, Ivory Coast, Kenya, Nigeria, and Malawi), and authoritarian regime (Sudan, Cameron, Mali, Angola and Egypt).

In the late 1990s, African states migrated from military to civil rule but it is saddening that some African countries have gone back to military rule as coups have become the order of the day. Schultes (2022) reported that in 2021 four successful coups took place and the affected African countries were Chad, Guinea, Mali, and Sudan. In 2022, a successful coup took place in Burkina Faso and a failed coup attempt in Guinea-Bissau. In the same vein, Powell & Thyne (2011) submit that African countries such as Burkina Faso, Guinea, and Mali have had a series of coups within the past 15 years. On his part, Baltoi (2023) reported that some parts of West Africa have had Coup d'états over the last three years- Mali (August 2020 and May 2021), Guinea (September 2021), and Burkina Faso (January and September 2022). Regional instability, poor governance, and a series of successful past coups are some of the factors responsible and if care is not taken, the other West African states will experience coups. Aly Tounkara argues that the "lack of integrity of leaders is responsible for security challenges, serve as fertile grounds for coups (cited in Baltoi, 2023). War, coups, and attacks on democratic institutions by illiberal incumbents weaken democratic practice (Gorokhovskaia, Shahbaz, & Slipowitz, 2023).

A successful coup d'état took place in Niger on 26 July 2023 in which President Mohamed Bazoum was placed under house arrest by his guard commander general Abdourahamane Tchiani and proclaimed himself as the leader of a new military junta. Fact Sheet (2023) reported that Niger has experienced continuous growth in jihadist activity since 2018, with a record year for violence in 2021 measured by fatalities while the number of political violence incidents increased further in 2022, the lethality of the violence has steadily declined, with a significant overall decrease in fatalities last year. In the first six months of 2023, political unrest decreased by an estimated 39% when compared to the previous six-month period from July to December 2022 attacks on civilians decreased by 49%, and resulting fatalities decreased by 16% operations by the Nigerien security forces increased by 32%, however, as part of a continuous effort to counter insecurity cases of looting and property destruction were the most common type of incident during this period, suggesting that militant groups such as IS Sahel and JNIM increasingly see Niger as a key target for resource extraction.

Another coup took place in oil-producing Gabon on 30th August, 2023. On the issue, Obangome (2023) reported that on Wednesday 30th August 2023 military officers declared they had seized power, placing President Ali Bongo (president of Gabon) under house arrest and naming a new leader after the Central African state's election body announced Bongo had won a third term. Hundreds of people celebrated the military's intervention in the streets of the Gabonese capital Libreville, while the United Nations, African Union, and France, Gabon's former colonial ruler which has troops stationed there, condemned the coup. Military officers have also seized power in Mali, Guinea, Burkina Faso, and Chad, erasing democratic gains since the 1990s and raising fear among foreign powers that have strategic interests in the region. "I am marching today because I am joyful. After almost 60 years, the Bongos are out of power," said Jules Lebigui, a jobless 27-year-old who joined crowds in Libreville. Thus, democratic practice in Africa is not entirely rosy as it is marred by some constraints such as coups, dirty politics and corruption. All this is a reflection of poor governance, which is an end condition of failure and collapse of governmental institutions and structures (Yagboyaju & Akinola, 2019).

Limiting Factors Against Democratic Practice in Africa

The limiting factors to be considered in this chapter are coups, dirty politics and corruption.

Coups

Coups d'état is the "greatest threat to the survival of democracy" (Marsteintredet & Malamud, 2019). As Powell & Thyme assert, coups are "overt attempts by the military or other elites within the state apparatus to unseat the sitting head of state using unconstitutional means. A coup attempt is defined as successful if the coup perpetrators seize and hold power for at least seven days" (cited in Mo Ibrahim Foundation, 2022). It signifies an unconstitutional seizure of power. Ordinarily, nobody in his or her right mentality would want to be ruled by the military because it is believed that the military is brutal. But in a situation like that of Niger where the military took over the government and the citizens were happy with the change in government, simply tells them how democratic elected leaders have failed woefully. In the same vein, Research Network Afro Barometer Surveys (2023) revealed that the number of people supporting democracy and elections in Africa has fallen. Only 68% of respondents across 34 countries preferred democracy to any other system of government, down from 73% a decade ago.

According to Anthony Butler, "In a democracy, you can say what you like as long as you do what you are told" (cited in Malone, 1990, p. 227). So, they should resort to fate under military rule rather than the rule of a pseudo-democracy. Military rule in a way, is not bad because citizens tend to behave well in a military rule than in a democratic system. Also, in some African countries, the death rate of civilians due to religious, political, and ethnic conflicts and insurgency in a democratic dispensation is higher than the one recorded during military rule. With the return of military rule, West Africa is affected most compared to other African regions.

Dirty Politics

There is no perfect political system anywhere in the world but when laid down electoral procedures are strictly observed and the voice of the citizens is respected, it is a kudos. Can this be said of African politics? Certainly not! African politics is fluctuating and the electoral means or avenues used for electing leaders into political offices, most times, are marred with violence, protest, hate speech, and character assassination by party members and supporters. This calls for serious interventions from international bodies.

The period of campaign in preparation for elections is always a busy one as efforts are put in place by political parties and actors to ensure their preferred candidates win. Campaign promises are an important aspect of representative democracy but some politicians go as far as using violent means to win elections. It is during campaigns that politicians or political aspirants are more committed to meeting the needs of their people to gain their trust, vote, or support. This is very disheartening as the electorate or voters are only seen as a means to an end rather than an end in themselves. Most African politicians make empty promises to the people, playing on people's intelligence. They come up with fascinating political manifestos that sound convincing but their actions afterwards contradict the promises they initially made before the election. Fake campaign promises and voters' inducements are some of the political means used by politicians or political aspirants to manipulate voters or the electorate. This undermines the credibility of an election. Must Africans continue in this kind of political deceit? The answer is no! There is always room for change and to do better.

Another disturbing area in African politics is the rebellious act of the losing parties when elections are over. Most times, the problem here is not the political aspirants or candidates per se but their party godfathers, members, and supporters. They invested so much resources campaigning for their preferred candidate(s) with the hope of being compensated with political appointments in the future. They ascribed titles to themselves such as senators, ministers, and commissioners even before the announcement of election results. They, therefore, become disappointed, and depressed when their preferred candidate(s) or party did not win. As such, they began transferring aggression; making the government unbearable for the declared winner or winning party. But this crisis can be resolved through the "policy of inclusiveness" on the part of the winning party in carrying everyone along. In other words, the winning party ought to allow even the opposition parties to contribute their quota to the progress of the nation.

A victorious president ought to know that he or she is elected to be president of a country and not his or her political party. The same goes for all political appointees. The attitudinal crisis in African politics is seen in the African attitude to politics and compromising agencies or institutions. One cannot imagine the deadly effects that would arise when electoral institutions, paramilitary architecture, and the judiciary organ allow themselves to be influenced by politicians or incumbent political leaders.

Elections, Fake Campaign Promises and Voters' Inducements

In response to the question, "Who will guard the guardians?" Gerald Pomper gave an outright answer: "Those who choose the guardians." But in what way? The answer is, via election (1968). According to Mmaduabuchi (2015), voting gives life to elections while elections give life to democracy (p. 222). Elections are central to the practice of democracy. They are the basis of democracy. Elections are processes through which people choose their leaders and indicate their preferred public policies and programmes by voting (Mmaduabuchi, 2015, p. 211). An election is an essential element of a democratic system of government, a means through which leaders are democratically elected. Elections are processes through which people choose their leaders and indicate their preferred public policies and programs by voting. Elections also serve as a means through which citizens of a given society reject those they do not want to be governed by or leaders who have not governed well. Elections are vital to the practice of democracy. They form the basis of democracy. According to Ranney (1974), elections are used to "establish popular control over public officials" and to "create popular support for leaders and policies".

Generally, elections have two functions: First, to provide a mechanism through which to punish poor-performing incumbents and in so doing to create incentives for better performance (Ferejohn, 1986); and second, to provide a mechanism through which voters can select high-quality leaders (Besley, 2005). Teshome-Bahiru (2008) opines that many elections have failed to produce democracy in Africa instead they produced fraudulent leadership while contributing to the erosion of legitimacy. Onoge (1997) argues that the demarcation project in Africa is essentially dominated by an emphasis on the type of government in place, with little or no consideration for the authentic participation of the people. Mbaku (2020) submits that in Africa, elections perform at least three important democratizing functions: They (1) help the continent build and sustain effective democratic institutions; (2) provide the people with an effective legal tool to constrain and guard the government and minimize impunity; and (3) enhance the ability of the people to change their government and bring into public service new and more energetic and effective political leaders. Nevertheless, for elections to perform these three important functions and do so effectively, these elections must (i) be regular, not infrequent; and (ii) fair, free, competitive, inclusive, transparent, and credible.

African politics is festooned with attitudinal crisis and the African person, one way or the other is influenced by the crisis. Political culture, according to Ake (1967), is the "system of empirical beliefs, expressive symbols, and values which define the situation in which political action takes place". For Walton and Smith (2000), political culture is "the individual's attitudes, beliefs and values about politics and the political system". African attitude towards elections and political offices is very shallow. Even though there are existing laid-down procedures on how elections should be conducted, political parties still want to have it their way or should we say, play politics in the African way, which undermines the ideals of transparent politics and a democratic system of government. Politics, for most African politicians, is a do-or-die duel. The politics of a country cannot and will not survive without transparent and legitimate institutions. Such a country or nation is on its way to total collapse. Further, it is no news that constitutional laws and bodies responsible for the conduct of elections in Africa are been compromised by the elites (political godfathers, and business tycoons, among others). They see themselves as demigods and can influence government decisions.

Election or campaign promises are necessary tools to guarantee victory in elections. In themselves, campaign promises are absolutely important and good but bad, when the issuer fails to deliver his part of the bargain between himself and the electorate and the citizens at large. Campaign promises provide a mechanism for voters to select among multiple equilibria in a repeated game, much like a focal point. Campaign promises affect voters' expectations about what policies will be chosen by an elected official, and they provide a benchmark for voters to link policy decisions with future re-election (Aragonès, Postlewaite, and Palfrey, 2007). Election campaign promises are formally expressed through a manifesto, which is essentially a list of policies that a political party says it will enact if it is voted into office at a general election. The word "manifesto" is a derivative of the Latin word, *manifestum*, which refers to a list of facts. It is "a published declaration of the intentions, motives, or views of the issuers, be it an individual, group, political party or government. Candidates make promises to signal to voters their intentions in office and voters evaluate candidates based on those promises" (Bonilla, 2021).

According to Hornby (2006), a manifesto is a "written statement in which a group of people, especially a political party, explains their beliefs and say what they will do if they win an election" (p.898). Before an election, each party will produce an official manifesto which will form the basis of its campaign. Manifestos serve a very important function because they are the main way of telling voters why they should give their vote to a particular political party. When a political manifesto is not actualized in the long run, the problem is not the manifesto itself but the issuer of the manifesto- the political party or candidate. Most times, their true intention is not the wording as contained in the manifesto but their selfish interests when elected into office. In this regard, their manifestos serve as a deceiving tool to the masses. And once they assume office, their "true nature" unveils; a nature of corruption, lordship, and dictatorship. No wonder Sean Hughes submits that "a politician is a person who has nothing to say but says it anyway" (cited in Malone, 1990, p. 227).

Another product of attitudinal crises in African politics is voters' inducements. Vote buying is an inducing item politicians use to persuade voters to do their bidding or to gain their support. It is of varied forms, viz. money, gifts, fake promises, and diabolic means, amongst others. Vote buying is the "direct exchange of benefit and material goods by the political elites to propel electoral support" (Carreras and

Irepoglu, 2013). It also includes "buying of the voting shares or payments made to voters to influence them to vote for a specific candidate" (Nichter, 2014). These rewards could include cash, goods, service, position, kind, or anything that benefits the said receiver to sway them over (Nichter, 2014). Vote buying is also an economic transaction just like buying and selling commodities such as shoes, bags, and foodstuff based on demand and supply so as the electorates are willing to sell, candidates are also available to buy (Fredrick and Andreas, 2005). It is pertinent to say that vote buying cuts across all countries be it developed or developing countries but it differs in manifestation, level, or magnitude.

Approaches to vote buying could be payment for a vote and vote for payment (Adetoye, and Omilusi, 2016; Onuoha and Ojo, 2018). In the former, vote buying is greatly based on trust the buyer puts on the seller while in the former, vote buying is based on trust the vote seller puts on the buyer. (Onuoha and Ojo, 2018). Factors responsible for vote buying are poverty, lack of trust in the government, lack of voter education and enlightenment, and lack of operation of electoral laws and sanctions (Bratton, 2008; Carreras and Irepoglu, 2013; Jensen and Justesen, 2014).

Corruption

Corruption is the nefarious manner through which people particularly those not qualified seek preferential or special favour through offering or accepting of bribes, gifts, and kickbacks (Aimola, 2003, p. 42). It is the "misuse of entrusted power for private benefits" (Agbibboa, 2012). According to Hornby (2006), corruption is dishonest or illegal behaviour, especially of people in authority (p. 329). It is an abuse of public office. Plato was right to say that "when people of corrupt minds labour for the state, the state will start degenerating because the corruption of the state implies the corruption of the character of the citizens" (cited in Baker, 1979). In the same vein, Achebe (1988) asserts, "Without doubt, corruption has permeated the African society and anyone who can say that corruption in Africa has not become alarming is either a fool, a crook, or else does not live in this continent." Corruption is one of the ways poor governance manifests itself in African economies (Kimenyi & Mbaku, 2011). Corruption is now a lifestyle for many in Africa, which is quite worrisome.

Resolving Attitudinal Crises in African Politics

African politics is marred with lots of constraints traceable to attitudinal crises intrinsic to all Africans whether leaders or the led. This concern can be addressed from two angles, viz. political office as service to humanity and why democratic governance matters.

Political Office, Call to Service, Not Lordship or Profession

The United States of America, for instance, has had several political leaders, presidents, and senators who returned to their private lives upon the completion of their tenure in office. But in Africa, the reverse is the case as political leaders prefer to die while in office. Even after they had reluctantly left office, they are still receiving government allowance (funds) for their past services. They have a sit-tight syndrome. This is an aberration of the highest order. A good number of African heads of state have moved to undermine term limits or rig elections to remain in power (Campbell and Quinn, 2021). In Africa, people see politics as a profession or a career, a self-enriching business, "politics of the belly" (Bayart, 1993). In the same vein, Okunloye (2017) speaks of monetized politics. Okunloye (2017) writes:

The monetization of politics refers to the conception, pattern of behaviours, and the relationship between/ among organizational activists, organizational contributors, opinion leaders, voters, and non-voters involving the use of different forms of giving and taking of monetary or material inducements to secure varieties of political patronage, allegiance, support or favour before, during and after intra-party or general elections in a political system. It may involve rent-a-crowd political rallies, press conferences, political processions/demonstrations of opposition or support, voting, manipulation of the voting procedure against or in favour of specific political parties and candidates, provision of security coverage/report to compromise the electoral process, etc. based on offered or accepted monetary or material inducements.

Seeing politics as a business venture is a misconception. Politics is not lordship, profession, or career but rather a call to serve humanity. A political office is a privileged office to give your best in serving your country or state. Also, some African leaders confused democracy with monarchy or dictatorship they desired to die in office. For instance, Teodoro Obiang Nguema Mbasogo of Equatorial Guinea spent 44 years in office, Omar Bongo Ondimba (Gabon 42 years), Paul Biya (Cameroon 41 years), Denis Sassou Nguesso (Republic of Congo 39 years), José Eduardo dos Santos (Angola 38 years), Gnassingbé Eyadéma (Togo 38 years), Yoweri Museveni (Uganda 38 years), Robert Mugabe (Zimbabwe 38 years), Félix Houphouët-Boigny (Ivory Coast 33 years), Isaias Afwerki (Eritrea 32 years), Mobutu Sese Seko (Democratic Republic of Congo 31 years), Idriss Déby (Chad 30 years), Hastings Kamuzu Banda (Malawi 30 years), Omar al-Bashir (Sudan 30 years), Mathieu Kérékou (Benin 28 years) and Ismaïl Omar Guelleh (Djibouti 24 years) (Klobucista & Ferragamo, 2023). In a democratic dispensation, a political office is not monarchical or hereditary. In other words, democracy is not a monarchical or dictatorial system of government. It is not a lordship system as found in a monarchy where the king or queen or the royal house has absolute power.

Democracy, so to speak, is the government of the people where power lies with the people and not the elected leaders per se. The people are the true leaders while the elected leaders are servants to the people. They are representatives of the people chosen by the people via elections based on the people's votes, for everyone cannot be a leader at the same time. For some, democracy means "meaningful political citizenship" (Grugel, 200). Heater (1964) sees democracy as a form of government, a way of life, or an attitude of the mind. To him, democracy is essentially a method of organizing society politically. He says "There are, it is suggested, five basic elements without which no community can call itself truly democratic. These elements are equality, sovereignty of the people, respect for human life, the rule of law, and liberty of the individual (Heater, 1964). As Ake (1990, p. 2) asserts, "Africa needs democracy not only because is desirable in itself but because it will greatly facilitate development. For him, authoritarianism is not conducive to economic growth in Africa because: (i) It turns politics into warfare, that is, siege mentality. (ii) The leaders are disconnected from their people and public policy dissociated from social needs. (iii) There is constant coercion of the people which has alienated them from the state. (iv) It permits great waste of human resources, the engine of development (cited in Anifowose and Enemuo, 2015). Democracy is now widely accepted as the best method to use for national government. It could also mean "a set of rights or an entire way of organizing the political and economic life of a state" (Catt, 1999).

Furthermore, a political office ought to be responsible responsive, and manned by people of integrity. It is not a child's play. It is not an office for wealth accumulation. On the issue of leadership, Achebe (1983) sees leaders as "role models whose behaviour and mannerisms are emulated by others. Leaders must be self-disciplined" (p. 1). According to Thomson (2010), many of the political elites in Africa, both incumbents and opposition, are only using multi-party democracy instrumentally. In other words, they support pluralism because it is a method of retaining or gaining power, not because they inherently believe in its moral value (pp. 259-260). This is the mentality of most Africans. It is all about political interests. No matter the interest, the interest of the common good should come first. When political candidates or aspirants win elections, they are been celebrated, receiving goodwill or congratulatory messages from people. A careful study of these congratulatory messages reveals that most of them are borne out of the wrong perception of what a political office is meant for. Congratulating political winners, given the wealth that awaits them, oh! It is their turn to enjoy, to make money, and to rule, to acquire power and their voice heard. An example is the utterance of the newly elected president of Nigeria, Bola Ahmed Tinubu who before the presidential election, publicly declared that "it is his turn to rule Nigeria" (*The Sun Nigeria*, 2 June 2022). What a remark! Is Nigeria now a piece of furniture? This is a clear indication of a wrong perception of what politics entails.

Plato was right to define justice as "the right ordering of the state, with every man keeping his appointed place" (cited in Lewis, 1970, p. 42). By implication, when the wrong set of people are in office, injustice prevails. Political leaders are representatives (especially senators and ministers) of their constituencies but some of them do not know what political representation entails. For them, it is about attending occasions and donating funds. This is wrong! Good representation means meeting the needs of the people as the people's interest should be paramount.

Why Democratic Governance Matters

Good governance and accountability are major indices for measuring the success of democratic practice. Democracy is not the only system of government practised in the world but its packages are so enticing and welcoming hold the people (the led) in high esteem. No wonder H. L. Mencken asserts that "democracy is too good to share with just anybody" (cited in Malone, 1990, p. 227). In Africa, democratic practice seems expensive as a lot of funds are needed to run it. That is why some people are agitating for its rejection, especially in Africa. For instance, in Nigeria, the allowance of political appointees is very high. According to Revenue Mobilizations Allocation and Fiscal Package (2023), the 36 State governors in Nigeria each earn a monthly basic salary of N2,223,705 a yearly pay of N11,540,896 as well as an annual leave allowance of N222,370.50. In the same country, medical workers and teachers are underpaid. As such, there is a need to review the take-home salaries of Nigerian political appointees. One way of dealing with this is to make their salaries less attractive. Mo Ibrahim Foundation (2022) identified security and rule of law, participation, rights and inclusion, foundations for economic opportunity, and human development as the four pillars of the overall governance score. The World Bank (1994) identified three distinct aspects of governance, viz. (i) the form of political regime; (ii) the process by which authority is exercised in the management of a country's economic and social resources for development; and (iii) the capacity of governments to design, formulate, and implement policies and discharge functions.

In its written memorandum to parliament on Democracy and Human Rights in Sweden's Development Cooperation, The Government of Sweden defines "good governance" as a good system of government encompassing the state's way of exercising its political, economic, and administrative powers. It maintains that both institutions and processes ought to be based on the principles of the rule of law and should be characterised by responsibility, openness, integrity, and efficiency (SIDA, 2002). Ogundiya (2020) argues that the matter of good governance is confined to culture and is system-bound in the sense that governance protects people's lives, caters to their culture, and ensures their co-existence. It is also based on the historical background that a nation's constitution is being formulated. The inability of those in control of political power to ensure proper management of social, economic, and social institutions constitutes bad governance. According to the World Bank (1992), characteristics of bad governance are Failure to ensure clear separation between what is public and private, thus, the inclination of diverting public funds to private gain; failure to establish a predictable framework for law and government behaviour in a way that is conducive to development or arbitrariness in application of rules and laws; excessive rules, functioning of markets and encourage rent-seeking; priorities that are inconsistent with development, thereby, leading to misallocation of resources and excessively narrow base for, or non-transparencies, decision-making.

According to SIDA (2022), key institutions of good governance are a democratic constitution, a government and a parliament with its controlling functions, a central bank, national and local authorities, an independent judiciary, independent mass media, and an active civil society i.e. the basic democratic institutions and processes. Through institutions, certain processes play a more central role in good governance, by reforms of public authorities, decentralization of budget processes, etc. Good governance entails that responsibility and transparency are reinforced and that real participation is fostered, which implies that the link with democracy becomes much clearer and that good governance reinforces democracy and vice versa. Strengthening good governance is thus in the long term to support the consolidation of democracy (SIDA, 2002).

CONCLUSION

Not all African countries are on the same pedestal when it comes to the idea of good governance. Some African nations have good democratic track records than others but on a general note, attitudinal crisis is the core problem in African politics. This problem involves all Africans, be it the leaders, and the governed. Attitudinal crisis refers to African wrong mindset and attitude toward politics, which undermines the principles of good governance. Thus, correcting the crisis will result in sustainable good governance in Africa. Okafor (2006) described the anomalies in African politics as "a politically unstable polity, which can be likened to a human mind that is unstable he/she lacks the capacity for the calm judgment and calculations required for success in life (p. 30). Both the leaders and the leaders are equally involved in this political mess. Fake campaigns or election promises and voters' inducements are tools in the hands of most African political parties and candidates to deceive and exploit the electorate. However, voters and the masses at large, cannot claim to be ignorant of politicians' Trojan horse. Everyone is equal before the law and ought to be patriotic to the core, putting the interest of their beloved state, nation, country, and continent first before individual, party, religious, and ethnic interests. There lies a great future for African politics if and only if Africans can change their wrong mentality and attitude towards elections and democratic practice.

REFERENCES

Achebe, C. (1983). *The Trouble with Nigeria.* Heinemann.

Adetoye, D., & Omilusi, M. (2016). Pains of Development and Electoral Politics in Nigeria's Democracy: Ekiti State in Perspective. *European Journal of Research in Social Sciences*, *4*(1), 27–33.

Adetula, V. A. O. (2011). *Measuring democracy and good governance in Africa: A critique of assumptions and methods.* HSRC Press.

Agbiboa, D. E. (2012). Saving the few, starving the many: How corruption underdeveloped Nigeria and how there is an alternative perspective to corruption cleanups. *Africa Today*, *58*(40).

Aimola, B. F. (n.d.). *Citizenship Education for National Re-orientation: A Handbook for Nigerians.* Loyce Graphic Printer & Publishers.

Ake, C. (1967). *A Theory of Political Integration.* The Dorsey Press, Inc.

Ake, C. (1990). *The case for democracy in The Carter Centre African governance in the 1990s: Objectives, Resources and Constraints.* The Carter Centre of Emory University.

Anifowose, R., & Enemuo, F. (2015). *Elements of Politics* (2nd ed.). Sam Iroanusi Publications.

Annan, K. (1999). *Preventing War and Disaster.* Annual Report on the Work of the Organization.

Aragonès, E., Postlewaite, A., & Palfrey, T. (2007). Political Reputations and Campaign Promises. *Journal of the European Economic Association*, *5*(4), 846–884. doi:10.1162/JEEA.2007.5.4.846

Aristotle. *Politics*, Book III, section 1279b.

Babatope, E. (1997). *The Struggle for Democracy in Nigeria.* Ebino Topsy.

Baltoi, D. (2023). *A deeper look into the West African Coup Wave.* Foreign Policy Research Institute.

Barash, D. P. (2001). *Understanding Violence.* Allyn and Bacon.

Barker, E. (1979). *Greek political theory: Plato and his predecessors.* Methuen and Co.

Bates, R. H. (2010). Democracy in Africa: A Very Short History. *Social Research*, *77*(4), 1133–1148. doi:10.1353or.2010.0036

Bayart, J. F. (1993). *The State in Africa: The Politics of the Belly.* Longman.

Besley, T. (2005). Political Selection. *The Journal of Economic Perspectives*, *19*(3), 43–60. doi:10.1257/089533005774357761

Bonilla, T. (2021). *The Importance of Campaign Promises.* Cambridge University Press.

Bratton, M. (2008). Vote buying and violence in Nigerian election campaigns. *Electoral Studies*, *27*(4), 621–632. doi:10.1016/j.electstud.2008.04.013

Campbell, J., & Quinn, N. (2021). What's happening to Democracy in Africa? Carreras, M and Irepoglu, Y (2013). Trust in elections, vote buying, and turnout in Latin America. *Electoral Studies*, *32*, 609–619.

Carreras, M., & Irepoglu, Y. (2013). Trust in elections, vote buying, and turnout in Latin America. *Electoral Studies*, *32*, 609–619.

Catt, H. (1999). *Democracy in practice*. Routledge. doi:10.4324/9780203270240

Dahl, R. (1995). *Modern Political Analysis*. Prentice Hall of India.

Economist Intelligence Unit. (2023). *Democracy Index 2022: Frontline democracy and the battle for Ukraine*. https://pages.eiu.com/rs/753-RIQ-438/images/DI-final-ver sion-report.pdf

Edeh, S. C. (2020). *Pillars of Democracy: 7 Essential Pillars of a Democratic Government*. https://bscholarly.com/pillars-of-democracy/

Fact Sheet. (2023). *Military Coup in Niger*. https://acleddata.com/2023/08/03/fact-sheet-military-coup-in-niger/

Ferejohn, J. (1986). Incumbent performance and electoral control. *Public Choice*, *50*(1), 5–25. doi:10.1007/BF00124924

Gorokhovskaia, Y., Shahbaz, A., & Slipowitz, A. (2023). *Marking 50 Years in the Struggle for Democracy*. Freedom in the World. Freedom House.

Grugel, J. (2002). *Democratization: A Critical Introduction*. Palgrave Macmillan.

Heater, D. B. (1964). *Political ideas in the modern world*. George G. Harrap & Co. Ltd.

Hornby, A. S. (2006). *Oxford Advanced Learner's Dictionary of Current English* (7th ed.). Oxford University Press.

Ibrahim, S. G., Oranyeli, S. O., & Bibi, F. I. (2021). Challenges of Democratization in Africa, North Asia. *International Research Journal of Business Economics & Management*, *5*(9). Advance online publication. doi:10.6947/2277-1018.2021.00009.8

International Institute for Democracy and Electoral Assistance. (2017). *The fundamentals of a constitution*. https://www.idea.int/sites/default/files/publications/the-fundamentals-of-a-constitution.pdf

Jensen, P. S., & Justesen, M. K. (2014). Poverty and vote buying: Survey-based evidence from Africa. *Electoral Studies*, *33*, 220–232. doi:10.1016/j.electstud.2013.07.020

Kimenyi, N. S. & Mbaku, J. K. (2011). Africa's war on corruption: foresight Africa: The continent's greatest challenges and opportunities. *The Brookings Institutions*, 30-32.

Klobucista, C., & Mariel Ferragamo, M. (2023). *Africa's 'Leaders for Life*. Council on Foreign Relations.

Lewis, J. (1970). *History of Philosophy*. The English Universities Press Ltd.

Linz, J. J., & Stephan, A. (1996). Towards Democratic Consolidated Democracy. *Journal of Democracy*, *7*(2), 45–57. doi:10.1353/jod.1996.0031

MacGregor, S. (2010). *The Politics of Poverty: Elites, Citizens and States: Findings from ten years of DFID-funded research on Governance and Fragile States 2001–2010*. A Synthesis Paper.

Maier, K. (2000). *This House has fallen: Nigeria in Crisis*. Westview.

Malone, A. (1990). Quotable quotes for quoters. *The Clarion (Guwahati).*

Marsteintredet, L., & Malamud, A. (2019). Coup with Adjectives: Conceptual stretching or Innovation in comparative research? *Political Studies*, 1–22. doi:10.1177/0032321719888857

Mbaku, J. M. (2020). Threats to democracy in Africa: The rise of the Constitutional Coup. Brookings.

Mmaduabuchi, G. S. (2015). Elections and voting behavior. In R. Anifowose & F. C. Enemuo (Eds.), *Element of Politics* (2nd ed., pp. 210–226). Sam Iroanusi Publications.

Mo Ibrahim Foundation. (2023). *2022 Ibrahim Index of African governance*. https://mo.ibrahim.foundation/iiag/downloads

National Open University. (2015). *Politics of Development and Underdevelopment*. The National Open University of Nigeria.

Nichter, S. (2014). Conceptualizing vote buying. *Electoral Studies*, *35*, 315–327. doi:10.1016/j.electstud.2014.02.008

Obangome, G. W. (2023). *Gabon officers declare military coup, President Ali Bongo detained*. Reuters. https://www.reuters.com/world/africa/gabonese-military-officers-announce-they-have-seized-power-2023-08-30

Ogundiya, I. S. (2020). Democracy and good governance: Nigeria's dilemma. *African Journal of Political Science and International Relation*, *5*(6), 201–208.

Okafor, V. O. (2005). *A Roadmap for understanding African Politics: Leadership and Political Integration in Nigeria*. Routledge.

Okunloye, R. W. (2017). Monetization of Politics and Elections in Fourth Republican Nigeria: Implications for Sustainable Democratic Governance. *KIU Journal of Social Humanities*, *2*(2A), 77–85.

Oluwole, V. (2023). *African nations leading in democracy index rankings*. Business Insider Africa.

Onoge, O. (1997). *The democratic imperative in Africa. Claude Ake Memorial lecture series no. 1.* African Centre for Democratic Governance.

Onuoha, F., & Ojo, J. (2018). *Practice and Perils of Vote Buying in Nigeria's Recent Election Pretoria.* African Center for the Constructive Resolution of Dispute.

Onwe, P. S. (2021). An examination of good governance and the state of security in Nigeria. In A. S. Ihuah & P. A. Idachaba (Eds.), *Philosophy and national security: Interrogations in a distressed nation* (Vol. 1, pp. 25–64). Eagle Prints.

Osaghae, E. (1988). *Political Analysis (POS 211).* UI External Studies Programme.

Pomper, M. G. (1968). *Elections in America*. Dodd, Mead & Company, Inc.

Potter, D. (2004). *Democratization, Good Governance and Development*. Allen Publishers.

Powell, J. M., & Thyne, C. L. (2011). Global Instances of Coups from 1950 to 2010: A New Dataset. *Journal of Peace Research*, *48*(2), 249–259. doi:10.1177/0022343310397436

Ranney, A. (1974). *The Governing of Men* (4th ed.). The Dryden Press.

Revenue Mobilizations Allocation and Fiscal Package. (2023). *Salary of Nigerian Governors, Deputy, Ministers, Senators*. https://nigerian.com/salary-nigerian-governors/

Schaffer, F. C., & Schedler, A. (2000). *What is Vote Buying? The Limits of the Market Model*. Lynne Rienner Publishers.

Schultes, I. (2022). *Western Africa's recent coups highlight the risk of trading off development for security, the rule of law, and rights*. Mo Ibrahim Foundation.

Schumpeter, J. A. (1950). *Capitalism, Socialism, and Democracy*. Harpers and Row.

Strong, C. F. (1963). *Modern Political Constitutions*. Academic Press.

Swedish International Development Cooperation Agency (SIDA). (2002). Good Governance. Division for Democratic Governance. Art.no:2845en, Sweden.

Taylor, I. (2018). *African politics: A very short introduction*. Oxford University Press. doi:10.1093/actrade/9780198806578.001.0001

Teshome-Bahiru, W. (2008). Democracy and elections in Africa: Critical Analysis. *International Journal of Human Sciences*, *5*(2). https://ssrn.com/abstract=1164829

Thomson, A. (2010). *Introduction to African Politics* (3rd ed.). Routledge. doi:10.4324/9780203857946

Transparency International. (2004). *Corruption Perceptions Index 2010*. Transparency International Press. www.unescap.org/pdd

Walton, H., & Smith, R. C. (2000). *American Politics and the African American quest for Universal Freedom*. Longman.

Wheare, K. c. (1966). *Modern Constitutions*. OUP.

World Bank. (1992). *Government and development*. International Bank for Reconstruction and Development.

World Bank. (1994). *Governance*. The World Bank's Experience.

Yagboyaju, D. A., & Akinola, A. O. (2019). Nigerian State and the Crisis of Governance: A critical Exposition. *SAGE Open*, *9*(3), 1–10. doi:10.1177/2158244019865810

ADDITIONAL READING

Akiba, O. (2023). *Political Change and Constitutionalism in Africa: Emerging Trends* (1st ed.). Routledge.

Huntington, S. (1991). *The Third Wave*. University of Oklahoma Press.

Mawere, M., & Nwanaka, T. R. (2015). *Democracy, Good Governance and Development in Africa*. Langaa RPCAG. doi:10.2307/j.ctvk3gmq7

Mudacumura, G. M., & Morcol, G. (2014). *Challenge to Democratic Governance in Developing Countries*. Springer. doi:10.1007/978-3-319-03143-9

KEY TERMS AND DEFINITIONS

African Politics: The practice of politics on the African continent.

Attitudinal Crises: Faulty attitude or myopic mindset.

Constitution: A supreme set of rules which governs a nation.

Democracy: Voice of the governed.

Good Governance: An exercise of authority over a group or nations on the platform of democratic principles.

Chapter 4
Stakeholder Engagement and Community Participation in Sustainable Development in Southern Africa

Maximino Costumado
University of KwaZulu-Natal, South Africa

José A. D. Chemane
University of KwaZulu-Natal, South Africa

ABSTRACT

This chapter highlights the role of stakeholder engagement and community participation in sustainable development and growth in Southern Africa. It emphasizes the relevance of inclusive collaboration and traditional knowledge to tackle the socio-economic and environmental challenges in the region. This chapter discusses adopting stakeholder engagement processes with a robust and inclusive community participation approach in projects and initiatives promoting sustainable growth and development in the Southern African region. Additionally, the chapter stresses the value of open communication channels and partnerships for fostering sustainable development. This chapter shares best practices and suggestions for all stakeholders involved in sustainable development initiatives by analyzing empirical evidence and case studies. It accentuates the need for inclusive strategies based on ethical cooperation, transparency, and gender equity that consider the voices of local communities and facilitate innovation to ensure a more equitable and sustainable future.

INTRODUCTION

The Southern Africa region boasts a remarkable cultural and geographical diversity with many countries, ethnic groups, and abundant natural resources. However, this rich composition is affected by challenges that prevent the region's achievement of sustainable development goals (SDGs). These challenges in-

DOI: 10.4018/979-8-3693-0477-8.ch004

clude economic disparities, environmental degradation, and social inequalities, as evidenced by recent studies (Mpofu, 2022; Wang & Huang, 2021). The pursuit of improved living standards for local and disadvantaged communities and the overarching achievement of sustainable growth and development depends on the active engagement of communities through collaborative efforts and robust partnerships among diverse stakeholders (Babu et al., 2020; Eweje et al., 2021). Globally, sustainability has assumed a central role in government interventions. Recent research highlights the wave of collaborative initiatives in Southern Africa to nurture sustainable growth and development (Chitakira et al., 2022; Lindner, 2023). Stakeholders from various sectors have come together with a shared commitment to address the challenges hindering progress towards SDGs within the region (Abiddin et al., 2022).

This chapter stresses the importance of stakeholder engagement and community participation in the success of sustainable development initiatives. These collaborative efforts not only provide local communities with a sense of ownership and empowerment but also leverage their profound knowledge of their unique realities (Mamokhere & Meyer, 2023; Rijal, 2023). Additionally, they serve as catalysts for identifying community needs, mobilizing resources, and devising practical solutions to address pressing issues (Rosen & Painter, 2019). Furthermore, stakeholder engagement and community participation foster social cohesion and inclusivity (Ferreira et al., 2019; Jewett et al., 2021), vital elements for ensuring the success and sustainability of projects. These collaborative efforts and active community involvement also provide mechanisms for conflict resolution, fostering a harmonious environment and enhancing accountability and transparency among the diverse project collaborators (Fiandrino et al., 2022; Sari, 2023; Tejedo-Romero).

This chapter explores stakeholder engagement practices and community participation in initiatives aimed at promoting sustainable growth and development across Southern Africa. At its core, the chapter recognizes the pivotal role played by stakeholders and local communities in shaping the direction and success of sustainable development initiatives. It emphasizes the significance of effective stakeholder engagement processes coupled with robust, inclusive community participation in projects and initiatives promoting sustainable growth and development in the region. The chapter begins with an introduction highlighting the relevance of stakeholder engagement and community participation in sustainable development. Subsequently, it delves into identifying and mapping critical stakeholders involved in the development process within Southern Africa while exploring historical and cultural perspectives on stakeholder and community participation in the region.

Moreover, this chapter examines the challenges of community participation in development projects, drawing inputs from real-world case studies and research findings. It culminates in a comprehensive analysis of successful interventions highlighting stakeholder engagement and community participation. It offers valuable lessons for policy formulation, innovation promotion, and guidance for practitioners and stakeholders engaged in initiatives to foster sustainable growth and development. This chapter serves as a repository of insights into best practices for stakeholder engagement and community participation in sustainable growth and development in Southern Africa. It concludes with actionable recommendations directed at policymakers, practitioners, and organizations, facilitating improved future initiatives that promote collaboration and knowledge-sharing among diverse stakeholders.

BACKGROUND

Southern Africa is a dynamic and culturally diverse region with numerous countries, each with its history, challenges, and potential. Notably, the continent of Africa is undergoing a significant demographic transformation, with a majority of its population being female youth. Projections indicate a substantial population increase in Africa, expected to surpass 1.8 billion by 2050, up from nearly 1.2 billion in 2020 (Guttal, 2021). However, like many parts of the world, Southern Africa grapples with various issues that hinder the achievement of sustainable development goals. These challenges are exacerbated by the effects of climate change, leading to natural disasters such as land erosion, droughts, storms, flooding, and rising sea levels, which in turn impact the region's pursuit of sustainable development (Chingono & Mbohwa, 2023; Steiner, 2019). Consequently, Southern Africa is characterized by impoverished communities, lacking access to essential services, and being highly vulnerable to the adverse effects of climate change. A continuing trend of rural-urban migration and population growth further highlights the importance of finding sustainable approaches to enhance development planning processes and ensure social and economic benefits for local and marginalized communities while also promoting environmental preservation and community resilience (Gibbens & Schoeman, 2020; Varela et al., 2022).

The goal of long-term prosperity, economic growth, and the well-being of Southern Africa's burgeoning youth population comes with substantial challenges. These include economic disparities, environmental degradation in deforestation, habitat loss, and water scarcity, all exacerbated by climate change (Nguyen et al., 2023; Onebunne & Okechukwu, 2021). Social inequalities, including unequal access to quality education, healthcare, food security, and limited employment opportunities, further complicate the region's agenda toward sustainable growth and development (Mukumbang et al., 2020; Ngumbela et al., 2020).

Globally, sustainability has emerged as a central focus in both governmental policies and international agendas. The famous 1987 report, "Our Common Future," released by the World Commission on Environment and Development (WCED) from the United Nations (UN), formally defined sustainable development as an approach that addresses present needs without jeopardizing the ability of future generations to meet their own (WCED, 1987). This commitment to sustainability gained momentum with the UN Sustainable Development Goals (SDGs), universally adopted in 2015, signifying a dedicated pledge to fostering sustainability, equity, and prosperity worldwide, particularly in developing regions like Southern Africa (Chopra et al., 2022). Despite the active involvement of stakeholders across sectors, integrating the sustainability agenda into all phases of community interventions remains a challenge (Babu et al., 2020; Eweje et al., 2021; Saha et al., 2022; UN, 1992).

Integral to sustainable development initiatives is the fundamental pillar of community participation, emphasizing active and effective collaboration during project planning and implementation. This collaborative process involves open dialogues, a profound respect for diversity, and a keen sensitivity to the perspectives of all stakeholders, considering the intricate economic, social, and environmental dynamics of the local context (Pawar, 2017). Beyond facilitating collaboration, community participation is a potent tool for rebalancing power dynamics, ensuring that the voices and perspectives of local communities carry equal weight alongside those in positions of authority (Tosun, 2000, as cited in Sebele, 2010).

Community participation enhances local communities' quality of life and fosters a sense of ownership and responsibility for preserving local natural assets, thereby promoting tourism development (Tosun, 2006). However, this chapter contends that while stakeholder engagement and community participation are vital for the success of sustainable development initiatives in Southern Africa, caution is essential due to the potential unseen, subtle, hidden, and sometimes harmful agendas of diverse development partners.

Striking a fair balance between fulfilling all partners' needs and achieving project success efficiently and effectively is crucial. In this chapter, we explore the transformative potential of community participation in Southern Africa's sustainable growth and development initiatives, delving into empirical evidence and case studies to unveil the tangible impacts and implications of these collaborative efforts on local communities, their well-being, and the conservation of their cherished natural resources.

FINDINGS

In this section, we unveil the invaluable findings derived from our comprehensive examination of stakeholder engagement practices and community participation within initiatives aimed at fostering sustainable growth and development in the dynamic landscape of Southern Africa. Our findings represent the culmination of rigorous research and analytical work on the multifaceted aspects of stakeholder engagement and community involvement within this region. We seek to offer a unique perspective on the complex cover of development dynamics through meticulous data collection and analysis.

This journey through our findings is organized to reveal crucial insights into key themes and patterns and present critical observations that have emerged throughout our exploration. As we navigate these findings, we will highlight the essence and significance of stakeholder engagement and community participation in Southern Africa. Within these findings, we will delve firstly into the process of identifying and mapping stakeholders, then we will explore the historical and cultural context of community participation in Southern Africa, elucidate the roles and contributions of stakeholders to the development process, and explore the benefits, challenges, and opportunities that arise when these elements converge. Our findings will be further enriched by real-world case studies from the Southern African region, providing tangible examples of the impact of stakeholder engagement and community participation. Moreover, we will engage in a thoughtful discussion on the promising strategies and best practices that hold the potential to advance this region toward a future characterized by sustainable growth and development.

UNVEILING STAKEHOLDER IDENTIFICATION AND MAPPING PROCESS

Key stakeholders involved in the development agenda of Southern Africa hold diverse interests, making it essential to identify and map these partners effectively. Stakeholder mapping, a visual methodological process, has proven indispensable in identifying and categorizing stakeholders based on their interests and influence (Aligica, 2006; Reed and Cuzon, 2015). This mapping process requires a tailored approach to identify relevant actors with local knowledge and an entrusted interest in forming effective partnerships to enhance local development and promote sustainability within Southern Africa. Recent studies emphasize the importance of involving stakeholders with significant influence, recognition, and engagement in initiatives addressing issues affecting impoverished communities (Sahoo et al., 2023). Through this stakeholder mapping process, critical actors are identified to facilitate collaborative efforts in promoting sustainable development within the region as shown in Table 1.

Table 1: Stakeholder mapping example based on representation

Stakeholder Group	Name, Position and Organization	Role						
		Decision makers	Implementers	Coordinators	Knowledge provider	Financers	Lobbyists	Gatekeepers
SH1: Authorities	Regional Coordinator, Contingency Agency		X	X				
	Municipal Council, Municipality X	X	X					
SH2: Political Representatives	Union Representative						X	
	Elected Town Council Representative	X					X	
SH3: Civil Society	Representative of association for local inhabitants			X	X			
	House owner				X			X
SH4: Private Sector	Insurance Company	X			X		X	
	Private Company				X		X	
SH5: Research Community	Climate Adaptation Unit, government agency			X	X			
	Researcher University				X			
SH6: NGOs	Transboundary Commission			X	X			

Source: Barquet, Segnestam, and Dickin (2022:11)

While stakeholders must represent only one segment of society to avoid conflicts of interest, they can assume multiple roles within established partnerships (Gregory et al., 2020). Table one above substantiates the findings by Gregory et al (2020) by describing different stakeholders assuming one or more roles in the development process. Effective methods to identify key stakeholders in the development agenda include literature reviews, document analysis, interviews, focus groups, and surveys (Barquet et al., 2022; Reed et al., 2009; Fritz et al., 2018; White et al., 2017).

HISTORICAL AND CULTURAL DIMENSIONS OF COMMUNITY PARTICIPATION

The importance of active community participation in the decision-making processes of developmental initiatives gained prominence through the advocacy of multilateral agencies such as the United States Agency for International Development (USAID), the World Bank, and the United Nations (UN) during the late 1960s and early 1970s. The objective was to ensure equitable benefits for all stakeholders, with a particular emphasis on the well-being of local community members (Catley, 1999). Community participation in local development initiatives within the Southern Africa region is deeply rooted in its historical, social, and political fabric (Barrow, 2002; Williams, 2006). While these communities have a long history of exclusion and land expropriation, along with limited participation in land management and governance processes, communal land management practices have been an integral part of the region's landscape since ancient times, including pre-colonial and colonial eras (Barrow et al., 2002; Kangalawe et al., 2014).

During these times, local authorities, actively involving community members, held decision-making power and were responsible for the sustainable management of land use systems and conservation efforts. Colonial governments, in collaboration with traditional leadership, imposed regulations governing the use and exploitation of natural resources, aiming to promote the sustainable utilization of the country's resources and enhance the well-being of local communities. Examples include the Native Reserves Forest Produce Act in Zimbabwe and the establishment of village forest areas in Malawi, Uganda, and Tanzania, managed by local authorities to foster local ownership and sustainable use of forest resources (Barrow et al., 2002). Additionally, the Southern African region inherited the institution of Traditional Tribal Councils from colonial governance. These councils, led by local community leaders, exercise authority over communal property, such as land and mining, often making decisions on behalf of local communities, albeit with limited decision-making power (Claassens & Matlala, 2014). In Lesotho, regulatory norms introduced during the colonial era, such as the Native Administration Proclamation of 1938 and the Land Husbandry Act No. 22 of 1969, legitimized the power of tribal chiefs to manage and protect natural resources for the benefit of local communities (Shackelton & Campbell, 2000).

Cultural practices in Southern Africa encompass a complex web of socially related behaviours, rituals, religion, education systems, gender roles, and social and family practices. These practices inform people's behaviours, economic production, social organization, and participation in development initiatives (Sen, 2004). In rural settings, these cultural practices deeply immerse themselves in the daily dynamics of society, influencing the extent of community participation (Khadiagala, 2001; Landes, 2000).

A growing body of research highlights the socio-cultural factors influencing participation across Southern African communities. Customs, traditions, beliefs, and norms significantly impact community participation, particularly women's involvement, due to deeply rooted beliefs and taboos that lead to exclusion from specific community-based initiatives (Oloo, 2013). This exclusion extends to ownership rights and benefits, further marginalizing segments of society, particularly women (Tamale, 2004), which show the relevance of applying African traditional practices and beliefs to foster an active participation of all community members in the local development practice. The philosophy of ubuntu, deeply ingrained in Southern African traditions, profoundly shapes social relations and stakeholder engagements at various levels within the region. Ubuntu, centred on the principles of personhood, community, and interdependence, seeks consensus and common ground, elevating notions of community and hospitality over individualism (Makgoba, 1997). It expands understanding of social order systems, valuing hierarchy, formality, and gender roles and promoting a symbiotic relationship between the individual and the group (Moemeka, 1996).

In summary, community participation has evolved in the Southern African region, bearing the imprints of historical, social, and political dynamics. From pre-colonial traditions of collective decision-making to the struggles for liberation and post-colonial governance efforts, community participation remains a potent force shaping the region's development trajectory. Understanding these historical and cultural perspectives is essential for fostering inclusive, sustainable, and community-driven approaches to governance and development in Southern Africa.

SIGNIFICANCE OF STAKEHOLDER ENGAGEMENT

In recent years, there has been a growing emphasis on the concept of stakeholders, particularly within the domains of public and management theory and practice (Bryson, 2003). Stakeholder engagement has emerged as a critical concept primarily used to identify individuals, communities, or groups that are perceived to have the potential to influence or be influenced by an organization's pursuit of its objectives. For instance, Freeman's groundbreaking work in 1984, titled "Strategic Management: A Stakeholder Approach," defines stakeholders as those entities with the power to impact or be affected by an organization's goal attainment. Furthermore, Mitchel et al. (1997) have delineated two perspectives regarding stakeholders: one considers them as 'claimants,' while the other characterizes them as 'influencers.'

The concept of stakeholders as 'claimants' has attracted substantial attention in managerial contexts because it encourages managers to extend their focus beyond just the influencers. It emphasizes the importance of addressing the needs and demands of stakeholders with a legitimate interest in achieving the organization's goals (see Bryson, 2004). Additionally, stakeholders have been categorized into two groups: internal stakeholders, such as influencers, who are directly involved in project execution, and external stakeholders, like claimants, whose impact on the project is more indirect (Olander, 2006). This dual categorization helps organizations distinguish between those stakeholders intimately tied to their operations and those with a more peripheral influence. Furthermore, strategic management emphasizes identifying the claims, individuals, groups, and organizations integral to a company's structure (Mitchel et al., 1997; Freeman, 1984). This approach ensures that organizations consider the broader societal context in which they operate and recognize their responsibilities towards various stakeholders.

In addition to this managerial perspective, ethics plays a crucial role in shaping the stakeholder discourse. The ethical perspective views stakeholders as citizens with the right to determine or influence an organization's or project's processes to meet their needs, particularly in public policy. This perspective provides a framework for proactive engagement with citizens, fostering participatory governance, equity, and transparency (Ridley & Jones, 2002; Rowe & Shepherd, 2002). For example, the construction sector has actively contributed to the ethical dimension of stakeholder engagement. On the one hand, it utilizes stakeholder engagement to capture knowledge, enhance project users' sense of ownership, mitigate conflicts, foster innovation, and facilitate partnership mediation processes (Creative et al.). On the other hand, ethics-driven stakeholder engagement promotes inclusive decision-making processes, enhances equity, encourages local decision-making, and builds social capital (ibid). In summary, stakeholders have evolved significantly in recent years, containing managerial and ethical perspectives.

This evolution underlines the importance of recognizing stakeholders' diverse interests and roles in shaping organizational and project outcomes while highlighting the ethical imperative of inclusive and transparent engagement with stakeholders for the betterment of society. Different perspectives on stakeholder engagement vary in their approaches to inclusivity. Some viewpoints highlight individuals or groups with significant power, emphasizing their ability to respond, negotiate, and generate substantial changes that can shape an organization's productivity (Eden and Ackermann, 1998, cited in Bryson, 2003). In contrast, others advocate for a perspective that prioritizes empowering those with less power, thereby promoting democratic practices and social justice to give a voice to the marginalized (Bryson, 2003; Lewis, 1991). Another critical aspect of stakeholder engagement revolves around the concept of social learning. This entails diverse stakeholders coming together to exchange knowledge, self-reflecting on each other's values, and collaboratively creating shared visions and objectives (ibid).

Given stakeholders' diverse interests, conducting engagements with ethical considerations becomes imperative (McAdam et al., 2005). Therefore, ethical stakeholder engagement carries significant implications for public policy, reinforcing equity and empowerment (Involve, 2005; Ridley & Jones, 2002). It also legitimizes compromises that may arise in multiple stakeholder engagements, ensuring transparency as the basis for equitable outcomes (Kaatz et al., 2005). Moreover, aligning managerial processes with stakeholder engagement as part of project decision-making processes can enhance the sense of project ownership. In the long run, this contributes to the project's success, quality, and maintenance and ensures its long-term sustainability, particularly concerning sustainable built environments (Shepherd & Bowler, 1997; Shindler & Cheek, 1999).In the context of sustainable development, there is a consensus that it primarily focuses on the social choices that communities and individuals face, especially during the project's initial operational stages when all stakeholders gain an understanding of the proposed solutions to be adopted in the project's implementation phase (Hardi & Zdan, 1997; Devuyst, 2000).

ROLES AND CONTRIBUTIONS OF STAKEHOLDERS

In pursuing sustainable growth and development, the global South, particularly the Southern Africa region, grapples with many social, economic, and environmental challenges. These challenges require a collaborative effort from an array of stakeholders, each characterized by diverse interests, resources, and levels of influence. This section discusses the multifaceted roles undertaken by these stakeholders within initiatives designed to drive sustainable growth and development. At the core of sustainable development projects lies the vital role of stakeholders in shaping a collective vision and planning activities containing the perspectives of various community groups engaged in the development process (Flint, 2013). Stakeholders, alongside local decision-makers, often collaborate, drawing upon their unique expertise to generate accurate and credible knowledge essential for the successful execution of programmatic activities (Clark et al., 2016; Edelenbos et al., 2011).

Resource mobilization stands as another pivotal mission that propels the work of stakeholders. This mission encompasses both economic and non-economic assets. It involves diverse actors, including NGOs, governments, the private sector, and national and international agencies, all actively engaged in activities to promote sustainable global development (Barua, 2020; Batti, 2014). However, it is essential to acknowledge the financial challenges in achieving the 17 SDGs. Reports from ECOSOC CHAMBER (2018) indicate an annual investment requirement of \$5–7 trillion, with a global financial gap of \$2.5 trillion per year, posing a potential threat to the world's commitment to achieving the SDGs by 2030.

The design and implementation of robust monitoring and evaluation (M&E) processes are crucial to effectively address the challenges of mobilizing resources for sustainable development initiatives. These processes should involve a diverse group of stakeholders to monitor project progress and ensure the effective implementation of action plans. An illustrative example is the participation of diverse stakeholders, including government authorities, producers, consumers, community managers, and volunteers, in the M&E of Globally Important Agricultural Heritage Systems (GIAHS) action plans (Jiao et al., 2022). This collaborative approach guarantees the conservation of land use systems and landscapes with vital biological biodiversity, thereby contributing to sustainable development goals (Koohafkan & Delacruz, 2011). Furthermore, stakeholders play an indispensable role in advocacy and policy influence, exerting their influence to advance the cause of sustainable development goals (Ascoli & Benzaken, 2009; Kestin et al., 2017; WHO, 2018a; WHO, 2018b). This engagement extends beyond project implementation, shaping policies and advocacy efforts that resonate with the broader objectives of sustainable growth and development.

As we delve deeper into these multifaceted roles of stakeholders, this section aims to provide a comprehensive understanding of their impact on shaping sustainable growth and development trajectory within the Southern Africa region and beyond. A good example within the Southern African Development Community (SADC), is the actions to curb the effects of climate change by the Agricultural and Food Security (CCFS) organ of the Agricultural Development Coordination (ADC) which embarked on a pioneering project aimed at addressing the profound challenges posed by climate change in the realm of agriculture. This forward-thinking initiative strategically employs methodologies to comprehensively map and understand the intricate landscape of stakeholders in the agricultural sector.

Conceptually, it facilitates the identification of key players, sheds light on the dynamics of power, uncovers the myriad interests that drive these stakeholders, and casts a spotlight on the often-overlooked vulnerable groups. Moreover, it unravels the relationships among stakeholders and elucidates how they interconnect, ultimately influencing policy formulation and implementation (Chevallier, 2020). Each member state within the SADC has diligently established comprehensive national policies and strategies to combat climate change and bolster the agricultural sector, often inspired by or aligned with the overarching framework of SADC's Food, Agriculture, and Natural Resources (FANR) body. These national policies and strategies, as explored in detail in Chevallier (2020: 19-23), set the stage for coordinated efforts at the regional level.

Consequently, this ambitious undertaking has empowered the SADC's CCFS organ to pinpoint the agricultural sector's critical stakeholders, unveiling their roles and the nature of their intricate interrelations. The resulting insights serve as a valuable resource for understanding the complex web of actors shaping the future of agriculture and climate resilience within the SADC. In Table 2, we summarize some of the identified categories of stakeholders and provide a glimpse into their pivotal roles within the SADC framework.

Table 2. Stakeholder categories and roles

Stakeholder Category	Role played
Grassroots/Community-based organisations	Hub local perspectives, indigenous knowledge and wisdom, channel the voice of the people on the ground
Commercial/Private players	Build partnerships, promote innovation, economic perspectives, and resources
Financial institutions	The financing of projects, prospect long-term investment risks; provide market solutions
Regional economic communities	Plan towards regional development, integration and coordination, and regional leadership; set the bodies' agenda
Government	It develops policies, and legislation and provides leadership and the strategic direction to be taken
Multilateral organizations	Deal with transnational development, cooperation, financial and technical support, decision-making and setting the agenda at a transnational level
Media and Journalists	Advocate, share information, raise awareness and provide alternative means of knowledge-sharing
Scientific communities and academia	Knowledge generation and information based on evidence
Managers of local resources and labourers	Generate incomes and improve livelihoods, promote good practices and knowledge around local farming, sustainable management and natural resources exploration
Civil society	Advocates, shares information, raises awareness, provides advice and builds capacities, elevates agents of change, ensures people's voices are heard, identifies affected and/or interested people in different societal issues

Source: Adapted from Chevallier et al. (2020)

Civil society emerges as a potent voice within this dynamic landscape. Civil society organizations can vocalize grievances, advocate for marginalized segments of society, raise awareness about gender inequalities, and forge networks through the media and journalism. As Bilal (2017) suggests, member state institutions should orchestrate opportunities for key stakeholders to connect and cultivate relationships. This should create an enabling environment where the voices of both the private sector and civil society resonate at every stage of the policy cycle. This engagement, however, must align with each stakeholder's unique incentives and interests (Bilal, 2017: 4) to drive climate change-related initiatives effectively. Understanding how each stakeholder stands to gain or contribute throughout the entire cycle of engagement is essential. Only through this holistic approach can the region realize its vision and effectively navigate the challenges posed by climate change and agriculture.

Cultural tourism, particularly in the context of tourist hunting, has offered valuable insights into stakeholder engagements. Countries like Zambia, Tanzania, and Botswana in the SADC have crafted their hunting industries to position the state as both the owner of wildlife and the regulator of tourist hunting activities within customary land (Lewis & Jackson, 2005). However, customary land laws in these regions are grounded in communalism, emphasizing collective decision-making over individual interests (Akpa-Inyang & Chima, 2021). This communal approach conflicts with state and corporate interests, creating complexities and disputes among multiple stakeholders with ill-defined roles. Challenges emerge, particularly regarding co-management, ownership of resources and revenue, and the vulnerability of wildlife to various threats (Lewis & Jackson, 2005; Gujadhur, 2001).

The sharing of resources and revenue generated from activities in communal lands challenges the principles of communalism, especially when local communities are excluded from management and decision-making processes. This disregard for indigenous communities by the state and other stakeholders exposes inequalities and forms of marginalization despite these communities' rightful ownership of land (Lewis & Jackson, 2005). Community-based initiatives have enabled government authorities, the private sector, and local communities to promote community participation in wildlife conservation collaboratively. Programs such as the Communal Areas Management Programme for Indigenous Resources (CAMPFIRE) in Zimbabwe, ADMADE in Zambia, and the Chobe Enclave Conservation Trust in Botswana (Lewis & Jackson, 2005) exemplify community-based initiatives grounded in principles of cooperation between local communities and states.

Community participation in sustainable ecotourism development is exemplified by the Isimangaliso Wetlands Park, located on the east coast of KwaZulu-Natal South Africa, an institution mandated to protect the site's world heritage values while enhancing the economic development, restitution, and social justice of local communities (Zaloumis, 2007, as cited in Magi, 2007). From this case study, two significant outcomes related to community participation emerge. Firstly, the engagement between the Park and local authorities led to the resettlement of lands to specific community members who had lost them in 1895 when the area was designated as a game reserve. During this period, the Park's management expanded its mandate to include the involvement of park dwellers in its daily activities. Secondly, the Isimangaliso community became an active stakeholder in the park, directly participating in its planning, development, and management (Magi, 2007). This meant local communities had a substantial say in the Park's decision-making processes. While some findings from this study indicated that certain local community members perceived their participation in the Park's ecotourism development as hostile, there were also beliefs that, overall, stakeholder involvement in co-management practices, the restoration of some land to the native population, and the Park's integration of both private and communal land were counted as successful (Magi, 2007). Communities residing near Gorongosa National Park in Mozambique play an active role in conservation efforts, reaping the rewards of ecotourism initiatives. Their involvement extends to integral decision-making stages throughout the planning and execution of conservation projects, as highlighted in the study conducted by Matos et al. (2021).

CHALLENGES PREVENTING SUSTAINABLE DEVELOPMENT

The SADC was established with a dual mission that includes the promotion of regional peace and fostering sustainable development, aiming to lift its citizens out of poverty while upholding principles of freedom and social justice (Bilal, 2017). Recently, the SDGs have taken centre stage on the agendas of SADC member states. The region is home to nearly 345 million inhabitants, with half its population comprising young individuals living in impoverished rural areas (Chevallier et al., 2020). Despite commonalities in cultural traits, history, water systems, ecosystems, road and railway networks across the region (ibid), and an ambitious agenda for regional integration and cooperation, progress in the region has been slow (Bilal, 2017).

Historically, community participation has served as a valuable tool for addressing diverse issues within different settings. For instance, during colonialism, there was a prevailing perception that development was a self-reliant exercise, with participation considered a civic duty for citizens (Dhliwayo, 2007). In the post-colonial era (1960s-1970s), marked by political participation, the emphasis shifted towards establishing state hegemony and managing rural communities. During this period, we also witnessed the rise of emancipatory participation and liberation movements, actively engaging in social action against structured oppression. Moreover, in the 1990s, participation initiatives focused on exclusion and mainstream development, with discussions on alternative development options gaining momentum. During this era, attention to promoting participation as a fundamental right has increased. As top-down projects and planning began to stumble, particularly in the 1980s, community participation in development gained momentum to empower people, capture indigenous knowledge systems, and enhance the sustainability and efficiency of initiatives. The essence of participation has been centred on building trustworthy networks and associations, fostering greater civic engagement, and creating conducive conditions for economic growth (Croese & Duminy, 2023; Hickey & Mohan, 2004).

A significant obstacle to sustainable development in southern Africa arises from cultural barriers deeply ingrained in traditions, customs, beliefs, and norms (Eni et al., 2022). These entrenched cultural influences have contributed to the region's slow progress, with specific belief systems, rituals, and norms perpetuating discriminatory and exclusionary practices, particularly affecting marginalized groups like women (Eni et al., 2022; Nyasimi et al., 2009: 474). Cultural practices encompass various socially-linked behaviours, including rituals, idioms, religious traditions, educational systems, gender roles, and family customs. These practices shape people's behaviours and impact economic production and social organization (Sen, 2004). In rural settings, these cultural norms manifest in everyday events, influencing individuals' decisions regarding participation in community-related matters, including development initiatives (Khadiagala, 2001; Landes, 2000). Consequently, these cultural practices give rise to issues related to gender inequality and discrimination, particularly affecting vulnerable groups such as women. In southern Africa, women continue to encounter biases rooted in cultural norms and patriarchal traditions, creating substantial challenges for their meaningful participation in the region's development and poverty alleviation efforts (ibid).

Cultural practices have adversely affected women's involvement by perpetuating beliefs and taboos in rural societies, leading to exclusionary practices that deprive certain social groups, like women, of their rights to ownership or benefits from community resources (Oloo, 2013). These exclusionary practices further aggravate women's barriers to active participation and engagement in the region's development goals (Tamale, 2004). This example vividly illustrates the consequences of limited community participation in decision-making and control over processes and resources, which ultimately led to exclusionary policies. An example from South Africa illustrates collaborative efforts to address the pressing issue of land reform. The primary goal of these efforts is to rectify the historical imbalances in land distribution and ownership within the country. However, this goal has encountered significant challenges that hinder its effectiveness (Jansen & Kalas, 2020). One prominent obstacle is the need for more capacity and effective communication among stakeholders involved in the land reform process. This organizational and operational capacity deficiency needs to improve the coordination of efforts and the seamless exchange of crucial information among government departments, local communities, and other relevant parties. The authors further stated that limited financial resources at various local administrative levels pose a substantial challenge. The need for more funds can significantly hamper the implementation of land reform initiatives, ultimately hindering progress toward achieving a more equitable distribution of land resources.

BEST PRACTICES TO PROMOTE SUSTAINABLE GROWTH AND DEVELOPMENT

The achievement of sustainable growth and development in the Southern Africa region requires the identification and implementation of interventions that are tailored to the unique challenges and opportunities of the region. In recent years, Southern Africa has witnessed a significant surge in collaborative efforts, signalling a growing commitment to promoting sustainable growth and development in the area (Cole & Broadhurst, 2022

A combination of innovative strategies and collaborative efforts is required to effectively address the complex challenges that arise from stakeholder and community engagement in local initiatives. One of the best practices involves promoting inclusive stakeholder engagement, with the participation of all relevant parties in the process. Jansen & Kalas (2020) further suggest that the success of a multi-stakeholder partnership hinges on building trust, addressing power asymmetries, enhancing financial support, nurturing conditions for capacity building, and promoting transparency and accountability within decision-making processes. Another exemplary approach to promoting the engagement of research and academic institutions in Ghana, South Africa, and Zimbabwe to pursue sustainable development and growth is the implementation of transdisciplinary (TD) research. This approach allows multiple stakeholders to collaborate in mapping out best practices and solutions for sustainability (Thondhlana et al., 2021). TD projects implemented in Ghana (Kumasi), South Africa (Durban and Makhanda), and Zimbabwe (Harare) under the support of the LIRA2030 program aim to understand and promote urban sustainability in diverse socioeconomic locations. These projects emphasize the importance of applying collective knowledge from academics, practitioners, and communities to design effective and localized solutions for addressing current and emerging challenges while facilitating mutual learning among project partners.

The SADC region has led initiatives to promote regional socioeconomic cooperation and integration. This is achieved by enabling effective communication and partnerships among member states and allowing stakeholder engagement at various levels (Garwe & Gwati, 2018; Muboko, 2017). These interventions ensure that regional and national policies are responsive to the needs of the people, especially those from marginalized groups such as women and indigenous communities. Studies also suggest that recognizing the Southern African region's abundant natural resources and their impact on advancing economic growth requires implementing policies and regulations that balance economic interests with environmental conservation (Ghisellini et al., 2016; Liu et al., 2022). For instance, community-based conservation initiatives like the CAMPFIRE in Zimbabwe empower communities to benefit financially from wildlife conservation efforts while promoting sustainable practices (Jali, 2022).

Other noteworthy best practices in the Southern African region to promote sustainable growth and development focus on activities to empower women and promote gender equality while challenging unfavourable cultural norms that hinder women's participation in development initiatives (Gressel et al., 2020; Ndonga et al., 2021). By championing women's rights and empowerment, development partners contribute to social justice and economic growth (Resurrección et al., 2019). Studies conducted in South Africa highlight the pivotal role of female entrepreneurs in poverty reduction and unemployment alleviation (Maziriri et al., 2019), showcasing their contributions to fair leadership practices, innovation, research and development efficiency, job creation, competitiveness, productivity, and the establishment of new economic sectors in the country (Nxopo, 2014). Therefore, interventions to provide women with access to quality education, healthcare, and financial capital will empower them to participate in the region's development (Mkandawire et al., 2021). Moreover, implementing awareness campaigns and policy reforms is essential to challenge discriminatory norms and taboos that limit women's participation in the development process (Vyas-Doorgapersad, 2020).

Furthermore, advancing the sustainability agenda in the Southern African region necessitates diversifying its economic sectors and promoting innovation through the active involvement of multiple stakeholders, both from the region and developed countries (Grant et al., 2020; Pandey et al., 2022). This is crucial as the region heavily relies on the mining and agriculture sectors, which still require the application of modern and innovative technologies to drive economic growth and enhance the living conditions of most of its population living in poverty. In a positive development, Erika and Mario (2014) highlighted that SADC countries were actively involved in establishing robust innovation networks. These networks encompassed research institutes, higher education institutions, think tanks, and other organizations capable of generating pertinent knowledge to promote development.

Investing in research and development, fostering a culture of innovation, and supporting small and medium-sized enterprises (SMEs) stand out as best practices for achieving economic diversification. Embracing innovation and entrepreneurship enables Southern Africa to tap into emerging industries such as renewable energy, information technology, and eco-tourism, creating job opportunities and bolstering economic resilience.

DIRECTIONS FOR FUTURE RESEARCH

As Southern Africa actively establishes partnerships to fulfil its vision of achieving sustainable growth and development by 2030, several critical directions for future research can significantly contribute to these ambitious goals. These research areas promise to provide valuable inputs and inform policies and strategies tailored to the region's unique challenges and opportunities. Efforts should be directed towards a deeper engagement with sustainable resource management, exploring innovative approaches encompassing conservation, resource allocation, and the sustainable utilization of natural resources. The aim is to balance economic development and the goal of environmental preservation.

Furthermore, as the impacts of climate change continue to escalate within the region, research on resilience strategies tailored to Southern Africa's distinct vulnerabilities becomes crucial. This assertion aligns with the insights of Enqvist and Ziervogel (2019), with a particular focus on South Africa's unique context. Inclusive innovation must remain at the forefront of research priorities. It is vital to ensure that marginalized groups, including women and indigenous communities, actively participate in and benefit from technological advancements, promoting equity and progress. In addition, efforts to refine effective stakeholder engagement frameworks should persist, enhancing decision-making processes and outcomes. As Pale et al. (2021) highlight, a crucial suggestion involves future research about power discrepancies among governments at various administrative levels and assessing the influence of marketization and legislation on economic growth.

Gender equality, economic diversification, and transboundary cooperation demand further research attention, as articulated by Dogan et al. (2023). This entails immersing into the analysis of the connection between economic diversity and related topics, including industrial policy, technological sophistication, technological change, innovation, structural transformation, and environmental sustainability, particularly bioeconomy and circular economy studies. Future studies should also explore knowledge transfer and interaction between countries, encompassing global research and higher education institutions.

This chapter's authors also suggest that the investigation of Practical strategies for promoting youth empowerment and evaluating education's pivotal role in shaping social and economic development should be prioritized. This involves assessing existing policies and initiatives and identifying areas for improvement. The preservation and integration of indigenous knowledge and traditional practices into modern sustainability efforts is an emerging research area with immense potential to enrich sustainable development initiatives. Realizing the region's sustainable and prosperous future necessitates a collaborative, multidisciplinary approach that actively engages local and international stakeholders in pursuing these shared aspirations.

CONCLUSION

The analysis found that stakeholder engagement and community participation are crucial to the success of initiatives working to achieve sustainable development goals. Actions to promote sustainable growth and development should involve a diverse and inclusive group of stakeholders dedicated to collaborating ethically, openly, and with mutual respect. Partners in local development efforts must be willing to capacitate, transfer knowledge and skills, adequately respond to each member's needs and aspirations, and focus on empowering local communities to participate actively in the development process. The chapter identified challenges affecting stakeholders' performance and project success, including a lack of finances, effective coordination and collaboration, lack of technical skills and training opportunities, lack of transparency, corruption and mismanagement, political conflicts, and poor access to technology. The active participation of various community actors in initiatives promoting sustainable growth and development would bring different perspectives and solutions to assist in curbing some of the identified challenges.

The findings also indicated that collaborative efforts should be open with mutual dialogue between diverse stakeholders to guarantee a sense of ownership and active community members' participation in decision-making. Project partners must share relevant information with the general audience promptly and transparently. In addition, the chapter demonstrated that stakeholder engagement processes should consider and hear all partners' and community members' perspectives, guarantee capacity-building opportunities, and promote cooperation and long-term partnerships that address local communities and vulnerable groups' needs and aspirations. The chapter findings also determined that to guarantee effective coordination and preparedness of local and disadvantaged community members to participate in development initiatives actively, a set of strategies must ensure the local's participation in all the project stages. These strategies included strengthening the capacity of social networks and community-based organizations to protect local communities' rights and offer technical skills training opportunities to enhance local communities' abilities to engage in project implementation tasks professionally, ethically and confidently.

Lastly, the chapter found that interventions that engage different partners in designing and implementing income-generation projects will likely contribute to the region's sustainable economic growth and improve communities' quality of life. These projects must directly benefit the disadvantaged members of the community to enable their resilience, self-dependency, and abilities to balance long-term socio-economic and environmental benefits. The focus should be on incorporating traditional and local values and knowledge to promote communities' commitment to execute their tasks with a high sense of duty, confidence in their abilities, values, and respect for their traditions. Several communication channels must inform communities about available training and job opportunities using two-way communication, allowing community members to voice their opinions and request information about the projects freely. Thus, community members will actively monitor project progress by sharing feedback and concerns about its processes and outcomes. The findings will help strengthen stakeholder engagement and community participation in initiatives to achieve sustainable development goals. Project partners will be empowered with knowledge and skills to participate in the project's decision-making actively and equally, implementation, monitoring, and evaluation stages, irrespective of their socioeconomic background.

REFERENCES

Abiddin, N. Z., Ibrahim, I., & Abdul Aziz, S. A. (2022). Non-governmental organizations (NGOs) and their part towards sustainable community development. *Sustainability (Basel)*, *14*(8), 4386. doi:10.3390u14084386

Akpa-Inyang, F., & Chima, S. C. (2021). South African traditional values and beliefs regarding informed consent and limitations of the principle of respect for autonomy in African communities: A cross-cultural qualitative study. *BMC Medical Ethics*, *22*(1), 1–17. doi:10.118612910-021-00678-4 PMID:34391415

Aligica, P. D. (2006). Institutional and stakeholder mapping: Frameworks for policy analysis and institutional change. *Public Organization Review*, *6*(1), 79–90. doi:10.100711115-006-6833-0

Ascoli, K., & Benzaken, T. (2009). *Public policy and the promotion of corporate social responsibility.* BSR. http://www. bsr. org/research/reports-bycategory. cfm

Babu, M. M., Dey, B. L., Rahman, M., Roy, S. K., Alwi, S. F. S., & Kamal, M. M. (2020). Value co-creation through social innovation: A study of sustainable strategic alliance in telecommunication and financial services sectors in Bangladesh. *Industrial Marketing Management, 89*, 13-27. doi:10.1016/j.indmarman.2020.06.003

Bal, M., Bryde, D., Fearon, D., & Ochieng, E. (2013). Stakeholder engagement: Achieving sustainability in the construction sector. *Sustainability (Basel)*, *5*(2), 695–710. doi:10.3390u5020695

Barquet, K., Segnestam, L., & Dickin, S. (2022). *MapStakes: a tool for mapping, involving and monitoring stakeholders in co-creation processes.* Stockholm Environment Institute. doi:10.51414ei2022.014

Barrow, E. G., Clarke, J., Grundy, I., Jones, K.R., & Tessema, Y. (2002). *Analysis of stakeholder power and responsibilities in community involvement in forest management in Eastern and Southern Africa* (No. 9). IUCN.

Barua, S. (2020). Financing sustainable development goals: A review of challenges and mitigation strategies. *Business Strategy & Development*, *3*(3), 277–293. doi:10.1002/bsd2.94

Batti, R. C. (2014). Challenges facing local NGOs in resource mobilization. *Humanities and Social Sciences*, *2*(3), 57–64. doi:10.11648/j.hss.20140203.12

Bell, S., Morse, S., & Shah, R. A. (2012). Understanding stakeholder participation in research as part of sustainable development. *Journal of Environmental Management*, *101*, 13–22. doi:10.1016/j.jenvman.2012.02.004 PMID:22387326

Bilal, S. (2017). *SADC institutional capacity to deliver on its mandate*. Paper prepared for the SADC Strategic Ministerial Retreat - "The SADC We Want", 12-14 March 2017, Kingdom of Swaziland.

Bryson, J. M. (2003). *What to do when stakeholders matter: A guide to stakeholder identification and analysis techniques*. London School of Economics and Political Science.

Bryson, J. M. (2004). What to do when stakeholders matter: Stakeholder identification and analysis techniques. *Public Management Review*, *6*(1), 21–53. doi:10.1080/14719030410001675722

Catley, A. (1999). *Methods on the move: A review of veterinary uses of participatory approaches and methods focusing on experiences in dryland Africa*. International Institute for Environment and Development.

Chamber, E. C. O. S. O. C. (2018). *Financing for SDGs: Breaking bottlenecks of investment from policy to impact*. The United Nations.

Chevallier, R., Gosling, A., & Chesterman, S. (2020). Structures, policies and stakeholder landscape relevant to climate change and agriculture in the SADC Region. SADC Futures: Developing Foresight Capacity for Climate Resilient Agricultural Development Knowledge Series. CCAFS Report. Wageningen, the Netherlands: CGIAR Research Program on Climate Change. *Agriculture & Food Security*.

Chingono, T. T., & Mbohwa, C. (2023). Disasters in Selected Emerging Economies. In Supply Networks in Developing Countries: Sustainable and Humanitarian Logistics in Growing Consumer Markets (pp. 31-44). Emerald Publishing Limited. doi:10.1108/978-1-80117-194-620231003

Chitakira, M., Nhamo, L., Torquebiau, E., Magidi, J., Ferguson, W., Mpandeli, S., Mearns, K., & Mabhaudhi, T. (2022). Opportunities to improve eco-agriculture through transboundary governance in transfrontier conservation areas. *Diversity*, *14*(6), 461. doi:10.3390/d14060461

Chopra, M., Singh, S. K., Gupta, A., Aggarwal, K., Gupta, B. B., & Colace, F. (2022). Analysis & prognosis of sustainable development goals using big data-based approach during COVID-19 pandemic. *Sustainable Technology and Entrepreneurship*, *1*(2), 100012. doi:10.1016/j.stae.2022.100012

Claassens, A., & Matlala, B. (2014). Platinum, poverty and princes in post-apartheid South Africa: new laws, old repertoires. In G. M. Khadiagala, P. Naidoo, D. Pillay, & R. Southhall (Eds.), *New South African Review* (Vol. 4). Wits University Press. doi:10.18772/22014047632.12

Clark, W. C., Van Kerkhoff, L., Lebel, L., & Gallopin, G. C. (2016). Crafting usable knowledge for sustainable development. *Proceedings of the National Academy of Sciences of the United States of America*, *113*(17), 4570–4578. doi:10.1073/pnas.1601266113 PMID:27091979

Cole, M. J., & Broadhurst, J. L. (2022). Sustainable Development in Mining Communities: The Case of South Africa's West Wits Goldfield. *Frontiers in Sustainable Cities*, *4*, 87. doi:10.3389/frsc.2022.895760

Croese, S., & Duminy, J. (2023). Co-producing urban expertise for SDG localization: The history and practices of urban knowledge production in South Africa. *Urban Geography*, *44*(3), 538–557. doi:10.1080/02723638.2022.2079868

Devuyst, D. (2000). Linking impact assessment and sustainable development at the local level: The introduction of sustainability assessment systems. *Sustainable Development (Bradford)*, *8*(2), 67–78. doi:10.1002/(SICI)1099-1719(200005)8:2<67::AID-SD131>3.0.CO;2-X

Doğan, B., Rao, A., Ferraz, D., Sharma, G. D., & Shahzadi, I. (2023). What do we learn from Nexus between trade diversification and structural change: Informing the future about climate action and Sustainability. *Environmental Science and Pollution Research International*, 1–20. PMID:37486468

ECOSOC Chamber (2018). *Financing for SDGs: Breaking bottlenecks of investment from policy to impact*. The United Nations.

Edelenbos, J., Van Buuren, A., & van Schie, N. (2011). Co-producing knowledge: Joint knowledge production between experts, bureaucrats and stakeholders in Dutch water management projects. *Environmental Science & Policy*, *14*(6), 675–684. doi:10.1016/j.envsci.2011.04.004

Eni, O., Nnam, M. U., & Udu, E. A. (2022). The Right to Participate in Political and Decision-Making Process under the Maputo Protocol: Normative Masculinity and Nigerian Women. *The Age of Human Rights Journal*, (18), 397–423. doi:10.17561/tahrj.v18.6633

Enqvist, J. P., & Ziervogel, G. (2019). Water governance and justice in Cape Town: An overview. *WIREs. Water*, *6*(4), e1354. doi:10.1002/wat2.1354

Erika, K.-M., & Mario, S. (2014). *UNESCO Science Report: Towards 2030*. UNESCO.

Eweje, G., Sajjad, A., Nath, S. D., & Kobayashi, K. (2021). Multi-stakeholder partnerships: A catalyst to achieve sustainable development goals. *Marketing Intelligence & Planning*, *39*(2), 186–212. doi:10.1108/MIP-04-2020-0135

Ferreira, V., Barreira, A. P., Loures, L., Antunes, D., & Panagopoulos, T. (2020). Stakeholders' engagement on nature-based solutions: A systematic literature review. *Sustainability (Basel)*, *12*(2), 640. doi:10.3390u12020640

Fiandrino, S., Scarpa, F., & Torelli, R. (2022). Fostering social impact through corporate implementation of the SDGs: Transformative mechanisms towards interconnectedness and inclusiveness. *Journal of Business Ethics*, *180*(4), 959–973. doi:10.100710551-022-05189-9

Flint, R. W. (2013). *Practice of Sustainable Community Development A Participatory Framework for Change*. Springer. doi:10.1007/978-1-4614-5100-6

Freeman, R. E. (1984). *Strategic management: A stakeholder approach*. Pitman.

Freeman, R. E., Kujala, J., & Sachs, S. (2017). *Stakeholder engagement: Clinical research cases*. Springer. doi:10.1007/978-3-319-62785-4

Garwe, E. C., & Gwati, L. (2018). The role of international and regional quality assurance bodies. *Higher Education Research*, *3*(1), 15–22. doi:10.11648/j.her.20180301.14

Ghisellini, P., Cialani, C., & Ulgiati, S. (2016). A review on circular economy: The expected transition to a balanced interplay of environmental and economic systems. *Journal of Cleaner Production*, *114*, 11–32. doi:10.1016/j.jclepro.2015.09.007

Gibbens, M., & Schoeman, C. (2020). Planning for sustainable livelihood development in the context of rural South Africa: A micro-level approach. *Town and Regional Planning, 76*(1), 14–28. doi:10.18820/2415-0495/trp76i1.2

Govender van-Wyk, S., & Wilson, D. (2009). Sustainable Tourism on Commonages: An Alternative to Traditional Agricultural-based Land Reform in Namaqualand, South Africa. In Sustainable tourism in Southern Africa: Local communities and natural resources in transition. Academic Press.

Grant, R., Carmody, P., & Murphy, J. T. (2020). A green transition in South Africa? Sociotechnical experimentation in the Atlantis Special Economic Zone. *The Journal of Modern African Studies, 58*(2), 189–211. doi:10.1017/S0022278X20000208

Gray, B. (1989). *Collaborating: Finding Common Ground for Multiparty Problems*. Jossey-Bass.

Gregory, A. J., Atkins, J. P., Midgley, G., & Hodgson, A. M. (2020). Stakeholder identification and engagement in problem structuring interventions. *European Journal of Operational Research, 283*(1), 321–340. doi:10.1016/j.ejor.2019.10.044

Gressel, C. M., Rashed, T., Maciuika, L. A., Sheshadri, S., Coley, C., Kongeseri, S., & Bhavani, R. R. (2020). Vulnerability mapping: A conceptual framework towards a context-based approach to women's empowerment. *World Development Perspectives, 20*, 100245. doi:10.1016/j.wdp.2020.100245 PMID:32835139

Gujadhur, T. (2001). *Joint Venture Options for Communities and Safari Operators in Botswana*, CBNRN Support Programme Occasional Paper No. 6. SNV/IUCN.

Guttal, S. (2021). Re-imagining the UN Committee on World Food Security. *Development, 64*(3-4), 227–235. doi:10.105741301-021-00322-z PMID:34703165

Hardi, P., & Zdan, T. (1997). *Assessing Sustainable Development: Principles in Practice*. International Institute for Sustainable Development.

Hickey, S. (2004). *Participation: From tyranny to transformation: Exploring new approaches to participation in development*. Zed books.

Honey, M. (1999). *Ecotourism and Sustainable Development: Who Owns Paradise?* Island Press.

INVOLVE. (2005). *People and participation: how to put citizens at the heart of decision-making*. INVOLVE. https://www.involve.org.uk/resources/publications/practical-guidance/people-and-participation-how-put-citizens-heart-decision

Jamal, T., & Stronza, A. (2009). Collaboration theory and tourism practice in protected areas: Stakeholders, structuring and sustainability. *Journal of Sustainable Tourism, 17*(2), 169–189. doi:10.1080/09669580802495741

Jani, V., De Wit, A. H., & Webb, N. L. (2022). Evaluating the relevance of the CAMPFIRE principles to wildlife utilization in northern Zimbabwe. *African Journal of Wildlife Research, 52*(1), 56–71. doi:10.3957/056.052.0056

Jansen, L. J., & Kalas, P. P. (2020). Improving governance of tenure in policy and practice: A conceptual basis to analyze multi-stakeholder partnerships for multi-stakeholder transformative governance illustrated with an example from South Africa. *Sustainability (Basel)*, *12*(23), 9901. doi:10.3390u12239901

Jewett, R. L., Mah, S. M., Howell, N., & Larsen, M. M. (2021). Social cohesion and community resilience during COVID-19 and pandemics: A rapid scoping review to inform the United Nations research roadmap for COVID-19 recovery. *International Journal of Health Services*, *51*(3), 325–336. doi:10.1177/0020731421997092 PMID:33827308

Jiao, W., Yang, X., & Min, Q. (2022). A review of the Progress in globally important agricultural heritage systems (GIAHS) monitoring. *Sustainability (Basel)*, *14*(16), 9958. doi:10.3390u14169958

Kaatz, E., Root, D. S., Bowen, P. A., & Hill, R. C. (2006). Advancing key outcomes of sustainability building assessment. *Building Research and Information*, *34*(4), 308–320. doi:10.1080/09613210600724608

Kangalawe, R. Y., Noe, C., Tungaraza, F. S., Naimani, G., & Mlele, M. (2014). Understanding of traditional knowledge and indigenous institutions on sustainable land management in Kilimanjaro Region, Tanzania. *Open Journal of Social Sciences*, *4*(13), 469.

Kestin, T., van den Belt, M., Denby, L., Ross, K., Thwaites, J., & Hawkes, M. (2017). *Getting started with the SDGs in universities: A guide for universities, higher education institutions, and the academic sector*. Academic Press.

Khadiagala, L. S. (2001). The failure of popular justice in Uganda: Local councils and women's property rights. *Development and Change*, *32*(1), 55–76. doi:10.1111/1467-7660.00196

Koohafkan, P., & Delacruz, M. (2011). Conservation and adaptive management of globally important agricultural heritage systems (GIAHS). *Journal of Resources and Ecology*, *2*, 12–13.

Kujala, J., & Sachs, S. (2019). The practice of stakeholder engagement. In J. Harrison, J. Barney, & R. E. Freeman (Eds.), *The Cambridge handbook of stakeholder theory* (pp. 121–140). Cambridge University Press. doi:10.1017/9781108123495.014

Landes, D. S. (2000). Culture Makes Almost All the Difference. In Culture Matters: How Values Shape Human Progress. Basic Books.

Lewis, C. (1991). *The Ethics Challenge in Public Service: A Problem-Solving Guide*. Jossey-Bass.

Lewis, D., & Jackson, J. (2005). Safari hunting and conservation on communal land in southern Africa. People and Wildlife, Conflict or Co-existence? 9, 239. doi:10.1017/CBO9780511614774.016

Lindner, R. (2023). Green hydrogen partnerships with the G lobal South. Advancing an energy justice perspective on "tomorrow's oil". *Sustainable Development (Bradford)*, *31*(2), 1038–1053. doi:10.1002d.2439

Liu, H., Saleem, M. M., Al-Faryan, M. A. S., Khan, I., & Zafar, M. W. (2022). Impact of governance and globalization on natural resources volatility: The role of financial development in the Middle East North Africa countries. *Resources Policy*, *78*, 102881. doi:10.1016/j.resourpol.2022.102881

Magi, L. M. (2007). To create or conserve, that is the question: The case of St. Lake Lucia. *Journal of Tourism & Hospitality (Los Angeles, Calif.)*, *4*(2), 1–12.

Makgoba, M. W. (1997). Mokoko, the makgoba affair: A reflection on transformation. Florida Hills, South Africa: Vivlia.

Mamokhere, J., & Meyer, D. F. (2023). *Towards an Exploration of the Significance of Community Participation in the Integrated Development Planning Process in South Africa*. Academic Press.

Matos, A., Barraza, L., & Ruiz-Mallén, I. (2021). Linking conservation, community knowledge, and adaptation to extreme climatic events: A case study in Gorongosa National Park, Mozambique. *Sustainability (Basel)*, *13*(11), 6478. doi:10.3390u13116478

Maziriri, E. T., Mapuranga, M., Maramura, T. C., & Nzewi, O. I. (2019). Navigating on the key drivers for a transition to a green economy: Evidence from women entrepreneurs in South Africa. *Entrepreneurship and Sustainability Issues*, *7*(2), 1686–1703. doi:10.9770/jesi.2019.7.2(62)

Mbigi, L., & Maree, J. (1995). *Ubuntu: The spirit of African transformation and management*. Sigma Press.

McAdam, R., Hazlett, S., & Casey, C. (2005). Performance management in the UK public sector: Addressing multiple stakeholder complexity. *International Journal of Public Sector Management*, *18*(3), 256–273. doi:10.1108/09513550510591542

Mitchell, R. K., Agle, B. R., & Wood, D. J. (1997). Toward a theory of stakeholder identification and salience: Defining the principle of who and what really counts. *Academy of Management Review*, *22*(4), 853–886. doi:10.2307/259247

Mkandawire, E., Mentz-Coetzee, M., Mangheni, M. N., & Barusi, E. (2021). Enhancing the Glopan Food Systems Framework by Integrating Gender: Relevance for Women in African Agriculture. *Sustainability (Basel)*, *13*(15), 8564. doi:10.3390u13158564

Mpofu, F. Y. (2022). Green Taxes in Africa: Opportunities and challenges for environmental protection, sustainability, and the attainment of sustainable development goals. *Sustainability (Basel)*, *14*(16), 10239. doi:10.3390u141610239

Muboko, N. (2017). The role of transfrontier conservation areas and their institutional framework in natural resource-based conflict management: A review. *Journal of Sustainable Forestry*, *36*(6), 583–603. doi:10.1080/10549811.2017.1320224

Mukumbang, F. C., Ambe, A. N., & Adebiyi, B. O. (2020). Unspoken inequality: How COVID-19 has exacerbated existing vulnerabilities of asylum-seekers, refugees, and undocumented migrants in South Africa. *International Journal for Equity in Health*, *19*(1), 141. doi:10.118612939-020-01259-4 PMID:32819364

Ndonga, D., Chihaka, S., & Fielder, A. (2021). Integration of gender practices and promotion of diversity in customs and trade: The case of East and Southern Africa. *World Customs Journal*, *15*(1).

Ngumbela, X. G., Khalema, E. N., & Nzimakwe, T. I. (2020). Local worlds: Vulnerability and food insecurity in the Eastern Cape province of South Africa. *Jamba (Potchefstroom, South Africa)*, *12*(1), 1–10. doi:10.4102/jamba.v12i1.830 PMID:32832036

Nguyen, T. T., Grote, U., Neubacher, F., Do, M. H., & Paudel, G. P. (2023). Security risks from climate change and environmental degradation: Implications for sustainable land use transformation in the Global South. *Current Opinion in Environmental Sustainability, 63*, 101322. doi:10.1016/j.cosust.2023.101322

Nwosu, P. O. (2009). Understanding Africans' conceptualizations of intercultural competence. The SAGE handbook of intercultural competence, 158-178.

Nxopo, Z. (2014). *The Role of Government in Empowering Female Entrepreneurs in the Western Cape, South Africa* [Master's dissertation]. Cape Peninsula University of Technology, Cape Town.

Nyasimi, M., Okang'a, J., Mutuo, M., & Masira, J. (2009). Change from within: Engaging local communities in achieving the Millennium Development Goals in Sub–Sahara Africa. *Omertaa J. Appl. Anthropol*, 474-494.

O'Dwyer, M., & Gilmore, A. (2015). Value and alliance capability and the formation of strategic alliances in SMES: The impact of customer orientation and resource optimization. *Journal of Business Research, 87*, 58–68. doi:10.1016/j.jbusres.2018.02.020

Olander, S. (2007). Stakeholder impact analysis in construction project management. *Construction Management and Economics, 25*(3), 277–287. doi:10.1080/01446190600879125

Oloo, J. O., Makenzi, P. M. D., & Mwangi, J. G. P. (2013). Influence of traditions/customs and beliefs/norms on women in tree growing in Siaya County, Kenya. *Global Journal of Environmental Science and Technology, 1*(1), 1-6.

Onebunne, J. I., & Okechukwu, S. (2021). African Ecological Crisis and Education. *Journal of African Studies and Sustainable Development.*

Pandey, N., de Coninck, H., & Sagar, A. D. (2022). Beyond technology transfer: Innovation cooperation to advance sustainable development in developing countries. *Wiley Interdisciplinary Reviews. Energy and Environment, 11*(2), e422. doi:10.1002/wene.422

Pawar, M. (2017). The need for enhanced community participation. *Future Directions in Social Development*, 79-98.

Perold, H. (2006, November). Volunteering as a strategy to foster civic participation among youth in southern Africa. In *Presentation made to XIX IAVE World Volunteer Conference on Volunteering for Peace in Multicultural Societies, Delhi* (pp. 10-13). Academic Press.

Phale, K., Li, F., Adjei Mensah, I., Omari-Sasu, A. Y., & Musah, M. (2021). Knowledge-based economy capacity building for developing countries: A panel analysis in Southern African Development Community. *Sustainability (Basel), 13*(5), 2890. doi:10.3390u13052890

Pillay, I. (2021). The impact of inequality and COVID-19 on education and career planning for South African children of rural and low-socioeconomic backgrounds. *African Journal of Career Development, 3*(1), 7. doi:10.4102/ajcd.v3i1.36

Reed, M., & Curzon, R. (2015). Stakeholder mapping for the governance of biosecurity: A literature review. *Journal of Integrative Environmental Sciences, 12*(1), 15–38. doi:10.1080/1943815X.2014.975723

Reed, M. S., Graves, A., Dandy, N., Posthumus, H., Hubacek, K., Morris, J., Prell, C., Quinn, C. H., & Stringer, L. C. (2009). Who's in and why? A typology of stakeholder analysis methods for natural resource management. *Journal of Environmental Management, 90*(I5), 1933-1949. doi:10.1016/j.jenvman.2009.01.001

Resurrección, B. P., Bee, B. A., Dankelman, I., Park, C. M. Y., Haldar, M., & McMullen, C. P. (2019). *Gender-transformative climate change adaptation: advancing social equity.* GCA.

Ridley, J., & Jones, L. (2002). *User and public involvement in health services: a literature review.* Partners in Change.

Rijal, S. (2023). The Importance of Community Involvement in Public Management Planning and Decision-Making Processes. *Journal of Contemporary Administration and Management, 1*(2), 84–92. doi:10.61100/adman.v1i2.27

Rosen, J., & Painter, G. (2019). From citizen control to co-production: Moving beyond a linear conception of citizen participation. *Journal of the American Planning Association, 85*(3), 335–347. doi:10.1080/01944363.2019.1618727

Rowe, R., & Shepherd, M. (2002). Public participation in the new NHS: No closer to Citizen Control? *Social Policy and Administration, 36*(3), 275–290. doi:10.1111/1467-9515.00251

Roy, I. (2002). 2AHIFA? JELAI. *Economic and Political Weekly*, 3591.

Saha, M., Varghese, D., Bartindale, T., Thilsted, S. H., Ahmed, S. I., & Olivier, P. (2022). Towards Sustainable ICTD in Bangladesh: Understanding the Program and Policy Landscape and Its Implications for CSCW and HCI. *Proceedings of the ACM on Human-Computer Interaction, 6*(CSCW1), 1-31. 10.1145/3512973

Sahoo, K. C., Sahay, M. R., Dubey, S., Nayak, S., Negi, S., Mahapatra, P., Bhattacharya, D., Del Barrio, M. O., & Pati, S. (2023). Community engagement and involvement in managing the COVID-19 pandemic among urban poor in low-and middle-income countries: a systematic scoping review and stakeholders mapping, *Global Health Action, 16*(1), 2133723.

Sari, A. R. (2023). The Impact of Good Governance on the Quality of Public Management Decision Making. *Journal of Contemporary Administration and Management, 1*(2), 39–46. doi:10.61100/adman.v1i2.21

Shackelton, S., & Campbell, B. (2000). *Empowering communities to manage natural resources: case studies from Southern Africa.* Division of Water, Environment and Forestry Technology.

Shepherd, A., & Bowler, C. (1997). Beyond the requirements: Improving public participation in EIA. *Journal of Environmental Planning and Management, 40*(6), 725–738. doi:10.1080/09640569711877

Shindler, B., & Cheek, K. A. (1999). Integrating citizens in adaptive management: A propositional analysis. *Conservation Ecology, 3*(1), 9. doi:10.5751/ES-00112-030109

Steiner, A. (2019). Climate change, environment, and sustainable development in Africa. In *African Economic Development* (pp. 93–110). Emerald Publishing Limited.

Tamale, S. (2004). Gender trauma in Africa: Enhancing women's links to resources. *Journal of African Law*, *48*(1), 50–61. doi:10.1017/S0021855304481030

Tejedo-Romero, F., Araujo, J. F. F. E., Tejada, Á., & Ramírez, Y. (2022). E-government mechanisms to enhance the participation of citizens and society: Exploratory analysis through the dimension of municipalities. *Technology in Society*, *70*, 101978. doi:10.1016/j.techsoc.2022.101978

The World Commission on Environment and Development-WCED. (1987). *Our Common Future*. Oxford University Press.

Thondhlana, G., Mubaya, C. P., McClure, A., Amaka-Otchere, A. B. K., & Ruwanza, S. (2021). Facilitating urban sustainability through transdisciplinary (TD) research: Lessons from Ghana, South Africa, and Zimbabwe. *Sustainability (Basel)*, *13*(11), 6205. doi:10.3390u13116205

Tosun, C. (2006). Expected nature of community participation in tourism development. *Tourism Management*, *27*(3), 493–504. doi:10.1016/j.tourman.2004.12.004

United Nations Conference on Environment and Development. (1992). *Earth Summit Agenda 21*. The United Nations Programme of Action from Rio. UN. Available from: http://www.un.org/esa/ dsd/agenda21/index.shtml

Varela Pérez, P., Greiner, B. E., & von Cossel, M. (2022). Socio-Economic and Environmental Implications of Bioenergy Crop Cultivation on Marginal African Drylands and Key Principles for a Sustainable Development. *Earth (Basel, Switzerland)*, *3*(2), 652–682. doi:10.3390/earth3020038

Vyas-Doorgapersad, S. (2020). Gender equality in the sport sector: The case of selected Southern African countries. *International Journal of Social Sciences and Humanity Studies*, *12*(1), 207–221.

Wang, Q., & Huang, R. (2021). The impact of COVID-19 pandemic on sustainable development goals– a survey. *Environmental Research*, *202*, 111637. doi:10.1016/j.envres.2021.111637 PMID:34233155

White, D. D., Jones, J. L., Maciejewski, R., Aggarwal, R., & Mascaro, G. (2017). Stakeholder analysis for the food-energy-water nexus in Phoenix, Arizona: Implications for nexus governance. *Sustainability (Basel)*, *9*(12), 2204. doi:10.3390u9122204

Williams, J. J. (2006). Community Participation. *Policy Studies*, *27*(3), 197–217. doi:10.1080/01442870600885982

World Health Organization. (2018a). A vision for primary health care in the 21st century: towards universal health coverage and the Sustainable Development Goals (No. WHO/HIS/SDS/2018.15). World Health Organization.

World Health Organization. (2018b). WHO water, sanitation and hygiene strategy 2018-2025 (No. WHO/CED/PHE/WSH/18.03). World Health Organization.

Zaloumis, A. (2007). A name for a miracle. *Isimangaliso News, 1*(1), 1-10.

ADDITIONAL READING

Debrah, J. K., Teye, G. K., & Dinis, M. A. P. (2022). Barriers and challenges to waste management hindering the circular economy in Sub-Saharan Africa. *Urban Science (Basel, Switzerland)*, *6*(3), 57. doi:10.3390/urbansci6030057

Kaler, J. (2002). Morality and strategy in stakeholder identification. *Journal of Business Ethics*, *39*(1/2), 91–99. doi:10.1023/A:1016336118528

Muhamad Khair, N. K., Lee, K. E., & Mokhtar, M. (2020). Sustainable city and community empowerment through the implementation of community-based monitoring: A conceptual approach. *Sustainability (Basel)*, *12*(22), 9583. doi:10.3390u12229583

Oliveira-Duarte, L., Reis, D. A., Fleury, A. L., Vasques, R. A., Fonseca Filho, H., Koria, M., & Baruque-Ramos, J. (2021). Innovation Ecosystem framework directed to Sustainable Development Goal# 17 partnerships implementation. *Sustainable Development (Bradford)*, *29*(5), 1018–1036. doi:10.1002d.2191

Pretorius, O. R., Drewes, J. E., & Gumbo, T. (2022). Evidence to Inform Resilience Policy in the SADC: Current Limitations and Future Research Areas. *WORLD (Oakland, Calif.)*, *3*(3), 449–469. doi:10.3390/world3030024

World Health Organization. (2015). *From MDGs, millennium development goals to SDGs, sustainable development goals*. WHO.

KEY TERMS AND DEFINITIONS

Community Participation: Refers to the dynamic and meaningful engagement of local communities in initiatives to advance socio-economic development. This engagement spans all stages of the development lifecycle, from project inception to implementation, ensuring that the community's voices, contributions, and aspirations are integrated into the process.

Inclusive Participation: The practice of engaging individuals or organizations in activities or initiatives to facilitate the successful implementation of a development project or program, ensuring a diverse and comprehensive representation of stakeholders.

Stakeholder Engagement: Is a collaborative and inclusive process wherein multiple partners establish constructive relationships to tackle shared challenges affecting their communities. It entails voluntary partnerships among individuals and organizations united by the common goal of addressing specific community-based issues.

Sustainable Development: Represents the collaborative efforts of diverse stakeholders engaged in the planning and execution of projects to enhance the well-being of local communities while safeguarding natural resources, ensuring their availability for future generations without depletion or harm.

Traditional Knowledge: Refers to the knowledge, practices, and beliefs inherited from indigenous communities, which serve to enhance and inform interventions aimed at advancing sustainable development strategies.

Chapter 5
From Rhetoric to Reality:
Strengthening Peacebuilding Through Women's Leadership in Nigeria

Comfort Fatimoh Sheidu
https://orcid.org/0000-0002-9203-5600
University of Abuja, Nigeria

Hosea Olayiwola Patrick
https://orcid.org/0000-0001-8022-9099
McMaster University, Canada

ABSTRACT

The role of women in peacebuilding has largely been underrepresented and marginalized. This chapter explores the potential of women's leadership in peacebuilding in Nigeria and how their participation can strengthen the peace-building processes. Using desktop review approach, the chapter investigates the obstacles such as patriarchal attitudes and structural barriers to women's leadership in peacebuilding. It argues that increasing women's participation is critical to strengthening peacebuilding in Nigeria. This necessitates a multifaceted strategy that addresses structural barriers to women's participation. It concludes that women's peace-building leadership is critical for achieving long-term peace and security in Nigeria and by extension Africa. However, turning rhetoric into reality necessitates a collaborative effort on the part of all stakeholders. It necessitates a commitment to gender equality and women's empowerment, as well as an understanding of the unique perspectives and contributions that women can bring to peace-building efforts.

INTRODUCTION

Man is innately indulgent, which explains his never-ending search for a peaceful environment void of insecurity (Salaudeen & Gombi, 2019). Nigeria is one of the nations in the globe that has gone through and continues to experience violent conflict, necessitating the adoption of various methods to address the issue. These strategies include peacekeeping missions, truth and reconciliation commissions, panels

DOI: 10.4018/979-8-3693-0477-8.ch005

of inquiry and others (Olaitan, 2018; Patrick *et al.,* 2022). According to Jah et al. (2022), these processes of peace have been mainly controlled by men throughout history, with barely any involvement of women. This is a consequence of patriarchal cultural practices, gender inequality, and other factors that pervade peacebuilding. It is important to note that "gender" is a crucial idea in peacebuilding and peacekeeping because it addresses social norms that result in differentiated treatment of males and females. This is prevalent in situations involving resource distribution, services and goods, and rewards derived from resources – resulting in different developmental effects on men and women (Kimani & Kombo, 2010). Also, Agbalajobi (2010) contends that in conflict situations, men and women are confronted with new roles and shifting expectations based on gender. Their sociological and biological disparities have an impact on peacekeeping (Iteyo & Mumbi, 2020).

Garba (2016) argues that women's participation in peacebuilding is a concept that is just starting to gain traction in Nigeria. Indeed, since the outbreak of violent conflicts in Nigeria, Nigerian women's participation in peacebuilding remains severely underutilised. And uneven, with women taking the initiative for peacebuilding only at the grassroots level, despite being victims of such violent conflicts (Garba, 2016). Violence based on gender is well-known to be on the rise in conflict-affected communities, but the specific causes of the problem remain unknown (Desai & Mandal, 2021). As a result, women's leadership is increasingly being recognized as an important factor in promoting global peace and stability.

Nigeria, Africa's most populous country, has a complicated history defined by religious conflicts, ethnic strife, and political insecurity (Bamidele, 2020). These factors have fuelled periods of armed conflict in various parts of the country (See Olagbaju & Awosusi, 2019; Ngwoke & Ituma, 2020; Afolaranmi, 2021; Sheidu & Patrick, 2023). As a result, various peacebuilding efforts involving governmental, non-governmental, and international actors have been launched. Despite these efforts, achieving long-term peace is still an enormous challenge (Sharifi et al., 2021).

The establishment of women's leadership in peacebuilding cannot be overemphasised in the context of Nigeria, a nation that has witnessed constant violence and conflicts ranging from resource conflicts by farmers and headers in the Middle Belt (Sheidu & Patrick, 2023) to religious and political conflicts in the North and South among others (Afolaranmi, 2021). It is worth noting that when women get involved in peace processes and decision-making, the outcomes are more long-term (Adjei, 2019). Women offer distinct views, and experiences, as well as abilities for conflict resolution, prevention, and reconstruction. In addition, Haider (2009) agrees that women frequently prioritize social cohesion, community building, and long-term development, all of which are critical components of fostering long-term peace. Knowing the factors that impede or promote women's leadership in peacebuilding is therefore critical for developing effective initiatives and strategies in Nigeria. As a result, the study intends to examine the situation of women's leadership in peacebuilding, examining current challenges, opportunities, and strategies for strengthening their role in translating rhetoric into real outcomes.

METHODOLOGY

This chapter adopts a qualitative desktop approach to explore the research focus of the study. By this, a systemic scoping review method (see Hosea and Khalema, 2020) was adopted using a convenience sampling of literature that addresses peacebuilding approaches in general, community participation in peacebuilding and more specifically, women's participation in peacebuilding efforts in Nigeria. Using the base year of 1997 to 2023, we used the Scopus search engine to filter relevant literature to the study themes. Of this, 5109 pieces of literature were found on peacebuilding. From this number, only 376 literature jointly addressed peacebuilding and women themes while only 20 literature covered the 3 central themes of our study (Peacebuilding, women and leadership). In total, 73 articles were triangulated, sorted, and analysed for thematic relevance to the study aim. The data gathered were then thematically analysed.

BACKGROUND

Historical Overview

The United Nations first introduced the concept of peacebuilding as a measure to recognise as well as encourage structures that are inclined to fortify and solidify peace to avoid a conflict relapse (Chinkin & Charlesworth, 2008). As argued by Adeogun and Muthuki (2018), this meant that where conflict had ended, peacebuilding efforts were needed, which included revitalising the infrastructures and institutions of countries destroyed by conflict, along with endeavours to bring those who were involved in the conflict together to minimise the possibility of a recurrence. Peacebuilding refers to measures that aim to prevent the onset or return of violent conflict by fostering long-term peace (Hanachor & Echezu, 2021). It involves individual and group responsibilities, as well as reconciliation processes that aid in minimising or avoiding the occurrence of armed conflict. (Goyol, 2019).

Peacebuilding entails a wide range of methods, techniques, and phases required to transform relationships into more friendly and peaceful. It encompasses a wide variety of tasks related to capacity development, peace-making, as well as social transformation. (Olaifa, 2017). According to Porter and Every (2009), peacebuilding is a lengthy procedure that occurs following a cease in violent conflict. In a broader sense, peacebuilding is a process that seeks to avert conflict from recurring by tackling the immediate and remote causes and consequences via reconciliation and the establishment of institutions (Parlevliet, 2010). This is a collection of physical, social, and structural efforts that are frequently incorporated into post-conflict recovery and rebuilding efforts (Mbella et al., 2018).

Women were actively involved in conflict resolution within the communities they lived in during Nigeria's pre-colonial era. Women's organisations, such as the Igbo "I-Ita" groups and the Tiv "Mgba-Mgba" associations, provided significant opportunities for women to participate in mediation and peacebuilding endeavours (Omitola et al., 2021). These groups played important roles in addressing conflicts, encouraging reconciliation, and preserving social harmony. According to Pereira (2005), the colonial period in Nigeria saw major shifts in the roles of women in society. The involvement of women expanded with the emergence of Western education and the impact of missionary activities. Women's groups, such as the 1929 Aba Women's Riots, displayed women's collective opposition to oppression by colonisers and served as social change catalysts (Kuumba, 2006). Nigerian women continued to contribute to peacebuilding efforts after independence. Women's roles were especially visible during the Biafra-Nigeria civil war (1967-1970) when women played vital functions as peace activists and negotiators (Falola & Ezekwem, 2016).

The transition to civilian governance in Nigeria in 1999 heralded a new era in women's involvement In peacebuilding. Whereby, according to Goetz and Jenkins (2016), women's organizations began pushing for gender equality, women's rights promotion, and involving them in procedures for making decisions. As a result, the Nigerian government took the initiative in peacekeeping through its policies and institutional frameworks. International structures, such as United Nations Security Council

Resolution 1325 on Women, Peace, and Security (UNSCR 1325), have affected Nigerian women's engagement in peacebuilding efforts. (Nduwimana, 2006). Willett (2010) contends that the resolution calls for increased women's participation in the resolution of conflict, prevention of conflict, and post-conflict reconstruction decision-making procedures This prompted Nigeria's government to create the National Action Plan on Women, Peace, and Security in 2017 to guide the implementation of UNSCR 1325, which acknowledges the relevance of gender equality and women's involvement in peacebuilding (Adefisoye & Adefisoye, 2019).

In Nigeria, it is becoming evident that women perform an important role in peacebuilding. As rightly argued by Obonyo (2014), humanitarian support, the elimination of arms, and hostage swaps are all crucial in the effort of peacebuilding. For ages, women served essential functions in peacekeeping, primarily as conventional peace activists and as praise singers for men while in wars as motivation to guarantee their victory (Olaitan, 2023). There are tales in all societies about women who have taken on leadership roles as peace agents in their communities. It is therefore important to note that it is not possible to achieve long-term peace while ignoring a significant portion of the population. Women play a critical role in fostering tolerance and peaceful action, as they instruct the first lessons in life (Michau et al., 2015). Olaitan (2023) agrees that women can exert influence on their husbands by instilling honesty and dignity in their homes.

Despite these advances, women in Nigeria continue to face major obstacles to fully engaging in peacebuilding processes. Women's leadership in peacebuilding continues to be hampered by socio-cultural norms, biased practices, and inadequate access to resources and decision-making positions (Olufade, 2013). This is why Ojo (2022) contends that women are frequently seen as helpless targets of armed conflict, as opposed to as change agents whose abilities and potential can be utilized in peacebuilding. Women are often relegated to inactive roles, and their contributions to peace reconstruction, community rehabilitation, and national reconciliation are overlooked (Ojo, 2022). Women's absence and neglect from structured peace-building processes, overall, imply that they are excluded from public life. Women are frequently viewed as the targets of armed conflict as opposed to agents of peacebuilding (Island, 2013).

However, recently, the involvement of women in the peace procedure has brought much-needed peace to many countries around the world, including Nigeria (O'Reilly et al., 2015). It has become obvious that without women's involvement, lasting peace may never be attained, or perhaps not in the timeframes desired. Women's position in Peacebuilding contributes to the steady transition of a conflict-affected society to a more balanced and stable state (Mofya, 2022). Therefore, women's contributions to peacebuilding have enormous potential to improve the entire process. Furthermore, given the magnitude of suffering that women typically face in armed conflict, it is appropriate that they engage actively in these processes (O'Reilly et al., 2015). Thus, involving women in peacebuilding processes is an essential step in showing women's acceptance as members of the governing system. Instructively, De Coning (2020) asserted that such inclusion has come to be regarded as an essential component of a long-term transition from armed conflict to peace. Women's involvement in peacebuilding processes demonstrates that women can make a significant socio-economic and political difference during peace transitions.

CHALLENGES FACED BY WOMEN LEADERS IN PEACEBUILDING

For a long time, women leaders lacked sufficient power to have an impact on peace negotiations. The position of women in peacebuilding has become more prominent lately due to combined attempts to tackle the leadership role of women and peacebuilding issues. However, achieving the ideal of ensuring equal and complete involvement of women in positions of leadership remains a challenge. Here are some of the challenges that women in peacebuilding face;

Patriarch System Leading to Gender-Based Discrimination and Stereotyping

Nigerian society is rife with stereotyping and discrimination as a result of its patriarchal system (Olonade et al., 2021). This patriarchy positioned women beneath status men. According to Hossen (2020), men rule, intimidate, and abuse women in the patriarchal structure of social order. Women are subordinated in the patriarchal system, which results in their low status and inadequate accessibility to financial and political resources (Bourque & Warren, 2010). In essence, it involves women's feeling powerless and discriminated against. Men have an advantage over women because they perceive them differently. (Sultana, 2010).

The patriarchal system consists of factors that seek to limit the roles of women while promoting the argument that men are superior to women (Hossen, 2020). A society founded on a culture that fails to recognize women as equal partners with men cannot allow women to participate in leadership positions. This demonstrates that patriarchy as a system has a significant impact on women's self-actualization in society. This continues to exist because Nigeria depends greatly on tradition, which constitutes one of the country's founding principles; tradition pervades and presents itself in various forms (Olaitan, 2018). Peacebuilding constitutes one of the ways it has come into effect because a woman's belief as most vital as a housekeeper and that she should be seen rather than heard, has discouraged women's active engagement in peacebuilding operations.

The patriarchal system has a great impact on women's engagement in the peacebuilding process. According to Sultana (2010), one of the difficulties that the patriarchal system creates is the challenge of reconciling a woman's duties to her family and her effective participation in peacebuilding procedures. Women in conventional cultures are liable for managing their households and caring for their children because patriarchal customs recognise women's only position as wives and mothers, leaving very little opportunity for women to participate in leadership or peacebuilding processes (Parreñas, 2009). Kassa (2015) argues that the subordination by men affects women by denying them the necessary experience to engage in activities aimed at promoting peace. Women are typically marginalized in conventional societies, and they lack social support for their involvement in peacebuilding activities. (Olaitan, 2018). Olonade et al. (2021) assert that the patriarchal system pervades into discrimination and stereotyping of women, resulting in a lack of active engagement of women in positions of leadership, which affects the issue of peacebuilding. This is a result of the belief in Nigerian society that the male gender is superior to the female gender, which frequently trumps the problem of women's freedom of preference (Sultana, 2010). For example, in Nigeria's recently concluded 2023 general elections, the turnout of women in elective positions was very low, allowing men to dominate. The 10th National Assembly, which was recently inaugurated, has women in 3 of 109 Senate seats (2.7%) and 17 of 360 House of Representatives seats (4.7%), representing 4.2% of the 469-member Assembly. In general, the elections produced a low number of women in elective positions. Nigeria remains at the bottom of the list in terms of the number of women in African parliaments, based on current figures for the 10th National Assembly (Ajodo-Adebanjoko, 2021). Garba (2016) contends that when women are underrepresented in the political space, particularly as legislators, it is highly challenging to enact gender-sensitive laws that will free women to live their lives to the fullest. A society that fails to improve gender equality will unavoidably struggle to thrive in concerns regarding equality of involvement in peacebuilding (Olaitan, 2018).

Hence, these biased practices and stereotypes perpetuate inequality, strengthen gender norms, and reduce women's chances for success in various aspects of life, particularly in peacebuilding. To address gender-based discrimination and stereotypes, it is necessary to challenge societal norms, promote gender equality, and create inclusive environments in which individuals can succeed irrespective of their gender. This includes dismantling the patriarchy, encouraging awareness and education, maintaining equal chances for all, and promoting inclusive and varied representations in every facet of life.

Lack Of Access to Resources and Decision-Making Position

Decisions have been delegated to a tiny group of male leaders (Corner, 1997). As previously stated, the patriarchal system is hostile to women's participation in formal peacebuilding activities and decision-making. The structure is unconstitutional since decision-making is dominated by men and leaves out women (Hossen, 2020). As a result, women are barred from holding positions of leadership in formal peacebuilding endeavours. In addition, restrained access to formal peacebuilding processes is prompted by an absence of leadership influence and assets as argued by Bourque and Warren (2010).

Involvement of women in decision-making and post-conflict processes has been low in Nigeria (Ogege, 2009). This might be clarified by the social and cultural constraints imposed on women, which allow them to be pushed to the background. Ogege (2009) contends that the pushing of women to the background, even regarding issues that directly affect them, such as armed conflict and insecurity spreads from their homes into general society. In this regard, Bourque and Warren (2010) argue that women have no means of obtaining resources unless they have a say in decision-making, and women will continue to be marginalized unless they are given access to resources and the institutions that shape social norms and attitudes. It is critical to point out that when women get an opportunity to make decisions, they are often able to prevent conflict from escalating. The lack of women in official peace talks and decision-making bodies limits their capacity to shape peace agreements (Paffenholz, 2018). The absence of women from important decision-making processes limits their perspectives and experiences, resulting in peace processes that may overlook gender-specific issues and fail to fulfil women's needs.

Women leaders frequently face a lack of financial resources, technical assistance, and networks, which limits their ability to execute and maintain peacebuilding plans. Sultana (2010) argues that disparities in access to resources may hinder women from fully realising their leadership potential and effectively carrying out their peacebuilding activities. The efforts of women in peacebuilding are frequently ignored. Women in Nigeria are denied equal access to resources such as land, as well as small to medium-sized business co-ownership is limited. (Bako & Syed, 2018). Women's participation in the labour force is increasing around the world, but this hasn't altered their situation or eliminated economic disparity against them. Women continue to face economic marginalization, which limits their ability to play roles of leadership in peacebuilding. As Hora (2014) notes, women face significant challenges in many societies owing to a lack of access to assets as well as leadership positions. This inequality perpetuates power imbalances and limits individuals' ability to fully engage in social, economic, and political spheres (Milazzo & Goldstein, 2019).

Addressing the absence of access to resources and decision-making positions calls for multi-level collaboration. This involves carrying out gender equality policies and programmes, ensuring equal opportunity for education and skill development, creating inclusive economic opportunities, promoting quotas and affirmative action measures, as well as challenging societal norms.

Institutional and Systemic Barriers

The lack of political will on the part of the government to address women's marginalisation only adds to the problem, as evidenced by the government's indifferent behaviour towards encouraging women in positions of leadership (Olaitan, 2018). The Nigerian government is active in policy formulation, but policy execution is an important issue that must be addressed. Okoronkwo-Chukwu (2013) contends that the country ratified the 30% affirmative action for women in political positions passed by the 1995 Beijing Women's Conference, but the percentage of women in politics remains low. Currently, no woman holds any of the four highest positions of authority in the country: President, Vice President, Senate President, or Speaker of the House of Representatives. No female governor in any of Nigeria's 36 states, and the dream of having the first female governor, Mrs Aishatu Dahiru Binani, in Adamawa state in the 2023 governorship election was snuffed out and buried in the sands of politics. Aishatu Binani faced strong opposition from conservative groups in Adamawa state due to her gender. According to reports, some Islamic clerics in the state cautioned their followers not to vote for a woman to lead them and not to set a precedent for their Muslim women.

Institutional and systemic barriers are structural impediments and discriminatory practices embedded in social, political, and economic systems that perpetuate inequality and limit women's leadership opportunities (Beck et al., 2022). Therefore, Ahmed (2022) argues that these impediments make the environment undesirable for women's full inclusion, representation, and advancement in peacebuilding. Inadequate representation narrows the scope of gender-specific issues, perspectives, and needs, perpetuating systemic biases and reinforcing existing inequalities. Discriminatory practices in areas such as employment, education, inheritance, property rights, and political participation are examples of these biases (Aluko, 2015). Such institutionalized biases limit women's ability to access resources, decision-making positions, and advancement opportunities Hudson (2006) notes that One of the barriers to women's leadership participation in Nigeria is officials' inability to design a comprehensive structure to include women as mediators, counsellors, experts, and observers in formal delegations during peacebuilding processes. This structure should promote women's significant participation and achieve equal participation in leadership endeavours. Institutional hurdles, such as limited access to political party structures, nomination processes, and electoral systems that do not promote gender equality, all contribute to women's underrepresentation in leadership (Kiamba, 2009). One of the key initiatives toward improving the empowerment of women and gender disparities in societies that have experienced conflict is to institutionalise the methods required for women to participate in leadership positions and initiatives aimed at terminating conflicts and building peace.

To address these issues, comprehensive efforts must be made to promote gender equality, address structural barriers, and create an enabling environment for women's leadership in peacebuilding. Women's marginalisation in political leadership, as well as their continued exclusion from decision-making positions, has left many women feeling insecure about their abilities and preventing them from participating in any form of politics (Bako & Syed, 2018). The insistence on women's traditional roles not only limited their political chances but also raised mistrust of women's capacity in politics, increased their lack of confidence in themselves, and strengthened patriarchal forces that pushed women out of governance and positions of leadership (Aluko, 2015). Even though women's inclusion is supported in many world constitutions, Nigeria, like many other countries, has yet to put it into action. It is extremely difficult to change women's situations without government incentives, which include promoting women's representation and meaningful participation, providing targeted support and resources, as well as challenging gender norms and stereotypes faced by women leaders.

Strategies for Strengthening Women's Leadership in Peacebuilding

Strengthening women's leadership in peacebuilding necessitates a multifaceted approach that addresses both systemic barriers and the specific challenges that women face in the field. Here are some strategies for empowering women and strengthening their leadership roles in peacebuilding:

Engaging Men and Traditional Leaders in Supporting Women's Leadership in Peacebuilding

Engaging men and traditional leaders to advocate gender equality, challenging patriarchal norms, and creating an atmosphere that allows for women's full involvement in peacebuilding is critical (Kidane, 2014). Policymakers, community leaders, and traditional leaders, for example, can be urged to show support for women's leadership and actively mentor women leaders Olaitan (2018) notes that men in positions of power and influence can use their positions to promote gender-responsive policies, create opportunities for women's participation, and assist women in gaining access to resources and decision-making positions. This can be accomplished by conducting sensitization programmes to educate men and traditional leaders about the value of women's leadership in peacebuilding (Jendia, 2020). Men and traditional leaders can be encouraged to support women's leadership by engaging them in dialogue and providing them with accurate information.

It is worth noting that traditional leaders frequently wield significant power within their communities. Jendia (2020) notes that it is critical to engage them in discussions about women in leadership and the significance of gender equality in peacebuilding. It will be critical to seek their support and collaboration in challenging discriminatory practices and norms that hinder women's leadership opportunities.

Therefore, encouraging men in positions of power and traditional leaders to promote gender equality has the potential to transform community attitudes and behaviours. A more inclusive and gender-equal environment for women's leadership in peacebuilding can be created with men and traditional leaders as allies, supporters, and advocates (Kidane, 2014). This collaborative approach acknowledges that gender equality in leadership is a shared responsibility that necessitates the involvement and backing of all members of society.

Capacity Building Programmes for Women in Peacebuilding

Following the enactment of UN Resolution 1325, the majority of work on Nigerian women including them in peacebuilding processes, was done within academic circles and women, peace, and conflict-related organisations (Garba, 2016). However, little has been done to prepare women for leadership roles in official peacebuilding processes, particularly in nations that are developing. Aside from women being excluded from peace processes, the issue of women's capacity building is crucial. Cabeza-García et al. (2019) note that Women should be incorporated into economic leadership roles and pushed into becoming entrepreneurs by expanding their ability to obtain extensive and equitable financial products and services such as credit and loans. Financially supportive government policies for women will increase their participation in leadership positions. McKay (2004) argues that financial insecurity, impoverishment, prejudice, and exploitation impede women's participation in peacebuilding activities. Civil society organizations ought to be urged as well to address women's economic problems by reaching out to rurally disadvantaged women, poor women, and uneducated women and assisting them in gaining access to economic resources, thereby improving their prospects for leadership positions in peacebuilding tasks (Garba, 2016).

Capacity-building programmes would facilitate networking and collaboration opportunities for women peacebuilders. Creating structures for women leaders to share their experiences, form alliances, and foster peer support can help to strengthen their collective voice and influence (Van Eerdewijk et al., 2017). These programmes should promote cross-sector collaboration, including collaboration with civil society organisations, government agencies, and international actors involved in peacekeeping efforts. It should also include assisting female leaders in understanding and incorporating gender perspectives into their peacebuilding efforts. This can be accomplished through gender analysis training, recognition of gender-based power dynamics, prevention of gender-based violence, promotion of gender equality in decision-making processes, and maintaining women's participation and representation in peacebuilding initiatives (Avis, 2021).

Unless and until women have the means to engage in these processes through capacity building, their contributions will be insignificant, particularly in formal processes. In Nigeria, particularly in conflict-prone areas, women cannot make significant improvements to long-term peace. (Garba, 2016). Hence, by successfully carrying out these capacity-building programmes, women peacebuilding leaders can improve their skills, confidence, and effectiveness in contributing to long-term peace processes. These programmes are critical for advancing gender equality and creating more inclusive and effective peacebuilding initiatives.

International and Regional Collaboration for Advancing Women's Leadership in Peacebuilding

International and regional cooperation is critical in improving the role of women in peacebuilding by encouraging collaborative efforts, sharing best practices, and promoting gender equality on an international basis (Olonisakin et al., 2010). The role of women in peacebuilding has gained popularity in recent years as a result of international agencies working together to address the issues of women's leadership and peacebuilding. The United Nations Security Council Resolution 1325 on Women, Peace, and Security, as well as the Beijing Declaration on Affirmative Action, have provided the most impetus (Garba, 2016). The global community, and even the Nigerian government, acknowledged this unequivocal call for greater women's participation in all peacebuilding processes. The United Nations Security Council recognized not only the devastating and unusual effects of violent conflicts on women but also the urgent need for their full inclusion in peacebuilding as argued by Dharmapuri (2012). The UN reaffirmed the significance of women's roles in conflict prevention, resolution, and peacebuilding, emphasising the significance of their full and equal involvement in all attempts to foster peace, while also emphasising the need to expand their role in peacebuilding (Dharmapuri, 2012).

Though many of international law's gendered structures remain, international law allows women to claim a right to participate in decision-making and develops a structure that evaluates policies in that regard (Chinkin & Charlesworth, 2008). An array of instruments of law developed in recent years have come together to form an extensive rights-based global framework for the rights of women, which has been adopted by the majority of African governments. The Convention on the Elimination of All Forms of Discrimination Against Women (CEDAW), the Protocol to the African Charter on Human and People's Rights on the Rights of Women in Africa, UN Security Council Resolution 1325, the Southern African Development Community (SADC) Declaration on Gender and Development with its Addendum on the Prevention and Eradication of Violence Against Women, and the Heads of State Solemn Declaration on Gender Equality in Africa are just a few examples (Chinkin & Yoshida, 2020). It's also worth noting that the UN Established a Peacebuilding Commission, which emphasised the crucial function of women in peacekeeping. Regardless of getting widely recognised as a political watershed for women who engage in peacebuilding, a lot of these global legal structures are merely rhetorical agreements because this progress has not culminated in watershed achievement for women peacebuilding leaders as asserted by Chinkin and Charlesworth (2008). Instead, women's exclusion from peacebuilding activities has become the norm rather than the exception, and when they are included, it is often piecemeal.

As a result, international and regional collaboration should prioritize support for local women-led peacebuilding initiatives, such as giving technical assistance, financing, and capacity-building assistance to grassroots organizations, community-based groups, and women-led initiatives engaged at the local level. It is equally important to foster collaboration between countries and regions through South-South and North-South partnerships. This entails sharing experiences, exchanging expertise, and forging cross-regional alliances to improve understanding and develop context-specific approaches (Ghaebi, 2017). South-South collaboration allows countries facing similar challenges to share knowledge and strategies, whereas North-South collaboration allows for learning from best practices and experiences in different contexts. As a result, international and regional collaboration is critical for advancing women's roles as leaders in global peacebuilding. Organisations and actors can pool their resources, expertise, and networks to foster a supportive environment, promote policy changes, and ensure long-term efforts to support women leaders and promote gender equality in peacebuilding processes by collaborating (Montgomery et al., 2012).

CONCLUSION AND RECOMMENDATIONS

Women are frequently underrepresented at decision-making levels and in peace negotiations and agreements. To maintain peace, stakeholders must include women at all stages of the peacebuilding process (Goyol, 2019). Regardless, men control many official peacebuilding processes, and women are on the receiving end of conflicts (Hossen, 2020). Various attempts have been made to ensure that a gender perspective plays an important role in preserving peace. The expectation that peacebuilding will be carried out by global legal standards is inadequate to ensure that women's rights are protected equally with those of men (Chinkin & Charlesworth, 2008). Even if it is merely rhetoric, international organisations, governments, and civil society are increasingly supporting women's peace action. The challenge now is determining how to ensure that these policy instruments are implemented in such a way that women are truly partners in the process.

To achieve long-term peace in Nigeria, women must be fully included in all peace processes, and obstacles to the full engagement and involvement of Nigerian women in peacebuilding must be removed. Nigerian society may realise the full abilities of women leaders and pave the way for equitable and lasting peace by investing in capacity-building programmes, challenging gender stereotypes, encouraging women's participation, and creating supportive environments. Hence, by closing the gap between rhetoric and reality, society can get closer to achieving gender equality, social justice, and long-term peace. Empowering women as peacebuilding leaders is not only an issue of fairness and rights for all; it also serves as an essential strategy for creating a more peaceful, prosperous, and fair world for all. On this basis, the following recommendations are suggested.

1. The government should ensure that gender equality is actively incorporated into all scheduled measures, including laws, policies, and programmes, in every field and across all levels of the economic, political, and social realms. Adoption of certain laws tackling gender stereotypes and inequalities, intimidation and harassment of women, violence against women, discrimination against women, impunity and its effect on women, justice administration, such as the availability of justice, as well as backing for human rights mechanisms. Women's participation in informal peace processes should be acknowledged and capitalized on. Considering that these are frequently small-scale initiatives focused at the local level, they may be critical in altering people's attitudes, creating possibilities for more formal peace processes, and serving as a significant driver for change.
2. Equal rights of women to education should be prioritized. Education should be a tool used to instil understanding, principles, and attitudes to reorient people's perceptions of women's roles in promoting peace. Human dignity, respect for the individual, integrity, patriotism, and loyalty are examples of positive attitudes and values. This is critical for freeing people from cultural shackles that limit women's prospects and potential, as well as preventing behaviours that may lead to disintegration and disunity.
3. Communities should be encouraged to raise awareness and educate themselves about the importance of women's leadership in peacebuilding. To challenge stereotypes, promote gender equality, and encourage support for female leaders, public campaigns, workshops, and educational programmes should be implemented. Community involvement is critical for fostering an inclusive culture that accepts women in leadership roles. The community should also contribute to raising gender awareness and reviewing the provisions of laws that sustain bias against women, as well as constitutional and judicial reforms, election involvement, and access to and influence over financial resources, education, and training.
4. Increasing investment in comprehensive capacity-building programmes for female peacebuilding leaders. These programmes should emphasise leadership development, conflict resolution, negotiation, and analysis of gender. Training in advocacy, networking, and mentorship should also be provided to improve women's effectiveness and impact on peacebuilding initiatives. Hence, governments, international organisations, and donors should prioritise funding for women-led organisations, grassroots initiatives, and capacity-building programmes. Long-term funding is essential for maintaining the impact and continuity of women's leadership efforts.

Nigeria can strengthen women's leadership in peacebuilding, create a more inclusive and equitable society, and contribute to long-term peace and development by implementing these recommendations. To achieve long-term change, these actions necessitate the commitment and collaboration of government entities, civil society organisations, international partners, and the larger community.

REFERENCES

Adefisoye, T. O., & Adefisoye, I. (2019). Nigeria and the implementation of the United Nations Security Council Resolution 1325 on women, peace and security. *Journal of Public Administration and Development Alternatives*, *4*(1), 16–29.

Adeogun, T. J., & Muthuki, J. M. (2018). Feminist perspectives on peacebuilding: The case of women's organisations in South Sudan. *Agenda (Durban, South Africa)*, *32*(2), 83–92. doi:10.1080/10130950.2018.1450572

Adjei, M. (2019). Women's participation in peace processes: A review of literature. *Journal of Peace Education*, *16*(2), 133–154. doi:10.1080/17400201.2019.1576515

Agbalajobi, D. T. (2010). The role of women in conflict resolution and peacebuilding. *Understanding Africa's contemporary conflicts*, 233.

Ahmed, S. A. (2022). *The role of women in reconciliation and peace building process in Somalia= Somali'de uzlaşma ve barış inşa sürecinde kadınların rolü.* Sakarya Üniversitesi.

Ajodo-Adebanjoko, A. (2021). Giving Voice to the Voiceless: The Challenges of Women Legislators in Nigeria's National Assembly. *Two Decades of Legislative Politics and Governance in Nigeria's National Assembly: Issues, Achievements, Challenges and Prospects*, 317-343.

Aluko, Y. A. (2015). Patriarchy and property rights among Yoruba women in Nigeria. *Feminist Economics*, *21*(3), 56–81. doi:10.1080/13545701.2015.1015591

Avis, W. (2021). *Incorporating Gender Perspective in Peace Operations since 2018*. Academic Press.

Bako, M. J., & Syed, J. (2018). Women's marginalization in Nigeria and the way forward. *Human Resource Development International*, *21*(5), 425–443. doi:10.1080/13678868.2018.1458567

Bamidele, S. (2020). Ethnic conflict and the politics of spoils in Nigeria. *Social Change*, *50*(4), 569–583. doi:10.1177/0049085720964280

Beck, M., Cadwell, J., Kern, A., Wu, K., Dickerson, M., & Howard, M. (2022). Critical feminist analysis of STEM mentoring programs: A meta-synthesis of the existing literature. *Gender, Work and Organization*, *29*(1), 167–187. doi:10.1111/gwao.12729

Bourque, S. C., & Warren, K. B. (2010). *Women of the Andes: patriarchy and social change in two Peruvian towns*. University of Michigan press.

Cabeza-García, L., Del Brio, E. B., & Oscanoa-Victorio, M. L. (2019). *Female financial inclusion and its impacts on inclusive economic development.* Women's Studies International Forum.10.1016/j.wsif.2019.102300

Chinkin, C., & Yoshida, K. (2020). *40 years of the convention on the elimination of all forms of discrimination against women*. Academic Press.

Chinkin, C., & Charlesworth, H. (2008). Building Women into Peace: the international legal framework. In *International Law and the Third World* (pp. 243-264). Routledge-Cavendish. 10.1016/j.wsif.2019.102300

Corner, L. (1997). *Women's participation in decision-making and leadership: A global perspective.* A paper presented at a conference on Women in Decision-making in Cooperative held by the Asian Women in Cooperative Development Forum (ACWF) and the International Cooperative Alliance Regional Office for Asia and the Pacific (ICAROAP).

De Coning, C. (2020). Adaptive peace operations: Navigating the complexity of influencing societal change without causing harm. *International Peacekeeping*, *27*(5), 836–858.

Desai, B. H., & Mandal, M. (2021). Role of climate change in exacerbating sexual and gender-based violence against women: A new challenge for international law. *Environmental Policy and Law*, *51*(3), 137–157. doi:10.3233/EPL-210055

Dharmapuri, S. (2012). Implementing UN security council resolution 1325: Putting the responsibility to protect into practice. *Global Responsibility to Protect*, *4*(2), 241–272. doi:10.1163/187598412X639728

Falola, T., & Ezekwem, O. (2016). *Writing the Nigeria-Biafra War.* Boydell & Brewer. doi:10.1017/9781782047735

Garba, G. K. (2016). *Building women's capacity for peace building in Nigeria.* Academic Press.

Ghaebi, M. R. (2017). The Role of South-South Cooperation in Realization of the Right to Development: The Way Forward. *Int'l Stud. J.*, *14*, 169.

Goetz, A. M., & Jenkins, R. (2016). Agency and accountability: Promoting women's participation in peacebuilding. *Feminist Economics*, *22*(1), 211–236. doi:10.1080/13545701.2015.1086012

Goyol, Y. I. (2019). The role of women in peacebuilding: Liberia in perspective. *International Journal of Development and Management Review*, *14*(1), 123–135.

Haider, H. (2009). *Community-based approaches to peacebuilding in conflict-affected and fragile contexts.* Academic Press.

Hanachor, M., & Echezu, B. C. (2021). Contributions of faith-based organizations towards peace building for sustainable community development in Rivers State, Nigeria. *International Journal of Education, Learning and Development*, *9*(3), 11–18.

Hora, E. A. (2014). Factors that affect women participation in leadership and decision making position. *Asian Journal of Humanity, Art and Literature, 1*(2).

Hosea, P., & Khalema, E. (2020). Scoping the nexus between climate change and water-security realities in rural South Africa. *Town and Regional Planning*, *77*, 18–30.

Hosea, P., & Khalema, E. (2020). Scoping the nexus between climate change and water-security realities in rural South Africa. *Town and Regional Planning*, *77*, 18–30.

Hossen, M. S. (2020). Patriarchy practice and women's subordination in the society of Bangladesh: An analytical review. *Electronic Research Journal of Social Sciences and Humanities*, *2*, 51–60.

Hudson, H. (2006). *Human security and peacebuilding through a gender lens: Challenges of implementation in Africa.* JSTOR.

Island, S. (2013). Legal analysis on. *Violence Against Women.*

Iteyo, C., & Mumbi, A. (2020). Challenges and opportunities of women's peace building activities in Nairobi county Kenya. *Journal of Public Policy and Administration*, *5*(1), 47–61.

Jah, E. A., Kurmi, A. N., Paul, T. S., & Henry, L. H. (2022). Women and peace processes in Nigeria. *Wukari International Studies Journal*, *6*(1), 13–13.

Jendia, C. (2020). Conspicuously absent: Womens role in conflict resolution and peace building in northern Uganda in the context of United Nations resolution 1325. *Journal of Law and Conflict Resolution*, *11*(1), 1–14. doi:10.5897/JLCR2019.0285

Kassa, S. (2015). Challenges and opportunities of women political participation in Ethiopia. *Journal of Global Economics*, *3*(4), 1–7. doi:10.4172/2375-4389.1000162

Kiamba, J. M. (2009). Women and leadership positions: Social and cultural barriers to success. *Wagadu Volume 6. Journal of International Women's Studies*, *10*(1), 89.

Kidane, Y. (2014). Women's leadership role in post-conflict peacebuilding process. *Journal of African Union Studies, 3*(2-3), 87-101.

Kimani, E. N., & Kombo, D. K. (2010). Gender and poverty reduction: A Kenyan context. *Educational Research Review*, *5*(1), 24.

Kuumba, M. B. (2006). African women, resistance cultures and cultural resistances. *Agenda (Durban, South Africa)*, *20*(68), 112–121.

Mbella, M. R. E., Yari, A. F., & Sama-Lang, R. B. (2018). Youths and Peacebuilding in Africa: Socio-Political & Economic Exclusion and the Role Youths Play in Peacebuilding in Africa. *Young African Leaders Journal of Development*, *2*(1), 8. doi:10.32727/24.2018.33

McKay, S. (2004). Women, human security, and peacebuilding: A feminist analysis. *Conflict and human security: A search for new approaches of peacebuilding, 19*, 152-170.

Michau, L., Horn, J., Bank, A., Dutt, M., & Zimmerman, C. (2015). Prevention of violence against women and girls: Lessons from practice. *Lancet*, *385*(9978), 1672–1684. doi:10.1016/S0140-6736(14)61797-9 PMID:25467577

Milazzo, A., & Goldstein, M. (2019). Governance and women's economic and political participation: Power inequalities, formal constraints and norms. *The World Bank Research Observer*, *34*(1), 34–64. doi:10.1093/wbro/lky006

Mofya, T. N. (2022). Role of Women in Peace Building in Zambia: Case of Northern Province. *International Journal of Conflict Management*, *3*(1), 61–95. doi:10.47941/ijcm.1010

Montgomery, A. W., Dacin, P. A., & Dacin, M. T. (2012). Collective social entrepreneurship: Collaboratively shaping social good. *Journal of Business Ethics*, *111*(3), 375–388. doi:10.100710551-012-1501-5

Nduwimana, F. (2006). *United Nations Security Council Resolution 1325 (2000) on Women, Peace and Security Understanding the Implications, Fulfilling the Obligations. Office of the Special Adviser on Gender Issues and Advancement of Women.* OSAGI.

Ngwoke, P. N., & Ituma, E. A. (2020). Ethno-religious conflict and sustainable development in Nigeria. *Hervormde Teologiese Studies*, *76*(4).

O'Reilly, M., Súilleabháin, A. Ó., & Paffenholz, T. (2015). *Reimagining peacemaking: Women's roles in peace processes*. Academic Press.

Obonyo, J. A. (2014). A gendered critique of women in peace and conflict situations in Africa. *Research on Humanities and Social Sciences*, *4*(26), 87–96.

Ogege, S. O. (2009). Conflict resolution and peace building: the gender question in the Niger delta crisis in Nigeria. *African Research Review, 3*(5).

Ojo, O. (2022). More than victims: The roles of women in conflict resolution and peacebuilding in Nigeria. *KIU Interdisciplinary Journal of Humanities and Social Sciences*, *3*(2), 92–111.

Okoronkwo-Chukwu, U. (2013). Female representation in Nigeria: The case of the 2011 general elections and the fallacy of 35% affirmative action. *Research on Humanities and Social Sciences*, *3*(2), 39–46.

Olagbaju, O. O., & Awosusi, O. E. (2019). Herders-farmers' communal conflict in Nigeria: An indigenised language as an alternative resolution mechanism. *International Journal of Multidisciplinary and Current Research, 7*.

Olaifa, O. (2017). Curbing violent extremism through peace building in Nigeria. *Journal of US-China Public Administration*, *14*(4), 221–223.

Olaitan, Z. (2023). Feminist Rethinking of the Representation of African Women in Peacebuilding: A Theoretical Analysis. *African Journal of Gender Social Development*, *12*(1), 185.

Olaitan, Z. M. (2018). *Women's Participation in Peace Processes in Nigeria*. Challenges and Prospects.

Olonade, O. Y., Oyibode, B. O., Idowu, B. O., George, T. O., Iwelumor, O. S., Ozoya, M. I., Egharevba, M. E., & Adetunde, C. O. (2021). Understanding gender issues in Nigeria: The imperative for sustainable development. *Heliyon*, *7*(7), e07622. doi:10.1016/j.heliyon.2021.e07622 PMID:34377858

Olonisakin, F., Barnes, K., & Ikpe, E. (2010). *Women, peace and security: translating policy into practice*. Routledge. doi:10.4324/9780203837085

Olufade, A. O. (2013). Nigerian Women, Politics and the National Identity Question. *American Educational Research Journal*, *1*(3), 161–170.

Omitola, B., Akinrinde, O. O., & Omitola, A. (2021). Traditional Institutions and Socio-economic Development in Nigeria: A Critical Analysis. *Journal of Law and Legal Reform*, *2*(4), 539–552. doi:10.15294/jllr.v2i4.48587

Paffenholz, T. (2018). Women in peace negotiations. *Gendering diplomacy and international negotiation*, 169-191.

Parlevliet, M. (2010). Rethinking conflict transformation from a human rights perspective. *Human rights and conflict transformation: The challenges of just peace*, 15-46.

Parreñas, R. S. (2009). Transnational mothering: A source of gender conflicts in the family. *North Carolina Law Review*, *88*, 1825.

Patrick, H. O., Ugwanyi, J. I., Akuche, A. B., & Mba, C. C. (2022). Federalism and the Politics of Restructuring in Nigeria (Vol. 19).. African Renaissance. https://journals.co.za/doi/abs/10.31920/2516-5305/2022/19n3a12

Pereira, C. (2005). Domesticating women? Gender, religion and the state in Nigeria under colonial and military rule. *African Identities*, *3*(1), 69–94. doi:10.1080/14725840500065937

Porter, E., & Every, D. (2009). Peacebuilding: Women peaceworkers. In Mediation in the Asia-Pacific Region (pp. 47-65). Routledge.

Salaudeen, A., & Gombi, D. D. (2019). Gender Mainstreaming in Peace Building and Conflict Resolution in Nigeria: North East in Focus. *KIU Journal of Social Sciences*, *5*(1), 139–146.

Sharifi, A., Simangan, D., Kaneko, S., & Virji, H. (2021). The sustainability–peace nexus: Why is it important? *Sustainability Science*, *16*(4), 1073–1077. doi:10.100711625-021-00986-z PMID:34149938

Sheidu, C. F., & Patrick, H. O. (2023). Climate Change and Open Grazing impact on Agricultural production in Benue State, Nigeria. *African Journal of Public Administration and Environmental Studies*, *2*(1), 29–52.

Sheidu, C. F., & Patrick, H. O. (2023). Climate Change and Open Grazing impact on Agricultural production in Benue State, Nigeria. *African Journal of Public Administration and Environmental Studies*, *2*(1), 29–52.

Sultana, A. (2010). Patriarchy and women s subordination: a theoretical analysis. *Arts Faculty Journal*, 1-18.

Van Eerdewijk, A., Wong, F., Vaast, C., Newton, J., Tyszler, M., & Pennington, A. (2017). *White paper: A conceptual model on women and girls' empowerment*. Academic Press.

Willett, S. (2010). Introduction: Security Council Resolution 1325: assessing the impact on women, peace and security. *International Peacekeeping*, *17*(2), 142–158. doi:10.1080/13533311003625043

Afolaranmi, A. O. (2021). Conflict Resolution Strategies in Resolving Religious Conflict in Nigeria. *Academia Letters*, 2.

Section 2

Barriers and Advancement of Democratic Practice

Chapter 6
Advancing Democratic Governance Through Political Accountability in the SADC Region

Levy Ndou
https://orcid.org/0000-0001-7018-2557
Tshwane University of Technology, South Africa

ABSTRACT

The African continent and the SADC region have embraced the basic principles of democratic governance such as political accountability. Through democratic governance, governments exercise their power in the advancement of social, economic, and political development. To achieve this democratic mandate, bureaucracy should be held politically accountable through formal and informal mechanisms. Despite the monarchs in Lesotho and Eswathini, SADC has the traceable record of upholding democratic governance through the promotion of elections. Elections in any democratic order are regarded as the pillar of democracy. This tendency is juxtaposed to citizens' expectations of their leaders to discharge their responsibilities based on good governance principles of accountable, social justice, impartiality, equality, and equity. It goes without saying that ethical and accountable leadership is needed to deal with governance challenges such as corruption and democratic deficit.

INTRODUCTION

This chapter focuses on the concept of democratic governance and how it is exercised in the current political and governance landscape. Much focus is given to the SADC region with specific reference to Botswana, South Africa, and Zimbabwe. The relationship and interconnection between the leaders and the citizens are articulated to provide insight into the importance of involving citizens in the running of government. Institutions that support democratic governance are explained and how they strengthen governance and accountability. Citizen's participation in the establishment and the running of govern-

DOI: 10.4018/979-8-3693-0477-8.ch006

ment is central to democratic governance. According to Tamayaoc, (2014), governance is a concept of democracy in how government and civil society agree on meeting the needs of the citizens. This chapter also evaluates the effectiveness of existing mechanisms meant to ensure democratic governance and political accountability thrive in the SADC region. Both formal (legislative oversight) and informal (protests) mechanisms will be used to hold political elites accountable. In this chapter, Botswana, Zimbabwe and South Africa are used as case studies to wrestle with issues of democratic governance and political governance.

Democratic governance has now become a common feature of our governance system in Africa. The chapter aims to highlight the state of democratic governance in the SADC region. This chapter is important for the government, civil society, academic institutions, students including researchers. The chapter outlines the practical significance of democratic governance in SADC. Literature which includes, books, articles, newspapers, constitutions and acts from Botswana, South Africa and Zimbabwe including observation has been utilised to collect data. Institutions that support democracy and governance are looked at and analysed for their relevancy in democratic governance and accountability.

BACKGROUND

SADC region

The African continent and the SADC region have embraced the basic principles of democratic governance such as political accountability. Through democratic governance, governments exercise their power in the advancement of social, economic and political development (UNDP, 2007). To achieve this democratic mandate, bureaucracy should be held politically accountable through formal and informal mechanisms (Heywood, 2019). Despite the monarchs in Lesotho and Eswatini, SADC has a traceable record of upholding democratic governance through the promotion of elections. Elections in any democratic order are regarded as the pillar of democracy. Citizens in the SADC region are afforded human suffrage which makes democracy to be stronger. An interesting phenomenon about the elections in the region is that they are generally open, free, transparent, and fair. However, despite the confirmation relating to regular and fair elections by political parties, the electoral commissions, and the elections observers, there is a growing tendency within SADC to unethical conduct resulting in rigging and violence. At the heart of the democracy is the elections to form a government and political accountability. This tendency is juxtaposed with citizens' expectations of their leaders to discharge their responsibilities based on good governance principles of accountability, social justice, impartiality, equality and equity. Ethical and accountable leadership is needed to deal with governance challenges such as corruption and democratic deficit.

Democratic governance and political governance are fundamental in consolidating a developmental state. For SADC countries to advance developmental states based on political accountability as the cardinal principle of good governance, democratic mechanisms aimed at engaging citizens on governance and policy-related matters are imperative. These mechanisms are vital in holding bureaucratic accountability, guaranteeing good governance and maintaining political stability (Oluwatosin, 2017). The different systems that are created to encourage the citizens to participate in democratic governance will be explored to determine their relevance in the current democratic governance setup in the SADC region. The laws and regulations which are created for democratic governance will be looked at. Political governance is an important element of political accountability. The important areas to be looked at will be the institutions that are created to strengthen political governance. In the context of South Africa and Botswana, the political sentiments are about the institutions created to strengthen democracy. These are the institutions that are associated with political governance which are the Public Protector, The Auditor General, the Independent Electoral Commission, and the Human Rights Commission amongst others. Their role in the strengthening of governance and accountability is of great importance. Governance and accountability work well when the affected citizens are part of the decision-making process. Section 118 of the South African constitution gives the government an obligation to consult with the citizens on matters that affect them. To provide context, role players in the government decision-making process will be looked at including the impact that they make. Civil society has the potential to mobilize and conscientize citizens about government decisions and their implications. Their role in making the government accountable is crucial as they provide meaningful contributions to the governance and accountability of the state.

Countries in the SADC region appear to have accepted and accommodated the concept of democratic governance. Democratic governance entails the direct and indirect involvement of the citizens in the running of the government. People are at the centre of decision making and they are constantly consulted by the government on matters that concern them. Section 118 of the South African Constitution makes a requirement for the government to receive public input on all legislative and policy matters. In Zimbabwe, Civil society groups are actively involved in the government decision-making process (Chikerema: 2013). There is a huge space to accommodate civil and political liberties and institutional pluralism. People are allowed to organise themselves, accept responsibilities and become involved in local decision-making (Reddy: 1999). The same can be said about Botswana which allows citizens to take part in the governance of the country though at a minimal level as compared to South Africa and Zimbabwe (Mfundisi: 2006)

Defining Democratic Governance and Political Accountability

Democratic governance is defined as a system in which people have the authority to deliberate and decide on legislation and to choose the governing officials of their choice. The expectation is that in democratic governance institutions that are open, responsive, and accountable are built. Government serves the needs and preferences of the citizens therefore; citizens are allowed to freely participate in the affairs of the government. According to Rotberg (2004), democratic governance is the delivery of political goods to the citizens and the better the quality of that delivery and the greater quality of political goods being delivered the higher the level of governance. People in many societies associate democratic governance with inclusion and consultation. As stated by Jerome and Nel (2022) democracy in its very nature is inclusive and societies are to thrive on their participation in democratic processes. As stated by Obayori (2009), democracies in modern times must be participatory and this requires the popular participation of all people not only in the national elections but also on issues that affect their daily lives.

Botswana, South Africa, and Zimbabwe are considered democratic and they have regular elections which are free and fair. These countries, encourage citizens to participate in the governance and decision-making processes which talk to political accountability. Obayori (2009) states that democracy in its nature, is inclusive and societies are to strive on their participation in democratic processes. According to Gberevbie (2014), democracies in modern times must be participatory and this requires the popular participation of all people, not only at national elections but also those issues affecting their daily lives. Section 152 of the South African Constitution states that government must provide communities with a democratic and accountable government. Elected leaders are expected by the citizens to be accountable and take them along on the programmes of government.

PRINCIPLES OF DEMOCRATIC GOVERNANCE

Public Political Participation

Participation is a principle of democratic governance which is popular amongst the ordinary citizens. When government give citizens the authority to make decisions on what they want, they feel valued. They feel that they are part of the governance of the state. Therefore, public participation is not just about participation only, it is a constitutional obligation. The legitimacy of government actions is based on the level of public participation levels of government. The principle of citizen participation brings the government and the citizens together to discuss how they could meet the needs of the people (Tamsyaoc: 2024). The same principle of citizen participation is being used in Botswana. According to the Afro Barometer of August 2018, 67% of the Batswana population gets involved in the public participation initiatives in that country. The citizens and government at different levels appear to be on the same page regarding citizen participation as an important principle of democratic governance. In his study on public participation in Harare, Mapfumo Linos (2019) has indicated that "public participation can play an important role in addressing developmental, governance and administrative challenges being faced by governments".

Fair Conduct of Elections

Elections are a central element of democracy throughout the world. The situation in Botswana demonstrates an indication of active citizens when it comes to elections. 71% per cent of the Botswana population actively participates in the elections. (Afro: 2018). According to the Zimbabwean Electoral Commission, 68% of the population participated in the elections in 2023, while 32% could not be accounted for. In the 2019 general elections in South Africa, 66.1% of the eligible voters participated in the election . Beyond voting, citizens participate in community meetings more than once a year. Of great concern would be the 7% which has no interest in the politics of Botswana.

The same can be said about South Africa. Both Botswana, South Africa and Zimbabwe have regular elections which are generally declared as free and fair. Citizens in these countries, participate in the elections regularly to elect the leaders of their choice. Five years are set aside for elections in these countries which are regular and conducted in a conducive environment.

Responsiveness

Since the birth of democracy in South Africa, regular, free and fair elections have been held which is a sign of political stability. In South Africa, and Botswana, the Independent Electoral Commission (IEC) while in Zimbabwe there is the Zimbabwe Electoral Commission (ZEC) which administers elections. The electoral commission in these countries is generally considered independent and capable. Elections observers from SADC have generally been satisfied with the election process in these countries. The elections to be considered free and fair should meet the following requirements:

- All eligible citizens have the right to vote.
- Every vote has equal weight.
- The ballot is secret, and citizens cast their ballot without fear of reprisal.
- The electoral body is independent.
- Media is free, independent and competent so that voters have accurate objective information about the candidates and the issues.
- Freedom of association is protected, and candidates and voters are free to gather and campaign and canvass for their preferred candidates.
- There is freedom of speech and voters can express their political views without fear of reprisal if they do not break the law. (section 7 SA Constitution)

There are contradictory views about the elections in Zimbabwe. In the case of Zimbabwe, Aaron Rwodzi (2017) argues that despite the elections being held per the country's constitution, they are not free and fair. According to Chikwanha-Dzenga (pp11), Zimbabweans feel that the post-independent dispensation accords them more political rights than under the white minority regime. Most citizens feel freer to express themselves, join political organizations, choose candidates or parties of their choice at elections and are less fearful of being arrested by the police for no apparent offence.

Efficiency and Effectiveness

This is referred to as the government's ability to provide acceptable service with the least expenditure of time, materials, and money. Efficiency and effectiveness pursue the relationship between inputs, outputs, and outcomes (Farrel,1957). Considerations given for efficiency are:

- Increasing productivity, production,
- Activities in the business environment,
- Society's expectations regarding the degree to of citizens need coverage.

Efficiency and effectiveness have a close relationship with the systems theory which is depicted by the interaction between the societal environment and an abstract political system which processes or converts demands and supports into outputs, producing an overall stability or homeostasis (Jackson RJ & Jackson D: 1997). According to David Easton, this study entails the search for clinical processes that govern political structures. This is the process that deals with the relationship between the leaders and followers. Citizens make demands or raise concern to the government and the government respond by doing whatever they can be able to do. Of course, many other factors like the budget must be looked at before doing what the citizens expect.

At the local government level, which is the case in the selected countries, the government has created mechanisms for participation and accountability. Municipalities are required to establish ward committees to enhance participatory democracy at the local government level. (Patience: 2022)

Openness and Transparency

Section 1 of the South African Constitution talks about openness transparency and accountability as the founding values of the constitution. An open government is transparent, accessible to anyone, anytime, anywhere, and responsive to new ideas and demands. Transparency is used as a means of holding public officials accountable and fighting corruption. Citizens see democratic governance as a tool in which all government activities are done openly, and all government information should be made available for all citizens. When the government allows people to access information, the government become accountable to the public.

The accountable government has to ensure that it communicates regularly with the citizens. There are different mechanisms that the government may use to communicate e.g., newspapers, portals for citizens, use of adverts on radio and television and calling public meetings to engage with the citizens. The government may also foster a culture of transparency. In so doing citizens will feel that they are not left behind on matters of government. The finances of government should be accounted for and that will be an indication that the government is accountable to the people. In the process, the governments should always be available to get the views of the citizens. In so doing citizens feel valued by the government.

THE IMPORTANCE OF DEMOCRATIC GOVERNANCE

Botswana formerly known as Bechuanaland gained its independence on 30 September 1966. Before gaining independence, Botswana was a British protectorate and one of the poorest and least developed states in the world. Zimbabwe formerly known as Rhodesia gained its independence in 1980 from Britain. Led by the likes of Robert Mugabe and Kenen Banana, and others a fight for liberation was finally won that gave birth to what is known as Zimbabwe today. As for South Africa, independence was gained in 1960 from the British government but the Apartheid government was in place until 1994 when a democratic government was established. Pre-1994 most of the South Africans who were mainly blacks were oppressed and they did not have rights under the apartheid government. It would be correct to argue that real democracy was attained in 1994 in South Africa. (Landsberg :2020 pp4)

Democracy in Botswana is generally considered the way of life, a cultural expectation, and a treasure. There is a general commitment to ensure that the will of the people is observed. In Botswana, democracy is founded on the principles already practised in the Setswana culture such as;

- "Botho" Humility.
- "Therisano" - Consultation
- "Puso ya batho ka batho" - Government of the people by the people
- "Mafoko a kgotla a mantle other"- Free speech
- "Morero"- Dialogue. (Botswana.gov.za 08/12/2021).

In Zimbabwe, democracy is associated with the liberation from the oppressive white rule. It is seen as the opening of an era in which Zimbabweans would be able to rule themselves and run their affairs without foreign influence. Both in Botswana and South Africa, democracy is closely associated with rights.

Democracy and Rights

The constitutions of Botswana, South Africa, and Zimbabwe, all speak about the rights of all citizens. The citizens of these countries only started to enjoy their rights through the independence they got from their past oppressive regimes. After the first elections of independence, human suffrage had to be guaranteed to all citizens. Citizens associate democracy with universal suffrage which they did not get while they were oppressed. SADC countries have a reputation for conducting regular, free, and fair elections regularly. There could be some dissatisfactions in some isolated instances but generally, elections are considered free and fair by the SADC elections observers. Of more importance, the trend has developed that all the necessary efforts and resources are put in place to ensure that elections are conducted regularly in the region.

Democracy is known for ensuring that the citizens' rights are protected. The supremacy of the constitution and the rule of law is primary for the success of democracy. The conduct of citizens and their behaviour is constantly based on the constitution (Jackson R & Jackson D: 1997). It therefore means that democracy creates an environment of law, order and stability which is based on the supremacy of the constitution.

The concept of equality is circumscribed mainly in democracies. The emphasis is on equality of political rights, participation, gender equality and equality before the law. Equality would mean that citizens are treated equally without any form of discrimination which is based on race, culture, religion, gender and background. There have been efforts to strengthen the fight against equality specifically gender equality by many countries especially in the SADC region. The gender commission has been established to specifically focus on issues related to gender discrimination. In South Africa, the government has gone to the extent of establishing the Department of Women, Children and People with Disabilities in the Presidency. The role is to champion issues related to gender inequality and develop strategies to solve such challenges. The Republic of Zimbabwe has section 4 (80) of the Zimbabwe constitution which states the rights of women:

1. Every woman has full and equal dignity of the person with men, and this includes equal opportunities in political, economic and social activities.
2. Women have the same rights as men regarding the custody and guardianship of children, but an Act of Parliament may regulate how those rights are to be exercised.
3. All laws, customs, traditions, and cultural practices that infringe the rights of women conferred by this Constitution are void to the extent of the infringement.

Citizens see democracy as a huge shift from oppressive systems to a system where they can express themselves freely and participate in the governance system.

INSTITUTIONS FOR POLITICAL GOVERNANCE

The Constitutions in the SADC region provide for constitutional democracy and list the rights to which the people of these countries are entitled. To give substance to these Constitutional rights, independent institutions have been established to promote rights and to strengthen constitutional democracy. These institutions are found in South Africa, Botswana, and Zimbabwe.

Auditor General

The Auditor General is charged with the primary oversight/ assurance role of ensuring accountability within the three arms of government. The Auditor General is required by law to examine and report annually to parliament on the accounts of ministries, departments, Provincial, regional, and state-owned, enterprises and statutory boards. It is the taxpayers' watchdog, ensuring that their taxes are well spent. It promotes accountability, helps fight corruption and prevents waste.

The Public Protector

This is the institution that works very closely with the people on the ground. It is an institution that is created to be patient and listen to complaints from citizens without any discrimination or favour. In South Africa, The Public Protector is established according to the Act 23 of 1994. It receives and investigates complaints from the public about the government. Some functions include (but are not limited to): The power to investigate any conduct of government or administration that is seen as improper/ prejudiced. Their main objective is to defend democracy and its citizens.

There are cases in which the Office of The Public Protector has investigated high-profile politicians in South Africa. (Secure in Comfort, Report No25 Of 2013/14). The Public Protector investigated former President Jacob Zuma in 2013 and the former president was found guilty of unethical conduct. It was established by the Public Protector that the former president unduly benefitted from the upgrades at his personal property. In that regard, he was ordered to pay back, some of the money due to the state. This is a demonstration that the office of the Public Protector is required to do its work without any fear or favour.

Human Rights Commission

Some governments that claimed democracy were oppressive and did not grant citizens their rights. Democracy, as a system of government should be credited for the promotion and the protection of human rights. To live and enhance the protection of human rights, SADC states have established the Human Rights Commissions in their respective states. Since its establishment by Constitutional Mandate, the South African Human Rights Commission has dedicated itself to:

- Raising awareness of human rights issues;
- Monitoring and assessing the observance of human rights;
- Education and training on human rights;
- Addressing human rights violations and seeking effective redress.
- Protect people against abuse of power and maladministration by the State and public institutions and by officials of those institutions.

The same mandate that the SAHRC has is the same as in other states in the region. There is an emphasis on the celebration of rights with responsibilities. That talks to that when you are enjoying your rights you should not infringe on other people's rights.

In the case of Zimbabwe, most citizens feel that post-independent dispensation accords them more political rights than under the white minority regime. They feel much freer to express themselves, join political organizations, to choose a candidate or a party of their choice at elections and they are less fearful of being arrested by the police for no apparent offence (Chikwanha-Dezenga AB, Masungure E, Madzingira N; IDASA, 2001)

There is considerable progress related to the white minority regime and the current democratic system in Zimbabwe. A much larger proportion of adult citizens report an improvement in terms of the freedom to join a political organization of their choice. They mostly feel that they are enjoying their freedom to make their choice and they are not forced by anyone.

Independent Electoral Commission

Act 51 of 1996 makes the provision for the establishment and the composition of an electoral Commission to manage elections for national, provincial and local legislative bodies and to make provision for the establishment of the composition and powers, duties and functions of an electoral court. The mandate of the electoral commission is to ensure that they run elections regularly. The primary function as outlined in section 190(1) of the SA constitution, is to manage elections at all levels of government; to ensure that elections are free and fair and to declare the results of the elections in as short time as possible. The Zimbabwe Electoral Commission (ZEC) and the Independent Electoral Commission (IEC) have the mandate to ensure that the elections are free and fair. Sufficient support is given to the electoral commission for efficiency and effectiveness. There is a reasonable amount of money budgeted to ensure that the Electoral Commission does not have financial strain while performing its duties.

ELECTIONS AND POLITICAL ACCOUNTABILITY

Elections as earlier discussed in this chapter are a cornerstone of democracy in many countries in the SADC region. Politicians are put in government through elections based on the party manifestos that they present during the election period. Elections are a tool used by the electorate, to seek accountability from the politicians. The process of elections is an essential requirement of any political system that hopes to be regarded as possessing democratic credentials (D Caramani; 2007). The assumption is that when politicians have done well in government, they can still be put back in office because they would have impressed the voters. There are mechanisms used by politicians to account for the voters.

According to Jackson (1997), elections do much more than simply determine who will form the next government. Elections have an important role in providing a routine mechanism for recruiting and selecting individuals to occupy seats in representative institutions. That is the reason there are campaigns when elections are held. It is done to ensure that when citizens vote, they know what the political parties and individuals who are standing stand for.

Elected governments claim that they have a mandate from the voters. Most of the things they do, they claim that they are doing them for the citizens. Elections and electoral processes legitimize the government (Caraman 2008: pp182). The government that is put in place through the popular wish of the government have the authority to make decisions on behalf of the citizens. The elections in SADC are generally competitive. Competitive elections allow periodic opportunities for smaller parties and independent candidates to express themselves and air their views on many issues affecting the citizens. Electoral processes provide a safety valve, allowing voters to express dissatisfaction with the major parties and register their protest by voting for fringe parties or candidates.

Elections

Elections are the methods of assessing preferences through votes and they are important for democracy (Garner R 2009). It makes citizens know and understand what is happening in their daily political lives and they develop the desire to get involved in the political processes. A strong civil society underpins democracy (Hugo et al., 1995). Article 12 of the Universal Declaration on Democracy adopted by the Inter-Parliamentary Union in 1997 outlines that: "The key element in the exercise of democracy is the holding of free and fair elections at regular intervals enabling the people's will to express it" (Inter-Parliamentary Union, 1997)

Political parties strive to ensure that they are as representative as possible to appeal to the electorate. Electoral legislation is silent on the nomination procedures that parties should follow to select when compiling their party lists. The different political parties have their internal processes that they follow to select candidates. Members of the political parties come with candidates from different constituencies or branches until a final list is submitted to the electoral body. In the case of proportional representation political parties are represented based on the number of votes accumulated during the elections (IEC)

In the case of Botswana, South Africa and Zimbabwe, elections are held regularly and they have constantly been declared free and fair. The constitutions of all these countries guarantee the rights of all citizens to participate freely in the election process. Guidelines are there to participate in the elections. The requirements are generally accepted by the citizens as a reasonable tool to govern elections (Chikwanha-Dzenga;2001)

Political Party Funding

There are a lot of resources required for the proper functioning of the political parties. Political parties coordinate their activities regularly. They also must recruit members to join the party and also have to ensure that there is constant contact with the members and supporters (Caramel:225). All these activities require financial resources. Most political parties rely on donations and affiliations for their financial support. Businesses and individuals make donations to political parties for them to run their affairs. Individuals when they join political parties, pay affiliation fee which is used to run party activities.

In South Africa and Zimbabwe, political parties that are represented in parliament get funding to run their political party activities. Some rules and guidelines govern the use of the money that parties get from parliament. South Africa has gone a step further by introducing the Political Party Funding Act of 2018. In Zimbabwe, it is the Political Parties Funding Act (1992) of Zimbabwe. This act provides guidelines on how parties are supposed to be funded and receive donations. It encourages transparency from political parties themselves. Section 6 of the act stipulates that "The accounting officer of a political party of a legislature must annually, within three (3) calendar months of the end of the financial year, disclose any funding of represented political party". Section 7 further states that political parties should disclose donations received by political parties.

State funding of political parties in Botswana remains a contested issue after more than fifty years of independence. No law provides for the funding of political parties. According to the afro barometer, there are calls by stakeholders including civil society and opposition parties to provide for such funding to enhance democracy.

Good Governance

According to Cameron (2004), "Good governance is strengthening democracy; ensuring respect for human rights and rule of law; promoting transparency and capacity of the state to deliver." It should be understood in the context of putting citizens first in whatever the government does or intends to do. There is no way good governance can be discussed without introducing the ethical principle of accountability. It is argued by Cameron (2004:59) that "accountability is an important element of governance". He further states that accountability promotes good governance. The constitution of the Republic of South Africa, 1996 subsection 91(1) and 92(2) calls for accountability from the President, Deputy President, and cabinet ministers as individuals and collectively. It is argued that good governance is needed to stop corruption. It is further argued that where there is good governance, there is prosperity. The constitution is clear about what individual accountability entails. According to Rautenbach & Malherbe (2004:178), individual accountability entails the following:

- A duty to explain to parliament how the powers and duties under his or her control have been exercised and performed.
- A duty to acknowledge that a mistake has been made and to promise to rectify the matter.
- Duty to resign if personal responsibility has been accepted.

Accountability implies that parliament should be given full information and disclosure for parliament and the citizens to know the truth. Where mistakes have taken place, there should be an acknowledgement and openly and plans must be undertaken to remedy the situation (Rautenbach and Malherbe, p. 78). Elements for good governance are inclusive of a) accountability; b) transparency; c) responsiveness; d) equitable and inclusive; e) effective and efficient; and f) follows the rule of law.; g) consensus Oriented and finally h) participatory.

Citizens Expectations

When politicians campaign for elections, they articulate their ideology and make promises to the electorate. Campaigns are dominated by the identification of the problems and challenges facing society and parties seek to provide solutions to such. The expectation from the citizens is always that the politicians will provide better lives for them and solutions to the problems will be provided. Citizens expect their leaders to be the source of solutions to their challenges. They expect leaders that have ethics and honesty when leading them. Citizens expect leaders who are open, transparent and accountable. (D. Plaatjies: 2013) Leaders are expected to set an example for good governance and act in a manner that is consistent with good governance at all times. Leaders are expected to set an example for good governance and should act by the law. International Organization of Supreme Audit Institutions (INTOSAI) working with the International Monetary Fund (IMF), the World Bank, the International Federation of Accountants (IFAC), International Budget Partnership (IBP) has been established to evaluate how more and more transparency can be achieved, to make the difference in the citizens lives. These are areas that require attention as they boost the character of good governance in government and the citizens.

ROLE PLAYERS IN ACCOUNTABILITY

Parliament

Members of parliament are elected by the citizens during elections. Countries in the SADC region have regular uninterrupted elections to elect their representatives in government. In both South Africa and Botswana, the president is elected by the parliament while in Zimbabwe, the president is directly elected by the citizens during elections. Though the elections differ on the election of the president, he/she remains accountable to parliament. In the case of Botswana and South Africa, the president is elected by parliament and he/she must be accountable to parliament. Regular sessions are arranged for the president to go and account to parliament on what the government is doing. Members of parliament use that as an opportunity to make the president accountable for his/her actions.

Parliament has committees that are created to ensure that the executive is accountable. Most of the work of government is done in the parliamentary committees. Each state department has a committee set up for the minister and the department to be accountable. Members of parliament monitor and evaluate the progress that is made in different state departments. It is in this context that accountability is exercised by parliament.

Interest Groups

Organisations outside the government have a role to play in making the government accountable. They are the recipients of government services, and they are directly affected by government decisions. Interest groups may resemble political parties, but their leaders are not elected by the public, and they are not responsible to the public. (Roskin M: 1997 pp 185) Interest groups differ based on the reasons for their existence. Some are religious organisations, youth, professional, business, and cultural groups. They are organised based on their interests and they also try to influence government decision making. They attend and participate in the meetings arranged by the government, and they propose government.

They use different mechanisms to influence or force the government to make some decisions. They do it in different ways including the following: picketing, demonstration, marching, writing memos, and striking. They try and use any method that will make their voice heard by the government. According to Ogudare D 2023:pp70), strikes and public protests can reshape government direction to meet the needs of the citizens.

Media

Most people in the developed world rely on the media for information including government information. The media plays a role in informing the citizens about the developments in the government. People get to know what is happening in government through the media. Citizens read newspapers daily and they listen to the radio for the news and they rely on the television for political news. There are radio stations that read the news every hour and people rely on them for information. The media lets people know the plans of the government and its policies. In some instances, senior government officials including ministers are invited for talk shows on the radio. In that way, citizens are made to know what the happening in government. In some instances, citizens are allowed to directly speak with government officials on the talk shows.

The government use the media for accountability. During the Covid-19 lockdown in South Africa in 2020-2022, citizens in South Africa relied on the media for government information. Regular media briefings by the Minister of Health were conducted and the media was the carrier of the news to the citizens. Regular updates by the president of South Africa Mr Cyril Ramaphosa were done through the media. Government utilises the media by calling, press conferences, media briefings and writing statements to the media. In so doing the information easily gets to the citizens.

Judiciary

The judiciary plays the central role of adjudication. Countries in the SADC adhere to the principle of the supremacy of the constitution and the rule of law. The judiciary plays the role of ensuring that they interpret the law. They help in assisting citizens and the government about the importance of respecting and upholding the law. In whatever government does, the law has to be respected and no government decision should contradict the law. Government decisions should be based on the law and they should at all times follow the legal framework. In case there are misunderstandings amongst the other arms of the state, they refer to the judiciary for adjudication.

Legal opinions are constantly sought when the decision is to be taken. That is done to avoid contradicting the law since the law is superior. The judiciary acts independently and it serves in the interest of the constitutional democracy. The judiciary is always making decisions without fear or favour. They work only in the interest of justice and the Constitution.

CONCLUSION

There is progress relating to how democracy is developing in the SADC region. There is an acceptance of democratic governance and the institutions that support democracy are functioning well. Citizen's participation in the governance of the state appears to be gaining momentum in the region. There is still room for improvement in the SADC region. The involvement of citizens in decision-making is an important step in the development of democratic governance in the region. Active citizens have a huge role to play in our body politic as they make the politicians to be always focused on their responsibilities. Citizens play a critical role in assisting the government to make decisions that encompass the views of the citizens.

REFERENCES

Cameron, W. (2004). Public Accountability: Effectiveness, equality and ethics: worlds apart. *Canadian Journal of Political Science*, *38*(4), 1003–1028.

Caramani, D. (2008). Comparative Politics (2nd ed.). Academic Press.

Chikerema, A.F. (2013). Citizen Participation and Local Democracy in Zimbabwean Local Government System. *Journal of Humanities and Social Science, 13*(2), 87-90.

Chikwanha-Dzenga, Masunugure, & Madzingira. (2001). *Democracy and national Governance in Zimbabwe: A country survey Report*. IDASA.

Constitution of the Republic of South Africa. (1996). Government Printers.

Farrell, M.J. (n.d.). The measurement of Productive Efficiency. *Journal of the Royal Statistical Society, 120*(3), 253-290.

Friedman, S. (2008). We met the and he is us: Domestic politics and South Africa's role in promoting democracy. *African Journal of International Affairs, 11*(2), 29–53. doi:10.4314/ajia.v11i2.57263

Garner, R., Ferdinand, P., & Lawson, S. (2009). *Introduction to Politics*.

Gberevbie, D. E. (2004). Democracy, democratic Institutions and Good Governance in Nigeria. *Eastern Africa Social Science Research Review, 30*(1), 133–152. doi:10.1353/eas.2014.0005

Heywood, A. (2002). *Politics* (2nd ed.). Palgrave.

Hussein, Z. (2018). *Democratic Accountability*. Dawn.

Jackson RJ & D, (1997), *A Comparative Introduction to Political Science*. Prentice Hall.

Landsberg, C., & Graham, C. (2017). *Government and Politics in South Africa- Coming of age* (5th ed.). Pretoria Van Schaik Publishers.

Mandaza, I. (1991). *The one party state and democracy: The Zimbabwe debate*. Academic Press.

Mapfumo, L. (2019). *Public Participation and Collaborative Governance in Zimbabwe flea Markets: A case study of the City of Harare*. Academic Press.

Merdith, M. (2018). Mugabe misrule. And how it will hold Zimbabwe back. *Foreign Affairs, 97*(2), 129–138.

Mfundisi, A. (2006). Civic Participation and Voting Patterns in Botswana. *Journal of African Elections*.

Obeyori, F. (2009). Poverty and Underdevelopment: Threat to participatory democracy. *The Constitution: A Journal of Constitutional Development, 9*(3), 17-25.

Ogudare, Y. D. (2023). *Governance and Public Protests*. IGI Global.

Patience, J.J., & Nel, D. (2022). *Governance, Democracy and Accountability from a Network Governance Perspective within the City of Ekurhuleni*. Academic Press.

Plaatjies, D. (2013). *Protecting the inheritance: Governance and Public Accountability in Democratic South Africa*. Academic Press.

Political Parties Finance Act. (1992).

Political Party Funding Act (2018). Act No 6 of 2018.

Public Protector Act. Act 23 of 1994.

Rautenbach, I. M., & Malherbe, E. F. (2004). *Constitutional law*. LexisNexus Butherworth.

Reddy, P.S. (1999). *Local government and democratisation: A review of the Southern African Region.* Juta & Co.

Roskin, M., Cord, R. L., Medeiros, J. A., & Jones, W. S. (1997). *Political Science: An introduction.* Prentice -Hall, International.

Rwodzi, A. (2017). *Democracy Governance and Legitimacy in Zimbabwe since the November 2017 Military Coup*. Academic Press.

Secure in Comfort. (2013/14). *Report no 25 of 2013/14.* Tamayaoc, M.J, Law Politics and Philosophy. http://tamayaosbc.wordpress.com

Tamayaoc, M.J, Law Politics and Philosophy. http://tamayaosbc.wordpress.com.

Vaole, O. O. (2017). *The democratic Coup dëtat*. Oxford University Press.

Venter, A., & Landsberg, C. (2010). *Government and Politics in South Africa.* Van Schaik.

Chapter 7
Corruption as an Obstacle to Socio-Economic and Political Justice in Zimbabwe

Menard Musendekwa
https://orcid.org/0000-0002-6644-8727
Reformed Church University, Zimbabwe

ABSTRACT

In Zimbabwe, it has long been believed that corruption is the main barrier to economic growth. Corruption has frustrated all chances for socio-economic and political justice in Zimbabwe. The democratic space has also been shrunk as evidenced by judicial failure to affect reasonable punishment on perpetrators of corruption. This chapter examines recorded incidents of corruption in Zimbabwe that have not received the proper attention, resulting in the deterioration of socioeconomic and political justice.

INTRODUCTION

Corruption has long been seen as the greatest obstacle to economic success in Zimbabwe. All attempts at socioeconomic and political justice in Zimbabwe have been thwarted by corruption. The judiciary's reluctance to impose just punishment on corrupt officials is more evidence of the shrinkage of the democratic space. This chapter examines instances of corruption that have been reported but not properly investigated in Zimbabwe, which has led to a decline in socioeconomic and political justice.

International organisations like the United Nations and the European Union blame the Zimbabwean government for poor governance, political polarisation and corruption that led to hyperinflation (Bratton & Masunungure 2008; Hanke 2008; Makochekanwa 2016:1250-1260; Maunganidze et al 2021:2). In 2011, the United States listed Zimbabwe as the sixth failed state in the world and the ruling elites blame sanctions from the western countries. This research acknowledges that Zimbabwe has been facing a socio-economic and political crisis that has led to hopelessness, even after independence. A nation's progress is hampered by corruption at the expense of individual interests. Although Zimbabwe's issues

DOI: 10.4018/979-8-3693-0477-8.ch007

are multifaceted, corruption is the main barrier to economic liberation (Mutanda 2014:1). The main culprits of corruption have been fingered as the political players at the expense of the majority citizenry. Zimbabwean economy has been under years of depression since independence in 1980.

It may not be appropriate to attribute sanctions as a major factor in the decline of the Zimbabwean economy. Although sanctions were applied on selected political leaders and institutions in 2002, corruption existed long before that (Matanda 2014:3). So, it is reasonable to consider corruption as one key factor in the current development impasse (Marango 2018:57). Particularly since corruption shrunk the democratic space for the Zimbabwean populous. Corruption therefore is the final nail in the coffin, even though sanctions are one of the economic huddles.

In Zimbabwe, family fragmentation and poverty appear to have taken the place of ambitions for a decent life (Wini-Dari and Damauswa 2016:154; Bonga, Chiminya, and Mudzingiri 2015:11). Despite all promises for economic liberation that were inspired by the achievement of political freedom, they have all been dashed. Due primarily to corruption, the country experienced economic stagnation and regression (Masango 2016). Corruption has dominated all sectors of society with the political players as the main culprits. According to Bonga, Chiminya, and Mudzingiri (2015:11), corruption "explodes and harms the economy." All efforts of economic recovery are futile as the justice and democratic system is manipulated for individual gains over against the majority of Zimbabweans. Thus, one significant barrier to economic growth is corruption.

Several variables, such as the struggle for power politics of political patronage, political violence, and the emergence of special interest groups like women in politics, Youth Action Groups, and indigenous Business Groups, are mentioned by Muzurura (2016:3) as having fostered an increase in corruption. Gaining political influence through economic monopolisation by the ruling elites is at the heart of all these elements.

Defining Corruption

The Latin word corrupter, which is closely related to the English words "destroy," "mar," and "bribe," is the source of the English word "corruption" (Cresswell 2010:103; Chiweshe and Mahiya 2021:73). Bribery, fraud, extortion, embezzlement, abuse of power, and nepotism or favouritism are examples of corruption (Thabani 2017:286). Corruption includes any unethical behaviour that violates social standards through deceptive actions that limit the ability to uphold economic fairness. The intricacy of the situation arises when the authorities themselves are unfair and corrupt if they implement laws that are harmful to just practices. According to the UNDP (2010), the operational definition of corruption is the abuse of authority for personal benefit. A corrupt culture no longer values morality, virtue, or integrity. The situation deteriorates. Such a civilization starts to degenerate and embarks on its path of self-destruction. Selfishness. The two basic reasons for corruption are avarice and greed. According to Musingafi et al. (2011), political corruption refers to state officials abusing their positions of authority for illegal personal gain. If corruption can be regarded as a political enterprise, it is a confirmation that corruption is rooted in the abuse of power.

The definition of corruption in Zimbabwe is characterised by the misuse of public office for personal benefit This may also include grand corruption, also referred to as political corruption, because it has harmed Zimbabwe's whole political and governmental systems. This sort of corruption occurs when individuals abuse their power or influence to benefit themselves, and their allies, or to keep hold of political power at the expense of the wealth of the State and the welfare of its citizens. The state's obligation to respect, protect, and uphold rights—which are tied to the rights of people and the wider public—is undermined by this kind of corruption (Muyambwa 2018).

In Zimbabwe, bribery, extortion, nepotism, patronage, and grand venality are the most common ways that corruption manifests itself. Other ways that it abuses power include other types of abuse as well. Zimbabwe was placed 157th out of 176 countries in the 2018 Corruption Index. According to estimates, corruption costs Zimbabwe an estimated $1 billion annually, which harms its ability to thrive economically and socially (Takawira 2017: 204).

The first move of corruption in Zimbabwe is notable through the perpetuation of colonialism after the independence struggle under the guise of neo-colonialism

The former colonisers typically view neo-colonialism as the imposition of new kinds of colonialism. In Zimbabwe, the political establishment continued colonialism.

(Idemudia 2016:188). Mutumbuka (1981:xiii) describes neo-colonialism as the transition from colonialism as a situation whereby colonialism takes a new guise in which third-world countries are often worse when corruption and self-enrichment undermine freedom and truth. Colonialism imbued the colonial spirit of self-aggrandizement that made African leaders adopt colonialism at its worst. The colonial baton stick has been handed over to the indigenous people who perpetuated the oppressive structures of domination (Musendekwa 2016:107).

According to Lawman (2013:217), hope for a better Africa is undermined by corruption, bribery and inefficiency.

Corruption has been regarded as the number one obstacle to economic prosperity in Zimbabwe. Corruption undermines the national development at the expense of individual interests. The word corruption is an English word derived from the Latin word *corrupter* closely related to the words "destroy", "mar" and "bribe" (Cresswell 2010:103; Chiweshe and Mahiya 2021:73). Corruption encompasses issues of bribery, fraud, extortion, embezzlement, abuse of power and nepotism or favouritism (Thabani 2017:286).

According to Osoba (1996:372), corruption is a type of antisocial behaviour by an individual or social group that bestows unfair or fraudulent benefits on its perpetrators, violates established legal norms and the nation's moral ethos, and is likely to undermine or lessen the ability of the legitimate authorities to fully provide for the material and spiritual well-being of all members of the society in a just and equitable manner.

Corruption encompasses all unethical practices that go against the norms of society through fraudulent practices that undermine the capacity to practice economic justice. The complexity of the matter is when the authorities are the ones who are corrupt and unjust. If the authorities institute policies that are detrimental to just practices, corruption would have become central to economic degradation.

BACKGROUND

Reflection on the Zimbabwean Landscape of Crisis

Since 1980, when Zimbabwe gained its independence, under Robert Mugabe's leadership, the nation has been in a state of upheaval. Emmerson Dambudzo Mnangagwa, his successor, accomplished very little, if anything, to reform the dishonest political system. According to Nyambi (2013:183), there are many depictions of the Zimbabwean crisis in the years after 2000. This argument shows that the narratives can be understood in a variety of ways. Any definition offered by dissenting voices has been disregarded and may even result in victimisation. By placing the blame on the old colonisers, the ZANU-PF asserted control over the narrative. According to Nyambi (2013:183), the ZANU-PF's argument is unfounded because the government was not duly elected. Following several closely contested elections, the legitimacy of ZANU-PF was questioned.

Despite the country's economic collapse, Zimbabwe also experienced a legitimacy crisis as a result of the Mugabe era's worsening living conditions and hotly contested elections, particularly in 2008 when Mugabe was still in power and in 2018 when Mnangagwa was elected president (Dzimiri 2017:52). A humanitarian crisis that the state created was made worse by hurried African Union (AU) and Southern African Development Cooperation (SADC) initiatives (Dzimiri 2017:50).

President Mnangagwa's military-assisted coup against President Robert Mugabe in 2017 did not result in significant change. Instead, there was a rise in the number of social and economic problems. Mnangagwa did not hold office as a duly elected head of state. The much-anticipated independence was not achieved by the new administration, which instead increased the hardship that had already existed under Mugabe (Lamarche, Toysen, & Wishart 2019:14).

Zimbabwe's context in the twenty-first century is marked by crises (Dzimiri 2017:51). According to some academics (Mude & Chigora 2013:27; Fenga & Wepener 2018:1–8), it is a socioeconomic and political crisis. The "Zimbabwean Crisis" is how other academics refer to it (Chitando 2010:199; Maposa, Sibanda, and Makahamadze 2011:250; Rugwiji 2017:16; 2020:6; Paradza 2019:1-8; Moyo 2013:68). International bodies including the United Nations and the European Union hold the Zimbabwean government accountable for the hyperinflation that resulted from corruption, political polarisation, and poor governance (Bratton & Masunungure 2008; Hanke 2008; Makochekanwa 2016:1250–1260; Maunganidze et al 2021:2The ruling elite has blamed the sanctions imposed by western nations for Zimbabwe's position as the sixth failed state in 2011. This study highlights how corruption among the political elites led to socioeconomic and political catastrophe in Zimbabwe even after independence, which demoralised the populace.

The current study indicates that the Zimbabwean issue first manifested itself, particularly between 1997 and 2008. According to some, Zimbabwe was in a state of crisis during this time, and some literary works have referred to it as the "post-2000 hegemonic masculinities" (Tembi 2006:12–18). Men's loss of control bred aggression towards women and acts of violence. The Zimbabwean state established the dominant hegemonic masculinity after the year 2000. Depending on the historical or political context, masculinities are thought to produce oppressive, repressive beliefs or even liberating ones (Tembi 2006:18).

It is also important to note that the ruling party is accused of supporting political violence, eroding democracy, and weakening the rule of law (Ndlela 2005:74). After decades of British colonial domination, independence brought back native elites to run the country (Musendekwa 2018:6). Therefore, independence did not bring forth the expected freedom but instead created a new kind of reliance.

Zimbabwe's ZANU-PF administration has been viewed as a barrier to the country's desired level of prosperity. A major economic crisis resulted from the unanticipated payment of the 1997 compensation and pensions for liberation war veterans and the country's subsequent suspension from the Commonwealth (Kanyenze, Chitambara & Tyson 2017:3, Cox 2005:35-36). Concerning the US dollar, the value of the Zimbabwean dollar fell by 71, or 5% (Kanyenze, Chitambara, & Tyson 2017:3). Zimbabwe's unforeseen spending on the war in the DRC in August made corruption more likely (Kanyenze, Chitambara & Tyson 2017:3), which made the situation worse. According to this study, the majority of Zimbabweans' already precarious living situations were made worse by bad government policies. Corruption in the Zimbabwean government's policies prevented peaceful resolutions to the country's crisis. To crush any forms of resistance, the administration also continued draconian colonial-era laws (Vao News, October 27, 2009).

Since the country's independence, the ZANU-PF administration has failed. "Poor governance, economic mismanagement, loss of international community support following repeated human rights violations and manipulated electoral processes and failed elections, all compounded by periods of drought" are some of the factors that have contributed to these failures, according to Besada and Moyo (2008). Because of Mugabe's failings, a crisis developed, forcing people who had little to gain from his rule to rebel by casting their eyes towards a potential saviour in the future. Such resistance encounters counterresistance through "patriotic rhetoric of sovereignty" and revives the spirit of liberation in which the "patriots" are hailed as the world's greatest liberators (Hammar, McGregor, & Landau 2010:263).

The Fast Track Land Reform Programme (FTLRP), which displaced white commercial farmers, was the most divisive and widely denounced fraudulent programme. As a result, the United Nations (UN) and Western nations imposed specific sanctions on political figures. The FTLRP had a significant negative impact on the nation's agricultural industry. (Sachikonye 2002:14; Gunda 2018:13). Although the programme was successful in gaining access to land, the resultant collapse of Southern Africa's once-prosperous breadbasket hampered agricultural production.

Economic challenges, political unrest, victimisation, and unemployment prompted a large-scale flight of Zimbabweans to other nations. More than three million professionals departed the nation in search of asylum or work prospects abroad. Accordingly, Zimbabwe has been ranked 10th out of 157 countries in terms of brain drain between 2000 and 2019 (Lamarche, Toysen, & Wishart 2019:10). Therefore, this researcher sees exile as one indication of the Zimbabwean issue. If Daniel 9 is viewed as literature that fervently yearns for restoration, then exiled Zimbabweans place their faith in a foreign land.

The severity of the issue in Zimbabwe is best and accurately captured by Caputo (2016:72), who claims that it is currently impossible to have hope in democracy or its public institutions because of how deeply and thoroughly it has been tainted by money. Politicians who are completely beholden to the wealthy interests funding their political careers cannot be trusted. When judges are chosen based on political ideology, it is impossible to trust in the independence of the legal system.

It is impossible to have hope in democratic elections when political campaigns focus on deceit rather than truth, on destroying the reputations of the opponents, on doing everything possible to discourage the least powerful people from voting, and when voting districts are rigged.

Caputo defends the likelihood of hopelessness in a totalitarian regime. Money is used by political figures to further their objectives. Even the judges are appointed per their political ideas, leading to the capture of the judiciary and the manipulation of the entire system that oversees free and fair elections.

Mugabe had an imperial view of political independence. Being in positions of political authority required embracing the colonial rulers' imperial dominance. The response to opposition politics that gained strength at the start of the twenty-first century worsened the situation in Zimbabwe, making it once more vulnerable to despondency.

Additionally, it is claimed that the Lancaster House Constitution protected the interests of white farmers (Yeros 2012:5). White farmers failed to give the land back to the native population, thereby prolonging the colonial occupation. Since 1980, the nationalist administration has held white farmers responsible for impeding development. Yeros (2012:5) claims that the nationalist government was made up of a petty-bourgeoisie class that betrayed the masses by sustaining imperialist capitalism. Nationalism then acts as a corrupt neo-colonialist actor. According to Mulinge and Lesetedi (1998:17), neo-colonialism upholds the colonial era's legacy. They also link corrupt institutions and practices that date back to colonialism.

One of the colonial legacies that haunted the nation of Zimbabwe long after the liberation fight was racism, which sparked the Gukurahundi and the invasion of white-owned farms. According to Mlambo (2013:56), the British controlled the Rhodesian government and refused to select ministers from other countries. Thus, racism was a result of British colonialism. According to Mlambo (2013:57), one example of a racist policy was the colour bar, which protected some employment for white people while excluding black people from running for office and "reducing them to second-class citizens."

In a letter to Mugabe published in Nehanda Radio (Dec 2013: 80), Joshua Nkomo criticised Mugabe for continuing to uphold corrupt colonial legislation. Mugabe employed some of the legal measures that the colonial administration had previously used to suppress the native population. Why does Mugabe continue to uphold laws like the Law-and-Order Maintenance Act, the Unlawful Organisation Act, and the Emergence Powers Act that were put in place by previous governments specifically to repress and oppress Zimbabwe's black population and to be used in opposition to their efforts to fight for independence, social justice, the enjoyment of freedom, and human rights? You now appear to justify the use of these infamous laws to deny his people the rights they are entitled to.

Under Robert Mugabe's leadership, Zimbabwe's new government upheld the colonial era's imperial cocoon. That was done to maintain the colonial era's oppressive structures. According to Musendekwa (2016:83), the continued abuse of indigenous people led to a worsening of living conditions after the country gained independence. Another illustration is Liberia, one of Africa's first sovereign governments. At the time of independence, the government didn't outlaw the slave trade; instead, it kept executing slaves.

The indigenous administration in Zimbabwe kept the colonial legacies alive and may have even made them worse (Ranger 2007:162). To safeguard the interests of the governing elites, Mugabe's government allegedly dealt with political opponents using colonial structures. Mugabe, who was imprisoned during the independence fight, followed in the footsteps of the white colonial authority, which was his predecessor in power. Leaders in Mugabe's government have endured abhorrent oppression. Mugabe, who had liberated the country, became an oppressor by siding with the colonial authority (Mwananyanda, Amnesty International, 6 September 2019). The indigenous administration in Zimbabwe upheld and may have even exacerbated the colonial legacy (Ranger 2007:162). According to reports, Mugabe's administration dealt with political opponents using colonial methods to uphold the interests of the ruling class. Mugabe, who was imprisoned during the independence war, followed in the footsteps of the white colonial authorities who came before him. Leaders who had endured dreadful oppression made up Mugabe's government. By siding with the colonial authority, Mugabe—who had previously liberated the country—became an oppressor (Mwananyanda, Amnesty International, 6 September 2019).

Hegemony results from the implementation of laws that continue to violate the rights of the people and support the accumulation of riches by the ruling class. The Public Order and Safety Bill in Zimbabwe is one instance where such behaviour is prohibited while ignoring the dishonest tactics used by the political ruling elites. The same law forbids disparaging the presidential persona in any way. Another illustration is the Access to Information Bill, which (Vao News, 27 Oct 2009) imposed restrictions on journalists' rights to shield the corrupt practices of the ruling elites. These laws serve comparable purposes as the colonial government's statutes.

After Mugabe's departure, the issue of power struggles persisted. Before Mugabe was removed from power, ZANU-PF split into two significant factions. One faction appeared to support Mugabe's continued rule, while the other advocated for his appointment of a successor.

There was even a forecast that the end of Mugabe's reign might result in several post-Mugabe scenarios, such as the hand-picking of a successor, his death, a coup, or chaos, demonstrating how deeply felt Mugabe's corrupt rule was (Todd & Stewart 2006:22). Future forecasts not only inspired hope but also political despondency.

There was even a forecast that the end of Mugabe's reign might result in several post-Mugabe scenarios, such as the hand-picking of a successor, his death, a coup, or chaos, demonstrating how deeply felt Mugabe's corrupt rule was (Todd & Stewart 2006:22). Future forecasts not only inspired hope but also political despondency.

The Zimbabwean Legal Framework on Corruption

Zimbabwe is currently dealing with a remarkable rise in governmental corruption, which might further choke off a rapidly contracting economy, in addition to dwindling FDI inflows. On the World Bank's ease of doing business scale, the nation was placed 161 out of 189 in the world in 2016, whereas its main commercial rivals South Africa, Botswana, and Zambia are ranked 74, 71, and 98 respectively. It has frequently been claimed that excessively high levels of official corruption, which affect how easy and expensive it is to conduct business, are the likely reason for poor FDI inflows (WB, 2016). Zimbabwe's Perception of Corruption Index (CPI), according to Transparent International (2015), is 21 compared to South Africa's 44, Zambia's 38, and Botswana's 68.

Zimbabwe's industrialisation has halted, and this lack of progress has been partially attributed to the difficulties in getting enough FDI. In absolute terms, FDI flows to the Sub-Saharan African Region have grown since the early 1990s, according to UNCTAD (2014).

The amount of foreign direct investment (FDI) in the region increased from US$36.7 billion in 1990 to US$108.5 billion in 2000, and it reached US$474 billion as of 2013 (World Bank, 2015). Zimbabwe, however, has not benefited from the FDI influx into the area. In actuality, the nation only drew US$1.4 billion, or less than 1% of the total for Sub-Saharan Africa, of the total inward stock of FDI to the region (UNCTAD, 2014). FDI declined in Zimbabwe. 2014). Between 2010 and 2013, FDI in Zimbabwe stayed around USD 400 million. In comparison to Southern African countries like Mozambique, which received US$5,9 billion in 2013, South Africa, and Zambia, which garnered US$8.1 billion and US$1.8 billion respectively, this amount is incredibly small.

According to Duri (2020) The SADC Protocol against Corruption, the first anti-corruption agreement in Africa, was adopted on August 14, 2001, and it came into effect on August 8, 2003. It offers strategies for preventing and combating corruption in the public and private sectors. 14 years after gaining independence, Zimbabwe passed its first anti-corruption law. In 1994, the Parliamentary and Ministerial Code of Conduct, which established rules of conduct for lawmakers, went into effect. Although it was a rather thorough piece of law, the hotly contested Anti-Corruption Commission of Zimbabwe (ACCZ) was never named (Zinyama, 2013).

Money and property used in conjunction with or as the proceeds of crime could be confiscated before 2005 under the Serious Offences (Confiscation of Profits) Act (1990). The State Procurement Board was founded by the Procurement Act of 57 of 2001 and is in charge of managing public procurement contracts on behalf of purchasing bodies. It also oversees the procurement process and looks into potential violations of the procurement process (ISS, 2004).

Zinyama (2013) believes that the Bank Use Promotion and Suppression of Money Laundering Act (Chapter 24, Art. 24) prevents money laundering by SOEs, particularly those in the financial sector, while the Public Finance Management Act (Chapter 22, Art. 19) establishes a legal framework for the financial management, corporate governance, and auditing requirements for SOEs. The Criminal Law (Codification and Reform) Act of 2004 created bribery and corruption offences, such as domestic active and passive bribery (Articles 170 and 174), abuse of functions (Articles 174), as well as embezzlement in the public and private sectors (Articles 113). In addition, it defines a "statutory body" to include SOEs.

The Anti-Corruption Commission Act outlines several requirements for the Commission in terms of preventing corruption, including (1) monitoring and examining the practises, systems, and procurement practises of public and private sector institutions; (2) instructing, advising, and supporting any officer, agency, or institution in the elimination or minimization of corruption; (3) assisting in the development of practices, systems, and procurement procedures of public and private, (4) to offer recommendations on how to make anti-corruption laws stronger, and (5) to urge the government to ratify pertinent international legal agreements designed to fight corruption. The Attorney General's Office, the National Prosecuting Authority, the Zimbabwe Republic Police, the Financial Intelligence Unit (within the Reserve Bank of Zimbabwe), the National Economic Conduct Inspectorate, and the Public Service Commission are additional organisations important to the fight against corruption in Zimbabwe (Ncube, 2011).

(Duri 2020) noted that 2018 saw TI Zimbabwe conduct a review of the nation's anti-corruption laws. The adoption of whistleblower laws, the enactment of a thorough anti-money laundering law, the independence of the anti-corruption commission, and the instruction and training of law enforcement agents were among the important anti-corruption concerns on which suggestions were made.

To effectively combat corruption, it almost always necessitates shifting political, economic, and social authority away from those who stand to gain from the status quo, according to UNDP (2010). In light of this, how do decision-makers implement anti-corruption institutional and policy changes during the process of post-conflict state-building?

The fiduciary risk resulting from the misuse of their funds and the requirement to account for these funds to their constituency is the biggest corruption-related concern for contributors. The additional concern of donors not to endanger the peace is another factor.

Even though funders, diplomats, UN agencies, and the World Bank all want to see corruption reduced, they frequently avoid discussing it with governments because they believe it to be unsolvable, too sensitive, or both, particularly in the initial years following a conflict. Donors anticipate that the overall trend will show some progress over time, even though specific signs are difficult to come across due to data limitations. Donors may withdraw or reduce their support in the absence of demonstrable attempts or progress in this area rather than confront the problem head-on (Musingafi, Chadamoyo, Dumbu 2013).

According to Crane–Charef, (2015) Zimbabwe ratified the African Union Convention on Preventing and Combating Corruption in 2006, the SADC Protocol Against Corruption in 2004, and the UN Convention Against Corruption in 2007.

Crane-Charef (2015) noted that the Zimbabwe Anti-Corruption Commission (ZACC) was founded by the government in 2004 to fight corruption. The Anti-Corruption Commission Act, which was revised in 2013, further explains the ZACC's duties. The ZACC was formed by the Zimbabwean Constitution. A state-owned company, the ZACC reports to the minister of home affairs. The Commission is in charge of looking into and making public instances of corruption in both the public and private sectors. The Attorney General's Office, the National Prosecuting Authority, the Zimbabwe Republic Police, the Financial Intelligence Unit (within the Reserve Bank of Zimbabwe), the National Economic Conduct Inspectorate, and the Public Service Commission are additional organisations important to the fight against corruption in Zimbabwe.

Table 1.

Period	Company	Description of Corruption	The amount involved in United States Dollars
1988	Willowvale Motor Industry	Ruling party officials corrupt usage of privileges to buy vehicles and resell them at exorbitant prices	
1999	VIP Land Grab		
2010	United Passenger's Company Bribery Scandal		
2008-2014	Airport Road Scandal		
2010	Diamond	Prejudice	2.7 billion
2012	Zimbabwe Schools Examination Council		
2012	Zimbabwe Mining Development Corporation Diamond Scandal	Money remitted against the total sales	45 million remitted. 800 million total sales meaning 765 million was not remitted.
2013	Premier Service Medical Aid Society (PSMAS) a parastatal company	Unrealistic Salary hike per month	Group Chief Executive 230 000 Group Financial Manager 200 000 Group Operations Executive 122 000 Eight Senior Directors 60 000 per director Three Middle Managers 30 000, 22 000 and 15000 respectively
2013	Zimbabwe Broadcasting Corporation Pricing Scandal	Unrealistic Salary hikes for directors while other staff members go without salaries for 7 months	Happison Muchechetere getting US$40 000 per month and US$250 000 housing allowance
2013	Air Zimbabwe Insurance Scandal		
2014	Zimbabwe Electricity Supply Scum		
2016	Mining revenue		US$15 Billion
2016	Zimbabwe Manpower Development Fund (ZIMDEF)	ZIMDEF Scandal involved the then Minister of Higher Education and his deputy who diverted money from student support	US$430 thousand.
2020	Covidgate Scandal	Minister of Health and Childcare Obadia Moyo inflated prices of COVID-testing kits	60 million
2023	Al Jazeera Gold Mafia	Illicit gold dealing among the elite rulers	

Numerous obstacles stand in the way of the Zimbabwe Anti-Corruption Commission's (ZACC) ability to combat corruption effectively. Political interference, a lack of operational independence, the politicisation of corruption investigations, a lack of qualified employees, and insufficient funding are some of the problems. Similar difficulties are being faced by the National Prosecuting Authority (NPA), which prosecutes corrupt defendants. The Prosecutor-General lamented in a statement from the first quarter of 2018 that few corruption cases were being prosecuted due to a lack of political will, human ability, and financial support (Hodzi 2018: 1). According to Marumahoko (2020), President Mnangagwa set up a special anti-corruption team in his office with the responsibility of looking into and prosecuting corruption cases in reaction to the ZACC and NPA's failure to contain corruption. The effectiveness of this unit in the fight against corruption is yet to be determined. Because it has become so entrenched, only genuine anti-corruption initiatives based on essential strategies have a higher chance of doing so in Zimbabwe.

Examining Corruption in Zimbabwe

There was even a forecast that the end of Mugabe's reign may result in several post-Mugabe scenarios, including the hand-picking of a successor, his death, a coup, or chaos (Todd & Stewart 2006:22). This shows how deeply felt Mugabe's corrupt rule was. Future projections sparked both hope and political anguish in addition to optimism. It is hard today to have hope in democracy, in the public institutions of democracy, when the democracy has been corrupted root and branch by money, according to Caputo (2016:72), who best captures the severity of the problem in Zimbabwe. Politicians who are completely beholden to the wealthy interests funding their political careers cannot be trusted. When judges are chosen based on political ideology, it is impossible to trust in the independence of the legal system. When political campaigns focus on deceit rather than the truth, on destroying the reputations of opponents, on doing everything necessary to discourage the least powerful people from voting, and when voting districts are rigged, it is hard to have hope in democratic elections.

Caputo (2016) defends the likelihood of hopelessness in a totalitarian regime. Money is used by political figures to further their objectives. They even pick judges based on their political ideas, which results in the judiciary being captured and the entire system that oversees free and fair elections being manipulated. In Zimbabwe, the government is accused of influencing the legal system to run unfairly.

The focus was on Mnangagwa's dedication to fighting corruption, poor leadership, and terrible governance. His choice of ministers, his stance towards corrupt elites, and his selection of competent leadership were all under close examination. In each of these areas, he utterly failed. In yet another public relations gimmick, he appointed and kept corrupt cabinet ministers, some of whom he has since sought to jail. In his office, he established an anti-corruption team, but it has done nothing. He has let well-connected, wealthy elites maintain monopolistic control over the lucrative gasoline supply contract for the nation, including Kuda Tagwirei's Sakunda. He has permitted the Reserve Bank to be used to provide connected elites with preferential access to foreign exchange, which it then expatriates, launders, or sells at a premium on the black market in an arbitrage scheme. He permitted the theft of $3 billion from the "command agriculture" subsidies programme, the majority of which went to Sakunda (Ndlovu-Gatsheni Ruhanya 2020).

In Zimbabwe corruption has become a normal way of life (Wini-Dari and Damauswa 2016:154). Corruption has penetrated all sectors of human existence, best depicted by Bonga, Chiminya and Mudzingiri (2015:11) as affecting "the ocean that we swim in and the air we breathe and as a result, poverty and family disintegration replaced the aspirations for a decent life and a hopeful future". The Zimbabwean economy has since been one of the worst in the world. Despite all aspirations that were borne from the acquisition of political independence, all hopes for economic emancipation have been undermined. Paradoxically, the nation witnessed economic stagnation and regression mainly due to corruption (Masango 2016) Bonga, Chiminya and Mudzuri (2015:11) describe corruption as "exploding and damaging the economy". Thus, corruption becomes one major obstacle to economic growth. This section explores corruption as the main cause of economic collapse in Zimbabwe.

Muzurura (2016:3) highlights several factors that stimulated an increase in corruption including "the struggle for power politics of political patronage, political violence and the emergence of special interest groups like the women in politics, Youth Action Groups and indigenous Business Groups". Central to all these factors is obtaining political millage by monopolisation of the economy by the ruling elites.

Between 1998 and 2000 Zimbabwe witnessed a decrease in the Perception index from 42% to 8% (Muzarura 2016:2). By 2020 Zimbabwe was listed at number 157 out of 180 making it to be one of the top 20 countries in corruption.

War Veterans

In Zimbabwe, corruption increased as a result of the benefits given to veterans of foreign wars. Zimbabwe's ZANU-PF administration became a barrier to the country's desired development. A serious economic crisis resulted from the unanticipated payment of the 1997 compensation and pensions for liberation war veterans and the country's subsequent suspension from the Commonwealth (Kanyenze, Chitambara, and Tyson 2017:3 & Cox 2005:35-36). In comparison to the US dollar, the Zimbabwean currency lost 71, or 5% of its value (Kanyenze, Chitambara, and Tyson 2017:3). Zimbabwe's unanticipated August investment in the conflict in the Democratic Republic of the Congo (DRC) worsened the situation (Kanyenze, Chitambara, and Tyson 2017:3). According to this study, the majority of Zimbabweans' already precarious living situations were made worse by bad government policies. Government policies in Zimbabwe discouraged peaceful resolutions to the country's crisis.

Corruption crept into various sectors. That also includes the payment of war victim's compensation for the liberation war veterans. After payment of compensation for physical disabilities, a further claim was made for those with post-traumatic stress disorder. Dr Chenjerai Hunzvi, a government medical doctor was also the leader of the War Veterans Association. He distributed forms to be completed. He further granted compensation to everyone without any further medical examination. Fraudulent claims of war veterans and some government officials were circulated in independent media exposing widespread corruption by March 1997. The government stopped paying compensation and in July the government set up a commission to investigate (Kriger 2005:257). Upon investigation, the War Veterans made further claims of compensation. The matter was then taken up by the commission which reported in 1998 reported that among those interviewed there was gross exaggeration of war-related injuries. Since such cases involved high-profile people, little was done.

Marange Diamond US$15 billion scandal

Zimbabwe has experienced one of the greatest losses since the discovery of diamonds in Marange. Revenue worth 15 billion United States dollars and raw diamonds disappeared without any trace in 2016 (Wini-Dari and Hamauswa 2016:152); Muquyi & Chimwara 2019:445). The state president then, acknowledged that great loss. No further investigations were revealed. Under a normal and democratic system, such a level of corruption should have been investigated and brought the culprits to book. Zimbabwe has experienced unprecedented levels of corruption in a country with the majority of citizens are in great poverty. Such huge sums of money could have potentially changed the lives of Zimbabweans but simply disappeared and could not be accounted for.

COVID-Gate Scandal

The COVID-19 scandal is a COVID-19 procurement scandal involving overcharging COVID-19 testing kits. The scandal involved US$60 million by the Minister of Health and Child Care, Dr Obadaih Moyo and Delish Nguwaya founder of Drax Internation (Mutumwa and Ufuwoma 88; Tshabangu, 2021:487). Some commentators claim that the scandal involved the powerful political elites a matter that was published and commented on by an independent award-winning journalist, Hopewell Chingono before being thrown into custody for several months before trial. Hopewell ballooned news that had appeared on Zimlive that implicated the high-profile elite politicians from the ruling party, revealing the democratic deficiencies in the Zimbabwean governing system.

According to Mabuza (9 June 2020 Zimlive), the government had concealed a corrupt procurement tender of COVID-19 medical equipment worth US$60 million from a company linked to the First Family. That was followed by the detention of Delish Nguwaya who is purported to be the owner of Drax International Company (Whiz 14 June Zimlive). On the 19th of June Obadia Moyo was detained (Mathuthu 19 2020 June Zimlive). The following day he was released on bail (Banya 20 June 2020 Zimlive). The justice system in Zimbabwe was revealed to be undemocratic. When corruption implicates the elite politicians it is very unlikely that they are held accountable. Rather those who publish the news are eventually incarcerated and tortured. Moreover, elite politicians tend to attribute corruption to people of the low class continually preserving the untouchable political elites (Wini-Dari and Hamauswa 2016:154). The democratic space was severely undermined and diminished.

Research has revealed that corruption in Zimbabwe has been institutionalised that what is abnormal is normalised and accepted as the rule of the game. Chiweshe and Mahiya (2021:77) corruption has penetrated daily activities that include payment of bribes, for passing examinations or acquiring a driver's licence, bribery of police officers at roadblocks, bribing immigration officers, hiring youth militia to instigate political violence and use of illicit means to get money. Consequently, corruption has led to a spiral of economic death rendering all sectors of the economy dysfunctional.

Gold Mafia

According to Transparency International Zimbabwe (2023), the first episode of the Gold Mafia documentary on Al Jazeera titled "The Laundry Service", published on March 23, 2023, suspected illegal financial flows from Zimbabwe are revealed. This includes severe charges of abuse of diplomatic immunity, illegal gold dealing, corruption, and money laundering in the mining industry. Transparency International urges additional investigation and the implementation of the necessary changes by the Financial Intelligence Unit, Zimbabwe Republic Police, and Zimbabwe Anti-Corruption Commission to put an end to such actions in the nation.

The documentary was made after the 2022 Corruption Perceptions Index was published, which indicated widespread corruption in Zimbabwe with a mere 23 out of 100 points. Grand corruption and other scandals continue to surface, harming the nation from the standpoint of investors and development partners. These numbers, along with the alarming documentary discoveries, demonstrate the need for the government to step up its efforts to combat corruption and money laundering.

In Southern Africa, several gold smuggling gangs assist criminals in laundering hundreds of millions of dollars while enriching themselves and pillaging their countries, according to a four-part investigation by Al Jazeera's Investigative Unit (I-Unit) The Gold Mafia study reveals why the precious metal is so attractive as a tool for those with substantial quantities of unreported riches to transform shady money into gleaming clean, seemingly lawful money. They accomplish this by utilising a convoluted network of businesses, false identities, and fraudulent documents.

In Southern Africa, several gold smuggling gangs assist criminals in laundering hundreds of millions of dollars while enriching themselves and pillaging their countries, according to a four-part investigation by Al Jazeera's Investigative Unit (I-Unit).

The research also reveals Zimbabwe's top officials' involvement in money laundering and smuggling, which aids the nation in evading the crushing effects of Western sanctions. The fact that gold trafficked from one country may end up in the form of cash placed in offshore accounts of front businesses halfway around the world highlights the global dimension of these crimes.

The documentary emphasises how cartels are increasingly collaborating with people and organisations in Zimbabwe to transport illicit funds by using shell corporations and anonymous trusts in tax havens and other covert jurisdictions. Large-scale exports of gold and other precious minerals as well as organised crime are made possible by this pernicious link. The documentary specifically highlights instances of purported under-invoicing and under-declarations by registered gold dealers to Fidelity Printers and the Zimbabwe Revenue Authority, indicating much greater losses than previously thought. both money laundering and corruption. As a result, the nation is less able to develop crucial infrastructure, meet the requirements of the populace, or deal with pressing problems. To address this, the government of Zimbabwe should improve the mutual legal aid agreements it has with other concerned jurisdictions. They must also make sure that these organisations are equipped to handle requests for reciprocal legal help (Transparency International Zimbabwe 2023)

Transparency International Zimbabwe (2023) added that it is alarming since the documentary implies that authorities do not thoroughly research prospective investors, even licenced gold traders. The information provided by the disclosures could be used to dismantle organised crime groups that are actively smuggling gold and laundering cash out of Zimbabwe and other particular African nations. In the interim, while the claims are being investigated, law enforcement, anti-corruption organisations, and regulatory bodies should immediately cancel the gold export and trading licences granted to the accused people and businesses.

Uebert Angel, one of Zimbabwe's top ambassadors, proposed to utilise his diplomatic powers to bring more than $1 billion in illicit funds into the nation. President Emmerson Mnangagwa chose Uebert Angel to promote investment from Europe and North America. Henrietta Rushwaya, the head of the Zimbabwe Mining Association and Mnangagwa's niece, played a crucial role in his plans. Rushwaya advised Al Jazeera reporters that they could leave Zimbabwe with an equivalent quantity of gold by parking their cash at Fidelity, a gold refinery run by the nation's central bank (Al Jazeera's Investigative Unit [I-Unit]).

News24 (06 Mar 2023) reports that a publicised yet unscreened Al Jazeera investigation exposing the illegal gold trade and corruption involving powerful elites and politicians in Zimbabwe has caused a public relations crisis in the government and ruling party circles.

According to News 24 (06 March 2023), this has compelled Reserve Bank of Zimbabwe governor John Mangudya to speak out and make it clear that the country's targeted sanctions have no impact on its ability to conduct business internationally. As a result, illegal businesses that claimed to be sanction-bursting were adopting backdoor methods for personal advantage.

CONCLUSION

In conclusion, this chapter has revealed that corruption in Zimbabwe has penetrated all sectors of society, becoming detrimental to democracy and economic justice in Zimbabwe. An examination of various corruption activities in Zimbabwe has revealed that most people and organisations that have been the main culprits are members of the ruling elite community. They manipulate the state laws for their material gain. Corruption has taken centre stage among political elites who further manipulate the political system at the expense of the majority of Zimbabwean citizens. Despite that the various cases involved political elites of the ruling party in Zimbabwe, further manipulated the justice system in Zimbabwe. Those people involved in corrupt activities have been under the protection of the state.

It is therefore clear that corruption shrinks the socio-economic and political justice in Zimbabwe. Corruption should therefore be regarded as evidence of a lack of democracy. The involvement of political elites also implies that there can be more to it than the published cases as some cases are potentially swept under the carpet before reaching the media.

This research recommends that the state empower the state machinery to name and shame those corrupt leaders. Those who deserve to be detained should be detained and punished for their unscrupulous businesses. Further research is relevant since this research only picked a few cases that have frequented the media.

REFERENCES

Al Jazeera Investigative Unit. (2023). *Six Secrets Uncovered by Aljazeera's Gold Mafia investigation.* https://www.aljazeera.com

Bonga, W. G., Chiminya, J., & Mudzungiri, C. (2021). An Explanatory Analysis of the Economic and Social Impact of Corruption in Zimbabwe. *IOSR Journal of Economics and Finance(IOSR-JEF), 6*(1), 11-20.

Bratton, M., & Masunungure, E. (2007). Popular Reactions to State Repression: Operation Murambatsvina in Zimbabwe. *African Affairs, 106/422*(422), 21–45. doi:10.1093/afraf/adl024

Chitando, E. (2010). Equipped and ready to serve? Transforming theology and religious studies in Africa. *Missionalia, 38*(2), 197–210.

Chiweshe, M. K., & Mahiya, I. (2021). Corruption and the Morality of Everyday Life in Urban Harare, Zimbabwe. *Africa Today, 68*(1), 72–92. doi:10.2979/africatoday.68.1.04

Duri, J. (2020). *Overview of corruption and anti-corruption in sub-Saharan Africa*. Academic Press.

Dzimiri, P. (2017). African Multilateral responses to the crisis in Zimbabwe: A responsibility to protect perspective. *SRSA*, *39*(2), 50–77.

Gunda, M. R. (2018). At the Cross Roads: A call to Christians to act in faith for an alternative Zimbabwe. In *Bible in Africa Studies* (Vol. 21). University of Bamberg.

Hammar, A., McGregor, J., & Landau, L. (2010). Introduction. Displacing Zimbabwe: Crisis and construction in Southern Africa. *Journal of Southern African Studies*, *36*(2), 263–283. doi:10.1080/03057070.2010.485779

Hanke, S. H., & Kwok, A. K. (2009). On the measurement of Zimbabwe's hyperinflation. *The Cato Journal*, *29*, 364–353.

Hodzi, K. 2018. *The Prosecutor General's Speech (Guest of Honour) at the Occassion of the Mutare Anti-Corruption Commission Court.* https://jsc.org.zw/jscbackend/upload/Publications/prosecutor%20general%20speech.pdf

ISS. (2004). *Terrorism Legislation in Zimbabwe.* www.issafrica.org/cdct/mainpages/pdf/ Terrorism/Legislation/Zimbabwe/Zimbabwe%20Serious%20offences%20Confiscation%20of%20Profits%20Act%201990.pdf

Kanyenze, G., Chitambara, P., & Tyson, J. (2017). *The outlook for the Zimbabwean economy.Supporting Economic Transformation.* UkAid.

Lamarche, C; Toysen, T; & Wishart, A (2019). *The country that cannot collapse: Fragility Analysis of Zimbabwe: Policy recommendations for USAID.* Academic Press.

Marango, T., Francis, J., & Adgibolosso, S. (2016). Realities of Communication and Social Inclussion in Zimbabwe Local Government: A Case of the Eastern Chimanimani District. *Review of Human Factor Studies*, *22*(1), 104–128.

Marumahoko, S., & Chigwata, T. C. (2020). The idea of a new Zimbabwe post-Mugabe. *The History and Political Transition of Zimbabwe: From Mugabe to Mnangagwa*, 299-329.

Maunganidze, F., Bonnin, D., & Ruggunan, S. (2021). Economic Crisis and professions: Chartered Accountants in Zimbabwe. *SAGE Open*, *11*(1), 1–14. doi:10.1177/2158244021994802

Mazarura, J. (2016). Is Public Corruption the Main Cause of Low Foreign Direct Investment in Zimbabwe? *British Journal of Economic Finance and Management Sciences*, *13*(1), 1–18.

Mlambo, S. (2013). Becoming Zimbabwe or Becoming Zimbabwean: Identity Nationalism, or State-Building. *Africa Spectrum*, *1*(1), 49–70. doi:10.1177/000203971304800103

Moyo, N & Besada, H (2008). Zimbabwe in Crisis: Mugabe's Policies and Failures. *The Centre for International Governance Innovation Technical Paper*, *38*, 1-29.

Moyo, S. (2013). Regime survival stratergies in Zimbabwe in the 21st century. *AJPSIR*, *7*(2), 67–78.

Moyo, S., & Yeros, P. (2007). The Radicalised State: Zimbabwe's Interrupted Revolution. *ROAPE*, *34*(111), 103–121.

Mude, T., & Chigora, P. (2013). Promoting good governance in crisis ridden country: The Zimbabwean dilemma in the 21st century. *JASPS, 1*(1), 27–33.

Mulinge, M. M., & Lesetedi, G. N. (1998). Interrogating Our Past: Colonialism and Corruption in Sub-Saharan Africa. *Afri J Polit Sci, 3*(2), 15–28.

Muqayi, S., & Chimwara, O. (2019). The Sustainability of Diamond Mining in Zimbabwe. *The Sustainability Ethic in the Management of the Physical, Infrastructural andNatural Resources of Zimbabwe*, 423.

Musendekwa, M. (2016). Colonisation as an obstacle to Civilisation: a critical evaluation of Albert Schweitzer's Experiences and Observations. In I.J.J. Spangenberg & C. Landman (Eds.), The legacies of Albert Schweitzer reconsidered. Cape Town: AOSIS.

Musendekwa, M. (2018). Messianic characterisation of Mugabe as rhetorical propaganda tolegitimise his authority in crisis situations. *Studia Historiae Ecclesiasticae, 44*(3), 1–17. doi:10.25159/2412-4265/4059

Musingafi, M C, Chadamoyo, P., & Dumbu, E. (n.d.). Fighting corruption in post-conflict situations'. *International Journal of Innovative Research in Management, 4*(1), 12-24.

Musingafi, M. C., Mupa, P., Dumbu, E. (2011). Post-conflict reconstruction: A

Mutanda, D. (2014). The Impact of the Zimbabwean Crisis on the Parastatals. *International Journal of Politics and Good Governance, 5*(2), 1-14.

Mutumwa, W. T., & Ufuwoma, A. (2022). *Critical Journalism and Media Convergence During the COVID-19 Pandemic: Representation of Corruption in Zimbabwean Online News. In health Crisis and Media Discourses in Sub-Saharan Africa*. Springer.

Muyambwa, D. F. (2018). *Corruption as a violation of Human and People's Rights: Implications for Youth in Zimbabwe*. Academic Press.

Muzurura, J. (2016). Is public corruption the main cause of low foreign direct investment in Zimbabwe. *British Journal of Economics. Finance and Management Sciences, 13*(1), 1–18.

Mwananyanda, M. (n.d.). *Obituary: Robert Mugabe- 1924-2019, a liberator turned an oppressor*. https://www.amnesty.org/

Ncube, N. (2011). *Zimbabwe 2011*. Global Integrity Report.

Ndlela, N (2017). The African paradigm: The Coverage of the Zimbabwean Crisis in the Norwegian media. *Strategic Review for Southern Africa, 39*(2), 71-90.

Ndlovu-Gatsheni, S. J., Ruhanya, P., Ndlovu-Gatsheni, S., & Ruhanya, P. (2020). Postscript: A tale of broken promises. In *The history and political transition of Zimbabwe: From Mugabe to Mnangagwa* (pp. 389-398). News24. https://www.news24.com

Osoba, S. O. (1996). Corruption in Nigeria: Historical Perspectives. *Review of African Political Economy, 69*(69), 371–386. doi:10.1080/03056249608704203

Ranger, T. O. (2007). City versus state in Zimbabwe: Colonial antecedents of the crisis. *Journal of Eastern African Studies : the Journal of the British Institute in Eastern Africa*, *1*(2), 161–192. doi:10.1080/17531050701452390

Rugwiji, T. (2017). Land, farming and socio-economic crisis development in Yehud: A quest for sustainable development towards poverty reduction in Zimbabwe. *Scriptrura: Journal for Contextual Hermeneutics in Southern Africa*, *116*(1), 1–34.

Sachikonye, L. M. (2002). Whither Zimbabwe? Crisis & Democratisation: The Challenge of Transition Process in Zimbabwe. *ROAPE*, *29*(91), 13–20.

Takawira, T. (2017). Corruption and Bad Policies Repel Foreign Capital and Cause Domestic Capital to Flee: Is Jovanovic Right? *International Journal of Economics and Financial Issues*, *7*(5), 204–215.

Todd, M., & Stewart, P. (2006). After Mugabe: Applying post-conflict recovery lessons to Zimbabwe. *Africa Policy Journal*, *1*, 21–36.

Transperancy International Zimbabwe. (n.d.). *Aljazeera Gold Mafia Documentary Demonstrates Urgent Need to Combat Corruption in Zimbabwe*. Academic Press.

Tshabangu, T., & Salawu, A. (2021). An Evaluation of Constructive Journalism in Zimbabwe: A Case Study of the Herald's Coverage of the Coronavirus Pandemic. *Journal of African Media Studies*, *13*(3), 477–490. doi:10.1386/jams_00060_1

UNCTAD. (2014). *Foreign direct investments in Africa*. United Nations.

UNDP. (2010). *Fighting corruption in post-conflict and recovery situations: Learning from the past*. UNDP.

Zinyama, M. T. (2013). Efficiency and effectiveness in public sector auditing: An evaluation of the comptroller and auditor general's performance in Zimbabwe from 1999 to 2012. *International Journal of Humanities and Social Science*, *3*(7), 267–282.

ENDNOTE

1 The former colonisers typically view neo-colonialism as the imposition of new kinds of colonialism. In Zimbabwe, the political establishment continued colonialism.

Chapter 8
Decolonizing the Developmental Agenda:
A Prerequisite for African Democracy and Governance

Mohamad Zreik
https://orcid.org/0000-0002-6812-6529
Sun Yat-sen University, China

ABSTRACT

This chapter examines the colonial legacy, neo-colonial influences, and the fight for democratic government as root reasons of Africa's developmental issues. Institutional responses to these problems are examined, including the African Union (AU), the New Partnership for Africa's Development (NEPAD), and the African Peer Review. A decolonized perspective on development and political will are both emphasized. Relying on Walter Rodney's claims, this chapter stresses the significance of accountable governance, human rights, and civic engagement in addressing Africa's self-underdevelopment.

INTRODUCTION

The continent of Africa has a wide range of complex and long-standing development issues that may be traced back to the colonial era and beyond (Hopkins, 2019). These obstacles are multifaceted, showing up in the political, economic, and social sectors to create a tangled web of problems that have slowed the continent's development.

Many African countries' governments have struggled with democracy and good governance (Mangu, 2014). Despite great achievements made in the post-independence era, a democratic deficit characterized by political instability, corruption, weak institutions, and an often-glaring absence of the rule of law persists. The establishment of stable settings essential to sustained growth has been hampered by these political issues (Christensen & Laitin, 2019).

DOI: 10.4018/979-8-3693-0477-8.ch008

Poor infrastructure, minimal industrialization, high unemployment, and a reliance on primary commodities as exports are only some of the economic challenges the continent faces. A cycle of economic instability, characterized by slow growth and widespread poverty, has followed (Rekiso, 2017). Africa's capacity to steer its economic direction is hampered by the continent's high level of external debt and the negative effects of globalization (Asongu & De Moor, 2017).

Poverty, inequality, and social exclusion are persistent problems in many African countries (Modi, 2015). The repercussions of climate change and environmental degradation, as well as issues like inadequate access to quality education and healthcare, compound the continent's developmental challenges.

Further complicating these developmental issues is the fact that conflicts and post-conflict scenarios continue to plague large swaths of the continent, disrupting economic operations, diverting resources, and displacing populations.

Africa's path to development is complicated by a wide range of issues that call for collaborative, creative, and culturally sensitive solutions that take into consideration the continent's specific historical and contemporary situations.

The fight for democracy in Africa is intrinsically linked to the continent's colonial history and the continuing influence of neo-colonial powers (Zreik, 2021). Many of Africa's pre-colonial ethnic and regional disputes were exacerbated by the imposition of institutions and systems that didn't fit with them by former colonial powers (Somerville, 2017).

Post-colonial government has been plagued by ethnic struggle and warfare because of the arbitrary borders set during the colonial period, which often confined multiple ethnic groups within single states. Political instability and authoritarianism are common outcomes of the struggle for power and wealth inside these arbitrary borders.

The colonial legacy is also strongly felt in the business world. Instead of establishing varied, self-sustaining economies, African economies were predominantly constructed to serve the needs of the conquerors, with an emphasis on extracting resources for export (Wengraf, 2018). As a result, it is susceptible to swings in commodity prices and dependent on overseas markets.

These problems are made worse by neocolonial ideas. Many African nations' internal affairs are still meddled with by former colonial powers or international financial organizations, even though they have achieved legal independence (Schmidt, 2013). This meddling can weaken national sovereignty, distort economies, and keep autocratic and corrupt regimes in power.

In addition, the Western-style democracy that is transferred to Africa may not necessarily be compatible with the local social and cultural norms. This discrepancy can make it harder to consolidate democratic government by undermining the legitimacy of democratic institutions and processes (Youngs, 2015).

The history of colonialism in Africa, the impact of neocolonialism, and the fight for democracy all have complex and intertwined connections. One of Africa's greatest difficulties is overcoming these historical and ongoing influences to establish effective, responsive, and truly democratic governance systems.

BACKGROUND

Overview of Colonialism, Neo-Colonialism, and Apartheid in Africa

Colonialism, neocolonialism, and apartheid have left lasting traces on the political, economic, and social landscapes of Africa, shaping the course of the continent's history. The 'Scramble for Africa' began in the late 19th century and marked the beginning of colonialism in Africa. During this time, Europe was split up among competing European powers such as Britain, France, Portugal, Germany, Belgium, and Italy for control of resources and hegemony (Barnhart, 2016). As a result, new nations were created with borders and governments that didn't take into account preexisting ethnic or racial hierarchies. The colonial era was characterized by widespread discrimination against the indigenous population and massive resource exploitation throughout Africa (Feagin, 2013).

By the middle of the twentieth century, most African states had attained official political independence as a result of growing independence movements. However, the newly independent governments entered a global system in which their economic, political, and social institutions were mainly influenced by their former occupiers (Thomson, 2022). During this time, sometimes referred to as neo-colonialism, multinational financial institutions enforced unfair trade deals, debt, and foreign aid requirements on developing countries.

Apartheid, mostly in South Africa but also in Namibia, was a particularly violent manifestation of the colonial heritage in Southern Africa. From its inception in 1948 until the early 1990s, apartheid was a state-sanctioned system of racial segregation and discrimination in South Africa. Human rights abuses were rampant, as was economic and political persecution of the black majority, but there was also a strong undercurrent of resistance that ultimately helped advance the cause of human rights around the world (Neocosmos, 2010).

All three forms of imperialism—colonialism, neocolonialism, and apartheid—had a profound effect on Africa's history and continue to define the continent's current fights for democracy, human rights, and sustainable development. To make sense of Africa's current issues and develop viable solutions for its future, it is essential to have a firm grasp of the continent's history.

Analysis of the Systemic Imbalances Caused by These Historical Events

Colonialism, neocolonialism, and apartheid all had long-lasting and far-reaching consequences on Africa, and their legacy is still felt today. These inequalities permeate the societal, political, and economic institutions.

Many African countries have been left with political instability as a result of the colonial era's arbitrariness. Multiethnic states, where power struggles, ethnic conflicts, and civil unrest are commonplace, are a direct result of borders that fail to take into account people's racial or tribal identities. Moreover, the colonial administration style frequently imposed autocratic systems that clashed with preexisting indigenous government systems, a pattern that was often repeated by leaders after independence (Chlouba, Smith, & Wagner, 2022). This creates an environment where democratic principles, the rule of law, and transparent leadership are occasionally lacking.

Colonialism's concentration on extracting resources for export to the metropole is the economic foundation upon which structural inequities rest. As a result, many African economies became very sensitive to variations in global commodity prices due to a lack of industrialization and an over-reliance on commodity exports. Africa's potential to establish strong, diversified economies has been hampered by the neocolonial continuation of this oppressive economic system, which is often maintained through unfair trade agreements and crushing external debt (Abegunrin, 2009).

These historical events have reinforced discrimination and marginalization in today's society. The widespread lack of education and poor health outcomes that followed colonial authority is a direct result of the prioritization of colonizers over natives in the provision of social services. Apartheid was emblematic of this division because it deepened existing socioeconomic gaps along racial lines.

The exploitation of natural resources has resulted in serious environmental degradation and climate vulnerabilities, further impeding sustainable development due to structural imbalances.

A thorough familiarity with these historical causes and a dedication to policies that promote fairness, inclusion, and sustainability are necessary for resolving these systemic inequities. Unless such an approach is taken, it's unlikely that sustainable development and democratic government will be achieved in Africa.

IMPACT OF COLONIAL LEGACIES ON AFRICAN DEVELOPMENT

Examination of the Impacts on Political, Economic, and Social Spheres

Africa's political, economic, and social progress have all been hampered by the legacy left behind by colonialism. Colonialists' model of extractive and autocratic rule left a permanent mark on post-independence political systems. Ethnic tensions, power inequalities, and colonial-era styles of government have all contributed to the difficulty many African countries have had in establishing stable, democratic institutions (Christensen & Laitin, 2019). Civil wars, authoritarian governments, corruption, and weak institutions are all things that have been linked to these legacies, and they all serve as roadblocks to political progress.

Africa's economy is not diversified and is unduly reliant on global markets as a result of the colonial focus on extracting raw minerals and cash crops for export (Thomson, 2022). This dependence leaves African countries exposed to fluctuations in global commodity prices and hinders their capacity to pursue economically autonomous policies. In addition, economic development and modernization attempts were hampered by the colonial era's lack of significant expenditures in infrastructure and industrial capacity (Fox, 2014).

The social realm is likewise deeply scarred by colonial history. Social divides and inequities have their roots in the systematic devaluing of indigenous knowledge and culture, as well as in racial and ethnic prejudice. Colonial policies on education, which tended to favour a select few, have aided in perpetuating educational inequalities, which in turn have widened gaps in social and economic mobility (Blakemore & Cooksey, 2017). Furthermore, public health infrastructure and health outcomes were significantly impacted because health policies and systems throughout the colonial era were often aimed towards supporting the demands of the colonizer (Prince & Marsland, 2013).

The natural world was also not spared. Environmental damage brought on by intensive resource extraction during the colonial period adds to the difficulties of achieving sustainable development in the face of the effects of climate change.

These lingering impacts of colonialism are not only pervasive, but also deeply ingrained, and they present significant roadblocks to Africa's progress. To solve them, we need a decolonized development strategy that considers Africa's specific history and context in depth.

Discussion: Legacies and the Current Developmental Impasse

One of the keys to understanding Africa's developmental issues is the connection between colonial legacies and the continent's current developmental deadlock. The current challenges that African countries face can be traced straight back to these historical fingerprints.

Colonialism left a political legacy of authoritarian control, weak institutions, and a lack of democratic consolidation. This instability, corruption, and weakness all have their roots in the era of colonial authority. The colonial era left many African countries struggling to consolidate democratic government due to entrenched power structures and political traditions.

Colonial economies, which relied heavily on the export of raw goods, had far-reaching effects because of their extractive nature. Many African economies continue to place too much on a small number of export goods, leaving them exposed to swings in global commodity prices. Colonial-era underinvestment in industrialization and diversification, as well as infrastructure, prevented these economies from realizing their full potential. Many African countries' current economic woes can be traced back to this longstanding mode of economic organization (De Brauw & Bulte, 2021).

The colonial era's discriminatory practices bred the kind of entrenched societal disparities that still plague the world today. Many areas of Africa suffer from widespread illiteracy and poor health because of colonial neglect of local education and health services for the indigenous population (Abebe et al., 2021). As they hinder the growth of human capital and keep low-income patterns from breaking, social inequalities contribute significantly to the development impasse.

The key to Africa's sustained development lies in crafting models that reflect its intrinsic values, histories, and cultures. This calls for the establishment of a Decolonial Development Model (DDM) - a holistic approach that pivots from Western templates and dives into indigenous knowledge systems, community-centered policies, and localized solutions (Zreik, 2023).

The environmental degradation caused by colonial disregard for sustainable practices has increased Africa's sensitivity to climate change and hampered the continent's capacity for sustainable development (Tikly, 2019).

As a result, the current impasse in Africa's development is deeply entangled with the legacy of colonial control. It is essential to recognize and confront these historical legacies and work toward a development paradigm that fosters inclusiveness, sustainability, and self-reliance if we are to effectively address these difficulties.

Attempts at Resolving the Developmental Impasse

Introduction to Institutional Efforts at Continental and Regional Levels

Institutional attempts at both the continental and regional levels have been attempted to break the developmental deadlock. These initiatives seek to promote regional integration, sustainable development, and good governance while also addressing the systemic difficulties and structural inequities that have persisted since colonialism.

Among continental intergovernmental organizations, the African Union (AU) is the most prominent. The African Union (AU), which replaced the OAU in 2002, was founded on the idea of an "integrated, prosperous and peaceful Africa, driven by its citizens and representing a dynamic force in the global arena." Its goals include bolstering continental harmony, democratic rule, economic progress, social progress, and security (Joshua & Olanrewaju, 2017). Agenda 2063, a strategic framework for the economic and social transformation of Africa over the next half-century, is one of the AU's most important efforts (Nshimbi, Moyo, & Oloruntoba, 2018).

In 2001, the AU announced a comprehensive economic development program called the New Partnership for Africa's Development (NEPAD). To speed up economic cooperation and integration across Africa, NEPAD strives to create an overarching vision and policy framework (Tavares & Tang, 2011).

Significant roles in breaking the development deadlock are played by regional bodies as well. There are several regional organizations in Africa. Some examples are the Southern African Development Community (SADC), the Economic Community of West African States (ECOWAS), and the East African Community (EAC). These groups work to coordinate social development strategies among their member governments, promote peace and security, and increase economic integration.

These institutional endeavours are vital to Africa's aspirations to forge its path to development by harnessing the strength of solidarity and regional collaboration to meet the continent's difficulties. These groups are essential to the pursuit of sustainable development and democratic government in Africa, even though their efficacy varies and obstacles continue.

The Decolonial Development Model (DDM) champions a shift towards embracing Africa's intrinsic values and systems. It underscores the importance of leveraging indigenous knowledge, especially in sectors like agriculture and governance, blending them with contemporary practices for balanced progress. Central to the DDM is the crafting of community-driven policies that resonate with grassroots aspirations, ensuring marginalized groups aren't overlooked. Economically, it encourages a departure from Western paradigms, urging a focus on community cooperatives, localized commerce, and intra-African trade. Moreover, the DDM stresses reforming education to be rooted in Africa's rich history and innovations, fostering pride and purpose among the continent's youth.

Detailed Analysis of the African Union (AU), the New Partnership for Africa's Development (NEPAD), and the African Peer Review

Achieving sustainable development and democratic governance in Africa is a shared goal of the African Union (AU), the New Partnership for Africa's Development (NEPAD), and the African Peer Review Mechanism (APRM).

The African Union is the continent's highest political, economic, and social body. Its goals are to strengthen continental identity and promote peace, security, and economic integration across the continent (Fioramonti & Mattheis, 2016). It has, however, been criticized for what is seen as its ineffectiveness in resolving crises, with some claiming that it has been too slow to respond or lacked the requisite political will. Despite these setbacks, the AU has accomplished a great deal, helping to advance the pan-African agenda and contributing to peacekeeping efforts and global health programs.

NEPAD is an AU initiative designed to boost the continent's economy. Its goals are to end poverty, achieve sustainable development, and help Africa reclaim its rightful place in the global economy. NEPAD can do its work because of the cooperation it has with its member states, regional entities, and international organizations (Adogamhe, 2008). The organization has started several programs, including the Comprehensive Africa Agriculture Development Programme (CAADP) and the Programme for Infrastructure Development in Africa (PIDA). While NEPAD has had a mixed impact, it has been crucial in bringing Africa's development concerns to the forefront of the international conversation and in rallying support for the continent (Ahenkan & Osei-Kojo, 2014).

Another AU program that helps spread the word about excellent government is the APRM. It's a way for AU countries to evaluate their performance in terms of governance, and participation is entirely voluntary. Democracy and political governance, economic governance and management, corporate governance, and socioeconomic development are the four themes within which APRM assessments are organized (Hope, 2005). However, the structure it has offered for policy discourse, self-assessment, and peer learning among African countries has made it worthwhile despite reservations about implementation and the non-binding character of its recommendations.

The work of each of these organizations is essential if Africa is to break out of its current developmental rut. They are committed to African-led solutions and regional cooperation, notwithstanding the difficulties they encounter. Their perseverance exemplifies Africa's determination and ambition to determine its destiny.

The waves of military coups also challenge the effectiveness of continental and regional institutions in promoting democracy and preventing unconstitutional changes in government. The African Union's policy of 'non-indifference' regarding unconstitutional alterations of governance, while laudable on paper, often faces challenges in execution, largely due to political complexities and competing national interests (Diaby & Klingelschmitt, 2023).

Evaluation of their Effectiveness in Fostering Development and Democracy

There has been some discussion about whether or not the AU, the NEPAD, and the APRM are effective at promoting development and democracy in Africa. Through its peacekeeping deployments and conflict resolution initiatives, the AU has made tremendous progress in promoting peace and security. Its opposition to unconstitutional transitions of government is indicative of a growing dedication to democratic principles. Sceptics, however, point to things like a lack of political will among member nations, weak enforcement mechanisms, and inadequate finance as reasons why the AU has been ineffective (Tavares, 2009). Despite the laudable nature of the AU's mission and objectives, the organization's ability and resources continue to need development.

NEPAD has demonstrated promise as a means of resolving Africa's development problems. Critical areas, like as infrastructure and agricultural development, have received increased attention because of initiatives like the Programme for Infrastructure Development in Africa (PIDA) and the Comprehensive Africa Agricultural Development Programme (CAADP). Inconsistent execution, a lack of ownership among African nations, and insufficient money are only a few of the problems that have hampered NEPAD's efficacy (Niyonkuru, 2016). Although NEPAD has re-energized Africa's development agenda, the success of its programs and objectives relies on the dedication of member states.

The APRM has received acclaim for its novel strategy in assessing governance, for fostering accountability, and for creating a forum for peer learning and experience sharing. Voluntary involvement, selective compliance, and the recommendations' lack of binding force all mitigate the system's potential (Bhatia, 2021). While the APRM has sparked discussions on governance policy and inspired some positive changes, its full potential has yet to be realized.

Key Factors in African Underdevelopment

Discussion on the Lack of Political Will

The lack of political will on the part of many African leaders and governments is a major contributor to the continent's stagnant development. The absence of political will takes many forms and has serious consequences for Africa's economic future.

In the first place, insufficient political will frequently leads to ineffective institutions and administration. Lack of dedication from political leadership has prevented the complete development and reform of institutions in many African countries. This has led to inefficient government agencies, widespread corruption, and the breakdown of law and order (Mmereki, Baldwin, & Li, 2016). Lack of political will to implement anti-corruption laws and encourage openness, for example, has allowed corruption, a widespread problem in many African countries, to go virtually unchecked (Ittner, 2009).

If political will is lacking, there is a higher chance that development initiatives will be inconsistent and unstable. Because they may be politically controversial or difficult to implement, much-needed reforms are often postponed or abandoned. It is impossible to make substantial headway in resolving developmental difficulties without a firm commitment to consistent and sound policy-making.

In addition, the benefits of regional and continental cooperation have not been fully realized due to a lack of political will. The AU and regional economic communities like ECOWAS and SADC are examples of structures for collaboration, although they have been hampered by a lack of commitment from member nations. For instance, a lack of political will at the national level has prevented the implementation of many AU decisions and resolutions (Arthur, 2017).

The absence of political will undermines efforts to strengthen democracies. The institutionalization of democracy is difficult if political leaders are not fully invested in and dedicated to democratic principles and practices. Inadequate political competition, restrictions on civil liberties, and frequent abuses of human rights are just some of the democratic weaknesses that result from this.

Overcoming Africa's underdevelopment will require tackling this difficult problem of a lack of political will. Developing a culture of responsibility, advocating for democratic norms, and fortifying civil society are all necessary steps. Better governance, more efficient institutions, and the kind of socioeconomic progress that Africa so desperately needs may be achieved with a strong and sustained political will.

Necessity of Decolonizing Democratic Development

Decolonizing democratic development is crucial for long-term success in Africa. It includes abandoning the imported Western models of government and development, acknowledging the lasting effects of colonialism, and developing a more localized, situationally appropriate strategy that places a premium on African expertise, experience, and cultural variety.

Multiparty elections, a division of powers, and a written constitution are all examples of procedural aspects of democracy emphasized by Western models. These are crucial, yet they might not take into account the nuances and complexities of life in Africa. Further, the adoption of such models without thorough consideration of the local environment can lead to the collapse of conventional government structures, societal fragmentation, and the establishment of a democratic veneer without substance.

Recognizing and appreciating indigenous political systems and institutions is essential for decolonizing democratic growth. Consensus-building, broad engagement, and solidarity are common features of traditional African administrative structures. By adopting these guidelines, African nations can create a democratic system that better reflects the needs and aspirations of its citizens.

The narratives and discourses around development are also being reevaluated as part of this process. The Western-dominated development rhetoric typically views Africa as a problem that has to be solved or a gap that must be filled (Lorenzini, 2014). A decolonized development strategy, on the other hand, would place more emphasis on Africa's capabilities, agency, and strengths. Self-sufficiency, local creativity, and environmentally sound methods consistent with Africa's cultural values and long-term interests would all benefit from this. Decolonizing development also requires redressing colonial-era injustices and inequities at the institutional level. Land and economic redistribution, resolving societal disparities, and restoring Africans' sense of dignity and identity are all called for.

The Decolonial Development Approach (DDA) advocates for a shift from externally imposed developmental blueprints to models anchored in African realities, history, and aspirations. At its core, the DDA emphasizes the importance of integrating indigenous knowledge systems into modern developmental strategies. This means giving precedence to grassroots-driven policies that reflect the genuine needs of African communities. It encourages economic strategies that don't merely mimic Western models but resonate with the continent's unique socio-economic dynamics. Furthermore, education under the DDA would be refashioned to centre on Africa's rich history, innovations, and future aspirations, ensuring that the next generation is equipped with a sense of identity and purpose. This approach is not just about reclaiming Africa's past, but about forging a path to a future that is intrinsically African in its design and execution.

Critical Engagement With Walter Rodney's Assertion of Europe's Role in Africa's Underdevelopment

Understanding the processes of colonialism and its ongoing repercussions on the African continent is essential for critically engaging with Walter Rodney's argument of Europe's responsibility for Africa's underdevelopment. Rodney contended in his landmark study "How Europe Underdeveloped Africa" that the continent's economic and social underdevelopment was caused by the colonial exploitation of Africa by European powers (Rodney, 2018).

According to Rodney, Africa's self-sufficient economy and social structures were disturbed by Europe's conquering efforts, which included the extraction of natural resources, the enslavement of people, and the imposition of foreign political and economic systems. He pointed out that as a result of these actions, African economies were restructured to benefit European interests, and African cultures became extremely reliant on their colonial overlords. Rodney suggested that Africa's underdevelopment could be traced back to this reliance.

Recognizing the enormous and continuing repercussions of colonialism on Africa's developmental trajectory is essential for critical engagement with Rodney's statements. Africa's social, economic, and political landscapes have been profoundly impacted by the extractive nature of colonial economies, the underfunding of indigenous education and health facilities, and the dismantling of traditional government structures (Norgaard 2019). Without question, these elements have played crucial roles in forming the developmental obstacles that Africa still faces today.

While Europe's colonial past is certainly a factor in Africa's current condition of underdevelopment, it is only part of the story. Africa's development problems are exacerbated by several reasons, including postcolonial government failures, intra-African wars, and global economic trends (Flahaux & De Haas, 2016).

An in-depth and nuanced comprehension of Africa's underdevelopment is essential, as is made clear by Rodney's work. It requires reflection, with an awareness of both internal and exterior processes. This perspective is crucial for developing development policies that consider both the injustices of the past and the reality of today in Africa.

Decolonization and Africa's Place in the Global Economy

Historically, the decolonization process had implications that reached far beyond political independence. Africa's economic trajectory was and continues to be, significantly influenced by its colonial past. Post-independence, many African nations inherited economies structured around extractive industries that served the colonial metropole. This economic model limited diversification and positioned Africa primarily as a supplier of raw materials to global markets, rather than a producer of finished goods. The global economic system, largely shaped by Western interests, perpetuated these trade dynamics, often disadvantaging African states (John, Messina, & Odumegwu, 2023).

In contemporary times, despite strides in diversification and industrialization, many African economies remain reliant on primary commodity exports. The challenges of this dependency became starkly evident during global events like the 2008 financial crisis and the recent COVID-19 pandemic, where fluctuations in global commodity prices and disruptions in supply chains had disproportionate impacts on Africa (Vos, McDermott, & Swinnen, 2016).

However, recent years have also seen a renewed drive across Africa to reposition its role in the global economy. With initiatives such as the African Continental Free Trade Area (AfCFTA), there's a concerted effort to enhance intra-Africa trade, fostering resilience against global economic shocks. Yet, the decolonial perspective argues that for Africa to truly find an equitable place in the global economic system, there needs to be a conscious move away from economic models and global trade norms that have colonial residues. Instead, Africa should champion economic systems that prioritize its unique socio-cultural context, resource endowments, and development aspirations (Panse, Fyall, & Alvarez, 2021).

The decolonial development model aligns with this perspective. By emphasizing indigenous knowledge systems, community-centred policies, and economic models rooted in African realities, the DDM seeks not just to break free from the legacy of colonial economic structures, but to redefine Africa's role in the global economic order. By doing so, Africa can transition from a historically peripheral position to one of agency, partnership, and co-creation in the global economy.

Towards a Democratic and Developmental Africa

The Imperative of Introspective Analysis of Africa's Self-Underdevelopment

If we want to see genuine democracy and progress in Africa, we must examine the continent's state of underdevelopment. This critical evaluation of internal processes in Africa that contribute to its underdevelopment extends beyond the assessment of external issues such as the legacy of colonialism.

The term "Africa's self-underdevelopment" describes the internal obstacles to development inside African cultures and governments. There is a lack of openness in government as well as internal tensions and authoritarian tendencies (Flahaux & De Haas, 2016). Even while colonial history has left its mark on Africa's problems, the continent's internal problems must be addressed before it can move forward on the road to progress and democracy.

Poorly functioning and corrupt institutions have hampered progress in Africa. Corruption at high levels prevents money from being spent on public services, deepening poverty and inequality. The public's trust is eroded and developmental programs are less likely to be put into action when there is poor governance, which is characterized by weak institutions, inadequate accountability, and a lack of transparency (Hopper, Lassou, & Soobaroyen, 2017).

Recent years have seen a concerning resurgence of military coups in various African nations, with countries like Mali, Guinea, and Sudan experiencing abrupt political shifts (Taruvinga, 2023). These events underline the fragile nature of democratic institutions in parts of the continent, and the persistent challenges that many African nations face in ensuring stable, accountable governance.

Emerging literature suggests that while some coups may stem from a genuine desire to correct perceived governance flaws (Thompson, 2023), many are driven by elite power struggles, regional influences, and in some cases, international geopolitical interests (Pogodda, Richmond, & Visoka, 2023). The recurrence of these coups suggests a deeper structural issue that challenges the traditional development and governance models, further necessitating the importance of a decolonial approach.

Development attempts in Africa have also been severely hampered by internal and external wars. Inequalities in wealth and opportunity, racial and religious tensions, and power disputes are common causes of war. They cause massive human suffering, economic disruption, and population displacement (Flahaux & De Haas, 2016).

In addition to these problems, the continued disregard for democratic ideals and human rights is a serious obstacle. Electoral fraud, repressing the opposition, and restricting civil freedoms are all undemocratic actions that undermine democratic governance and slow progress (Rakner, 2021).

Facing these internal pressures calls for dedication to institution building, accountability promotion, and the protection of democratic principles and human rights. To overcome these obstacles, introspective introspection is becoming increasingly important as Africa charts its course towards development. Africa can only make progress toward a more democratic and prosperous future if its people heal from the wounds they have inflicted on themselves.

Argument for Greater Emphasis on Accountable Governance, Human Rights, and the Empowerment of Civic Engagement

Africa must prioritize accountable governance, human rights, and the facilitation of civic involvement if it is to attain a sustainable and equitable developmental trajectory. These three factors all work together to form the basis for a more democratic and prosperous Africa.

Transparent and ethical government is only possible when public officials are held accountable for their decisions and actions. It requires strong institutions that can uphold the rule of law, effective anti-corruption measures, and a well-developed system of checks and balances. Responsible leadership is essential for progress because it boosts confidence in government, encourages productive investment, and creates conditions that encourage economic and social development (Zreik, 2022).

Human rights observance is also essential. Human rights are essential to the functioning of a democratic society and have a direct bearing on progress. Along with civil and political rights, the Universal Declaration of Human Rights also guarantees the right to social, economic, and cultural development. Human rights are important because they protect people from being mistreated, help communities stay peaceful, and strengthen bonds between people (Iriye, Goedde, & Hitchcock, 2012).

Finally, encouraging citizens to take part in shaping a more democratic and prosperous Africa is crucial. Citizens who are given the means to engage in political, economic, and social life are better equipped to hold their leaders accountable, shape public policy, and grow their communities. Citizens who take part in government are more likely to feel represented, to be creative and resourceful in finding solutions to problems, and to have their development needs addressed.

Africa can be propelled toward a more democratic and progressive trajectory by the interplay of accountable governance, human rights, and empowered civic involvement. That development is people-focused, rights-based, and controlled by accountability and transparency principles is what this method guarantees. The development difficulties in Africa may be met and the continent's full potential can be realized thanks to its emphasis on resilience, inclusion, and sustainable growth.

For the Decolonial Development Model (DDM) to thrive, it requires governments to champion its principles through public sensitization, ensuring widespread understanding and buy-in. Essential to its rollout are collaborative spaces where community figures, academics, and decision-makers can co-create policies reflecting DDM's ethos. Implementing robust monitoring and evaluation systems will help gauge its real-world impact and facilitate course corrections. Further bolstering its potential, forging strategic alliances between African countries, grounded in their shared history and culture, is paramount to advancing the DDM vision.

Concluding Thoughts on How to Foster a Truly Democratic and Developmental Africa

Creating a more democratic and prosperous Africa is a difficult challenge requiring a varied strategy. It requires facing both the current internal forces that hinder progress and the historical legacies of underdevelopment.

Africa's current developmental trajectory owes a great deal to the legacies of colonialism and neo-colonialism. Fostering a new narrative of development that places a premium on Africa's potential, agency, and resilience, and seeking justice and equity are all necessary steps in getting there.

Concurrently, the internal causes like corruption, bad governance, and internal conflicts that contribute to Africa's self-underdevelopment must be addressed. This necessitates a dedication to establishing reliable institutions, encouraging transparent leadership, and maintaining the rule of law.

Human rights and civic engagement play an essential role in Africa's progress toward a more democratic and prosperous future. Protecting human rights promotes growth-friendly conditions and upholds people's inherent worth and dignity. To ensure that all people's concerns are heard and met, civic engagement must be encouraged through various means.

The role of continental and regional institutions in promoting democracy and progress is crucial. However, they will only be useful if their member nations are willing to carry out the policies that have been agreed upon and maintain democratic standards.

In the end, it takes the determination and dedication of all parties involved - governments, civil society, and citizens - to make Africa a more democratic and progressive place. This involves serious self-examination, creative problem-solving, and a dogged pursuit of justice, tolerance, and human rights. The promise of an affluent, democratic, and developing Africa is within grasp, bringing hope and inspiration to future generations despite the difficulty of the path.

CONCLUSION

This chapter analyzed the post-colonial effects, the fight for democratic government, and the need to decolonize the developmental agenda as they pertain to Africa's current developmental deadlock. It highlighted the profound and ongoing effects of colonialism, neocolonialism, and apartheid on Africa's sociopolitical and economic realms and established a connection between the continent's contemporary developmental and governance issues and these historical imbalances.

Institutions like the African Union, New Partnership for Africa's Development, and the African Peer Review, were among those studied. Despite the promising potential of these endeavours, they have not been fully realized due to a lack of political will and, to a lesser extent, competent and accountable governance structures. It also examined Walter Rodney's claim that Europe is responsible for Africa's underdevelopment, critiquing its virtues and shortcomings.

This chapter stated that Africa's unique socio-cultural setting necessitates a departure from enforced Western forms of governance and that this departure is essential to decolonizing democratic progress. The need for Africa to confront its internal difficulties, such as corruption, weak governance, and internal conflicts, was also stressed, underscoring the significance of introspective examination.

The chapter highlighted the importance of accountable leadership, human rights protection, and citizen empowerment in Africa's quest for democracy and progress. The key to changing Africa's development trajectory lies with these factors and a stronger emphasis on institutional capacity building.

It acknowledges that there is still much to be done. There has to be more study done to learn about the specific developmental dynamics in Africa. This requires in-depth research that takes into account the interplay of historical, sociocultural, and political elements that have shaped Africa's progress. Specifically, more study needs to be done to unpack the complexities of decolonizing development and democracy, looking at how indigenous systems of governance and locally driven development initiatives can be used to promote growth and development.

To further ensure that responsible government, human rights, and civic engagement are at the centre of Africa's development agenda, policy directions need to be refocused. Institutional improvement, more openness, and less corruption should all be goals of policymaking. To foster growth, it is necessary to devise plans for mending internal divisions and strengthening social bonds.

It also urges governments to show more political will to carry out measures for regional and continental development. Accelerating the continent's transition to democracy and development requires increased cooperation and coordination across African states.

Finally, regular residents and members of civil society must be brought into the development process as soon as possible. Citizens with agency can drive change by calling their leaders to account and propelling initiatives for local improvement.

Adopting the Decolonial Development Model doesn't negate the relevance of global partnerships or external insights. Instead, it emphasizes the centrality of African agency in the development discourse. It's a call for Africa to navigate its development trajectory using a compass calibrated by its own historical, cultural, and socio-economic realities.

REFERENCES

Abebe, R., Aruleba, K., Birhane, A., Kingsley, S., Obaido, G., Remy, S. L., & Sadagopan, S. (2021, March). Narratives and counternarratives on data sharing in Africa. In *Proceedings of the 2021 ACM conference on fairness, accountability, and transparency* (pp. 329-341). 10.1145/3442188.3445897

Abegunrin, O. (2009). *Africa in global politics in the twenty-first century: A Pan-African perspective*. Springer. doi:10.1057/9780230623903

Adogamhe, P. G. (2008). Pan-Africanism revisited: Vision and reality of African unity and development. *African Review of Integration*, *2*(2), 1–34.

Ahenkan, A., & Osei-Kojo, A. (2014). Achieving sustainable development in Africa: Progress, challenges and prospects. *International Journal of Development and Sustainability*, *3*(1), 162–176.

Arthur, P. (2017). Promoting security in Africa through regional economic communities (RECs) and the African union's African peace and security architecture (APSA). *Insight on Africa*, *9*(1), 1–21. doi:10.1177/0975087816674577

Asongu, S. A., & De Moor, L. (2017). Financial globalisation dynamic thresholds for financial development: Evidence from Africa. *European Journal of Development Research*, *29*(1), 192–212. doi:10.1057/ejdr.2016.10

Barnhart, J. (2016). Status competition and territorial aggression: Evidence from the scramble for Africa. *Security Studies*, *25*(3), 385–419. doi:10.1080/09636412.2016.1195620

Bhatia, R. (2021). *India–Africa Relations: Changing Horizons*. Taylor & Francis. doi:10.4324/9781003044550

Blakemore, K., & Cooksey, B. (2017). *A sociology of education for Africa* (Vol. 8). Routledge. doi:10.4324/9781315412733

Chlouba, V., Smith, D. S., & Wagner, S. (2022). Early statehood and support for autocratic rule in Africa. *Comparative Political Studies*, *55*(4), 688–724. doi:10.1177/00104140211036031

Christensen, D., & Laitin, D. D. (2019). *African states since independence: Order, development, and democracy*. Yale University Press.

De Brauw, A., & Bulte, E. (2021). *African farmers, value chains and agricultural development*. Springer International Publishing. doi:10.1007/978-3-030-88693-6

Diaby, A., & Klingelschmitt, N. (2023). De Facto Sovereignty and Multilateral Sanctions for a Return to Constitutional Order in a Context of Regional Armed Conflict: The Case of Mali. In *War, State and Sovereignty: Interdisciplinary Challenges and Perspectives for the Social Sciences* (pp. 185–207). Springer Nature Switzerland. doi:10.1007/978-3-031-33661-4_9

Feagin, J. (2013). *Systemic racism: A theory of oppression*. Routledge. doi:10.4324/9781315880938

Fioramonti, L., & Mattheis, F. (2016). Is Africa really following Europe? An integrated framework for comparative regionalism. *Journal of Common Market Studies*, *54*(3), 674–690. doi:10.1111/jcms.12307

Flahaux, M. L., & De Haas, H. (2016). African migration: Trends, patterns, drivers. *Comparative Migration Studies*, *4*(1), 1–25. doi:10.118640878-015-0015-6

Fox, S. (2014). The political economy of slums: Theory and evidence from Sub-Saharan Africa. *World Development*, *54*, 191–203. doi:10.1016/j.worlddev.2013.08.005

Hope, K. R. Sr. (2005). Toward good governance and sustainable development: The African peer review mechanism. *Governance: An International Journal of Policy, Administration and Institutions*, *18*(2), 283–311. doi:10.1111/j.1468-0491.2005.00276.x

Hopkins, A. G. (2019). *An economic history of West Africa*. Routledge. doi:10.4324/9780429400582

Hopper, T., Lassou, P., & Soobaroyen, T. (2017). Globalisation, accounting and developing countries. *Critical Perspectives on Accounting*, *43*, 125–148. doi:10.1016/j.cpa.2016.06.003

Iriye, A., Goedde, P., & Hitchcock, W. I. (Eds.). (2012). *The human rights revolution: an international history* (Vol. 3). Oxford University Press.

Ittner, S. (2009). *Fighting corruption in Africa: A comparative study of Uganda and Botswana* [Doctoral dissertation]. Deutsche Universität für Verwaltungswissenschaften.

John, O. I., Messina, G. M., & Odumegwu, A. C. (2023). The Effects of Neocolonialism on Africa's Development. *PanAfrican Journal of Governance and Development*, *4*(2), 3–35. doi:10.46404/panjogov.v4i2.4846

Joshua, S., & Olanrewaju, F. (2017). The AU's Progress and Achievements in the Realm of Peace and Security. *India Quarterly*, *73*(4), 454–471. doi:10.1177/0974928417731639

Lorenzini, S. (2014). Comecon and the South in the years of détente: a study on East–South economic relations. *European Review of History: Revue européenne d'histoire, 21*(2), 183-199.

Mangu, A. M. (2014). The African Union and the promotion of democracy and good political governance under the African Peer-Review Mechanism: 10 years on. *African Review (Dar Es Salaam, Tanzania)*, *6*(1), 59–72. doi:10.1080/09744053.2014.883757

Mmereki, D., Baldwin, A., & Li, B. (2016). A comparative analysis of solid waste management in developed, developing and lesser developed countries. *Environmental Technology Reviews*, *5*(1), 120–141. doi:10.1080/21622515.2016.1259357

Modi, I. (2015). Social exclusion and inequality: Challenges before a developing society. *Sociological Bulletin*, *64*(1), 3–14. doi:10.1177/0038022920150101

Neocosmos, M. (2010). *From Foreign Natives to Native Foreigners. Explaining Xenophobia in Post-apartheid South Africa: Explaining Xenophobia in Post-apartheid South Africa: Citizenship and Nationalism, Identity and Politics*. African Books Collective.

Niyonkuru, F. (2016). Failure of foreign aid in developing countries: A quest for alternatives. *Business and Economics Journal*, *7*(3), 1–9.

Norgaard, K. M. (2019). *Salmon and acorns feed our people: Colonialism, nature, and social action*. Rutgers University Press.

Nshimbi, C. C., Moyo, I., & Oloruntoba, S. O. (2018). Borders, informal cross-border economies and regional integration in Africa-an introduction. *Africa Insight*, *48*(1), 3–11.

Panse, G., Fyall, A., & Alvarez, S. (2021). Stakeholder views on sustainability in an urban destination context: An inclusive path to destination competitiveness. *International Journal of Tourism Cities*, *7*(4), 895–915. doi:10.1108/IJTC-10-2020-0225

Pogodda, S., Richmond, O. P., & Visoka, G. (2023). Counter-peace: From isolated blockages in peace processes to systemic patterns. *Review of International Studies*, *49*(3), 491–512. doi:10.1017/S0260210522000377

Prince, R. J., & Marsland, R. (Eds.). (2013). *Making and Unmaking Public Health in Africa: ethnographic and historical perspectives*. Ohio University Press.

Rakner, L. (2021). Don't Touch My Constitution! Civil Society Resistance to Democratic Backsliding in Africa´ s Pluralist Regimes. *Global Policy*, *12*(S5), 95–105. doi:10.1111/1758-5899.12991

Rekiso, Z. S. (2017). Rethinking regional economic integration in Africa as if industrialization mattered. *Structural Change and Economic Dynamics*, *43*, 87–98. doi:10.1016/j.strueco.2017.10.001

Rodney, W. (2018). *How europe underdeveloped africa*. Verso Books.

Schmidt, E. (2013). Foreign intervention in Africa: From the Cold War to the war on terror (No. 7). Cambridge University Press.

Somerville, K. (2017). *Africa's long road since independence: the many histories of a continent*.

Taruvinga, G. R. (2023). The Resurgence of Military Coups in Africa: The Case of West Africa and the Sahel. In *Contemporary Issues on Governance, Conflict and Security in Africa* (pp. 147–157). Springer Nature Switzerland. doi:10.1007/978-3-031-29635-2_9

Tavares, R. (2009). *Regional security: The capacity of international organizations*. Routledge. doi:10.4324/9780203874059

Tavares, R., & Tang, V. (2011). Regional economic integration in Africa: Impediments to progress? *South African Journal of International Affairs*, *18*(2), 217–233. doi:10.1080/10220461.2011.588826

Thompson, B. S. (2023). Impact investing in biodiversity conservation with bonds: An analysis of financial and environmental risk. *Business Strategy and the Environment*, *32*(1), 353–368. doi:10.1002/bse.3135

Thomson, A. (2022). *An introduction to African politics*. Taylor & Francis. doi:10.4324/9781003031840

Tikly, L. (2019). *Education for sustainable development in the postcolonial world: Towards a transformative agenda for Africa*. Routledge. doi:10.4324/9781315211343

Vos, R., McDermott, J., & Swinnen, J. (2022). COVID-19 and global poverty and food security. *Annual Review of Resource Economics*, *14*(1), 151–168. doi:10.1146/annurev-resource-111920-013613

Wengraf, L. (2018). *Extracting profit: Imperialism, neoliberalism and the new scramble for Africa*. Haymarket Books.

Youngs, R. (2015). *The Puzzle of non-western democracy*. Brookings Institution Press.

Zreik, M. (2021). China and Europe in Africa: Competition or Cooperation?. *MJIR| Malaysian Journal of International Relations, 9*(1), 51-67.

Zreik, M. (2022). Contemporary geopolitics of Eurasia and the Belt and Road Initiative. *Eurasian Research Journal, 4*(1), 7–26. doi:10.53277/2519-2442-2022.1-01

Zreik, M. (2023). Harnessing the Power of Blockchain Technology in Modern China: A Comprehensive Exploration. In L. Ferreira, M. Cruz, E. Cruz, H. Quintela, & M. Cunha (Eds.), *Supporting Technologies and the Impact of Blockchain on Organizations and Society* (pp. 94–112). IGI Global. doi:10.4018/978-1-6684-5747-4.ch007

KEY TERMS AND DEFINITIONS

African Continental Free Trade Area (AfCFTA): A trade agreement among African Union member states aiming to create a single market followed by free movement and a single-currency union.

Commodity Dependency: A state where a nation's or region's economy relies heavily on the export of a limited number of primary commodities for a significant proportion of its revenue and foreign exchange.

Decolonial Development Model (DDM): An approach to development that emphasizes the importance of breaking free from historical colonial influences, focusing on indigenous knowledge, community-driven initiatives, and economic models rooted in local realities.

Decolonization: The process by which colonies become independent from their colonizing powers, often involving political, cultural, and economic shifts.

Extractive Industries: Industries that remove non-renewable resources from the Earth, such as mining and logging. Historically, many African economies were built around these industries during colonial times.

Global Economy: The interrelated economies of the world's countries, considered as a single economic system influenced by global events and decisions made by multinational corporations and governments.

Grassroots Development: A bottom-up approach to development where local communities identify and address their own needs, ensuring interventions are tailored to specific cultural and contextual realities.

Indigenous Knowledge Systems (IKS): The understandings, skills, and philosophies developed by societies with long histories of interaction with their natural environment.

Neocolonialism: A system in which former colonial powers maintain economic, political, and cultural influence over former colonies, typically through economic mechanisms and international relations.

Post-Colonialism: An academic discipline that deals with the cultural legacy of colonialism and imperialism, focusing on the human consequences of the control and exploitation by colonized people and their lands.

Chapter 9
Political Apathy as a Challenge of Democratization in Africa:
An Assessment of General Elections in Nigeria

Hezekiah Usman
Ahmadu Bello University, Nigeria

Hosea Olayiwola Patrick
https://orcid.org/0000-0001-8022-9099
McMaster University, Canada

ABSTRACT

The place of political participation in the democratization process in Africa necessitates understanding the motivation for participation as an integral component for democracy. For Nigeria and Africa, this is crucial for the emergence of good governance and the development of democratic processes and governance. This chapter explored political participation in Nigeria and the issues of political apathy as a challenge of the democratization process. Using a desktop review technique, the chapter explored the causes of political apathy and its possible effect on Nigeria's democratization process as a template for Africa. While the factors and impacts identified in this chapter for political apathy in Nigeria are not exhaustive, the implication for the democratization process is significant. Therefore, there is a need for all stakeholders, governments, and citizens alike to embrace proactive measures in curtailing political apathy in Nigeria and, by inference, Africa's democratization process.

INTRODUCTION

In all democratic nations worldwide, the challenges associated with political apathy negate the essence of democratic governance. It is an irrefutable fact that the fascinating and unique feature of democracy is the power it confers on the citizenry to not only choose their leadership but also influence the formation

DOI: 10.4018/979-8-3693-0477-8.ch009

and direction of policies. This implies that democracy would be unattractive and dreary if the people who are the major component of democracy become apolitical or fail to exercise this right of choosing their leaders during periodic elections. On this basis, Usman (2023) rightly observes that democracy is in jeopardy when its' popular component – demos (Greek: *the people*) is undermined. Adekoya (2019) asserts that democracy appears to be a failure when the populace is indifferent about who emerges victorious in the electioneering process. All these assertions reveal the significance of the people in democratic governance because democracy is primarily about the people.

Political apathy implies nonchalant and lackadaisical feelings towards political issues such as electioneering, public opinion aggregation, and policy formulation, as well as turnout and participation in political processes and activities and civic engagement with government. Political apathy is usually assessed in the context of voter involvement and engagement in the electoral process. Fagunwa (2015:6) perceives "apathy as a deficient response, indifference and nonchalance in electioneering." The expression of these feelings for citizens in a given country during elections, according to Okafor, Odigbo & Okeke (2022), sheds light on the level at which representative democracy may be derailing.

Political apathy has become a global problem (I-IDEA 2016: Chukwudi, 2022). It is even more a worrisome trend in the democratization process, especially in Africa (Andriani & Escudero-Loaiza, 2021; Dobbs, 2021; Obiagu *et al.*, 2021). All over the world, the diminution in political participation seems to be a general phenomenon (Fagunwa, 2015). It is generally argued that "voter turnout has been dropping worldwide for the last 30 years and has reached alarmingly low levels in some countries" (Beregovskiy, 2019: 1). The decline in electoral participation is evident in most democracies globally (Blais, 2000; Gray & Caul, 2000). This informs Moliki & Dauda's (2014) argument on the universal increase in voter apathy. That is the absence of citizens' involvement and nonchalance towards civic obligations and political activities. Using America as a case in point, Beregovskiy (2019) posits that millions of Americans, despite living in a country acclaimed as one of the best democracies in the world, have never voted in their entire adult lives. In comparison with Europe, which records an average of 70% voter turnout in any presidential election, the U.S. voter turnout is always less than 60% in the same election.

The situation of political apathy is even more perturbing in African countries. For example, the International Institute for Democracy and Electoral Assistance (I-IDEA) (2014:43) reports on the rate of voter turnout across elections in Africa is worthy of note. While Zimbabwe had about 32% voter turnout in the 1996 presidential election, Nigeria's 2019 presidential election recorded 35%, while Cape Verde, Egypt, and Mali recorded 36%, 41%, and 43%, respectively. Others with equally low voter turnout in major elections in Africa include Sudan and Sao Tome and Principe (46%), the Democratic Republic of Congo (45%), Cote d'Ivoire (53%), Algeria and Mozambique (49%). This situation has become a serious concern because there is no democracy without the people. The essence of democracy is the opportunity it confers on the citizens to govern themselves or to choose who governs them in a representative democracy. As espoused by Abraham Lincoln, the conceptualization of democracy as the 'government of the people' (in terms of makeup and ownership), by the people (in terms of process), and for the people (in terms of the responsibility of government)' voting provides the necessary credence to democracy (Abdulrazak & Abdulmalik, 2020).

Although, the factors responsible for plummeting voter turnout differ from country to country. For example, in the United States, logistical issues and voting legislation negatively impact on voters' turnout (Hill, 2009). Buttressing this, Beregovskiy (2019) argued that the voting system operational in the United States has uncommon characteristics as compared to other global democracies, such as voting on a weekday and non-automatic voter registration. These factors, among others, account for America's low voter turnout. In Africa, the situation is different. Several studies have also identified a deficiency of mobilization, weather conditions on election day, lack of civic engagement, indecision on preferred candidates, lack of transparency, timing, ethnic affiliation, political party loyalty, political marginalization, failed campaign promises, lack of accountability, as well as the nature violence characteristics of electioneering processes in Africa as probable factors spurring the continuous rise in voter apathy during an election. (Aloysius *et al.*, 2019; Gberevbie, 2014; Fowler, 2003; Morrow, 2015; Fagunwa, 2015).

The situation is even worse in the 2023 general elections in Nigeria. It was recorded that Nigeria experienced the lowest voter turnout (INEC 2023). The Independent National Electoral Commission (INEC) reports (2023) that, out of over 93 million registered voters, only 24.9 million, representing 26.7%, voted during the presidential election. According to the report, it was only in 2003 that Nigeria recorded the highest voter turnout of 69%. Since then, it has been a nosediving trend, and this is a problematic situation for a nation that is bedevilled with a high rate of unemployment, poverty, corruption, infrastructural decay, violent conflicts in almost all the regions of the federation, etc. This implies that there is a general sense of dissatisfaction among the people, which then affects their input into the political system (Chukwudi, 2022).

Political apathy is one of the foremost challenges of the democratization process globally. The global regression of political apathy occurs in parallel with the emergence of many vociferous voices of scholars about the state of democracy around the world. As Diamond (2015:152) rightly posits: "low levels of voter participation are additional signs of democratic ill-health." For Oluwagbohunmi (2020), it is a "worrisome impediment to the electoral process." This chapter, therefore, contributes to the burgeoning literature on political apathy in Africa and its implication on the democratization process using Nigeria as a case study. In doing so, the chapter is structured into eight sections. The first section is the introduction, providing a context to the chapter's subject matter. This is followed by a background and conceptual discourse and a snapshot of the methodology adopted for the chapter. A theoretical discourse section then follows this. Forming the findings sections, the next section explores the historical context of voter apathy in Nigeria. The sixth section examines factors that cause political apathy in Nigeria. The seventh section considers the effects of political apathy on the democratization process in Nigeria, and the last section provides a summary and conclusion of the chapter.

METHODOLOGY

The chapter adopts a systemic desktop review technique to explore political apathy and democratization processes using Nigeria as a Case study (see Webb *et al.*, 2015). Data were sources using a convenience simple random sampling to collect literature from archival sources. The selected sample data were based on their relevance to the subject matter of discourse (see Emerson, 2015; Sharma, 2017). Keywords such as 'Democratization,' 'Political Apathy,' 'Election,' and 'Nigeria' were used interchangeably and collaboratively to elicit data for the study from search engines such as Scopus and Google Scholar. Archival materials from organizational sources such as the Nigerian Independent National Electoral Commission (INEC), among others, were also used to source relevant data for the study. The data were coded and thematically analyzed to allow for coherent discourse and insights into the rationale, cause, and impact of political apathy in Africa using Nigeria as a litmus example.

BACKGROUND

Conceptual Discourse on Political Apathy

The concept of political apathy, unlike many concepts in social sciences, is less controversial. However, it is tidier to separate 'political' from 'apathy' and then treat the latter as a separate conceptual category, as its meaning is indispensable to the discourse. Apathy refers to a state of indifference or lack of motivation, interest, or emotional investment in a particular issue, activity, or situation. Apathy is "the mental state of not caring much about something or anything at all. It is the suppression of passion, emotion, or excitement for something" (Nuka, Kia & Nwibor, 2015:161). An individual is described as apathetic when there is a lack of emotion or motivation in any aspect of human life (cultural, social, religious, political, etc.). Hence, we have cultural apathy, religious apathy, political apathy, etc. However, the focus of this chapter is on political apathy.

Political apathy, therefore, refers to a lack of interest, engagement, or active participation in political affairs. According to Nuka *et al.* (2015:162), "Political apathy is expressed and measured by the degree of political phobia and non-participation in political activities in a country." For Chukwudi (2022:33), political apathy is seen as "the totality of all forms of withdrawal, unwillingness to be part of socio-political activities of the country with the belief that it won't add value or make a difference in the observed state of the society." Given this assertion, the connotation of political apathy goes beyond just absence during elections. It also encompasses apathy in the forms of civic engagement and contributions to society, listening and dialogue apathy, reading and information gathering apathy, among others. In essence, apathy breeds the situation whereby citizens harbour negative feelings towards the government and those in authority in terms of little or no expectation of performance; hence, there is no gain in commitment or any form of involvement in political activities of the state (Chukwudi, 2022:33).

Political apathy is "the lack of psychological involvement in public affairs, emotional detachment from civic obligations and abstention from political activity" (INEC & FES, 2011: 15). It is seen as the overall drop in citizens' engagement in the political activities of a particular nation or territory (Fagunwa, 2015). A distinction must be made between voter apathy and political apathy. Voter apathy is an aspect or a subdivision of political apathy, and it refers to a situation when eligible voters are reluctant or, in many cases, deliberately take avoiding actions in participating in elections (Okafor, Odigbo & Okeke, 2022). While voter apathy is unconcern feelings towards an election, political apathy is a feeling of indifference towards political issues such as electioneering, policy-making, civic engagement and political leaders, public opinion aggregation, attendance and involvement in political functions and activities. Given this assertion, it is safe to say that while political apathy connotes total disregard in terms of interest in all political activities, voters' apathy is a narrower concept that connotes just disinterest in the voting and electioneering process. For context, therefore, a citizen can be politically active (and be involved in activities such as public opinion aggregation policy formulation, among others, and yet refuse to turn out for voting. This means that political apathy is bigger (not equal to) voters' apathy. However, by being involved in voting, one can safely say the individual is politically active. This is why political apathy can be assessed in the context of voter participation in the electoral process (voter turnout). Hence, in this work, the two concepts will be used interchangeably.

Theoretical Discourse

Despite several efforts made by the government, political parties, civil society organizations, the media, etc., to ensure citizens' involvement and participation in governance and politics in Nigeria, a significant majority lack interest in such participation despite it constituting a major thrust of representative democracy. As Adewale & Musa (2023) opined, it is unhealthy for any democratic system to have a significant level of citizens' non-participation in its political activities. Given this, several scholars have postulated several theories to explain the reasons for the loss of interest and enthusiasm for civic engagement in the political process. For example, Nuka *et al.* (2015) posit within the framework of elitist theory to argue that political apathy is caused by electoral violence in Nigeria. Their view is predicated on the assumption that issues of governance, elections, and political participation are determined, controlled, and championed by the elites who monopolize political power and retain it by any means necessary. In essence, the electoral processes are typically manipulated in the interest of the elites. Here, the idea of "any means necessary" or the notion of the "ends justify the means" is employed to ensure political domination and victories at the poll. By this, violence and electoral rigging are carried out in an attempt to retain political power. Given these postulations, one can argue that the expectation of violence influences political apathy behaviour by the electorates in Nigeria.

Other scholars, such as Idike (2014) and Chukwudi (2022), have used system theory to explain political apathy in Nigeria. According to these scholars, while several units and subsystems are making the Nigerian state a system as a whole, the Nigerian government is likened to a gatekeeper within the transformation mechanism of the system. The integrity of the gatekeeper as a subsystem within the whole determines the output and the feedback to and from the system. The reaction of the people (in terms of feedback to the system) is expressed in discontent as strike actions, protests, terrorism, political violence, and the latest bush in Nigeria referred to as the '*Japa*' syndrome1. Political apathy is, therefore, within this argument, a direct reaction in terms of feedback from a failed system.

In his book, "Economic Theory of Democracy," Downs (1957) conveyed the "Rational Choice Theory" to explain citizens' lethargic feelings towards the political process. This theory has been used in recent times to explain the rationale for voters' turnout in elections. In essence, the rational choice theory accentuates the justification for voting and non-voting in an election. It argued that voting is done in an election process by the electorates to maximize gains (Geys, 2006). Before any type of election, voters evaluate the expected gains of voting and abstention. If the advantages of voting to the cost of the same exercise, the propensity of the voter to vote becomes high. While this is true, the propensity to vote may be low if the voters perceive at any point within the electioneering process that their participation is inconsequential to the final result of the election. With this notion in mind, the tendency to abstain from the entire voting process, leading to political apathy, is significantly high (Ebenezer, 2017). Therefore, Downs' rational choice theory emphasizes that the profitability or unprofitability of voting as perceived by the voters would determine the level of participation or apathy experienced within a political system.

In Western democracies or developed nations, issues that could influence the propensity to vote include factors such as distance to the polling station, duration needed to contemplate the voting choice, weather during the election, registration requirements, education and income of voters etc. (Wolfinger & Rosenstone, 1980). Narrowing in on education and income as probable factors to determining political apathy, Feddersen & Pesendorfer (1996,1999) postulated using the game theory model that voters' turnout would increase due to better access to information.

However, several pebbles of criticism have been thrown at Downs' rational choice model. For example, Dowding (2005) faulted this model because it lacks consistency in explaining voter turnout rate. For Kirchgassner (2003), the rational choice model failed to explain abstention due to alienation, that voters failed to vote in an election because they are alienated from the democratic process and benefits and that the more alienated the voters are, the less probable they are to participate in an election. Matsusaka (1995) also faulted Downs' rational choice theory for not recognizing the influence of information in determining voting patterns, notably in the modern age of digital technology and social media interactions and interconnectivity. Despite these shortcomings, however, the theoretical contributions of the rational choice theory cannot be over-emphasized in explaining the unenthusiastic and languid feelings towards the political process.

In replicating the rational choice model in Nigeria, Ebenezer (2017) identifies the cost of voting in an election, which includes the risk of assassination or any form of harm liable to occur because of activities such as thuggery, sporadic shootings, bomb targets among others on elections days. In addition, the general perception held by many a citizen that the dividend of democracy in terms of accountable governance, infrastructural development, and corrupt-free government is impossible could trigger political apathy. Ebenezer (2017) agrees with Downs' rational choice model and the criticism by Kirchgassner (2003) that the motivation determining voters' decision to participate in voting is determined by the maximization of benefits. Hence, voters would abstain from voting when they realize the inconsequentiality of their votes in deciding the outcome of an election. On this basis, Ebenezer (2017) justifies the postulations of the Rational Choice Theory and the Political Alienation Theory of non-voting with the Theory of Democratic Deprivation (TDD) in proffering an explanation for political apathy in Nigeria.

In the Political Alienation Theory of non-voting, Kirchgassner (2003) identifies the inconsequentiality of voters, lack of political accountability, and total disconnect from the proposed policies of political parties (alienation) could most likely contribute to abstention from voting by a prospective voter. This implies that abstention from voting is caused by alienation. Although this may be true, it does not limit the fact that alienated voters are more likely to vote, as Downs' Rational Choice Theory argues.

To connect these two viewpoints within the context of political apathy, especially voter turnout, Ebenezer (2017) espoused the theory of Democratic Deprivation. The theory argues that "when people are deprived of democratic dividends in a democratic dispensation due to lack of political accountability, they tend to react either negatively or positively to either establish a sense of dissatisfaction to such democratic system (regime) by distancing from participating in any activity or aggressively work towards changing such democratic dispensation for the better" (2017:647).

The deprivation can create outcomes that could be either positive or negative (Ebenezer, 2017; Nweke & Etido-Inyang, 2018). Positive Democratic Deprivation is "when the existing democratic dispensation or governance structure does not provide the desired dividend of democracy, is not accountable, cannot protect lives and property, lacks the provisions of sustainable development and does not improve on the standard of living of the people; the people (voters) react positively by democratically turning out en mass to vote out such government in a free, fair and credible election" (Ebenezer, 2017:647). He attributes this to Downs's (1957) postulation that the more alienated the voters are, the more probable they turn out to vote. Negative Democratic Deprivation, on the other hand, "arises when the existing democratic dispensation or governance structure does not provide the needed democratic dividends, is not accountable, cannot protect lives and property of the people, does not guarantee sustainable development and cannot better the living standard of the people; the people (voters) react by not wanting to be part of the electoral and political process which results in apathetic feelings towards political and electoral process, possibly with the assumption that their votes will not count and that they cannot change such government through the electoral process" (Ebenezer, 2017:648). He attributes this to Kirchgassner's (2003) argument that the more alienated the voters are, the less probable they turn out to vote in an election. The theory of Negative Democratic Deprivation (NDD) is due to the general frustration, lack of confidence in the credibility of the electoral process as well and the skepticism between the government and the governed, which breeds political apathy. This chapter, therefore, adopts the Theory of Democratic Deprivation to explain how political apathy is a challenge to the democratization process in Africa by using Nigeria's 2023 general elections as a case in point.

Historical Context of Voter Apathy in Nigeria

The historical context of Nigeria is indispensable in the understanding of political apathy. Nigeria is sandwiched between different regime types and has experienced political instability, including military coups and authoritarian rule (Suberu, 2009; Usman & Patrick, 2020). Political instability has long-lasting effects on political participation and civic engagement (Adewale & Musa, 2023). The issue of voters' apathy is not strange to the Nigerian political sphere as this can be traced since from the electoral principles in 1922. The first election in 1923 was limited to the provinces of Lagos and Calabar, excluding a significant portion of the population from participating. Only adult males who met income suffrage requirements were eligible to vote, leading to widespread alienation and apathy among Nigerians. The introduction of the policy of regionalism in 1946 further influenced the dynamics of voter apathy. Regional elections were held in 1955, with different suffrage conditions in different regions. While universal suffrage was prevalent in the southern regions, the northern region preferred male-adult suffrage. However, even in the regions with more inclusive suffrage, some conditions undermined enthusiasm for participation (Adigwe 1975). In the Eastern region, for example, voters were required to pay taxes or rates for specific periods and meet residency requirements. In the Northern region, only male taxpayers had the right to vote. While the indirect voting system was practised in the regional House of Assembly.

These stringent conditions of the franchise, the lack of standardization in electoral law and process, and the absence of proper election management mechanisms and organization contributed to the alienation of voters. Ethno-religious practices, such as the non-involvement of Muslim women in the political process, also played a role in limiting participation. However, there was a significant shift in voter turnout during the December 12, 1959, election, with a turnout of 79.5 per cent of registered voters. Several factors influenced this unprecedented participation. The euphoria surrounding the impending political independence of Nigeria in 1960 played a crucial role in motivating voter turnout. The election was seen as a crucial step towards achieving political freedom from colonial rule.

Additionally, the rise of ethnic-regional political parties like the Action Group in Western Nigeria, the National Council of Nigeria and Citizens in Eastern Nigeria, and the Northern People's Congress in the North mobilized their respective regional electorates for the historic election. The establishment of the Electoral Commission of Nigeria (ECN) further facilitated voter awareness and civic engagement. The ECN was responsible for enfranchising eligible voters, setting eligibility conditions for candidates, and organizing credible elections (Adewale & Musa, 2023).

The historical dynamics and pattern of voter apathy in Nigeria have been characterized by periods of high enthusiasm followed by disillusionment and decreasing voter turnout. The first national election in 1964 and the Western regional election in 1965 were marred by irregularities, boycotts, and violence, which led to a reversal of the growing trend of voter enthusiasm. These events resulted in thirteen years of authoritarian rule from 1966 to 1979 and entrenched a culture of voter distrust among the Nigerian electorate. In an attempt to reawaken optimism toward the democratic process, General Murtala/Obasanjo's regime introduced measures such as the creation of states, the Constitutional Drafting Committee, local government reform, and the lifting of the ban on partisan politics. These reforms aimed to foster democratic transition and included the adoption of a democracy model in the 1979 Constitution, which mirrored the U.S. presidential system. However, despite these efforts, the first Nigerian Presidential election in 1979 witnessed widespread voter apathy, with only a 35.25% voter turnout. Factors contributing to this apathy included the irregularities and violence of previous elections, the lingering effects of the Nigerian civil war, and concerns about the political elite as candidates (Idris, Shuaibu & Aliyu, 2023).

The four-year experiment with the American presidential system from 1979 to 1983 failed to meet the general expectations of national development as conceived by the Constitution and the general population. The ruling and opposition political parties became increasingly desperate to consolidate power, leading to violence and further apathy in the 1983 national elections. The military intervened again in December 1983, further dampening voter enthusiasm. However, the optimism of Nigerians towards elections was reignited by the democratic and constitutional reforms initiated by Gen. Ibrahim Babangida's regime from 1985 to 1993. Reforms such as the 1987 Political Bureau report, the promulgation of the 1989 constitution, and reformed election management increased a sense of patriotism and civic responsibility.

Table 1 reveals trends in voter participation in Nigerian electoral history before the fourth republic.

Table 1. Voter Participation from 1959 to 1993

Year	Population	Registered voters		Votes cast		
		Registered Voters	% of registered voters to the population	Total number of votes	% of votes cast on the registered voters	% of votes cast on the Population
1959	30,400,000	9,043,404	29.7	7,628,847	79.5	23.7
1964	55,600,000			5,761,483		10.4
1979	77,841,000	48,499,091	62.3	17,098,267	35.25	22
1983	89,022,000	65,304,818	73.4	25,430,096	54.0	28.6
1992	88,514,501	38,866,336	43.9	16,909,871	43.5	19.1
1993	88,514,501	39,000,000	44.1	14,293,396	36.6	16.1

Source: Adapted from Africa Elections, 2022.

Table 1 shows that the 1959 and 1964 general elections were characterized by the strong need to take control of the pre-independence preparations and the immediate post-independence power struggles (Idris *et al.*, 2023). However, the only fair elections in terms of voter turnout were in 1959, just before independence, and in 1979, just before the military temporarily withdrew. In addition, there was a lot of violence and fraud during the 1964 and 1983 federal elections. More interestingly, the outcome of the 1983 elections led to military involvement, which remained the sole practical, albeit unlawful, method of ousting unpopular governments (Campbell, 1994). Despite the subsequent annulment of the 1993 presidential election, voter turnout in the February 1999 presidential and National Assembly elections reached an impressive 52.3%, driven by the desire for democratic rule after years of authoritarianism. This is revealed in Table 2.

Table 2. Voter Participation in Presidential Elections from 1999 to 2023

Year	Population	Registered voters	Votes Cast	Valid	Invalid
1999	108,258,359	57,938,945	30,280,052 (52.3%)	29,848,441	431,611
2003	129,934,911	60,823,022	42,018,735 (69.1%)	39,480,489	2,538,249
2007	131,859,731	61,567,036	35,708,881 (58%)	35,397,517	
2011	155,215,573	73,528,040	39,469,484 (54%)	38,209,978	1,259,506
2015	181,562,056	67,422,005	29,432,083 (44%)	28,587,564	844,519
2019	208,679,114	84,004,084	28,614,190 (34.0%)	27,324,583	1,289,607
2023	230,842,743	93,522,272	24,965,218 (27%)	24,025,940	939,278

Source: Adapted from Institute for Democracy and Electoral Assistance, 2023

The 2003 presidential election marked the first democratic transition of power under a civilian government. Interestingly, voter turnout rose to 69.1% from the previous election in 1999 at 52.3%. However, the elections were marred by infractions, thuggery, and arson, contributing to a sense of voter distrust. Since then, voter turnout has kept nosediving. In the 2007 presidential election, it was 58%; in 2011, it was 54%; in 2015, it was 44%; in 2019, it was 34%; and the worst in the history of Nigeria was the 2023 presidential election which was 27%. The decline in voter turnout in a country bedevilled with a high unemployment rate, poverty, corruption, infrastructural decay, and violent conflicts in almost all the regions of the federation is dismaying. What, then, are the possible factors responsible for the regressive political participation?

Causes of Political Apathy

Political apathy has become a global problem, and it is a challenge to the democratization process in both developed and developing nations (Bukusi, 2022; Manoel *et al.*, 2022; Dupuy & Prakash, 2022). Globally, there are several factors responsible for political apathy, although these factors may vary from country to country. For example, in the United States, the weather during the election, registration requirements, the duration needed to ponder about one's voting decision, relative distance to the polling stations to residence, voting on a weekday, voting regulations and other logistical issues lowered voter turnout. (Wolfifinger & Rosenstone, 1980; Hill, 2009; Beregovskiy, 2019). In Africa, the situation is different. However, several empirical research studies have established the correlation between age, education, and access to the Internet and voter turnout (Snyder, 2011; Fowler, 2013; Tolbert & Mcneal, 2016; Alelaimat, 2019).

Seanego & Mogoboya's (2019) study with South Africa as a case study argued that the people's perceptions of government as not meeting or adding significant values to their lives spur apathy towards voting in any election. In a similar study in Zambia, Mutaka & Nkandu (2020) espoused that the failure to honour campaign promises coupled with failure to change leadership, electoral violence, age eligibility, religious beliefs, inadequate voting hours and lack or insufficient voters' literacy and education are accounted as factors for voter apathy. In the case of Ghana, Yeboah-Assiamah (nd) argued that since 1988, Ghana has decentralized to advance the democratic involvement of its citizens and improve service delivery, but after over three decades of its use, there is no recorded success in achieving the set goals on participation and voter turnout has been kept low as a result. In the case of Ghana, the structure for achieving democracy has been laid, but its failure has brought about political apathy experienced in Ghana.

Correspondingly, in Nigeria, Falade (2014), Amanyie, Bariledum & Lucky (2015) and Micheal (2018), studies all postulated a correlation between electoral violence and voter apathy. Their studies argued that political apathy is a by-product of electoral violence. This directly produces a negative impact on the electoral process and eventual outcome. For context's sake, electoral violence is any form of threat that arises from the electoral process. It includes but is not limited to, any form of action ranging from the forced displacement of a specific group of voters to the exchange and distribution of hate-speech leaflets, protests, riots, political assassinations, and targeted violent attacks (Burchard 2015; Okafor, Odigbo & Okeke, 2022). It could occur before, during and after elections. The political actors use thugs, and in some cases, they utilize security agencies to perpetuate violence. This negative occurrence and the attitude of the 'do or die' by politicians explained the rationale for the negative use of security agencies in the manipulation of the electoral process. For instance, the militarization of elections in Nigeria emboldens violence, which in itself leads to the loss of lives, intimidation of voters, and the manipulation of the system for the selfish ambition of a few elites.

In some cases, politicians use thugs to intimidate and truncate the people's consent. In buttressing this assertion about Nigeria, Okafor *et al.* (2022:94) argued that "Hoodlums and soldiers were seen disrupting the electioneering process in general elections." These politicians do this because they have failed in their campaign promises and, therefore, resort to violence to win votes. This situation has led to a lack of interest and an apathetic attitude of eligible voters to the democratic process (Onwuama, 2019; Odigbo & Okafor, 2019; Usman, 2023).

Buttressing further on electoral violence, Ijere (2015:31), cited in Usman (2023), copiously describes the nature of Nigerian politics when he states that "in Nigeria, a power struggle is fierce, divisive and militarized. Retaining power is more through neo-patrimonial networks, state capture, militarisation and coercion. The "Us" versus "Them" ideology, the kind of politics that have to broaden the fault lines." In justifying the picture painted above, Obasanjo (2002) states that "we fight and sometimes shed blood to achieve and attain political power because, for us in Nigeria, the political kingdom has for too long been the gateway to the economic kingdom" (2002:50-51). This implies that the electoral violence in Nigeria is precipitated by the politicians who fight to capture the state's power to amass wealth.

Furthermore, research has revealed that individuals with higher education levels and income tend to exhibit higher levels of political participation and voter turnout (Verba *et al.*, 1995). Conversely, socio-economic disparities, including low educational attainment and poverty, can contribute to lower voter turnout and increased apathy among certain segments of the population. Fawole (2018) observes that high levels of poverty and income inequality resulting in socioeconomic marginalization are responsible for Nigeria's political apathy. At the root of political apathy in Nigeria are the issues of illiteracy, poverty and purposeful deception by some politicians (Chukwudi, 2022). The general public is unable to draw a connection between their underdevelopment and their lack of engagement in the electoral and political process (Fabiyi, 2010). As a result, many starving and politically indifferent citizens sell their Permanent Voters Card (PVC) to desperate politicians who are determined to manipulate and commit electoral fraud for as low as ten thousand naira (₦10,000) (Agbo, 2011; Folade 2014). They sell their voter cards, believing their votes do not count in elections.

Akiyemi (2019) posits that bad governance is the major factor for political apathy. Buttressing this, Usman and Patrick (2020) posit that Nigeria has remained a laggard in social, economic, and political developments because of bad governance. 'The practice of politics and governance in Nigeria appears disappointing' (Okafor *et al.*, 2022:91). The prevalence of corruption and the perception that politicians prioritize personal gain over public welfare have eroded trust in political leaders and institutions (Omotola, 2010). On this basis, the people lost interest in the political and electoral process. Additionally, broken promises and unfulfilled expectations have contributed to voter apathy. When citizens witness a pattern of unfulfilled political promises and the persistence of socioeconomic challenges, they can become disenchanted and disengaged from the political process (Musa, 2014). These factors, among others, have led to a loss of faith and trust in the political system and its ability to bring about positive change in Nigeria.

Another fundamental factor responsible for political apathy, as identified by Akiyemi (2019), is the lack of trust in the Electoral Management Bodies. Ekanem & Okafor (2018) define Electoral Management Bodies as those bodies or agencies involved in administering elections. In Nigeria, the management bodies include the Independent National Electoral Commission (INEC), Security agencies, as well as tribunals (Okafor *et al.*, 2022). According to Ekanem & Okafor (2018), the problem is poor management demonstrated by a lack of independence, political attachment, corruption, ingrained Nigerian culture and inadequate capacity in the electoral institutions. Experience reveals that successive electoral commissions in the country have either been pro-ruling parties or manipulated election results in favour of the highest bidding contestants.

In some cases, there is the feared assumption that INEC officials probably collaborated with politicians to rig elections. The lack of integrity in the electoral process erodes public trust in the institutions responsible for organizing elections (Omotola, 2014). This gave the citizens the sense that their votes did not count and that going to the polling unit to vote was viewed as a waste of time.

Effects of Political Apathy in Nigeria

The implications of political apathy to the Nigerian polity are enormous. The numerous dangers that emanate from political apathy among electorates in Nigeria have remained a clog in the wheel of the country's democratic consolidation and political development. It is safe to argue that these effects cannot be extensively or exhaustively covered in a single piece. Odeyemi (2014:5) distinctly posits that the stake of politics is very high in society since it goes more than governmental organizations and operations of the state and its institutions, and it is also critical and determinative of people's fate or fortune in life. In his words, "Politics has a role in determining who survives, who dies, who is favoured or sidelined, and who is lauded or vilified." This implies that the effect of political apathy is that people are no longer interested in determining who survives, who dies, who is favoured or sidelined, and who is lauded or vilified. It is a precarious situation and a clear threat to democracy once citizens refuse or decide to dissociate from political activities in their state or country. The attitude will end up bringing in mediocrity as leaders of the people (Chukwudi, 2022). We will attempt to summarize some of the major effects of political apathy in Nigeria.

1. Implication for democratic process and structure: It is an irrefutable fact that the growth and development of the democratic process depend extensively on the active participation of the citizenry. Since democracy is a game of numbers, subject to the creation of government by and for the people (Usman & Patrick 2020), any attempt or factor that dissuades such participation directly impacts democracy. In essence, the decline in the active participation of people in the democratic process would lead to the creation of 'reduced legitimacy' for elected officials. This can also impact the

government's responsibility for accountability and checks and balances as the structure to provide such checks is either eroded or non-existent due to the non-participation of people in the governance process.

2. Inadequate representation and voters' turnout: One obvious effect of political apathy is its lopsided impact on adequate government representation. As more and more people become disinterested or disillusioned with and about political processes, the implication on voters' turnout and eventual representation is always negative. The implication of political apathy would naturally imply that more and more people become unconcerned with the governance process, leading to a continuous decline in voter turnout (Nuka *et al.*, 2015). Political apathy not only led to a continuous decline in voter turnout but also led to lopsided misrepresentation in terms of demography and interest. This misrepresentation implies the disempowerment of a significant proportion of the citizenry in the state's political process.
3. Implication for social cohesion: A society's socio-political and economic prosperity and growth are enhanced by the level of social cohesion enjoyed by the arrears of diverse ethnic and social groups (Patrick, 2020). Nigeria's socio-ethnic configuration makes social cohesion a crucial ingredient for peace and development. Given this, one can argue that political apathy would contribute to the disconnection of citizens from the state's political activities, weakening the sense of community and comradeship that active participation would have fostered for the polity.
4. The propensity for authoritarianism: The continuous seat-tight syndrome of post-independence African leaders and the recent sway of military junta experience across Africa (in Mali, South Sudan, Burkina Faso, Chad, and more recently, Niger Republic) embodies the implication of political apathy in Africa. The propensity for an authoritarian government's rise is more pronounced when there is a conscious absence of citizen participation in polity. This is brought to be by the lack of government accountability to the governed as espoused by the rule of law, which has been a fundamental aspect of the democratic process (Folade 2014).
5. The proliferation of fake news and misinformation: The rise in populism and left-wing movements has become a global political reality. The implication of political apathy in this sense is the reinforcement of these movements and the proliferation of misinformation among the citizenries. The continuous apathy of the people as a result of mere laziness to source factual information or a general disinterest in the affairs of the state may provide a viable breeding ground and opportunity for mischievous individuals to propagate fake news and misinformation capable of creating greater risk to the state and governance process in general.
6. Implication on leadership configuration and national identity: A direct implication of political apathy is the propensity of incompetent leaders to emerge from the electioneering process (Chukwudi, 2022). This would result from little resistance or lack of checks necessary to vet the competency of leaders before their emergence. Since democracy is a summary of a people's government created for and by the people, the absence of the people in creating such a government may imply that those left to handle the affairs of the state may be unlearned of the same society. The propensity of the emergence and rulership of such incompetent leaders would result from political apathy in creating and monitoring governance structures and processes.

DIRECTION FOR FUTURE RESEARCH

It is an irrefutable fact that the engine room for democracy is developed on the foundation of people's participation. This chapter is an attempt to diagnose the problem of passive democratic participation prevalent in the African polity. By this, future research would be the investigation of active parameters needed in terms of policy and practice in ensuring and motivating active political engagement for sustainable growth and development of democracy and governance in Africa as a whole. Also, an exploration of the correlation between voting patterns, participation of youth and their demographic and parental affiliation, as well as what motivates the younger generation to be involved or become apathetic toward politics, is worthwhile future research.

CONCLUSION

The implication of popular and active participation in democratization cannot be relegated in terms of importance. For Nigeria and Africa, this is crucial for the emergence of good governance and the development of democratic processes and governance. This chapter explored political participation in Nigeria and the issues of political apathy as a Challenge of the Democratization Process. Using a desktop review technique, we explored the causes of political apathy and its possible effect on Nigeria's democratization process as a template for Africa. While the factors and impacts identified in this chapter for political apathy in Nigeria are not exhaustive, the implication for the democratization process is significant. Therefore, there is a need for all stakeholders, government, and citizens alike to embrace proactive measures in curtailing political apathy in Nigeria and, by inference, Africa's democratization process. By effect, while civic education is crucial, an inclusive and conducive political atmosphere must be created to steer the participation of citizens in public affairs. Also, transparency and accountability in governance, as well as the promotion of inclusive and participatory democracy, must be encouraged as standard norms at all levels of society.

REFERENCES

Adekoya, R. (2019). Democracy has failed in Nigeria when voters no longer care who wins. https://www.theguardian.com/commentisfree/2019/mar/01/democracy-failed-nigeria-turnout presidential-election

Adewale, F. B., & Musa, Z. A. (2023), 'Voter Apathy and its Implication for Democratic Consolidation in Nigeria' Being text of a chapter presented at the third International Conference of the Department of Political Science and International Studies, Ahmadu Bello University, Zaria on "Beyond Sustainable Elections: Interrogating the Challenges of Leadership and Governance in Nigeria." July 9th – 12th, 2023.

Akiyemi, S. (2019). *Voter apathy: a threat to democracy in Nigeria*. Retrieved from: http://democracy-inafrica.org/voter-apathy-threat-democracy-nigeria/

Alelaimat, M.S (2019). Factors affecting political participation (Jordanian universities students' voting: Field study 2017-2018). *Review of Economics and Political Science*. . doi:10.1108/REPS-05-2019-0072

Aloysius, I. S., Edeh, E. C., Emma, A. O., Onwe, O. S., & Ernest, E. N. (2019). Voting apathy among the Nigerian electorates in 2019 general elections: The role of INEC, issues and the way forward. *International Journal of Business and Management Invention*, *8*(12), 64–74.

Amanyie, N. S., Bariledum, K., & Lucky, N. B. (2015). Electoral violence and political apathy in Nigeria: Issues and challenges. *British Journal of Humanities and Social Sciences*, *13*(1), 155–173.

Andriani, L., & Escudero Loaiza, M. M. (2021). Institutional trust and corruption: Evidence from Latin America. *Revista Debates*, *15*(1), 247–274. doi:10.22456/1982-5269.112643

Beregovskiy, A. (2019). *Effect of the two-party system on voter turnout in the United States of America* [Master of Arts Thesis]. The Johns Hopkins University.

Blais. (2000). *To Vote or Not to Vote – The merits and limits of rational choice theory*. University of Pittsburgh Press.

Bukusi, A. D. (2022). Why you must vote in an African democracy. *American Journal of Leadership and Governance*, *7*(1), 19–28. doi:10.47672/ajlg.942

Campbell, I. (1994). Nigeria's Failed Transition: The 1993 Presidential Election. *Journal of Contemporary African Studies*, *12*(2), 179–199. doi:10.1080/02589009408729556

Chukwudi, C. E. (2022). Governance Factor and Effects of Political Apathy in Nigerian Political Culture: A Prognostic Analysis. *Socialscientia: Journal of Social Sciences and Humanities, 7*(4).

Diamond, L. (2015). Facing up to the democratic recession. *Journal of Democracy*, *26*(1), 41–55. doi:10.1353/jod.2015.0009

Dobbs, K. L. (2021). Active on the street but apathetic at the ballot box? Explaining youth voter behavior in Tunisia's new democracy. *British Journal of Middle Eastern Studies*. Advance online publication. doi:10.1080/13530194.2021.1962243

Downs, A. (1957). *An economic theory of democracy*. Harper and Row.

Dupuy, K., & Prakash, A. (2022). Why restrictive NGO foreign funding laws reduce voter turnout in Africa's national elections. *Nonprofit and Voluntary Sector Quarterly*, *51*(1), 170–189. doi:10.1177/0899764019897848

Ebenezer, L. (2017). Political accountability and voter turnout in Nigeria's elections (1999-2016). *Quarterly Journal of Contemporary Research*, *5*(2), 135–146.

Ebenezer, L. (2017). Trend analysis of voter turnout in Nigeria's elections (1999-2016) [Nigeria Edition]. *African Social and Educational Journal*, *6*(2), 198–209.

Ebenezer, L. (2018). *Political accountability and voter turnout in Nigeria's elections (1999-2015)* [PhD thesis]. University of Port Harcourt.

Emerson, R. W. (2015). Convenience sampling, random sampling, and snowball sampling: How does sampling affect the validity of research? *Journal of Visual Impairment & Blindness*, *109*(2), 164–168. doi:10.1177/0145482X1510900215

Fabiyi, O. (2009). Apathy of Nigerian Voters Worrisome- Iwu. In Falade, D. A Political Participation in Nigerian Democracy: A Study of Some Selected Local Government Areas in Ondo State, Nigeria. *Global Journal of Human-Social Science: F. Political Science (Wellington, N.Z.), 14*(8), 16–23.

Fagunwa, T. (2015). *Voter apathy and Nigeria's electioneering process: a synopsis on 2015 general elections*. Academic Press.

Falade, D. A. (2014). Political participation in Nigerian democracy: A study of some selected local government areas in Ondo State, Nigeria. *Global Journal of Human & Social Science: f Political Science, 14*(8), 17–23.

Fawole, O. I. (2018). The Role of Poverty and Income Inequality in Voter Apathy: Evidence from Sub-Saharan Africa. *Journal of African Elections, 17*(1), 109–126.

Feddersen, T. J., & Pesendorfer, W. (1996). The Swing Voter's Curse. *The American Economic Review, 86*(3), 408–424.

Feddersen, T. J., & Pesendorfer, W. (1999). Abstention in Elections with Asymmetric Information and Diverse Preferences. *The American Political Science Review, 93*(2), 381–398. doi:10.2307/2585402

Fowler, A. G. (2013). *Five Studies on the Causes and Consequences of Voter Turnout* [Doctoral dissertation]. Harvard University.

Gberevbie, D. E. (2014). Democracy, democratic institutions and good governance in Nigeria. *Eastern Africa Social Science Research Review, 30*(1), 133–152. doi:10.1353/eas.2014.0005

Geys, B. (2006). National theory of voter turnout: A review. *Political Studies Review, 4*(1), 16–35. doi:10.1111/j.1478-9299.2006.00034.x

Hill, D. (2009). *American Voter Turnout: An Institutional Perspective (Transforming American Politics)*. Routledge: Westview Press.

Idris, S., Shuaibu, M., & Aliyu, Y. (2023). *Voter Dissatisfaction, Leaders' Performance Evaluation, and Voters Turnout in Nigeria's Fourth Republic*. Paper presented at the third International Conference of the Department of Political Science and International Studies, Ahmadu Bello University, Zaria on "Beyond Sustainable Elections: Interrogating the Challenges of Leadership and Governance in Nigeria." July 9th – 12th, 2023.

INEC. (2023). *Voters Turnout in 2023 Presidential Election*. Retrieved June 23, 2023, from www.inec.org

INEC & FES. (2011). *Voter apathy and the 2011 elections in Nigeria: a research report*. INEC & FES Publication.

International IDEA. (2016). *Voter Turnout Trends around the World*. International IDEA.

International IDEA. (2020). *Voter Turnout since 1990 in Africa: A Global Report*. International IDEA.

Kirchgassner, G. (2003). *Abstention because indifference and alienation and its consequences for party competition: a simple psychological model*. University of Gallen: Economics Discussion paper 12.

Madu, A. Y., & Abdulmalik, T. A. (2020). *An assessment of factors responsible for voter apathy in Africa: Empirical evidence from 2019 Nigerian presidential election.* The International Seminar on Regional Politics, Administration and Development 2020 (INSORPAD2020), STISIPOL Raja Haji, Riau, INDONESIA, 14-15.

Manoel, L., Costa, A. C., & Cabral, P. (2022). Voter turnout in Portugal: A geographical perspective. *Papers in Applied Geography*, *8*(1), 88–111. doi:10.1080/23754931.2021.1958251

Mataka, B., & Nkandu, M. O. (2020). The effects of voter apathy on the growth of electoral democracy in Zambia with a special focus on Kabwe central constituency. *Global Journal of Advanced Research*, *7*(3), 81–87.

Micheal, O. E. (2018). Politics and governance: A critique of the 2019 Nigeria presidential election. *International Journal of Academic Research in Public Policy and Governance*, *5*(1), 50–70.

Moliki, A. O., & Dauda, K. O. (2014). Political apathy, electoral process and Nigeria's democracy: A study of the 2014 Ekiti governorship election. TASUED. *Journal of Applied Education and Vocational Research*, *12*(1).

Morrow, S. (2015*). Causes of low voter turnout of the Hispanic Population in South-West Texas* [Doctoral dissertation]. Walden University.

Musa, A. A. (2014). Political parties and democratic consolidation in Nigeria. In *Democracy and Development in Nigeria*. Palgrave Macmillan.

Obiagu, U. C., Udeji-Okpalaku, C. O., & Udeh, C. O. (2021). The Undermining Consequences of Inconclusive Elections on Democratic Consolidation in Africa: Interrogating Nigerian Elections, 2011-2019. *African Journal of Democracy and Election Research*, *1*(2), 7–40.

Odigbo, J., & Okafor, C. O. (2019). State militarization of election and management of electoral process in Nigeria's 2019 general elections. *Kwararafa Journal of Contemporary Research*, *7*(1), 69–83.

Okafor, O. C., Odigbo, J., & Okeke, C. R. (2022). Two Decades of Electoral Democracy: Voter Apathy and Democratization Process in Nigeria. Social Sciences and Education Research Review, 9(1).

Oluwagbohunmi, M. F. (2020). Political Apathy: A Worrisome Impediment to Electoral Process in Nigeria. International Institute for Science, Technology and Education, 4(4).

Omotola, J. S. (2010). Political liberalization and democratization in Africa: Theoretical perspectives and methodological approaches. In *The Democratization Project in Africa*, Accomplishments, Challenges, and Prospects. Palgrave Macmillan.

Omotola, J. S. (2014). Governance and corruption in Nigeria: The way forward. In *Good Governance and Development in Nigeria*. Palgrave Macmillan.

Patrick, H. O. (2020). Winning hearts and minds; fostering inclusiveness through community development tactics in South Africa. In P. Kariuki, M. Goyayi, & S. Mhlongo (Eds.), *Social Cohesion in the Last Decade: Taking Stock to Inform the New Decade* (pp. 119–161). Democracy Development Program. Atlas Printers.

Seanego, M. J., & Mogoboya, M. J. (2019). *Factors contributing to the decline of votes in South Africa: A case study of Mankweng community.* The 4th Annual International Conference on Public Administration and Development Alternatives 03 - 05 July 2019.

Sharma, G. (2017). Pros and cons of different sampling techniques. *International Journal of Applied Research, 3*(7), 749–752.

Snyder, R. E. (2011). The impact of age, education, political knowledge and political context on voter turnout. *UNLV Theses, Dissertations, Professional Papers, and Capstones.* https://digitalscholarship.unlv.edu/thesesdissertations/1400

Suberu, R. T. (2009). *Federalism and ethnic conflict in Nigeria.* United States Institute of Peace Press.

Tolbert, C. J., & Mcneal, R. S. (2016). Unraveling the effects of the Internet on political participation. *Political Research Quarterly, 56*(2), 175–185. doi:10.1177/106591290305600206

Usman, H. (2023). *The Nexus between Democracy and Conflict in Nigeria's Fourth Republic.* Paper presented at the third International Conference of the Department of Political Science and International Studies, Ahmadu Bello University, Zaria on "Beyond Sustainable Elections: Interrogating the Challenges of Leadership and Governance in Nigeria." July 9th – 12th, 2023.

Usman, H., & Patrick, H. O. (2020). Democracy, Good Governance, And Development in Nigeria: Familiar but Strange Bedfellows. In *Reinvigorating Nigerian Universities for Sustainable Development* (pp. 470–499). Ajayi Crowder University Press.

Verba, S., Schlozman, K. L., Brady, H. E., & Nie, N. H. (1995). Citizen activity: Who participates? What do they say? *The American Political Science Review, 89*(3), 271–294.

Webb, J. A., Miller, K. A., Stewardson, M. J., de Little, S. C., Nichols, S. J., & Wealands, S. R. (2015). An online database and desktop assessment software to simplify systematic reviews in environmental science. *Environmental Modelling & Software, 64*, 72–79. doi:10.1016/j.envsoft.2014.11.011

Wolfifinger, R. E., & Rosenstone, J. S. (1980). *Who Votes?* Yale University Press.

Yakubu, Y. A. (2012). Democracy and Political Apathy in Nigeria (1999-2011). *European Scientific Journal, 8*(20), 38–48.

Yeboah-Assiamah, E. (n.d.). *Low Voter Turnout and Poor Participation in District Level Elections in Ghana: Towards a new Explanation.* https://www.academia.edu/8922082/Low_Voter_Turnout_and_Poor_Partictipation_in_District_Level_Elections_in_Ghana_Towards_a_new _Explanation

ENDNOTE

1 "Japa" is a popular buzzword in the 'everyday' Nigerian lingual used to commonly refer an escapism attempt by any means necessary to leave the supposed economic and social hardship experienced by Nigerians in Nigeria. The 'japa' syndrome in essence is therefore the popular drive by many a Nigerian to leave the country for better economic life outside Nigeria as economic migrants masqueraded in several other migrant typologies.

Chapter 10
Tunisia's Struggle for Democratic Consolidation:
Obstacles, Opportunities, and Political Culture Post Arab Spring

Akash Bag
https://orcid.org/0000-0001-8820-171X
Adamas University, India

Souvik Roy
Adamas University, India

Ashutosh Pandey
Adamas University, India

ABSTRACT

The Arab Spring, the wave of protests that swept over the Middle East and North Africa in 2011, failed to impose democracy there. However, only in Tunisia did the Arab Spring result in a democratic change in 2011. Tunisia has been dealing with several difficulties since the country's democratic transition, including political unrest and terrorist assaults. This study looks at Tunisia's political growth between 2011 and 2022 to determine the chances and challenges for the country to consolidate its democracy. Using a case study approach and Samuel P. Huntington's theory of democratic consolidation, the study has identified two barriers to democratic consolidation: the democratic government's inability to deliver economic reforms and the political elite's unwillingness to work together to find solutions. Since the political elite has used Tunisia's economic woes to gain undemocratically more power, the study also explains the failure of democratic consolidation with the absence of the formation of a democratic political culture in the nation.

DOI: 10.4018/979-8-3693-0477-8.ch010

INTRODUCTION

The Middle East and North Africa are regions where democracy has generally had difficulty gaining a foothold (Cavatorta, 2018, pp. 364–365). While the third wave of Democratization swept Eastern Europe and Latin America, the Middle East and North African countries remained undemocratic. Although some democratic features have been introduced in some countries in the Middle East and North Africa, it has not threatened the authoritarian regimes in the regions (El-Husseini, 2015). Political scientists have long described the Middle East and North Africa as authoritarian and anti-democratic regions, while questions about why the regions have been slow to start their democratization processes have arisen (El-Husseini, 2015). However, something happened in 2011 that surprised most academics specializing in Middle Eastern politics, namely when popular demonstrations demanding democracy and social reforms spread in several Middle Eastern countries and resulted in the resignation of several dictators (Gause, 2011). The protests were named the Arab Spring and gave hope that the region would begin its democratization process (Cavatorta, 2018, pp. 364–365).

Despite the hope for Democratization in the Middle East associated with the Arab Spring, it did not democratize the region. Only in Tunisia, where the Arab Spring began, did the protests lead to the establishment of a liberal democracy, highlighted as particularly successful and unique in the region (Cavatorta, 2018, pp. 364–365). The popular uprising in Tunsis was named the Jasmine Revolution and symbolized democratic change in the Middle East and North Africa (El-Khawas, 2012). Despite the successful transition to democracy, the political situation in Tunisia after the Jasmine Revolution has been characterized by high polarization in the country, outbreaks of terrorist attacks, and political instability. In addition, the inefficient state apparatus and the centralized bureaucracy have hindered the stabilization of democracy (Trisnaningtyas, 2022). Thus, Tunisian democracy has been described by researchers as fragile and threatened by authoritarian tendencies (Günay & Sommavilla, 2019).

Democracy in Tunsisen received a new and serious challenge in July 2021 due to a series of decisions introduced by the President, which he called emergency measures. The President dissolved Parliament and dismissed the prime minister, which plunged the country into a political crisis (Nassif, 2022). Several scholars have likened the President's introduction of these decisions to a coup d'état, as these decisions were undemocratic and unconstitutional. (Nassif, 2022). The President's actions in 2021 have negatively affected the consolidation of democracy in Tunisia, and the country has had to drop in ranking as free 71/100 in 2021 to partially free 64/100 in 2022 in the Freedom House democracy survey (Freedom House, 2022). Political developments in Tunisia since 2021 raise questions about the consolidation of democracy in Tunisia after a decade of transition to democracy. Has the consolidation of democracy in Tunisia failed? And if so, why? What are the prospects for democracy and its consolidation in Tunisia? These questions, as well as the difference between the promising development towards democracy in 2011 and the recent political developments in Tunisia, arouse the interest to investigate and analyze the political developments after 2011 to find out and understand what obstacles and opportunities exist to consolidate democracy in Tunisia.

The purpose of the chapter is to study the political development in Tunisia in the period 2011-2022 to investigate and analyze obstacles and opportunities for the consolidation of democracy in Tunisia after the transition to democracy in 2011. To fulfil the purpose of the study, the following questions are asked:

1) What explains the lack of consolidation of democracy in Tunisia?
2) What are the obstacles to the consolidation of democracy in Tunisia?
3) What are the conditions for the consolidation of democracy in Tunisia?

BACKGROUND

Concept Overview

During this section, the concepts of democracy, Democratization, and consolidation will be presented and clarified. The purpose of doing so is that these concepts are often used in the literature, which means that the concepts are ambiguous, and there are also different opinions in research about what democracy and Democratization mean (Grugel & Bishop, 2013, p. 5).

Democracy

The concepts of democracy and Democratization are central in political science, but despite that, the two concepts are contested and used in different ways in the literature (Miller et al., 2012). It is impossible to study Democratization without studying democracy because democrats are often the starting point for studies of Democratization. Sometimes, the concept of democracy is taken for granted and is not discussed in depth. However, it is important to define and clarify the concept of democracy because the definition of democracy determines when the transition to democracy is considered complete and which system is to be consolidated (Miller et al., 2012). Within democratization research, researchers have developed two definitions of democracy, namely the minimal democracy definition and the maximal democracy. Within the minimal definition of democracy, democracy is defined as a procedural system built on free and fair elections, and within the minimal definition, democracy has been associated with electoral democracy.

The researcher Joseph Schumpeter is a prominent name among the advocates of a minimal definition of democracy (Erdmann, 2011). He has argued that a democratic form of governance exists in societies where the institutional structures force those who seek to gain the power to compete for the people's votes openly and that people's rights to express themselves and choose for themselves are protected. Joseph Schumpeter views democracy as a political struggle between elites and that the free, fair, and regular elections are intended to serve as a way for the people to keep the elites under control. Therefore, fair, free, and regular elections are essential for a functioning democracy (Knappe, 2017). Other leading political science researchers, such as Samuel P. Huntington and Seymour Martin Lipset, have also used the minimal definition. The minimal definition of democracy has been criticized by other political scientists, including David Bethman, who criticizes that democracy is equated with free and fair elections (Erdmann, 2011). He believes it is wrong to equate democracy as a system with democracy as an end. He believes that in this way, democracy as a system acquires a value in itself without considering the values or social norms that democracy intends to fulfil.

The maximum definition of democracy includes the whole of society. Democracy is only achieved when all relationships and spheres are democratic in society. This applies to political, economic, and social issues. The maximum definition of democracy emphasizes that fair and free elections are only the foundation of a democratic society, which a range of other fundamental freedoms and democratic rights should follow. The maximum democracy definition is associated with liberal democracy. The political scientist Robert Dahl is a vocal proponent of the maximum perspective in democracy definition. Robert Dahl presents seven democracy criteria that characterize a democratic system.

1. Elected representatives.
2. Free and fair elections.
3. Universal and equal suffrage.
4. The right to stand for election.
5. Freedom of expression
6. Access to alternative information.
7. Free organizations.

Dahl claims that in empirical reality, no state fulfils the ideal of democracy. Instead, Dahl developed the concept of Polyarchy, which refers to the closest a country can get to full democracy. Polyarchy is not an ideal but a definable type of society. Not all of the seven criteria presented by Dahls need to be met in a country for it to be considered democratic. Thus, one country can be more or less democratic than another.

Democratization

The research in Democratization is vast, and scholars have researched it for many decades. Since the time of Aristotle, scientists have tried to answer questions such as why some states are democracies while others are not. And why do some democracies tend to survive while others fail to do so? (Coppedge, 2012, p. 1). Although Democratization is one of the most important trends in the world, it is often misunderstood as a process of political change and questioned both in theory and practice. Namely, there are different opinions about the character and nature of democracy and Democratization (Grugel & Bishop, 2013, p. 5). The political scientist Samuel P Huntington argues that Democratization occurs in waves and defines it in his book The Third Wave: Democratization in the Late Twentieth Century (1991) as a group of transitions from non-democratic to democratic regimes that occur in specific periods that are significantly more than transitions in the opposite direction during the specific period. Huntington adds that a wave of Democratization often involves liberalization or partial Democratization in political systems that do not become fully democratic (Huntington, 1991, p.15).

According to Huntington (1991), the modern world has witnessed three waves of Democratization affecting a relatively small number of countries. Furthermore, Huntington argues that each of the first two waves of Democratization was followed by a reverse wave in which some but not all countries that had previously transitioned to democracy reverted to undemocratic rule (Huntington, 1991, p.15-16). Lauri Karvonen (1997) describes Democratization as a process that moves society or the state toward democracy. He likens Democratization to a path toward the goal, which is democracy. The researchers Jean Grugel & Matthew Louis Bishop (2014) argue in the book Democratization: A Critical Introduction that Democratization is often presented in limited terms where it is introduced as steps in a linear path towards liberal Western democracy where the process ends with adopting a market economy, building liberal democratic institutions and a strong independent civil society with a free press (Grugel & Bishop 2013, p. 10). Jean Gurgel & Matthew Louis Bishop (2014) believe that this definition of Democratization misses broad philosophical questions about the meaning of democracy and Democratization (Grugel &

Bishop 2013, p. 10). Therefore, Jean Gurgel & Matthew Louis Bishop (2014) argue for a more critical approach to democratization and present democratization as a non-linear, long-term, and inevitably partial process where democracy can always be improved and developed. That approach does not see democracy and Democratization as value-neutral, but it considers many forms of democracy, including the Western one (Grugel & Bishop 2013, p. 10).

Consolidation

Consolidated democracy is a term often used in democracy studies. When the concept is used often, it can become ambiguous (Erdmann, 2011). Therefore, it is important to present and clarify what the concept of consolidated democracy means. A consolidated democracy is perceived as the desirable end goal of the democratization process. Within the political science literature, several aspects have been raised regarding the issue of consolidated democracy. These aspects address the system's legitimacy, the longevity of the democratic institutions, and the lack of major structural changes; however, scholars do not agree on how consolidated democracy should be characterized (Erdmann, 2011). Juan Linz and Alfred Stepan develop a definition of a consolidated democracy that includes behavioural, attitudinal, and constitutional dimensions. They identify a consolidated democracy as a political regime where democracy is a complex system of institutions, rules, and patterned incentives, and disincentive incentives have become "the only game in town" (Linz & Stepan, 1996).

Behaviorally, democracy is consolidated when no significant national, social, economic, political, or institutional actors spend significant resources trying to overthrow the democratic system and create an undemocratic regime (Linz & Stepan, 1996). Attitudinally, democracy is consolidated when most of the population, even amid deep economic crises and deep dissatisfaction with the existing rulers, believes that democratic procedures and institutions are the most appropriate ways to govern collective life. Constitutionally, a democratic regime becomes consolidated when state and non-state forces become accustomed to resolving conflicts within democratic institutions, procedures, and laws (Linz & Stepan, 1996). When the three dimensions are combined, democracy is consolidated so that it has widespread legitimacy and support among all actors in society, and that support is so entrenched that the democratic system appears as a matter of course. So, democracy has gained value in itself (Linz & Stepan, 1996).

Larry Diamond emphasizes that consolidation is a process of achieving a widespread and profound level of legitimation in society so that all significant political actors at both elite and mass levels believe that democracy is better for society than any other real alternative that they can imagine (Diamond, 1996), Samuel P Huntington argues in his book The Third wave: Democratization in the Twentieth century (1991) that the essential aspect of a democracy is that the people should be able to choose their regents in regular, free and fair elections. Consequently, a criterion of the consolidation of democracy should be the extent to which political elites and the public are convinced that their regents should be elected in this way. It means an attitude test on the development of democratic political culture. The second criterion is the extent to which political elites and the public select regents through elections. It involves a behavioural test of the Institutionalization of democratic practice in a country's political system (Huntington, 1991, pp. 257-258). According to Samuel P Huntington (1991), consolidated democracy in a country develops a democratic political culture when democratic political behaviour has been institutionalized (Huntington 1991, pp. 257-258).

Democracy in the Middle East

Researchers in political science have long pondered why democracy has failed to take hold in the Middle East and North Africa, and they have come up with various explanations. Some researchers have explained this phenomenon with the region's lack of a strong civil society and high illiteracy. On the other hand, some researchers point to the neighbourhood effect and highlight the peripheral location of the Middle East as the epicentre of democracy in the West (El-Husseini, 2015). A further explanation raised by the researchers is that in the Middle East and North Africa, there is an efficient and highly repressive state apparatus with the will and the capacity to inhibit any attempt at Democratization (Bellin, 2004). Some researchers have raised a cultural explanation for the phenomenon and claimed that Islam itself as a religion is incompatible with democracy and that Islam's influence on the political culture is the cause of the authoritarian features of the region's politics (El-Husseini, 2015). However, some scholars dismiss the argument that Islam is incompatible with democracy and emphasize that the democratic deficit in the Middle East should be explained by political factors rather than by Islam (Cevik, 2011). Examples of political factors that can explain the Middle East's democracy deficit are the rentier state model in oil-rich countries that do not need legitimacy from their citizens. In addition, there is a tight government grip on the economy in non-oil-rich countries and the lack of international support for democratic forces in the region due to the fear that it will develop into an Islamist political system (Cevik, 2011).

The outbreak of the Arab Spring in 2011 with demands for democracy showed that the popular will for democracy and freedom is high in a region considered immune to Democratization (El-Husseini, 2015). Researchers have pointed out some factors to the outbreak of the Arab Spring, for example, lack of legitimacy for states, poor economic development, and the role of social media and young people (Saidin, 2018). However, despite its extensive scope, the Arab Spring has failed to democratize the Middle East. Several factors have been pointed out regarding why the Arab Spring has failed to democratize the region. Researchers have argued that Arab countries are still underdeveloped to maintain democratic systems, while there are relatively low literacy rates and literacy levels compared to other countries in the world as well as the absence of tolerance in the political culture of Arab countries (Masoud, 2015). An exception to this pattern was Tunisia which, after all, could transition from an authoritarian rule to democracy after the Arab Spring (Masoud, 2018). The unique democratic transition that took place in Tunisia has led scholars to ask the question of why Tunisia succeeded in transitioning to democracy while other countries in the Middle East failed. There are various explanations for Tunisia's unique transition towards democracy in the Middle East. For example, the research points out that Tunisia's Democratization was inevitable due to the country's relatively large middle class and proximity to Europe and Tunisia's relatively liberal culture (Masoud, 2018). In addition, other factors are highlighted, such as a politically neutral and narrow army and the lack of deep ethnopolitical divisions in the country (Rivera-Escartin, 2022).

THEORETICAL UNDERPINNINGS

The study's theoretical framework is based on Samuel P Huntington's (1991) definition of a consolidated democracy, which he presents in his book The Third Wave of Democratization in the late twentieth century (1991). The choice of Samuel P Huntington's criteria for a consolidated democracy is justified because he starts from a minimalist perspective that highlights basic but essential criteria for democracy

(Huntington, 1991). Without these criteria, a form of government can hardly be seen as a democracy. Furthermore, for analytical reasons, the minimal perspective is a more useful and applicable analytical instrument than the maximal perspective. A further justification is that using a definition of a consolidated democracy based on the minimalist perspective is more appropriate in the Tunisian case because democracy in Tunisia is new and young democracy in a region that has rarely had any democratic states, which makes it difficult to set ideal and more normative demands from the maximum democracy perspective on democracy in Tunisia. In that way, Huntington's criteria for a consolidated democracy built on the minimalist perspective enable the analysis to capture genuine opportunities and obstacles for democracy and its consolidation in Tunisia (Huntington, 1991).

Huntington constructed two criteria that characterize a consolidated democracy. According to Huntington, the first is the development of democratic political culture, and the second is the Institutionalization of democratic political behaviour. When these two criteria are met, democracy is considered consolidated (Huntington 1991, pp. 257-258). The first criterion (development of democratic political culture) constitutes an attitudinal test for democratic culture within the country, and the second criterion (Institutionalization of democratic political behaviour) constitutes a behavioural test of democratic practice in the country's politics (Huntington 1991, pp. 257-258).

The Development of Democratic Political Culture

The development of democratic political culture focuses on the relationship between the effectiveness/performance and legitimacy of the governments of the new democracies. Thus, the degree to which political elites and the public believe in the value of a democratic system. Democratic governments that are ineffective in performance have low legitimacy, and democratic governments that have low legitimacy cannot be effective in their work (Huntington 1991, p. 258). Huntington argues that the legitimacy of democratic governments rests both on performance and effectiveness in solving difficult economic problems and on the processes and procedures underpinning their formation. That new democracies fail to solve difficult economic problems does not automatically mean they will collapse (Huntington 1991, p. 258). Huntington believes that the stability of democratic regimes rests, first, on the ability of the political elite (party leaders) and military leaders, as well as the economic elite, to work together to solve the problems facing their society and refrain from exploiting these problems for their own material or political advantage. The second on which the stability of democratic regimes rests is the public's ability to distinguish between support for democracy as a political regime and support for the performance of democratic governments (Huntington 1991, p. 260).

Institutionalization of Democratic Political Behavior

Samuel Huntington argued that the disenchantment problem common to New Democrats manifested itself behaviorally in four ways. Firstly, through cynicism, subservience, and withdrawal from politics. Second, voters voted for other options through a backlash against existing politicians who tried to be transformed. Third, this disappointment was sometimes expressed through an anti-establishment reaction against the entire political establishment, and voters tend to choose political alternatives outside the prevailing establishment (Huntington 1991, p. 265-266). Finally, a more extreme backlash against the entire democratic system by disaffected political figures, parties, and military leaders against the entire democratic system (Huntington 1991, p. 268).

Huntington notes that anti-establishment backlash and backlash against incumbent politicians and political parties are traditional democratic responses to failed politics. Huntington argues that democracy is consolidated to the level that these traditional democratic responses are institutionalized (Huntington 1991, p. 265-266). Huntington develops a criterion to measure this consolidation. Huntington calls the criterion the two-turnover test, and it is based on whether the party or group that takes power in the first election during the transition period to democracy loses in later elections and leaves power to those who won the election. In addition, those who won this election must peacefully leave power to those who win in later elections (Huntington 1991, p. 266-267). Huntington states that the first democratic transfer of power is of symbolic importance and that democracy is based on the willingness of those in power to relinquish power due to elections. The second transfer of power shows two important aspects. The first aspect is that many political leaders in society are committed enough to leave power when they lose in elections. The second aspect is that the elite and the public operate within the democratic system (Huntington 1991, p. 267). Huntington emphasizes that the two-turnover test is a difficult and tough test of democracy that many democratic countries took a long time to fulfil (Huntington 1991, p. 267).

METHODOLOGY

The method used in implementing this study is a consuming case study. In theory-consuming studies, a single case is at the centre, and the researcher's task is to use existing theories and explanatory factors in the field to try to explain what happened in that specific case. Thus, a case study is an empirical investigation that studies a current phenomenon in its real context, particularly when the boundaries between the phenomenon and the context are unclear. The case study method is used in several different situations to contribute to the collective knowledge of, among other things, political, social, or organizational phenomena. The case study method is a common research strategy in the social sciences and contributes to maintaining real events' whole and meaningfulness. A case study is a well-defined aspect or example of a historical event that constitutes a phenomenon of scientific interest that the researcher selects for analysis.

Thus, a case can be a revolution, a government regime, or an economic system (George & Bennett, 2005, pp. 17-18). In this chapter, Tunisia constitutes a unique case of the democratization process after the Arab Spring. The case study of Tunisia is theoretically grounded through the use of democratization theory, which is important in formulating and justifying the research problem. A justification for choosing a case study method in this paper is that the author is interested in interpreting the results in a particular case and studying a delimited country. This is appropriate for a case study as the focus is on a concrete social context, and the researcher has little control over the studied situation. In addition, the case study method has clear advantages when studying a current event. In this chapter, the consolidation of democracy in Tunisia is the current event under study.

TUNISIA'S POLITICAL DEVELOPMENT BEFORE 2011

Tunisia became an independent state in 1956 from France after a long struggle for independence that began in the early 20th century and intensified after the end of World War II. In 1957, Tunisia was proclaimed a republic after being ruled by a royal family with roots in the 18th century. The key figure

Habib-Bourguiba, the leader of the Néo-Destour party with roots in the independence struggle, became Tunisia's first president (Vatthauer & Irene, 2017). Habib-Bourguiba later came to dominate the country's politics and introduced a series of important laws, including the right to vote for women and increased social rights. In 1961, Habib-Bourguiba introduced socialism in Tunisia, and as a result, central control of the economy was initiated, and industries and banks were nationalized. In 1963, Habib-Bourguiba introduced a one-party state where his party, Néo-Destour, became Tunisia's only legal party. In 1975, Habib-Bourguiba became President for life after changes to the Constitution. During the early 1980s, Tunisia went through an economic crisis that led to riots put down by the regime. Prime Minister Zine Al-Abidin Ben Ali deposed 1987 President Habib-Bourguiba due to his advanced age (Paciello, 2011). Ben Ali began his time in power with domestic political liberalization and an apparent multi-party system that tolerated some opposition parties as long as they did not threaten his regime.

Other opposition parties were banned, and their leaders were imprisoned or forced into exile. In all the presidential elections held during Ben Ali's era, only he could run for the presidency (Paciello, 2011). The population tolerated Ben Ali's regime for many years in exchange for economic growth and stability. But there was a hidden popular dissatisfaction with state corruption (Vatthauer & Irene, 2017). In the early 2000s, the cost of living increased, as did inflation in Tunisia. In addition, the financial crisis came in 2008, which also affected the economy badly (Perkins, 2004, p. 215). The pent-up popular discontent against corruption, unemployment, and increased living costs expressed itself when the street vendor Mohammed al-Bouazizi committed suicide on December 17, 2010, in protest against corruption and unemployment in the country (Günay & Sommavilla, 2019). Al-Bouazizi's suicide led to widespread protests around Tunisen and eventually to the Jasmine Revolution. The Jasmine Revolution ended Ben Ali's regime, forcing him to flee the country, thus beginning Tunisia's democratic transition (El-Khawas, 2012).

ANALYSIS

This chapter seeks answers to the study's questions, and the analysis is carried out using the study's analytical framework. In addition, the analysis will be structured by assigning each theoretical concept its section. The next sub-section deals with the theoretical concept of democratic political culture, which focuses on the legitimacy and performance of democratic governments. The concept focuses on the population's ability to distinguish between support for democracy as a form of government and support for the performance of democratic governments. In addition, the concept focuses on the ability of the political, military, and economic elite to work together to solve the country's problems without exploiting the problems to expand their political or material power. Therefore, the analysis will focus on these three main aspects: the political elite, the population, and the economy. The analysis includes the economy because it characterizes the country's problems in Tunisia, and the difficult economic situation was a reason for the population's uprising in 2011 (Rivera-Escartin, 2022). Since the focus of the study extends from 2011 – 2022, the analysis is also structured chronologically: 2011-2014, 2015-2019, and 2020 – 2022.

DEMOCRATIC POLITICAL CULTURE

The Period 2011-2014

The Political Elite

Tunisia's democratization process towards democracy began after the 2011 revolution and was characterized by broad compromises and a high spirit of consensus between secular parties and moderate Islamist parties. In January 2011, shortly after the country's dictators fled, there were discussions between various opposition parties about how to relate politically to each other and the old political elite from the authoritarian era on whether the parties should take a revolutionary path or a more moderate path. In the end, the moderate path won in the discussions between the parties. Subsequently, three main political parties consisting of moderate Islamists Ennhada and secular parties of the Congrès pour la République (CPR) and Ettakatol came to lead the transition towards democracy based on the idea of consensus, consensus, and power sharing. (Rivera-Escartin, 2022). The country's first free and fair elections were held in October 2011, and a commission called the National Constituent Assembly (NCA) was elected to combine the executive and legislative powers and draft a new constitution for the country. Although the moderate Islamist party Ennahda won the most seats in the NCA elections, the party chose to form a coalition government with the secular parties Ettakatol and Congrès pour la République (CPR) in which power was shared between the three main parties. CPR was given the presidency, Ettakatol got the chairmanship of the NCA, and Ennahda got the prime ministership (Yardimci Geyikci & Tür, 2018).

In 2013, Tunisia was rocked by terrorist attacks when extreme Islamists assassinated two leading politicians from the left. Secular parties called for strikes and demanded the resignation of the government. At the beginning of 2014, the government, then dominated by moderate Islamists, chose to resign, and a new neutral and technocratic government was formed (Yardımcı- Geyikçi & Tür, 2018). The work to adopt a new constitution in the country was also characterized by a high level of cooperation between the various parties, especially in Western articles that touch on the relationship between the state, religion, and civil liberties. Secular parties and conservative Islamists agreed to consider Tunisia a civil state and emphasize the rule of law. In addition, the parties agreed to introduce consensus democracy and separation of powers in the Constitution (Rivera-Escartin, 2022). In 2014, a constitution was adopted with a large cross-party majority, and the Constitution was described as progressive and unique in the region. The Constitution also adopted semi-presidentialism with clear principles of power distribution between the President, the prime minister, and the speaker. After the adoption of the Constitution, presidential elections were held where a candidate from the secular party, Nida Tounes, won the election, and a coalition government between secular and moderate Islamist parties was formed (Rivera-Escartin, 2022).

Despite the socio-economic and security challenges during the transitional phase toward democracy in Tunisia, the political elite in Tunisia managed to work together to lead Tunisia toward democracy. It was facilitated by the military remaining politically neutral while not attempting to exploit the country's problems to achieve political goals. The willingness to compromise and consensus politics also contributed to a relatively calm transition period where political parties prioritize long-term goals over short-term and narrow interests. The political elite in Tunisia showed during the period 2011-2014 a high level of cooperation despite ideological differences.

The Economy

Regarding the economic situation in post-revolution Tunisia, no significant improvements have been achieved since 2011. Economic growth was extremely slow, with an average growth of 1.8% between 2011 and 2015. In addition, unemployment registered figures such as 15.3%, which increased to 39% for those under the age of 25 (Yardımcı- Geyikçi & Tür, 2018). In applying the theoretical concept of democratic political culture to Tunisia, it can be stated that despite the failure of the new democratic regime in the country to achieve socio-economic improvements, neither the political elite nor the military elite took advantage of the socio-economic situation to expand its power during the transition phase.

The Population

Regarding the attitude of the Tunisian people to democracy after the transition to democracy, survey figures have shown a significant degree of dissatisfaction with both the political parties and the democratic system. Support for democracy decreased from 63% in 2012 to 48% in 2014. In addition, the percentage of those who found a stable government, even without democracy, to be more beneficial has gone up to 62% compared to 38% in 2012 (Yardımcı- Geyikçi & Tür, 2018). These figures show the dissatisfaction of the Tunisian people with democracy and the performance of the democratic governments after the transition to democracy, especially considering the economic aspect, where no improvements have been made. When applying the theoretical concept of democratic political culture, it can be stated that the Tunisian people can distinguish between support for democracy as a form of governance and the inefficiency of democratic governments during 2011-2014 is deficient as support for democracy has decreased during this period. It is important to point out that dissatisfaction with the economic situation was an important reason for the Jasmine Revolution in 2011. Considering the reduced support for democracy during this period, it can be stated that no development of democratic political culture can be identified.

The Period 2015-2019

The Political Elite

The Tunisian model built on consensus and understanding between secular parties and moderate Islamist parties that paved the way for Tunisia's Democratization after the revolution has been praised internationally. The Tunisian National Dialogue Quartet, which is an organization of civil society groups, received the Nobel Peace Prize in 2015 for its decisive role in achieving a political compromise between the parties in Tunisia during the transition to democracy (Yardımcı-Geyikçi & Tür, 2018). While consensus politics and broad compromises contributed positively to Tunisia's transition towards democracy in 2011-2014, in 2015, the country's political system began to show functional deficiencies in making and implementing political decisions and reforms (Yarmidcı-Geyikçi & Tür, 2018). The country's political system created several veto players that limited the government's room for manoeuvre, especially regarding economic reforms. Governments that ruled Tunisia between 2015-2016 had difficulties dealing with the country's economic and political problems. This is due to internal splits between the coalition parties and insufficient political support for the reforms. For example, a law on the autonomy of the central bank was passed by only two votes in the Parliament due to the lack of support from the government's coalition party (Yardımcı-Geyikçi & Tür, 2018).

In addition, terrorist attacks perpetrated by extreme Salafists in 2015 led the then-president to declare a state of emergency. Periodically renewed states of emergency gave the executive more authority at the expense of Parliament. The declaration of a state of emergency has been followed by a strict anti-terror law that has limited constitutionally guaranteed political freedoms in the country (Günay & Sommavilla, 2019). In this way, the fight against extremism and terror has become an effective tool for monitoring and controlling political opposition. President Essebsi used the fight against terrorism as an opportunity to expand his powers contrary to the Constitution's prescribes. President Essebsi has, on several occasions, placed himself in the prime minister's and government's responsibilities (Günay & Sommavilla, 2019).

Even during the period 2016-2019, the political elite in Tunisia continued to have difficulties cooperating to reach agreements to make and implement decisions. Conflicts between the parties prevented coalition governments from implementing reforms promised to the population. Tunisian politics began to be increasingly characterized by political deadlock and the use of vetoes by various political parties (Rivera-Escartin, 2022). In addition, in connection with the presidential and parliamentary elections in 2019, polarization increased in the country where the Parti Destourien Libre party (PDL), which is against the 2014 constitution, gained increased support. The political situation worsened when the President, the prime minister, and the speaker came into conflict regarding their constitutional boundaries, which also hindered reforms and the consolidation of democracy in Tunisia (Rivera-Escartin, 2022).

In addition, the political deadlock and conflicts between the parties have led to the deterioration of the legitimacy of the political parties, which in turn favoured populism (Rivera-Escartin, 2022). Radical parties from secular and Islamist circles gained increased influence in Parliament due to internal divisions within the main political parties. Even President Kais Saied, who won the 2019 election as an independent candidate, built his political campaign on anti-establishment discourse (Rivera-Escartin, 2022). He has advocated a traditional law and order policy and a radical direct democracy (Salem & Brumberg, 2020). Since his installation as President, President Kais Said has had conflicts with the speaker and various prime ministers regarding the power to nominate ministers and control the security service (Nassif, 2022).

It can be stated that conflicts between the political elites about how the country's problems should be solved began to arise in 2015 after the adoption of the Constitution. The ability to cooperate between the political elites began to deteriorate more and more and was replaced by veto tactics, which were made possible thanks to the principle of power distribution and consensus politics in the country's political system. These veto tactics inhibited the government's ability to make important decisions and reforms, making governments increasingly ineffective. The fight for democracy and the common fear of the return to authoritarianism united the political parties despite ideological differences. However, when the common threat was gone, conflicts arose within the political elite that seemed to have difficulty showing the same cooperation and consensus they showed during the transition to democracy to overcome these conflicts. These conflicts within the political elite affected the effectiveness of governments in addressing the country's problems and negatively impacted the consolidation of democracy in Tunisia.

Another problem that harmed the consolidation of democracy in Tunisia is the fight against terrorism. The fight against terrorism has curtailed several basic political freedoms due to the state of emergency and anti-terror laws. In addition, the then-president's attempt to use the fight against terrorism to expand his power also hurt the consolidation of democracy in Tunisia. It shows that the political elite in Tunisia has tried to exploit the country's problems to expand their power illegally, contrary to the development of a democratic political culture, which is essential for the consolidation of democracy. In applying the theoretical concept of democratic political culture in Tunisia during 2015-2019, we find shortcomings in developing a democratic political culture in the country.

Economy

Regarding the economy, GDP per capita in Tunisia in 2015-2019 decreased from 2544 US$ in 2014 to 3571.9 US$ in 2019. Also, Tunisia registered an annual growth rate of 1% between 2015 and 2019, the same as in 2014 (World Bank Open Data, 2022). Moreover, unemployment has recorded levels of 15.1% between the years 2014 and 2019 (World Bank Open data, 2022). No economic improvement could be registered between 2015 and 2019, which means the democratic governments have continued to be as ineffective in the economy as they were between 2011 and 2014. The fight against terrorism that began in 2015 has also affected the Tunisian economy negatively. Large sums of money that would have been invested in fighting poverty and unemployment have instead been invested in fighting terrorism, further worsening Tunisians' economic situation (Günay & Sommavilla, 2019). This, in turn, means a failure for the democratic governments that have not been able to respond to the population's demands for improved socio-economic conditions.

The Population

Regarding the population's view of democracy during 2015-2019, Survey surveys conducted in 2015 show a positive view of democracy and its implementation. A majority of Tunisians have expressed that the Arab Spring has had a positive impact on Tunisia (Lekalake, 2017). In addition, public demand for democracy and satisfaction with its implementation have increased. In addition, most Tunisians prefer democracy as a form of government more than any alternative form. Moreover, more than three-quarters of Tunisians would disapprove of Islamist rule without elections or political parties. The percentage of citizens who think that Tunsisen is a complete democracy or a democracy with fewer problems has increased from 27% in 2013 to 38% in 2015 (Lekalake, 2017).

Interestingly, while no significant economic improvement has occurred during the period 2011-2019 in Tunsisen, and the economic problems have remained the same, there has been an increase in support for democracy between 2015-2019, unlike the period 2011-2014. It shows that the Tunisian people's dissatisfaction is not with democracy as a form of government, but the real dissatisfaction is with the democratic government's inability to solve the country's problems and respond to the population's demands for improved economic conditions. When applying the theoretical concept of the development of democratic political culture in the period 2015-2014 in Tunisia, we find that the public's ability to distinguish between support for democracy as a form of governance and support for governments that come through democratic elections has been able to be identified and increased in comparison to the period 2011 -2014.

The Period 2020-2022

The Political Elite

Even after 2019, the political situation in Tunisia continued to be highly polarized, with conflicts between parties in the Parliament and between the President, the prime minister, and the speaker, which led to the continued political deadlock that hindered reforms. The conflicts between the branches of executive power and the legislature were about, among other things, the law for creating the constitutional court, the nomination of ministers, and different interpretations of the Constitution (Rivera-Escartin, 2022). In his interpretation of Article 80 of the Constitution, the President dismissed the prime minister on July 25, 2021, suspended and dissolved Parliament, and ordered military forces to cordon off Parliament to prevent members from gathering (Nassif, 2022). Article 80 of the Tunisian Constitution empowers the President to take exceptional measures when there are threats to the country's security and independence. However, the article provides for consultation with the Prime Minister, the speaker of the Parliament, and the President of the Constitutional Court; however, the President did not do so.

In addition, despite the Constitution providing for the existence of the constitutional court, no constitutional court has been able to be formed in Tunisia. The President defended his actions by complaining about the government's inability to deal with the country's severe economic problems, the handling of the COVID-19 pandemic, and the political paralysis in the country's political system (Nassif, 2022). In addition, the President issued a decree that gave him additional powers and repealed several sections of the Constitution. The President later announced that he intends to call a referendum for a new constitution in July 2022, followed by new parliamentary elections in the same year (Nassif, 2022). The President's actions in July 2021 are signs of a failed consolidation of democracy in Tunisia (Rivera-Escartin, 2022). For the first time since the transition to democracy, the country's economic problems were used by the political elite, namely the President, to expand their powers illegally. In addition, the Tunisian President used the army to implement his decisions, a serious development in Tunisia after the 2011 revolution. While the military refused to obey the dictatorship's order to shoot at protesters during the 2011 revolution, they agreed to support the President's actions in 2021 (Nassif, 2022).

It shows that the lack of cooperation among the political elite to reach agreements to solve the country's problems contributed to the President's exploitation of these problems by illegally expanding his powers together with the military who stepped forward in the tense political scene of the country. These factors contributed to a failed consolidation manifested in the President's actions in July 2021. The constant conflicts within the political elite and, especially between the President, the Prime Minister, and the speaker of the Parliament, have created an environment where populism and extremism from both secular and Islamist sides have flourished. In addition, the President's actions represent very, very changed game rules in the political spectrum in Tunisia and a serious development after the 2011 revolution. It is the first time since the transition to democracy that an actor within the political elite uses non-democratic means to achieve political change and violates the idea of consensus that characterizes the transition to democracy. The President's use of military troops to implement his decisions in July 2021 marked the end of the military's neutrality in politics. When applying the theoretical concept of the development of democratic political culture, we find that the development of democratic political culture is lacking in Tunisia.

A referendum to amend the Constitution according to the President's plan was held in July 2022, and the result was affirmative with 96%; however, with a turnout of 31%, the Constitution came into force (McDowall, 2022). The new Constitution strengthens the power of the President at the expense of Parliament and the prime minister. They give the President the power to appoint the Prime Minister and other ministers on the proposal of the Prime Minister. In addition, the President can dismiss the government or any of its members. In addition, the Constitution provides that the President exercises executive power with the government's help (Perry, 2022). The new Constitution has created a significantly weaker parliament than the 2014 constitution. For example, the new Constitution refers to legislative, executive, and judicial functions rather than powers. In addition, the President has the right to submit proposals to Parliament, which have priority. In addition, the new Constitution would create a regional council as a second chamber of Parliament. However, the Constitution provides few details on how it would be elected or its powers (Perry, 2022).

On December 17, 2022, Tunsisen held a parliamentary election following the President's original plan after the suspension of the Parliament in July 2021 and the introduction of the new Constitution in July 2022 (Volkmann, 2022). The new parliamentary election takes place with a new electoral system and a new electoral law introduced by the President. The new electoral law stipulates that candidates may only run as individuals through parties and not through party lists. In addition, candidates must be able to finance their campaigns without support from the state or political parties. Most opposition parties have boycotted the parliamentary election and criticized the new electoral law and system, claiming that the new election continues the President's intention to further expand his power with a weak parliament (Volkmann, 2022). The preliminary election results show a historically low voter turnout of 8.8% of 9.2 million eligible citizens. As a result of the extremely low voter turnout, opposition parties have called on the country's President to resign immediately, saying that the President has lost his legitimacy. However, a second round of elections will be arranged after the low turnout, and the final results are not expected to be announced until January 2023 (Aljazeera, 2022).

Finance

The Tunisian economy has suffered an extreme decline due to the Covid-19 pandemic in 2020 -9.2%. In addition, the recovery of the economy in 2021 has been slow. Unemployment has increased by 3.3% to reach 18.4% in 2021. The percentage of unemployed is particularly high among young people and women (World Bank, 2021). Public debt has taken up 84% percent of Tunisia's GDP in 2021. In addition, the war in Ukraine has worsened the socio-economic situation in Tunisia further, with increased commodity prices and demand for energy products. In addition, inflation has increased in Tunisia, reaching 8.1% in June 2022 (World Bank, 2022). Tunisia's economic situation during 2020-2022 has worsened with the Covid-19 pandemic and the war in Ukraine. At the same time, the governments in Tunisia, both during this period and before, have not agreed on introducing and implementing reforms to the economic situation. Conflicts within the political elite (the President, the prime minister, the speaker) have prevented the country from starting reforms of the economy. In addition, governments' failures to respond to population demands have given the President an excuse to undemocratically dissolve Parliament and dismiss primary ministers, strengthening his grip on power.

The Population

Figures from polls conducted at the end of 2021 show that most Tunisians support the President's actions in July 2021, including the suspension of Parliament. The surveys also show that most of the Tunisians included in the surveys see the President's actions more as a way to stop the political paralysis in the country's political system than a political coup (Arab Barometer, 2022). In addition, a majority say that the existing political system needs to be replaced or undergo major changes. Regarding the view of democracy, most people believe that democracy is the best form of government or the only feasible form of government (Arab Barometer, 2022). It can be stated that while the Tunisian people still have faith in democracy as a sustainable form of governance against authoritarianism, they also have a deep dissatisfaction with the political paralysis that prevails in the country's political system and inhibits economic and political reforms. The President has skillfully exploited the deep discontent in a populist way in justifying his actions in July 2021. The President aimed to end the political paralysis in the country's political system, inhibiting necessary reforms. However, the President's decision in 2021 meant more power to the President and an increasingly authoritarian rule in Tunisia. In Tunisia, the governments that have come after the transition to democracy have been ineffective in addressing the country's problems. Despite that and the President's decision in 2021, Tunisians still show their commitment and faith in democracy. In addition, results from the last parliamentary elections in December 2022, with an extremely low turnout of only 8.8%, show the dissatisfaction of Tunisians with the authoritarian direction led by the President since 2021. The election result confirms the Tunisians' faith and commitment to democracy as a form of government and their ability to distinguish between their dissatisfaction with ineffective democratic regimes and democracy. When applying the theoretical concept of developing a democratic political culture in Tunisia in 2020-2022, we find that the population, unlike the political elite, has developed a democratic political culture.

Table 1. Analysis results of the development of democratic political culture in Tunisia 2011-2022.

Democratic political culture	Operational indicators
Not fulfilled	Cooperation between the political elite, military leaders, and economic elite to solve the country's problems and refrain from exploiting them for its own political or economic interest.
Fulfilled	The public's ability to distinguish between support for democracy as a political regime and support for the performance of democratic governments.

The next section deals with the theoretical concept of institutionalizing democratic political behaviour. The concept focuses on whether the anti-establishment reaction and reaction against the existing parties are institutionalized within the democratic system. When these responses are institutionalized, democracy is considered consolidated. The two-turnover test is one way to measure the Institutionalization of the anti-establishment reaction and the reaction against the existing parties. It is based on those in power respecting election results and being willing to leave power according to these in two rounds. When a country passes this test, democratic political behaviour is institutionalized. The analysis in the next section will focus on seeing if the anti-establishment reaction and reaction against the existing parties are institutionalized in Tunisia and if Tunisia has floated the two-turnover test.

INSTITUTIONALIZATION OF DEMOCRATIC POLITICAL BEHAVIOUR

Tunisia distinguished its transition to a democratic system because the country held three free and fair presidential elections in 2011, 2014, and 2019, where these three elections were respected and accepted by all within the political elite. In addition, the three presidents have come from 2 different political parties and independents (Rivera-Escartin, 2022). Thus, Tunisia has gone through the two turnover tests presented by Samuel Huntington (1991), a requirement for the Institutionalization of democratic political behaviour. As Huntington describes, Tunisia has passed this test, showing that the elite and the public operate within the democratic system (Huntington 1991, p. 267). The fact that Tunisia has passed the test shows that Tunisia has fulfilled a requirement for democratic consolidation according to the study's theoretical framework. In Tunisia, the anti-establishment reaction and the reaction against the existing parties have also become institutionalized through two other aspects: firstly, by the fact that the legitimacy of the traditional parties has decreased and that other extreme and populist parties have gained increased support and thus increased influence in the Parliament. Secondly, by the fact that the current President has run as an independent candidate for the presidency and won it with some anti-establishment elements in his election campaign (Rivera-Escartin, 2022). These two aspects show that the Tunisian people have transformed their dissatisfaction with the establishment into a legitimate democratic reaction and thus show that they profess faith in the democratic system and operate within it. And that the population considers elections legitimate and legal methods to achieve political change without using other non-democratic methods. This, in turn, means that democracy has gained a foothold among the people, confirmed by surveys showing that most Tunisian citizens still believe in democracy as the main form of government (Arab Barometer, 2022).

Table 2. Analysis results of Institutionalization of democratic political behaviour

Institutionalization of democratic practices in the country's politics.	Operational indicators
Fulfilled	When a party that wins the first election in the transition and comes to power loses in a later election and hands over power to those who win the election, they leave power in a later election to the party that wins the election.

DISCUSSION

Tunisia is an interesting case to study from the perspective of Democratization, especially considering that Tunisia was the only country in the Middle East and North Africa that succeeded in transitioning to democracy after the Arab Spring in 2011. The study of Tunisia from a democratization perspective becomes more interesting by studying the development ten years after the transition to democracy to follow up and find out the state of democracy in the country. The study hoped to contribute to the collective knowledge of the political phenomenon of the consolidation of democracy in Tunisia. So, what has this study contributed? The study followed the political development in Tunisia from 2011-2022 with a theory of Democratization and managed to identify obstacles and explanations for the empirical case of a failed democratic consolidation. In addition, the study has tested a minimalist theory that also made it possible to come up with criticism in areas where the theory has shown shortcomings in the explanation.

The study's theoretical framework has been Samuel P Huntington's definition of consolidated democracy. This definition is based on a very minimalist view of democracy. This definition is useful in the analysis and captures the basic and essential aspects of a consolidated democracy. It considers the political elite, the population, and the procedures of democracy. However, certain shortcomings have been observed during the study, which can lead to the analysis bypassing essential factors and also becoming limited and narrow. For example, the great focus on repeated free and fair as a requirement for the consolidation of democracy. Even though Tunisia has undergone the two turnover tests, democracy in Tunisia cannot be considered consolidated; moreover, repeated free and fair elections do not guarantee a consolidated democracy. In Tunisia, the current President has come to power through free and fair elections, but this has not prevented him from taking authoritarian measures. Therefore, repeated free and fair elections should be a necessary condition for democracy rather than a requirement for a consolidated democracy.

Another flaw in Huntington's definition is that it overlooks other important aspects of a consolidated democracy, such as the role of democratic institutions, civil society, and the rule of law. However, other researchers have taken the role of democratic institutions in their definition of a consolidated democracy, such as (Linz & Stepan, 1996). It is in this sense that Huntington's definition is considered limited. Another way that could have improved the analysis in this study and overcome this limitation would have been to perform the analysis based on a more comprehensive definition. However, despite its limited definition, Huntington's definition has nevertheless highlighted essential aspects of a consolidated democracy and answered the study's questions. Furthermore, despite Huntington's minimalist definition, Tunisian democracy has not passed these minimalist and basic requirements for a consolidated democracy, which shows that it may not pass a more comprehensive definition. Finally, as has been pointed out before, Tunsisen is an interesting case to study from a democratization perspective, and here, future research can contribute a lot. For example, future research would study democracy in Tunisia concerning Islam or political Islam because previous research has pointed to religion, especially Islam, as an obstacle to democracy, but this has not been found in the material for this study.

CONCLUSION

The purpose of the chapter was to study the political development in Tunisia in the period 2011-2022 to examine and analyze obstacles and opportunities to consolidate democracy in Tunisia during 2011-2022. To fulfil the purpose of the study, the following questions have been asked: What explains the lack of consolidation of democracy in Tunisia? What are the obstacles to the consolidation of democracy in Tunisia during the period? What are the conditions for democracy in Tunisia?

What Are the Obstacles to The Consolidation of Democracy in Tunisia?

The main obstacle to the consolidation of democracy in Tunisia is the inability of democratic governments to deliver reforms and solutions to Tunisia's economic problems. Ten years after the transition to democracy, the democratic governments have been unable to improve the country's economy. It is important because, in Tunsisen, the economy has been a source of legitimacy during the authoritarian era. In addition, dissatisfaction with the economy was a reason for the revolution in 2011 (Vatthauer & Irene, 2017). Consequently, the economic factor being ignored by the democratic governments in Tunsisen hinders the consolidation of democracy in the country. Another obstacle to the consolidation of democracy is the lack of cooperation and consensus among Tunsis's political elite to solve the country's economic problems during the consolidation phase and in the post-revolutionary era, unlike what they showed during the transition phase, which was a prerequisite for Tunisia's successful transition to democracy. Constant conflicts between the political parties have created a political deadlock in the country's political system, where the parties use vetoes to block various bills, which has prevented the implementation of reforms. In addition, populist and extreme forces have exploited the constant conflicts within the political elite to delegitimize them and offer the population a more attractive authoritarian alternative with order and efficiency instead of disorder and inefficiency.

What Explains the Lack of Consolidation in Tunisia During the Period?

What explains the lack of consolidation of democracy in Tunisia, based on Samuel Huntington's (1991) definition of a consolidated democracy, has been captured in the lack of development of a democratic political culture in the country. Democratic political culture refers to the extent to which the public and the elite believe in the value of the democratic system, that is, that the elite cooperates to solve the country's problems and do not exploit them to expand their power and that the public can distinguish between support for democracy as a political regime and the support of democratic governments' performance (Huntington, p. 259-360). Based on the analysis, it has been shown that the political elite in Tunisia do not believe in the value of the democratic system because the country's political elite has failed to cooperate to solve the country's problems and have exploited them to increase their power undemocratically. In Tunsisen, the political elite has taken advantage of the country's economic problems to expand their power in ways that are against the Constitution. In addition, the political elite (the President) has taken support from the army to expand its power. It shows that the political elite has not developed a democratic political culture and thus does not believe in the value of the democratic system. However, the analysis has shown that the public believes in the value of the democratic system, and this has been proven with the help of surveys that show that Tunisians believe in democracy as the main form of governance despite ineffective democratic governments (Arab Barometer, 2022).

What Conditions Exist for Democracy in Tunisia?

The political system in Tunisia is at a crossroads between autocratization and consolidation of the democratic gains achieved since 2011. Each direction has its contributory factors that are strengthened and weakened by the evolution of the current political situation. The positive conditions for the consolidation of democracy are found in the fact that the political elite has respected all elections held in the country and that presidents have been willing to leave power according to election results. Another positive condition for the consolidation of democracy is that the population still believes in democracy as the main form of government despite the severe economic problems they suffer from and the tense political situation in Tunisia. In addition, the Tunisian people have clearly shown their dissatisfaction with the authoritarian and populist direction that the President has led since July 2021, with a historically low turnout in parliamentary elections held in December 2022. The people of Tunisia, who led the country to Democratization in 2011, may well end the development towards an authoritarian rule now and in the future.

As for the prerequisites for the development of the authoritarian direction, some prerequisites must be mentioned. The new Constitution adopted in 2022 is a prerequisite for developing an authoritarian rule in Tunisia. Because the new Constitution provides for increased power for the President at the expense of Parliament and the government. The role of the government and Parliament has been weakened in the new Constitution, and therefore, they have limited opportunities to influence or limit the policies pursued by the President. Another prerequisite for developing authoritarianism in Tunisia is the military's role in politics, which emerged as a supporter of the President's decision in 2021. The military's involvement in politics is hardly positive for democracy, especially in the case of Tunisia, where the military has traditionally been politically neutral. The military's support for the policies pursued by the President strengthens the President's grip on power and makes it difficult for the President's power to be challenged by the democratic forces in the country.

The trend towards authoritarianism is also determined by how the President who holds the most power under the new Constitution uses this power in practice, for example, if the power is used to limit the basic democratic rights provided for in the Constitution. If so, Tunisia may be back in the authoritarian era again. The current political situation in Tunisia suggests that the political crisis in the country will worsen shortly. It is because the opposition in the country has increasingly, since the extremely low turnout in the last parliamentary elections, questioned the legitimacy of the President and called for his resignation. However, knowing that these calls rarely lead to the resignation of incumbents, it suggests that the President is waiting for the final results of the second round of elections, which will not be announced until January 2023. Even if the results of the second round of elections raise the turnout more than that of the first election round, it is no guarantee that the legitimacy of the Parliament or the President will be increased. Finally, there is a risk that Tunisia's democracy will end up in a hybrid regime where democracy is written in the Constitution but not applied in reality.

REFERENCES

Aljazeera. (2022). *Tunisia set for runoffs after low turnout parliamentary elections*. https://www.aljazeera.com/news/2022/12/19/runoffs-due-in-most-tunisian-districts-in-parliament-election

Arab Barometer. (2022). *Arab Barometer Wave VII – Arab Barometer*. https://www.arabbarometer.org/surveys/arab-barometer-wave-vii/

Bellin, E. (2004). The Robustness of Authoritarianism in the Middle East: Exceptionalism in Comparative Perspective. *Comparative Politics*, *36*(2), 139–157. doi:10.2307/4150140

Cavatorta, F. (2018). The Middle East and North Africa. In *Democratization* (pp. 364–383). Oxford University Press.

Cevik, S. (2011). Myths and Realities on Islam and Democracy in the Middle East. *Estudios Politicos*, *0*(38), 121–144. doi:10.17533/udea.espo.10057

Coppedge, M. (2012). *Democratization and Research Methods*. Cambridge University Press., doi:10.1017/CBO9781139016179

Diamond, L. (1996). Is the Third Wave Over? *Journal of Democracy*, *7*(3), 20–37. doi:10.1353/jod.1996.0047

El-Husseini, R. (2015). Is gender the barrier to democracy? Women, Islamism, and the "Arab spring.". *Contemporary Islam*, *10*(1), 53–66. Advance online publication. doi:10.100711562-015-0324-4

El-Khawas, M. (2012). Tunisia's Jasmine Revolution: Causes and Impact. *Mediterranean Quarterly*, *23*(4), 1–23. doi:10.1215/10474552-1895357

Erdmann, G. (2011). *Transition from Democracy.: Loss of Quality, Hybridisation and Breakdown of Democracy*. German Institute of Global and Area Studies (GIGA). https://www.jstor.org/stable/resrep07511

Freedom House. (2022). *Tunisia: Freedom in the World 2022 Country Report*. Freedom House. https://freedomhouse.org/country/tunisia/freedom-world/2022

Gause, F. G. (2011, July 1). Why Middle East Studies Missed the Arab Spring. *Foreign Affairs, 2011*(July/August). https://www.foreignaffairs.com/articles/middle-east/2011-07-01/why-middle-east-studies-missed-arab-spring

George, A. L., & Bennett, A. (2005). *Case studies and theory development in the social sciences*. MIT Press. http://bvbr.bib-bvb.de:8991/F?func=service&doc_library=BVB01&doc_number=013153145&line_number=0001&func_code=DB_RECORDS&service_type=MEDIA

Grugel, J., & Bishop, M. L. (2013). *Democratization: A Critical Introduction*. Bloomsbury Academic. doi:10.4135/9781446286227

Günay, C., & Sommavilla, F. (2019). Tunisia's democratization at risk. *Mediterranean Politics, 25*(5), 1–9. doi:10.1080/13629395.2019.1631980

Huntington, S. P. (1991). *The third wave: Democratization in the late twentieth century*. University of Oklahoma Press. https://opac.eui.eu/client/en_GB/default/search/detailnonmodal/ent:$002f$002fSD_ILS$002f0$002fSD_ILS:392477/one

Knappe, H. (2017). Participatory and Deliberative Democracy: From Equality Norms to Argumentative Rationalities. In Doing Democracy Differently (pp. 45–76). Verlag Barbara Budrich. doi:10.2307/j.ctvbkk41f.8

Lekalake, R. (2017). *Beyond the Arab Spring: Will economic and security challenges further test Tunisia's democracy?* [Policy paper]. Afrobarometer Policy Paper. https://www.afrobarometer.org/publication/pp40-beyond-arab-spring-will-economic-and-security-challenges-further-test-tunisias/

Linz, J., & Stepan, A. (1996). Toward Consolidated Democracies. *Journal of Democracy, 7*(2), 14–33. doi:10.1353/jod.1996.0031

Masoud, T. (2015). Has the Door Closed on Arab Democracy? *Journal of Democracy, 26*(1), 74–87. doi:10.1353/jod.2015.0013

Masoud, T. (2018). Review Chapter: Why Tunisia? *Journal of Democracy, 29*(4), 166–175. doi:10.1353/jod.2018.0071

McDowall, A. (2022, August 17). Tunisia constitution giving President wider powers comes into effect. *Reuters*. https://www.reuters.com/world/africa/tunisia-constitution-giving-president-wider-powers-comes-into-effect-2022-08-16/

Miller, L. E., Martini, J., Larrabee, F. S., Rabasa, A., Pezard, S., Taylor, J. E., & Mengistu, T. (2012). Democratization and Democracy Promotion: Trends, Theories, and Practices. In *Democratization in the Arab World* (pp. 9–34). RAND Corporation. https://www.jstor.org/stable/10.7249/mg1192rc.10

Nassif, H. B. (2022). Coup in Tunisia: Why the Military Abandoned Democracy. *Journal of Democracy, 33*(1), 27–39. doi:10.1353/jod.2022.0002

Paciello, M. C. (2011). *Tunisia: Changes and Challenges of Political Transition*. Istituto Affari Internazionali (IAI). https://www.jstor.org/stable/resrep09864.7

Perkins, K. (2004). *A History of Modern Tunisia*. Cambridge University Press.

Perry, T. (2022, July 25). Factbox: What's in Tunisia's new Constitution? *Reuters*. https://www.reuters.com/world/africa/whats-tunisias-new-constitution-2022-07-25/

Rivera-Escartin, A. (2022). Tunisia's democratisation process: When 'consensus democracy' undermines democratic consolidation. *Third World Quarterly*, *43*(2), 414–431. doi:10.1080/01436597.2021.2015315

Saidin, M. I. S. (2018). Rethinking the 'Arab Spring': The Root Causes of the Tunisian Jasmine Revolution and Egyptian January 25 Revolution. *International Journal of Islamic Thought*, *13*(1). Advance online publication. doi:10.24035/ijit.06.2018.007

Salem, M. B., & Brumberg, D. (2020). Tunisia's Endless Transition? *Journal of Democracy*, *31*(2), 110–124. doi:10.1353/jod.2020.0025

Trisnaningtyas, J. P. N. (2022). Forecasting Tunisia's Future: A Lesson Learned from the Past. *Ijd-Demos*, *4*(1), 1. Advance online publication. doi:10.37950/ijd.v4i1.208

Vatthauer, J.-P., & Irene, W.-F. (2017). *Economic and social challenges in Tunisia: Continuity in times of political change*. Peace Research Institute Frankfurt. https://www.jstor.org/stable/resrep14477.5

Volkmann, E. (2022). *Why are Tunisia's parliamentary elections so controversial?* https://www.aljazeera.com/news/2022/12/17/why-tunisia-elections-controversial-explainer

World Bank. (2021). *Tunisia Economic Monitor: Economic reforms to navigate out of the crisis*. https://documents1.worldbank.org/curated/en/454631642741750737/pdf/Executive- Summary.pdf

World Bank. (2022). *Tunisia Economic Monitor: Navigating the crisis during uncertain times*. https://documents1.worldbank.org/curated/en/099515309022233400/pdf/IDU0f8cf 9a5703e950485f0b-2d0025e156f8091d.pdf

World Bank Open Data. (2022). *Tunisia*. https://data.worldbank.org/country/tunisia

Yardimci Geyikci, S., & Tür, Ö. (2018). Rethinking the Tunisian miracle: A party politics view. *Democratization*, *25*(5), 1–17. doi:10.1080/13510347.2017.1422120

ADDITIONAL READING

Benstead, L. J. (2022). Tunisia: The Challenges of Party Consolidation and the Specter of Authoritarian Reversal. In L. Blaydes, A. Hamzawy, & H. Sallam (Eds.), *Struggles for Political Change in the Arab World* (pp. 272–298). University of Michigan Press. https://www.jstor.org/stable/10.3998/mpub.12237894.18

Huber, D. (2012). *Democracy Building since the Arab Spring: In Need of "Diversification."* German Marshall Fund of the United States. https://www.jstor.org/stable/resrep18646

Lecha, E. S., & Dokos, T. (2011). *Mediterranean 2020: The Future of Mediterranean Security and Politics*. German Marshall Fund of the United States. https://www.jstor.org/stable/resrep18845

Marzo, P. (2016). *Why Youth Empowerment Can Sustain Tunisia's Democratic Consolidation*. Istituto Affari Internazionali (IAI). https://www.jstor.org/stable/resrep09847

Miller, L. E., & Martini, J. (2013). Democratization in the Arab World: A Summary of Lessons from Around the Globe. In *Democratization in the Arab World* (pp. 1–42). RAND Corporation. https://www.jstor.org/stable/10.7249/j.ctt5hhstf.3

Miller, L. E., Martini, J., Larrabee, F. S., Rabasa, A., Pezard, S., Taylor, J. E., & Mengistu, T. (2012a). Lessons from Past Transitions and Policy Implications. In *Democratization in the Arab World* (pp. 293–342). RAND Corporation. doi:10.7249/RB9673

Miller, L. E., Martini, J., Larrabee, F. S., Rabasa, A., Pezard, S., Taylor, J. E., & Mengistu, T. (2012b). The Arab World on the Eve of Change. In *Democratization in the Arab World* (pp. 35–54). RAND Corporation. doi:10.7249/RB9673

Ratka, E., & Wahlers, G. (2017). *On the Emergence of an Arab Democracy: Social Divides and Political Compromises in Tunisia*. Konrad Adenauer Stiftung. https://www.jstor.org/stable/resrep10034.6

Szmolka, I. (2015). Exclusionary and Non-Consensual Transitions Versus Inclusive and Consensual Democratizations: The Cases of Egypt and Tunisia. *Arab Studies Quarterly*, *37*(1), 73–95. doi:10.13169/arabstudquar.37.1.0073

KEY TERMS AND DEFINITION

Arab Spring: A series of popular uprisings and demonstrations that swept across several countries in the Middle East and North Africa in 2011. The protests aimed to challenge autocratic rule and demand democratic reforms, resulting in significant political changes in some countries.

Authoritarian Regime: A political system characterized by centralized power, limited political freedoms, and often the suppression of opposition and dissent. Authoritarian regimes typically lack democratic institutions and mechanisms for checks and balances.

Autocratization: The process by which a country that previously showed democratic characteristics or progress experiences a decline in democratic norms, institutions, and practices, resulting in a gradual shift toward authoritarian rule or hybrid regimes.

Consolidation of Democracy: The process of strengthening and stabilizing democratic institutions, practices, and norms within a country. Consolidation ensures that democratic changes become deeply rooted and enduring, resisting challenges to democratic governance.

Constitutional Changes: Revisions or amendments to a country's Constitution, which outlines the fundamental principles and rules of governance. Constitutional changes can significantly impact the distribution of power, political institutions' functioning, and individual rights protection.

Democratic Political Culture: The shared attitudes, beliefs, values, and behaviors within a society that support and promote democratic principles, such as a commitment to the rule of law, tolerance of political differences, and a belief in the legitimacy of democratic institutions.

Democratization: The process of transitioning a political system from autocratic or authoritarian rule to a more democratic and participatory form of governance, involving the establishment of democratic institutions, respect for human rights, and including citizens in decision-making processes.

Hybrid Regime: A political system that displays a mix of democratic and authoritarian features, often characterized by formal democratic structures (such as elections), significant restrictions on political freedoms, and a lack of genuine competition.

Jasmine Revolution: Refers to the popular uprising and protests that took place in Tunisia in 2010-2011, leading to the ousting of President Zine El Abidine Ben Ali and the establishment of a democratic government. It symbolizes the successful democratic transition in Tunisia amid the broader Arab Spring movement.

Political Elite: A group of influential individuals who hold significant power, often due to their positions in government, political parties, or other influential organizations. The political elite plays a crucial role in shaping policies and determining the direction of a country's political development.

Section 3

Democracy, Trade, and Economy

Chapter 11
Democracy, Trade, and Economic Growth:
The Challenge of Managing Foreign Exchange in Nigeria

Shafiu Ibrahim Abdullahi
https://orcid.org/0000-0003-3471-4493
Bayero University, Kano, Nigeria

Mansur Idris
Bayero University, Kano, Nigeria

ABSTRACT

The chapter analyses factors that influence exchange rate in Nigeria during the period of democracy by using generalized method of moments (GMM) and Granger causality tests for analyses. The democratic system of governance is associated with reduction in arbitrariness, policy continuity, protection of property rights, human rights, freedom, free market, community development, consensus, and human development. The results of the analysis show that GDP growth and FDI have long-run inverse relationships with foreign exchange while export and consumption have long-run positive relationships with foreign exchange.

INTRODUCTION

May 29th of every year marks Nigerian democracy day. Before May 29th 1999, Nigeria had experienced prolonged military rule for most of its independence period. The other periods of democratic rule in Nigeria are 1960 to 1966 and 1979 to 1983. Around the world, democracy has gained wide acceptance when compared with what was obtainable decades back (Guseh and Oritsejafor, 2007). Nigeria and Africa are not left behind in embracing a democratic system of governance. The democratic system of governance is associated with a reduction in arbitrariness, policy continuity, protection of property

DOI: 10.4018/979-8-3693-0477-8.ch011

rights, human rights, freedom, free market, community development, consensus and human development (Sen, 1999; MacEwan, 1999). Along this line, democracy has been classified as the best system of governance over dictatorship and another authoritarian form of governance. According to Sen (1999), political freedom can have a major role to play in providing incentives and information in the solution of acute economic needs. Adam Smith has famously emphasized the freedom inherent in a market economy which contrasts it with a planned economy. It is widely accepted that economic development must champion human and social development for it to be democratic. Thus, democracy shall be the ultimate goal of economic development.

The over two decades of democracy may have been responsible for the growth of import in the Nigerian economy; where the urgency to win the election may have forced politicians to bow to electorate pressure, who desire cheaper import over costly domestically produced goods and services. This shall be viewed together with high population growth and the death of domestic industry. The amount of Nigerian imports has grown since the return to democracy, and so also has the deterioration in Nigerian foreign exchange. In any economy where import is higher than export foreign exchange will automatically deteriorate. Inflation may have also grown since the return to democracy, which also goes hand in hand with deterioration in foreign exchange and interest rates. Part of the inflation is caused by imported inflation from abroad, due to the high cost of import. But, at the same time, the banking sector, GDP, FDI and consumption may have grown exponentially. According to Fraj, Bouchoucha and Maktouf (2020), exchange regimes play an important role in decisions to strengthen political and economic stability. Recently, excessive borrowings and deficit budgeting by the Nigerian government have resulted in balance of payment problems. These have a direct connection with the foreign exchange problem. Under a democratic regime, people can protest the negative consequences of devaluation of currency; but this is difficult to do under non democratic regime. Generally, some democracies in Africa have proven themselves to be poor when it comes to controlling foreign trade; opposition from the people and fear of losing election makes it even more challenging. African countries such as Kenya, South Africa and Ghana have experienced currency deterioration in recent years.

Achievement of an equilibrium exchange rate has become difficult to achieve for developing economies of Africa. Some economists have viewed the equilibrium exchange rate as unobservable (Aliyu, 2011). It is generally acknowledged that exchange rate misalignment has serious negative effects on macroeconomic fundamentals. Akinlo and Yinusa (2007) noted that of all the prices in an economy, the exchange rate occupies a strategic position due to its role in linking an open economy with the world economy. The exchange rate is the link between domestic and international prices. The fluctuation in exchange rates is a reflection of changes in domestic and foreign fundamentals. The exchange rate has effects on prices, investments, balance of payment, import, export, employment and interest rate. Poor and unstable foreign exchange policy has also been blamed for the death of local industries in Nigeria. Country risk plays an important role in making a nation's currency fall in value. Countries such as Somalia and Afghanistan with high country risk tend to have depreciated currencies. The heightened insecurity in Nigeria, the 2015 change of government and the collapse in oil revenue of 2014-18 might have contributed to the rapid collapse in the value of Naira against other currencies. The above factors have contributed to an increase in the country risk associated with Nigeria. Some studies such as that of Yildirim and Ivrendi (2016) and Akindiyo and Olawole (2015) have shown that currency depreciation is responsible for recession and high inflation. Other studies such as that of Pandey (2013) and Birgul and Sevcan (2016) have shown that currency depreciation leads to an improvement in trade balance. Work by Fontaine (2005) shows that deterioration in economic fundamentals and the pursuit of lax monetary policy contribute to currency crises.

The recent changes in the design of Nigeria's Naira (that were supposed to last between November 2022 to January 2023) had temporarily caused the value of Naira to further depreciate against the Dollar. This occurred because people were changing Naira into other assets pending the time the new legal tender would hit the ground running. Some empirical works such as that of Ajibola et al (2020) have predicted that currency substitution is associated with foreign exchange volatility. Unpredictability in exchange rates has been widely acknowledged to be very detrimental to the external sector of any economy. Exchange rate volatility has become the norm all over the world, since the wide adaptation of flexible exchange regimes beginning from the 1970s. In Nigeria, the era of volatility in the exchange rate began right from the introduction of the Structural Adjustment Program (SAP) in 1986. The persistent misalignments that have to do with exchange rate appreciation or depreciation are a good reflection of the exchange rate crisis. Exchange rate policy in developing economies such as Nigeria is very sensitive and controversial; it has always been the subject of controversy. One can safely say that exchange rate and inflation are the two most watched and difficult of all the major macroeconomic goals.

Achievement of exchange rate stability has always been the cornerstone of macroeconomic policy of governments around the world. Before the advent of the SAP economic policy framework, Nigerian monetary authorities were accused of maintaining non-competitive and overvalued Naira. But, for most of the period after SAP, the monetary authorities were equally accused of undervaluing the Naira and the poor management of the exchange rate of the Naira against other currencies. Recently, the Nigerian government has pursued an import reduction strategy (especially food-related imports) and has devalued the Naira as well as tried to expand the production of tradable goods, but its ability to generate a stable macroeconomic environment has been weakened by declining term of trade, fluctuations in the international market for its major export crude oil, high inflation and unstable interest rate regime. The attempt to substitute imported goods with made-in-Nigeria goods while maintaining a devalued Naira is seen as not very wise. To make good use of the devalued Naira, the Nigerian government must push for export expansion. All the variants of foreign exchange policies adopted by the Nigerian government over the years were aimed at achieving exchange rate stability, reducing the widening premium, conserving external reserves, and minimising speculative tendencies of authorized dealers (Akpan and Atan, 2011).

Nigeria has been a huge import-dependent economy that depends on imports for a large share of its needs (Abdullahi, 2018). Nigerians' love for foreign-made goods and services is legendary; Nigeria imports everything from cars, TVs, and textiles to health tourism and foreign education. Proponents of the abolition of the fixed exchange rate in 1986 and its replacement with a flexible exchange rate have argued that the fixed exchange system is fraught with high distortions, inefficiency and misallocation of resources. These have resulted in an excessive balance of payment disequilibrium (Aliyu, 2011). Nigerian foreign exchange rate has always been at the mercy of the highly volatile international crude oil market; where the interplay between demand and supply, war and diplomacy play a key role in setting prices. Since Nigeria gets most of its foreign earnings from the sale of crude oil in the international market, there will be direct and indirect links between the price of and the amount of crude oil exported from Nigeria with its domestic currency exchange rate value. This is where the foreign reserve comes in; the size of the Nigerian foreign reserve has played an important role in moderating this relationship. Whenever the foreign reserve is huge, the foreign exchange tends to be stable compared to when the reserve is low. An exchange rate crisis has been defined as episodes of exchange rate depreciation to the tune of 15 to 30 per cent (Laeven and Valencia, 2008).

This chapter finds out the major factors that influence foreign exchange in Nigeria since the return to democracy in 1999. Hence, the paper tests the influence of GDP, consumption, foreign direct investment, export, money supply, domestic investment, interest rate and inflation on foreign exchange in Nigeria during the period 1989 to 2019 with a specific focus on 1999 to 2019; using GMM model and Granger causality test. The main objective is to find out the main factors that determined foreign exchange management during the period of the study with an emphasis on the democratic period. Democracy is emphasized in this work because the economic management pattern in a democratic system generally differs from what is obtainable under a nondemocratic system. This is the major point of departure from most works on foreign exchange management that tend to underplay the role of democracy. The chapter is divided into several subsections which include: introduction, democracy and economic development, literature review, theoretical framework methodology, discussion of results and conclusion.

BACKGROUND

Democracy and Economic Development

Checks and balances in a democratic system of governance ensure the reduction of arbitrary government intervention, lower the risk of policy changes and strengthen property rights protection (North & Weingast, 1989). There is no consensus among scholars on the role of democracy in promoting economic growth and development; while one side believes that democracy promotes economic growth the other side says otherwise (Sen, 1999; MacEwan, 1999). Guseh and Oritsejafor (2007) noted that several studies have observed that historically, democracies tend to grow out of free market economies. Ghosh, Gregoriou and Mitra (2013) have noted that democracy has a positive effect on economic growth. Aisen and Veiga (2011) found that higher degrees of political instability are associated with lower growth rates of GDP

per capita. Neo-liberal economic thinkers such as Milton Freidman have promoted free enterprises and liberal democracy as one sure ticket to economic progress. However, thinkers and political leaders such as Singapore's Lee Kwan Yew see democracy and political freedom as a hindrance to economic growth and development. In Africa and around the world, the era of structural adjustment program (SAP) came together with the push for developing countries to adopt democracy as a means of governance. But for about one to three decades both experiments have failed to achieve their full aims. It was only in later years when countries adopted the systems of their own volition that some of these experiments began to take off successfully. But up to now, the two systems have a long way to go in Africa; as many countries are ruled under dictatorship, and liberal economic policies are impeded by government interventions. According to Mac Ewan (1999), despite the rhetoric about neo-liberalism and democracy, developed countries of Europe and America have practised different kinds of government interventions before arriving at where they are today. It was not just a free market all the way. In Nigeria, since the return to democracy in 1999, the number of universities has increased, and so also the number of graduates from these schools. But, the poverty rate has fluctuated from one high point to another; so also the value of Naira continues to depreciate; with the increase in population also comes an increase in the number of primary health care centres. However, the growth in the number of medical doctors has not kept phase with the growth in the population.

Amartya Sen (1999) in his book 'Development as Freedom' has asked the question; 'what should come first; removing poverty and misery, or guaranteeing political liberty and civil right?' This question is important when one looks at poor countries in Africa and elsewhere around the developing world. Shall Africa pursue economic development in place of democracy or the other way around? Is it possible for Africa to have it both ways: democracy and economic development? According to Sen (1999), "While we must acknowledge the importance of democratic institutions, they cannot be viewed as mechanical devices for development. Their use is conditioned by our values and priorities and by the use we make of the available opportunities for articulation and participation. The role of organized opposition groups is particularly important in this context." Democracy shall promote sustainable economic development not just any kind of development. Development that comes at the expense of the environment is not desirable. Just like economic progress that damages the natural environment could hardly be categorized as progress, change that destroys social bonds in society and undermines the basis of their security would not be consistent with any positive concept of development (Mac Ewan, 1999). Sen (1999) has defined development as consisting 'of the removal of various types of unfreedom that leave people with little choice and little opportunity of exercising their reasoned agency'. But democracy, according to Diamond et al., (1990), is a "system of governance that meets three essential conditions: meaningful and extensive competition among individuals and organized groups (especially political parties) for all effective positions of government powers, at regular intervals and excluding the use of force; a highly inclusive level of political participation in the election of leaders and policies, at least through regular and fair elections, such that no major (adult) social group is excluded; and a level of civil and political liberties—freedom of expression, freedom of the press, freedom to form and join organisations—sufficient to ensure the integrity of political competition and participation".

Okolie et al. (2021) in an analysis on the link between democracy and development have blamed the short period of four years between elections as causing too much pressure on the economies of poor countries. Guseh and Oritsejafor (2007) have examined the impact of government size, political freedom and openness of the economy on economic growth in Nigeria. They employed a generalized least squares regression model, using annual data from 1960 to 2000. The result shows that the effect of political freedom on economic growth is not statistically significant; the result for the size of the government shows that an increase in the size of the government leads to slower economic growth and trade openness has a positive effect on economic growth. Faraj, Bouchoucha and Maktouf (2020) explore the relationship between political stability and economic growth with an emphasis on the role of exchange rate. They used ordinary least squares (OLS), Generalized least squares (GLS) and system generalized method of moments (GMM) models for the analysis. The study is based on a panel of 50 countries of which 21 are developed while 29 emerging during the period 1996-2013. The study found that political stability is not important in explaining economic growth, while exchange rate flexibility negatively affects the economies of emerging countries but boosts economic growth in developed countries. The results also indicate that political stability goes with a flexible exchange rate regime. The results show that the nature of the exchange rate regime plays a crucial role in the decision to strengthen political and economic stability. Ifarajimi and Onyejiuwa (2017) examined exchange rate fluctuation, stock market performance and economic growth in Nigeria under democratic dispensation. The study covers the period from 1999 to the second quarter of 2016. The study used VAR Granger Causality and Block Exogeneity Wald Tests, and the VAR approach for variance error decomposition and impulse function response functions. The results show that the variables do not have the power to predict real growth. However, the exchange rate has causal feedback from growth rate, stock market, money supply and government capital expenditure. However, the study revealed that exchange rate shocks are crucial factors in explaining economic growth and growth in the stock market in the long run.

Volatility

Salisu (2011) has analysed volatility in exchange rates in Nigeria covering the period 1999 to 2011 using daily returns. The paper evaluates the volatility under the democratic regime of four years namely 05/29/1999 – 05/28/2003; 05/29/2003 – 05/28/2007; and 05/29/2007 – 05/28/2011. The result indicates that the behaviour of the exchange rate tends to change over short periods with inconsistent leverage effects and persistence of shocks. Aliyu (2011) estimated the long-run behavioural equilibrium real exchange rate in Nigeria using the Vector error correction model. The results of the analysis show that most of the long-run behaviour of the real exchange rate could be explained by terms of trade, index of crude oil volatility, index of monetary policy performance and government fiscal stance. Akintunde, et al, (2019) examine determinants of the exchange rate in Nigeria by comparing the official exchange rates with the parallel market rates starting from the post-SAP era using quarterly time series data for the period 1986 to 2017. The potential determinants of the exchange rate were identified as; GDP, inflation, interest rates, imports, oil exports, non-oil exports, and reserves. The result shows that GDP, inflation, interest rates non-oil exports, oil exports and reserves are the main determinants of official exchange rates, while inflation, non-oil exports and GDP determine the parallel exchange rates. Umoru (2013) estimates monetary models of exchange rate determination in Nigeria. The results show that inflation expectations of economic agents are important determinants of exchange rate volatility in Nigeria. Adenekan, et al, (2019) investigate the impact of Naira-to-dollar exchange rate volatility on Naira exchange rate returns. The study estimated an AR(5)-TGARCH (1,1) model to examine whether there is an asymmetry in the time path of the Naira exchange rate volatility. The findings showed that exchange rate volatility leads to depreciation in the Naira value. Olamide (2018) assessed the efficiency of the Nigerian foreign exchange market. The study also tests whether the past exchange rate affected the current exchange rate. The study covered the period from 1985 - 2016. The data were analysed using the Fully Modified Ordinary Least Square Approach (FMOLS). The findings of the study showed that oil price, GDP, inflation rate, and interest rate have positive relationships with the exchange rate; while money supply (M2) has a negative relationship with the exchange rate. However, previous exchange rate returns have a negative and insignificant relationship with current exchange rate returns.

Ozekhome (2021) investigates the determinants of real exchange rates in Nigeria during the period 19812019. The study used cointegration and dynamic error correction model (ECM) techniques for analysis. The results show both a shortrun dynamic and a longrun equilibrium relationship between real exchange rate and its determinants. The main determinants of the exchange rate in the study are output capacity, trade openness, net capital inflow, real interest rate, government expenditure and inflation. Increased output capacity, greater degree of openness, increased net capital inflows and high real interest rate lead to exchange rate appreciation. But, an increase in government expenditure and a high inflation rate, on the other hand, causes exchange rate depreciation. The study further shows that money supply is positively related to the exchange rate, albeit weakly. Ajibola, et al (2020) investigates the relationship between exchange rate volatility and currency substitution in Nigeria. The paper used the Autoregressive Distributed Lag (ARDL) model, accounting for the presence of structural breaks. The findings show a positive relationship between exchange rate volatility and currency substitution both in the short- and long-run. This implies that higher real exchange rate volatility is associated with an increased level of currency substitution. Shuaibu, et al, (2022) estimate the factors that influence export in Nigeria during the period 1989 to 2019 using the ARDL model for the analysis. It findings show that foreign exchange inflation and government expenditure negatively affected exports; while interest, trade openness, domestic credit and agriculture positively affected exports.

Akpan and Atan (2011) investigate the effect of exchange rate on real output growth in Nigeria; using quarterly series for the period 1986 to 2010. The results show that exchange rate depreciation affects both output and money supply. Atoi, et al, (2021) examine the money market and foreign exchange market dynamics in Nigeria with data from January 2007 to August 2019. The study used dynamic conditional correlation GARCH (DCC-GARCH) and unrestricted bivariate BEKK-GARCH (1, 1) for the analysis. The results reveal that interest rate and exchange rate are dynamically linked, negatively. The effects of shock spillover are bi-directional across the markets. The results show the influence of the foreign exchange market in the Nigerian economy. Yakubu, et al, (2019) investigated the impact of exchange rate volatility on trade flows in Nigeria. The study used monthly data for the period 1997 – 2016, using GARCH and ARDL models for analysis. The study found that exchange rate volatility affected trade flows negatively in the short-run but not in the long-run.

Framework

The behaviour of an economy depends on the exchange rate it is using (Mankiw, 2007). This implies that the choice of exchange rate regime affects the nation's exchange rate value. According to Reed (1996), World Bank strategies on foreign trade and liberalization were responsible for poor countries' vulnerability to changes in international terms of trade and falling income. While, the IMF has championed the use of exchange rate policies to redress government deficits and current account imbalances (Reed, 1996). Under a floating exchange rate, capital inflow from abroad has two main effects. One, it leads to the reduction in domestic interest rate; two, it leads to appreciation in domestic currency. Under a floating exchange rate, monetary policy influences income by changing the exchange rate rather than the interest rate. An increase in money supply leads to a reduction in interest rate while at the same time causing depreciation in foreign exchange. A floating exchange rate allows monetary authorities to pursue other goals instead of focusing on maintaining a particular fixed rate. Under the old Bretton Woods system governments of the world agreed to fix exchange rates. This happened in the early 1970s. The oil shock of 1974 with the global recession that came with it forced nations around the world to adopt a floating exchange rate (Reed, 1996). It is assumed that under flexible exchange rates, an equilibrium rate of exchange prevails that clears the market and ensures a balance of payment equilibrium. Before the world ditched the gold standard in the 1970s as a means of determining exchange rates, nations around the world operated fixed exchange rates. Under a fixed exchange rate, the rate is determined by the monetary authorities; on the other hand, a flexible exchange rate is determined by market forces. Under a fixed exchange rate system, monetary policy is geared toward maintaining the fixed rate. Usually, Monetary policy is ineffectual under a fixed exchange rate. Under this system, the Central Bank surrenders control over the money supply (Mankiw, 2007). A devaluation of currency expands exports and income; while revaluation reduces exports and income under a fixed exchange rate system. It is understood that if the price level of one country rises relative to that of another country, the equilibrium value of its currency will fall relative to that of other countries (Lipsey and Chrystal, 2005). The theory of purchasing power parity (PPP) is based on the equality of purchasing power between nations. It says that the exchange rate between two nations is determined by their relative price levels. PPP assumes that the free movement of merchandise would bring about parity between the purchasing powers of the money of different nations, as also indicated by respective national price levels.

Since the founding of the Central Bank of Nigeria in March 1958 the maintenance of external value of Naira has remained its major task. CBN has adopted different types of foreign exchange systems to guarantee stability and ensure the attainment of its macroeconomic objectives. The enactment of the Exchange Control Act of 1962 led to the introduction of rigid control in the management of Nigerian foreign exchange. The system was dismantled with the introduction of SAP in 1986 (Nwaoba, 1999). It is argued that during the era of fixed exchange rate the Naira was overvalued (Adenikinju and Alabi, 1997). The adaptation of a flexible exchange rate in Nigeria in the 1980s was aimed at boosting the export base of the country. A flexible exchange rate was introduced in Nigeria in September 1986 (Adenikinju and Alabi, 1997). SAP was central to the introduction of flexible exchange rates. Nigeria introduced the Second-Tier Foreign exchange market (SFEM) and later transformed it into a Foreign exchange market (FEM) in July 1987. Later on in 1989, FEM was transformed into the interbank foreign exchange market (IFEM). Thereafter, the government adopted the Dutch auction system in February 1993. In 1994, the government again settled in favour of allocating foreign currency itself and the use of a single legal exchange rate. Between 1995 to 2000, Nigeria made use of the Autonomous Foreign Exchange market (AFEM) and Inter-Bank Foreign Exchange market (IFEM) to achieve foreign exchange market stability with little success. The introduction of the Dutch Auction System (DAS) in 2002 has led to some measure of success in the foreign exchange market and the achievement of some level of stability in the market (Umoru, 2012). The turbulence in the market under a free-floating exchange rate justifies the intervention of the Central Bank from time to time to stabilize the market. Depreciation of domestic currency is justified based on the fear that continued capital inflow may negatively affect exports. Huge depreciation has implications for servicing foreign debts. Ghosh et. al. (2014) have noted that countries with a flexible exchange rate regime should avoid non-conventional monetary easing (via the foreign exchange market), while those with fixed exchange rates should not undertake any depreciation without in-depth consultations with agencies such as the International Monetary Fund (IMF). This brings us to the major theoretical anchor of this chapter, according to the Mundell-Fleming model:

$$Y = C(Y\text{-}T) + I(r^{*}) + G + NX(e) \tag{1}$$

$$M/P = L(r^{*}, Y) \tag{2}$$

Where Y = income, C = aggregate consumption, T = taxes, I = Investment, r^{*} = equilibrium interest rate, G = government purchases, NX = net export, and e = real exchange rate. Equation (1) shows equilibrium in the goods market, and equation (2) shows equilibrium in the money market. The model explains the aggregate demand curve for an open economy. Changes in economic fundamentals as a cause of exchange rate misalignment go hand in hand with appreciation or depreciation of currency. Changes in fiscal and monetary policies affect the fundamentals of an economy, thereby causing the real exchange rate to attain or deviate from its fundamental equilibrium exchange rate (FEER). Hence;

$$e = f_t + \frac{LE\left(dl_t\right)}{d_t} \quad \partial > 0 \tag{3}$$

Where, e = exchange rate, f = economic fundamental, L = interest rate elasticity of money demand, E = expectations operator

Data and Methodology

Data

Data for the study was sourced from the Central Bank of Nigeria and the World Bank for the period 1989 to 2019. The period is chosen because it falls within the period that Nigeria adopted a flexible exchange rate (post SAP adaptation era); which allows us to measure the factors that shape the exchange rate during the period of the study. The period is important as two-thirds of it falls within the democratic system of governance that started in 1999. The period witnessed the adaptation of different exchange rate systems by Nigeria. The data is annual time series data for a total of nine variables. The variable data includes gross domestic product (GDP), aggregate consumption, foreign direct investment (FDI), export, money supply, domestic investment, interest rate and inflation. Foreign exchange is the dependent variable and is represented by Naira-Dollar exchange rates. GDP represented changes in the size of the Nigerian economy. Consumption is represented by gross consumption in the economy. FDI represented the aggregate foreign investment inflows into Nigeria. FDI has the effect of appreciating domestic currency while depreciating that of the originating country (Lipsey and Chrystal, 2005). Export represented the aggregate export from Nigeria to the rest of the world. The money supply is represented by broad money (M2). Domestic investment is assumed to come out of domestic savings since FDI represents investment coming from abroad. The variable interest rate represents the annual interest rate prevailing in the domestic economy. Inflation shows the official annual inflation rate. In macroeconomic research, the exchange rate has been widely seen as endogenous in developing countries. Factors seen as responsible for this include the widespread exchange control practice by these economies. Other factors include time series properties of exchange rate and the behaviour of economic agents operating in the market (Devereux, 1997; and Aron, et al, 1997).

Model

The model is in line with that of Akpan and Atan (2011), Edwards and Sebastein (2000) and Akintunde, et al, (2019), though it is adjusted to suit the present purpose. The Nigerian economy is seen as a small open economy like all other developing economies, competing in a highly globalized world. The model measures the effects of gross domestic product (GDP), aggregate consumption, foreign direct investment (FDI), export, money supply, domestic investment, interest rate and inflation on foreign exchange in Nigeria between the periods 1989 to 2019.

FX = f(GDP, consumption, FDI, export, money, investment, interest and inflation)

$$FX = \delta_0 + \delta_1 GDP + \beta_2 cons + \delta_3 FDI + \delta_4 exp + \delta_5 mone + \delta_6 inv + \delta_7 int + \delta_8 inf + \mu \tag{4}$$

Where, FX = foreign exchange, GDP = gross domestic product, cons = aggregate consumption, FDI = foreign direct investment, exp = export, mone = money supply, inv = domestic investment, int = interest rate, inf = inflation.

Methods of Analysis

Granger Causality

A variable *X* is theorized to be Granger-cause *Y* if it can be demonstrated that those *X* values can show statistically significant results about future values of *Y*. A model of Granger causality looks like this:

$$\Delta Y_t = \sum_{i=1}^{n} \alpha_i \Delta Y_{t-i} + \sum_{j=i}^{n} \beta_j \Delta X_{t-j} + u_{1t} \tag{5}$$

$$\Delta X_t = \sum_{i=1}^{n} \gamma_i \Delta X_{t-i} + \sum_{j=i}^{n} \delta_j \Delta Y_{t-j} + u_{2t} \tag{6}$$

Eq. (5) shows current value of ΔY is related to past values of itself as well as past values of ΔY. Eq. (6) postulates that ΔX is related to past values of itself and ΔY.

GMM Model

Generalized Method of Moments (GMM) is an important econometric method of analysis that uses both linear and non-linear models with applications in economics and finance. It was first formulated by Hansen (1982) and has since then become widely applicable in applied econometric research. One of the advantages of GMM is that it does not require complete knowledge of the distribution of the data. In models where there are more moment conditions than parameters, GMM provides an easier way to test the specification of a proposed model. This feature is unique to GMM. The GMM technique is generally preferred due to its ability to generate unbiased estimators even with lagged dependent variables serving as instruments. It avoids biased results due to the correlation between the error term and the lagged endogenous variables. It also has the potential of getting consistent parameter estimates even in the presence of measurement error and endogenous right-hand side variables in a system equation estimation procedure. GMM is used to measure the short-run and long-run relationship between foreign exchange and the independent variables in the study. The GMM method also minimizes a certain norm of the sample averages of the moment conditions.

To apply GMM, the moment conditions shall be:

$$m(\theta_0) \equiv E\left[g(Y_t, \theta_0)\right] = 0 \tag{7}$$

Where E – expectation, Y_t – generic observation; m(Θ) ≠ 0: $\Theta \neq \Theta_0$

The GMM estimator can be written as follows:

$$\widehat{\varnothing} = \arg\min \left(\frac{1}{T} \sum_{t=1}^{T} g(Y_t, \varnothing) \right)^T \widehat{W} \left(\frac{1}{T} \sum_{t=1}^{T} g(Y_t, \varnothing) \right) \tag{8}$$

Stylized Facts

The summary statistic shows that foreign exchange has a high standard deviation which further confirms the level of volatility in the Nigerian foreign exchange market. The same high standard deviation can also be noticed in the case of FDI; this testifies to the uneven nature of FDI inflow into Nigeria. The results of skewness show that inflation is the most skewed variable in the study followed by money supply. This shall not be surprising since inflation and money supply are two sides of the same coin. Monetary economics tells us that inflation is a purely monetary phenomenon. Hence, this explains the comovement in skewness between the two. Inflation and money supply also have the first and second highest Jarque-bera, respectively.

Table 1. Summary Statistics

	FX	GDP	INFL	INTR	INVS	MONEY	FDI	EXP01	CONS
Mean	117.9877	2.91E+11	19.30258	12.11607	5.87E+10	8.57E+12	3324.705	3.52E+10	2.53E+11
Median	125.8100	2.58E+11	12.56000	10.82000	4.92E+10	2.13E+12	2190.680	2.54E+10	2.52E+11
Maximum	306.9200	5.11E+11	72.84000	23.99000	1.49E+11	3.49E+13	8914.890	7.24E+10	4.25E+11
Minimum	7.360000	1.37E+11	5.390000	4.704871	2.21E+10	4.34E+10	775.2500	1.48E+10	8.48E+10
Std. Dev.	89.71435	1.35E+11	17.59917	5.231871	3.42E+10	1.06E+13	2480.922	1.81E+10	1.26E+11
Skewness	0.606559	0.420756	1.805065	0.822377	0.819853	1.027243	0.998735	0.486959	0.077444
Kurtosis	2.762328	1.591340	4.990633	2.821002	2.746348	2.745608	2.706714	1.744299	1.370954
Jarque-Bera	1.973850	3.477767	21.95272	3.535622	3.555926	5.535604	5.264713	3.261847	3.458803
Probability	0.372721	0.175716	0.000017	0.170706	0.168982	0.062800	0.071909	0.195749	0.177391
Sum	3657.620	9.04E+12	598.3800	375.5981	1.82E+12	2.66E+14	103065.9	1.09E+12	7.86E+12
Sum Sq. Dev.	241459.9	5.47E+23	9291.921	821.1743	3.50E+22	3.37E+27	1.85E+08	9.80E+21	4.78E+23
Observations	31	31	31	31	31	31	31	31	31

Source: authors' analysis using Eview

Since 1989 when this data started, the value of the Naira against the Dollar has fallen this confirms the non-competitiveness of the Naira and the weak position of the Nigerian economy among others around the world. The value of Naira, particularly, falls sharply during the period of democracy, as one can see from the graph. This trend is not arguing well for the Nigerian economy, Nigerian fiscal and monetary authorities must put changes in place that will reverse the trend. GDP too has been trending upward during the period. In the past, the size of Nigerian GDP was behind that of South Africa and Egypt, but today Nigeria is the largest economy in Africa; though at the same time, it has continued to witness growth in its population. One should have expected Nigerian foreign exchange to stabilize and the Naira to appreciate concerning GDP, but that seems not to be the case. Inflation has come down from its galloping level of the 1990s, but it is still not as low and stable as found in matured economies. The interest rate has fallen when compared with the height it attended in the 1990s, but it is still high enough and not favourable for sustainable economic growth and development. The domestic investment level has trended upward until recently when it started to fall. Since the 1990s money supply has continued to grow at a higher rate than in any period in the past. FDI has trended upward but with increasing intensity during the 2000s then started to fall during 2010s. The growth in FDI somehow mimics the growth in domestic investment during the period. Both export and consumption have trended upward almost at a similar rate. This has also been the growth pattern of GDP and money supply during the period.

It is clear from the graph that all these variables have trended upward during the period of democracy except inflation and interest rate. While foreign exchange has fallen sharply against the Dollar during democracy, GDP has increased; domestic investment has grown too, and so also are money supply, exports and consumption. Foreign direct investment achieved a steep rise during the democratic period and then fell. The comparison between the period of military rule (1989-1999) and the period of democracy (1999-2019) further brings into light the sharp difference between the two periods in terms of the performance of the Nigerian economy. The economy has done better during democracy than military rule.

Figure 1. Variables trends
Source: authors' analysis using Eview

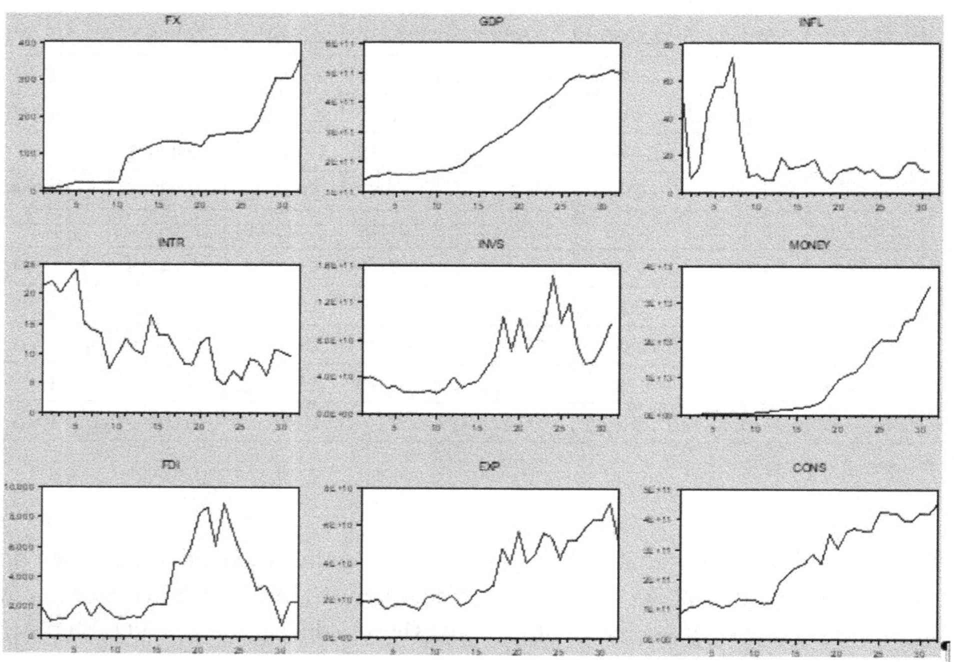

RESULTS AND DISCUSSION

The result of the Granger causality test shows that there are two ways to causality between foreign exchange and the rest of the variables in the study. Granger causality tests only provided short-run causality between variables. However, the GMM model provides long-run causality and dynamism between variables.

Table 2. Granger causality analysis

Null Hypothesis:	Obs	F-Statistic	Prob.
GDP does not Granger Cause FX	30	2.29904	0.1212
FX does not Granger Cause GDP		0.65795	0.5267
INFL does not Granger Cause FX	29	1.32472	0.2846
FX does not Granger Cause INFL		1.64623	0.2138
INTR does not Granger Cause FX	29	1.76154	0.1933
FX does not Granger Cause INTR		0.25861	0.7743
INVS does not Granger Cause FX	29	0.38925	0.6818
FX does not Granger Cause INVS		3.01754	0.0678
MONEY does not Granger Cause FX	29	1.76283	0.1931
FX does not Granger Cause MONEY		2.25271	0.1269
FDI does not Granger Cause FX	30	0.24872	0.7817
FX does not Granger Cause FDI		1.99627	0.1569
EXP01 does not Granger Cause FX	30	1.72249	0.1991
FX does not Granger Cause EXP01		1.21278	0.3143
CONS does not Granger Cause FX	30	2.25697	0.1256
FX does not Granger Cause CONS		2.72323	0.0851

Source: authors' analysis using Eview

This chapter's main aim is to find out variables that help in explaining foreign exchange behaviour in Nigeria. It measures the effects of gross domestic product (GDP), aggregate consumption, foreign direct investment (FDI), export, money supply, domestic investment, interest rate and inflation on foreign exchange in Nigeria. The findings of the long-run study using GMM show that GDP growth and FDI have an inverse relationship with foreign exchange while export and consumption have a positive relationship with foreign exchange. This result is in line with some of the findings in Ozekhome (2021), Akintunde, et al, (2019) and Olamide (2018). The rest of the variables which are inflation, interest, investment and money supply are not statistically significant. The inverse relationship between FDI and foreign exchange means that growth in FDI might have led to an appreciation in the value of Naira during the study period. This result is expected theoretically since any growth in foreign direct investment which comes with Dollar investment into Nigeria would automatically lead to appreciation in the value of the Naira against the US Dollar. The positive relationship between export and exchange rate which means the exchange rate has continued to depreciate in relation to the Dollar means that export growth is very insignificant in leading to appreciation in Naira. This called for the boosting of exports especially non-oil exports to strengthen the value of Naira. The positive relationship between consumption and foreign exchange is a pointer to the Nigerian's dependence on consumption of imported goods and services. This has been the case for many years since Nigeria does not have the industrial base to produce most of the things that it requires. In terms of agricultural production Nigeria has a long way to go to become self-reliant in agricultural production.

Table 3. GMM results

Dependent Variable: FX				
Method: Generalized Method of Moments				
Date: 11/06/22 Time: 21:06				
Sample (adjusted): 2 31				
Included observations: 30 after adjustments				
Linear estimation with 1 weight update				
Estimation weighting matrix: HAC (Bartlett kernel, Newey-West fixed				
bandwidth = 4.0000)				
Standard errors & covariance computed using estimation weighting matrix				
Instrument specification: FX(-1) GDP(-1) INFL(-1) INTR(-1) INVS(-1) MONEY(-1) FDI(-1) EXP01(-1) CONS(-1)				
Constant added to the instrument list				
Variable	**Coefficient**	**Std. Error**	**t-Statistic**	**Prob.**
GDP	-1.58E-09	6.63E-10	-2.389406	0.0263
INFL	0.552493	0.637625	0.866486	0.3960
INTR	-5.640449	2.940990	-1.917874	0.0688
INVS	-1.63E-10	1.05E-09	-0.154581	0.8786
MONEY	-1.07E-12	5.14E-12	-0.208417	0.8369
FDI	-0.029485	0.013541	-2.177435	0.0410
EXP01	8.04E-09	1.77E-09	4.549791	0.0002
CONS	1.56E-09	6.64E-10	2.345148	0.0289
C	79.38147	113.0853	0.701961	0.4904
R-squared	0.768241	Mean dependent var		121.6753
Adjusted R-squared	0.679952	S.D. dependent var		88.82634
S.E. of regression	50.25154	Sum squared resid		53029.57
Durbin-Watson stat	1.783771	J-statistic		2.107352
Instrument rank	10	Prob(J-statistic)		0.146593

Source: authors' analysis using Eview

CONCLUSION AND RECOMMENDATIONS

This chapter analyses the factors that influence the exchange rate in Nigeria during the period 1989 to 2019 which precisely falls after the introduction of SAP. The chapter paid special attention to the period of democracy (1999-2019). In the academic literature, there is a contradicting view regarding the relationship between democracy and economic development. One view sees democracy as causing economic growth; while the other says democracy does not cause economic growth. But the democratic system has spread all around the world and has become a reference point. The work used the GMM model and Granger causality for the analyses; in addition, the chapter carefully studies how the data trended. GMM result provides long-run causality between variables; while Granger causality provides short-run causality. The result of the Granger causality test shows that there are two ways to causality between foreign exchange and the rest of the variables in the study. The results of the GMM analysis show that GDP growth and FDI have long-run inverse relationships with foreign exchange while export and consumption have long-run positive relationships with foreign exchange. The rest of the variables which are inflation, interest, investment and money supply are not statistically significant in the long run. But, in the short run foreign exchange is affected by gross domestic product (GDP), aggregate consumption, foreign direct investment (FDI), export, money supply, domestic investment, interest rate and inflation.

The implication of this is that Nigerian monetary authorities aiming to achieve short-run targets in the foreign exchange market can use these variables. However, some of the policy implications of the GMM model study include that the effects of money supply, inflation and interest rate on foreign exchanges are ambiguous. More empirical studies are needed to pinpoint the actual effects of these on foreign exchange in the long run, though they can be used to achieve short-term objectives. Hence, monetary authorities shall be cautious in using money supply, inflation and interest rates to influence the foreign exchange market in the long run. Nigerian authorities shall consider the foreign exchange market when designing macroeconomic policy to avoid negative situations from arising. A situation where foreign exchange is forgotten in pursuing less important economic goals by the authorities will continue to do damage to the Nigerian economy. Finally, there is a need to improve the overall management of the foreign exchange market in Nigeria. Overall, the study has shown that some variables have done well during the democratic period, while others have not performed so well. Despite this, African countries shall further push for democracy across the continent, as its economic advantages far outweigh any disadvantages it may have. Economic growth will indeed help the growth of democracy in Africa, as much as democracy will help boost economic growth across the continent.

REFERENCES

AbdullahiS. I. (2018). *Nigerian economy: business, governance and investment in period of crisis.* doi:10.2139/ssrn.3310120

Adenekan, A. T., Sanni, G. K., & Itodo, A. I. (2019). Investigating the Impact of Exchange Rate Volatility on Naira Exchange Rate in Nigeria. *Central Bank of Nigeria Economic and Financial Review.*, *57*(3), 17–38.

Adenikinju, A. F. & Alabi, G. A. (1997). The impact of exchange rate instability on Nigerian non oil exports. *Journal of Social and Management Studies, 3-4*, 1-21.

Aisen, A., & Veiga, F. J. (2011). *How Does Political Instability Affect Economic Growth?* IMF Working Paper, WP/11/12.

Ajibola, I. O., Udoette, S. U., Muhammad, R. A., & Anigwe, J. O. (2020). Currency Substitution and Exchange Rate Volatility in Nigeria: An Autoregressive Distributed Lag Approach. *CBN Journal of Applied Statistics*, *11*(2), 1–28.

Akindiyo, O., & Olawole, A. (2015). Devaluation of Nigerian Naira: Bane or Panacea? *Review of Public Administration and Management.*, *4*(8), 98–123.

Akinlo, A. E., & Yinusa, D. O. (2007). Exchange Rate versus Capital Account Liberalization in Nigeria: Some Important Issues. *CBN Economic and Financial Review.*, *45*(4), 69–89.

Akintunde, Y. W., Ebunoluwa, O. O., Jelilov, G., & Haruna, T. M. (2019). Determinants of Exchange Rate in Nigeria: A Comparison of the Official and Parallel Market Rates. *The Economics and Finance Letters*, *6*(2), 178–188. doi:10.18488/journal.29.2019.62.178.188

Akpan, E. O., & Atan, J. A. (2011). Effects of Exchange Rate Movements on Economic Growth in Nigeria. *CBN Journal of Applied Statistics*, *2*(2), 1–14.

Aliyu, S. U. R. (2011). *Real Exchange Rate Misalignment: An Application of Behavioural Equilibrium Exchange Rate (BEER) to Nigeria.* Central Bank of Nigeria Occasional paper No. 41.

Aron, J., Elbadawi, I., & Kahn, B. (1997). *Determinants of Real Exchange Rate in South Africa.* CSAE Working Paper, WPS/ 97 – 16, CSAE.

Atoi, N. V., & Nwambeke, C. G. (2021). Money and Foreign Exchange Markets Dynamics in Nigeria: A Multivariate GARCH Approach. *CBN Journal of Applied Statistics*, *12*(1), 109–138. doi:10.33429/Cjas.12121.5/6

Birgul, C., & Sevcan, G. (2016). Marshall-Lerner Condition Analysis: Turkey Case. *Economics, Management, and Financial Markets*, *11*(1), 272–283.

Devereux, M. B. (1997). Real Exchange Rates and Macroeconomics: Evidence and Theory. *The Canadian Journal of Economics. Revue Canadienne d'Economique*, *30*(4), 773–808. doi:10.2307/136269

Diamond, L., Linz, J. J., & Lipset, S. M. (1990). Introduction: Comparing experiences with democracy. In L. Diamond, J. J. Linz, & S. M. Lipset (Eds.), *Politics in developing countries: Comparing experiences with democracy* (pp. 1–38). doi:10.1515/9781685853150-002

Edwards, S. (1989). *Real Exchange Rates, Devaluation and Adjustment: Exchange Rate Policy in Developing Countries.* MIT Press.

Faraj, H. F., Bouchoucha, N., & Maktouf, S. (2020). *Political stability and economic growth: the role ofexchange rate regime.* MPRA Paper No. 104586. https://mpra.ub.uni-muenchen.de/104586/

Fontaine, T. (2005). *Currency Crises in Developed and Emerging Market Economies: A Comparative Empirical Treatment.* IMF Working Paper, WP/05/13, January.

Ghosh, A. R., Jonathan, D. O., & Mahvash, S. Q. (2014). *Exchange Rate Management and Crisis Susceptibility: A Reassessment.* IMF Working Paper, WP/14/11, January.

Ghosh, S., Gregoriou, A., & Mitra, A. (2013). *On the Role of Democracy in the Ethnicity-Growth Relationship: Theory and Evidence*. Working Paper, Brunel University.

Guseh, J. S., & Oritsejafor, E. (2007). Government size, Political freedom and Economic growth in Nigeria, 1960-2000. *Journal of Third World Studies*, *24*(1), 139–165.

Hansen, L. P. (1982). Large Sample Properties of Generalized Method of Moments Estimators. *Econometrica*, *50*(4), 1029–1054. doi:10.2307/1912775

Ifarajimi, G. D., & Onyejiuwa, D. C. (2017). Exchange Rate Fluctuation, Stock Market Performance And Economic Growth In Nigeria Under Democratic Dispensation. *International Journal of Innovative Research and Advanced Studies*, *4*(1), 270–277.

Laeven, L., & Valencia, F. (2008). *Systemic Banking Crises: A New Database*. IMF Working Paper 08/224.

Lipsey, R., & Chrystal, A. (2005). *Economics*. Oxford University Press.

MacEwan, A. (1999). *Neo-liberalism or Democracy? Economic strategy, markets, and alternatives for the 21st century*. Zed Books.

Mankiw, N. G. (2007). *Macroeconomics*. Worth publishers.

North, D. C., & Weingast, B. N. (1989). Constitution and Commitment: The Evolution of Institutional Governing Public Choice in Seventeenth Century England. *The Journal of Economic History*, *49*(4), 803–832. doi:10.1017/S0022050700009451

Nwaoba, P. I. (1999). Critical factors affecting Nigeria's foreign exchange flows. *CBN Economic & Financial Review, 37*(3), 1-17.

Okolie, A., Nnamani, K. E., Ezirim, G. E., Enyiazu, C., & Ozor, A. C. (2021). Does liberal democracy promote economic development? interrogating electoral cost and development trade-off in Nigeria's fourth republic. *Cogent Social Sciences*, *7*(1), 1918370. doi:10.1080/23311886.2021.1918370

Olamide, A. O. (2018). Foreign Exchange Market Efficiency in Nigeria (The Past and Current Exchange Rate Returns). *Sumerianz Journal of Economics and Finance*, *1*(1), 14–21.

Ozekhome, H. O. (2021). Determinants of Real Exchange Rate in Nigeria: An Empirical Investigation. *Asian Journal of Economic and Finance*, *3*(4), 487505.

Pandey, R. (2013). Trade Elasticities and the Marshal Lerner Condition for India. *Global Journal of Management and Business Studies,* 423-428.

Reed, D. (1996). *Structural adjustment, the environment, and sustainable development*. Earthscan publications.

Salisu, A. A. (2011). Modelling and Forecasting Exchange Rate Volatility in Nigeria: Does One Model Fit All? *Central Bank of Nigeria Economic and Financial Review*, *49*(3), 1–30.

Sen, A. (1999). *Development as Freedom*. Anchor Books.

Shuaibu, M., Adamu, M. B., Abdullahi, S. I., Shehu, K. K., & Buba, S. I. (2022). International Trade and Export Dynamics in Nigeria: An ARDL Vector Error Correction Analysis. *Journal of Humanities. Arts and Social Science*, *6*(1), 50–61. doi:10.26855/jhass.2022.01.005

Umoru, D. (2012) Empirical investigation of the determinats and dynamic adjustment of the real exchange rate in Nigeria. In Studies in the state of the Nigerian economy. Department of economics, Umar Musa Yar'adua University, Katsina.

Umoru, D. (2013). Monetary models and exchange rate determination: The Nigerian Evidence. *International Journal of Development and Management Review*, *8*(1), 172–197.

Yakubu, M. U., Sani, Z., Obiezue, T. O., & Aliyu, V. O. (2019). Empirical Investigation on Exchange Rate Volatility and Trade Flows in Nigeria. *CBN Economic and Financial Review*, *57*(1), 23–46.

Yildirim, Z., & Ivrendi, M. (2016). Exchange Rate Fluctuations and Macroeconomic Performance: Evidence from four Fast-Growing Emerging Economies. *Journal of Economic Studies (Glasgow, Scotland)*, *43*(5), 678–698. doi:10.1108/JES-01-2015-0010

Chapter 12
Foreign Direct Investment and Economic Growth in Developing Countries:
The Prospect and Bane

Opeyemi Idowu Aluko
Ajayi Crowther University, Oyo, Nigeria

Oluwole Ayodeji Aluko
Federal Airport Authority, Nigeria

ABSTRACT

Countries of the world require financial capital for economic growth and development. It lubricates the wheels of the economy for development. The developed countries of the world held on to continuous capital investments in the economy and these resulted in rapid economic growth. The case of most developing countries is different. They do not have sufficient capital to be invested in their economy; therefore, they need to depend on the external hands of the developed countries. The research question is, What is the prospect and bane of foreign direct investment on the economy? The theoretical framework of dependency theory is used to analyse the prospect and bane of foreign direct investment. The methodology adopted utilises data from the World Bank, which is analysed using descriptive techniques. The chapter concludes that over dependent on the foreign direct investment will make the recipient countries as an extension of the donor countries.

INTRODUCTION

All countries of the world need a strong capital base for virile economic growth and development. Capital is an essential ingredient which lubricates the wheels of the economy to achieve rapid growth. A country with huge sums of such capital base will possess a strong economy which will enable it to explore other channels of development while a country with little or poor capital base will possess a weak economy

DOI: 10.4018/979-8-3693-0477-8.ch012

which will be handicapped to devilled into major developmental enterprises that will lead to economic, social, and political growth. Capital is therefore necessary for every country to lubricate the wheels of the economy for development.

It is obvious that the developed countries of the world held on to continuous capital investments in the economy and this results in rapid economic growth in most cases in Europe, America and a few countries in Asia and Latin America. The case of most developing countries such as those in Africa, Asia, the Middle East, and Latin America is different. There is little to invest as capital and the little is mostly diverted to patronage of patrons and clients' relationships (Aluko 2017). This has made such countries depend on the mercies and moral reasoning of the developed countries to send in foreign capital for their local development. These occur in different forms such as economic loans, gifts, charities, and expertise-advised investments, especially in the form of foreign direct investments (FDI).

Foreign direct investment is mobilised and scouted for by many developing countries. This includes the direct investment by an external country in an agreed or predetermined sector of the recipient country's economy to achieve a certain end which might be different to both the donor and the recipient countries at the same time. These capital investments are needed for the economy to strive from a little stage to a developed stage. Foreign direct investment like most loans from developmental institutions such as the World Bank, International Monetary Fund (IMF) and other donor agencies is strictly attached to some terms and conditions. These terms and conditions must be met and obeyed to be in the good book of the donor agencies.

In most cases, these conditions might be unfavourable to the welfare of the country's economic development in the long run. Some of the unfavourable imposed policies by the donor institutions include stiff tax regimes, privatisation and commercialisation of major assets of the state, deregulation of major sectors and devaluation of the country's currency among other policies. The recipient countries do not have many choices due to their conditions of lack of sufficient capital to be invested in their economy therefore they need to depend on the external hands of the developed countries.

The research question this Chapter seeks answer to is what is the prospect and bane of foreign direct investment on the recipient countries' economy? It is widely believed that the sole purpose of an investor in an investment is to make a gain but should this be to the detriment of the recipient communities? The benefits that most recipient nations harnessed, did it commensurate with the visible and the invincible, known and unknown losses? The theoretical framework of dependency theory is used to analyse the prospect and bane of foreign direct investment. The methodology adopted utilises data from the World Bank which was analysed using descriptive techniques.

BACKGROUND

Foreign Direct Investment

Foreign direct investment (FDI) is made into a business or a sector by an individual or a company from an overseas country. It is different from portfolio investment, which is made more indirectly into another country's economy by using financial instruments, such as bonds and stocks. World Economic Report (2007), Olusanya (2013) and Osei, and Kim (2023) conceived it as an investment involving a long-term relationship and reflecting a lasting interest and control by a resident entity in one economy (foreign direct investor or parent enterprise) in an enterprise resident in an economy other than that of the foreign direct investor (FDI Enterprise or affiliate enterprise or foreign affiliate). FDI implies that the investor exerts a significant degree of influence on the management of the enterprise resident in the other economy or economies.

There are various levels and forms of foreign direct investment, depending on the type of companies involved and the reasons for investment. A foreign direct investor might purchase a company in the target country utilizing a merger or acquisition, setting up a new venture or expanding the operations of an existing one. Other forms of FDI include the acquisition of shares in an associated enterprise, the incorporation of a wholly owned company or subsidiary and participation in an equity joint venture across international boundaries. FDI has three components: equity capital, reinvested earnings and intra-company loans (UNCTAD 2012, Aluko, Opoku, Ibrahim, and Kufuor, 2023). In a different prospect, Morisset (2000) and Agwu, (2014) from economic perspectives argue that FDI is a type of investment that involves the injection of foreign funds into an enterprise that operates in a different country of origin from the investor. Investors are granted management and voting rights if the level of ownership is greater than or equal to 10% of ordinary shares. Shares ownership amounting to less than the stated amount is termed portfolio investment and is not considered FDI.

The Organization for Economic Cooperation and Development (2008) opined that FDI Provides a means for creating direct, stable and long-lasting links between economies. Foreign direct investment (FDI) is an investment made by a company or individual in one country in business interests in another country, in the form of either establishing business operations or acquiring business assets in the other country, such as ownership or controlling interest in a foreign company (Anyanwu 2017; Kasemsap 2017; Amendolagine, Hansen, Lema, Rabellotti, and Ribaudo, 2023). Foreign direct investments are distinguished from portfolio investments in which an investor merely purchases equities of foreign-based companies. The key feature of foreign direct investment is that it is an investment made that establishes either effective control of, or at least substantial influence over, the decision-making of a foreign business.

Desbordes, and Wei, (2017), Kasemsap (2017) and Camara (2023) also noted that foreign direct investments are commonly made in open economies, as opposed to tightly regulated economies, that offer a skilled workforce and above-average growth prospects for the investor. Foreign direct investment frequently involves more than just a capital investment. It may include the provision of management or technology as well. Foreign direct investments are commonly categorized as being horizontal, vertical or conglomerate in nature. A horizontal direct investment refers to the investor establishing the same type of business operation in a foreign country as it operates in its home country, for example, a cell phone provider based in China opening up stores in Nigeria.

A vertical investment is one in which different but related business activities from the investor's main business are established or acquired in a foreign country, such as when a manufacturing company acquires an interest in a foreign company that supplies parts or raw materials required for the manufacturing company to make its products (Danakol, Estrin, Reynolds, and Weitzel, 2017; Investopedia 2017; Camara, 2023). Meunier, (2017) also noted that a conglomerate type of foreign direct investment is one where a company or individual makes a foreign investment in a business that is unrelated to its existing business in its home country. Since this type of investment involves entering an industry the investor has no previous experience, it often takes the form of a joint venture with a foreign company already operating in the industry.

THEORETICAL FRAMEWORK

Dependency Theory

Dependency Theory was developed in the late 1950s by Raul Prebisch. Prebisch and his colleagues were troubled by the fact that economic growth in the advanced industrialized countries did not necessarily lead to growth in the poorer countries. Indeed, they also suggested that economic activity in the richer countries often led to serious economic problems in the poorer countries. This was contrary to the opinion of the neoclassical theory, which had assumed that economic growth was beneficial to all (Pareto optimality) even if the benefits were not always equally shared.

Osvaldo (1969) purported that dependency is an explanation of the economic development of a state in terms of the external influences--political, economic, and cultural--on national development policies. Theotonio (1971) also perceived dependency as a historical condition which shapes a certain structure of the world economy such that it favours some countries to the detriment of others and limits the development possibilities of subordinate economics. This is an emphasis on the historical dimension of the dependency relationships in his definition. Dependency theory advocated an inward-looking approach to development and an increased role for the state in terms of imposing barriers to trade, making inward investment difficult and promoting nationalisation of key industries.

Prebisch's explanation for the phenomenon was that when poor countries export raw materials and or primary commodities to the rich countries, the rich countries then manufacture products out of those commodities and sell them back to the poorer countries. The "Value Added" of manufacturing a usable product always cost more than the primary products used to create those products (Ferraro 2008). Therefore, poorer countries would never be earning enough from their export earnings to pay for their imports. This makes them always depend on the rich countries to supply their basic needs as the finished goods to them.

Prebisch therefore suggested that the poorer countries should embark on programs of import substitution, exchange goods for services, or other products so that they need not purchase the manufactured products from the richer countries. The poorer countries would still sell their primary products on the world market, but their foreign exchange reserves would not be used to purchase their manufactures from abroad. This will reduce the level of dependency on the rich countries by the poor ones. But the question is how feasible is this breakoff? The major problems that the poor countries will encounter are; the small and lean nature of the internal markets of the poorer countries which may not be sufficient to support the economies of scale used by the richer countries to keep their prices low.

Also, the political will of the poorer countries to transform from being primary product producers and exporters to finished goods exporters and to what extent do the poorer countries have control of their primary products, particularly in the area of selling those products abroad? Therefore, dependency theory explains the persistent poverty and dependency status of poorer countries. The traditional neoclassical approach of the dependency theory opined that the poorer countries were late in coming to solid economic practices and that as soon as they learned the techniques of modern economics, then the poverty would begin to subside. However, Marxist theorists of the dependency theory only perceived persistent poverty as a consequence of capitalist exploitation.

Dependency theory believes that the character of the international system is comprised of two sets of states, variously described as dominant/dependent, centre/periphery or metropolitan/satellite. The dominant states are the advanced industrial nations in the Organization of Economic Co-operation and

Development (OECD) such as the United States of America, the United Kingdom, Russia, France, and Germany among others. The dependent states are those states of Latin America, Asia, and Africa which have low *per capita* and poor gross national products (GNPs) and which rely heavily on the export of a single commodity for foreign exchange earnings (Bodenheimer 1971; Aluko and Aderinola, 2019). They also assumed that external forces are germane to the economic activities within the dependent states. These external forces include multinational corporations, international commodity markets and foreign assistance among others.

Andre Gunder Frank (1972) one of the earliest dependency theorists views the capitalist system as enforcing a rigid international division of labour which is responsible for the underdevelopment of many areas of the world. The dependent states supply cheap minerals, agricultural commodities, and cheap labour, and serve as the repositories of surplus capital, obsolescent technologies, and manufactured goods. For the dependency theorists, underdevelopment is a wholly negative condition which offers no possibility of sustained and autonomous economic activity in a dependent state.

METHODOLOGY

The methodology adopted utilises data from the World Bank. Two Sample sizes are selected. The first is the foreign direct investments for 1970 and 2015 of five regions of the world such as the Arab World, the European Union, the Latin America and Caribbean, the Middle East and North Africa and Sub-Saharan Africa. The second sample size is the randomly selected countries of developing countries in Africa. This includes; Nigeria, South Africa, Sudan, Kenya and Morocco. The foreign direct investment data collected for 1970 and 2015 were analysed using descriptive techniques.

DATA PRESENTATION AND ANALYSIS OF ECONOMY GROWTH

Foreign Direct Investment, Net Inflows (BoP, Current US$)

(International Monetary Fund, Balance of Payments database, supplemented by data from the United Nations Conference on Trade and Development and official national sources).

Table 1. Showing FDI to selected regions of the world

World Regions FDI	1970	2015
Arab World	155,910,000	35,484,089,184
European Union	4,029,972,127	554,876,979,520
Latin America & Caribbean	615,103,000	256,646,044,965
Middle East & North Africa	225,950,000	49,002,815,022
Sub-Saharan Africa	706,575,988	42,230,921,200

Source: The World Bank 2023

Figure 1. Showing FDI to selected regions of the world

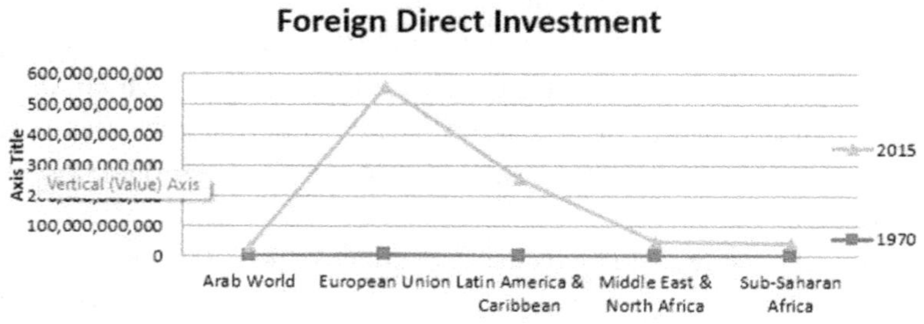

From Table I and Figure 1 above, the FDI to the Arab world in 1970 was very low but this witnessed a drastic change in 2015 but this was still below that of Sub-Saharan Africa and Middle East and North Africa. This implies that the rate of capital investment in their economy has improved to a somewhat high level which has transformed their economy from a poor to a rich economy. The FDI in the European Union in 1970 was that of Sub-Saharan Africa, Middle East and North Africa, Latin America and the Caribbean and the Arab World put together and in 2015 the capital investments still surpassed the four regions put together. This implies that the European Union is typically a richer region than the rest of the world. The FDI to Latin America and the Caribbean is slightly lower than that of Sub-Saharan Africa in 1970 but this was largely exceeded in 2015 by a great margin of growth and development. This implies that the extent of capital investment inform of FDI to this region has contributed to the transformation of this region of the world.

This phenomenon is similar to that of the Middle East and North Africa which were lower than the Sub-Saharan Africa FDI in 1970 but the rate of the investments slightly surpasses that of the Sub-Saharan Africa. This (among other factors as the political will of the leaders of each country and regional unions to develop such regions accounts for the) growth difference among the regions of the world and the present rate of development and dependency among the regions. The line graph depicts that the 1970 foreign direct investments to all the regions of the world were very low to those of 2015 which witnessed a tremendous improvement. The European Union region of the world revealed a virile economic growth and development has the highest marginal difference and the Arab World has the poorest economic development in terms of FDI followed by Sub-Saharan Africa and Middle East and North Africa respectively.

Table 2. Showing FDI in selected countries in Africa

Selected Countries FDI	1970	2015
Nigeria	205,000,000	3,128,591,679
South Africa	333,605,988	1,521,139,945
Sudan	1,660,000	1,736,764,247
Kenya	13,800,000	1,437,000,004
Morocco	20,000,000	3,252,913,902

Source: The World Bank 2023

Figure 2. Showing FDI in selected countries in Africa

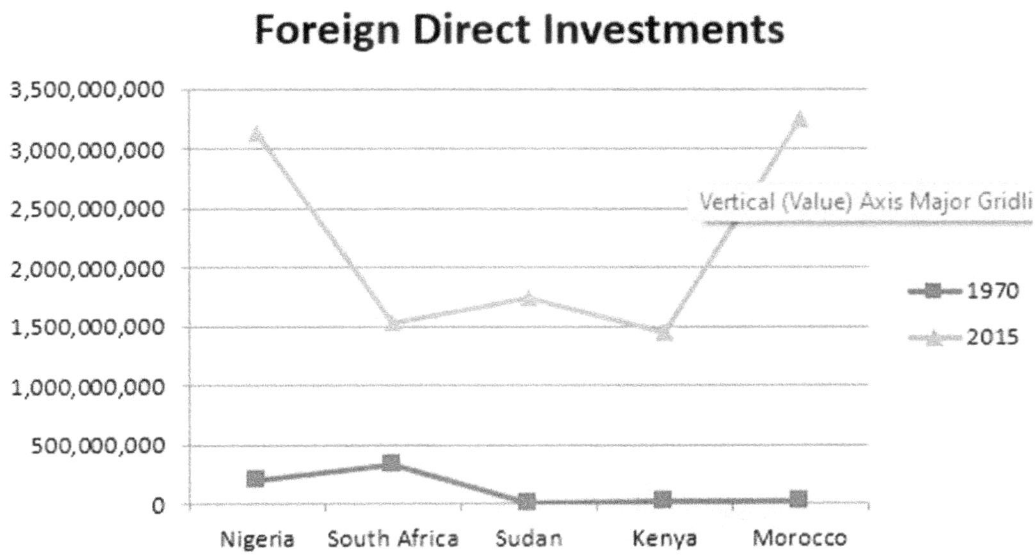

From Table II and Figure 2 above, the FDI to Nigeria in 1970 was very high and this trend was sustained in 2015 to the extent that it is the highest next to South Africa in the selected countries. However, these have not translated into rapid economic growth and development. This may largely be due to the political will of the leaders in addressing the most germane issues of development in the country. The FDI in South Africa in 1970 was the highest in Africa but in 2015 the capital investments dropped to a low point than Nigeria. This is a paradox because the reductions in South Africa's FDI have not reduced her economic growth and development as seen in Nigeria. This may be due to the political will of South Africa's leadership to grow the economy with indigenous resources prudently. The FDI in Sudan and Kenya was far lower than that of Nigeria and South Africa in 1970 but not too low in 2015. This implies that capital investment in the form of FDI to this region has contributed to the economic growth and development of these countries.

This phenomenon is similar to that of Morocco which had lower FDI than Nigeria and South Africa in 1970 but the rate of the investments slightly surpasses that of Nigeria and South Africa. The country has a more emphatic growth and development than many countries in Africa. This no doubt is not a result of huge FDI alone but other factors as the political will of the leaders of the country to develop her economy cannot be jettisoned. The line graph depicts that the 1970 foreign direct investments to all the countries were very low to those of 2015 which witnessed a tremendous improvement. The Nigerian and Moroccan economies were the highest recipients of the FDI but were not evenly developed due to differences in the political structures. Morocco and the South have a virile economic growth and development despite South Africa having lower FDI like those of Sudan and Kenya respectively.

In Figure 3, it is observed that FDI was better off in Eastern and Southern Africa since 2015 than in Western and Central Africa. This is due to the good governance and evidence of democratic evidence in the economy and in the attraction of foreigners to invest in their economy than that of their West Central African counterparts. However, by 2022, the World Bank data shows that both had reduced to an almost equal level. This is due to the global pandemic that resulted in world economic meltdown.

Figure 3. Showing FDI in Africa (East and South; West and Central)

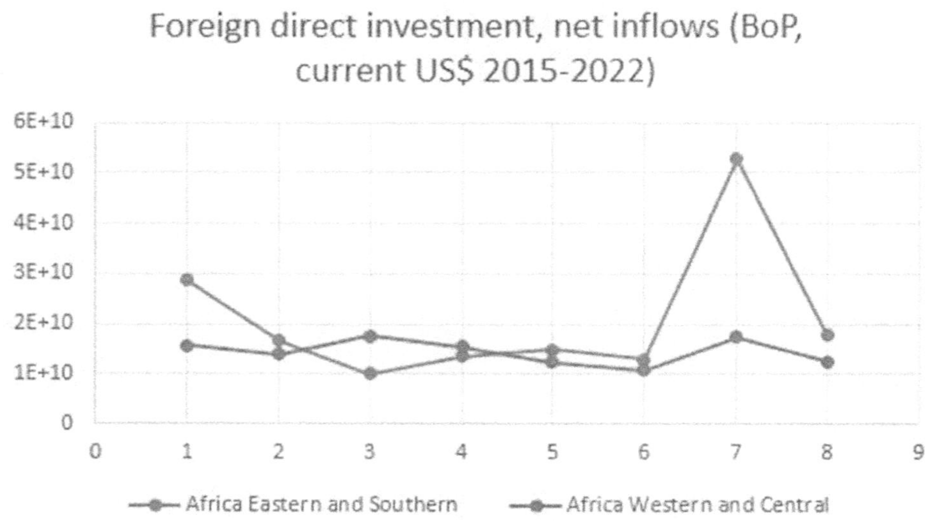

PROSPECT AND BANE OF FOREIGN DIRECT INVESTMENT

Foreign direct investment has a lot of prospects for the host or recipient nation and the donor country. At the same time, it has its banes for both the host or recipient nation and the donor country. Some of the prospects include capital, technology and management benefits among others.

Capital

Multinational enterprises (MNEs) invest in long-term projects, taking risks and repatriating profits only when the projects yield returns. The free flow of capital across nations is likely to be favoured by many political economists since it allows capital to yield the highest rate of return. Many MNEs are usually very large and diverse in operations. By their large size and financial strength, have access to financial resources not available to host country firms. MNEs may find it easier to borrow money from capital markets than host-country firms would (Hill, 2000; Aluko 2017; Osei and Kim, 2023).

Bosworth and Collins (1999); Jenkins and Thomas (2002) and Aluko et al (2023) argue that FDI can contribute to economic growth not only by providing foreign capital but also by crowding in additional domestic investment; so it increases the total growth effect of FDI. Feldstein (2000) emphasized several advantages that are related to unrestricted capital flows, such as International flows of capital reduce the risk faced by owners of capital by allowing them to diversify their lending and investment. The global integration of capital markets can contribute to the spread of best practices of corporate governance, accounting rules, and legal traditions. The global mobility of capital limits the ability of governments to pursue bad policies.

Technology

The crucial role played by technological progress in economic growth is more pronounced in the economies of industrialised nations. Technology can stimulate economic development and industrialization. Hill, (2000) and Kwakwa, Adzawla, Alhassan, and Oteng-Abayie, (2023) noted that it can take two forms, both of which are valuable. Technology can be incorporated into a production process such as the technology for discovering, extracting and refining crude products or it can be incorporated into a product such as personal computers.

However, many countries lack the research and development resources and skills required to develop their own native product and process technology. Kurtishi-Kastrati (2013) noted that technologies that are transferred to developing countries in connection with foreign direct investment tend to be more modern and environmentally friendly than what is locally available. Moreover, positive externalities have been observed where local imitation, employment turnover and supply-chain requirements led to more general environmental improvements in the host economy.

Management

FDI helps in the management of knowledge and the transfer of knowledge. This will increase the existing stock of knowledge in the host country through labour training, the transfer of skills, and the transfer of new managerial and organizational practices. Foreign management skills acquired through FDI may also produce important benefits for the host countries. The beneficial offshoot effect arises when local personnel who are trained to occupy managerial, financial and technical posts in the subsidiary of a foreign MNE leave the firm and help to establish local firms.

Lall and Streeten (1977) and Amendolagine et al (2023) emphasized that training received by foreign companies sometimes may be considered under the general heading of organization and management, meaning that the host country will benefit from the managerial superiority of MNCs. Lall and Streeten (1977) and Dunning, 1993 also listed three kinds of managerial benefits of foreign direct Investments; Managerial efficiency in operations arising from better training and higher standards; Entrepreneurial capability in seeking out investment opportunities and externalities arising from training received by employees such as technical staffs, executive officers, accounting Clark and so on.

Other viable advantages of Foreign Direct Investment in any economy include; a general stimulation of the economic development. The target countries' economic development creates a more conducive environment for the investor and benefits for the local industry. It also makes international trade to be easy. Industries that usually require their presence in the international markets to ensure their sales and goals are achieved will be completely satisfied with FDI.

Foreign direct investment also creates new jobs, as investors build new companies in the target country, and create new opportunities. This may usually lead to an increase in income and sometimes more buying power for the people, which in turn leads to an economic boost.

Another prospect of the FDI is the development of human capital resources which helps to strengthen democracy. Human capital is the competence and knowledge of those able to perform labour, known as the workforce. The attributes gained by training and sharing experience would increase education and positively affect the overall human capital of a country. Foreign direct investment also allows resource transfer and other exchanges of knowledge, where various countries are given access to new technologies and skills. The facilities and equipment provided by foreign investors can increase a workforce's productivity in the target country and increase the target country's income. With more jobs and higher wages, the national income normally increases and economic growth is spurred to a reasonable height.

The banes of FDI are almost equivalent to the prospects in both the host and the donor country. FDI, even more than other types of capital flows, has historically given rise to these conflicting views because FDI involves a controlling stake by often large MNEs over which domestic governments fear and have little power. The controversies have mostly focused on the inward, that FDI, due to sensitivity often exert foreign control over domestic industries. In small economies, large foreign companies can and often abuse their influence due to their dominant market positions. Countries facing increased inflows of FDI have often experienced unease. Many developing countries have until recently been wary of inward FDI. The alleged economic effects include balance of payments deficits, reduced domestic research and development, diminished competition, crowding-out of domestic firms and lower employment, the potentially harmful environmental impact of FDI, especially in the heavy industries and the effects on competition in national markets.

Another major bane of FDI is job loss; In the case of FDI by Japanese auto companies in the US, some argue that the jobs created by this investment have been more than offset by the jobs lost in US-owned auto companies, which have lost market share to their Japanese competitors (Agwu, 2014). However, as a consequence of such substitution effects, the net number of new jobs created by FDI may not be as great as initially claimed by an MNE (Hill, 2000; Agwu, 2014). In the case of the Republic of Macedonia, the high unemployment represents the biggest economic problem and it has a direct effect on low economic growth and the small number of newly opened workplaces. The restructuring process of the enterprises in the course of the transition resulted in increased unemployment in the short run (Agwu, 2014; Aluko and Aderinola, 2019; Aluko and Oluwadele, 2023).

Unhealthy competition; Although FDI can boost competition, it is mostly to the detriment of the host governments. The subsidiaries of foreign MNEs may have greater economic power than local competitors. If it is part of a large international organization, the foreign MNEs may be able to draw on funds generated elsewhere to subsidize its costs in the host market, which could drive local companies out of business and allow the firm to monopolize the market. This concern tends to be greater in countries that have few large firms of their own in most less developed countries.

The negative balance of payments set against the initial capital inflow that comes with FDI must be the subsequent outflow of earnings from the foreign subsidiary to its parent company. Such outflows show up as a debit on the capital account. This therefore leads to hindrance to domestic investment. Domestic investors will focus their resources elsewhere other than the investor's home country. It also has a negative influence on exchange rates. Foreign direct investments can occasionally affect exchange rates to the advantage of one country and the detriment of another. This depends on the level of risk in the political system.

FDI in many instances results in higher costs of investments and exports. Things might be so expensive to the extent that exportation might be of more benefit than FDI. If the FDI is not well planned, because it is capital-intensive it can sometimes become very risky or economically non-viable. This will in turn constitute a negative impact on the country's investment if foreign exchange rates and direct investment products are banned in some foreign markets. Olusanya, (2013) opined that most importantly for developing countries, FDI may constitute modern-day economic colonialism and political neo-colonialism. Many countries at least those with a history of colonialism, believes that foreign direct investment result in some kind of modern-day economic colonialism, exploitation and neo-colonialism which exposes host countries to external control and aggression.

CONCLUSION

The Chapter concludes that over dependent on foreign direct investment by a country will make the recipient countries a mere extension of the donor countries. Governance and democracy will be better when there is a control or balance of trade to prevent neo-colonialism in developing countries. Therefore, there must be some drastic measures in reconciling the banes of FDI on the host country. Given these, there is a need to rethink on the existing policies in the locales. Policy recommendations to the government and other private indigenous investors include the following; the government must concentrate on providing the basic infrastructures to support the local organized private sector that are ready to invest domestic funds into the economy. This can be achieved if a favourable environment with tax-friendly, stable rates and effective unbiased monopoly-like market competition policies are made.

The response to private initiatives by the government must be more proactive to more favourable policies targeting specifically the locals as opposed to foreigners. Many investors regard political and economic stability, availability of natural resources and a large and growing market as important factors to attract foreign direct investment. This means that all of these incentives should be further used to domesticate capital projects and domestic investments in a global environment. Other incentives which the government and other policy actors must consider for domestic economic growth and development to ensue and be boosted in the country include the following; low transactions and business costs for labour and trade regulations, entry and exit rules, location and environment regulation and a favourable Subcontract services to local firms.

Other essential policy notes include the support for quality assurance and technical extension to small and medium-scale enterprises (SMEs). Human capital with diverse modern skills enhancement and a reasonably low cost of infrastructure such as efficient communications system, power rates and transportation links may be systematically built upon. A transparent merger and acquisition of firms, industries and other means of production either from the government to the private ownership or the reversal. Similarly, open policies on export activities such as free trade and free foreign exchange regimes may be created to maximize economies of scale.

REFERENCES

Agwu, E. (2014). Foreign Direct Investments: A Review from The Nigerian Perspective. *Research Journal of Business & Management, 1*(3).

Aluko, O. A., Opoku, E. E. O., Ibrahim, M., & Kufuor, N. K. (2023). Put on the light! Foreign direct investment, governance and access to electricity. *Energy Economics*, *119*, 106563. doi:10.1016/j.eneco.2023.106563

Aluko O.I. (2017). Political Economy of Crony Inequality Among Nations: A Study on Capitalism and Socialism. *Journal of Community Development Research (Humanities and Social Sciences), 10*(2).

Aluko, O. I., & Aderinola, G. (2019). E-Governance and Corruption Impasse In Nigeria: A Developmental Expedition Synopsis. In R. Abassi & A. Ben Chehida Douss (Eds.), Security Frameworks in Contemporary Electronic Government (pp. 129-149). Hershey, PA: IGI Global. doi:10.4018/978-1-5225-5984-9.ch006

Aluko, O. I., & Oluwadele, L. B. (Eds.). (2023). *Insights and Explorations in Democracy, Political Unrest, and Propaganda in Elections*. IGI Global. doi:10.4018/978-1-6684-8629-0

Amendolagine, V., Hansen, U. E., Lema, R., Rabellotti, R., & Ribaudo, D. (2023). Do green foreign direct investments increase the innovative capability of MNE subsidiaries? *World Development*, *170*, 106342. doi:10.1016/j.worlddev.2023.106342

Andre, G. F. (1972). The Development of Underdevelopment. In J. D. Cockcroft, A. G. Frank, & D. Johnson (Eds.), *Dependence and Underdevelopment* (p. 3). Anchor Books.

Anyanwu, J. C. (2017). Foreign direct investment. Handbook of Globalisation and Development, 131.

Bodenheimer, S. (1971). Dependency and Imperialism: The Roots of Latin American Underdevelopment. In *Readings in U.S. Imperialism*. Boston: Porter Sargent.

Bosworth, B.P., & Collins, S.M. (1999). Capital flows to developing economies: implications for saving and investment. *Brookings Papers on Economic Activity*, 1.

Camara, A. (2023). The effect of foreign direct investment on tax revenue. *Comparative Economic Studies*, *65*(1), 168–190. doi:10.105741294-022-00195-2

Danakol, S. H., Estrin, S., Reynolds, P., & Weitzel, U. (2017). Foreign direct investment via M&A and domestic entrepreneurship: Blessing or curse? *Small Business Economics*, *48*(3), 599–612. doi:10.100711187-016-9792-z

Desbordes, R., & Wei, S. J. (2017). The effects of financial development on foreign direct investment. *Journal of Development Economics*, *127*, 153–168. doi:10.1016/j.jdeveco.2017.02.008

Dunning, J. (1993). *Multinational Enterprises and the Global Economy*. Addison-Wesley.

Feldstein, M. (2000). *Aspects of Global Economic Integration: Outlook for the Future*. National Bureau of Economic Research. NBER Working Paper No.7899.

Hill, C. (2000). *International Business - Competing in the Global Marketplace*. Irwin McGraw-Hill.

Investopedia. (2017). *Foreign Direct Investment – FDI*. http://www.investopedia.com/terms/f/fdi.asp#ixzz4kYzUFivt

Jenkins, C., & Thomas, L. (2002). *Foreign Direct Investment in Southern Africa: Determinants, Characteristics and Implications for Economic Growth and Poverty Alleviation, Globalization and Poverty Project*. University of Oxford.

Kasemsap, K. (2017). Foreign Direct Investment. Handbook of Research on Economic, Financial, and Industrial Impacts on Infrastructure Development, 239.

Kurtishi-Kastrati, S. (2013). The Effects Of Foreign Direct Investments For Host Country's Economy. *European Journal of Interdisciplinary Studies, 5*(1).

Kwakwa, P. A., Adzawla, W., Alhassan, H., & Oteng-Abayie, E. F. (2023). The effects of urbanization, ICT, fertilizer usage, and foreign direct investment on carbon dioxide emissions in Ghana. *Environmental Science and Pollution Research International*, *30*(9), 23982–23996. doi:10.100711356-022-23765-4 PMID:36331739

Lall, S., & Streeten, P. (1977). *Foreign Investment, Transnationals and Developing Countries*. Macmillan. doi:10.1007/978-1-349-02290-8

Meunier, S. (2017). Integration by stealth: How the European Union gained competence over foreign direct investment. *Journal of Common Market Studies*, *55*(3), 593–610. doi:10.1111/jcms.12528

Morisset, J. (2000). Foreign Direct Investment in Africa: Policies Also Matter. *Transnational Corporations, 9*(2).

Olusanya, S. (2013). Impact of Foreign Direct Investment Inflow on Economic Growth in a Pre and Post Deregulated Nigeria Economy. A Granger Causality Test (1970-2010). *European Scientific Journal*, *9*(25).

Osei, M. J., & Kim, J. (2023). *Financial development and the growth effect of foreign direct investment: Does one size fit all?* International Economics.

Osvaldo, S. (1969). National Development Policy and External Dependence in Latin America. *The Journal of Development Studies*, *6*(1).

Theotonio, D. (1971). The Structure of Dependence. In *Readings in U.S. Imperialism.* Boston: Porter Sargent.

UNCTAD. (2012). *World Investment Reports. United Nations Conference on Trade and Development.*

World Bank. (2017). *Foreign direct investment, net inflows (BoP, current US$) International Monetary Fund, Balance of Payments database, supplemented by data from the United Nations Conference on Trade and Development and official national sources.* www.worldbankdata.org

Chapter 13
Rural Startups in an Emerging Market:
An Examination of the Entrepreneurial Ecosystem in Rural Areas of Uganda

Isaac Wasswa Katono
https://orcid.org/0000-0002-6106-3078
Uganda Christian University, Uganda

ABSTRACT

This study investigates factors that constrain the development of rural startups in the Ugandan rural entrepreneurial ecosystem in light of the importance of entrepreneurship in reducing poverty worldwide. Based on a review of the literature on entrepreneurial ecosystems, necessity, and opportunity entrepreneurship plus a range of theoretical approaches, the study demonstrates that the characteristics of the rural population, the social cultural context, and the lack of physical infrastructure greatly constrain the start and growth of rural startups. Recommendations as to what should be done to promote rural startups are proposed.

INTRODUCTION

There is a consensus in the literature that a positive relationship exists between the creation of new entrepreneurial projects and the development of a region or country (Audretsch & Keilback, 2007). According to Sutter et al., (2019), entrepreneurship has the potential to alleviate rural poverty. In their review of over 200 articles from 77 journals covering the period 1997-2017, these authors' analysis reveals three different perspectives through which entrepreneurship alleviates poverty. The first is poverty alleviation through entrepreneurship as remediation (actions that address immediate resource concerns). This perspective assumes that poverty is a result of a lack of resources, thus a provision of these resources will enable entrepreneurship to flourish. The second perspective is that of reform (actions that address institutional changes). It assumes that markets are potential engines of poverty alleviation, hence the

DOI: 10.4018/979-8-3693-0477-8.ch013

issue of market access comes to the fore. The third perspective is revolution (actions that change the underlying capitalist assumptions of business). This perspective argues that poverty alleviation will occur if different economic models are devised and scaled through entrepreneurship.

Do Entrepreneurs Need Democratic Space?

Entrepreneurs should subscribe to the basic tenets of economic democracy, without which they would not survive. Democracy guarantees the right of everyone to participate in social-economic activities, and to own and use private property (Ummatovich et al., 2020). According to Gomez and Korine (2008), there is an iterative bond between work and private property, which means that people can only acquire property through work i.e., work legitimizes private property. Hence entrepreneurs need an efficient policy concerning the efficient and rational use of labor, which can only be guided by effective legislative laws as those espoused in a democratic environment. Democracy enables the creation and fostering of competition, or a market economy; this competitive environment fosters innovation, as entrepreneurs fight to attract and retain customers, to the benefit of society (Ummatovich et al., 2020). In effect, entrepreneurs do influence the socio-economic life of a community through the formation of a market economy.

Necessity and Opportunity Entrepreneurship

Entrepreneurship has two major categories: necessity and opportunity entrepreneurship. Block et al., (2015) argue that primary motivations for one starting a business are important for strategy, as some founders start a business out of necessity because they have no other way of getting an income (necessity entrepreneurs), while other founders launch a business under less restrictive or compelling conditions (opportunity entrepreneurs). The necessity aspect has strong connotations for the motivational, human development and resource endowments of the business and hence its nature, future and impact on economic growth (Kautonen & Palmross, 2010). Opportunity entrepreneurship is more prevalent in high-income countries and is linked to economic growth, while necessity entrepreneurship occurs more in low-income countries and is linked to low growth; this is probably because people in high-income countries have more safety nets (social welfare) and a more developed labour market, hence they do not feel the need to start a business (Reynolds et al., 2002).

Block et al. (2015) further argue that strategies pursued by a new venture are influenced by the motivations of their founders and the particular situations in which they find themselves. Since their motivation is to find a job or an income, necessity entrepreneurs usually pursue a cost leadership strategy rather than a differentiation strategy (they lack the resources to make their businesses unique). Why is this the case? First, necessity entrepreneurs may have little time in which to plan their ventures. Second, they may have fewer capital or knowledge-based resources that can enable them to craft a differentiated product or service (Denceker et al., 2009). In other words, necessity entrepreneurs are less likely to have the knowledge, education and skills that can enable them to pursue a differentiation strategy. They may have to resort to family labor for example to enable them to produce products cheaply. In light of their situation and motivation, they may not make a significant impact on economic growth. The challenge of African governments is to produce more opportunity-driven entrepreneurship even in the rural areas, and also provide the conditions that spur firms to grow.

The shift from need-based entrepreneurship to more opportunity-driven entrepreneurship requires the development of a favourable entrepreneurial ecosystem to alleviate poverty in rural remote areas. An entrepreneurial ecosystem is defined as the support platform for the creation and growth of new enterprises (Flores & Kovacs, 2018). ANDE (2013) argues that entrepreneurship can improve the livelihoods of people who live in rural areas, "*if it can evolve beyond the informal, necessity-based entrepreneurship that is currently prevalent in many emerging economies to opportunity-based firm creation led by managers that intend to grow their businesses and generate increased employment and sustainable income for the poor*". Hence a supportive entrepreneurial ecosystem is a prerequisite in the bid to realize SDG 1. The attainment of development goals and higher living standards by developing African countries will depend on their ability to foster entrepreneurship and promote innovation (Oyelaran-Oyeyinka & Lal, 2016). There is plenty of evidence in the literature in support of the notion that entrepreneurship spurs economic growth as espoused in this paper. For example, Stephens and Partridge (2011) in their study of the Appalachian region found that positive outcomes of entrepreneurship in fostering economic growth are reinforced by the existence of many opportunity entrepreneurs, as opposed to necessity entrepreneurs.

Constraints in the Entrepreneurial Ecosystem in Rural Areas

Research on African entrepreneurship is limited (Sherriff & Muffatto, 2015), hence little is known about African entrepreneurial ventures (Igwe & Icha-Ituma, 2020). While many approaches to local economic development have evolved in the recent past, economic development based on local entrepreneurship is increasingly gaining momentum in the research, policy, and practice spheres. The motivation to stimulate economic growth and job creation through entrepreneurship can be traced to the work of Birch (1979), who argued that job creation was not coming from large companies, but rather from small independently owned businesses in the US. Since then, government interest in entrepreneurship and small business development to bolster economic growth and stem rising unemployment has increased the world over. In agreement, the Africa Commission (2009) calls upon Africa to embrace entrepreneurship and considers macroeconomic factors which influence job creation and entrepreneurship as a panacea to unemployment.

Therefore, in the bid to promote economic development, and alleviate the scourge of poverty haunting its peoples, African nations must focus on the development of entrepreneurship in both urban and rural areas. Unfortunately, there is concern that the current economic environment in Africa is breeding more necessity entrepreneurs than opportunity entrepreneurs (Amin, 2010). Hence, a key question is what constraints does the entrepreneurial ecosystem impose on the development of entrepreneurship in Africa? To answer these and other questions, there is a need to examine the entire entrepreneurial ecosystem (Motoyama & Watkins, 2014), thus, Igwe and Icha-Ituma (2020) call for more rigorous research on entrepreneurial ecosystems on this continent, given that general research on this subject is both underdeveloped and under-theorized (Spiegel, 2015).

Focusing on rural areas and Uganda in particular, this study reviews the literature on entrepreneurial ecosystems to examine the constraints to rural start-ups in SSA. The rest of this article is organized as follows. The next section presents the theoretical basis of entrepreneurial ecosystems, followed by a brief on the methodology used to conduct this study in section three. Section four presents some of the root causes of poverty in Uganda, while section five presents constraints to rural entrepreneurship imposed by the cultural ecosystem, the economic environment in rural areas, and the legal, political, and educational context follow in that order. A presentation on implications and recommendations wraps up the paper in section six.

BACKGROUND

First, it is important to note that there is no agreed definition of entrepreneurship (Baum et al., 2007). However, the focus of this paper is the examination of the entrepreneurial ecosystem, this paper adopts a definition emphasizing the context in which entrepreneurship occurs: Thornton (1999, p.20) defines entrepreneurship as the "*creation of a new organization which occurs as a context-dependent, socio and economic process*". This definition is based on the emphasis of Gartner (1988) i.e., starting an enterprise, According to Wennekers and Thurik (1999 p.34), "*entrepreneurship has to do with individuals, both with their traits and actions (roles)*".

The History of Entrepreneurship and Economic Growth

This section traces the link between entrepreneurship and economic growth as viewed by various schools of thought. The role of entrepreneurship in fostering economic growth has been a subject of debate by entrepreneurship researchers and economic theorists for a long time. Cipolla (1981) and Thurik et al., (2008) affirm that economic growth cannot be understood without considering the role of entrepreneurship and that a lack of entrepreneurship is directly related to low rates of innovation (Acs et al., 2013). In this regard, Wennekers and Thurik (1999) in Table I below, trace the role of entrepreneurship in economic growth as perceived by scholars in different domains.

From a historical perspective and focusing on the dynamic role of the entrepreneur in the economy, the taxonomy of entrepreneurship theories can be coalesced into three major traditions, each originating from Richard Cantillon (Hébert & Link, 1989). First is Schumpeter (1942) who views the entrepreneur as a creator and source of destruction. Second, the neo-classical growth approach is concerned with how supply and demand influence producers of goods and services within an economic system in determining equilibrium. Scholars within this realm have agreed that there is no space for entrepreneurship when the economy is in equilibrium because all resources are deployed efficiently (Glancey & McQuaid, 2000). Third, is the Austrian school whose economic model is based on methodological individualism (the notion that individual motivation, beliefs, values desires and actions explain social phenomena) and subjectivism (things do not have inherent value, but have value because individuals desire them, hence value is a feature of the appraiser) as the pillars of economic science (Andrieu, 2010). In Austrian thought, entrepreneurs drive the economy by determining the uses of the factors of production (Mises, 1949).

Endogenous growth models e.g., Lucas (1988) added human capital accumulation and knowledge capital to the growth models. "*By assuming that some knowledge was nonrival and nonexcludable, the explanatory power was greatly increased. However, the models lacked an agent that combined and applied the new knowledge with other factors of production to generate growth. In short, the models were entrepreneurless*" (Henrekson et al., 2021 p. 1). Economic history paints a picture of the role of entrepreneurship in the historical analysis of economic growth (Wennekers & Thurik, 1999; Thurik, 2007). In their review of the economic history of Europe, these authors assert that culture and institutions played a key role in the 'rise and fall of nations. For example, the decline of Great Britain was driven by the cultural and institutional environment in that country becoming less conducive to the growth of entrepreneurship. On the other hand, the Asian Miracle (the economic development of the Asian Tigers) is ascribed to the emergence of entrepreneurship, encouraged and sanctioned by the government. Hofstede (1995) points to the long-term value orientation of these countries as a possible contributor to this Asian Miracle.

The Porter (1990) analysis summarizes the role of entrepreneurship in economic development in industrial economics. In this view, four conditions govern the competitiveness of nations, and consequently the sustainability of productivity and growth. These four conditions are first the factor conditions made up of both natural resource endowments, cheap unskilled labour and factors such as skills, networks and infrastructure; second are the demand conditions, which are composed of the nature of buyer needs, the size and pattern of growth and mechanisms of transferring domestic requirements to foreign markets; the third is the presence of supporting industries, while the fourth refers to the nature and structure of domestic rivalry.

Finally, evolutionary economics as advocated for by Nelson and Winter (1982) does not explicitly state the role of the entrepreneur in economic growth, however, Eliasson (1995) asserts that the major production factor is competence capital personified in people. Such capital accumulates through education and on-the-job learning (Wennekers & Thurik, 1999: Thurik, 2007).

Table 1. Assessment of the role of entrepreneurship, drawn from several fields of research.

Field of literature	Specific Domain	Competition	Innovation	Firm start-ups	Importance of entrepreneurship for economic growth
Historical views	Schumpeter/Baumol Neo-classical Austrian	++ ++ ++	+++ + +	+ 0 0	++ + ++
Endogenous growth theory		+	+++	0	+
Economic History		++	+++	+	+++
Management Literature		+	+++	++	+++
Industrial economics	Porter	+++	+++	++	+
Evolutionary economics	Eliasson	+++	+++	+++	+++

Source: Wennekers & Thurik (1999 p. 50).
0 Not present in the writings.
+ Implicitly present in the writings.
++ Explicitly present in the writings.
+++ Pivotal element in the writings.

Knowledge Spillover Theory

The knowledge spillover theory of entrepreneurship (KSTE) developed by Marshall (in Audretsch et al., 2019) and later extended by scholars like Arrow (1962) and Romer (1986) is concerned with the contextual variables that influence entrepreneurship, shifting attention away from the firm to the individual actor or the entrepreneur (Acs et al., 2013). This theory advances the microeconomic foundation of endogenous growth theory and provides a framework that accounts for differences in growth rates between regions (Acs et al., 2013). According to this theory "*the context in which decision making is derived can influence one's determination to become an entrepreneur ....in particular if the context is rich in knowledge, entrepreneurial opportunities are generated from those ideas that are created; entrepreneurs put these ideas to good use (commercialize these ideas) and hence act as a conduit for the knowledge spill over and innovation, eventually enhancing the economic performance of a region*" (Acs et al., 2009). According to Acs and Szerb (2006), entrepreneurship contributes to economic growth by acting as a mechanism that permeates the knowledge filter, commercializing ideas that may not have been possible; thus, entrepreneurship makes a unique contribution by providing this missing link to economic growth (Armington, 2006).

Emergence of the Small Firm

Economic history shows the dominance of large firms characterized by economies of scale and mass production in the 19th century. However, the emergence of small firms (and entrepreneurship) started in the 1970s, and with it an increase in employment share. While there are so many reasons in the literature for this shift, Piore and Sable (1984) posit that the instability of markets led to the demise of mass production and the ushering in of small firms. Audretsch and Thurik (2000) assert that the shift toward a knowledge-based economy (and possible knowledge spillovers) is the force behind the shift from large to small business i.e. the rebirth of small firms is a result of technological opportunities made possible by information technology. Small businesses are a vehicle for entrepreneurship, contributing to employment, and social and political stability and are also an innovative and competitive force (Wennekers & Thurik, 1999: Thurik, 2007).

Acs et al., (2013) view economic development as a consequence of two models: a managed economy and an entrepreneurial economy. While both models attempt to explain the occurrence of economic growth through entrepreneurship, their foundations vary. The managed economy is characterized by stability, specialization, homogeneity, scale, certainty and predictability while the entrepreneurial economy is characterized by flexibility, turbulence, diversity, novelty, innovation, linkages and clustering (Audretsch & Thurik, 2004). Acs et al., (2013) provide three factors that link entrepreneurship to economic growth. The first is the shift from the managed economy to the entrepreneurial economy, the most important aspect of which is the changing and growing role of small firms as drivers of growth (Foelster, 2000). The second factor is the role of innovations, the job generation processes and institutional arrangements. The third factor is the role of entrepreneurial capital in fostering growth and this occurs in several ways. Audretsch and Thurik (2004), as well as Thurik (2007), propose that the first avenue is through knowledge spillovers, the second one is by creating a competitive environment (Porter, 1990), and the third is by creating diversity among firms (Cohen & Klepper, 1992).

ENTREPRENEURIAL ECOSYSTEM THEORY

Cluster and RIS Theory

The entrepreneurial ecosystem has two distinct streams of literature, each premised on a different theoretical approach, but sharing common roots in ecological systems thinking, by focusing on the interdependence of actors in a given community to create value (Acs et al., 2017). The first is the regional development literature, while the second is the strategy literature. The former examines ecosystems to account for differences in the socioeconomic performance of regions, clusters, industrial districts and regional innovation systems (Stam & Spiegel, 2017), while the latter focuses on business ecosystems or forms of economic coordination in which firm ability to create and appropriate value is contingent upon various groups of actors that provide complementary products and services (Williamson & De Meyer, 2012). Adner (2017) asserts that business ecosystems are the group of partners that should be brought into alignment for a value proposition to be realized in a given market; this alignment of various actors in the community is important for firms to create value (Acs et al., 2017).

The industrial district's view which focuses on the division of labour within an industry can be traced to Marshall (1920) who pays attention to the interaction between the populace and firms within a region (Becattini, 1990), while the cluster view refers to the collection of firms in a given area e.g., specialized suppliers, service providers and firms in related industries all of which may compete but also cooperate (Porter, 1988). Lastly, the regional innovation system (RIS) refers to networks that link knowledge producers such as universities to innovative firms within a region. Such linkages enhance knowledge spillover within the region, thus improving the innovativeness of the firms therein (Cook et al., 1997).

The Process Theory of Entrepreneurial Ecosystems

Spigel and Harrison (2017) posit that the literature on entrepreneurial ecosystems (EE) is typological and atheoretical and fails to explain how EE influences the entrepreneurial process. Consequently, these authors advance a process theory of entrepreneurial ecosystems. "*Rather than seeing ecosystems as tangible things, they can better be understood as ongoing processes through which entrepreneurs acquire resources, knowledge and support increasing their competitive advantage and ability to scale up (p.158). In this sense, we can talk about ecosystem processes as the mechanisms through which start-ups and scale-ups gain a competitive edge from their regional environments*". Ecosystems are viewed as processes: how ecosystems are reproduced and transformed over time and are driven by three major processes: The first process is resource creation (e.g., entrepreneurial knowledge, financial capital, successful mentors, skilled workers) which are created or attracted over time by entrepreneurial activity and public investment. The second process is resource recycling, within an ecosystem, while the third process is the flow of resources between actors. Process theory "*provides an important point of departure from the cluster and RIS theories of ecosystems and helps our understanding of entrepreneurship as a contextually embedded phenomenon.*"

Poverty in Africa

Africa is the poorest continent on this planet, despite its resource endowment of human and material (Addae-Korankye, 2014). Poverty in Africa has been increasing in the last two decades, despite numerous efforts by many African governments in conjunction with the Bretton Woods institutions to curb it. According to Ndaguba and Hanyane (2019 p.7), "*the persistence of poverty in Sub-Saharan Africa is allegedly because the approach used by the IMF and the World Bank for Poverty alleviation is not appropriate, hypocritical, misleading and fallacious*". This assertion is based on the fact that while the blueprints used to restart growth in other parts of the world facing similar predicaments as Africa faces today emphasized independence from these institutions, the prescriptions for restarting growth in Africa are in the opposite direction: Africa should be dependent upon these institutions. Evidence abounds to the effect that poverty has been growing steadily in Africa since the share of poverty in the region is above 600 million (Beegle et al., 2016; World Bank., 2008) as evidenced in Figure 1 below.

Figure 1. Rising poverty in SSA in millions
Source: Ndaguba and Hanyane (2018)

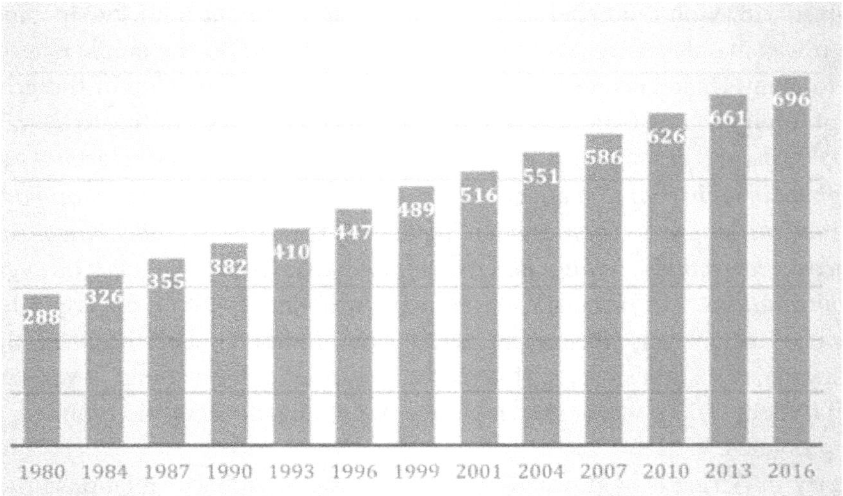

According to Eyoh and Sandbrook (2001), the economic crises facing SSA countries in the 1970s and 1980s led to the dwindling of commercial loans and foreign investment, thus forcing many SSA governments into the arms of the IMF and World Bank. The flow of financial aid depended on the recipient government's subservience to structural adjustment programs that funded government and development programs. Hence the governments of these countries resigned the shaping of economic and social policies to these external bodies (Mkandawire & Soludo, 1999). What caused the economic and social crises that led to this scenario? At independence, most SSA states depended on the exportation of raw materials and the contribution of manufacturing to their GDP was negligible (Eyoh & Sandbrook, 2001). Hence the rain-dependent peasant agricultural production in these countries could not withstand the exigencies of the weather like severe draught. Besides this, the colonial administration period in these countries like Uganda, for example, failed to produce entrepreneurs who would spearhead industrial development (Kennedy, 1988), since the colonialists feared that the emergence of an African entrepreneur would threaten political stability due to the eruption of socio-economic divisions, thus enacting policies that favoured European and Indian over indigenous African businesses. Consequently, most African states remained dependent on the export of agricultural raw materials even after independence, making them vulnerable to external shocks such as rising oil prices, falling commodity prices on the world market and global recession (Eyoh & Sandbrook, 2001).

Another major cause of inequalities and poverty is that the structural adjustment reforms that were implemented did not address the needs of the community due to a lack of consultation, because many governments' economic decisions were determined by international financial institutions (Muriisa, 2005). According to Ndaguba and Hanyane (2018), the neo-liberal ideology on which SAPs were based called for a free market approach in the economy even in vital areas such as education and health. The adoption of such policies resulted in inequalities in income, with the skilled workers having higher wages than the non-skilled workers (Ndou, 2012). A major policy included in the structural adjustment programs was the privatization of public enterprises, a process of increasing the efficiency of the private sector or any policy move to foster private sector development (Saiji Naya, 1990). A major intention of the privatization drive was to make the "*Southern countries become able to pay the debts owed to the Northern donors*" (Muriisa, 2005, p.122).

There are mixed views on the benefits of privatization, particularly to low-income earners in an economy. Since it was mainly foreigners who had the funds to bid for the public enterprises that were being divested, to many Ugandans for example this new form of ownership of the private companies was a new form of foreignization (Mamdani cited by Muriisa, 2005). According to Dumba-Sentamu and Mugume (2001), "*Although privatisation was intended to result in fiscal benefits and equity-enhancing outcomes through income distribution effects, there are concerns that privatisation has hurt the socio-economic welfare of the majority. There is a feeling that there has been inadequate participation of the locals in the process, hence their feeling robbed of national assets that were built through accumulation of taxpayers' contributions.*" In summary, the billions of dollars spent on poverty alleviation in SSA have had little or no effect, because the recipients of the programs do not participate in their formulation (Ndaguba & Hanyane, 2018); besides, problems are identified at the national level, and implemented at the local level (Ndou, 2012), which may lead to a wrong diagnosis of the problem, resulting in the creation of new problems.

Further, poverty in Africa is aggravated by the "core and periphery" relationships, in which poor nations that form the periphery (Africa) have little or no say in global issues including global business compared to the few core countries that have the economic muscle to prescribe the policies that determine the fate of the periphery countries. Lastly, poverty in the African continent is also a result of poor management systems, political machinations, corruption and bad leadership, wars and insurgencies, poor infrastructure, and cultural and structural factors, plus a lack of ability by the poor to influence social processes among others (Addae-Korankye, 2014).

Poverty in Uganda

The Uganda Bureau of Statistics (UBOS), the body mandated to collect and disseminate data in this country has computed a multi-dimensional poverty index (MPI) based on Alkire and Foster (2011), which is a holistic measure of the multi-dimensionality of poverty (UBOS, 2022). MPI is a measure of both the prevalence (incidence) and intensity (breadth) of poverty, based on four dimensions namely health, living standards, employment and financial inclusion. At the national level, the incidence of multidimensional poverty (the percentage of people who are multidimensional poor or the poverty rate or headcount ratio) was estimated at 42.1 per cent. The average intensity of poverty (the average percentage of dimensions in which poor people are deprived, or the average deprivation score of poor persons) was estimated at 54.5 per cent, implying that on average, the poor are deprived in 2.2 dimensions. The rural multidimensional headcount ratio and MPI were estimated at 50.2 per cent and 0.78 respectively, which is approximately three times larger than that of urban areas (19.7 per cent and 0.108 respectively). These MPI measures imply that a large number of people in this country are poor in at least two dimensions of the four measured and that the majority of these live in rural areas. Hence to achieve SDG 1, which calls for the elimination of poverty in all its forms everywhere, there is a need to understand the drivers of economic growth in lagging regions since governments in many parts of the world invest a significant number of resources in trying to bring about economic growth to these regions, but most often with limited success (Stephens et al., 2013). These authors add, "*Economic theory does not provide clear guidance when it comes to identifying growth factors in lagging regions—especially if they are rural and remote*" (p.778).

Leadership and Poverty in Uganda

Focusing on Uganda, a major problem this country has had is the leadership issue (a poor democratic culture) which has wasted immense resources, caused untold suffering of the people, impaired economic growth and brought the country firmly in the grip of the IMF. Starting in 1966 just after independence in 1962, the country was engulfed in a political crisis that saw the ushering of a Republican Constitution after a spate of bloodletting in which Milton Obote deposed the Kabaka of Buganda and other monarchies and declared Uganda a Republic. This is referred to as the Obote 1 period. This crisis led to the Ushering in of the Idi Amin regime through a coup de tat (1971 -1979), during which period the country witnessed the expulsion of the Asians (skilled entrepreneurs) from this country, an economic crisis, and a dictatorship of unprecedented imagination in which over 200,000 people were brutally murdered. Amin was deposed in 1979 by a joint force of Ugandan rebels and the Tanzanian army after Amin attacked Tanzania and claimed parts of that country. In 1980 the new government, The Military Commission led by Paulo Muwanga organized multi-party elections which were worn by the Uganda People's Congress, UPC and Milton Obote, thus ushering in the Obote 2 regime. The results of these elections were disputed by a section of Ugandans who launched a guerilla war to dislodge the new government. The Obote 2 regime was overthrown by the guerillas in 1986 under the National Resistance Movement (NRM) which has ruled the country since then to-date. Although NRM has managed to establish a level of tranquillity during this 37-year reign, there have been spates of rebel activity in this country, like was the case of the Joseph Kony war in the Northern part of the country which lasted 18 years (1987-2006) and brought this region in near total ruin (Fisher, 2014). In a nutshell, while the issue of poverty in Uganda can be blamed on structural adjustment policies of the IMF as espoused by Ndaguba & Hanyane (2018), most of the blame goes to governance issues that have resulted in wastage of human and other resources in acts of war and violence for the last 60 years much to the neglect of both rural and urban areas.

Method for Selecting Study Materials

Based on Page et al., (2021) this study utilized the PRISMA-P approach to set eligibility conditionalities for inclusion of articles, reports, and other material in the study, plus the search plan for these required items. Starting with suitability conditionalities, items that were included in this study were those that emphasized entrepreneurial ecosystems and economic growth in the developing world. To enable comparison, studies from developed countries were suitable for this review if they concentrated on entrepreneurial ecosystems and their impact on startups. As for study design, both qualitative and quantitative studies were acceptable for inclusion. Study sources were electronic databases such as Google Scholar, government websites, UN agency websites and university academic repositories. The search plan was based on the employment of keywords. Boolean operators used were AND, OR and NOT. Approximately 30 journal articles were reviewed, besides relevant reports from ministries, statistical abstracts from the Uganda Bureau of Statistics (UBOS), and reports from private bodies like the Uganda Manufacture Association (UMA) and the Private Sector Foundation (PSF).

THE ENTREPRENEURIAL ECOSYSTEM FACETS IN RURAL AREAS IN UGANDA

This section examines the major constraints that hinder the establishment and development of rural startups in Uganda and makes several major arguments.

Characteristics of the People in Rural Areas

As earlier stated, poverty is a big problem in this country with 40.3 million people and a GDP per capita of $878 (UBOS, 2022). Over 10 million people live below the poverty line and the majority of these are living in rural areas (UNHS, 2017). In terms of employment, the overall employment rate in this country in 2016/17 was 9.2%, with females experiencing a higher level of unemployment (14%) compared to males (6%). On the other hand, labour underutilization focuses on issues of insufficient labour absorption. The composite measure of youth labor underutilization for example stands at 38%. On the other hand, the education level of people in employment is low, with just about 23% having completed secondary school or post-secondary training, while 64% of the working-age population who had no formal education were women. Overall, the proportion of people in occupations requiring high qualifications including professional occupations, technicians and associate professions is low (9%). In effect, rural populations have a very low level of education, which means they lack the necessary skills that can enable them to participate in opportunity entrepreneurship through the pursuit of a differentiation strategy, thus they remain as necessity entrepreneurs. UNHS, 2017 estimates that 64% of the working population is engaged in agriculture, forestry and fishing. The above statistics show that the poor people who live in rural areas and are mostly engaged in peasant agriculture, cannot provide a good market (effective demand) for industrial goods even if these goods were manufactured near them.

Lack of Markets

Markets act as catalysts for the development of entrepreneurial ecosystems (Spigel, 2015). A global entrepreneurship monitor study (GEM, 2011) cited in Bakashaba (2018) established that the key challenges faced by Ugandan business people that translate into poor performance include limited markets, unstable commodity prices, little value addition if any and lack of access to market information. Uganda being an agricultural country should have strong markets for products produced in rural areas such as mangoes, pineapples etc. Unfortunately, these markets are lacking and lead to the exploitation of producers by middlemen.

Corruption as a Deterrent to Rural Entrepreneurship

Corruption is another problem that this country faces. According to the Inspector General of Government Report (2021), corruption is one of the major obstacles hindering the development of this country. It is reported that the total cost of corruption annually in taxation is UGX 1.36 billion, the loss in unpaid user fees is UGX 478 billion, while corruption in royalties is estimated at UGX 868 billion. On the other hand, the annual loss in environmental resources due to corruption is estimated at UGX 2.28 trillion, while the cost of environmental pollution and degradation totals UGX 5.36 billion. The existence of corruption implies a weakness of governance in general. There is a raging debate about the relationship between corruption and the development of the informal economy (Ouedraogo, 2017), defined as all activities providing goods and services that are unregulated and hardly fit into any contemporary economic category. Some scholars (Johnson et al., 1997) view corruption as a compliment to the informal economy and also a tax on the entrepreneur, which forces him/her further into the informal economy. Yet other scholars view corruption and shadow markets as substitutes (Dreher et al., 2009). Either way, this paper views corruption as a hindrance to the development of opportunity entrepreneurship, since it pushes the cost of doing business up, thus stifling opportunity. The electoral process in Uganda is not free from corruption either (Faller 2015), thus ushering in decision-makers who may not have the interests of the country at heart.

Social Cultural Context

The importance of culture in the economic development of nations is highlighted in many scholarly works and many international change agents are focusing on culture as a resource to be mobilized in the fight against poverty on the African continent (Munene et al., 2000). Therefore, the study of culture is important because differences in behaviour in various societies are dictated by culture (Linan & Chen, 2009). According to Spigel (2015 p.3), there are two major cultural attributes of entrepreneurial ecosystems: cultural attitudes and histories of entrepreneurship. Aoyama (2009) posits that regional cultures shape acceptable entrepreneurship practices and norms. First, cultural beliefs and values legalize peoples' views about entrepreneurship, portraying it as a possible career path, or being seen as something one can only embrace when there is nothing else to do (Kibler et al., 2014). A culture that supports entrepreneurship activities is thus built in a society that views entrepreneurship as a possible career path. Second, the success histories of some outstanding entrepreneurs are very helpful in confirming to those who may be in doubt that entrepreneurship can be a rewarding career path (Feldman et al., 2005). "This helps ensure a stable supply of new entrepreneurs and further legitimizes the status of risk-taking within the region's culture" (Spigel, 2015 p.5).

Culture constrains the development of entrepreneurship in Uganda (Katono, 2020). This is because the African value orientation does not favour the development of a firm entrepreneurial orientation i.e., risk-taking, proactiveness and innovativeness (Pretorius & Van Vuuren, 2002). The examples below highlight how this happens in a rural setting. In a collective setting like Uganda (Hofstede, 1980) power distance and uncertainty avoidance may be the key constraints to entrepreneurship especially in rural areas where traditional views reign high. First in a collective setting people live in groups and abide by group norms (Hofstede, 1980). People with a collectivist orientation tend to be driven by socio-oriented goals, not individualistic achievement-oriented goals (Triandis, 1995). Group membership has roles, obligations and duties that go with it and harmonious relations must be maintained so group members do not lose face (Joy & Kolb, 2009).

Uncertainty Avoidance

The central thrust of this dimension is that the future is unknowable and always will be (Hofstede 1980). Low uncertainty-avoidant cultures hold the notion that conflict and competition can co-exist constructively in an environment of fair play, while uncertainty-avoidant cultures view conflict and competition as dysfunctional and thus as something that needs to be avoided (Mueller & Thomas, 2001). Entrepreneurs in low uncertainty avoidance societies will most likely spot more opportunities in the external environment (and hence be more proactive) compared to those in high uncertainty-avoidant cultures (Thomas

& Mueller, 2001). In addition, communities that harbour high degrees of ambiguity intolerance are usually resistant to innovation and prefer a stable environment (Kreiser et al., 2010). Proactive behaviour is a characteristic of people who perceive situations in a manner that enables them to take action in a desired direction rather than be passive onlookers who wait for changes to engulf them (Fryer & Payne, 1984). Claes and Ruiz-Quintanilla (1998) posit that high uncertainty avoidance hinders the development of divergent opinions, and is a barrier to innovative ideas, self -esteem and belongingness, all of which combine to inhibit proactive behaviour.

Power Distance

The key premise on which the power distance dimension of culture is based is that people are not equal in life, and some communities accept these inequalities yet other societies downplay them as much as possible (Hofstede, 1983). These inequalities put power and resources in the control of those in privileged positions in high power distance cultures, hence the individual is not allowed to do what he/she thinks is right but is given guidance (by those with the power) to do what they think is socially right and proper (Joy & Kolb, 2008). Thus, people in such cultures lack both the freedom and autonomy to walk independent paths (Kreiser et al., 2010). This should have a profound impact on entrepreneurial opportunities and the intentions of the less privileged. For example, a student may not start a business because those who have power over him or her think it is not proper to do so. The social-cultural context of also affects graduate intentions to start a business (Katono, 2020). Graduates who hail from these rural areas may not want to start a business in these areas because it is shameful to do so. People regard such a graduate as a failure (Omagor & Mubiru, 2014).

Given the inherent inequality between men and women, particularly in collective societies such as Uganda, power distance will most probably impact negatively women's risk-taking and proactiveness and hence their entrepreneurial proclivity. This assertion is supported by Glick (2006), who finds a positive correlation between power distance and gender inequality, arguing that countries rated high on power distance also portray high levels of gender inequality. In such countries, not only does gender inequality exist, but it is also legitimized and enforced. This gender inequality is likely to translate into a difficult environment and suppress women's entrepreneurship. In high power distance societies, knowledge is the preserve of a few, and information is hoarded. Hence the lower-end people may not have the resources / experiences (knowledge since it is the preserve of the elite) that promote the development of a business venture.

Gender and Entrepreneurship

Cultural values and norms give birth to gender roles and stereotypes, on which the decision for determining occupations that are regarded as appropriate for each sex are premised (Shinnar et al., 2012). Gender stereotypes are the extensively held outlooks about what defines a given sex (Eagly et al., 2000) and play a descriptive role (outlining what men and women are) and a prescriptive one or outlining norms and behaviours that should go with each sex (Heilman, 2001). Thus, gender stereotyping assigns jobs that are regarded as suitable for each sex i.e., feminine or masculine (Heilman, 1983) thus contributing to the gender gap or inequality between males and females in various societies. There is a gender gap in entrepreneurship in Uganda, just as is the case in other East African countries. This is because within the Ugandan collective society are common strands of gender inequality enshrined in in patriarchal beliefs

(Mirembe & Davies, 2001). Kaleeba et al., (in Mirembe & Davies, 2001) posit that Ugandan society is also patrilineal. This means that women are subservient to their fathers and later to their husbands. Besides, in a patriarchal society, women are rarely granted inheritance as a norm of the patrilineal philosophy. Mungai and Ogot (2012) provide an elaborate presentation of the role of culture in constraining women's entrepreneurship in neighbouring Kenya. Therefore, just as elsewhere, the assertion that "gender differences are especially evident in entrepreneurial careers" (Sánchez, & Licciardello, 2012, p.8) is indeed true for Uganda.

Social Networks

The importance of social networks and social capital is highlighted in many entrepreneurship studies (Spiegel, 2015). Social capital is defined as "assets within networks" (Lin, 1999 p. 28). Networking is strongly correlated with a proactive entrepreneurial orientation (Morrison, 2002). First, entrepreneurs make use of informal networks (family, friends) to assist them in various activities, thus opportunities will come to those who have positioned themselves strategically within such networks (Aldrich & Zimmer, 1986). For example, Khavul et al., (2009) note that entrepreneurs in East Africa rely on strong family ties to start and run their businesses. Networks act as conduits through which information and new knowledge about opportunities pass (Owen-Simith & Powell, 2004) and also greatly influence the way issues are perceived (De Carolis & Saparito, 2006).

This paper argues that the social environment in the rural areas in Uganda may not be conducive to the development of networks that foster the development of entrepreneurship. This could be because the creation of new ventures requires a pre-existence of connections among entrepreneurs, investors, and other entrepreneurial actors as well as a sufficient level of trust among various parties to foster cooperation and the sharing of scarce resources (Kwon et al., 2013), all of which may not be in existence in a rural setting. Hence rural settings lack a network of venture capitalists who are willing to invest in new ventures; there is also a glaring lack of skilled workers in rural networks, a lack of mentors and "deal makers" or people with a high level of social capital, who build connections between entrepreneurial actors and thus enable firms to grow (Feldman & Zoller, 2012). Also of importance is the lack of trust in rural networks, especially with issues of money.

THE INFRASTRUCTURAL ISSUES

Spigel (2015) notes that there are other infrastructural issues which may contribute to the development of entrepreneurial ecosystems. The first of these are universities, which provide two main resources to an entrepreneurial ecosystem. In the first instance, universities develop new technologies that create entrepreneurial opportunities (Lawton et al., 2014) and the other is that they develop the human capital of a region, while also fostering a change in the mindset of students imploring them to start new ventures or work with them. According to the National Council for Higher Education (NCHE, 2019) Uganda now has a total of 51 universities, 9 public and 43 private. While these institutions are doing a good job, their underfunding inhibits their operations, especially the private ones that rely on fee collections for their operations. Spigel (2015) also notes that support services, policies and the existence of strong markets go a long way in stimulating venture startup and growth. First, as will further be explained below, in the case of Uganda support services such as law firms, accountants and human resource advisors are lacking in the rural areas and are too expensive for the rural communities. The other issue is do these communities know what to do with them? Second, policies provide the legal and political context in which entrepreneurs operate. While many policies have been put in place by the Ugandan government, a comprehensive study to assess the impact they have on rural entrepreneurship is lacking. What is obvious is that some of these policies are retrogressive, such as the sugar policy which seeks to streamline sugar production in the country, but ends up in severe bio-diversity loss and food insecurity of the sugar-growing families (Mwavu et al., 2016).

Physical Infrastructure

Sullivan and Sheffrin (2003) define infrastructure as organisational structures and physical amenities that are needed by the community in general. These infrastructures include industries, buildings, roads, bridges, health services, governance, and many others. These authors assert that infrastructure development is needed as it affects the demand and supply side of economic activities. Hence development of basic infrastructure such as roads is essential for the development and well-being of both rural and urban communities (Simkova, 2008). Infrastructural development is also related to the quality of social services in areas such as education, health and the quality of life of rural communities in general. Egbetokun (2009) asserts that basic infrastructure is an essential part of rural development strategies as it is integrated with all other aspects, including agriculture, education, health, nutrition, electricity and clean water. Basic infrastructural development in rural areas can be viewed as a solution for inequality and social justice problems in rural areas in general.

While many studies have been done to demonstrate the relationship between entrepreneurial infrastructure and other contexts (Wiklund et al., 2009), very few studies have examined physical infrastructure as one of the drivers of entrepreneurial activity (Audretsch et al., 2015) and most of these have been done in the west (Ngoma et al., 2021). Ahmed and Donovan (1992), distinguish between hard infrastructure, soft infrastructure, physical infrastructure, social infrastructure, economic infrastructure and institutional infrastructure. This paper mainly refers to physical and financial infrastructure. Previous studies (Calderon & Serve, 2010) posit that poor infrastructure in sub–Saharan Africa, stifles entrepreneurial activities. Uganda is no exception to this fact. What is clear from the literature is the fact that the effect of physical infrastructure on entrepreneurial activity is an issue that has received little attention from scholars (Bennett, 2019). Ngoma et al., (2021), carried out a study in an attempt to bridge this gap in Uganda and summarize the importance of physical infrastructure thus:

"Road infrastructure also increases the interconnectivity of markets and the market actors therein which further improves the environment of doing business. Ultimately, the costs of doing business reduce further, markets expand and business thrives" (Ngoma et al., 2021 p. 605).

Considering the above, infrastructural issues are a major detriment to the development of entrepreneurship in rural areas in Uganda. Starting with roads, the total paved national road network is just about 5,016 km (UBOS, 2022), while the proportion of paved to national roads totals 24.1%. Access to electricity in rural areas is as low as 26.7%. Apart from this, electricity supply is also vital in ensuring the quality of life among rural communities. This is in line with previous studies done in this area, for example, a study by Bose, Uddin and Mondal (2013). The limited access to electricity has affected the delivery of social services, constrained the development of small-scale industrial and commercial enterprises and adversely affected larger-scale industrial and commercial investment (African Development Bank, 2015).

In summary, the multiplier effect of infrastructural developments cannot be underestimated. An important finding of the Ngoma et al., (2021) study is that there is a significant relationship between the infrastructural developments with both the EO (risk-taking, proactiveness and innovativeness) and entrepreneurial activity. The results of their hierarchical regression confirmed significant positive effects of infrastructure development on entrepreneurial activity

Financial Infrastructure

Like in most developing countries, Uganda's financial sector is largely underdeveloped and concentrated in urban areas, leaving the majority of the agricultural producers in the rural population with no access to financial services (Mpuga, 2010). According to this author, "*There is a notable absence of formal financial institutions (banks) in the rural areas, which consider smallholders as high-risk and costly customers. The closure of the Co-operative Bank in 1998, which had 14 rural branches, and the privatization of the state-owned Uganda Commercial Bank (UCB— now Stanbic Bank Ltd), which operated 65 branches and 2 agencies countrywide (Akampumuza, 2007) worsened the rural credit situation. Several credit institutions have emerged to fill the lacuna created by the absence of a formal financial sector*" (Mpuga, 2010 p.117). Hence, access to credit by the rural populations and other indigenous people has increasingly become increasingly difficult due to the high lending rates by commercial banks. The Ugandan Head of State recently publicly expressed regret for the sale of UCB to Stanbic which took place in 1999 (URN, 2023). Further, there is a marked difference between men and women in the use of ICTs in Uganda (NITA 2017), which constrains the development of e-commerce; this gender digital divide just as in other developing countries is especially a cause for worry, because many women cannot use the internet, due to affordability, low education levels, and technological digital illiteracy among others (Abima et al., 2021).

THE INEFFECTIVENESS OF SOME GOVERNMENT PROGRAMS

The GOU recognizes the importance of SMEs in both rural and urban areas in the economic development of the country, and many programs have been put in place to assist these organizations in various ways, for example, the plan for modernization of agriculture (PMA), Business Uganda Development Scheme BUDS, Microfinance Outreach Plan, the UNIDO master crafts programme, Jua Kali Initiative among others (Turyahikayo, 2015). The services rendered by these programs range from the formulation of policies and programs to the provision of inputs such as finance, training, marketing, entrepreneurship and management; despite all this, these businesses close at an alarming rate (Bakashaba, 2018). The lack of multi-sectoral linkages is the major problem of these programs (Oteh, 2010). Further, there are concerns over the distribution of these incentives and resources to all intended beneficiaries (Turyahikayo 2015). For example, "*the level of support provided varies from one geographical area to another, causing-over provision and under-provision in others when applied uniformly, which results in a lack of integration and appropriate networking in the economy; it is also established that some of these support organizations do not treat small businesses like they do treat the other big businesses in the economy*"

(Bakashaba, 2018). Hence much more needs to be done by the government for example drafting policies aimed at the protection of SMEs in Uganda, such as those aimed at access to finance (Turyahikayo, 2015).

Land Tenure

Land tenure is another hindrance to rural startups as the proportion of the adult population with secure land rights, with legally recognized documentation and who perceive their rights to land as secure by sex and by type of tenure is 36% (UBOS, 2022). According to Tebajjukira (2009), 59000 people were forcefully evicted from their land between 2007 -2009. Security of tenure is a prerequisite for getting a loan from a financial institution. It is very difficult for rural people to meet that requirement and hence get any funding from a formal lending institution. Newspapers are awash with stories on land evictions in Uganda (Wandera & Nabukenya, 2023). In the Albertine region of Uganda (Bunyoro) where oil was discovered, land conflicts have reached a scale of threatening agricultural production, where for example an ex-minister is pitted against 4000 residents who are on the verge of expulsion from this land (Adong et al., 2020). These authors further argue that ethnic divisions and corruption in land institutions further escalate the land conflicts in Uganda, thus hindering rural startups.

CONCLUSION

This study went out to investigates some of the constraints to rural startups in Uganda, by examining the entrepreneurship ecosystem in these areas, which provides us with a lens for understanding how regional transformation can occur through entrepreneurship (Wurth et al., 2021). The study begins by exploring the status of poverty in this country and then goes on to draw a theoretical link between entrepreneurship and economic growth in the literature. Most of the entrepreneurship carried out in the rural areas of this country is necessity entrepreneurship. The move from this type of entrepreneurship to opportunity entrepreneurship is found to be constrained by the characteristics of the rural population, social-cultural variables and physical as well as financial infrastructural constraints among others. The study also notes that the lack of democratic space is greatly responsible for the underdevelopment of this country, especially the rural areas where the fighting has taken place since independence from the British colonial government in 1962.

The study argues that there must be deliberate policies put in place by the government to foster democratic space and attract opportunity entrepreneurs in rural areas, in line with reform and revolutionary perspectives of entrepreneurship, since some of its policy initiatives are found to be ineffective. The more entrepreneurial firms that are located in rural areas, the better for the population there. The government must also try as much as possible to raise the educational standards of the people in these areas, as a means to improving their attitude towards more opportunity-driven entrepreneurship.

The fight against corruption which wastes immense national resources must be strengthened. not only in business but also in electoral processes to boost the democratization of the country. While a large number of people are engaged in the informal economy as a means of survival, many studies assert that corruption pushes these people there, hence their capacity to graduate into opportunity entrepreneurship is curtailed. This is especially so in rural areas that are gripped in poverty. Lastly, weak government regulations against dumping of cheap quality goods in Uganda hurt rural startups (Bakashaba, 2018) just like many other unsustainable marketing practices that are rampant in this country. While the paper does not claim to exhaust all the constraints in the entrepreneurial ecosystem in the rural areas of Uganda, it is hoped that the paper sets a platform upon which further debate in this topical area can be anchored.

There is a need to conduct more research into how other infrastructural issues affect entrepreneurship in rural areas. For example, the link between digitalization and rural entrepreneurship needs to be investigated. While all the recommendations of the Entrepreneurship policy framework (Audretsch et al., 2007) may not apply to economies like Uganda, a few may be relevant. This needs to be investigated.

REFERENCES

Abima, B., Engotoit, B., Kituyi, G. M., Kyeyune, R., & Koyola, M. (2021). Relevant local content, social influence, digital literacy, and attitude toward the use of digital technologies by women in Uganda. *Gender, Technology and Development*, *25*(1), 87–111. doi:10.1080/09718524.2020.1830337

AcsZ. J.AudretschD. B.BraunerhjelmP.CarlssonB. (2004). The missing link: The knowledge filter and entrepreneurship in endogenous growth. *Available at* SSRN 667944.

Acs, Z. J., Audretsch, D. B., & Lehmann, E. E. (2013). The knowledge spillover theory of entrepreneurship. *Small Business Economics*, *41*(4), 757–774. doi:10.100711187-013-9505-9

Acs, Z. J., Stam, E., Audretsch, D. B., & O'Connor, A. (2017). The lineages of the entrepreneurial ecosystem approach. *Small Business Economics*, *49*(1), 1–10. doi:10.100711187-017-9864-8

Acs, Z. J., & Szerb, L. (2007). Entrepreneurship, economic growth and public policy. *Small Business Economics*, *28*(2-3), 109–122. doi:10.100711187-006-9012-3

Addae-Korankye, A. (2014). Causes of poverty in Africa: A review of literature. *American International Journal of Social Science*, *3*(7), 147–153.

Adner, R. (2017). Ecosystem as structure: An actionable construct for strategy. *Journal of management, 43*(1), 39-58. *Agricultural Sustainable Practice.*, *1*(2), 69–70.

Adong, M., Opio, M., & Mwesigwa, D. (2020). Consequence of Land Conflicts to Small-Holder Farmers in Masindi District, Mid-Western Uganda. *Journal of Agricultural and Rural Research*, *5*(1), 36–46.

Africa Commission. (2009). *Realizing the Potential of Africa's Youth: Report of the Africa Commission.* Author.

African Development Bank. (2015). *Uganda Rural Electricity Access Project 285-300.* Available afdb.org

Aidis, R. (2017). Do institutions matter for entrepreneurial development? IZA World of Labor, 334. Bonn: Institute for the Study of Labor (IZA). doi:10.15185/izawol.334

Akampumuza, J. (2007). *The Management of Uganda's Privatisation Since 1982* [PhD thesis]. University of London.

Aldrich, H., & Zimmer, C. (1986). Entrepreneurship through social networks. In H. Aldrich (Ed.), *Population Perspectives on Organizations* (pp. 13–28).

Alkire, S., & Foster, J. (2011). Counting and multidimensional poverty measurement. *Journal of Public Economics*, *95*(7–8), 476–487. doi:10.1016/j.jpubeco.2010.11.006

Amin, M. (2010). *'Necessity vs opportunity entrepreneurs in the informal sector', Enterprise Analysis Unit.* World Bank.

Aoyama, Y. (2009). Entrepreneurship and regional culture: The case of Hamamtsu and Kyoto, Japan. *Regional Studies*, *43*(3), 495–512. doi:10.1080/00343400902777042

Arrow, K. (1962). The Economic Implication of Learning by Doing. *The Review of Economic Studies*, *80*(3), 155–173. doi:10.2307/2295952

Aspen Network of Development Entrepreneurs (ANDE). (2013). *Entrepreneurship ecosystem diagnostic kit.* https://www.aspeninstitute.org/publications/entrepreneurial

Audretsch, D., Heger, D., & Veith, T. (2015). Infrastructure and entrepreneurship. *Small Business Economics*, *44*(2), 219–230. doi:10.100711187-014-9600-6

Audretsch, D. B., Grilo, I., & Thurik, A. R. (2007). Explaining entrepreneurship and the role of policy: a framework. The handbook of research on entrepreneurship policy, 1-17.

Audretsch, D. B., & Keilback, M. (2007). The Localisation of Entrepreneurship Capital, Evidence from Germany. *Papers in Regional Science*, *863*(3), 351–365. doi:10.1111/j.1435-5957.2007.00131.x

Audretsch, D. B., & Thurik, R. (2001). What's new about the new economy? Sources of growth in the managed and entrepreneurial economies. *Industrial and Corporate Change, 10*(1), 267-315. . 1. 267 doi:10.1093/icc/10

Bakashaba, R. (2019). *Entrepreneurial income and barriers to firm growth: a study of rural small and medium enterprises in Uganda* [Doctoral dissertation]. University of Reading.

Baum, J. R., Frese, M., Baron, R. A., & Katz, J. A. (2007). In J. R. Baum, M. Frese, & R. A. Baron (Eds.), *The Psychology of Entrepreneurship* (pp. 1–18). Lawrence Erlbaum.

Becattini, G. (1990). The Marshallian industrial district as a socio-economic notion. In F. Pyke, G. Becattini, & W. Sengenbeiger (Eds.), *Industrial districts and inter-firm co-operation in Italy*. International Institute for Labour Studies.

Beegle, K., Christiansen, L., Dabalen, A., & Gaddis, I. (2016). *Poverty in a rising Africa: Overview.* World Bank. doi:10.1596/978-1-4648-0723-7

Bennett, D. L. (2019). Infrastructure investments and entrepreneurial dynamism in the US. *Journal of Business Venturing*, *34*(5), 991–993. doi:10.1016/j.jbusvent.2018.10.005

Birch, D. G. (1979). *The job generation process.* University of Illinois at Urbana-Champaign's Academy for Entrepreneurial Leadership Historical Research Reference in Entrepreneurship.

Block, J. H., Kohn, K., Miller, D., & Ullrich, K. (2015). Necessity entrepreneurship and competitive strategy. *Small Business Economics*, *44*(1), 37–54. doi:10.100711187-014-9589-x

Bose, T. K., Uddin, M. R., & Mondal, A. (2013). Impacts of electricity access to rural SMEs. *International Journal of Managing Value and Supply Chains*, *4*(4), 17–28. doi:10.5121/ijmvsc.2013.4402

Calderon, C., & Serven, L. (2010). Infrastructure and economic development in Sub-Saharan Africa. *Journal of African Economies*, *19*(Suppl_1), i13–i87. doi:10.1093/jae/ejp022

Cipolla, C. M. (1981). *Before the industrial Revolution: European Society and Economy, 1000–1700* (2nd ed.). Cambridge University Press.

Claes, R., & Ruiz-Quintanilla, S. A. (1998). Influences of early career experiences, occupational group, and national culture on proactive career behavior. *Journal of Vocational Behavior*, *52*(3), 357–378. doi:10.1006/jvbe.1997.1626

Cooke, P., Uranga, M. G., & Etxebarria, G. (1997). Regional innovation systems: Institutional and organisational dimensions. *Research Policy*, *26*(4-5), 47. doi:10.1016/S0048-7333(97)00025-5

Ddumba, S., & Mugume, A. (2001). *The Privatization Process and its Impact on Society*. In Uganda National NGO Forum/Structural Adjustment Participatory Review Initiative, Kampala.

De Carolis, D. M., & Saparito, P. (2006). Social capital, cognition, and entrepreneurial opportunities: Atheoretical framework. *Entrepreneurship Theory and Practice*, *30*(1), 41–56. doi:10.1111/j.1540-6520.2006.00109.x

Dencker, J. C., Gruber, M., & Shah, S. K. (2009). Individual and opportunity factors influencing job creation in new firms. Academy of Management Journal, 52(6). doi:10.5465/amj.2009.47084648

Dreher, A., Kotsogiannis, C., & McCorriston, S. (2009). How Do Institutions Affect Corruption and the Shadow Economy? *International Tax and Public Finance*, *16*(6), 773–796. doi:10.100710797-008-9089-5

Egbetokun, O. A. (2009). Provision of rural infrastructures in Oyo State of Nigeria. *Journal of Ekonomie*, *11*(1), 26–32.

Eliasson, G. E. (1995). *Economic Growth Through Competitive Selection*. Paper presented at 22nd Annual EARIE Conference 3–6 September 1995.

Eyoh, D., & Sandbrook, R. (2003). Pragmatic neo-liberalism and just development in Africa. *States, markets, and just growth: Development in the twenty-first century*, 227-57.

Faller, J. K. (2015). The system matters: Corruption and vote choice in Uganda. *Commonwealth and Comparative Politics*, *53*(4), 428–456. doi:10.1080/14662043.2015.1094891

Feldman, M., Francis, J., & Bercovitz, J. (2005). Creating a cluster while building a firm: Entrepreneurs and the formation of industrial clusters. *Regional Studies*, *39*(1), 129–141. doi:10.1080/0034340052000320888

Feldman, M., & Zoller, T. D. (2012). Dealmakers in place: Social capital connections in regional entrepreneurial economies. *Regional Studies*, *46*(1), 23–37. doi:10.1080/00343404.2011.607808

Fisher, J. (2014). Framing Kony: Uganda's war, Obama's advisers and the nature of 'influence' in Western foreign policy making. *Third World Quarterly*, *35*(4), 686–704. doi:10.1080/01436597.2014.924068

Flores, K. M. G., & Kovács, J. K. (2018). Defining the entrepreneurship ecosystem. *SEA-Practical Application of Science*, (18), 299–306.

Foelster, S. (2000). Do entrepreneurs create jobs? *Small Business Economics*, *14*(2), 137–148. doi:10.1023/A:1008141516160

Fryer, D., & Payne, R. (1984). Proactive behaviour in unemployment: Findings and implications. *Leisure Studies*, *3*(3), 273–295. doi:10.1080/02614368400390231

Gartner, W. B. (1988). "Who is an entrepreneur?" is the wrong question. *American Journal of Small Business*, *12*(4), 11–32. doi:10.1177/104225878801200401

Glancey, K., McQuaid, R., & Campling, J. (2000). *Entrepreneurial economics*. Macmillan. doi:10.1057/9780333981245

Hébert, R. F., & Link, A. N. (1982). *The Entrepreneur: Mainstream Views and Radical Critiques*. Praeger.

Heilman, M. E. (2001). Description and prescription: How gender stereotypes prevent women's ascent up the organizational ladder. *The Journal of Social Issues*, *57*(4), 657–674. doi:10.1111/0022-4537.00234

Henrekson, M., Johansson, D., & Karlsson, J. (2021). *To be or not to be: The entrepreneur in endogenous growth theory*. IFN Working Paper No. 1385, 2021

Hofstede, G. (1980). *Culture's Consequences: International Differences in Work-related Value*. Sage.

Hofstede, G., & Hofstede, G. J. (1995). *Allemaal andersdenkenden: Omgaan met cultuurverschillen* [Cultures and Organizations: Software of the Mind]. Contact.

Igwe, P. A., & Icha-Ituma, A. (2020). A review of ten years of African entrepreneurship research. *Research handbook on entrepreneurship in emerging economies*.

Johnson, S., Kaufmann, D., Shleifer, A., Goldman, M. I., & Weitzman, M. L. (1997). The unofficial economy in transition. *Brookings Papers on Economic Activity*, *1997*(2), 159–239. doi:10.2307/2534688

Joy, S., & Kolb, D. A. (2009). Are there cultural differences in learning style? *International Journal of Intercultural Relations*, *33*(1), 69–85. doi:10.1016/j.ijintrel.2008.11.002

Katono, I. W. (2020). *Cultural predictions of entrepreneurial orientation and the moderating role of entrepreneurial competencies on graduate entrepreneurial intentions: A cross-sectional survey of East Africa*. https://scholar.google.com/citations?user=HQE6PycAAAAJ&hl=en&oi=sra

Kautonen, T., & Palmroos, J. (2010). The impact of a necessity-based start-up on subsequent entrepreneurial satisfaction. *The International Entrepreneurship and Management Journal*, *6*(3), 285–300. doi:10.100711365-008-0104-1

Kennedy, P. (1988). *African Capitalism: The Struggle for Ascendancy*. Cambridge University Press.

Khavul, S., Bruton, G. D., & Wood, E. (2009). Informal family business in Africa. *Entrepreneurship Theory and Practice*, *33*(6), 1219–1238. doi:10.1111/j.1540-6520.2009.00342.x

Kibler, E., Kautonen, T., & Fink, M. (2017). Regional social legitimacy of entrepreneurship: Implications for entrepreneurial intention and start-up behaviour. In *Entrepreneurship in a Regional Context* (pp. 57–77). Routledge. doi:10.4324/9781315691985-4

Knight, F. (1921). *Risk, Uncertainty and Profit*. Houghton Mifflin.

Kreiser, P. M., Marino, L. D., Dickson, P., & Weaver, K. M. (2010). Cultural influences on entrepreneurial orientation: The impact of national culture on risk taking and proactiveness in SMEs. *Entrepreneurship Theory and Practice*, *34*(5), 959–983. doi:10.1111/j.1540-6520.2010.00396.x

Kwon, S.-W., Heflin, C., & Ruef, M. (2013). Community social capital and entrepreneurship. *American Sociological Review*, *78*(6), 980–1008. doi:10.1177/0003122413506440

Lawton Smith, H., Chapman, D., Wood, P., Barnes, T., & Romeo, S. (2014). Entrepreneurial academics and regional innovation systems: The case of spin-offs from London's universities. *Environment & Planning*, *32*(2), 341–359.

Lin, N. (1999). Building a network theory of social capital. *Connections*, *22*(1), 28–51.

Liñán, F., & Chen, Y. W. (2009). Development and Cross-Cultural application of a specific instrument to measure entrepreneurial intentions. *Entrepreneurship Theory and Practice*, *33*(3), 593–617. doi:10.1111/j.1540-6520.2009.00318.x

Lucas, R. E. Jr. (1988). On the Mechanics of Economic Development. *Journal of Monetary Economics*, *22*(1), 3–42. doi:10.1016/0304-3932(88)90168-7

Manggat, I., Zain, R., & Jamaluddin, Z. (2018). The impact of infrastructure development on rural communities: A literature review. *International Journal of Academic Research in Business & Social Sciences*, *8*(1), 637–648. doi:10.6007/IJARBSS/v8-i1/3837

Mirembe, R., & Davis, L. (2001). Is schooling a risk? Gender, power relations and school culture in Uganda. *Gender and Education*, *13*(4), 401–416. doi:10.1080/09540250120081751

MKandirwe, T., & Soludo, C.C. (1999) Our Continent, Our Future: African Perspectives on Structural Adjustment. Trenton, NJ: Africa World Press.

Morrison, A. (2000). Initiating entrepreneurship. In *Enterprise and Small Business: Principles, Practice and Policy*. Prentice Hall.

Motoyama, Y., & Watkins, K. (2014). *Examining the connections within the start up ecosystem*. Kauffman Research Series on City, Metro, and Regional Entrepreneurship.

Mpuga, P. (2010). Constraints in access to and demand for rural credit: Evidence from Uganda. *African Development Review*, *22*(1), 115–148. doi:10.1111/j.1467-8268.2009.00230.x

Mueller, S. L., & Thomas, A. S. (2001). Culture and entrepreneurial potential: A nine country study of locus of control and innovativeness. *Journal of Business Venturing*, *16*(1), 51–75. doi:10.1016/S0883-9026(99)00039-7

Munene, J. C., Schwartz, S. S., & Smith, P. B. (2000). Development in Sub-Saharan Africa: Cultural influences and managers' decision behavior. *Public Administration and Development*, *20*(4), 339–351. doi:10.1002/1099-162X(200010)20:4<339::AID-PAD139>3.0.CO;2-#

Mungai, E. N., & Ogot, M. (2012). Gender, culture and entrepreneurship in Kenya. *International Business Research*, *5*(5), 175-183.

Muriisa, R. (2005). *The Privatisation Experience in Uganda: Prospects and Challenges in its Implementation. In The potentiality of 'developmental states' in Africa: Botswana and Uganda compared.* CODESRIA.

Mwavu, E. N., Ariango, E., Ssegawa, P., Kalema, V. N., Bateganya, F., Waiswa, D., & Byakagaba, P. (2016). Agrobiodiversity of homegardens in a commercial sugarcane cultivation land matrix in Uganda. *The International Journal of Biodiversity Science, Ecosystem Services & Management*, *12*(3), 191–201. doi:10.1080/21513732.2016.1177595

National Information Technology Authority Survey 2017/18 Report. (n.d.). https://www.nita.go.ug/sites/

NCHE. (2018/19). State of higher education and Training in Uganda. A Report on Higher Education Delivery and Institutions, Kampala.

Ndaguba, E. A., & Hanyane, B. (2019). Stakeholder model for community economic development in alleviating poverty in municipalities in South Africa. *Journal of Public Affairs*, *19*(1), e1858. doi:10.1002/pa.1858

Ndou, D. N. (2012). *An investigation into the reasons for failure of community-based projects at Folovhodwe, Limpopo* [Doctoral dissertation].

Nelson, R. R., & Winter, S. G. (1982). *An evolutionary theory of economic change*. Harvard University Press.

Ngoma, M., Ntale, P. D., & Castro, M. (2021). Entrepreneurial activity in the Albertine Graben region of Uganda: The role of infrastructure development and entrepreneurial orientation. *World Journal of Entrepreneurship, Management and Sustainable Development*, *17*(3), 601–615. doi:10.1108/WJEMSD-04-2020-0028

Omagor, C., & Mubiru, P. (2014). Courage, Purpose and Entrepreneurship. *International Journal of Business and Social Science*, *5*(6), 239–246.

Oteh, A., (2010). *Making capital markets work for SMEs in Africa*. A paper presented as the key note address of the 2010 Kikonyogo Capital Markets Award on 6th May 2010.

Owen-Smith, J., & Powell, W. (2004). Knowledge networks as channels and conduits: The effects of spillovers in the Boston biotechnology community. *Organization Science*, *15*(1), 5–21. doi:10.1287/orsc.1030.0054

Oyelaran-Oyeyinka, O., & Lal, K. (2016). Structural transformation in developing countries: cross regional analysis. *United Nations Human Settlements Program (UN-Habitat), 1.*

Page, M. J., McKenzie, J. E., Bossuyt, P. M., Boutron, I., Hoffmann, T. C., Mulrow, C. D., Shamseer, L., Tetzlaff, J. M., Akl, E. A., Brennan, S. E., Chou, R., Glanville, J., Grimshaw, J. M., Hróbjartsson, A., Lalu, M. M., Li, T., Loder, E. W., Mayo-Wilson, E., McDonald, S., ... Moher, D. (2021). The PRISMA 2020 statement: An updated guideline for reporting systematic reviews. *International Journal of Surgery*, *88*, 105906. doi:10.1016/j.ijsu.2021.105906 PMID:33789826

Piore, M., & Sable, C. (1984). *The Second Industrial Divide: Possibilities for Prosperity*. Basic Books.

Porter, M. (1990). *The Comparative Advantage of Nations*. Free Press. doi:10.1007/978-1-349-11336-1

Porter, M. E. (1998). *On competition*. Harvard Businesss School Press.

Porter, M. E. (1998). Clusters and the new economics of competition. *Harvard Business Review*, (November-December), 77–90. PMID:10187248

Pretorius, M., & Van Vuuren, J. (2002). *The Contribution of Support and Incentive Programs to Entrepreneurial Orientation and Start up Culture in South Africa. Presented At South African Entrepreneurship and Small Business Association Conference*, Sun City.

Reynolds, Bygrave, Autio, Cox, & Hay. (2002). *Global Entrepreneurship Monitor, 2002 Executive Report*. Babson College, London Business School and Kauffman Foundation.

Romer, P. (1986). Increasing Returns and Economic Growth. *The American Economic Review*, *94*, 1002–1037.

Romer, P. M. (1990). Endogenous Technical Change. *Journal of Political Economy*, *98*(5, Part 2), 71–102. doi:10.1086/261725

Rupasingha, A., & Stephan, J. G. (2013). Self-Employment and Local Economic Performance: Evidence from US Counties. *Papers in Regional Science*, *92*(1), 141–161. doi:10.1111/j.1435-5957.2011.00396.x

Sánchez, J. C., & Licciardello, O. (2012). Gender differences and attitudes in entrepreneurial intentions: The role of career choice. *JWEE*, (1-2), 7–27.

Sheriff, M., & Muffatto, M. (2015). The present state of entrepreneurship ecosystems in selected countries in Africa. *African Journal of Economic and Management Studies*, *6*(1), 17–54. doi:10.1108/AJEMS-10-2012-0064

Shinnar, R. S., Giacomin, O., & Janssen, F. (2012). Entrepreneurial perceptions and intentions: The role of gender and culture. *Entrepreneurship Theory and Practice*, *36*(3), 465–493. doi:10.1111/j.1540-6520.2012.00509.x

Simkova, E. (2008). *The sustainable development of rural areas and the role of tourism*. Academic Press.

Spigel, B. (2017). The relational organization of entrepreneurial ecosystems. *Entrepreneurship Theory and Practice*, *41*(1), 49–72. doi:10.1111/etap.12167

Spigel, B., & Harrison, R. (2018). Toward a process theory of entrepreneurial ecosystems. *Strategic Entrepreneurship Journal*, *12*(1), 151–168. doi:10.1002ej.1268

Stam, E., & Spigel, B. (2017). Entrepreneurial ecosystems. In R. Blackburn, D. De Clercq, J. Heinonen, & Z. Wang (Eds.), *The SAGE Handbook of Small Business and Entrepreneurship*. SAGE.

Stam, F. C., & Spigel, B. (2016). Entrepreneurial ecosystems. *USE Discussion Paper Series, 16*(13).

Stephens, H. M., & Mark, D. P. (2011). Do Entrepreneurs Enhance Economic Growth in Lagging Regions? *Growth and Change, 42*(4), 431–465. doi:10.1111/j.1468-2257.2011.00563.x

Stephens, H. M., Partridge, M. D., & Faggian, A. (2013). Innovation, entrepreneurship and economic growth in lagging regions. *Journal of Regional Science, 53*(5), 778–812. doi:10.1111/jors.12019

Stiglitz, J. E. (2000). Whither Reform. In *Annual World Bank Conference on Development Economics,* 1999. Washington DC: World Bank.

Sullivan, A., & Sheffrin, M. S. (2003). *Economics: Principles in action*. Pearson Prentice Hall.

Sutter, C., Bruton, G. D., & Chen, J. (2019). Entrepreneurship as a solution to extreme poverty: A review and future research directions. *Journal of Business Venturing, 34*(1), 197–214. doi:10.1016/j.jbusvent.2018.06.003

Tebajjukira, M. (2009), *60,000 evicted in the last two year.* New Vision.

Thomas, A. S., & Muller, S. C. (2000). A case for comparative entrepreneurship: Assessing the relevance of culture. *Journal of International Business Studies, 31*(2), 387–301. doi:10.1057/palgrave.jibs.8490906

Thorton, P. (1999). The Sociology of Entrepreneurship. *Annual Review of Sociology, 25*(1), 19–46. doi:10.1146/annurev.soc.25.1.19

Thurik, A. R. (2009). Entreprenomics: Entrepreneurship, economic growth and policy. *Entrepreneurship, Growth and Public Policy, 10*(6), 219-249.

Turyahikayo, E. (2015). Challenges faced by small and medium enterprises in raising finance in Uganda. *International Journal of Public Administration and Management Research, 3*(2), 21–33.

UBOS. (2022). *Multi-dimensional Poverty Index*. Multidimensional Poverty Index Report 2022 – Uganda | OPHI.

Uganda Bureau of Statistics. (2017). *Uganda National House Survey UNHS 2017*. Author.

Uganda Bureau of Statistics UBOS. (2022). *Statistical Abstract*. UBOS.

Ummatovich, K. M., Erkinjonovich, O. S., & Rahimovna, S. F. (2019). The Role Of Small Business And Private Entrepreneurship In Civil Society. *Frontiers in Finance & Economics, 16*(2).

Wandera, D., & Nabukenya, N. (2023). *Nabakooba cautions Luweero RDC over contested land, halts boundary opening*. Monitor Publications. Available at https://www.monitor.co.ug/uganda/news/national/nabakooba-cautions-luweero-rdc-over-contested-land-halts-boundary-opening

Wennekers, S., & Thurik, R. (1999). Linking entrepreneurship to economic growth. *Small Business Economics, 13*(1), 27–55. doi:10.1023/A:1008063200484

Wiklund, J., Patzelt, H., & Shepherd, D. A. (2009). Building an integrative model of small business growth. *Small Business Economics*, *32*(4), 351–374. doi:10.100711187-007-9084-8

Williamson, P., & De Meyer, A. (2012). Ecosystem advantage. *California Management Review*, *55*(1), 24–46. doi:10.1525/cmr.2012.55.1.24

Williamson, T. (2003). *Targets and results in public sector management: Uganda case study*. Overseas Development Institute.

World Bank. (2008). *More people living below poverty line*. Author.

Wurth, B., Stam, E., & Spigel, B. (2022). Toward an entrepreneurial ecosystem research program. *Entrepreneurship Theory and Practice*, *46*(3), 729–778. doi:10.1177/1042258721998948

Chapter 14
Continental Integration and Trade in the Southern African Development Community (SADC)

Ndwakhulu stephen Tshishonga
University of KwaZulu-Natal, South Africa

ABSTRACT

This chapter is concerned with the Southern African Development Community (SADC) and its trade potential to increase continental integration in Africa. The chapter argues that SADC has the potential not only to increase continental integration, but also as the building block for AfCTA to realise its vision of promoting continental economic integration, equitable human development, and advance African institutional development. Regional theory was adopted to comprehend the role, shared interests, challenges, and goals among SADC member countries. The chapter found that SADC region is endowed with natural, cultural, and human resources, but lacks state capacity, cooperation, and integration to optimize such resources. The chapter is qualitative in nature and uses systematic literature review to deliberate on the role and challenges faced by SADC in increasing continental integration and further forge socio-economic development between and within its members.

INTRODUCTION

Historically, the African continent is not only endowed with natural resources but is also considered to have a demographically youthful content (Honwana, 2013). Africa's history is intrinsically interwoven to the decades of imperialism and colonialism, and European domination which created borders and territorial boundaries envisaged today (Zahorik, 2018). Through the Berlin Conference of 1884-1885, Africa was auctioned and demarcated among colonial powers and foreign political and socio-economic systems were used to exploit its resources to benefit Europe (Gumede & Oloruntoba, 2018). The Scramble for Africa saw Africa being sliced up like a cake with Germany, Italy, Portugal, and Britain

DOI: 10.4018/979-8-3693-0477-8.ch014

having a bigger share of the cake (Southall, 2010). Thus, the Scramble for Africa made the European nations believe that Africa was discovered, hence, colonies were created for exploitation and settlement (Pakenham, 1991). From this colonial-historical perspective, Africa became the satellite of European powers through imperial expansion and capitalist industrialisation. For Ghai (2014), colonialism was a device used by colonisers to exploit Africa's resources for imperial benefit.

Africa is economically handicapped by the Western imposition and the adoption of neo-liberal economic policies (Amtaika, 2017). Colonialism in particular created strategies that exploit African natural resources. Thus, the Scramble for Africa was a resources-driven agenda to exploit Africa's mineral wealth with Bretton Woods Institutions (IMF and World Bank) being the "new frontiers" in post-World War II (Landsberg, 2018, p. 16). Africa is endowed with an abundance of both human and natural resources; however, the paradox is that Africa is one of the poorest continents in the world. Neo-liberal economic policies are blamed for contributing towards poverty and inequality with the South-based nations bearing the brunt (World Bank Group, 2018). It can be argued that Africa is caught up in a conundrum in terms of which economic approaches or models to adopt for economic freedom in the 21st century. Due to various factors, political freedom as envisaged by former President of Ghana, Kwame Nkrumah has not yielded economic fruits for the African continent. Economically, impoverished Africa re-affirms How Europe underdeveloped Africa to How Africa perpetuated its underdevelopment, socially, economically, politically, and culturally (Tshishonga, 2022).

At the centre of Africa's socio-economic woes is the self-serving leadership with corruption as its modus operandi. While some SADC nations are on the developmental path, most of them are on the verge of being failed states characterised by governments' inability to develop economic policies, stimulate growth, enforce laws and deliver service (Schwella, 2017). The marketisation of neo-liberal economic policies underpinned by capitalist modes of production sees the state being removed from the centre of directing economic planning and implementation (Carroll & Jarvis, 2017). By conforming to market-driven economic policies, Africa not only harvests slow economic development but is also embroiled in universal liberalisation, privatisation and deregulation perpetuated by global capitalism (Stubbs, 2017). Most African nations are bureaucratised with political and business elites in coalitions driven by material and ideological forces as well as state-capital relations. For the economy to grow in the SADC, and to generally benefit its citizens, state-directed development should deviate from conventional capitalist economic models in favour of regional integration and economy with balanced local investments (Feketha, 2019). Thus, within the continent, the adoption of neo-liberal policies has engendered structural inequality and inequality which violate human rights, and equal right to dignity and respect (Therborn, 2019).

Attempts to reverse this dire economic situation in Africa saw the emergence of regional bodies such as the Arab Maghreb Union (UMA), Common Market for Eastern and Southern Africa (COMESA), Community of Sahel-Saharan States (CEN-SAD), Eastern African Community (EAC), Economic Community of Western African States (ECOWAS), Intergovernmental Authority on Development (IGAD) and Southern African Development Community (SADC) (Nkala & Monyae, 2023; Wright, 2017, p.181). These formations are not only recognised by the African Union (AU) but were also established to forge the unification of Africa in its quest to end the looting of African resources (Burger, 2016). Although these regional communities were created to deal with the economic impasse in most of the African countries, they found themselves having to deal with peace and security issues as democracy and economic development cannot geminate roots in a crime-ridden environment. This chapter relied heavily on secondary data obtained from books, book chapters, accredited journal articles and government documentation and policies. Research engines such as Google Scholar, Scopus and ScienceDirect were mainly utilized to comprehend the notion of regional economic integration and its role and challenges within the SADC region.

BACKGROUND

History of SADC and its role as a sub-regional body

The Southern African Development Coordinating Conference (SADCC), which later became the Southern African Development Community (SADC), was founded in 1980 (Mlambo, 2015). The origin of SADC is traceable to the colonial efforts to coordinate anti-colonial campaigns by liberation movements including the newly independent African states (Mashimye, 2023). According to Schenoni (2017), Angola, Botswana, Lesotho, Malawi, Mozambique, Swaziland, Tanzania, Zambia, and Zimbabwe were the first nine member nations that signed the SADC Treaty in 1980, establishing the organization. This regional group aimed to support and coordinate regional collaboration on development initiatives (Lisakafu, 2017). Chigudu (2021) notes that these nations aimed to lessen their reliance on South Africa economically. Additionally, they hoped to encourage member states to work towards financial independence and economic integration.

SADC was formed with the initial goal of reducing South Africa's economic dependency on apartheid and forging connections to create fair regional integration. Southern African nations joined together to create the SADC in the 1980s (Mlambo, 2015). Saurombe (2010) notes that SADC was founded to undermine South Africa's dominance in the area. Its founding was a crucial turning point in Southern Africa's regional integration aspirations. The founding fathers of SADC had a goal to advance collaboration and unity among its member nations and to handle important concerns including trade, economic growth, and social advancement (Sonn, Plessis, Vuuren, Marais, Wagener and Roman, 2021). According to Stapel, Panke and Söderbaum (2023), the SADC changed its name to the SADC in 1992. Although it would be reasonable to expect that such a move would have strengthened member-state integration, there has been little progress in solving the problems that member states are facing (Mlambo, 2015). Namibia joined the Southern African sub-regional organisation in August 1992 after declaring its independence and gaining its freedom from South African domination two years earlier in 1990 when it subsequently became the SADC's fifth member (Nagar and Paterson, 2013). After its first democratic election in 1994 institutionalized apartheid ended resulting in the formal collapse of the Frontline States, and South Africa joined the Community two years later (Nagar and Paterson, 2013).

With shifting dynamics and difficulties in the area, SADC's function as a sub-regional entity has changed through time. As a sub-regional organisation, SADC is critical in encouraging commerce, integration, and regional development in the Southern African sub-region (Zondi, 2023). The SADC's role in fostering commerce within the sub-region, according to various sources, is critical.

Theory of regionalism

Regionalism theory is the study of and evaluation of the political, economic, and social interactions between nations or governments within a certain geographical region (Söderbaum, 2012). According to Börzel (2016), the theory of regionalism is significant because it allows people to make perceptions of the world and learn more about the phenomena of regionalism. The notion of regionalism recognizes that countries or states within a certain area share interests, challenges, and goals. Regionalism is designated as the process of building multilateral institutions to enhance political, security and integration among states (Heywood, 2019; Khadiagala, 2008). Thus, regionalism entails a complex combination of attitudes, loyalties and thoughts that makes people identify their region (Todaro & Smith, 2020). Regionalism can be politically stimulated when cross-border trading and the perceived need for closer cooperation are accepted by member states, and when the government reacts to these internal and external forces using trying to find a transnational level of governance.

The theory of regionalism is anchored on socio-economic integration and trade arrangements based on the movement of goods and people including opportunities to pool of resources for the common good (Mashimbye, 2023). According to this view, countries may solve these common concerns and attain common goals by joining coalitions of regional nations and organizations (Söderbaum, 2004). The theory of regionalism is important because it explains how actors within a region react to causative events and how regions are constituted (Söderbaum, 2012). Essentially, regionalism theory enables the coordination of social, economic and political activities with geographical regions (Heywood, 2019). Within the context of the African Union and its AfCFTA, the theory of regionalism (political and economic or security) is key in promoting cooperation and economic opportunities within and amongst African nations. Thus, for Africa including the SADC region to benefit from the available resources and to sustain economic growth, the elimination of tariffs and non-barriers is imperative for the promotion of the movement of capital and labour across national borders (Nkala & Monyane, 2023). However, this theory was criticised for being market-orientated and not developmental hence it failed to advance socio-economic and socio-cultural development (Oloruntoba, 2023).

PROFILE OF SADC COUNTRIES AND THEIR ECONOMIC POTENTIAL

The Southern African Development Community (SADC) is a Southern African regional economic association that seeks to advance economic cooperation and integration among its member nations (Aniche, and Ukaegbu, 2016). According to Rosenberg, Strauss and Isaacs (2021), about 16 countries made up SADC, each having a distinct potential for economic growth. Thus, SADC countries are diverse geographically, culturally, socially, economically and politically. The map below reflects the countries under the SADC region.

However, this diversity poses both opportunities and challenges for political, cultural and economic integration and development within the SADC region. This region is endowed with challenges, diverse economic opportunities, and natural resources.

South Africa

South Africa is the SADC region's largest economy and is considered one of the most heavily industrialized on the continent (Amos, 2010). It is one of the biggest exporters of gold, platinum, and other natural resources (Onyebukwa, 2021). According to Antin (2013), the mining industry continues to be South Africa's most closely scrutinized economic sector and has been crucial in luring international investment and fostering top global firms. South Africa's significance as a regional and continental centre, as well as its vital role in the expansion of human capital in the area, needs to be understood in the context of its comparative advantages in comparison to other African and global South nations (Amos,

2010). South Africa's economic and political dominance in Southern Africa is unquestionable (Amos, 2010). According to Hlongwane and Daw (2023), South Africa has one of the highest levels of public debt among developing economies, which hinders its capacity to react to shocks and satisfy expanding social and development needs.

Figure 1. Map of SADC Countries
Source: *https://www.google.com/search?q=map+of+SADC+nations&rlz=1C1CHBD.*

Botswana

The mining sector has been an important industry in Botswana's economy, accounting for a large share of both imports and exports (Malefane and Odhiambo, 2016). Botswana's government has prioritized diamond production since diamond exports have historically been a substantial contribution to the country's economic prosperity (Malindini and Mackett, 2018). Rankopo and Diraditsile (2018) assert that in light of the country's socioeconomic growth record after gaining independence in 1966, rising from the most impoverished nation to an upper middle-income country in under 40 years, Botswana has been widely hailed as an example of an African achievement story.

Siphambe (2004) notes that Botswana is a one-of-a-kind instance in the area and throughout Africa in that it did not implement the World Bank/International Monetary Fund-supported SAPs. The main reason was that the country's economy was performing well. Harvey (1992), affirms that Botswana has consistently run significant payment surpluses, except a brief spell in 1981/2. The country has a good balance of payments position, and it has amassed substantial foreign exchange reserves and the accumulated reserves cover approximately 36 months of imports of goods and services (Siphambe, 2004).

Namibia

The principal goal of SADCC was to diminish the region's economic reliance on apartheid South Africa and to enable them to successfully support Namibia's independence and South Africa's democratization (Mbuende, 2014). Vatuva, Filippelli, Gujar, Iyer & Udayaganesan (2022) point out that the essential natural resources that Namibia possesses consist of water, land, livestock, plants and animals, minerals, and fisheries. However, the Bank of Namibia (2019) notes that there has been a recession in Namibia's economy since 2016. The nation's economy has mostly been built on the extraction of natural resources with no valuable addition (Heyns, 2022). In light of the economic downturn and unsustainably high expenditure, Namibia is exceptional in that it is a developing nation that has tightened its financial belt and reduced spending even before the Coronavirus outbreak (Heyns, 2022).

Swaziland (Eswatini)

Eswatini is a small landlocked country with a growing economy that depends significantly on South Africa (Malefane, 2021). Mdlovu (2021) concurs with Malefane that Eswatini's lilangeni currency is tied to the South African rand to maintain stability in the economy. Dlamini (2019) states that the Eswatini economy is heavily dependent on the agriculture sector. Marazza, Campanale, WUR, and Balugani (2021) add that following its separation from the British Empire in 1968, the Kingdom of Eswatini had diverse economic expansion centred on agricultural growth in cotton, maize, and sugarcane as well as policies that encouraged private and international investment. However, Dlamini (2019) notes that Eswatini experiences significant levels of poverty; as a result, it is attempting to develop the agricultural sector to reduce hunger and poverty.

Lesotho

Lesotho is a nation that depends significantly on South Africa for its economic growth. (Lundahl and Petersson, 2019). The implementation of the NSDP saw the Lesotho government making some progress in enhancing the atmosphere for investment and constructing essential infrastructure (Arenas, Engel, Kotschwar and Maliszewska, 2018). Lall (2005) claims that Lesotho is lacking in resources, a nation within South Africa, and is currently the continent's top supplier of clothing to the US. Tsoeu-Ntokoane, Kali and Lemaire (2022) add that the country operates in an open economy where its key exports are textiles, water, and diamonds. South Africa and the United States (US) are its top trade partners, with the former serving as its principal trading partner (Damane and Sekants,2022).

Zambia

According to the Republic of Zambia (2013), after independence in 1964, the country acquired a dual economy consisting of a mining industry with cutting-edge technology and expensive equipment and an agricultural sector made up of a combination of commercial agriculture and small-scale farming. Chibbonta, Mayondi and Mulenga (2022) note that copper export has given the nation export income, tax income, and jobs. Mtiki (2022) asserts that with the money from selling copper, Zambia experienced stability and economic prosperity. However, Chibbonta, Mayondi and Mulenga (2022) argue that Zambia's economic development has slowed down in recent years after years of notable economic growth and attaining middle-income status in 2011.

Zimbabwe

Since the economic collapse and the implementation of the land reform program, the mining sector of Zimbabwe's economy has been a key contributor to the GDP of the country (Zikiti, 2016). According to Mwatwara, Mujere and Mkodzongi (2022), mine operations have been carried out throughout the nation's history, including artisanal gold mining. Calfucura (2018) states that Zimbabwe primarily depends on natural resources, which are essential to a variety of nature-based tourist industries. Siakwah, Musavengane and Leonard (2020) add that tourism significantly contributes to Zimbabwe's economic growth. Due to infrastructure and financial constraints, some of the abundant minerals are not properly utilized (Chamber of Mines, 2013).

Angola

Given that Angola possesses one of the largest and most diverse mining resources in all of Africa, mining there offers a lot of economic potential (De Almeida, 2019). Angola's GDP growth has ranked among the greatest in the world in the first ten years of the twenty-first century (Quixina and Almeida, 2014). It is commonly acknowledged that natural resources, particularly oil but also diamonds, are important to the Angolan economy (International Monetary Fund 2014). Quixina and Almeida (2014) claim that the oil industry, which accounts for more than 50% of Angola's GDP and is fuelled by the rise in oil prices has been the country's major engine of growth.

Mozambique

Mozambique is one of the least complicated economies in the world (Sørensen, Estmann, Sarmento and Rand, 2020). Pereira (2009) attests that Mozambique has gone through financial difficulties brought on by the switch to a market economy. Even with the high growth rates of recent years, the economy of this country continues to be among the least complicated in the world (Sørensen, Estmann, Sarmento and Rand, 2020). Nevertheless, average individuals who used to receive access to free education and healthcare, stabilized pricing, and employment have seen a significant improvement in their quality of life because the country transitioned to a market economy (Pereira, 2009).

Tanzania

Tanzania's economy is mostly reliant on agriculture and has a lower-middle income level (Moyo, Simson, Jacob and De Mevius, 2012). Lyatuu, Nie and Fang (2015) highlight that Tanzania has recently experienced sustained economic growth, which has aided in raising overall living standards. According to the World Bank (2021), Tanzania officially transitioned to a lower-middle-income country classification in July 2020, marking the culmination of two decades of consistent progress.

Malawi

Malawi is one of the world's poorest nations (Dossani, 2012). Tobacco, tea, and raw sugar have historically been Malawi's top foreign exchange producers (Said and Singini, 2014). According to Ndala and Pelser (2019), the small- and medium-sized enterprise sector employs 92% of the people in Malawi, whether they are working for themselves, their families, or running their enterprises. Since independence, Malawi has struggled to convert brief economic expansions to long-term, sustained growth (Said and Singini, 2014). Ndala and Pelser (2019) argue that Malawi is not a developed nation, and its citizens struggle to make ends meet on less than a dollar a day. Dossani (2012) asserts that if poverty is measured by GDP per capita, Malawi continues to be one of the world's poorest nations, which is explained by high poverty census ratios.

DR Congo

The official economy of the Congo was nearly exclusively dependent on mining minerals, especially copper and diamonds, before independence in 1960 (Lawal, 2022). The DRC's principal economic resource is its mineral resources, which account for about 90% of export revenue (Lawal, 2022). Since 2001, the DRC's economic and financial development has been accelerating. However, the World Bank Group (2018) contends that despite the country's remarkable natural resource richness, political instability accounts for the continued low standard of living among Congolese citizens. Koyame and Clark (2002) argue that the Democratic Republic of the Congo's (DRC) conflict has had terrible effects on the country's economy, but it has also had an impact on the whole of the central African area. Qi *et al.* (2022) claim that given the DRC's robust economic growth and a wealth of mineral and agricultural resources, there are still wide gaps in social and economic standing.

Mauritius

Mauritius has developed a solid growth-oriented development pattern despite being a tiny, economically precarious and resource-poor island (Moraghen, Seetanah and Sookie, 2023). Following its independence in 1968, Mauritius' economy has developed from a low-income, mono-crop economy to a middle-income and well-diversified economy (Mahadea, 2023). Behuria (2023) notes that Mauritius has a diverse economy, a strong financial sector, and significant tourism and industrial sectors. Moraghen, Seetanah and Sookia (2023) assert that the nation's efforts to diversify its economy have also been effective, enabling the country to transition from a sugar-based economy to one that includes a wider range of services.

Zafar (2011) notes that sugar, tourism, textiles and clothing, financial services, and fish processing have all been recognized as potential drivers of development for the country. Moraghen, Seetanah and Sookia, (2023) affirm that the expansion of its economy into services, manufacturing, exports, jewellery, and a burgeoning offshore financial sector, Mauritius has demonstrated its ability to embrace new industries. Nevertheless, the World Bank claims that the country's poverty rate is comparatively low in comparison to other emerging economies (Fauzel, Seetanah & Sannassee, 2016).

Seychelles

Schutter and Hicks (2019) note that due to its distant location in the Indian Ocean, and innovative role in advancing the Blue Economy, Seychelles occupies a special place in Africa. Yusheng, Atuahene Agyapong, Bentum-Micah and Konadu Aboagye (2019) add that tourism and fishing are the primary sources of income for Seychelles. Senaratne, Zimbroff and Stevens (2021) also note that the country has reaped substantial advantages from its maritime resources over time, with the growth of fisheries, tourism, trade, and internal and international ships that promote trade.

Madagascar

Madagascar is one of the world's poorest nations with a multitude of difficulties (Rakotondramaro and Andriamasy,2016). Sarrasin (2006) ascertains that despite being rich in biodiversity and natural resources, Madagascar has economic difficulties. Cope (2002) notes that Madagascar has one of the world's biggest ilmenite deposits, as well as significant amounts of chromite, coal, iron, and uranium. According to Rakotondramaro and Andriamasy (2016), the country boasts an abundance of tourist attractions, from animal watching to beach vacations and cultural interactions, providing visitors with a wide range of activities that aid its economy.

Comoros

The economy of Comoros is centred on subsistence farming and fishing, and there are natural resources (Golub and Varma, 2014). However, Shaaban, Ramzy and Sharabassy (2013) point out that due to its tiny size and location, there has been little industrial growth. Anyanwu and Salami (2021) argue that the Comoros has arguably one of the smallest and lowest economies in the world.

FINDINGS AND ANALYSIS

Socio-Economic Analysis of SADC Member States

The profiles above reflect the 16 SADC member states and their varied geo-political and economic environments as well as their socio-political opportunities and challenges. SADC integration is underpinned by eight (8) development priorities: 1) food security, land and agriculture; 2) economic development and poverty alleviation; 3) infrastructure and services; 4) industry, trade, investment and finance; 5) human resource development, science and technique; 6) natural resources and environment; 7) social welfare, information and culture; and 8) political, diplomacy, international relations, peace and security (Zondi, 2023, p. 93). These 8 priorities are the fundamental pillars established to advance a developmental regional integration aimed at the eradication of poverty, entrenching democratic governance with citizen participation and region-building processes (Zondi, 2023). Within the SADC region, challenges of deepening poverty, widening unemployment, lack of social and economic development, insecurity and instability, enduring inequality and systematic subjective violence are worrisome (Nkondo, 2023). However, these challenges are complementary to each other and are reinforced in undermining the potential of socio-economic and political development. Addressing these challenges demands the SADC nations to advance and enhance regional integration and solidarity.

Addressing these challenges can pave the way for the SADC region to achieve its agenda in pursuing developmental regional integration for integrated development. the table below depicts the economic potential in the form of resources. Effective utilisation of these resources could boost the economic development and integration within the region.

Table 1. SADC Nations & their Economic Potential

SADC COUNTRIES	MAJOR PRODUCTION
South Africa	Gold, platinum, and other natural resources
Botswana	Diamond
Namibia	Water, land, livestock, plants and animals, minerals, and fisheries
Swaziland (Eswatini)	Cotton, maize, and sugarcane
Lesotho	Textiles, water, and diamonds
Zambia	Copper mining industry
Zimbabwe	Nature-based tourist industries
Angola	Natural resources oil & diamonds
Mozambique	Aluminium, shrimp, and cotton
Tanzania	Agriculture
Malawi	Tobacco, tea, and raw sugar
Democratic Republic of Congo	Mining minerals, especially copper and diamonds
Mauritius	Sugar, tourism, textiles and clothing, financial services, fish processing
Seychelles	Maritime resources
Madagascar	Chromite, coal, iron, and uranium
Comoros	Subsistence farming and fishing, and there is little natural resources

SADC and African Continental Free Trade Area (AfCFTA)

The African Continental Free Trade Area (AfCFTA) is a free area of trade that provides a unique opportunity for regional countries to competitively develop their economies and integrate into the global economy, promote inclusion, and reduce poverty (Maliszewska *et al.,* 2020). Through AfCFTA, a single market has been created for the flow of goods and services as well as capital and business travellers (Signe, 2019). The African Continental Free Trade Area (AfCFTA) is a free area of trade that provides unique opportunities for regional countries to competitively develop their economies and integrate into the global economy, promote inclusion, and reduce poverty (Maliszewska *et al.,* 2020). Although Africa has made considerable progress in the past decades, especially in raising living standards and reducing poverty, AfCFTA as a negotiated agreement is expected to provide stimulus for reforms that will boost productivity and job opportunities. Farahat (2016) claims that AfCFTA; 's agreement has three targets: which are rules and procedures for the settlement of disputes, trade in goods, and trade in services. Various regional bodies inclusive of SADC are an integral endeavour for Africa. Trade plays a decisive role in economic growth and development. Todaro and Smith (2020, p. 634) identified six functions of trade in development such as; a) important stimulator of economic growth; b) promote greater international and domestic equality; c) help countries to achieve development through promoting and rewarding sectors in the economy; d) internationalise prices and costs of production through the principle of comparative advantage and finally e) promotion of growth and development through out-ward policy intervention and self-reliance. These functions are key in democratising the political economy of nations especially those in the African continent.

The fundamental goals of the SADC, form a free trade area to accomplish development and economic progress, reduce poverty, raise the standard of living for Southern Africans, and help the underprivileged via regional integration (Asuelime and Enaifoghe, 2018). The SADC Free Trade Area aims to satisfy the following demands of the private sector and other regional stakeholders; cheaper consumer products and inputs, more job opportunities, more foreign direct investment and joint ventures, and the development of regional value (Saurombe, 2011). For Moyer, Kabandula, Bohl and Hanna (2021), the fundamental goal of the AfCFTA is to establish a single marketplace for goods and services to promote the free movement of people and investments and to provide the groundwork for a Continental Customs Union.

The signing of the African Continental Free Trade Agreement (AfCFTA) has sparked considerable trade potential in Africa, which might result in the continent's intra-trade levels dramatically improving, hence enhancing the economic well-being of Africans (Pasara and Diko, 2020). According to Ndonga, Laryea and Chaponda (2020), the African Continental Free Trade Area (AfCFTA) accord is hailed as a key tenet and engine for the continent's industrialization, economic expansion, and development that is sustainable. Simo (2020) notes that Africa has made tremendous progress toward regional and continental integration with the implementation of the African Continental Free Trade Area (AfCFTA), which took effect on May 30, 2019.

However, Mlambo, Thusi, Zubane and Mlambo (2022) argue that for AfCFTA to be implemented successfully, certain additional difficulties and flaws must be fixed. Moyer, Kabandula, Bohl and Hanna (2021) criticise the AfCFTA because it is restricted and facilitated by the activities of other governments in the international system. Ndonga, Laryea and Chaponda (2020) affirm that even though the AfCFTA addresses several non-tariff barriers, including technical trade barriers, customs procedures, import fees, and sanitary and phytosanitary measures; it fails to address several other issues that plague African countries' international trade performances, such as insufficient infrastructure and low output and efficiency. Bassey (2023) pointed out that the AfCFTA's effective implementation might promote regional integration, promote equitable human development, and advance African institutions' development plans, such as Agenda 2063.

Role of SADC in Continental Trade and Integration

The SADC is crucial to the integration and trade of the continent (Tanyanyiwa and Hakuna, 2014). According to Saurombe (2011), one of the most significant legal documents governing SADC's works on trade is the SADC Protocol on Trade, which was formed in 1996 and updated in 2010. SADC is also aiming to deepen regional integration through various efforts like as infrastructure development and energy and water resource coordination (Al-Saidi and Hefny, 2018). Southern Africa's economy has recently become more efficient as a result of these measures, attracting more investment and creating job opportunities (Saurombe, 2011). SADC is anchored on the vision and mission which advocate for a holistic and developmental approach to regional integration. The mission of SADC is:

To promote sustainable equitable economic growth and socio-economic development through efficient productive systems, deeper co-operation and integration, good governance and durable peace and security (Zondi, 2023, p. 92).

The objectives of SADC are to:

Enhance the standard and quality of life of the peoples of the region, promote self-sustaining development and collective self-reliance, ensure productive utilisation of natural resources, achieve complementarity between national and regional policies and strategies; and strengthen the affinities between the peoples of the region (Zondi, 2023, p. 92).

For Habiyaremye (2020), SADC is constructing regional transportation infrastructure such as ports, trains, and highways. As a result, Mutambara (2009) claims that transporting goods and services from one part of the region to other parts of Africa will be more convenient and less costly. Beny and Snyder (2012) maintain that cross-border business will become more inexpensive if expenditures and delays are reduced. According to Habiyaremye (2020), it will be simpler to ensure that the region has a steady supply of these critical resources, which are critical for economic progress.

Anticipated SADC Challenges

One of the main issues that affect the SADC's security and development is poverty (Lisakafu, 2017). Simkins (2021) notes that a significant portion of the population in the SADC lives in poverty and is unhappy with the economies' heterogeneity which creates an unequal economic environment (Mapuva, 2014). Regional leaders' inability to uphold their commitments to the rule of law is contributing to the erosion of democracy that the SADC area is currently experiencing (Lisakafu, 2017). Rekindling political will and establishing a fresh, impartial space for citizen engagement and confidence in many facets of the nation's governing process are additional challenges for the SADC body (Aeby, 2019). Chigudu (2021) holds that structural and political obstacles must be solved if SADC is to guarantee long-term economic growth. According to Lisakafu, (2017), one of the challenges is connected to a concerning tendency of constitutional revisions intended to extend the terms of current presidents, which cause tensions in Africa and the SADC region. Policies and protocols exist; however, they are far from being implemented due to the lack of synchronisation and, compliance and reciprocation of trade rules and principles (Okafor, 2018). The absence of shared political beliefs among SADC member nations is the sixth obstacle (Lisakafu, 2017). Similar to other continental RECs, SADC; 's underperformance is due to a low level of compliance by its member states. Within the region, tariffs and failure to foster economic cooperation and sector-level competition are some of the surmountable challenges (Signe, 2019). Within the region, the quest and aspiration to build and promote regional solidarity, and integration and further widen the domestic markets is undermined by the absence of effective policy (Akafor, 2023). Ineffective structures for coordinating national actions, ineffective coordination by the SADC Secretariat; inadequate consultation among stakeholders at national levels, inadequate monitoring and evaluation of implementation; and resource constraints (in Zondi, 2023, p. 104). Many African countries belong to multiple regional economic communities (RECs) and that to Signe (2019) limits the efficiency and effectiveness of these regional bodies.

In addition to the political fragmentation and lack of political will in most of the SADC nations, the realisation of a nation-state is further hampered by the prevalence of poverty, unemployment and socio-economic inequality (Nkondo, 2023). Conflicts and misgovernance amongst some of the SADC members not only render both political and economic integration impossible but also undermine the region's efforts to consolidate cross-border trading. Within the region imposed tariffs and visa issues remain unsolved barriers towards promoting economic and social development and integration for regional self-sufficiency, self-sustainment and self-reliant development (Khadiagala, 2023). The goals and vision of AfCFTA cannot be realised while African nations are still operating on restrictive visa policies as opposed to open visas (Matlosa, 2023). Another huge challenge is that African economic powerhouses such as South Africa are reluctant to accept the free movement of persons (for social and economic) hence, its integration hegemony, xenophobic and Afrophobic tendencies against fellow Africans (Tshishonga, 2022). This point was reiterated by Hirsch (2021) who argues that South Africa's political and economic dominance is a threat to integration and efforts of free movement of people, free trade and freedom to choose where to live or work. Oloruntoba (2023) argues that the market approach to regional integration has failed to enhance economic development broadly on the continent and SADC in particular. The current RECs are based on neo-liberal theory and put more emphasis on accessing markets as opposed to being developmental, thus, taking socio-cultural, environmental and technical dements. Intra-trade in Africa and the SADC region is low and countries continue to import outside the continent.

DIRECTIONS FOR FUTURE RESEARCH

Considering the prevalence of poverty, unemployment and economic underdevelopment in Africa, there is continental pressure for financial and infrastructure investment and efficient utilisation of existing resources for Africa's development. Imperative in addressing these challenges, interdisciplinary research within SADC is needed that prioritises building adequate infrastructure, transport, and communication networks as the building blocks for SADC trade for increased integration. Such research will be instrumental in sparking interest among the SADC countries and Africa at large to create friendly trading regulatory environments, policies and governance culture that attract and facilitate both private and public investments for African economic growth and development. This will entail advancing Africa's development and economic prosperity through the promotion of Afro-centric trading networks and sustainable markets. This can be achieved by easing immigration policies and visas as a point of departure towards building local and regional markets for its products and sustainable economic growth.

CONCLUSION

It is against socio-political fragmentation, economic dependency and underdevelopment in Africa that this chapter deliberated on the merits and demerits of integration with particular focus on the SADC region. For socio-economic boosting sectors and development within the region, theoretical evidence pointed out that the African Continental Free Trade Area (AfCFTA) could be a good platform for African countries to advance free trade, market access, capital mobility and investment for Africa's economic development and prosperity. Importantly, the chapter profiled the different stages of economic growth and struggles among SADC countries and argues that through broader trading and the apex of the African Continental Free Trade Area (AfCFTA), Africa could accelerate free and intra-trade.

The chapter acknowledged the importance of establishing the superstructure such as the RECs, SADC and other regional bodies in Africa. However, the lack of micro-states' capacity and political will as well as power relations and closed visa policies and tariffs are the major stumbling blocks for realising developmental integration within the SADC region. Both roles and challenges faced SADC region were identified and discussed within the prevailing dynamics and environment conducive to either undermining or building a capable regional community. To ameliorate some of the challenges to effective integration in Africa and SADC in particular, the chapter argues for multilateralism to foster mutually beneficial economic integration amongst member states. Fundamentally, the removal of tariffs and the creation of a conducive trading environment for free trading is recommended if SADC is to maximise its economic potential. Finally, the chapter recommends regional integration innovation through the effective use of Artificial Intelligence and capability packages brought by the Fourth Industrial Revolution (4IR).

REFERENCES

Aeby, M. (2019). *SADC–the southern arrested development community?: Enduring challenges to peace and security in Southern Africa*. Nordiska Afrikainstitutet.

Al-Saidi, M., & Hefny, A. (2018). Institutional arrangements for beneficial regional cooperation on water, energy and food priority issues in the Eastern Nile Basin. *Journal of Hydrology (Amsterdam)*, *562*, 821–831. doi:10.1016/j.jhydrol.2018.05.009

Amos, S. (2010). The role of South Africa in SADC regional integration: The making or braking of the organization. *J. Int'l Com. L. & Tech.*, *5*, 124.

Amtaika, A. (2017). The particularistic and Universality of political Cultural Beliefs and Values: Western Liberalism, Islamic Fundamentalism and African Theoretical Perspectives. In A. Amtaika (Ed.), *Culture, Democracy and Development in Africa*. Pan-African University Press.

Aniche, E. T., & Ukaegbu, V. E. (2016). Structural dependence, vertical integration and regional economic cooperation in Africa: A study of Southern African Development Community. *African Review (Dar Es Salaam, Tanzania)*, *8*(2), 108–119. doi:10.1080/09744053.2016.1186866

Antin, D., (2013). The South African mining sector: An industry at a crossroads. *Economy Report South Africa*, (2013), 1-22.

Anyanwu, J. C., & Salami, A. O. (2021). The impact of COVID-19 on African economies: An introduction. *African Development Review*, *33*(1), S1. doi:10.1111/1467-8268.12531 PMID:34149237

Arenas, G., Engel, J., Kotschwar, B., & Maliszewska, M. (2018). *Supporting Lesotho's economic diversification and trade integration: structural transformation through greater export competitiveness*. World Bank. doi:10.1596/30178

Asuelime, R. A., & Enaifoghe, A. O. (2018). Southern African Regional and Economic Integration: The free trade zone strategy for South Africa? *Journal of African Union Studies*, *7*(2), 85–107. doi:10.31920/2050-4306/2018/v7n2a5

Bank of Namibia. (2019). *GDP by activity: Annual percentage changes*. Annual Report.

Bassey, O.B. (2023). *Leadership and the Success of African Integration and Development Agenda: Juxtaposing the African continental free trade area-AfCFTA and Agenda 2063*. Academic Press.

Behuria, P. (2023). The political economy of a tax haven: The case of Mauritius. *Review of International Political Economy*, *30*(2), 772–800. doi:10.1080/09692290.2022.2069144

Beny, L. N., & Snyder, M. (2012). Analysis of the Republic of South Sudan's Accession to the East African Community: Benefits, Detriments and Recommendations. *U of Michigan Public Law Research Paper*, (337).

Börzel, T. A. (2016). Theorizing regionalism. The Oxford handbook of comparative regionalism, 41-63.

Burger, P. (2016). *Getting It Right: A New economy for South Africa. Santon*. Review Publishing.

Calfucura, E. (2018). Governance, land and distribution: A discussion on the political economy of community-based conservation. *Ecological Economics*, *145*, 18–26. doi:10.1016/j.ecolecon.2017.05.012

Carroll, T., & Jarvis, D. S. L. (2017). Disembedding Autonomy: Asia after the Developmental State. In T. Carroll & D. S. L. Jarvis (Eds.), *Asia after the Developmental State: Disembedding Autonomy* (pp. 3–48). Cambridge University Press. doi:10.1017/9781316480502.002

Chibbonta, W., Mayondi, M., & Mulenga, R., A. (2022). *Reflection on Zambia's Development Strategies since Independence-1964 to 2021*. Academic Press.

Chigudu, D. (2021). Economic Integration in Southern Africa through SADC's Revised Priorities (2015-2020) for Sustainable Development: A Mirage? *J. Legal Ethical & Regul. Isses*, *24*, 1.

Cope, L. W. (2002). Madagascar mining—open for business. *Engineering and Mining Journal*, *203*(4), 24.

Damane, M., & Sekantsi, P. (2018). The Sources of Unemployment in Lesotho. *Modern Economy*, *9*(5), 937–965. doi:10.4236/me.2018.95060

De Almeida, L. D. C. T. (2019). Diamond Export and Economic Growth in Angola. *International Journal of Academic Research in Business & Social Sciences*, *9*(9). Advance online publication. doi:10.6007/IJARBSS/v9-i9/6382

Dlamini, L.N. (2019). *Determinants of commercial orientation and the level of market participation by women maize farmers in Eswatini*. Academic Press.

Dlamini, T. S., Mlipha, S., Mohammed, M., & Sacolo, T. (2018). Path to economic recovery and sustainable growth in the Kingdom of Eswatini. *African Review of Economics and Finance*, *10*(2), 3–9.

Dossani, S. (2012). Malawi: A development puzzle? *Global Majority E-Journal*, *3*(1), 20–32.

Farahat, M. A. (2016). African Continental Free Trade Area: Policy and Negotiation Options for Trade in Goods. In *UN Conference on Trade and Development* (*Vol. 2*). Academic Press.

Fauzel, S., Seetanah, B., & Sannassee, R. V. (2016). A dynamic investigation of foreign direct investment and poverty reduction in Mauritius. *Theoretical Economics Letters*, *6*(2), 289–303. doi:10.4236/tel.2016.62033

Feketha, V. (2019, Nov. 12). *Message to African Economies.* Mercury, p. 6.

Ghai, Y. P. (2014). State, ethnicity and economy in Africa. In Ethnic Diversity and Economic Instability in Africa. Cambridge University Press.

Golub, S., & Varma, A. (2014). Fishing exports and economic development of least developed countries: Bangladesh, Cambodia, Comoros, Sierra Leone and Uganda. UNCTAD. Swarthmore College.

Gumede, V., & Oloruntoba, S. (2018). Regional Integration and African Renaissance: Moving Beyond the Rhetoric. In C. Landsberg (Ed.), *Africa Rising Up: Perspectives on African Renewal* (pp. 245–258). Real African Publishers.

Habiyaremye, A. (2020). *Fast tracking the SADC integration agenda to unlock regional collaboration gains along growth corridors in Southern Africa* (No. 2020/95). WIDER Working Paper.

Harvey, C., (1996). *Banking policy in Botswana: Orthodox but untypical.* Academic Press.

Heyns, E. (2022). *An analysis of effects of economic growth on the financial performance of Namibian listed companies* [Doctoral dissertation]. University of Namibia.

Heywood, A. (2019). *Politics* (5th ed.). Red Globe Press.

Hirsch, A. (2021). 'The African Union's Free Movement of Persons Protocol: Why has it faltered and how can its objectives be achieved? *South African Journal of International Affairs*, *28*(4), 497–517. do i:10.1080/10220461.2021.2007788

Hlongwane, N. W., & Daw, O. D. (2023). Determinants of public debt in South Africa: A Regime-Switching Approach. *International Journal of Economics and Finance Studies*, *15*(1), 142–163.

Honwana, A. (2013). The Time of Youth; Works, social Change and Politics in Africa. Kumarian Press.

International Monetary Fund. (2014). *Angola: Second Post-Program Monitoring*. IMF Country Report No. 14/81, March 2014.

Khadiagala, G. (2013). Theories and concepts of regional integration in Africa. In D. Monyae & S. Nkala (Eds.), The Quality for Unity: An Appraisal of Regional Integration in Africa (pp. 21-41). Sunnyside: Jacana Media Ltd.

Koyame, M., & Clark, J. F. (2002). The economic impact of the Congo War. In *The African stakes of the Congo war* (pp. 201–223). Palgrave Macmillan US. doi:10.1057/9781403982445_12

Lall, S. (2005). FDI, AGOA and manufactured exports by a landlocked, least developed African economy: Lesotho. *The Journal of Development Studies*, *41*(6), 998–1022. doi:10.1080/00220380500155254

Landsberg, C. (2018). Introduction: Bolstering pan-African Agency: From Africa Rising to Africa rising up! In C. Landsberg (Ed.), *Africa Rising Up: Perspectives on African Renewal* (pp. 15–36). Real African Publishers.

Lawal, A. (2022). *Professor Matthew Statler Economic Inequality: Perspectives, Policies, and Practices I*. Introduction.

Lisakafu, J. (2017). The Southern African Development Community and the Challenges of Southern Africa Regional Security. *Huria: Journal of the Open University of Tanzania, 24*(1), 163–190.

Lundahl, M. O., & Petersson, L. (2019). *The Dependent Economy: Lesotho and the Southern African Customs Union*. Routledge. doi:10.4324/9780429309984

Lyatuu, E.T., Nie, F., & Fang, C. (2015). *The role of agriculture in the economic growth and poverty reduction in Tanzania*. Academic Press.

Mahadea, D. (2023). Economic Progress, Poverty. The Nexus between Poverty and Corruption: Quo Vadis? 322.

Malatji, T. L. (2021). Unemployment and regional human mobility; all roads lead to South Africa. *African Journal of Development Studies, 11*(3), 169.

Malefane, M. R. (2021). Investigating the Core–Periphery Relationship in the Southern African Customs Union. *The Review of Black Political Economy, 48*(2), 190–205. doi:10.1177/0034644620963040

Malefane, M. R., & Odhiambo, N. M. (2016). The Evolution of Trade Policy in Botswana. *Global Journal of Emerging Market Economies, 8*(1), 22–34. doi:10.1177/0974910115613705

Malindini, K., & Mackett, O. (2018). Trade liberalisation and female employment in Botswana and South Africa. *GLOBUS Research Paper, 14*.

Maliszewska, M., van der Mensbrugghe, D., Pereira, M., Osorio-Rodarte, I., & Ruta, M. (2020). *The African Continental Free Trade Area: Economic and Distributional Effects*. Academic Press.

Maphiri, M., Matasane, M. A., & Mudimu, G. (2021). Challenges to the effective implementation of SDG 8 in creating decent work and economic growth in the Southern African Hemisphere: Perspectives from South Africa, Lesotho and Zimbabwe. In *Global Challenges to CSR and Sustainable Development: Root Causes and Evidence from Case Studies* (pp. 39–63). Springer International Publishing. doi:10.1007/978-3-030-62501-6_3

Mapuva, J. W. M. (2014). The SADC regional bloc: What challenges and prospects for regional integration? *Law, Democracy & Development, 18*(1), 22–36. doi:10.4314/ldd.v18i1.2

Marazza, D., Campanale, L., Wur, G.V.V., & Balugani, P.E. (2021). *Integrated study and modelling of the factors affecting small-scale subsistence farming in eSwatini (southern Africa) through the use of causal diagrams and agent-based models*. Academic Press.

Mashimye, R. (2023). The ideological roots of regional integration in Africa. In D. Monye & S. Nkala (Eds.), The Quality for Unity: An Appraisal of Regional Integration in Africa (pp. 43-64). Sunnyside: Jacana Media Ltd.

Matlosa, K. (2023). The free movement of persons and African integration. In D. Monye & S. Nkala (Eds.), The Quality for Unity: An Appraisal of Regional Integration in Africa (pp. 265-289). Sunnyside: Jacana Media Ltd.

Mbuende, K. M. (2014). Namibia and the southern African development community. Namibia's Foreign Relations: Historic Contexts, Current dimensions, and Perspectives for the 21st Century, 231-252.

Mdlovu, N. (2021). *Exchange rate pass-through to domestic prices under the common monetary area of Southern Africa: the case of Eswatini*. University of Johannesburg.

Mlambo, D.N. (2015). *The role of the SADC as a tool for regional integration in Southern Africa*. Academic Press.

Mlambo, V. H., Thusi, X., Zubane, S., & Mlambo, D. N. (2022). The African Continental Free Trade Area: Challenges and Possible Successes. *Latin American Journal of Trade Policy*, *5*(12), 75–106. doi:10.5354/0719-9368.2022.64897

Moraghen, W., Seetanah, B., & Sookia, N. U. H. (2023). The impact of exchange rate and exchange rate volatility on Mauritius foreign direct investment: A sector-wise analysis. *International Journal of Finance & Economics*, *28*(1), 208–224. doi:10.1002/ijfe.2416

MoyerJ. D.KabandulaA.BohlD.HannaT. (2021). Conditions for success in the implementation of the African continental free trade agreement. *Available at* SSRN 3941470. doi:10.2139/ssrn.3941470

Moyo, M., Simson, R., Jacob, A., & De Mevius, F. (2012). *Attaining middle income status-Tanzania: growth and structural transformation required to reach middle income status by 2025*. International Growth Centre, London School of Economics and Political Science.

Mtiki, L. (2022). Mineral Resource Management and Economic Growth: What Zambia Should Learn from Chile. *Journal of Economics, Finance and Accounting Studies*, *4*(2), 191–205.

Mutambara, T. E. (2009). Regional transport challenges within the Southern African Development Community and their implications for economic integration and development. *Journal of Contemporary African Studies*, *27*(4), 501–525. doi:10.1080/02589000903399488

Mwatwara, W., Mujere, J., & Mkodzongi, G. (2022). Between violence and negotiation: Gold-rushes, gang violence, and negotiated access in artisanal gold mining along Zimbabwe's Great Dyke. *The Extractive Industries and Society*, *11*(11), 101103. doi:10.1016/j.exis.2022.101103

Nagar, D., & Paterson, M. (2013). The History of Regionalism in Southern Africa: From SADCC to SADC. In *South Africa in Southern Africa* (pp. 9–12). Centre for Conflict Resolution. https://www.jstor.org/stable/resrep05170.6

Ndala, N. N., & Pelser, T. (2019). Examining the effectiveness of entrepreneurship policy implementation in Malawi. *Journal of Contemporary Management*, *16*(2), 234–255. doi:10.35683/jcm19036.34

Ndonga, D., Laryea, E., & Chaponda, M. (2020). Assessing the potential impact of the African continental free trade area on least developed countries: A case study of Malawi. *Journal of Southern African Studies*, *46*(4), 773–792. doi:10.1080/03057070.2020.1767888

Nkala, S., & Monyae, D. (2023). Introduction: Regional integration in Africa's development. In D. Monye & S. Nkala (Eds.), The Quality for Unity: An Appraisal of Regional Integration in Africa (pp. 1-17). Sunnyside: Jacana Media Ltd.

Nkondo, M. (2023). African lingua francas and African knowledge systems; A framework for regional integration. In D. Monye & S. Nkala (Eds.), The Quality for Unity: An Appraisal of Regional Integration in Africa (pp. 65-85). Sunnyside: Jacana Media Ltd.

Okafor, H. O. (2018). Multilateralism, regionalism, and the effectiveness of trade policy in sub-Saharan African. In C. Landsberg (Ed.), *Africa Rising Up: Perspectives on African Renewal* (pp. 197–209). Real African Publishers.

Oloruntoba, S. O. (2023). The state, Regional Integration, and Economic Development in Africa: Rethinking the Neo-Liberal Paradigm. In C. Landsberg (Ed.), *Africa Rising Up: Perspectives on African Renewal* (pp. 1211–1226). Real African Publishers.

Onyebukwa, C. F. (2021). The Dilemma of natural resources and upsurge of conflicts in Africa: A cursory look at the Marikana management approaches in South Africa. Political economy of resource, human security and environmental conflicts in Africa, 277-296.

Page, J. M. (2016). *Industry in Tanzania: Performance, prospects, and public policy* (No. 2016/5). WIDER Working paper.

Pakenham, T. (1991). *The Scramble for Africa: 1876-1912*. Jonathan Ball Publishers.

Pasara, M. T., & Diko, N. (2020). The effects of AfCFTA on food security sustainability: An analysis of the cereals trade in the SADC region. *Sustainability (Basel)*, *12*(4), 14–19. doi:10.3390u12041419

Pereira, J.C. (2009). *The impact of democracy in Mozambique: Assessing political, social and economic developments since the dawn of democracy*. Academic Press.

Qi, X., Zhu, Y., Wang, Y., He, Q., Hee, J., Chen, W., Takesue, R., & Tang, K. (2022). Socio-economic inequalities in children's nutritional status in Democratic Republic of the Congo in 2017–2018: An analysis of data from a nationally representative survey. *Public Health Nutrition*, *25*(2), 257–268. PMID:34615568

Quixina, Y., & Almeida, A. (2014). *Financial development and economic growth in a natural resource based economy: Evidence from Angola. FEP-UP*. School of Economics and Management, University of Porto.

Rakotondramaro, H., & Andriamasy, L. (2016). Multivariate Granger Causality among tourism, poverty and growth in Madagascar. *Tourism Management Perspectives*, *20*, 109–111. doi:10.1016/j.tmp.2016.08.005

Rankopo, M.J., & Diraditsile, K. (2018). Perspectives on pro-poor policies in Botswana: Issues, challenges and prospects for Social Work. *Human needs in the 21st century: Perspectives from Botswana and Germany*.

Republic of Zambia. (2013). Zambia Review (14th ed.). Ministry of Commerce, Trade and Industry.

Rosenberg, J., Strauss, I., & Isaacs, G. (2021). COVID-19 impact on SADC labour markets: Evidence from high-frequency data and other sources. *African Development Review*, *33*(S1), S177–S193. doi:10.1111/1467-8268.12528 PMID:34149243

Said, J., & Singini, K. (2014). *The political economy determinants of economic growth in Malawi*. Academic Press.

Sarrasin, B. (2006). The mining industry and the regulatory framework in Madagascar: Some developmental and environmental issues. *Journal of Cleaner Production*, *14*(3-4), 388–396. doi:10.1016/j.jclepro.2004.03.004

Saurombe, A. (2010). The role of South Africa in SADC regional integration: The making or braking of the organization. *Journal of International Commercial Law and Technology*, *5*(3), 124–131.

Saurombe, A. (2011). *Regionalisation through economic integration in the Southern African Development Community SADC (SADC)* [Doctoral dissertation].

Schenoni, L. L. (2017). Subsystemic unipolarities? Power distribution and state behaviour in South America and Southern Africa. *Strategic Analysis*, *41*(1), 74–86. doi:10.1080/09700161.2016.1249179

Schutter, M. S., & Hicks, C. C. (2019). Networking the Blue Economy in Seychelles: Pioneers, resistance, and the power of influence. *Journal of Political Ecology*, *26*(1), 425–447.

Schwella, E. (Ed.). (2017). *South African Governance*. Oxford University Press.

Senaratne, M., Zimbroff, A., & Stevens, J. T. (2021). An instrument to assess Blue Economy entrepreneurship ecosystems: A case study from the Seychelles. *Journal of the Indian Ocean Region*, *17*(2), 205–223. doi:10.1080/19480881.2021.1969516

Shaaban, I. A., Ramzy, Y. H., & Sharabassy, A. A. (2013). Tourism as a tool for economic development in poor countries: The case of Comoro Islands. *African Journal of Business and Economic Research*, *8*(1), 127–145.

Siakwah, P., Musavengane, R., & Leonard, L. (2020). Tourism governance and attainment of the sustainable development goals in Africa. *Tourism Planning & Development*, *17*(4), 355–383. doi:10.1080/21568316.2019.1600160

Signe, L. (2019). *African Development, African Transformation: How Institutions Shape Development Strategy*. Cambridge university Press.

Simkins, C. (2021). *The Southern African Development Community II – Economy: Levels, Growth, Structure, Income Distribution And Happiness*. Helen Suzman Foundation.

Simo, R. Y. (2020). Trade in services in the African Continental Free Trade Area: Prospects, challenges and WTO compatibility. *Journal of International Economic Law*, *23*(1), 65–95. doi:10.1093/jiel/jgz031

Siphambe, H.K. (2004). Botswana's economy and labour market: are there any lessons for SADC regional integration? *Development Southern Africa, 21*(2), 353-364.

Söderbaum, F. (2004). *The political economy of regionalism: the case of Southern Africa*. Springer. doi:10.1057/9780230513716

Söderbaum, F. (2012). Theories of regionalism. Routledge handbook of Asian regionalism, 11-21.

Sonn, I. K., Plessis, M. D., Vuuren, C. D. J. V., Marais, J. E., Wagener, E., & Roman, N. V. (2021, December 7). *Achievements and Challenges for Higher Education during the COVID-19 Pandemic: A Rapid Review of Media in Africa*. Academic Press.

Sørensen, B. B., Estmann, C., Sarmento, E. F., & Rand, J. (2020). *Economic complexity and structural transformation: the case of Mozambique* (No. 2020/141). WIDER Working Paper.

Southall, R. (2010). Scramble for Africa? Continuities and Discontinuities with Formal Imperialism. In R. Southall & H. Melber (Eds.), *A New Scramble for Africa? Imperialism, Investment and Development. Scottsville*. University of KwaZulu-Natal Press.

Stapel, S., Panke, D., & Söderbaum, F. (2023). Regional international organizations in Africa as recipients of foreign aid: Why are some more attractive to donors than others? *Cooperation and Conflict*, *58*(4), 00108367221147791. doi:10.1177/00108367221147791

Stubbs, R. (2017). The Origins of East Asian's Developmental States and the Pressures for Change. In *Asia after the Developmental State: Disembedding Autonomy* (pp. 51-71). Cambridge: Cambridge University Press. Retrieved October 13, 2023, from https://hsf.org.za/publications/hsf-briefs/the-southern-african-development-community-ii-economy-levels-growth-structure-income-distribution-and-happiness

Tanyanyiwa, V. I., & Hakuna, C. (2014). Challenges and opportunities for regional integration in Africa: The case of SADC. *IOSR Journal of Humanities and Social Science*, *19*(12), 103–115. doi:10.9790/0837-19124103115

Therborn, G. (2019). South African inequalities in a global perspective. In C. Soudien, V. Reddy, & I. Woolard (Eds.), *Poverty & Inequality: Diagnosis, Prognosis Responses* (pp. 31–41). HSRC Press.

Tshishonga, N. (2022). The Impact of South Africa's Immigration Policies on Intra-African Trade and Development. In I. Tshabangu (Ed.), *Interdisciplinary Approaches to the Future of Africa and Policy Development* (pp. 119–136). IGI Publisher. doi:10.4018/978-1-7998-8771-3.ch007

Tshishonga, N. (2022). Afrophobic-Induced Violence on African Immigrants in South Africa. In Fighting for Empowerment in an Age of Violence (pp. 87-104). IGI Publisher. doi:10.4018/978-1-6684-4964-6.ch005

Tsoeu-Ntokoane, S., Kali, M., & Lemaire, X. (2022). Energy democracy in Lesotho: Prioritising the participation of rural citizens. *Cogent Social Sciences*, *8*(1), 2012973. doi:10.1080/23311886.2021.2012973

Vatuva, A., Filippelli, G., Gujar, A. R., Iyer, S. D., & Udayaganesan, P. (2022). Coastal and Nearshore Minerals: Blue Economy Potential and Prospects. In *Blue Economy: An Ocean Science Perspective* (pp. 221–249). Springer Nature Singapore. doi:10.1007/978-981-19-5065-0_8

World Bank Group. (2018a). *Democratic Republic of Congo Systematic Country Diagnostic: Policy Priorities for Poverty Reduction and Shared Prosperity in a Post-Conflict Country and Fragile State*. World Bank.

World Bank Group. (2018b). *An Incomplete Transition Overcoming the Legacy of Exclusion in South Africa*. UCT Press.

Wright, N. (2017). *One Race, The Human Race, Now! Crest-Gauteng*. Wright Publishing.

Yusheng, K., Atuahene Agyapong, S., Bentum-Micah, G., & Konadu Aboagye, A. (2019). Impact of foreign direct investment inflows on economic growth in small island developing states (Seychelles). *Scholars Bulletin*, *5*(5), 273–277.

Zafar, A. (2011). Mauritius: An economic success story. Yes Africa can: Success stories from a dynamic continent, 91-106.

Zahorik, J. (2018). Ethiopia and the colonial discourse. In Colonialism on the Margins of Africa. Routledge.

Zikiti, B. (2016). *How can Zimbabwe leverage its mineral resources for economic recovery and sustainable growth* [Doctoral dissertation].

Zondi, S. (2023). The Southern African Development Community's pursuit of regional integration. In D. Monye & S. Nkala (Eds.), The Quality for Unity: An Appraisal of Regional Integration in Africa (pp. 89-108). Sunnyside: Jacana Media Ltd.

KEY TERMS AND DEFINITIONS

Africa: Is one of the continents (Asia, Latin America, and Europe) with 54 countries under the auspices of the African Union.

African Continental free Trade Area (AfCFTA): Is an agreement created as a free trade area encompassing most of Africa and was established in 2018 at eliminating barriers to trade in Africa by the African Continental Free Trade Agreement, eliminating barriers to trade in Africa.

African Union: The African Union was formed in 2001 replacing the Organization of African Unity (OAU) as a continental apex organization with currently 54 countries. The African Union was established to advance democracy, human rights and sustainable economic development for the African continent.

Developmental State: A state that prioritises sustained economic development through industrial development with political, social and policy dimensions as we as the sound relationship between public and private sectors.

Economic Integration: The integration that takes place through the amalgamation of economies or economic policies of tow or more counties in a region.

Free Trade: Involves the movement of goods and services either through importation or exportation without any barriers or restrictions such as tariffs and quotas.

Regional Integration: An integration is the process by which two or more nation-states agree to co-operate and work closely together to achieve peace, stability and wealth.

Section 4

Some Factors Influencing Democratic Practice in African States

Chapter 15
Democracy and Governance:
The Role of the European Union in Africa

Arindam Goswami
https://orcid.org/0009-0002-5493-5744
Amity University, Noida, India

Mukesh Shankar Bharti
https://orcid.org/0000-0002-3693-7247
Amity University, Noida, India

Shreesh Kumar Pathak
https://orcid.org/0000-0002-1332-013X
Amity University, Noida, India

ABSTRACT

The purpose of this study is to discuss the role of the European Union (EU) in Africa in the establishment of democracy. Many African countries need the help of Western democracy to pave the way for the democratization process on this continent. The aim of this study is to discover the leading role of the EU in Africa in providing assistance to build strong democratic institutions. Further, the EU as a democratic institution has played an important role in uniting the European countries under its democratic legacy and motivating them to adopt and implement the "Copenhagen Criteria" which are basic principles of the democratization process of the member states in Europe in this sense how the EU has been working on the implementation of the democratic ethos in African countries. On the other hand, the internal situation of African countries differs from that of EU Member States because many countries gained independence in the late 1990s and dozens of countries are in civil war crises in many regions.

DOI: 10.4018/979-8-3693-0477-8.ch015

INTRODUCTION

Promoting democracy and good governance on the African continent is a massive undertaking with far-reaching ramifications for regional stability, inclusiveness, and equitable development. The European Union (EU) appears as a significant player in the middle of the complicated tapestry of difficulties and possibilities that shape this endeavour, leveraging its influence to guide African states through the transformational path towards democratic government (Mathlouthi, 2019). This introduction serves as a springboard for a more in-depth examination of the multiple features that characterise the EU's key role in promoting democratisation in Africa. The story of Africa's transition to democratic government is one of perseverance, tenacity, and complexity. Following a history of colonisation, authoritarian governments, civil wars, and economic adversity, the desire for democratic governance has emerged as a beacon of hope for many African countries. Following independence, there was a strong desire to build government systems that prioritise public engagement, respect the rule of law, and protect human rights. However, the path to democracy has been hampered by complex problems including frail governmental institutions, deep-seated ethnic hostilities, and stark socioeconomic inequality. The persistence of bothersome issues such as corruption, political exclusion, and governance flaws continues to be a barrier to the realisation of stable democratic societies.

The importance of external support emerges as a critical aspect in fostering democratic values and institutions in the middle of this complicated setting. The European Union, a staunch supporter of democratic values, human rights, and the rule of law, has emerged as a key player in promoting democratic government (Khan et al., 2022). The European Union (EU) evolved from post-World War II attempts to avert additional conflicts and develop collaboration among European governments to become a platform for regional integration and peaceful cooperation. This evolution has given the EU a particular vantage point, effortlessly combining its constant commitment to democratic principles with the practical experiences gained through managing a varied range of member states. As the EU's commitment expanded beyond Europe's borders, Africa emerged as a critical focus of concern. The EU's democratic history, carefully established through collaborative efforts, resonates strongly with African states as they work hard to build viable democracies that meet their specific requirements. The EU portrays itself as an inspirational and realistic model for democratic institution-building by drawing careful parallels between the EU's past democratic evolution and the complicated issues encountered by African countries (Raimundo, 2020).

The primary goal of this lengthy piece is to explore the EU's multifaceted role in catalysing democracy and good governance in Africa (Khan et al., 2022). This investigation will cover a wide range of characteristics, reflecting the EU's multidimensional engagement, from intellectual assistance and extensive aid efforts to the subtle creation of institutions that promote the democratic ethos. Furthermore, the EU's praiseworthy involvement in mediation and conflict resolution will be scrutinised as vital components of its democratisation efforts in Africa. The article's heart will be supplemented with a qualitative comparative study aiming at uncovering the concrete impact of these sincere efforts on Africa's colossal job of institutional development. Furthermore, the study will go into theoretical frameworks that persuasively contextualise Africa's convoluted democratisation process. Visionaries such as Julius Nyerere, whose democratic theory is rooted in African communalism, and Samuel P. Huntington, whose seminal "third wave of democratisation" theory has provided profound insights into global democratisation trends, will be called upon to provide invaluable lenses through which to decipher Africa's intricate democratic trajectory. To acquire a better understanding, the essay will look at the Arab Spring, a series of anti-authoritarian rallies that resonated across North Africa and beyond, highlighting the delicate relationship between democratisation, political turmoil, and regional stability.

Nonetheless, the EU's involvement in Africa's democratisation is far from a straight line free of complexity and criticism. The paper will address these numerous difficulties, including fears of cultural imposition and the unintentional reappearance of neocolonial tendencies. In dealing with these complications, the paper aims to provide a complete appraisal that highlights not only the accomplishments but also the areas that require a more nuanced approach to the EU's participation. The African road towards democratic government is a story that intertwines progress and problems in a complex symphony. The EU appears as a vital agent for directing Africa towards the shores of democracy and good governance, bolstered by its democratic legacy and a reservoir of experiential wisdom gathered through time. The varied endeavours of the EU, its indelible imprint on the democratic fabric of African states, and the potential of joint efforts for realising democratic principles and shared wealth are vividly revealed via the complete lens of this study.

BACKGROUND

Democracy, the rule of law, and good governance are the core concepts of the modern state (Dandashly, 2017). These pillars provide the foundation for the state and its institutions, as well as the interaction and norms for people and governmental entities. Although these concepts have considerable overlap, unique characteristics may be identified. The notion of the legal basis for governmental action (Keukeleire & Delreux, 2014), as well as the duty to protect people's fundamental rights, are the foundations of the rule of law (Velluti, 2020). Democracy strengthens the rule of law and is particularly concerned with transparency and citizen involvement. The growth of democracy and the rule of law are only two facets of good governance; it also considers the executive branch's efficacy and accountability (Khan et al., 2022). These elements are sometimes classed as components of the social "rechtsstaat," however this undervalues the conceptual legal aspect. Good governance is critical since it is both a requirement of the government and a fundamental right. This contributes to the third pillar of good governance. (Addick, 2019).

The African theory of democracy can be considered to be prompted largely by the articulated works of Nyere which shaped the modern statecraft in Tanzania under his tenure (Masabo, 2023). In the middle of the twentieth century, statecraft was frequently considered a treasured bequest from previous colonial masters and employed in the service of democratic principles in Africa. As a result, Africans were generally seen as simple objects of public morality. Nyerere objected to this viewpoint by releasing a philosophy of democracy that incorporated specific indigenous African elements that may govern the Tanzanian statecraft (Nyerere, 1963). Nyerere stressed the need for democracy in administering government affairs while being distinctly African. In this, Nyerere propounded democracy in two folds to be exercised in Africa. The first is a direct democracy drawn from the roots of indigenous African communities to discuss important matters. The second is a modification of direct democracy in a larger community for which the idea of representative democracy was taken into consideration which was Western (Masabo, 2023). However, Nyerere's democratic theory was criticised due to the fact that he clearly suggested integrating the two systems in an intercultural liquid democracy framework that, in theory, would be represented by a single party.

After the Cold War ended, a wave of democratisation swept over Africa in the early 1990s (EPRS, 2017). The fall of single-party communist regimes in Eastern Europe and the former Soviet Union, which in turn severely discredited the existence of single-party (especially Marxist) political systems throughout Africa, were some of the trends that brought together several internal and external trends that were affecting the African continent (Schraeder, 1995). Multi-party democracy was incredibly uncommon on the continent before 1989, with very few exceptions, most African nations adopted multi-party elections in the 1990s. The emergence of significant democracies has not necessarily followed this significant political transition. In many locations, elections continue to be of low quality, which hinders the development of true political plurality. A dominating party's dominance has been entrenched in several nations. During the democratisation process, Africanists have felt both optimism and grief. Several early wins, most notably the hosting of a "national conference" in Benin in 1990, which culminated in the peaceful change of power from President Kerekou's Marxist dictatorship to a multiparty democracy, fuelled hope. The fact that beginning in 1992, Africa's democratisation process stalled and, in extreme cases like Rwanda and Somalia, devolved into violent ethnic war and state disintegration has added to a general sense of pessimism (Schraeder, 1995). Whether optimistic or pessimistic, only a few Africanists might disagree with the normative assumption of a democratisation process that replaces economically weak, authoritarian, one-party countries with more economically robust, democratic ones.

The wave of democratisation that swept over the African continent in the early 1990s had mixed results and did not result in long-term democratic progress in many countries (EPRS, 2017). Even though many African countries have experienced peaceful power transfers and democratic transitions, several of these countries conducted free elections, with some showing signs of democratisation. Authoritarian governments have strengthened their grip on power in recent years by manipulating elections, enacting constitutional modifications, and repressing the civil rights movement and opposition society. Most importantly, the African masses continue to adore democracy. Furthermore, the majority of Africans state that they want greater democracy than they already have, according to Afrobarometer surveys (EPRS, 2017). The thrive of democracy in Africa allowed the external actors who understand the need to promote democracy and good governance in the region (Isaac, 2013). Since the Cold War's conclusion, new issues have joined the development debate. With the move from a bipolar to a multipolar international system, a variety of new topics and processes were introduced into international development aid (Olsen, 1998). International aid donors began to speak out more actively on concerns like democracy and human rights after 1989. In a speech made in June 1990, British Foreign Minister Douglas Hurd argued that in emerging nations, economic growth and so-called "good governance" go hand in hand. To paraphrase Hurd, political plurality, an effective and honest administration, adhering to the law, and the development of more free and open economies are all essential to economic success (ODI, 1992).

During an event with African heads of state that same month, French President Francois Mitterrand stated that France would be less accommodating in the future when providing help to "regimes that have an authoritarian approach without accepting an evolution towards democracy." These statements sparked demands in Europe and other OECD countries for political reforms in developing countries towards Western-style democracy, and as a result, Europe and the EC/EU came to endorse the global trend of replacing "development" with "democracy" as one of the slogans of its development assistance in the course of the 1990s (Olsen, 1998). Cold War's conclusion led to the promotion of democracy and has become a "boom industry." At the same time, identifying the essential goals and features of the policy sector is difficult. Support for democratisation is provided within the auspices of human rights, the rule of law, good governance, and post-conflict peace-building efforts. It is supported by governments, multilateral organisations, (international) NGOs, political parties, and party-affiliated foundations (Cranenburgh, 2010).

Methodological Approach

This study is based on the qualitative approach of the discussion in the context of the establishment of democracy in African countries. This study employs a multimodal technique to extensively explore the effect of the European Union (EU) on strengthening democracy and decent governance in African states. The methodology consists of theoretical frameworks, inductive reasoning, empirical content analysis, and qualitative comparison analysis. By integrating several techniques, the study seeks to provide a holistic picture of the EU's contribution to advancing democratic institutions and practices throughout Africa. The qualitative comparative analysis (QCA) method is used in this study to elucidate the diverse ways and impacts of the EU's participation in Africa. QCA, which provides a methodical way of discovering the myriad factors determining how EU projects come out, may be used to investigate several variables. Through a survey of EU initiatives, aid programmes, and cooperation frameworks, this study explores patterns of success and barriers in the creation of democracy and good governance in African governments. Using an inductive technique, this study examines the bigger concepts of democracy and democratisation in Africa. The study seeks to discover general trends and concepts relating to democratic transitions in Africa by collecting data from a range of sources, including official papers, reports, and scholarly articles. This technique makes it easy to comprehend the numerous opportunities and challenges those African nations confront as they embark on the path to democracy. The empirical method comprises a detailed evaluation of data relevant to EU aid for African nations' institutional improvement. A large number of documents, including project reports, policy statements, and partnership agreements, will be thoroughly reviewed for content. The EU will employ a range of methodologies, policy aims, and critical subjects that will be thoroughly defined via this process to support democracy and good governance in Africa. By studying these documents, the research aims to assess the practical impacts of the EU's efforts on a local level.

Contextualising African Democracies

The journey of African states towards democratic government is a complex one intertwined with historical legacies left by centuries of colonialism and following ardent wars for liberation. The colonial experience imposed alien customs, languages, and governance systems on indigenous peoples, causing seismic upheavals in existing sociopolitical institutions and sparking deep ethnic rivalries. Colonial aftershocks reverberated over decades, leaving an indelible impression of economic exploitation, cultural displacement, and institutional instability (Keukeleire & Delreux, 2014). With the dawn of independence came not only the promise of emancipation but also the daunting task of establishing political systems that resonated with the complex fabric of cultural and socioeconomic subtleties unique to each African nation.

Across Africa, postcolonial transition narratives took an astonishing variety of paths. These varied from relatively smooth power transitions defined by negotiated settlements to prolonged, often murderous battles against entrenched authoritarian governments. A unifying aspiration for democratic government emerges as a recurring motif across this variety. This longing exemplified a strong desire for self-determination, participatory government, and the supremacy of the rule of law. However, the route to democratic administration is rarely a straight line, disrupted by multiple hurdles (Keukeleire &

Delreux, 2014). The emerging governments had the massive job of grafting democratic principles onto young institutions, managing complex ethnic cleavages, and reconciling diverse socioeconomic goals.

Africa's political landscapes are vividly defined by a rich diversity that reflects a patchwork of cultures, languages, and ethnicities covering the continent's wide width. This rich mosaic bears witness to Africa's multifaceted heritage and complicated history. However, it also poses significant problems to the development of inclusive and coherent democratic systems. Political elites' manipulation of ethnic affinities, along with the purposeful exploitation of identity politics, has periodically heightened tensions and jeopardised the possibilities for democratic consolidation. These divides have frequently been used to serve the goals of power-seeking institutions, undermining the peaceful cohabitation and participatory ethos that are the core of successful democracies (Bharti, 2022).

The effectiveness of the state apparatus is critical in the effort to establish a democratic government. The legacy of colonisation frequently left African republics with weak institutions that were ill-equipped to provide critical services and respect the rule of law. In certain circumstances, the fragility of these institutions has given fertile ground for the growth of authoritarian inclinations or governing systems that are incapable of efficiently responding to citizens' demands. As a result, the challenge of developing effective, responsible, and transparent state institutions emerges as a critical component of attaining democratic government (Keukeleire & Delreux, 2014).

The socioeconomic situation has a significant impact on the trajectory of democratisation on the African continent. Economic gaps, which are usually the result of historical injustices and exploitative colonial practices, pose enormous obstacles to the equitable allocation of resources and opportunity (Keukeleire & Delreux, 2014). Poverty, unemployment, and inequality may all contribute to political instability, providing ideal ground for populist and demagogic discourse. These socioeconomic trends intensify the challenges of sustaining long-term democratic institutions. On the other hand, inclusive and sustained economic growth serves as a foundation for political stability. Such expansion provides individuals with a real interest in the democratic process, reducing the attractiveness of alternative divisive ideologies.

The Arab Spring marked a watershed point in Africa's road towards democracy. This wave of demonstrations and revolutions that swept over North Africa and the Middle East in 2010-2011 had a profound impact on the region. The Arab Spring inspired ambitions for democratic administration that transcended geographical lines, fueled by profound disgust with authoritarian leadership, a strong yearning for economic fairness, and an unyielding demand for political reform. Tunisia, where Mohamed Bouazizi's self-immolation sparked the flames of revolution, emerged as a forerunner of change. The fall of entrenched dictatorships and the growth of popular movements highlighted a genuine desire for a democratic government that resonated well beyond Tunisia's borders.

However, the Arab Spring's aftermath highlighted the complex realities that support democratic transformations. While Tunisia navigated a relatively smooth route towards democratic consolidation, other countries faced turbulent paths, devolving into warfare, turbulence, and, in some cases, the reemergence of authoritarian leadership. The Arab Spring revealed the complicated interaction of democratisation, mass mobilisation, and the difficult task of establishing long-term democratic institutions (Keukeleire & Delreux, 2014). It sheds light on the multifaceted, context-specific character of democratisation processes, providing both enlightening lessons and cautionary stories for Africa's ongoing struggle for democratic government.

Among the intricate features of democratisation, the European Union (EU) emerges as a powerful external actor, providing critical assistance to African states' democratisation efforts. The EU is a trustworthy partner for African nations as they map their democratic paths, drawing on its own experience in state-building, regional integration, and the consolidation of democratic standards among its different member states. The EU seeks to stimulate democratic progress while understanding the multifaceted problems that drive the continent's democratisation journey through the interchange of intellectual dialogue, strategic developmental initiatives, and the building of institutional institutions. Africa's march towards democratic government weaves across the continent's complicated historical echoes, socioeconomic complexities, and diverse political landscapes. The interaction of ethnic identities, state capability, and economic paradigms shapes the democratisation trajectory. The historic Arab Spring serves as both an uplifting beacon and a sobering guidepost. Among these many facets, the European Union remains a consistent partner, navigating the maze of hurdles to promote democratic development within Africa's dynamic narrative. The pursuit of democratic values continues to develop via collaboration and concerted efforts, motivated by a collective aspiration for inclusive government and shared prosperity.

EU's Promotion of Democracy Post-Cold War

In the aftermath of the Cold War, the relationship between the European Union (EU) and Africa witnessed a dynamic evolution in the prominence and priority accorded to democracy and human rights within their cooperative endeavours. The initial period, spanning the 1950s to the 1960s, marked the establishment of the European Community and the concurrent attainment of independence by numerous African countries (Bharti, 2023; Gozzi, 2018). This phase saw the signing of agreements such as the Yaoundé I (1963–1969) and Yaoundé II (1969–1975), which prioritized economic relationships. In this context, development aid was perceived as a form of redress for colonial injustices, embodying a non-conditionality approach. The focus was primarily on fostering trade agreements, economic development, and mutual prosperity, particularly in regions with historical ties to European Community member states.

The subsequent era, spanning the 1970s to 1991, witnessed the European Community's institutional maturation, accompanied by a more explicit emphasis on democracy and human rights in EU development policies (Mathlouthi, 2019). This evolution was exemplified by the Lomé agreements, specifically Lomé III, which marked a normative shift in recognizing human rights as a defining aspect of European identity. However, as subsequent agreements emerged, these issues appeared to lose some of their salience in the discourse, although they were still nominally acknowledged. The third period, commencing in 1991, saw the reconfiguration of EU development policies, driven by factors including the deepening integration of the EU, the conclusion of the Cold War, and a desire to extend development cooperation beyond traditional partners (Sanches, 2020). This shift was underscored by key documents like the EU Council of Ministers Resolution in 1991 and the Maastricht Treaty of 1993, both of which entrenched the promotion of human rights and democracy as integral objectives in the EU's activities. Additionally, the EU's Common Foreign and Security Policy expressed its dedication to democratic governance, human rights, and the rule of law (Özçelik, 2018).

A pivotal turning point in linking development aid to human rights and democracy was the mid-term review of Lomé IV bis (Crawford, 1998; Hurt, 2003). This heralded the emergence of economic and political conditionality within the EU's development policy. Economic conditionality, involving policy adjustments for aid reception, had already been in play since the late 1980s through the International Monetary Fund and World Bank programs (Zimelis, 2011). Political conditionality, exemplified by the allocation of financial resources to encourage democratic governance and human rights, gained prominence as an effective tool for advancing these principles. Political conditionality progressed through two distinct generations since the end of the Cold War (Keukeleire & Delreux, 2014). The initial generation, during the 1990s, was characterized by a reactive and punitive approach, wherein donor countries used sanctions as threats to suspend or reduce aid in response to human rights violations and democratic regression. This approach exhibited mixed outcomes, with limited effectiveness and inconsistent application (Sanches, 2020).

In the new millennium, a second generation of political conditionality emerged, guided by an emphasis on governance issues. This phase sought a more selective allocation of aid, contingent on meeting political prerequisites. The European Commission introduced initiatives such as the Governance Incentive Tranche and Good Governance Contracts, reinforcing the importance of political reform in aid allocation. Additionally, the Cotonou Agreement (2000–2020) exemplified this approach, requiring adherence to democracy, good governance, and human rights for access to EU financial aid. This agreement marked an innovation over previous agreements by incorporating an enforcement mechanism that employed both positive and negative measures in response to human rights violations.

The launch of the Joint Africa-EU Strategy (JAES) in 2007, accompanied by partnerships like the one on Democratic Governance and Human Rights, underscored the shared belief in the vital role of democratic governance and human rights in achieving sustainable development. The JAES represented a comprehensive framework encompassing diverse levels and spheres of cooperation, including political dialogue, cultural exchanges, and economic collaboration. In terms of financial instruments, the European Development Fund (EDF) assumed a central role, supplemented by instruments like the European Neighbourhood Instrument, the Development Cooperation Instrument, and the European Instrument for Democracy and Human Rights (Sanches, 2020). Notably, from 2007 to 2016, a significant portion of EU development aid was allocated to supporting democratic principles, civil society engagement, women's equality, and other related areas. Additionally, the EU played an active role in electoral observation and support, overseeing a substantial number of elections across African and non-African countries (Sanches, 2020).

In sum, the evolution of EU-Africa relations in the post-Cold War era reflects a dynamic interplay between democracy, human rights, and development. This trajectory spans multiple periods, each marked by distinct shifts in priority and emphasis, ultimately leading to a more comprehensive and pragmatic approach to linking aid with democratic governance and human rights principles (Olsen, 1998). Democracy and human rights aren't solely shaped by internal factors; international aspects like aid distribution also play a crucial role (Sanches, 2020). Aid can act as a catalyst for enhancing democratic processes, values, and outcomes, including the protection of fundamental human rights. As discussed earlier, a significant portion of aid is directed toward development objectives, and the application of conditionality, particularly sanctions, often aligns with the donors' security or economic concerns. This dynamic might lead to instances where aid inadvertently obstructs democratization by supporting economic growth within authoritarian governments. The empirical analysis conducted in this context underscores the significance of aid and, more importantly, underscores the vital influence of domestic political institutions on the trajectory of democracy.

EU Tools to Support Democracy in Africa

To improve democracy on the African continent, the EU has implemented several initiatives in conjunction with its African partners (Cottey, 2012). Apart from having a democracy clause in bilateral agreements such as the Cotonou agreement, there are others to be discussed which facilitate the mechanism of the EU to support democracy in Africa.

Aligned with its goal of fostering collaboration and equality with African nations, the European Union (EU) prioritizes an approach centred on dialogue. This approach is also a fundamental aspect of the Cotonou Agreement, which includes specific clauses mandating regular political discussions between parties, encompassing topics such as democracy and human rights. Within Article 8 of this agreement, titled 'Political dialogue,' one of the primary aims of these exchanges is to proactively prevent scenarios that would necessitate invoking the essential elements clause. These dialogues are designed to cultivate a stable and democratic political atmosphere, encompassing consistent evaluations of progress concerning the upholding of human rights, democratic values, the rule of law, and effective governance. In practice, the EU engages with matters of democracy and human rights through its political and human rights dialogues with African nations, as well as with the continental entity, the African Union. Collaboratively with the African Union, the EU has conducted a total of 12 human rights dialogues, with the most recent occurring in January 2017 in Brussels (EPRS, 2017). Moreover, the EU conducts political dialogues with regional economic communities, such as ECOWAS in April 2017, and addresses issues connected to democratization within these interactions. Dialogues inclusive of civil society additionally hold significant potential in advancing democratization efforts. For instance, in Tunisia, a trilateral dialogue initiated in April 2016 between EU institutions, Tunisian civil society, and Tunisian authorities has been instrumental in reinforcing the democratic transition.

Utilizing development assistance proves to be a potent strategy for enhancing democracy. This aid can fortify the capabilities of governmental institutions, including the judiciary, foster civic education, bolster civil society, and support electoral procedures. The European Development Fund is a substantial financial tool directed primarily towards Sub-Saharan African nations and African regional bodies. Although distinct from the EU budget, it draws funding from contributions made by EU Member States, amassing over €30 billion within the 2014-2020 timeframe (EPRS, 2017). It champions democracy and effective governance through direct funding for initiatives aligned with these goals or indirectly, by leveraging the financial support's conditionality tied to democratic principles, notably in budget support. The African Union (AU) is a particular focus, with targeted programs fostering collaboration in democracy, good governance, and human rights. This collaboration intensified with a collaborative plan between the AU Commission and the EU, aiming to amplify backing for the Political Department's initiatives. The 2017 evaluation of the 11th European Development Fund reveals the integration of core values like human rights, democracy, and justice within programming, showcasing a robust role in their advancement. Successful outcomes, however, hinge on active involvement from African governments in driving political reforms (EPRS, 2017).

EU budget support is underscored by strong democratic prerequisites. This facet is critical in various Sub-Saharan African nations, granting them the authority to set priorities and oversee fund allocation without financial constraints. The region receives the largest share of EU budget support (47%). The criteria are underpinned by rigorous principles. Guidelines from 2017 emphasize the significance of upholding democratic and human rights standards, aligned with commitments outlined in relevant agreements (the democracy clause). Fragile states are approached with a longer-term perspective, leading to more lenient expectations concerning democratic standards. Furthermore, the European Instrument for Democracy and Human Rights (EIDHR) is a specialized tool, channelling funds towards civil society organizations and occasionally individual human rights defenders. Management occurs through calls for proposals overseen by the Commission or EU delegations, with direct grants in exceptionally challenging contexts (EPRS, 2017). While the EIDHR covers a range of activities pertinent to democracy, its ongoing Multiannual Action Programme specifically allocates resources to democracy, with a focus on enhancing the capabilities of political parties and parliaments.

The EU's Neighbourhood Policy (ENP) encompasses North African nations, as well as countries in Eastern Europe and the Middle East. The series of political protests that emerged in North Africa in 2010 led to an adaptation of the ENP to address new challenges (Keukeleire & Delreux, 2014). In 2011, a communication titled 'A New Response to a Changing Neighbourhood. A review of the European Neighbourhood Policy' proposed a partnership focusing on democracy and shared prosperity with Southern Mediterranean states. This new approach emphasized the concept of 'deep democracy,' which encompasses aspects like fair elections, freedom of expression and association, independent judiciary, anti-corruption measures, and democratic control over security forces (Bouris & Schumacher, 2017; Özçelik, 2018). A pivotal change introduced by the ENP review was the 'more for more' principle, where EU assistance prioritizes countries implementing effective reforms related to democratization and the rule of law. For instance, Tunisia, regarded as having made significant democratic progress (Khan et al., 2022), witnessed a substantial increase in EU financial support since 2011, making it the main beneficiary in the Southern Neighbourhood under the 'umbrella' program. EU contributions, including grants, macro-financial aid, and loans from the European Investment Bank, amounted to approximately €3.5 billion from 2011 to 2016.

The central challenge of the ENP lies in bringing about substantial political and economic transformations in the EU's neighbouring regions through equitable partnerships. However, it lacks the powerful leverage provided by enlargement prospects, which was present for states joining the EU in 2004-2007. The concern is that a focus on economic and security collaboration could overshadow the EU's commitment to promoting democracy and the rule of law (Teti, Thompson, & Noble, 2013). This dynamic was evident in pre-2011 relations with North African nations, where support was extended to autocratic regimes based on economic and security interests. The EU's democracy and human rights support policy might also be undermined by individual European states pursuing short-term economic and security goals with North African countries. The Arab Spring upheaval has led to caution around democratization due to potential conflict and instability. In this context, the EU needs to safeguard its values despite short-term considerations, as democratic societies are more stable and conducive to long-term economic growth. The issue of irregular migration further impacts the EU's influence in its relations with North African countries, especially Libya, where cooperation with local authorities is crucial to managing migration flows.

A more specialized tool for supporting democracy in the neighbourhood is the European Endowment for Democracy (EED), which funds initiatives in all North African countries. EED, a collaborative endeavour of EU Member States and institutions, is an independent entity that offers grants to actors driving democratic change, especially those not covered by other EU mechanisms. Notably, EED operates with high flexibility, allowing it to function effectively even in restrictive environments. Before 1989, only Botswana and Mauritius engaged in regular multi-party elections in Sub-Saharan Africa. Since 1990, nearly every African nation has embraced routine elections, with the EU actively supporting much of this democratic advancement. The EU has dispatched numerous Electoral Observation Missions (EOMs) to Africa, constituting 85 out of 185 EOMs between 1993 and 2017. These missions encountered varying election quality and democratic practices. To address subpar standards and ineffective electoral bodies, the EU adopted a comprehensive approach involving the entire electoral cycle. Concluding reports from EU EOMs provide suggestions to improve upcoming elections. Electoral Follow-Up Missions are deployed to evaluate progress on these recommendations, incorporating insights from diverse stakeholders. The decision to conduct subsequent EOMs in a country is influenced by its willingness to implement prior recommendations (EPRS, 2017).

Furthermore, the EU extends electoral support to strengthen electoral body capabilities, empower civil society in electoral processes, and enhance citizen education on election matters. In specific cases, like post-conflict scenarios, the EU has financially contributed to election administration. For example, in the 2011 general elections in the Democratic Republic of the Congo (DRC), the EU provided €47.5 million, with an additional €2 million for security enhancement. The EU has also significantly aided the African Union's electoral observation capabilities through the Pan-African Programme, offering €6.5 million in funding. EU EOMs are esteemed for their impartiality, enhancing election credibility, promoting peaceful electoral competition, and encouraging legal means for contesting outcomes. An evaluation report for the European Commission (covering EOMs from 2016 to January 2017) indicated that EU election observation efforts aid in detecting irregularities and fraud, deterring misconduct, boosting stakeholder confidence, and diminishing potential election-related conflicts. EOM findings also contribute to motivating electoral reform.

However, certain criticisms have emerged regarding the modus operandi and assessment of EOMs. Although they consistently highlight deficiencies and provide recommendations, these reports are sometimes deemed to lack a critical tone, as mentioned in the aforementioned report. Nevertheless, in cases of substantial shortcomings, as exemplified by Gabon in 2016, EU EOMs do articulate notable concerns. Many EOMs are situated in fragile or post-conflict states, where elections frequently signify a potential dawn of peaceful coexistence. Given the instability and inefficacy of institutions in such contexts, electoral imperfections are commonplace. Nevertheless, some experts perceive the overly acquiescent stance of EU EOMs toward substandard norms in these instances as possibly counterproductive for long-term democratization efforts (EPRS, 2017).

Jasmine Revolution, Arab Spring and Changes in EU's Approach

Since the Arab upheavals swept the Middle East and North Africa (MENA) in 2011, there has been considerable emphasis on the European Union's (EU) activities in the region, as well as its aims, ambitions, and reasons (Dandashly, 2017). With long-standing authoritarian administrations in Tunisia and Egypt tumbling apart in a matter of weeks, the wave of unrest that has swept over North Africa since 2010 has also jeopardised Europe's relationship with its southern neighbour. After some reluctance, the political discussion in Brussels and the EU member states was overwhelmingly in support of promoting the democratisation processes that followed the so-called Arab Spring. (Kruger & Ratka, 2014).

Although the Arab Spring has demonstrated how the European Union's efforts to foster democracy in the Mediterranean area need more effectiveness to produce political change in the Middle East and North Africa, the partnership on strengthening democracy among Arab despotic regimes, on the other hand, differs, enabling the EU varied degrees of influence over domestic institutional change related to political engagement, human rights respect, and the rule of law. According to a study of domestic partnership and transformation in Morocco and Tunisia from 2000 to 2010, the EU played a significant impact in assisting and maybe enhancing indigenous reform goals. The EU, on the other hand, is unable to initiate internal institutional reform. The extent of political liberalisation determines how well the national political agenda aligns with international reform demands. It symbolises many methods between political inclusion and exclusion and is thus a required condition for cooperation and change rather than the result of collaboration and transformation. (Hüllen, 2011). In this section, the responses made by the EU in the wake and aftermath of the Arab Spring, particularly in Tunisia, known as the Jasmine Revolution are discussed with the scope of cooperation and policy implications, the extent of engagement between North African nations, especially Tunisia, and the EU on domestic political reforms. Following that, it provides findings that may be explained by differing degrees of political liberalisation, resulting in the alignment of domestic politics with international demands. Furthermore, it provides implications on the EU tools for promoting democracy in the aftermath of the Arab Spring in the affected areas of Africa.

In reaction to the Arab uprisings, EU leaders such as Herman Van Rompuy, Jose Manuel Barroso, and Catherine Ashton visited Southern Mediterranean countries to underscore the EU's commitment to democratic and political transformation (European Commission, 2013). As a result of the new reality, the EU was compelled to tackle the new challenges of rapid and potentially hazardous change, prompting a rethinking of EU strategy in the region (Dandashly, 2015; Noutcheva, 2015). According to the European Commission, the uprisings highlighted early on the ineffectiveness of the EU's attempts to foster democracy, as well as the necessity for "greater flexibility and more tailored responses in dealing with rapidly evolving partners and reform needs" (European Commission, 2011). The 'more-for-more' concept, which links incentives to democratic improvements, is emphasised in the first EU joint message in response to the Arab uprisings (Dandashly, 2017). The EU highlighted this by announcing that it is willing to help the countries of the Southern Mediterranean achieve democracy through a Partnership for Democracy and Shared Prosperity (PfDSP). Given its comprehensive understanding of the aspirations of Southern Mediterranean peoples, the EU will respect the sovereignty and right to self-determination of its partner states (European Commission, 2011). Except for an emphasis on the EU's and its neighbours' stability, the ENP assessments did not materially alter cognitive frameworks for supporting democracy. In May 2011, the new ENP programme, which prioritises democracy, stability, and prosperity, was approved. The Commission stressed the importance of security and stability in its 2014 review of the ENP, as well as giving "vulnerable groups" additional focus in the area of strengthening democracy. The 2015 review emphasised the significance of the security-stability nexus by stating that the new ENP will prioritise stability throughout its mandate because the EU's own stability is founded on democracy, human rights, the rule of law, and economic openness. Since the framing remained vague, little has changed in terms of actual initiatives to strengthen democracy. The study recognised that the political will of the nation in question was critical to achieving positive conditionality. Another notable component of the 2015 review was the emphasis on civil society support, which faced problems in several of the target countries (Dandashly, 2017).

The EU Global Strategy (EUGS) lauded the EU's recently acquired pragmatism as well. To paraphrase, the EUGS asserted that responsible involvement will drive external activities with principled pragmatism in the coming years (EU Global Strategy, 2016). With the assistance of the EUGS, the EU "stops overestimating the transformative power of the EU" and establishes more realistic goals. The EU's new strategy for the MENA region calls for practical collaboration through functional multilateral efforts in areas like the economy, environment, crisis resolution, and peace treaties. Building upon previous agreements like the Union for the Mediterranean, the EU aims to enhance cooperation on security, infrastructure, and disaster management to address issues like terrorism, migration, and climate change impacts. While emphasizing security and hard power, the strategy shifts away from putting as much focus on democratization, aiming to foster it in more suitable nations like Georgia and Tunisia. The goal is to increase resilience, fight poverty, and encourage positive change over time (Dandashly, 2017). Finally, the three fundamental objectives defined in the agreements signed since the 1995 Barcelona Process, or the Euro-Mediterranean Partnership (EMP), remain the focus of EU cooperation with the expanding Southern Mediterranean. The EU's engagement highlights "human security" and is driven by EU regional security concerns, which are consistent with the EUGS, which states that the EU would work with its neighbours to enhance their resilience (EU Global Strategy, 2016). Initially rooted in the Western liberal democracy model, the EU's approach to democracy in the Southern Mediterranean now shows signs of adapting to partner needs post-uprisings (Dandashly, 2017). While security remains a concern, a change is evident with a shift toward a more flexible and inclusive democracy support approach that embraces diversity and complexity (Kurki, 2012).

Prior to the Arab upheavals, the EU's economic and security connections with Tunisia were stronger than those with any other country in the region, despite violations of democratic norms and increased restrictions on freedoms. Following Ben Ali's demise, the EU's view of Tunisia has shifted dramatically. In addition to justice and home affairs, which are prioritised due to their relevance for security and stability, there has been an increase in financing for "human security." The government started to modernise the court to meet popular expectations and the demands of the new era. Since Tunisia's independence in the mid-1950s, the court has not been free and has been plagued by corruption with the previous government stymied EU initiatives to help judicial reform (Dandashly, 2017). From 2011 to 2013, more than half of the EU's support for Tunisia (€278 million) was intended for the country's democratic transition and economic stabilisation. It allocated €167 million to programmes supporting Tunisians, notably those in underprivileged areas. Furthermore, the EU allocated €25 million to justice reform in 2011 and €15 million in 2014. Tunisia was the first country to receive money via the Support for Partnership, Reform, and Inclusive Growth (SPRING) programme, which was launched in 2011 and given a total of €155 million (European Commission, 2016). Along with sending an electoral Assessment Team to Libya, the EU increased its electoral aid by deploying election observation teams to Tunisia, Jordan, and Algeria. The EU gave technical assistance to local governments in Tunisia, Libya, Egypt, and Morocco to help them hold legislative and presidential elections. Tunisia received €3 million from the European Election Observation Mission to observe its elections. Furthermore, the EU "supported CSOs in educating the public and preparing domestic election observers." Aside from elections, the EU generously supports the growth of democratic institutions.

EU's priorities for Tunisia from 2011 to 2016 were threefold: supporting inclusive growth via socioeconomic reforms, strengthening democratic underpinnings, and promoting sustainable regional and local development (Dandashly, 2017). The European Neighbourhood Instrument (ENI) provided funds for certain goals. From 2014 to 2020, the expected indicative allocation for these sectors was around €115 million per year. Tunisia, in particular, earned €234 million for 2014-2015. The 'more for more' approach resulted in €50 million in additional financing in 2014 and €71.8 million in 2015, contingent on satisfactory outcomes (European Commission, 2016). In addition, the EU Council decided to enhance financial aid to €300 million in 2017 and future years until 2020, subject to Tunisia's commitment to change (Council of the European Union, 2016). In reaction to the post-revolutionary scenario, the EU increased its financing for cultural sectors and public administration reform by €25 million. Agreements worth €18.6 million were negotiated to support further phases of the Association Agreement. This promoted collaboration between Tunisian and European governments, to modernise Tunisian public administration (ENPI, 2015). Furthermore, the EU provided financial support for changes in the areas of justice, women's rights, media, culture, migration, and security (European Commission, 2016). It's worth noting that the EU kept democracy in mind as a counter-terrorism strategy, incorporating security and stability into conversations about political and democratic change. Following the 2015 attacks, negotiations were conducted in Tunisia, with the EU promising assistance for security sector reform. Following talks, the EU reaffirmed its commitment to assisting Tunisia in its battle against terrorism (EEAS, 2017).

When compared to its efforts in Egypt, the EU's attempts to foster democracy in Tunisia have made progress. Nonetheless, both situations recognise the significance of the security-stability link in the democratisation process. The EU applies positive conditionality constantly, incorporating both tangible and verbal features, and Tunisia has profited from the more-for-more approach. Despite making little progress, Egypt has received EU assistance. In Tunisia, involvement with Civil Society Organisations (CSOs) is more emphasised than in Egypt. This divergence is due, first and foremost, to security considerations. Egypt has more urgent terrorist dangers, and the Muslim Brotherhood's failure has prompted the EU to choose stability and security above democracy. Second, the EU's strategy in Tunisia varies owing to its involvement with new elites. The En-Nahda party in Tunisia forced the EU to reconsider its position on political Islam, permitting collaboration with certain Islamist CSOs and parties. Because of the Muslim Brotherhood's actions and the subsequent coup, this contrast is missing in Egypt. As a result, the EU considers its presence in Tunisia to be less dangerous to security and stability than its role in Egypt, demonstrating the EU's policy of adjusting its activities to each country's circumstances (Dandashly, 2017).

CONCLUSION

The chapter provides a foundation for how the European Union has worked to foster democracy and good governance in Africa. The European Union's diverse role in fostering democratic governance across Africa represents a dynamic and complex process. The EU serves as a guiding force by leveraging its commitment to democratic ideals, institutional strengthening, and dispute resolution. However, underlying complexity and objections, such as worries about cultural imposition and neo-colonial echoes, highlight the importance of circumspection. This interplay of achievements and difficulties highlights the EU's role in assisting Africa's democratic journey towards shared prosperity. Since the post-Cold War era, the European Union has promoted democracy in Africa through a diversified approach that includes political engagement, development aid, and electoral support. The history of EU-Africa ties has seen a change away from a concentration on economic partnerships and towards a more complete inclusion of democracy and human rights in development programmes. The EU's commitment to democratic governance and human rights has been institutionalised in procedures such as the Cotonou Agreement, leading to the application of conditionality principles in assistance disbursement. The European Development Fund, the European Instrument for Democracy and Human Rights, and the European Endowment for Democracy are among the EU's measures for promoting democracy in Africa. Furthermore, through its Electoral Observation Missions, the EU plays a critical role in monitoring and assisting elections, contributing to election legitimacy and encouraging peaceful electoral competition. While there are some complaints, the EU's initiatives demonstrate its commitment to promoting democratic growth on the African continent.

While the path to democratisation in Africa is a complicated one characterised by historical legacies, socioeconomic gaps, and nuanced political processes, the Arab Spring's transformational influence demonstrates the continent's hunger for democratic government. Among these many facets, the European Union's position as an external player is critical. The EU aspires to support democratic growth within Africa's particular environment by utilising its own experience and skills. The intersection of ethnic variety, state capability, and economic growth dictates the route to democratisation, and the EU's combined efforts help Africa's continued quest for inclusive governance and shared prosperity. The European Union's reaction to the problems and possibilities in the Middle East and North Africa area in the aftermath of the Arab Spring has been complicated and multidimensional. As it navigates the delicate dynamics of the post-uprising scene, the EU's participation in supporting democracy and fostering political transformation indicates a shift in policy. While the Arab Spring revealed the EU's prior efforts to instigate quick political change, it also resulted in a more pragmatic and flexible strategy. The EU's emphasis on "more for more" incentives, targeted solutions, and a greater emphasis on security-stability links represents a subtle shift in its strategy. The situation of Tunisia, exemplified by the Jasmine Revolution, exemplifies the EU's efforts to adapt its support to changing partner requirements while taking security concerns into account. The EU's commitment to promoting civil society, democracy, and inclusive prosperity is clear, even as it strikes a careful balance between security and democratic progress in a region characterised by various problems and ambitions.

Further promotion of democracy also weaves in, with efforts to enhance political stability and rights further enhancing the EU's engagement in Africa-EU relations. Over time, the European Union's (EU) effectiveness and influence in Africa-EU relations have consistently improved, particularly in terms of its authority, independence, and unity. Nevertheless, maintaining consistency remains a notable challenge for the EU to strengthen its role and efficacy in development policy and its interactions with Africa (Bharti & Goswami, 2023). The COVID-19 crisis went beyond health, impacting democracy, the rule of law, and security on both continents. Handling elections posed dilemmas: holding them was costly amid low turnout while postponing risked power extension. Instability stemming from this fuelled migration, urging intra-continental and inter-continental solutions. To sustain collaboration, a bilateral partnership based on shared political goals is crucial, moving beyond reactive foreign policy. This entails coordinated policies and budgets, shifting from a focus solely on financial aid to prioritizing joint political ambitions, like governance, justice, and anti-corruption efforts. This marks a positive initial step toward a mutually beneficial Africa-Europe partnership (Slim, 2020). Furthermore, A Joint Vision for 2030 was endorsed during the recent Brussels Summit in February 2022, emphasizing four main objectives towards enhancing relations. The Summit also emphasized revitalized collaboration in areas like peace, security, migration, and mobility, as well as a steadfast dedication to multilateralism within an international order guided by established rules, with the United Nations as a central component (Bharti & Goswami, 2023).

The departure of Niger's democratically elected President has dealt a major setback to the EU's efforts to address the dual challenge of security and development in the region. There is also considerable weakening of European efforts to aid Niger in tackling poverty, terrorism, and climate change concerns. Individuals will feel the negative impacts first in a country that relies heavily on foreign aid and now faces the potential of having that cash cut off permanently, according to experts (Jones, 2023). The EU to further promote democracy and good governance will have to address such issues in the following times to envision a more securitised Africa. Further developments will need observations concerning response from the EU and regional actors. Overall, the EU's role has been growing on the African continent to support better institutional development. The African Union (AU) and the EU work together to address recurring problems in various areas of African countries.

REFERENCES

Aid and Political Reform. (1992). Briefing Paper, Overseas Development Institute.

Bharti, M. S. (2022). The Development of China's Economic Cooperation in the Horn of Africa: Special Reference to the Belt and Road Initiative. *African Journal of Economics, Politics and Social Studies*, *1*(1), 17–30. doi:10.15804/ajepss.2022.1.12

Bharti, M. S. (2023). The Sustainable Development and Economic Impact of China's Belt and Road Initiative in Ethiopia. *East Asia (Piscataway, N.J.)*, *40*(1), 175–194. doi:10.100712140-023-09402-y PMID:37065271

Bharti, M. S., & Goswami, A. (2023). Geopolitical Perspective of the EU's Post-Pandemic Public Diplomacy Prospects and Challenges. In S. Kavoğlu & E. Köksoy (Eds.), *Global Perspectives on the Emerging Trends in Public Diplomacy* (pp. 24–49). IGI Global. doi:10.4018/978-1-6684-9161-4.ch002

Bouris, D., & Schumacher, T. (2017). *The Revised European Neighbourhood Policy*. Palgrave Macmillan. doi:10.1057/978-1-137-47182-6

Cottey, A. (2012). Regionalism and the EU's neighbourhood policy: The limits of the possible. *Southeast European and Black Sea Studies*, *12*(3), 375–391. doi:10.1080/14683857.2012.711090

Crawford, G. (1998). Human Rights and Democracy in EU Development Co-operation: Towards Fair and Equal Treatment. In M. Lister (Ed.), *European Union Development Policy*. Palgrave Macmillan. doi:10.1007/978-1-349-26858-0_10

Dandashly, A. (2015). The EU response to regime change in the wake of the Arab revolt: Differential implementation. *Journal of European Integration*, *37*(1), 37–56. doi:10.1080/07036337.2014.975988

Dandashly, A. (2018). EU democracy promotion and the dominance of the security–stability nexus. *Mediterranean Politics*, *23*(1), 62–82. doi:10.1080/13629395.2017.1358900

Erasmus Khan, D., Lagrange, E., Oeter, S., & Walter, C. (Eds.). (28 Nov. 2022). Democracy and Sovereignty. Brill | Nijhoff. doi:10.1163/9789004508712

European Commission. (2011). Joint Communication to the European Council, the European Parliament, the Council, the European Economic and Social Committee and the Committee of the Regions. A Partnership for Democracy and Shared Prosperity with the Southern Mediterranean. COM(2011) 200 final (Brussels).

European Commission. (2011). A New Response to a Changing Neighbourhood: A Review of European Neighbourhood Policy. *COM*, *2011*(303), 25.

European Commission. (2016). *Tunisia Financial Assistance Fiche*. Author.

European Commission. (2016). *European Neighbourhood Policy and Enlargement Negotiations (Tunisia), last updated 23 June 2016*. Available at https://ec.europa. eu/enlargement/neighbourhood/countries/tunisia/index_en.htm

European External Action Service. (2017). *Second High-level Political Dialogue on 'Security and Counter-terrorism': European Union and Tunisia Renew their Cooperation (Brussels).* Available at https://eeas.europa.eu/headquarters/headquarters-homepage/19207/second-high-level-political-dialogue-security-and-counter-terrorism-europeanunion-and-tunisia_en

Global Strategy, E. U. (2016). *Shared Vision, Common Action: A Stronger Europe*. European External Action Service.

Gozzi, G.J. (2018). *Critical Perspectives on Euro-Mediterranean Relations after the "Arab Spring"*. Academic Press.

Hüllen, V. V. (2012). Europeanisation through Cooperation? EU Democracy Promotion in Morocco and Tunisia. *West European Politics*, *35*(1), 117–134. doi:10.1080/01402382.2012.631317

Hurt, S. R. (2003). Co-operation and coercion? The Cotonou Agreement between the European Union and acp states and the end of the Lome´ Convention. *Third World Quarterly*, *24*(1), 161–176. doi:10.1080/713701373

Isaac, S. K. (2013). Rethinking the New ENP: A Vision for an Enhanced European Role in the Arab Revolutions. *Democracy and Security*, *9*(1-2), 40–60. doi:10.1080/17419166.2012.736308

Jones, M. G. (2023, August 4). *What the Niger coup means for Europe's relationship with the Sahel.* Euronews. https://www.euronews.com/my-europe/2023/08/04/what-does-the-niger-coup-mean-for-europes-relationship-with-the-sahel

Keukeleire, S., & Delreux, T. (2014). *The Foreign Policy of the European Union* (2nd ed.). doi:10.1007/978-1-137-02576-0

Krüger, L., & Ratka, E. (2014). *"A new response to a changing neighbourhood?": The Perception of European Policies in Tunisia after the Arab Spring*. Academic Press.

Kurki, M. (2012). *How the EU can adopt a new type of democracy support.* Fundación para las Relaciones Internacionales y el Diálogo Exterior - FRIDE, Working paper No. 112, Madrid.

Mathlouthi, N. (2019). *EU As a Normative Power in The Med Region: Democracy Promotion in Tunisia* [Thesis].

Noutcheva, G. (2015). Institutional governance of European Neighbourhood Policy in the wake of the Arab Spring. *Journal of European Integration*, *37*(1), 19–36. doi:10.1080/07036337.2014.975987

Olsen, G. R. (1998). Europe and the Promotion of Democracy in Post-Cold War in Africa: How Serious is Europe and for What Reason? *African Affairs*, *97*(388), 343–367. doi:10.1093/oxfordjournals.afraf.a007948

Özçelik, A. (2018). *A Litmus Test for Europe: EU Mediterranean Politics After the Arab Spring*. The World Community and the Arab Spring.

Raimundo, A. (2020). *From the Treaty of Rome to Cotonou.* The Routledge Handbook of EU-Africa Relations. doi:10.4324/9781315170916-8

Sanches, E. R. (2020). *Democracy and human rights promotion*. The Routledge Handbook of EU-Africa Relations. doi:10.4324/9781315170916-16

Schraeder, P. J. (1995). *Understanding the "Third Wave" of Democratization in Africa*. Academic Press.

Slim, H. C. (2020). Electoral process in Africa: The impact of COVID-19 and challenges for the EU. *European View*, *19*(2), 212–221. doi:10.1177/1781685820971223

Sour, L. (2017). Rethinking The Euro Med Policy: A Cooperative Approach in An Increasingly Transforming Region. *Romanian Review of Political Sciences & International Relations*, *14*(1).

Teti, A., Thompson, D. A., & Noble, C. (2013). EU Democracy Assistance Discourse in Its New Response to a Changing Neighbourhood. *Democracy and Security*, *9*(1-2), 61–79. doi:10.1080/17419166.2012.736311

Velluti, S. (2020). *The Role of the EU in the Promotion of Human Rights and International Labour Standards in Its External Trade Relations*. Academic Press.

Zamfir, I. (2017). *EU support to democracy and good governance in Africa* [Briefing]. European Parliamentary Research Service.

Zimelis, A. (2011). *Conditionality and the EU–ACP Partnership: A Misguided Approach*. Academic Press.

ADDITIONAL READING

Echagüe, A., Michou, H., & Mikail, B. (2011). Europe and the Arab uprisings: EU vision versus member state action. *Mediterranean Politics*, *16*(2), 329–335. doi:10.1080/13629395.2011.583760

Hanau Santini, R. (2013). The EU's democracy promotion in the Middle East and North Africa: compromising with security concerns? In S. Lucarelli, L. van Langenhove, & J. Wouters (Eds.), *The EU and Multilateral Security Governance* (pp. 123–139). Routledge.

Kourtelis, C. (2015). Assessing EU aid to the 'Southern Partners' of the European Neighbourhood Policy: Who benefits from the reforms in the agricultural and industrial sector? *Journal of Intervention and Statebuilding*, *9*(2), 190–211. doi:10.1080/17502977.2015.1020736

Pace, M. (2009). Paradoxes and contradictions in EU democracy promotion in the Mediterranean: The limits of EU Normative power. *Democratization*, *16*(1), 39–58. doi:10.1080/13510340802575809

Powel, T. (2009). The stability syndrome: US and EU democracy promotion in Tunisia. *Journal of North African Studies*, *14*(1), 57–73. doi:10.1080/13629380802383562

Schumacher, T. (2011). The EU and the Arab Spring: Between spectatorship and actorness. *Insight Turkey*, *13*(3), 107–119.

Tetchau, J. (2016). *The EU's New Global Strategy: Useful or Pointless?* Carnegie Europe.

KEY TERMS AND DEFINITIONS

Arab Spring: A series of protests and uprisings that occurred in various countries in the Middle East and North Africa in 2010-2011.

Cotonou Agreement: An agreement between the EU and African, Caribbean, and Pacific (ACP) countries.

ECOWAS: Economic Community of West African States

EDF: European Development Fund

EED: European Endowment for Democracy

En-Nahda Party: A political party in Tunisia.

ENP: European Neighbourhood Policy

EOM: Electoral Observation Mission

EU: European Union

EUGS: European Union Global Strategy

Lomé Agreements: A series of agreements between the EU and ACP countries, named after the city of Lomé in Togo.

OECD: Organisation for Economic Co-operation and Development

Union for the Mediterranean: An initiative to enhance cooperation between the EU and Mediterranean countries.

Chapter 16
South Africa's Hegemony and Its Quiet Diplomacy:
A Case of Zimbabwe During Thabo Mbeki Presidential Era

Daniel Nkosinathi Mlambo
Tshwane University of Technology, South Africa

ABSTRACT

This chapter assesses South Africa's quiet diplomacy in Zimbabwe during the tenure of Thabo Mbeki as president. After the colonial era, hegemonic powers have always been considered critical role-players within their specific continent or regions because of their robust economies, military might, and soft power credentials, abuse, especially from the ruling Zimbabwean African National Union (ZANU – PF) regime. Instead of acting on its neighbour, the Mbeki regime opted for the quiet diplomacy route. With South Africa entering the African political landscape after the apartheid era and becoming a member of the Southern African Development Community (SADC), many considered it the driving force regarding the political landscape in Africa, particularly Southern Africa. While the Mandela administration achieved some of this, many eyebrows were raised throughout Mbeki's era, particularly in his quiet diplomacy towards Zimbabwe.

INTRODUCTION

Some scholars (see Le Pere, 2014; Barber, 2005; Lipton, 2009; Qobo and Nyathi, 2016) from diverse disciplines have written extensively about South Africa's post-apartheid foreign policy and international Relations (IR), especially in Africa. This dominant narrative portrays post-apartheid South Africa as quickly having repositioned itself from its pariah status to exercising leadership in Southern Africa and Africa. Nevertheless, continental and international observers have often portrayed this positive shift from a positive and negative outlook, predominantly because of the change in its foreign policy, continuous social ills, and domestic politics. Over the years, South Africa has been at the forefront in championing

DOI: 10.4018/979-8-3693-0477-8.ch016

the need to restructure global institutions such as the United Nations Security Council, provision of peace and security (especially in Africa), including forums such as the G20 and Brazil, Russia, India, China, South Africa (BRICS) (Hendricks and Majosi, 2021).

The re-integration of post-apartheid South Africa into the international community resulted in the re-orientation and development of the country's foreign policy. Recent studies on hegemonic powers have provided patterns of disappointment or bewilderment about the gap between the expectations and the achievements of such states in their region. According to Ogunnubi and Isike (2015), since the celebrated entry of South Africa into the African democratic space, the subsequent insinuation has been the shift in the contours of power and leadership equations in Africa. Post-1994 and from the Mandela administration, South Africa's policy stance has always been African-centred and firmly focused on the Southern African region. However, when Thabo Mbeki assumed office in 1999, his foreign policy had a slight paradigm shift primarily driven by the African Renaissance doctrine. His assumption of office also came when Zimbabwe's political arena was shifting through the formation of the Movement for Democratic Change (MDC).

To Prys (2008), former US president George W. Bush had assigned South Africa (mainly through President Mbeki) to deal with the issues in Zimbabwe and for Pretoria to project its hegemonic influence in regional affairs. This brought significant political changes in Zimbabwe driven by Mugabe's Zimbabwean African National Union (ZANU–PF) and, in essence, numerous human rights violations and policy changes that were driven to protect the ruling regime's interests. This era introduced South Africa's quiet diplomacy protocol to the ZANU – PF administration when continental and international observers looked at hegemonic South Africa to take a stance on the political repercussions in Harare. South Africa is undoubtedly a Southern African hegemonic power and a leading powerhouse, mainly because of its superior power advantages, political and economic capabilities, and ideational membership within Africa. Therefore, a regional hegemonic power enjoys a measure of acceptance of its regional leadership, although it is not deemed a must for the existence of influence.

In IR, power is viewed as the broad capability to influence the behaviour of other actors in international interactions. It is essentially grouped into (1) hard (command/relational/objective) and (2) soft (ideational/co-option/structural/subjective) power. Thus, power is a significant ingredient of political relationships and is conceptualized in terms of who gets what, when, where, and how in the global political arena. Hard power means the allusion to the mobilization of tangible instruments of a country's resources encompassing military and economic materials. The importance of hard power concepts cannot be taken for granted as, in most cases, the hegemonic power of states is drawn from their hard power currencies (Ogunnubi, 2013). For this reason, this article explores South Africa's post-1994 hegemonic posture and quiet diplomacy in the Mbeki presidential era toward Zimbabwe.

The Beginning of a New Dawn: From Apartheid to Democracy and South Africa's New Foreign Policy Inspirations

In 2002, African scholars Korwa Adar and Rok Ajulu noted that the transformation in the continent after the end of the Cold War necessitated us to re-visit the methodological, theoretical, and scholarly facts underpinning the African state's foreign policy and foreign policy-making processes. This is because foreign policy draws attention to why certain decisions are taken; therefore, it is an inherently political process because it encompasses a range of actors, each with their objectives and interests. A robust understanding of a state's foreign policy is essential for any researcher. This is drawn from the fact that those whose IR is a speciality possess the perspective to assist states in forging relations and ensuring global peace. Mngomezulu (2020) espouses that understanding foreign policy is critical because a state's foreign policy choices have intense repercussions for relations among states. Post the apartheid dispensation, much of the scholarly work regarding South Africa, particularly in South Africa, has been driven by a clash of concepts, assumptions, and normative convictions.

Foreign policy is a complex issue, and so is finding a robust conceptual clarification to define it. Hence, it is pretty hard to pinpoint its meaning, key aspects, and features. For this article, I will borrow from Mkhize's (2008) definition, which asserts that foreign policy is some official external relations conducted by an independent actor (usually a state) in IR. It is a strategy that governments utilize to guide their actions in the international arena. To draw a nuanced evaluation of South Africa's foreign policy, it is essential that and concisely the historical character of governance is given some attention. South Africa has undergone two waves recently, namely apartheid and democracy. Apartheid was commonly witnessed before the 1994 era. At this time, South Africa's relations with its neighbours were at their downfall due to the destabilization policies of the National Party (NP) government. Thus, during this period, South African policymakers dedicated much of their attention to exploring military options to protect South Africa from external threats rather than forging diplomatic relations.

According to Welsh (1994), after the Sharpeville massacre in 1960, the apartheid government banned the ANC, forcing it to wage its struggle from exile. However, despite many hindrances, while in exile, the current ruling party sharply rose to continental prominence in the late 1980s, and at the time, the ANC enjoyed massive support both continentally and internationally. Post the apartheid era, South Africa's foreign policy shifted and was geared toward stimulating human rights, a belief in justice, and international peace (Mkhize, 2008). The intention of this article is not to draw an entire historical transition period from apartheid to democracy in South Africa; it tends to mention some of these events in passing concisely. This is because scholarly studies on democratic transition have zoomed into the fact that successful democratization primarily depends on economic development; thus, economic growth impedes obstacles to expanding democracy (Welsh, 1994).

Significant events in the 1980s preceded the end of white domination, including the continuous process of apartheid laws by the majority black population, the force from the international community, and the long commencement of political transformation by Pieter W. Botha. Hence, as the 1990s approached, continental and global observers enthusiastically anticipated South Africa's road to transition (Mlambo and Mlambo, 2021). The ANC entered the transition negotiations with the NP unprepared and not knowing what to expect. While in exile, the ANC theorized about governing the country; nevertheless, it never fully articulated its blueprint plans for South Africa when it assumed power. By 1990, it had only created three documents about foreign policy. These were (1) the Freedom Charter of 1955, (2) the Final Report of the Commission on Foreign Policy from the Kabwe Conference of 1985, and the 1989 Harare Declaration. However, these documents were never an accepted basis for the foreign policy of an aspiring political party or a liberation movement; they were just an essential list of intended principles.

Mlambo (2017) observed that the shift from apartheid to democratic rule placed mounting expectations on South Africa from domestic and international observers for Pretoria to lead in spearheading socio-economic growth in Africa. Since 1994, South Africa's foreign policy has undergone significant changes through various heads of state as successive democratic administrations have wanted to forge a new identity in the global system of states. This is also contending with the post-Cold War and domestic challenges, which have been destructive in the instant alteration of democracy. South Africa's foreign policy is underpinned by the realization of democracy, growth, development, and empowerment of the country's people, international solidarity and cooperation, non–alignment, multilateralism, developing a steady and prosperous continent, and solving the conflict by negotiation.

The most critical element for the ANC post-1994 was to wash away the apartheid-era image, particularly to its Southern African neighbours. The foreign policy of Mandela (1994 -1999) and Mbeki (1999 – 2008) were firmly projected to drive this idea forward. Mbeki's quest was to work towards African renewal and stimulating African initiatives for economic development, democratic governance, reclaiming of African identity, and asserting the continent's interests globally (Marumo and Chakale, 2018). Post-1994, South Africa's foreign policy has been characterized in many ways, which have included (1) realism, a realistic theory based (2) soft power, (3) smart power, (4) diplomatic (5) inconsistent (6) emphatic (7) self-interested (8) Ubuntu diplomats (9) pro east and (10) anti-west and hypocritical. The above shows a diversity of views that most people hold on South Africa's foreign policy from 1994 across various international relations and regionalization issues. One may deduce that South Africa opted for a development-driven foreign policy.

According to Landsberg (2005), this seeks to instate development within international policy agendas and strives for balance in world affairs among traditional concerns with the state and human security and development. Similarly, it seeks partnerships between developing states by incorporating development issues. I believe this was the right step to be taken by the post-1994 government in the sense that irrespective of South Africa's hegemonic stance, most African states are developing economies. They ought to work together to steer economic development and regional integration collectively.

DISSECTING A HEGEMONIC POWER: A SOUTH AFRICAN REFLECTION

A regional power should be prepared to use its economic and military stance to claim and steer regional leadership. This denotes the willingness to shoulder the role of a stabilizer in regional security affairs. Apart from this and in support, Flemes (2009) argues that this is driven by the notion that a regional power possesses other essential and needed assets such as market competitiveness, technology, infrastructure, geography, energy, and environmental and human development factors. The concept of hegemony may be credited to the works of Italian Marxist Antonio Gramsci in his series of Prison Notebooks written between 1929 and 1935. To him, hegemony means political leadership based on the leader's consent (Gramsci, 2011). In recent years, there has been growing scholarly research on hegemonic states, emerging or regional powers seen as being dominant within their geographical area and are assumed to robustly shape the natures and contours of regional integration and governance. Several scholarly attempts (see Alden and Soko, 2005; Habib, 2009; Alden and Le Pere, 2009; Ahwireng – Obeng and McGowan, 1998; Destradi, 2010; Ojakoroto and Adeleke, 2018) have been brought to the fore in international discourse to amply come up with a conceptual framework that will further grant us the platform to understand hegemonic powers, their behaviour, and regional political roles.

The continuous attention paid to these states has partially been driven by the changing political and economic factors such as military power, economy, and level of development. Drawing from this, Yilmaz (2010) contends that states that possess these attributes in the new world order can exercise their hegemonic status. From a Southern African perspective, South Africa has tried to influence its hegemonic standpoint over the years with both successes and failures. This occasionally forms part of the baggage accompanying major power status, as power disparities sometimes generate resistance and even discord rather than obedience and acceptance (Mlambo and Adetiba, 2020). Therefore, the establishment and understanding of hegemonic powers are fixed within a rational dynamic usually derived from a materialist account of states and power set within the framework of the international system as a whole. From this perspective, hegemonic powers are understood to be dedicated states as a means of overcoming their material deficiencies regarding structural power.

While hegemonic states are situated ideologically and materially within the dominant hegemonic paradigm, they are sometimes limited (by both power and disposition) in their capacity to act. Theoretical frameworks that drive regionalism, such as the hegemonic stability theory, clearly outline that the existence of a dominant country or hegemon is essential for states to cooperate. However, in most cases, this requires consent among other weaker states built and driven, amongst other things, by the acceptance and ideology as expressed by the hegemon (Alden and Viera, 2005). Like any other middle power such as Brazil, South Africa, India, and China share singularly complex relations within their respective regions, grounded in their dominant economic and military position relative to other states. Post the colonial and Cold War era, hegemonic states have had a prominent need to be involved and steer regional integration protocols. This is even true for developing continents such as Africa. In particular, this is even true when it concerns security issues, and post the 1960s, most African states have continued to endure conflict-related challenges and political instability.

Globally, it is somehow accepted that the behaviour and role of hegemonic powers are linked to the failure and success of regional integration. At the time, they do not perform in a way that is expected of them, particularly in developing regions. Thus, hegemonic states must be at the forefront concerning their utilization of mediation, preventive diplomacy protocols, peacekeeping, peace support operations, peacebuilding, and post-conflict reconstruction. This is further spearheaded by the fact that conflict challenges and development. From a hegemonic standpoint, the role of post-1994 South Africa's stance on peace may be attributed to its history and recent experience in the transition period from apartheid to democracy. Furthermore, this is drawn from the debt Pretoria owes its Southern African neighbours because of the support the ANC (while in exile) received from these states (Mlambo and Adetiba, 2020). Krapohl, Meissner, and Muntschick (2014) noted that in their own right, and since 1994, South Africa has tried to steer development and economic growth in the region with both successes and failures.

One may further ask what makes Pretoria stand out from other Southern African states. Bukae (2017) offers us some of the following reasons. Economically, South Africa is an undisputed leader regarding fundamental economic indicators, provision of services, infrastructural development and resource endowment, Gross Domestic Product (GDP), trade, and industrial and agricultural production. For Western nations, South Africa's democratic transition, liberal constitution, large economy, and voluntary renunciation of nuclear weapons confirm its hegemonic presence. Nevertheless, some states have often failed to accept South Africa's hegemonic presence, constantly questioning its credentials and portraying it as a self-interested hegemon that fails to wield needed regional leadership.

South Africa's Soft Power Credentials Post-1994

According to Sidiropoulos (2014), in the 21st century, there have been new ways of conducting diplomacy. While power is still seen as the central prism concerning how states interact, philosophies of power have changed in the last few decades. While a country's power is often measured through its hard power resources (military and economic), current developments in the global arena are allowing other diplomatic methods apart from hard power. Such power is what Nye (1990) refers to as soft power, and since the concept was coined by Nye a few decades ago, it has received increasing recognition in literature.

For Nye, a state must possess soft and hard power to maintain what he calls smart power. These must be driven by three elements political value (when it lives up to them, at home and abroad), foreign policies (when they are seen as legitimate and having moral authority), and culture (in places where it is attractive to others). Thus, states with soft power resources can rely on these to leverage international diplomatic interaction, which is vital in accepting regional hegemony. From an African perspective, not many states possess soft power credentials driven mainly by autocratic regimes, continuous conflicts, and marginalization from the global economy; however, South Africa possesses both hard and soft power credentials. Globally, it is becoming increasingly clear that any state's categorization as a hegemonic power has much to do with other actors' opinions of that state. In the modern era, recognition of a state's capacity and sway can be linked to its hard power resources and soft power credentials must be considered (Ogunnubi and Tella, 2017).

The demise of apartheid and South Africa's reintegration into the African and international political landscape gave it the platform to exercise its soft power credentials. South Africa presented these early signals of soft power with the charisma of the late Nelson Mandela, its constitutional order, and the Truth and Reconciliation Commission (TRC) success. Such examples further provided South Africa to demonstrate other soft power resources, including but not limited to its cultural output in the form of its entertainment industry, sporting events, education exchange, Ubuntu, peace diplomacy, and democracy promotion together with South Africa's non-state actors including its civil society and multinational institutions. Other elements that have massively contributed to the country's soft power resources have been its numerous peacekeeping missions in countries such as Burundi, Central African Republic (CAR) Comoros, the Democratic Republic of Congo (DRC), Ethiopia, Lesotho, Liberia, Madagascar, Mali, Rwanda, Somalia, South Sudan, Sudan, Zimbabwe, and Mozambique. Over the years, South Africa has made peace an essential element in its foreign policy through mediation and formulation of coalition governments (see Tella, 2021).

An essential element of soft power involves a non-coercive and political value; foreign policy and culture drive it. Thus, power is the ability to sway the behaviour of other states to get what you want. This could be done in numerous ways, including but not limited to persuading them with payments, coercing them with threats, or you can attract and co-opt a state to get regional influence. Thus, soft power is essential if a state possesses it; it becomes more attractive and influential in its region. We may draw soft power resources from two sources (see Table 1), namely international sources (foreign policy and action) and domestic sources (domestic policies and actions) while working with multiple sub-sources in between. These sources are essential in enhancing the image of a state's relation with others.

Thus, and drawing from the above table, soft power is essential in stimulating a state's influence over international observers and increasing its global status in the comity of nations. From a South African viewpoint, and like its other BRICS allies, South Africa can be viewed as a soft power state possessing the attributes to avoid the use of coercion and force in ensuring that the attractiveness of its ideas and preferences is reflected in the choices of other states, especially in Africa (Ogunnubi and Isike, 2015).

In essence, soft power has become necessary to complement hard power resources. South Africa possesses ample soft power resources; its continental and international reputation has grown tremendously post-1994, even though some continental observers have not accepted its regional hegemonic power. Again, and on a similar note, what has further dented this narrative are the continuous social ills still being faced, including unemployment, corruption, rising inequality, and xenophobia.

Table 1. Foundation of Soft Power

International Sources	Domestic Sources
Respect for international law, norms, and institutions.	**Culture** Pronounced social cohesion Elevated quality of life Freedom Sufficient opportunities Tolerance Attractive lifestyle
Fundamental reliance on multilateralism and disposition against excessive unilateralism.	**Political Institutions** Democracy Constitutionalism Liberalism/Pluralism A well-functioning government
Respect for international treaties and alliance commitments	
Willingness to sacrifice short-run national interests to contribute toward the collective good of liberal foreign economic policies.	

Source: Gallrotti (2011).

POLITICAL INSTABILITY AND DYNAMICS IN ZIMBABWE: THE MUGABE ERA

Independence, equality, and freedom, these democratic ideals were at the heart of the revolutionary rebellion of many black Zimbabweans against the British colonial power of Rhodesia (currently known as Zimbabwe). Post the colonial era, an essential element for most African states has been the issue of African sovereignty; however, this has appeared to be fragile and hard to achieve for most African states. Indeed, sovereignty has become a favourable option for most African leaders as it ushered in venues legitimized by international laws and conventions for gaining access to outside sources of wealth and a protective shield behind which sources and beneficiaries of that wealth could remain ambiguous. The lack of legitimate authority in African governments has contributed to the ever-increasing alienation of African citizens, and indeed, the continuing disarticulation of states and societies in much of the continent has exacerbated domestic pressure for democratization. To exemplify this, the Zimbabwean government's growing disregard for its citizens over the years and their right to expression and participation, together with growing threats to human needs, are at the core of civil unrest that has continued to erupt in Harare. Thus, Zimbabwe's governance crisis is situated in the regional dynamics of the political economy of conflict (MaClean, 2002; Howard-Hassman, 2010).

Since its independence in 1980, the late Robert Mugabe and his ZANU-PF have dominated the country's political arena and won the overwhelming majority of elections defeating the Zimbabwe African Peoples Union (ZAPU), which was spearheaded by Joshua Nkomo and became the country's first post-independence prime minister. His policies have always been driven by continuously holding into power upon assuming power. The country was bequeathed a British-style constitutional dispensation which provided for a parliamentary system of government with a prime minister as the head of government and a non-executive president as head of state. After independence, the country gradually moved from being a one-party dominant state to a multi-party state and then to a presidential state. However, years later, particularly in 1997, Zimbabwe faced major economic crises as fuel and food prices increased, unemployment increased, inflation accelerated, and there were increasing labour strikes. On a similar note and years down the line, the emergence of the opposition (the MDC) was also followed by the defeat of the government in the February 2000 referendum to modify the constitution, which was intended to empower the state to acquire commercial farms compulsory and without compensation (Arbab, 2006). Under the regime of Mbeki, whose ascension into the president's office in 1999 was paralleled by intensifying political and economic problems in Zimbabwe.

Globally, states such as CAR, Libya, Nigeria, and South Sudan still witness different forms of instability. While many states are still hampered by this phenomenon, in Southern Africa, Zimbabwe has been experiencing political turmoil for a long time and is not even showing any escape from this effect (Maraswa, Mongale, and Makgola, 2020). The political instability in Zimbabwe dates back to the 1960s. To draw a nuanced appraisal of contemporary power succession struggles and factionalism, it is appropriate to locate these political conflicts in a concise historical context; thus, some historical trends in nationalist and opposition politics must be clarified. Several studies of African opposition politics in Zimbabwe during both the colonial and post-colonial setting stress the importance of a triple legacy in undermining the development and growth of a democratic tradition. This encompasses the influence of the politics of citizen and subject, the authoritarian structures of colonial rule, and the communist politics of the liberation struggle with its attendant view that only liberation movements can represent the people's will.

According to Mungwari (2017), during the colonial era, nationalist politics was often characterized by violent ruptures between and within the nationalist parties. The 1963 split between ZAPU and its splitter organization ZANU brought numerous conflicts and mutual demonization that continued until the formation of the Patriotic Front on the eve of the 1979 Lancaster House conference. This massive deployment of state violence led to the formal subsumption or assimilation of ZAPU to the ruling ZANU-PF in the form of the 1987 Unity Accord. The continuation of Mugabe's ZANU-PF post this era was intimately connected to the re-organization of state structures and the role of violence and intimidation. Since gaining power, ZANU-PF did not just inherit the political economy of the white settler state but also the power of the colonial state, its monopoly of the use of force, and its security executive and legislative capacity. Since then and post-1999, Zimbabwe's political unrest has been chiefly based on the contestation between ZANU-PF and the MDC. Although the ZANU-PF has been the most dominant political party in the country's general elections over the years, the MDC's formation brought fierce competition for ZANU-PF (Mlambo and Ogunnubi, 2018).

South Africa's involvement with its SADC members may be traced back to the early 2000s when Zimbabwe's political woes had started after the ruling ZANU-PF had sought a constitutional referendum that took place on 12 and 13 February 2000 (McGregor and Primorac: 2010). This was to permit the taking of land (particularly from white farmers) with no compensation and grant the president (Robert Mugabe) more power while adding twelve more years to his presidential tenure. The MDC sought to oppose this latest draft constitution which it succeeded in doing (Mlambo: 2014). Furthermore, an excellent showing in the MDC's general elections in 2000 made ZANU-PF realize that the MDC was a severe threat to its governance in Zimbabwe (Miti: 2012). In 2000, severe internal complications in Zimbabwe arose: sanctions, cessation of aid, embassies of European and other countries being closed down, and a twelve-month suspension from the commonwealth (Miti: 2012; Alao: 2012). These factors ushered in South Africa as a negotiator to rectify the political and economic complications causing immense internal problems in Zimbabwe. Former South African president Thabo Mbeki, 1999-2008, in conjunction with Australia and Nigeria (the Commonwealth Triad), had the task of rectifying these political woes.

The political situation intensified in 2007, leading towards the country's general elections. This was when the MDC structures were attacked by what were deemed to be ZANU-PF associates. In the same year, on 11 March 2007, Morgan Tsvangirai and Lovemore Madhuku were also beaten and arrested by the police. Mlambo and Raftopoulos (2010) assert that in March 2007, at an Extraordinary Summit of Heads of State in Tanzania, South Africa was again mandated by the SADC to facilitate a dialogue between the ZANU – PF and the two structures of MDC (T) and MDC (N)[1]. Through rigorous mediation from South Africa, the ZANU–PF, and the two MDC formations, the president (Robert Mugabe) set the election date to 29 March 2008. The MDC (T) was considered victorious in these elections, obtaining 47.9% to ZANU-PF's 43.2%. Hence, with neither getting the required 50 % majority, a run-off was scheduled for 27 June 2008 (Cawthra: 2010).

However, citing MDC supporters' continuous abductions, beatings, and torture, Morgan Tsvangirai withdrew from the election run-off (Shakespeare and Petra: 2015). The SADC then asked South Africa to intervene urgently in the Zimbabwean crisis. The MDC was not entirely satisfied with South Africa facilitating the dialogue. This was mainly due to the relatively close ties between the ANC and the ZANU–PF that date back to the colonial era (Zondi: 2012). To Shakespeare and Petra (2015), apart from his government strategies, Robert Mugabe was still one of the most respected presidents in the SADC region. In addition, there is some unity between most revolutionary parties in Southern Africa. These include the Popular Movement for the Liberation of Angola (MPLA), the Mozambique Liberation Front (FRELIMO), the ANC, the Patriotic Front (PF) of Zambia, and Namibia's South West People's Organization (SWAPO). Their relations may be drawn from the colonial era, more notably to forming the FLS. Hence, one significant reason may be that the MDC was unhappy that South Africa was one of these parties ushered in to facilitate the dialogue between itself and ZANU-PF. Nevertheless, Thabo Mbeki was tasked to mediate a discussion between all involved parties. In handling the situation, Mbeki sought a diplomatic intervention rather than a violent approach, as Pretoria thought a forceful intervention might lead to even more authoritarian political suppression in Zimbabwe (Zondi: 2012).

The country was already experiencing high stagflation rates, with its inflation at 231 million per cent in 2008 (Berger: 2008). The dialogue between Mbeki, his team of facilitators, ZANU–PF, and the MDC was conducted in different locations in Southern Africa, which took several months of intense negotiations between the involved parties (Zondi: 2012). On 17 September 2008, a breakthrough was achieved when an agreement was reached in the Global Political Agreement (GPA)[2] , which became the foundation of the Government of National Unity (GNU) (Miti: 2012). The GPA included constitutional, security, legal, and economic improvements, power sharing, and reconciliation arrangements. In addition, the agreement resulted in the MDC's Morgan Tsvangirai becoming prime minister and Arthur Mutambara, his deputy, while Robert Mugabe retained his presidency (Cawthra: 2010). South Africa had already spent vast amounts of money rectifying Zimbabwe's internal problems. Between 2008 and 2009, Pretoria had already contributed ZAR 613 million from the African Renaissance Fund (ARF) to Zimbabwe. Zimbabwe's economy remains weak and vulnerable to potential shocks that might stimulate further political instability. Again, government suppression of fundamental freedoms continues, and past crises have produced waves of refugees that have burdened Zimbabwe's neighbours, especially South Africa. Such continuous instability may burden Pretoria, which continues to deal with its numerous internal social ills.

South Africa's Quiet Diplomacy Towards Zimbabwe

The aim of this chapter was not to provide or analyze all aspects of diplomacy; however, it intended to provide some of these aspects in the tenure of Thabo Mbeki especially in Zimbabwe. One of the pivotal doctrines of South Africa's government post-1994 was (and still is) to safeguard the country's security to enhance citizens' quality of life. Thus, the government must support all South African citizens abroad. Nevertheless, those who do business or travel outside the country must concede that South Africa's ability to shape the course of events in other states may be limited. South Africa's quiet diplomacy approach indicated its unwillingness to employ or project its power to impose solutions to African problems. This is despite the South African government prioritizing this in its post-1994 foreign policy and Mbeki's African renaissance project. The emergence of quiet diplomacy needs to be understood against the backdrop of the inability of states like Zimbabwe to provide a proper and decent environment for their people. The incapacity of such nation-states has, in turn, exposed the increasing appropriateness to ensure adherence to international norms and values of good governance, democracy, human rights, law and order, and justice (Dlamini, 2002). Thus, Mbeki's quiet diplomacy received much criticism, particularly in light of his state's commitment to the African Renaissance doctrine and good governance in Africa. This is because Mugabe persistently ignored the basic principles of democracy and the role of law, which will be influenced by a soft diplomatic approach to change (Mkhize, 2008). The crisis in Zimbabwe's political architecture has much scholarly attention, with scholars trying to understand its cause, extent, and consequences. One of these was the quiet diplomacy approach used by former president Mbeki during the crises that were taking place in Zimbabwe (Hamill and Hoffman, 2009). A pivotal duty for the ANC-led government is safeguarding the country's security to protect citizens from external shocks. Nevertheless, those doing business or travelling outside state borders must acknowledge that South Africa's ability to shape events in another state is limited. Thus, South Africa's quiet diplomacy further indicates its reluctance to engage or protect its power to impose solutions to African problems. Quiet diplomacy may be conceptualized as a combination of measures, including behind-the-scenes engagements, secret negotiations, and subtle coaxing.

Many observers noted South Africa lacked sound foreign policy articulation during the Mandela administration. This may have been drawn from several reasons, firstly, the new ANC government was inexperienced, and secondly still had to grapple with its domestic challenges and destabilization policies left by the NP regime. Nevertheless, in years to come, particularly in the Mbeki tenure (from 1999), the most inconsistent framework in South Africa's foreign policy was the notion of quiet diplomacy on the rule of law in Zimbabwe. Pretoria's position of Zimbabwe in this period was more concerned with regime security than the plight of millions of Zimbabweans (Nathan, 2005). In support, Coetzee (2004) noted that Mbeki's apparent resistance to robustly condemning Mugabe's increasing authoritarianism and breach of human rights violations was even more confusing.

To others, South Africa's decision to follow the quiet diplomacy route toward Zimbabwe should have been understood within Mbeki's vision of the African Renaissance. With his dream of a new Africa, Mbeki seemed to follow in the founders' footsteps of Pan – Africanism. Because of the failure of most African states to rectify Zimbabwe's internal political woes, the West had turned to South Africa as a direct neighbour, regional hegemon, and Zimbabwe's biggest trading partner (at that time) to put pressure on Mugabe's regime (see Malimela, 2010). However, Pretoria failed to apply pressure (through sanctions on Zimbabwe) but chose the quiet diplomacy route through constructive engagements. This brought with it a lot of criticism. However, international observers like George W. Bush and Gerhard

Schroeder appreciated (during their visit to South Africa) Mbeki's quiet diplomacy route as it kept open a channel for continuous communication between Mugabe and the outside world. Conversely, the policy was criticized for being too soft on Mugabe's regime.

As this did not bear the needed result, many concluded that Mbeki was driven by the historical ties of the ANC and ZANU–PF as both parties fought the same liberation struggle against colonialism and racism. Thus, South Africa and Zimbabwe are connected by a joint settler colony history of minority rule and liberation struggle, which still impacts both states' politics and economics in the modern era. In essence, South Africa's foreign policy against Zimbabwe has been driven by consistent failure and broken promises, and its quiet diplomacy also evoked much criticism. This is because quiet diplomacy is inconsistent with the high moral principles underlying South Africa's post-1994 foreign policy. Thus, South Africa has been criticized for not using its hegemonic position to protect the region (see Adelmann, 2004). This is because it was noted that South Africa, through its hard and soft power sources, had ample reasons to put more pressure on the Mugabe regime and adopt what Prys (2007) calls a louder style of diplomacy combined with economic sanctions. This would have assisted the Zimbabwean population, but South Africa viewed this as a better strategy than utilizing hard power because Mbeki had hoped that Zimbabwe would solve its problems. The quiet diplomacy doctrine expressed the idea that Zimbabweans should decide among themselves about the issues they internally faced without interfering in their internal matters. The significant ideology and values are also reflected in the fact that South Africa convened several meetings to acquaint Mugabe with the norms, rules, and guidelines which govern countries that are members of the SADC. However, in these meetings, Mugabe was unprepared to listen, and South Africa never forced him to comply (Mkhize, 2008).

Quiet Diplomacy: Is it a Feasible Diplomatic Mechanism in Africa?

Under Mbeki's tenure, South Africa was still trying to establish itself as a pivotal interlocutor for Africa and the global fora, a strong advocate of South-South solidarity and reform of the outdated global governance architecture, and a leader in the reconstruction of the continent's institutional architecture (Sidiropoulos, 2008). The post-Cold War context of African peace-making has been characterized by a conviction that the continent needs more relevant approaches to peace. Thus, the African solutions to African problems frequently resonate with regional and continental peace and security frameworks. This is because African leaders must take their destinies into their own hands by creating peace and human solidarity for themselves. Some scholars argued that by employing quiet diplomacy in engaging Mugabe's regime, South Africa demonstrated hegemonic naivety in failing to bring Mugabe under control. Thus, failing to bring or display effective regional leadership as expected. In scholarly circles, whether quiet diplomacy effectively resolves conflicts is a continuous topic for both continental and international observers, and this debate will always be heated. Over the years, South Africa has deployed numerous foreign policy treaties to resolve instability in most African countries, as alluded to earlier. Whichever direction it has taken to resolve such has also been criticized in certain quarters. Intervention factors in post-colonial Africa are becoming increasingly complex and hardly lead themselves to uniform and straightforward diplomatic formulas. To Dlamini (2002), the challenge is not always to deploy the most discreet diplomatic approach to achieve the required objective. Also, the absence of the public in mediation processes raises concerns over the viability of quiet diplomacy as a practical peace-making tool. This is because the involvement of citizens and civil society, in particular, could have assisted in legitimizing the conflict resolution process. However, the argument is that involving too many people might delay the mediation process, especially when many stakeholders are involved. Akokpari (2016) noted that in some instances, where mediation is often used as an instrument of diplomacy, negotiators are, in most cases, unskilled, lacking not only appropriate negotiating techniques but also, at times, naive about the background of the conflict.

The tendency of some African heads of state to emphasize, rather than criticize, culpable peers has not helped the outcome of diplomatic efforts. Another limitation of quiet diplomacy has to do with the fact that it confirms the logic of solidarity, fraternity, and sovereignty. The point is that the solidarity politics of juridical statehood takes precedence over the need to ensure freedom, the rule of law, and respect for human rights. These are the basic tenets of South Africa's foreign policy and the SADC peace and security framework (Mhango, 2012). Thus, quiet diplomacy affects peace in a way that when regional powers sometimes employ this type of mediation, they fail to consider that the general populace still suffers while negotiations are at play.

Similarly, the failure to take immediate actions such as sanctions grants states and leaders to feel that they have control over such mediation processes. The best scenario for some would be opening up the political space for increased and robust democratization in the country. The government should continuously push for economic reforms that would give the country the platform to turn around its fortune both in the short and long run. These norms should be tried and tested to promote and encourage democratic practices, good governance, and the rule of law.

Despite its uncertain political leadership, labour unrest, and economic weaknesses, South Africa remains the most suitable state to tackle Zimbabwe's issues and that of many African states. Moving forward, foreign policy and other cognate fields of governance in South Africa and other developing regions will one day come under significant pressure to become more progressive because of the changing dynamics of the political landscape. A challenge South Africa will continue to face is that many observers will pressure it to play a more hegemonic role in Africa. Its foreign policy will have to be adequately managed in the coming years. One may deduce that foreign policy-making is not easy for any government due to diverse factors, including opposing opinions to those assigned the task of articulating it, lack of resources to implement it, and continuous political changes in the global political landscape.

CONCLUSION

This article aimed to ponder South Africa's foreign policy and quiet diplomacy, particularly over Zimbabwe in the Mbeki era from 1999. The article rightfully shows that South Africa has been a hegemonic state both during and after the end of apartheid due to both its hard and soft power currencies. However, post-1994 presented it with the opportunity to shift its stance from hard to soft power due to its hegemonic position and driven by its foreign policy and peacekeeping initiatives. However, the quiet diplomacy it took in the Mbeki era was amply criticized by both continental and international observers considering that these brought many human rights violations in Zimbabwe, which South Africa was looked upon to swiftly amend and rectify irrespective of the ANC's close relations with ZANU-PF.

REFERENCES

Adelmann, M. (2004). Quiet diplomacy: The reasons behind Mbeki's Zimbabwe policy. *Africa Spectrum*, 249–276.

Ahwireng-Obeng, F., & McGowan, P. J. (1998). Partner or Hegemon? South Africa in Africa: Part one. *Journal of Contemporary African Studies*, *16*(1), 5–38. doi:10.1080/02589009808729619

Akokpari, J. (2016). The challenges of diplomatic practice in Africa. *Journal of Contemporary History*, *41*(1), 1–17.

Alao, A. (2012). *Mugabe and the Politics of Security in Zimbabwe*. McGill-Queen's Press-MQUP. doi:10.1515/9780773587748

Alden, C., & Le Pere, G. (2009). South Africa in Africa: Bound to lead? *Politikon: South African Journal of Political Studies*, *36*(1), 145–169. doi:10.1080/02589340903155443

Alden, C., & Soko, M. (2005). South Africa's economic relations with Africa: Hegemony and its discontents. *The Journal of Modern African Studies*, *43*(3), 367–392. doi:10.1017/S0022278X05001011

Alden, C., & Vieira, M. A. (2005). The new diplomacy of the South: South Africa, Brazil, India, and trilateralism. *Third World Quarterly*, *26*(7), 1077–1095. doi:10.1080/01436590500235678

Arbab, F. (2006). Impact of Mugabe's policies on the prospects for democracy in Zimbabwe. *Strategic Studies*, *26*(1), 147–179.

Barber, J. (2005). The new South Africa's foreign policy: Principles and practice. *International Affairs*, *81*(5), 1079–1096. doi:10.1111/j.1468-2346.2005.00503.x

Bukae, N. M. (2017). South Africa: A Benign or Malign Regional Hegemon? The Case of the 1998 South Africa-Led Military Intervention in Lesotho. *Lonaka Journal of Learning and Teaching*, *8*(1), 112–141.

Cawthra, G. (2010). *The role of SADC in managing political crisis and conflict: The cases of Madagascar and Zimbabwe*. Friedrich-Ebert-Stiftung Mozambique.

Coetzee, C. (2004). *South Africa's foreign policy of quiet diplomacy towards Zimbabwe: constructivism as a framework to highlight the contradictory norms of human rights and African solidarity* [Doctoral dissertation]. Stellenbosch University.

Destradi, S. (2010). Regional powers and their strategies: Empire, hegemony, and leadership. *Review of International Studies*, *36*(4), 903–930. doi:10.1017/S0260210510001361

Dlamini, K. (2002). Is Quiet Diplomacy an Effective Conflict Resolution Strategy? *South African Yearbook of International Affairs*, *3*, 171–178.

Flemes, D. (2009). Regional power South Africa: Co-operative hegemony constrained by historical legacy. *Journal of Contemporary African Studies*, *27*(2), 135–157. doi:10.1080/02589000902867238

Gallarotti, G. M. (2011). Soft power: What it is, why it's important, and the conditions for its effective use. *Journal of Political Power*, *4*(1), 25–47. doi:10.1080/2158379X.2011.557886

Gramsci, A. (2011). *Prison Notebooks, Volumes 1-3.* Academic Press.

Habib, A. (2009). South Africa's foreign policy: Hegemonic aspirations, neoliberal orientations, and global transformation. *South African Journal of International Affairs, 16*(2), 143–159. doi:10.1080/10220460903265857

Hamill, J., & Hoffman, J. (2009). 'Quiet diplomacy or appeasement? South African policy towards Zimbabwe. *The Round Table, 98*(402), 373–384. doi:10.1080/00358530902895584

Hendricks, C., & Majozi, N. (2021). South Africa's International Relations: A New Dawn. *Journal of Asian and African Studies, 56*(1), 64–78. doi:10.1177/0021909620946851

Howard-Hassmann, R.E. (2010). Mugabe's Zimbabwe, 2000-2009: Massive Human rights violations and the failure to protect. *Hum.RTS.Q., 32,* 898.

Krapohl, S., Meissner, K. L., & Muntschick, J. (2014). Regional Powers as Leaders or R ambos? The Ambivalent Behaviour of Brazil and South Africa in Regional Economic Integration. *Journal of Common Market Studies, 52*(4), 879–895. doi:10.1111/jcms.12116

Landsberg, C. (2005). Toward a Developmental Foreign Policy?: Challenges for South Africa's Diplomacy in the Second Decade of Liberation. *Social Research, 72*(3), 723–756. doi:10.1353or.2005.0041

Le Pere, G. L. (2014). Critical themes in South Africa's foreign policy. *Strategic Review of Southern Africa, 36*(2), 31.

Lipton, M. (2009). Understanding South Africa's foreign policy: The perplexing case of Zimbabwe. *South African Journal of International Affairs, 16*(3), 331–346. doi:10.1080/10220460903495181

Maclean, S. J. (2002). Mugabe at war: The political economy of conflict in Zimbabwe. *Third World Quarterly, 23*(3), 513–528. doi:10.1080/01436590220138402

Malimela, L. P. (2010). *Analyzing Thabo Mbeki's policy of quiet diplomacy in the Zimbabwean crisis* [Master's thesis]. University of Cape Town.

Maraswa, T., Mongale, I. P., & Mokgola, A. (2020). The ramifications of non-elite political instability on the Zimbabwean economy: Vecm analysis. *African Journal of Development Studies, 10*(3), 253–275. doi:10.31920/2634-3649/2020/10n3a13

Marumo, P. O., & Chakale, M. (2018). Mbeki on African Renaissance: A vehicle for Africa development. *African Renaissance, 15*(4), 179–191. doi:10.31920/2516-5305/2018/V15n4a9

McGregor, J., & Primorac, R. (Eds.). (2010). *Zimbabwe's new diaspora: Displacement and the cultural politics of survival* (Vol. 31). Berghahn Books.

Mhango, G. A. (2012). *Is Quiet Diplomacy in Consonance with Meaningful peace-making in SADC?* Lessons from Zimbabwe.

Miti, K. (2012). South Africa and conflict resolution in Africa: From Mandela to Zuma. *Southern African Peace and Security Studies, 1*(1), 26–42.

Mkhize, M. C. (2008). *Assessing South Africa's" quiet diplomacy" towards Zimbabwe: strengths and weaknesses* [Doctoral dissertation].

Mlambo, A., & Raftopoulos, B. (2010, April). The regional dimensions of Zimbabwe's multi-layered crisis: An analysis. In *Election processes, Liberation movements and Democratic change in Africa Conference*. CMI and IESE.

Mlambo, A. S. (2014). *A history of Zimbabwe*. Cambridge University Press. doi:10.1017/CBO9781139128919

Mlambo, D. N. (2017). *Regional supremacy or coalition? Evaluating South Africa's regional integration efforts within the Southern African Development Community (SADC)* [Doctoral dissertation]. University of Zululand.

Mlambo, D. N., & Adetiba, T. C. (2020). Post-1994 South Africa's peacekeeping and military intervention in Southern Africa, reference from the Democratic Republic of Congo (DRC) and Lesotho. *Journal of Public Affairs*, *20*(1), e1984. doi:10.1002/pa.1984

Mlambo, D. N., & Adetiba, T. C. (2020). South Africa and regional integration in Southern Africa post-1994: Realities, challenges, and prospects. *Journal of Nation-Building and Policy Studies*, *4*(1), 5–33. doi:10.31920/2516-3132/2020/v4n1a1

Mlambo, D. N., & Mlambo, V. H. (2021). To What Cost to its Continental Hegemonic Standpoint: Making Sense of South Africa's Xenophobia Conundrum Post Democratization. *Journal of Ethnic and Cultural Studies*, *8*(2), 347–361. doi:10.29333/ejecs/696

Mlambo, D. N., & Ogunnubi, O. (2018). South Africa's integration efforts within the Southern African Development Community: Regional supremacy or coalition? *Journal of Public Affairs*, *18*(4), e1856. doi:10.1002/pa.1856

Mngomezulu, B. (2021). *Foreign Policy Posture in Post-Apartheid South Africa: Consistencies and Ambiguities*. Cambridge Scholars Publishing.

Mungwari, T. (2017). *Representation of political conflict in the Zimbabwean press: The case of the Herald, the Sunday Mail, Daily News and the Standard, 1999-2016* [Unpublished PhD Thesis]. University of South Africa, Pretoria.

Nathan, L. (2005). Consistency and inconsistencies in South African foreign policy. *International Affairs*, *81*(2), 361–372. doi:10.1111/j.1468-2346.2005.00455.x

Nye, J. S. (1990). Soft power. *Foreign Policy*, (80), 153–171. doi:10.2307/1148580

Ogunnubi, O., & Isike, C. (2015). Regional hegemonic contention and the asymmetry of soft power: A comparative analysis of South Africa and Nigeria. *Strategic Review for Southern Africa*, *37*(1), 152.

Ogunnubi, O., & Tella, O. (2017). Framing South Africa's soft power through non-state sources. *Strategic Analysis*, *41*(5), 478–495. doi:10.1080/09700161.2017.1343228

Ojakorotu, V., & Adeleke, A. A. (2018). Nigeria and conflict resolution in the sub-regional West Africa: The quest for a regional hegemon. *Insight on Africa*, *10*(1), 37–53. doi:10.1177/0975087817735386

Olusola, O. R. (2013). *Hegemonic order and regional stability in Sub-Saharan Africa: a comparative study of Nigeria and South Africa* [Doctoral dissertation].

Prys, M. (2007, September). Regions, power, and hegemony: South Africa's role in Southern Africa. In *Sixth Pan-European International Relations Conference* (*Vol. 12*, p. 15). Academic Press.

Qobo, M., & Nyathi, N. (2016). Ubuntu, public policy ethics and tensions in South Africa's foreign policy. *South African Journal of International Affairs*, *23*(4), 421–436. doi:10.1080/10220461.2017.1298052

Shakespeare, H., & Petra, C. (2015). *Unpacking the Complexities of Mediation in Africa: Some Lessons from the SADC's Mediation Role in Zimbabwe between 2008 and 2013*. https://www.up.ac.za/media/shared/237/PDFs/International%20conference%202015/2.-s-hamauswa-paper-on-mediation.zp58697.pdf

Sidiropoulos, E. (2008). South African foreign policy in the post-Mbeki period. *South African Journal of International Affairs*, *15*(2), 107–120. doi:10.1080/10220460802636158

Sidiropoulos, E. (2014). South Africa's emerging soft power. *Current History (New York, N.Y.)*, *113*(763), 197–202. doi:10.1525/curh.2014.113.763.197

Tella, O. (2021). *Africa's Soft Power: Philosophies, Political Values, Foreign Policies and Cultural Exports*. Taylor & Francis. doi:10.4324/9781003176022

Welsh, D. (1994). *South Africa's Democratic Transition*. https://www.jstor.org/stable/24595472#metadata_info_tab_contents

Yilmaz, S. (2010). State, power, and hegemony. *International Journal of Business and Social Science*, *1*(3).

Zondi, S. (2012). *South Africa in Southern Africa: A perspective*. https://library.fes.de/pdf-files/bueros/mosambik/09403-no-8.pdf Accessed 17 June 2022

ENDNOTES

1. The MDC had split into two. The MDC (T) was run by Morgan Tsvangirai while the MDC (N) was that of Professor Arthur Mutambara.
2. Signed in September 2008 and effective from February 2009, the GPA was an accord between Zimbabwe's three main political parties, the ZANU-PF and the two MDC structures. It was a power-sharing agreement between these parties that aimed to address internal challenges (political and economic) facing Zimbabwe.

Chapter 17
The Role of Multilateral Development Banks in Anti-Corruption:
The Case of the African Development Bank

Lucky Madikiza
University of South Africa, South Africa

ABSTRACT

Billions of dollars in funding for infrastructure development are managed by multilateral development banks. Due to their function as development financiers, they are vulnerable to fraud and corruption, both internally inside their organizations and externally from political stakeholders given that they are frequently state-owned businesses. Historically, they have relied on national law enforcement agencies to investigate corruption-related activities. However, multilateral development banks (MDBS) have been acting more proactively in recent years to combat corruption. The African Development Bank is one of several global multilateral development banks that have started to play a role in recent years. This chapter discusses its work.

INTRODUCTION

Given the legacy of subpar infrastructures in Africa, infrastructure development is emerging as a crucial area for promoting African economic development. Development banks, who have long played a role as funders of big projects in infrastructure development, are among the major actors in this field. Given their position, these organizations oversee vast sums of money that can reach billions. Furthermore, these organizations are frequently state-owned. Their role has put them in a situation where they are prone to corruption, which could come from political role-players.

DOI: 10.4018/979-8-3693-0477-8.ch017

Development banks have come to understand that to fight corruption, they must be more proactive. The African Development Bank is highlighted in this chapter along with the initiatives it is doing to fight corruption. The chapter begins with a summary of development banks before concentrating on the African Development Bank and the strategies it is using to combat corruption both internally and externally in the social environment. It is intended that this preliminary review chapter will lead to more in-depth research studies that investigate how development banks may help the fight against corruption while also considering how they are put in a susceptible position to becoming corruption hotspots. Other anti-corruption role-players who do well to have a more intimate understanding of these institutions, potentially they represent partner entities in the fight against corruption.

THE CONCEPT OF DEVELOPMENT BANK

There have been arguments that there is no universally accepted definition of development banks (Xu et al., 2021). Although logically these types of organizations can be distinguished as distinct, the phrase "development banking" is occasionally used as a synonym for "development finance institutions" (Bruck, 2001, p. 10). Development banks are institutions that provide long-term financing for initiatives aimed at socio-economic development, according to definitions emerging from the United Nations system (Bunich et al., 2019, p. 2864).

Development banks, which are typically state-owned, are examples of a government financial system intervention to overcome a market failure where private finance is not readily available to help with the imperative to achieve national socio-economic goals such as poverty reduction (Thorne & du Toit, 2009, p. 678). In other words, they are banks that will provide financing for socio-economic development projects that cannot be normally financed by private banks or financiers for various reasons. Among other reasons, the private banking sector may not participate in funding development projects which carry a development mandate which has historically been the preserve of the government. Furthermore, the private banking industry, with no historic expertise in development finance, may also be reluctant to fund development projects that are associated with high inherent long-term risk (Bruck, 2001, p. 12).

With their unique mandate, a development bank represents a unique institution that must be considered differently from private commercial banks or investment banks. Instead, development banks are more focused on financing development projects or infrastructure development initiatives which are often key for socio-economic development. Somewhat similar to investment banks in their long-term financing, development banks provide long-term loans for development projects (Bruck, 2001, p. 10). Compared to commercial banks, they can provide long-term loans because of their distinctive features entailing "development-oriented mandates, long-term liabilities, the higher collateral value of their bond issuances, and the acquisition and dissemination of expertise in providing long-term loans to finance new industries" (Hu et al., 2022, p. 3). The closest resemblance in their mode of work would be micro-finance institutions, who similarly ply their trade in a market niche considered high-risk for commercial banks (Wang, 2017). Aside from funding development or infrastructure projects, development banks may also fund capital-intensive industries by providing loans for projects that stimulate industrial development or new industries as well as infrastructure development (Lazzarini et al., 2015; UNCTAD, 2016).

The modus operandi of development banks tends to be underpinned by two principles in their financing activities. Firstly, they will approve financing based on having considered an economic appraisal, and secondly, their need for intervention is based on being a lender of last resort when no other finance is available on reasonable terms (Bruck, 2001, p. 11). Further comparing them with their commercial bank counterpart, development banks are not designed to provide banking services or products for individuals such as short-term credit for vehicle finance, savings, or bank accounts. Typical clients of development banks, who tend to be state-owned entities, will include governments, state-owned entities, or private sector role-players who may be involved in large-scale infrastructure projects. As a result of them largely fulfilling a market failure intervention mandate, they also partially assist in financially supporting national development objectives. In their gap-filling focus to address market segments that private bankers may be ignoring or periodically neglecting, development banks will typically venture to finance enterprise start-ups, small-medium businesses, housing, or rural development projects, in addition to infrastructure projects (Gutierrez et al., 2011).

Given that development banks are tied to a developmental mandate and still have to be sustainable, they need to adopt a fine balancing act to continue to be financially sustainable. In developing a sustainable business model, they will on one hand complement government resources to fund development projects which accrue no cost recovery whilst also providing private funding for projects which may earn profitability (Thorne & du Toit, 2009, p. 678). Typically, unlike commercial banks, the development banking sector is not expected to pursue profit but to just ensure they manage resources in a way that helps them to keep afloat as an institution. In practice, it is often quite a difficult endeavour. For starters, development banks are typically non-deposit-taking banks in their original configuration. Therefore, they may not have a financial pool derived from customer transactions and have to mobilise financial resources from secondary sources. This may entail borrowing from financial international markets and then lending the money as loans for development projects. In the instance of multilateral development banks, they can secure finance from financial markets as they will be supported by guarantees of their member governments (Nelson, 2001). Other sources of funds may also include commercial banks, insurance companies, or pension funds (Bruck, 2001, p. 24).

Following our initial conceptual primer, we will now elaborate on the history and modus operandi of development banking to yield more insights into the nature and practices of these types of banking institutions.

ORIGINS, EVOLUTION, AND CHEQUERED PERFORMANCE OF DEVELOPMENT BANKS

The World Bank, the first and most well-known development bank, was founded in 1944 to fill a gap in the provision of international finance following World War Two, as the capital markets at the time were unable to provide investment capital to rebuild war-torn nations (Sherk, 1994, p. 45). Although they were organized as "industrial banks" that supported industrialization initiatives in Europe and the United States, Bruck (2001, p. 12) traces the formation of development banks before World War Two. In the years following World War Two, people thought about ways to rebuild war-torn nations and even historically non-industrial nations.

The "industry" mission was thus replaced with a more inclusive "development" mandate that also considered the economic requirements of developing nations outside of Europe (Sherk, 1994; Bruck, 2001). Market failure occurred in both situations which led to the formation of industrial banks and development banks. Before World War Two, there had been the Great Depression of 1930, during which time investment finance was difficult to come by even though an economic recovery was required (Bruck,

2001, p. 13). Investment capital was needed to repair war-devastated infrastructure in the wake of the Second World War, and there was concern that private capital markets wouldn't provide it, as they had during the 1930s economic collapse (Sherk, 1994, p. 45).

After the World Bank, regional banks like the Inter-American Development Bank, the Asian Development Bank, and the African Development Bank were formed. Other development banks, particularly those in developing nations, were mostly established in the 1950s and 1960s. The region-wide banks, also known as multilateral development banks, were created by at least two or more nations and have the responsibility of providing financial support to a group of nations that are part of a worldwide region.

These were developed by the same World Bank mandate to satisfy the needs of socio-economic development while anticipating market failure. They were established in developing country environments for a variety of reasons, including the desire of those nations to integrate into the global economy and post-colonial national development aspirations (Bunich et al. 2019, p. 2864). Instead of serving a region of nations globally, development banks may also have national mandates and be affiliated with certain nations; in this instance, they are referred to as national development banks. The Development Bank of Southern Africa, which has a mandate for southern African governments within the continent, is an example of a sub-regional bank that spans several nations within a worldwide region.

Development banks adopted diverse ownership structuring arrangements in various nations as the years went by. They would typically be state-owned, but some might give the private sector a stake in them, and some might even be entirely owned by the private sector, as was the case with the Industrial Development Bank of Turkey in the 1970s (UNCTAD, 2016, p. 10). When evaluating their performance, development banks have both achievements and failures. Due to a variety of governance and financial concerns, less-developed nations have seen considerable financial failure in the development banking industry (Thorne & du Toit, 2009, p. 680). How these entities should be financed is the initial and ongoing difficulty.

According to Thorne and du Toit (2009, p. 680), even well-managed banks must balance the awkwardly competing goals of guaranteeing financial viability and seeking social results. For Sapienza (2004, p. 358), it is not always obvious whether the reduced profitability of government-owned banks is a result of their broader societal objectives or fewer incentives. Despite being in a high-risk environment where dangerous long-term projects are funded, their operational success must be evaluated considering several potential criteria.

The failure or subpar performance of development banks should not, as is sometimes the case, be only attributed to the fact that they are controlled by the government. Some people believe that compared to private banks, government-owned banks are more prone to inefficiency. Several research studies have refuted this assertion. According to a case study done in Germany, there is no indication that private banks are more effective than those that are controlled by the government (Altunbas et al., 2001). Private banks are not necessarily more profitable than government banks, according to research (Micco et al., 2007).

It is expected that development banks, as autonomous organizations, will be able to raise money on the open markets or through other financial institutions. However, some development banks will get financial aid from the government. Government transfers do not always indicate a complete reliance on government subsidies, as the German Development Bank, KfW, has been known to receive transfers from the government to support interest rate subsidies to specific borrowers (De Luna-Martnez & Vicente, 2012, p. 11).

Identical to its counterparts in the commercial sector, development banks may experience inadequate governance, which occasionally may result in closure. In the case of private banks, a lapse in normally conservative risk management led to the sub-prime lending crisis in the United States, which precipitated the 2008 economic recession. The funding of long-term projects in a high-risk sector where the development outcomes or sustainability may not be realized is a constant challenge for the development banking industry. As a result, they made decisions to fund unprofitable initiatives, which resulted in irrecoverable sunken expenses for duplicated infrastructure projects. The effectiveness of projects the banks may have funded may occasionally go unmonitored (Carrasco et al., 2017).

CORRUPTION VULNERABILITIES FOR THE DEVELOPMENT BANKING SPHERE

The governance concern regarding development banks also relates to external pressures. These institutions, some of which are already held by the government, could be influenced by the government or, to put it more bluntly, by politics. Development banks may have seated members of the executive branch on their boards of directors. There have been arguments made both in favour of and against the participation of government officials.

The supporting argument contends that public employees are valuable in providing strategic direction on mandates, while the opposing argument contends that if they have excessive power, they may improperly influence the Board (De Luna-Martnez & Vicente, 2012, p. 20). Politicians have occasionally been seen as advantageous when working on projects. According to Hainz and Kleimeier (2012), "development banks provide a so-called 'political umbrella' because these banks can use their clout to influence governmental decisions and deter adverse events that would negatively affect the project's outcome."

They consequently shift from being solely commercial organizations to being ones that are situated in political and economic circumstances. Even though they are under the umbrella of the public sector, it is expected that they will work freely and abstain from political influence. However, the concern over political sway has consistently hung over state-owned businesses as a whole. There is proof that state-owned banks may generally be susceptible to political influence. Other studies have supported the existence of undue political influence in state-owned banks' lending practices. For instance, in Italy, lending decisions were influenced by the outcome of elections for a political party linked to the bank's top executive (Sapienza, 2004).

Results from a different study that focused on developing markets in the 1990s show that state-owned banks boosted lending during election years, suggesting that political considerations can affect their lending activities (Dinç, 2005). Even though they are vulnerable, development banks have occasionally been able to resist political pressure. Empirical findings from research on European development banks indicated that they were not always influenced by politics, such as when they might change their lending policies during election years (Frigerio & Vandone, 2020). Similarly, research conducted in Brazil about the BNDES, or Brazilian National Bank for Economic and Social Development, disproved the political theory that development banks might favour politically connected businesses that have poor performance (Lazzarini et al., 2015a).

THEORISING CORRUPTION IN THE CONTEXT OF STATE-OWNED ENTERPRISES

It is helpful to establish a theoretical grasp of corruption when talking about it regarding state-owned development bank businesses. Understandably, the phenomenon has drawn a lot of attention in the literature to provide theoretical answers because it is a cause for concern and an indication of institutional weakness. Many academic fields, including public administration, economics, and other social sciences, have attempted to offer theoretical justifications for the problem of corruption. Except for a summary of the theoretical landscape, this chapter does not aim to rehash the many hypotheses in the large corpus of corruption theory that currently exists. The discussion has mainly selected a small sample of the prominent perspectives to essentially capture the analytical frameworks that have been invoked in corruption issues. The Principal-Agent Theory, Collective Action Theory, and Institutional Theory are a few well-known theories that have shed light on corruption.

The Principal-Agent Theory approach, which emanates from institutional economics, considers the principal and the agent as the two main role players interfacing with corruption. Despite the principal being able to dictate the relationship's pay-off terms, Groenendijk (1997, p. 208) indicates that there would be an informational asymmetry advantage for the agent in the principal-agent relationship. As Gronedijk goes on to say, the agent's interests will differ from those of the principal, allowing the agent to use the information asymmetry advantage against the principal's interests for their profit. It is believed that there is an "agency" problem if the agent commits corrupt conduct to further their interests (Wawrosz, 2022, p. 5). This is because it is happening against the principal's wishes. The agent's propensity to engage in corruption must be addressed to change the relationship through an anti-corruption policy.

Heywood (2018) claims that political scientists, economists, sociologists, and international organizations like the International Monetary Fund (IMF) and the World Bank have all utilized the principal-agent concept as one of the most well-known anti-corruption frameworks. Therefore, it could be reasonable to suppose that development banks who are modelling their anti-corruption activities after those of the World Bank would also be implicitly using principal-agent theory tenets. In the scenario presented by Bislev (2018), multilateral development banks serve as the principals and interact with the agents—the recipients of funding—who are more inclined to engage in corrupt behaviour since they stand to gain more from the financial proceeds. A borrower-lender relationship exists in a sense, with the lender (the principal) vulnerable to the borrower (the agent), who may engage in corrupt activities. Anti-corruption initiatives influenced by the principal-agent approach may call for measures such as transparency and accountability of agencies to enable the principal to monitor and sanction the agent as well as efforts to align the principal's and the agent's goals (Walton & Jones, 2017, pp. 2–3).

Before Collective Action Theory emerged to offer an alternative explanation for corruption, the principal-agent model of corruption which had a long history in economic discourse and literature from other disciplines studying corruption. The Collection Action Approach views both principals and agents as potentially corrupt, in contrast to the Principal-Agent Framework, which places the burden of proof for corruption on "the agent" (Persson et al., 2013, p. 456). According to the Collective Action framework, "actors engage in corrupt behaviour not because they morally approve of it or do not understand the negative consequences for society at large, but because as long as they expect everyone else to play foul, they perceive the short-term benefits of engaging in corrupt behaviour to be greater than the costs" (Ibid, p. 457). Since everyone is aware of how ubiquitous corruption is in an institution, it almost becomes the accepted norm. According to Marquette and Peiffer (2015, p. 6), the Collective

Action theory "can make sense of the fact that in a setting where everyone is believed to be engaging in corruption, there are few incentives for individuals to abstain." According to Marquette and Peiffer's scenario, attempts to combat corruption that uses the principal-agent paradigm may be unsuccessful because the ostensibly "principled principal(s)" may be corrupt and will only care about themselves and their narrow interests (Persson et al., 2013, p. 451).

Therefore, more collectively focused strategies would be required for combating corruption in scenarios based on the Collective Action Theory premise. The collective and coordinated anti-corruption strategies are also known as "collective action" strategies and involve cooperative collaboration efforts across stakeholders to enlist weak individual players in an alliance of like-minded organizations (World Bank, 2008, p. 4). There are, however, some issues with the collective action strategy. First, according to Martinsson (2021, p. 274), institutional corruption's high sophistication level reduces opportunities for widespread collective action. Second, social groups that are most likely to suffer from the negative effects of institutional corruption are left out of the policy-making process and are less likely to take part in non-state-sanctioned collective action in the first place.

Aside from the Principal-Agent Theory and the Collective Action perspective, there is another corruption perspective that looks beyond individuals and groups. Institutional corruption, in the words of Lessig (2013, p. 2), "is manifest when a systemic and strategic influence, which is legal, or even currently ethical, undermines the effectiveness of the institution by diverting it from its purpose or weakening its ability to achieve its purpose, including, to the extent relevant to its purpose, weakening either the public's trust in that institution or the institution's inherent trustworthiness."

Failure to consider how corruption functions in specific social, economic, and political contexts has been criticized as a weakness of the principal-agent paradigm, which Institutional Theory solves (Martinsson, 2021, p. 272). Martinsson (2021, p. 274), who favours an institutional approach to combating corruption, also makes the point that while both the principal-agent and collective-action frameworks offer various approaches to the same problem, neither provides a comprehensive framework capable of addressing all mechanisms facilitating institutional corruption. Therefore, while corruption can happen on an individual level, it can also happen at the institutional level and involve external environmental elements. When corruption goes unpunished, there may be a perception that an institutional design is complicit in it (Wawrosz, 2022). Likewise, the institutional theory also emphasizes the need to understand the social context of corruption as well as proffering a framework of how corruption becomes entrenched in organisations, institutions, and society, even though there can be anti-corruption efforts (Luo, 2005).

The necessity to comprehend the social context of corruption is also emphasized by institutional theory, which also provides a framework for how corruption creeps into organizations, institutions, and society despite anti-corruption initiatives (Luo, 2005). Studies like those by Debski (et al., 2018), which link gender and culture in the practice of corruption in institutional contexts, are instructive in taking the context into account. Megaprojects and infrastructure public projects, which can also be supported by development banks, have been studied using the Institutional Theory. For instance, Institutional Theory is used in a study by Locatelli et al. (2017) to establish the concept of "corrupt project context" and examine the effects of the corrupt context in a large Italian company.

The institutional theory would be used to strengthen political institutions including the executive, legislature, and electoral processes to come up with anti-corruption measures. Even if institutions may be constructed, more anti-corruption measures may still be required. According to certain studies, establishing organizations to combat corruption might not be sufficient. In one instance, the World Bank and donor organizations played a key role in creating an institutional framework to fight corruption in Uganda, although the level of corruption did not significantly decrease (Rothstein, 2018).

The three theories—Principal-Agent, Collective Action, and Institutional Theory—might focus on various aspects of corruption and consequently have different methodologies, but they are not wholly incompatible. For example, Marquette and Peiffer (2015, p. 6) contend that both principal-agent and collective action approaches presuppose individual rationality, according to which people will commit corruption when it serves their interests and when they believe they won't be held accountable. Thompson (2018, p. 508) asserts that the collective action strategy can be used to combat institutional corruption if appropriately modified. The type and degree of corruption should be considered while putting each of the theories into practice.

For instance, the principal-agent concept may be used to describe corruption that takes place on a personal level. Institutional Theory, on the other hand, becomes a lens through which to analyze such an environment if there is institutional corruption, such as when a state agency or government department has widespread corruption. The collective action theory may offer some insights into situations where systemic corruption affects the entire society. In a way, many theories can be used by the subtleties of corruption that may be felt in a specific environment. Graaf (2007) contends that techniques for controlling corruption should be based less on rigid adherence to theory and more on what works in specific situations.

Indeed, the anti-corruption strategies that are suggested have always been influenced by corruption theory (Graaf, 2007, p. 76). This can lead to misalignments between corruption theory and real-world situations, which can lead to a theoretical mischaracterization of corruption. For example, this can happen when a collective action problem is initially thought of as a principal-agent problem (Persson et al., 2013). As some anti-corruption initiatives have been shown to fail (Graaf, 2007; Persson et al., 2013; Rothstein, 2018), the conclusion would be that other attempts may also fail if misinformed by the wrong theory.

MULTILATERAL DEVELOPMENT BANKS ROLE IN COMBATTING CORRUPTION

The African Development Bank

The African Development Bank (AfDB) was established in 1964 to assist the African continental region as independent African nations emerged from colonialism. The bank was intended to serve as an institutional vehicle for post-colonial Africa's socioeconomic growth. The African Development Bank (AfDB), which is similarly organized to the World Bank as a "Group," offers both concessional and non-concessional loans, which have less lenient conditions and market-based interest rates. The AfDB established the concessional window fund in 1973, which enables it to offer loans to companies in the private sector. The bank's window for concessional loans permitted non-regional countries to join and contribute. Consequently, countries like the US joined the fund in 1976 (Nelson, 2020, p. 3). By 1979, non-regional members of the bank included European countries as well as Canada, Japan, the United Arab Emirates, and Brazil (Krasner, 1981, p. 323). A contemplative question can be asked as to why the bank sought to invite participation from non-African countries. Essentially, the invitation to join non-African countries was prompted by the need for the AfDB to raise capital from wealthier countries, given its limited resources though this would be undertaken without diluting regional control (Krasner, 1981, p. 323).

Governance and Managing Political Influence

The AfDB is a multilateral development, and as with other similar continental institutions like the Inter-American Development Bank, it is officially owned and governed by all the borrowing countries of Africa (Wang, 2017, p. 113). Its ownership structure would suggest that it is close to political influence from African states, elite policymakers, and international advocacy networks which may be able to affect its policy standards (Park, 2023, p. 66). Given that the bank is controlled by African nations, there may be a worry that it would be too close to the continent's political governance issues to get involved. As a result, the bank's charter has been designed to prevent it from taking politics into account when making lending decisions (Bøås, 1998, p. 121).

Multilateral development banks frequently find themselves in a catch-22 situation. They have come under fire for meddling with national sovereignty when they set restrictions, but on the other side, it is expected of them not to turn a blind eye to violations of human rights (Head, 2004). The AfDB has had to walk a fine line between satisfying the demands of the extra-regional donor countries, whom the Bank depends on for capital increase, that it pay attention to governance issues, while also having to manage the concerns of political interference that may emerge from borrowing countries (Bøås, 1998, p. 121).

Consequently, the AfDB evaluated a report from its African Advisory Council in 1994 that suggested its involvement in promoting good governance and democracy, even if it had been reluctant to do so under the terms of its Charter. What became clear was that, while governance as a topic for the Bank could not be ignored, governance, as linked with democratization, individual political rights, and human rights, had to be avoided if the Bank were to adhere to its charter (Bøås, 1998, p. 128). Given the dilemma, the AfDB decided to embark on studies and knowledge exchange initiatives in Asian countries to gain some insight into how it could deal with governance matters. As Bøås further documents, participants at a workshop on governance and development from six of the region's high-performing economies—Hong Kong, Indonesia, Japan, South Korea, Singapore, and Taiwan—met in April 1995. Unsurprisingly, there was a great deal of concern among borrowers throughout the workshop's discussion that an ADB governance strategy would represent the preferences and experiences of donors. Participants in the session voiced concern that the definitions of governance focused on individual political rights and ignored Asian experiences of governance as communal economic rights. The AfDB subsequently settled on the economic dimension of governance, which defines good governance as sound developmental management and emphasizes collective economic rights, rather than the overtly political dimension of governance (democracy, individual political rights, and human rights) (Bøås, 1998, p. 129).

Given the recurrent concerns about the influence of Western donor countries, the institutional design of the AfDB has been configured to shield it from donors from other countries. For instance, to preserve its African identity, the leadership of the Board is made up of regional members, and the president must be a citizen of an African nation (Nyadera et al., 2022). Even though African governments as stakeholders oversee internal governance procedures, there is still a constant risk that the AfDB will be subject to pressure from donor Western nations.

AfDB's Anti-Corruption Approach

Internal Institutional Mechanisms

The AfDB has set up internal organizational functions to combat corruption. The Office of the Auditor General's Anti-Corruption and Fraud Division (ACFD) was set up to safeguard the integrity of all AfDB activities by looking into claims of staff misconduct, fraud, or corruption in AfDB operations, and fostering a professional culture that discourages corrupt activities among staff and regional member nations (Carrasco, Carrington & Lee, 2009, p. 12). In the contemporary era, AfDB runs a dedicated Integrity and Ant-Corruption Department. The Department oversees creating proactive countermeasures to lessen the likelihood of corruption in Bank Group operations and participates in sanctions decisions made against individuals and businesses found to be involved in corrupt practices in Bank activities based on its investigative findings (AfDB, 2010, p.3). The Department's activities are normally reported in an annual report-type format which is released every year. AfDB will also openly and periodically disclose entities that have been involved in corrupt practices. For instance, in one announcement in 2022, the African Development Bank Group announced that Entreprise de Commerce et de Construction Immobilière, a limited liability business, would be barred for nine months for dishonest practices, following an investigation by the Bank's Office of Integrity and Anti-Corruption (*African Development Bank debars Entreprise de Commerce et de Construction Immobilière for nine months for fraudulent practices*, 2022).

In another incident concerning 2006 and 2011, the companies, then known as Alstom Power Generation AG, Alstom Power GmbH, and Alstom Egypt for Power & Transport Projects S.A.E., engaged in two instances of corrupt practices and one instance of fraudulent practice in connection with the Bank-financed Suez Thermal Power Plant Project and the El Kureimat III Power Project, in Egypt. The Bank's Office of Integrity and Anti-Corruption issued a debarment period of about 48 months and the same debarment would also be implementable by the Asian Development Bank, the European Bank for Reconstruction and Development, the Inter-American Development Bank, and the World Bank Group, by the Agreement for Mutual Enforcement of Debarment Decisions (*Integrity in Development Projects: The African Development Bank and GE Power Reach Settlement on Legacy Alstom Misconduct,* 2019).

Additionally, AfDB has an Advisory Committee on Corruption and Fraud (the ACCF), whose main duty is to counsel AfDB's President on the conclusions of any final investigations and any suggestions regarding corrupt and dishonest behaviour (Seiler & Madir, 2012, p. 17).

If the AfDB President finds evidence of the alleged corruption, they may order the party in question to repay any loans they have received, halt the project they are involved in, launch internal investigations against any responsible bank employees, add the responsible contractor to a "black list," and refer the offending party to the relevant member state's law enforcement agency (Carrasco, Carrington & Lee, 2009, p. 13).

Participation in Coordinated Anti-Corruption Initiatives by Regional Development Banks

It is clear from the AfDB's institutional makeup that it has been institutionally modelled after the World Bank and is hence prone to adopt some of its methods (Park, 2023, p. 62). It also appears that institutional modelling based on the World Bank has become commonplace in anti-corruption procedures among multilateral development banks. The African Development Bank is known to have imitated the World

Bank's anti-corruption tactics, rules, and processes, as with other regional development banks (Deming, 2010, p. 883). In 2012, the AfDB approved its sanctions policies. In previous years, the AfDB's sanctions processes had involved using instruments entailing a zero-tolerance policy against corruption; procurement processes on goods; procedures for the use of consultants, and the Uniform Framework for Preventing and Combating Corruption (Madir, 2019, p. 64). The Uniform Framework for Preventing and Combating Corruption is a culmination of the joint International Financial Institution Anti-Corruption Task Force (IFI Task Force) established in 2006 which included several multilateral development banks, including the AfDB, who sought a harmonized and consistent approach to combat corruption. The Uniform Framework contained a common set of definitions of sanctionable conduct as well as common principles and guidelines for investigations that would direct how development banks would carry out investigations (Fariello & Daly, 2013, p. 109). The framework recognises four sanctionable practices including corrupt, fraudulent, collusive, coercive, or obstructive practices such as deliberately hiding information or evidence from an MDB (Seiler & Madir, 2012, p. 9).

The Uniform Framework is just one of various multilateral development banks' initiatives to provide uniform, universal frameworks for battling corruption. Other initiatives along these lines include the 2010 Agreement for Mutual Enforcement of Debarment Decision, which was signed by the Asian Development Bank, World Bank, and European Bank for Reconstruction and Development in addition to the African Development Bank. The agreement establishes a framework within which entities or individuals found to have engaged in misconduct in development projects funded by an international financial institution (an "IFI"), in cases where such an entity or individual has been barred for more than a year by one IFI, may be punished by the other participating development banks for the same misconduct (AfDB, 2012). In terms of the agreement, MDBs may impose several possible sanctions, ranging from the least severe option, a letter of reprimand, to the most severe, permanent debarment with other sanctions including conditional non-debarment, fixed-term debarment, and restitution or reimbursement, all of which may be subject to aggravating or mitigating factors such as the severity of misconduct or harm caused (Atta-Krah & Laryea, 2021, p.6).

Due to the MDBs' shared and coordinated approaches, the AfDB employs sanctions policies that are comparable to those of the other regional banks. The MDBs typically use a two-tier sanctions system that was first created by the World Bank. The AfDB's Integrity and Anti-Corruption Department investigates allegations of illegal behaviour as the first stage in the penalties process, just like the World Bank does. In the first review state, the Integrity and Anti-Corruption Department submits a report to the penalties Commissioner, who then decides whether to impose penalties if the allegations of sanctionable conduct are found to be true by a preponderance of the evidence (Atta-Krah & Laryea, 2021, p.4). Respondents will be given the chance to challenge the Sanctions Commissioner's decision before the Sanctions Appeals Board in the second stage of the process. The Board also evaluates the appeal (Ibid).

The shared sanctions regime among MDBs implies that organizations doing business with such entities would need to be aware of the mutual enforcement agreement where there is a potential for global sanctions even for an illegal activity conducted in a single nation (Seiler & Madir, 2012, p. 28). The consequences can be most dire for borrowing entities. For instance, both the World Bank and AfDB have a three-year debarment implying that any debarment longer than a year immediately results in a cross-debarment that forbids a corruption respondent from taking part in any bid or project managed, funded, or sponsored by any other MDB, including all government initiatives that make use of MDB finances (Atta-Krah & Laryea, 2021, p. 6). Organisations that have faced debarment will often be listed on the AfDB's website in the interest of transparency, which may, in turn, serve as an alert system to country-based law enforcement authorities. The multilateral development banks' harmonized sanctions approaches represent an acknowledgement of the need for a global, coordinated effort to tackle corruption and how the development banks have an opportunity to contribute by serving as both promoters and models of global best practices (Fariello & Daly, 2013, p. 112).

Facilitating a Knowledge Base on Corruption in African Contexts

Aside from internal organizational arrangements to combat corruption, including having a dedicated department and the AfDB's efforts to benchmark its sanctions practices with other MDBs, knowledge exchange is another layer of activity. Through initiatives including workshops, conferences, and the creation of working papers and research, the AfDB mobilises a range of actions to promote corruption awareness and guidance. The role of AfDB in knowledge facilitation is not an altogether unique activity to the institution. Multilateral development banks, such as the AfDB, have realized that, in addition to their roles as financial intermediaries, they must also play a significant role as knowledge intermediaries if they are to address the socio-economic development challenges in their jurisdictional areas so that the acquisition, promotion, transfer, and transformation of knowledge complement resource transfers of financial resources (African Development Bank, 2001, p. 150).

The African Development Bank's role in economic knowledge and policy research in Africa consists of three main components of policy co-ordination through country policy dialogues and sectoral policy formulation; development research and dissemination; as well as support for research institutions and capacity building (African Development Bank, 2001, p. 151). Typically, the AfDB's knowledge products include working papers, evaluation reports, country profiles, and other ad hoc publications which may include sponsored research.

Among the various topics covered by the AfDB's knowledge repository are country profiles of various African countries which focus on their governance arrangements, including national instruments to combat corruption. Such reports typically look at the governance situation of a country including how it advances accountability, transparency, and public participation as well as combatting corruption and money laundering. Within the report, the AfDB will typically advance a set of recommendations on how the governance arrangements could be improved. For example, in a country assessment of Cameroon, recommendations on how it could strengthen its anti-corruption efforts include relocating its National Anti-Corruption Observatory which was then housed in the Prime Minister's Office so that it could grant more independence and build its capacities as well as those of anti-corruption units set up in ministries (African Development Bank, 2004).

On an ongoing basis, AfDB also hosts and participates in workshops and conferences themed around the topic of corruption. In 2022, the bank participated in the International Anti-Corruption Conference (IACC), an annual conference held in Washington D.C, United States, and held a conference in partnership with the Association of Anti-Corruption Authorities in Africa (AAACA) held in Abidjan, Nigeria (PIAC, 2022).

Within the ambit of capacity building, AfDB also provides technical advisory support to African governments for institutional capacity building to enhance good governance and accountability. Examples of initiatives include the Public Finance Governance Support Project in Cameroon funded with UA 12.4 million, of which UA 11.6 million ADF loan and UA 820,000 ADF grant, which seeks to strengthen the institutional and organizational environment of public finance management including fighting against corruption and illegal financial flows (African Development Bank Group, 2022).

Partnerships With Other International Organisations

The AfDB has prioritized collaborations with other African and international players in the fight against corruption as one of its main focal areas across its range of responsibilities. Among the goals of its anti-corruption and integrity business unit is to engage with internal and external partners to combat fraud and corruption in the context of development (PIAC, 2022). To this end, the bank tries to collaborate with numerous regional and global organizations that have an anti-corruption role. In 2019, with the end goal of developing a continental information-sharing platform for anti-corruption investigations, the bank started negotiations with several anticorruption agencies in regional member countries aimed at formalizing bilateral relationships for exchanging information and referring corruption cases. In 2020, it achieved headway by signing memorandums of understanding with Kenyan and Nigerian anti-corruption organizations, among other developments (Atta-Krah & Laryea, 2021, p. 9).

Further partnerships have been advanced with various international organisations such as the Organization for Economic Cooperation and Development (OECD). In 2008, the Joint Initiative to Support Business Integrity and Anti-Bribery Efforts in Africa) was launched by the African Development Bank (AfDB) and the (OECD). The initiative sought to build African government capacities in enforcing anti-bribery laws and to improve public sector integrity. The *African Union Convention on Preventing and Combating Corruption*, the *United Nations Convention Against Corruption*, and the *OECD Convention on Combating Bribery of Foreign Public Officials* serve as the foundation for the initiative's work. Emerging from the joint OECD-AfDB initiative, knowledge resources that were borne include a publication that reviews business integrity and anti-bribery policies for 20 countries in Africa (OECD/African Development Bank, 2012). Another output stemming from the OECD-AfDB partnership is an *Anti-Bribery Policy and Compliance Guidance for African Companies* whose goal is to advise private businesses operating in African nations on how to avoid, identify, and deal with corruption in their commercial dealings, thereby reducing the supply side of bribery. The AfDB has also made various inroads to forge partnerships and working relationships with various African anti-corruption stakeholders including the Association of Anti-Corruption Authorities in Africa and the African Union as well as ad hoc collaborations with African governments, especially in institutional capacity-building initiatives.

THEORETICAL REFLECTIONS FROM THE CASE STUDY

The Principal-Agent, Institutional, and Collective Action theories were discussed earlier in this chapter. The AfDB's examination of anti-corruption efforts appears to show that all three approaches can be used to explain how it operates. According to the Principal-Agent Theory premise, corruption is frequently seen as a field in which the agent can engage. In the context of development banking, the principal is a development finance institution acting as a lender, and the agent is the borrower. We can infer from the sanctions frameworks that punitive actions, such as debarments among all the multilateral development banks, are implemented to isolate or expose a borrowing company (the agent) that has been charged with corruption. The sanctions regime usually goes to further lengths to punish an agent.

The question of what happens if a corrupt activity is committed with the knowledge of bank employees may then be raised. In this situation, institutional theory could be used to explain factors to reduce corruption within the company. For instance, the AfDB has a code of conduct that expressly forbids staff from engaging in acts of corruption as well as an internal whistleblowing procedure. Additionally, the bank can investigate corruption both internally and outside because of the existence of an anti-corruption department. The decision to establish an anti-corruption business unit inside the bank itself demonstrates the understanding that institutional measures must be used to combat corruption. Additionally, AfDB also participates in institutional capacity-building efforts external to the organization such as providing technical assistance and advisory support to anti-corruption agencies or regimes in the various African member countries. Its knowledge exchange platforms and initiatives point again to its commitment to empowering various institutions including governments and other organizational stakeholders with the capacity to combat corruption.

Regarding the AfDB's efforts to seek alliances with various international organizations and anti-corruption entities, the Collective Action Theory as a framework of study should be taken into consideration. As mentioned above, multilateral development banks have realized the necessity to coordinate their anti-corruption actions, for example through cooperative initiatives like the Uniform Framework that various development banks have joined. The World Bank and other development banks, including the African Development Bank, appear to have accepted this idea. Partnerships against corruption appear to be a major focus of AfDB initiatives. The necessity to involve a variety of societal players, even the business community and civil society, has been the focus of AfDB operations like conferences and capacity-building initiatives and speaks to the importance of involving these parties.

Thus, when considered as frameworks to combat corruption, the Principal-Agent, Institutional, and Collective Action theories can be collectively implemented, as the AfDB case study indicates. Theoretical discourse on corruption should allow for cross-referencing of different ideas at the intersection of theory and application because one theoretical framework might not always give enough support for the assessment and mitigation of corruption. Again, there might be more nuances of corruption that are best explained by one theoretical framework than another, but this shouldn't stop people from being aware of how corruption theory can be cross-pollinated to comprehend the complexities of corruption. According to the Collective Action hypothesis, should corruption become more sophisticated, the involvement of several stakeholders becomes more crucial. The Principal-Agent framework, however, may explain individualistic or micro-stage actions of corruption if they may be accruing at a small scale. There are quite a few different corruption theories that offer their points of emphasis in addition to the ones covered in this chapter. Since corruption tends to progress into more sophisticated methods that may not always be easily identified, the area of anti-corruption studies is best seen as a dynamic one in which we should go beyond comprehending only recent advancements.

RECOMMENDATIONS AND DIRECTIONS FOR FUTURE STUDIES

This chapter has shed light on the function of development banks in the fight against corruption, with the AfDB as a prime example. There are some indications of how these institutions could contribute to the fight against corruption. Firstly, they have developed a technical aptitude for comprehending financial transactions about development or infrastructure projects through their work as financiers. Due to their extensive institutional memory and the fact that financial institutions like the AfDB have been around since the 1960s, they have a great deal of knowledge about the financial side of development projects and how corruption can creep into project finance. The technical expertise on infrastructure projects including their financing could be an invaluable resource for government infrastructure development planning.

Secondly, development banks have developed networks and partnerships with other stakeholders within their various areas of responsibility over time, again because of their lengthy existence. Beyond just being funders, they have worked to rally other stakeholders to develop coordinated measures to fight corruption. They could be thought of as knowledge brokers who are ideally situated to offer governments and other stakeholders who are willing to address the issue of eradicating corruption research, technical, and advisory support. Governments would be wise to approach them for advice on institutional transformation and for research to support evidence-led actions for combating corruption given their role as facilitators of knowledge sharing. As stakeholder mobilizers, they serve as a centre where different anti-corruption stakeholders, including civil society, can congregate to exchange ideas and innovations through the numerous platforms that they may offer, such as seminars, conferences, or training programmes.

When we consider development banks as more than just financiers but also knowledge brokers, we can see that they make excellent partners for anti-corruption groups as repositories of technical assistance and research. Governments would do well to approach these entities for advisory support when contemplating anti-corruption initiatives. Development banks, however, are also susceptible to political sway because they play important roles in the political economy of development. The political will of governments to support them in their various tasks determines whether they can continue to exist as organizations as governments, which they report to, and are their main stakeholders.

For this chapter, it is clear that development banks have demonstrated a role in anti-corruption and may ultimately be key actors in the fight against corruption. Specifically, the African Development Bank is an institution worth observing in the African setting. More thorough studies analyzing their performance and the degree to which they have succeeded in eliminating corruption are required to fully comprehend their role. This chapter merely provided an overview. Further empirical research may produce more precise data on the reduction of corruption because of their actions or, more crucially, the amount of corruption that has been exposed because of their involvement or interventions. In the context of financial institutional contexts like the development finance fraternity occupied by development banks, there are additional opportunities for more academically oriented studies desiring to try out other corruption hypotheses not mentioned in the discussion.

CONCLUSION

The chapter examined the African Development Bank's function considering the multilateral development banks' broader mandate for participating in anti-corruption activities. Given the variety of functions these organizations can provide outside of only financial support, distinct roles—and even potential new ones—can be considered. The conversation also touched on a few theories on corruption that, taken as a whole, seem to provide some insight into how to combat corruption, as the African Development Bank case study illustrated. This proves that many corruption theories can be used to understand how corruption is dealt with in a singular setting.

In the future, national governments should hopefully take more seriously how development banks are emerging as key protagonists in the fight against corruption. Yet on the other hand, as largely state-owned entities, whose independence must be guarded, they remain vulnerable to corruption which may be influenced by the political environment.

REFERENCES

African Development Bank. (2001). A Note on the Contribution of the African Development Bank to Economic Knowledge and Policy in Africa. *African Development Review*, *13*(1), 145–172. doi:10.1111/1467-8268.00034

African Development Bank. (2004). *Cameroon—Country Governance Profile*. https://www.afdb.org/en/documents/project-operations/country-governance-profiles

African Development Bank. (2019). *Integrity in Development Projects: The African Development Bank and GE Power Reach Settlement on Legacy Alstom Misconduct*. Available: https://www.afdb.org/en/news-and-events/integrity-in-development-projects-the-african-development-bank-and-ge-power-reach-settlement-on-legacy-alstom-misconduct-19116

African Development Bank. (2022). *African Development Bank debars Entreprise de Commerce et de Construction Immobilière for nine months for fraudulent practices*. Available: https://www.afdb.org/en/news-and-events/press-releases/african-development-bank-debars-entreprise-de-commerce-et-de-construction-immobiliere-nine-months-fraudulent-practices-53730

Altunbas, Y., Evans, L., & Molyneux, P. (2001). Bank Ownership and Efficiency. *Journal of Money, Credit and Banking*, *33*(4), 926. doi:10.2307/2673929

Atta-Krah, K., & Laryea, T. (2021). *Multilateral development banks and sanctions*. Presentation available https://www.orrick.com/en/Events/2021/08/Multilateral-Development-Bank-Sanctions-and-Investigationspresentation

Bislev, A. (2018). *Analysis of Anti-Corruption measures in Multilateral Development Banks. Masters Thesis*. University of Aalborg. Available https://projekter.aau.dk/projekter/files/290704827/Analysis_of_anti_corruption_measures_in_multilateral_development_banks.pdf

Bøås, M. (1998). Governance as Multilateral Development Bank Policy: The Cases of the African Development Bank and the Asian Development Bank. *European Journal of Development Research*, *10*(2), 117–134. doi:10.1080/09578819808426720

Bruck, N. (2001). Development Banking Concept and Theory. In *Principles and practices of development banking*. ADFIAP-IDF.

Buiter, W., & Fries, S. (2002). *What Should the Multilateral Development Banks do?* Working Paper, 74. European Bank for Reconstruction and Development.

Bunich, G. A., Rovenskiy, Y. A., Akhvlediani, J. T., & Yuriev, Y. (2019). Regional Development Banks: Theory And Practice. *Opcion, 35*(19), 2861-2871.

Carrasco, Carrington, & Lee. (Eds.). (2009). Governance and Accountability: The Regional Development Banks. Boston University International Law Journal, 27(1), 58. doi:10.4324/9781315254098

De Luna-Martínez, J., & Vicente, C. L. (2012). *Global Survey of Development Banks*. The World Bank. doi:10.1596/1813-9450-5969

Debski, J., Jetter, M., Mösle, S., & Stadelmann, D. (2018). Gender and corruption: The neglected role of culture. *European Journal of Political Economy*, *55*, 526–537. doi:10.1016/j.ejpoleco.2018.05.002

Deming, S. H. (2010). Anti-Corruption Policies: Eligibility and Debarment Practices at the World Bank and Regional Development Banks. *The International Lawyer*, *44*(2), 871–885.

Dinc, I. (2005). Politicians and banks: Political influences on government-owned banks in emerging markets. *Journal of Financial Economics*, *77*(2), 453–479. doi:10.1016/j.jfineco.2004.06.011

Fariello, F. A., & Daly, C. C. (2013). Coordinating the Fight Against Corruption among MDBS: The Past, Present and Future of Sanctions. *The George Washington International Law Review*, 45.

Frigerio, M., & Vandone, D. (2020). European development banks and the political cycle. *European Journal of Political Economy*, *62*, 101852. doi:10.1016/j.ejpoleco.2019.101852

Graaf, G. D. (2007). Causes of Corruption: Towards a Contextual Theory of Corruption. *Public Administration Quarterly*, *32*(1), 39–86.

Groenendijk, N. (1997). A principal-agent model of corruption. *Crime. Crime, Law, and Social Change*, *27*(3/4), 207–229. doi:10.1023/A:1008267601329

Gutierrez, E., Rudolph, H. P., Homa, T., & Beneit, E. B. (2011). Development Banks Role and Mechanisms to Increase their Efficiency. *World Bank Policy Research Working Paper*, *5729*(July), 1–37. doi:10.1596/1813-9450-5729

Hainz, C., & Kleimeier, S. (2012). Political risk, project finance, and the participation of development banks in syndicated lending. *Journal of Financial Intermediation*, *21*(2), 287–314. doi:10.1016/j.jfi.2011.10.002

Head. (2004). For Richer or Poorer—Assessing the Criticisms Directed at the Multilateral Development Banks. *U. Kan. L. Rev.*, *54*(241).

Hu, B., Schclarek, A., Xu, J., & Yan, J. (2022). Long-term finance provision: National development banks vs commercial banks. *World Development*, *158*, 105973. Advance online publication. doi:10.1016/j.worlddev.2022.105973

Krasner, S. D. (1981). Power structures and regional development banks. *International Organization*, *35*(2), 303–328. doi:10.1017/S0020818300032458

Lazzarini, S. G., Musacchio, A., Bandeira-de-Mello, R., & Marcon, R. (2015a). What do state-owned development banks do? Evidence from BNDES, 2002-09. *World Development*, *66*, 237–253. doi:10.1016/j.worlddev.2014.08.016

Lessig, L. (2013). "Institutional Corruption" Defined. *The Journal of Law, Medicine & Ethics*, *41*(3), 553–555. doi:10.1111/jlme.12063 PMID:24088144

Locatelli, G., Mariani, G., Sainati, T., & Greco, M. (2017). Corruption in public projects and megaprojects: There is an elephant in the room! *International Journal of Project Management*, *35*(3), 252–268. doi:10.1016/j.ijproman.2016.09.010

Luo, Y. (2005). An Organizational Perspective of Corruption. *Management and Organization Review, 1*(01), 119–154. doi:10.1111/j.1740-8784.2004.00006.x

Madir, J. (2019). *What Process is Due – Sanctions Regimes of Multilateral Development Banks*. University of Westminster.

Marquette, H., & Pfeiffer, C. (2015). *Corruption and collective action*. The Developmental Leadership Program (DLP) and U4 Research Paper 32.

Martinsson, J. (2021). Combatting institutional corruption: The policy-centered approach. *Crime, Law, and Social Change, 75*(3), 267–280. doi:10.100710611-021-09934-5

Micco, A., Yanez, M., & Panizza, U. (2007). Bank ownership and performance. Does politics matter? *Journal of Banking & Finance, 31*(1). doi:10.1016/S0305-750X(01)00073-0

Nelson, P. J. (2001). Transparency mechanisms at the multilateral development banks. *World Development, 29*(11), 1835–1847. doi:10.1016/S0305-750X(01)00073-0

Nelson, R. M. (n.d.). *Multilateral Development Banks: Overview and Issues for Congress*. Academic Press.

Nyadera, I. N., Agwanda, B., Onder, M., & Mukhtar, I. A. (2022). Multilateralism, Developmental Regionalism, and the African Development Bank. *Politics and Governance, 10*(2). Advance online publication. doi:10.17645/pag.v10i2.4871

OECD/African Development Bank. (2012). *Stocktaking of Business Integrity and Anti-Bribery Legislation, Policies and Practices in Twenty African Countries*. Available: https://www.oecd.org/daf/anti-bribery/stocktakingofbusinessintegrityandanti-briberylegislationpoliciesandpracticesintwentyafricancountries

Park, S. (2023). The African Development Bank and the Accountability Policy Norm: Endogenous Change, Norm Conformance, and the Development Finance Regime Complex. *Global Governance: A Review of Multilateralism and International Organizations, 29*(1), 61–84. doi:10.1163/19426720-02901003

Persson, A., Rothstein, B., & Teorell, J. (2013). Why Anticorruption Reforms Fail-Systemic Corruption as a Collective Action Problem: Why Anticorruption Reforms Fail. *Governance: An International Journal of Policy, Administration and Institutions, 26*(3), 449–471. doi:10.1111/j.1468-0491.2012.01604.x

PIAC (Office of Integrity and Anti-Corruption) African Development Bank Group. (2022). *Annual Report*. Available: https://www.afdb.org/en/documents/integrity-and-anti-corruption-department-annual-report-2022

Rothstein, B. (2018). Fighting Systemic Corruption: The Indirect Strategy. *Daedalus, 147*(3), 35–49. doi:10.1162/daed_a_00501

Sapienza, P. (2004). The effects of government ownership on bank lending. *Journal of Financial Economics, 72*(2), 357–384. doi:10.1016/j.jfineco.2002.10.002

Seiler, N., & Madir, J. (2012). Fight Against Corruption: Sanctions Regimes of Multilateral Development Banks. *Journal of International Economic Law, 15*(1), 5–28. doi:10.1093/jiel/jgr037

Thompson, D. F. (2018). Theories of Institutional Corruption. *Annual Review of Political Science, 21*(1), 495–513. doi:10.1146/annurev-polisci-120117-110316

Thorne, J., & du Toit, C. (2009). A macro-framework for successful development banks. *Development Southern Africa*, *26*(5), 677–694. doi:10.1080/03768350903303183

Walton, G., & Jones, A. (2017). The Geographies of Collective Action, Principal-Agent Theory and Potential Corruption in Papua New Guinea. SSRN *Electronic Journal*. doi:10.2139/ssrn.2993709

Wang, H. (2017). New Multilateral Development Banks: Opportunities and Challenges for Global Governance. *Global Policy*, *8*(1), 113–118. doi:10.1111/1758-5899.12396

Wawrosz, P. (2022). How Corruption Is and Should Be Investigated by Economic Theory. *Economies*, *10*(12), 326. doi:10.3390/economies10120326

Xu, J., Marodon, R., Ru, X., Ren, X., & Wu, X. (2021). What are public development banks and development financing institutions? Qualification criteria, stylized facts, and development trends. *China Economic Quarterly International*, *1*(4), 271–294. doi:10.1016/j.ceqi.2021.10.001

Chapter 18
The Politicization of the Military and the Militarization of Politics:
A Case of Lesotho's Political–Security Discourse

Mahlakeng Khosi Mahlakeng
National University of Lesotho, Lesotho

ABSTRACT

One important notion regarding Lesotho's persistent political and security instability revolves around the politicisation of the military, which ultimately poses major threats to Lesotho's fragile democracy. The security sector, especially the military in Lesotho, is vulnerable to political influence to a point where they are to blame for their undue interference in the political arena. They tend to become involved directly and/indirectly in high-level political battles. Hence this reality is referred to as 'militarisation of politics' and 'politicisation of the military. This phenomenon of exasperating politics-military relations has led to the security sector being actively and openly involved and/or used in high-level political disputes. However, at the heart of Lesotho's culture of violence lies the historical trend of militarisation. This persistent culture of violence can be attributed to the historical relationship between politics and military, but more significantly to events following post-colonialization.

INTRODUCTION

Analytical literature[1] in Lesotho's politics-violence linkages suggests that a worrisome feature of Lesotho politics is the pervasive culture of violence. All assessments of the violent culture in Lesotho conclude that the nation's security services are to blame, particularly the military. The 2019 Global Peace Index (GPI), which places Lesotho at 103 out of 163 violent countries worldwide, is cited by Matlosa (2020, p. 3) to support the severity of the violent culture there (IEP, 2019, p. 9).

DOI: 10.4018/979-8-3693-0477-8.ch018

The politicisation of the security sector and the militarisation of politics are two big challenges to Lesotho's fragile democracy today. Although practically all of the security services are partially at fault for their improper meddling in politics, the military is by far the most important agency. Thus, this fact is known as "*politicisation of the military*" and "*militarisation of politics*" (Matlosa, 2020, p. 5).

Lesotho has a lengthy history of unrest and is currently dealing with the Lesotho Defence Force's (LDF) pollicisation (News24, 2017a). The politicisation of the security sector and/or the vulnerability of the security sector to political influence are two key ideas surrounding the ongoing political and security instability in Lesotho. Indeed, the security sector in Lesotho (i.e., the LDF and the Lesotho Mounted Police Service (LMPS)) is politicised; as a result, they frequently meddle in political affairs and engage directly or indirectly in high-level political conflicts, with one of these institutions or sectors supporting the government or the opposition, respectively (News24, 2017a). Thabane (2017a, p. 1) also expresses serious worries about the regularity of political unrest in Lesotho, particularly in post-colonial Lesotho.

High-level political issues frequently include, utilize, or are actively associated with the security sector. Namely, to repress political activism and either frighten, torture or assassinate politicians (News24, 2017a). Yet, this can be linked to post-colonial developments, but more importantly and to a greater extent, to the historical interaction between politics and the military. Even though Lesotho was under British colonial rule for 100 years (1868–1965), the establishment of strong political–military ties and the subsequent politicisation of the security sector can be attributed to the post–colonial period (1966–present) in Lesotho. This is particularly true of the early 1970s. In a similar vein, Matlosa (2020, p. 5) contends that Lesotho has long had a culture of violence dating back to the period immediately following independence.

According to Matlosa (2017b, p. 142) *one of the biggest threats to Lesotho's fledgling democracy today is the rising spectre of militarisation"*. In Lesotho, militarisation refers to three interconnected trends: (a) the use of force in politics (including the abuse of the military by political actors to gain an advantage over rivals); (b) the establishment of armed militias and vigilante groups by political parties, which primarily involve youth; and (c) the involvement of the security forces (especially the military) in politics along partisan lines to advance the military's corporate interests and/or in the interests of the state. The culmination of all these elements has resulted in a culture of violence that is deeply ingrained in Lesotho's political system (Matlosa, 2020, p. 5). The militarization of political life entails the prioritization of military goals and the military's influence over citizens (Heywood, 2007, p. 401).

Given that there are no tensions, conflicts, or disagreements caused by religious, ethnic, tribal, or racial factors in Lesotho, the level of instability is alarming. To the stability or volatility of Lesotho's security, political divisions (i.e., political ideologies of the left or the right and/or political interests) between indigenous actors for ruling are significant. Furthermore, several historical occurrences can be used to explain the tensions and/or instabilities that have characterized the current political-security discourse (Maundeni, 2010, p. 128).

Unfortunately, a lot of the writings on Lesotho's political instability as a result of the military becoming more politicised tend to analyse the country's ongoing political-military instability in isolation or without acknowledging the impact that historical events have on the country's current unstable environment.

The author recognises and accepts the colonial era's influence on implications for political instability in post-colonial Lesotho even if it is not part of this chapter's research. First, the politics and political activities that are crucial to the political-military instability in Lesotho have been highlighted as one of this chapter's primary central features (i.e., the historical foundation that supports the current political-military landscape). The second factor influencing this instability is political. Finally, the chapter stressed how a certain party-political objective ultimately led to the formation and entrenchment of a culture of a violent and politicised military.

This chapter intends to contribute to the literature that seeks to understand the underlying features of Lesotho's political instability. And it does this by focusing its attention on historical vis-à-vis contemporary issues which it deems imperative in understanding the inability of Lesotho to maintain a stable political and/or military environment. The chapter argues and will later indicate that "*Lesotho underwent certain historical political periods and equally developed a political culture that has become part and parcel of the larger contemporary political agenda*".

BACKGROUND

Lesotho is a sovereign democratic parliamentary constitutional monarch (Coakley, 2002, p. 19.1; Mahao, 2006; Mahlakeng, 2018). This is due to the existence of a monarch who acts as Head of State in contrast to being Head of government[2] and simply plays a ceremonial role and plays no part in the "*political affairs*" of the country (Proctor, 1969, p. 64; 'Nyane, 2016, p. 177). Lesotho is just over 30,000 km2 (11,583 sq mi) in size and has a population of around 2 million. Lesotho is one among a few enclave landlocked states[3] (i.e. surrounded by South Africa – bordered on the East by the Natal, on the South by the Cape, and on the West and North by the Free State) in the World (i.e. the Vatican and San Marino, both within Italy) (Sohn and Gustafson, 1984, p. 129; Lundahl *et al,* 2003, p.3) (see Figure 1).

It is the only autonomous state outside of the Italian peninsula and one of only three that are encircled by the territory of another nation, along with Vatican City and San Marino. Because of its physical isolation (i.e., being a landlocked enclave) and homogeneous population, Lesotho's socioeconomic and political behaviour presents a special situation for examination. Its issues with just social, economic, and political survival are grave and delicate (Sohn and Gustafson, 1984, p. 129). Furthermore, it is crucial to recognize that due to these traits, Lesotho is effectively a prisoner of geography and policy, respectively (Khadiagala and Lyons, 2001, p. 139), making the country's survival in international politics and security extremely precarious. Understanding these traits is crucial for understanding historical and modern political behaviour in light of the security environment.

The character and socio-political discourse of Lesotho is distinctive in two ways. First of all, Lesotho is a landlocked "enclave" state. So far as Africa is concerned, it is the only state with such an uncomfortable unique geographic landscape. This implies that it is completely encircled by a nation (South Africa), which makes its issues and survival in the world political economy more delicate and serious than those of other states because of its sole dependence on its surrounding neighbours for socioeconomic and political survival. And secondly, Lesotho was predominantly characterized by armed struggle before and after this geographic position, including the Lifaqane/ Difaqane/ Mfecane Wars (1818–1835) and the Anglo–Boer War (1899–1902). (Mothibe, 2002, p. 15; Mothibe and Ntabeni, 2002, p. 43). Consequently, military prowess became crucial to its political survival in this region.

Figure 1. Map of the Kingdom of Lesotho
https://www.mapsofindia.com/world-map/lesotho/

LESOTHO'S POLITICAL-SECURITY DISCOURSE AND ITS RELEVANCE

It is crucial to comprehend the aforementioned, but especially the postcolonial political and security nature of Lesotho, to comprehend the country's current political and security landscape about political and security instability. This will be extremely beneficial to all parties involved and policymakers (including civil society, governments, NGOs, and IGOs, etc.) in their efforts to offer viable short--, medium--, and long-term solutions to the country's ongoing political and security instability.

Historical Political-Security Context

The politicisation of the military in Lesotho is not a new phenomenon. Matlosa's (2020) article "*Pondering the Culture of Violence in Lesotho: A Case for Demilitarisation*" grapples with the entrenched culture of violence in contemporary Lesotho. He contends that the historical pattern of militarisation is at the root of the violent culture in Lesotho (Matlosa, 2020, p. 1). The current social, economic, political, peace and security situation in Lesotho is a result of events, situations and environment of Lesotho following independence from Britain in 1966. This political–military relation can be traced back and/or attributed to several historical socio-political events which can be categorised into two (2) notable eras. These include "*autocratic rule*" [1970-1986], and "*military rule*" [1986-1993].

Force, especially that of the security branch, was primarily employed in each of these times periods to "keep the political and social status quo" and to gain access to, preserve, and/or exercise government power. Understanding these occurrences and the post-colonial milieu will also address misunderstandings and disinformation among individuals taking part in peace-building processes, both of which have contributed to unsuccessful solutions. The nature and politics of post-colonial Lesotho are largely the basis of the current political agenda vis-à-vis political culture. What is later experienced in the current "*democratic civilian rule*" [1993-present] is a result and consequence of these two eras respectively.

Autocratic Rule [1970-1986]

Anti-colonial and/or nationalist movements that were structurally organized began to arise in the first decades of the 20th century as a form of global resistance against colonial control. This also applied to Lesotho, which at the time was a protectorate of Britain and was known as Basutoland. Political pressure forced Britain to relent and grant Lesotho independence (i.e. equality and native self-driven social, economic and political governance and control) (Weisfelder, 1974, p. 398). Yet, because the British preferred "chieftainship" (i.e., social, political, and economic entitlement) to "commoners" and wanted to continue controlling Lesotho's socio-political and economic affairs, political power belonged to and was equally vested in those who were monarchical (Nyeko, 2002a, p. 132).

As a result, the Basutoland National Party (BNP), afterwards known as the Basotho National Party and heavily influenced and led by local chiefs, was established in 1958–1959 under the influence of British–Catholics. Its main objective was to combat the radical socialist rhetoric of the Basutoland Congress Party (later renamed Basotho Congress Party) and its promotion of commoners' interests at the expense of chiefs, which threatened to undermine Britain's social, political, and economic interests (Thabane, 2002, p. 115). Like any other colonized area in Africa and the world, British colonial rule was beneficial due to its dominance over and exclusive control of internal issues (i.e. social, legal, security, political, and economic) (Nyeko, 2002b, p. 154-64).

The socio-political environment was characterised by "intense politically motivated military and/or police brutality" when Lesotho gained independence from the British Empire's 98-year reign [1868-1966]. Before achieving independence on October 4th, 1966, Lesotho held its first democratic elections in April 1965. The Marema-Tlou Party (MTP), afterwards known as the Marema-Tlou Freedom Party (MFP), which likewise opposed the ideological leaning of the BCP, and the BNP, led by Chief Jonathan Leabua, ran in the elections.

Out of a total of 60 parliamentary seats, the BNP won 31 to the BCP's 25 and the MFP's four, narrowly defeating the BCP. Leabua served as Prime Minister of the BNP and guided Lesotho toward independence (Nyeko, 2002b, p. 170). The opposition BCP and MFP, who now wanted independence delayed, protested the election results, claiming that the BNP had corrupted the process with the implicit cooperation of the British colonial authorities. After that, there were violent confrontations that claimed a lot of lives (Pule, 2002a, p. 179).

The creation of a security department was essential for upholding the Leabua-British 60s regime. Hence, using force (such as a police force or paramilitary force) has become the norm. Furthermore, the motivations were political. As a result, a "Police Mobile Unit" or "Paramilitary Police" was established (Pule, 2002a, p. 179). When the then-prime minister of Lesotho, Leabua Jonathan of the Basotho National Party (BNP), nullified the 1970 election, suspended the 1966 constitution, and controlled the country by decree until 1986, it was the PMU, led by a British officer named Fredrick Roach, that enabled the country's first coup (Pule, 2002b, pp. 234-6; Pherudi, 2018, p. 119; Matlosa, 2020, p. 5).

Following the elections in 1970, Mokhehle's BCP triumphed with 36 seats to the BNP's 23, while the MFP only managed to obtain one seat. Elections were annulled, though, and multiparty democracy in the nation was put on hold. Chief Jonathan took control and proclaimed an emergency. As a result, political activists (namely BCP members) were detained, tortured, and killed. King Moshoeshoe II was also exiled (Pule, 2002a, p. 174, p. 226-7).

Lesotho Paramilitary Force (LPF), also known as a "paramilitary youth league," was founded as a separate organization from the paramilitary police between the years (1970-1986). (Global Security, 2017b). In August 1979, the LPF was first referred to as an "army". To repress, intimidate, torture, and/or assassinate political activists and related activism, Leabua's government deployed and relied upon this army.

Military Regime [1986-1993]

Leabua was overthrown in a military coup led by General Metsing Lekhanya, nevertheless, in January 1986. This led to a military rule (1986–1991) that similarly relied on and employed military force to seize and preserve political power (Maundeni, 2010, p. 133). The LPF was renamed "*The Royal Lesotho Defence Force (RLDF)*" after the coup and was given the status of a defence force (Matlosa, 2020, p. 5). Similar tactics were employed by the army to stifle political activities, particularly that of the BCP (Pule, 2002a, p. 179). The 1986 coup's success also represented the army's important position in domestic power dynamics. In terms of political-military relations, this government and the subsequent period were symbolic since they successfully and legally (i.e., by "*1986 Order No. 4*") enacted rules that permitted military involvement in the cabinet while also outlawing political activities (Pule, 2002a, p. 188-193).

Colonel Elias Ramaema's military coup in 1991 that overthrew Lekhanya serves as another proof of the necessity of using military action to seize or gain access to political power. Even though Lesotho returned to democratic civilian control after this military regime [2nd May 1991–2nd April 1993], military force was increasingly used to advance domestic political goals and/or outcomes (Pule, 2002a, p. 195-6; Pule, 2002b, p. 240).

Contemporary Political-Security Context

Civilian Democratic Rule [1993-Present]

The RLDF changed back to the LDF following the 1993 change from military to democratic governance (Matlosa, 2020, p. 5). The militarization of politics and/or the pollicisation of the military, however, continued to be a problem and was harmful to the civilian democratic system.

Nowadays, military reliance and/or accusations of military politicisation are not unheard of under democratic civilian rule. A few facts serve as evidence for this. On the one hand, the administration of former Prime Minister Pakalitha Mosisili (2015–2017) has been questioned and widely perceived as having the support of the army, led by former LDF commander Lieutenant-General Tlali Kamoli. On the other hand, Lt. Gen. Maaparankoe Mahao, a former leader of the LDF, was thought to have supported PM Thomas Thabane's (2012–2015) administration (Matlosa, 2017b, p. 148). In essence, Lesotho's political elites believe that the security sector is crucial to influencing the allocation of power and resources, which is obvious from the large number of security personnel, civilians, and official casualties that have resulted from the process (eNCA, 2015; News24, 2017a; Pherudi, 2018, p. 121-2).

The intensity and depth of the political-military relations are evidenced by the assassinations of the LDF's commanders (Lt. Gen. Mahao and Motšomotšo in 2015 and 2017, respectively) and military personnel in less than two years. The murder of the second commander in 2017 (Motšomotšo), despite numerous peace-building initiatives by different stakeholders and policy-makers to stabilize the political and security situation in the nation after the assassination of Mahao in 2015, also highlights the misunderstanding and/or ignorance of the entrenched historical political-military relations, which leads to failed and/or poor solutions in their respective initiatives (Aerni-Flessner, 2017. News24, 2017b).

The military's significant role in Lesotho's culture of violence is notable for being closely related to intra-party struggles for control of the state. This helps to explain why military crimes increase in frequency before and after elections, in particular. The military was involved in more political violence immediately following the elections in 1993, 1998, and 2015. One would be excused for mistaking the LDF for a political party based on these case studies of post-election violence with significant military involvement (Matlosa, 2020, p. 7).

For instance, before the establishment of the current democratic civilian government, Lieutenant-General Tlali Kamoli of the LDF's armed forces was perceived as generally supporting the policies of former Prime Minister Pakalitha Mosisili (Matlosa, 2017b, p. 148). On the other side, former LDF commander and late Lt. Gen. Maaparankoe Mahao was thought to have supported PM Thomas Thabane's (2012–2015) administration (Aerni-Flessner, 2017; Allison, 2017; Pherudi, 2018, p. 122).

Since 2012, when the political class started to reinvest in the military for access to the state apparatus and/or a protracted stay in power, there have been clear and significant indications of this (Matlosa, 2017b, p. 143). First, the then-prime minister Mosisili named Major General Tlali Kamoli as the LDF's commander on March 15, 2012, which resulted in his promotion to the rank of "*Lieutenant-General*" (i.e., three (3) months before the May 26 general elections). Yet, considering the closeness of the elections and Mosisli's failure to win power, such a crucial security appointment raises issues and worries about political activism, which is unrestricted when one considers the past politico-military backdrop of Lesotho. Second, after the election, Thomas Thabane formed the first coalition government in Lesotho with the help of his ABC, Metsing's LCD, and Thesele 'Maseribane's BNP. Thabane first affirmed Kamoli in his position but eventually fired him. After that, he named Brigadier Maaparankoe Mahao as the LDF's new leader. In response to these events, Mosisili vehemently criticized this dismissal in public (Sejanamane, 2016, p. 1; Matlosa, 2017b, p. 143-4).

Drawing from Susan Willet's (1998), "*Demilitarisation, Disarmament and Development in Southern Africa*" article, Matlosa (2020, p. 2) supports the idea of 'demilitarisation' as a way in which Lesotho can redress the negative effects of militarisation. He claims that Lesotho needs to demilitarize to shift away from its current violent culture and toward one of peace. According to Willet (1998, p. 412), demilitarisation is an '*all-encompassing concept, which attempts to deconstruct the ideological and institutional structures and reassert civil control over the organs of state and the economy*'.

FINDINGS

In the civilian democratic rule period, Lesotho came to experience certain political practices that either controlled and/or hindered the operational effectiveness of the armed forces. Motseki *et al* (2020, p. 3) argue that the LDF became politically influenced, and thus served and ensured the interests of legislators. For almost three decades, the military in Lesotho has been considered to be one of the major internal factors for political instability (Matlosa, 2005, p. 85). As a result, Lesotho's civil-military relations have deteriorated substantially in the previous decades, resulting in an increase in political intervention by military personnel, fragmentation within the armed services, and a broken military professional ethos.

To a larger extent, the military in Lesotho would make clear demonstrations of favour for political views or parties, emphasizing to subordinates that following such choice is better for professional survival and advancement. As a result, when someone in the chain of command displays support for partisan beliefs in front of a group of subordinates, that group is unsure whether it must concur or risk being disobedient or disrespectful.

The military, for the most part, bears major responsibility for maintaining its apolitical nature. However, civilians play an important role in the military's political neutrality, frequently refraining from asking or advocating military support for political choices. This is especially critical for the most senior civilian political leaders in the chain of command: the defence minister and/or the Prime Minister. In both hierarchy and law, everyone in uniform is subordinate to these two officials. Abstaining from partisan advocacy in front of uniformed audiences is a key way for civilian leaders to preserve the armed forces' professional, apolitical nature, and, via them, the health of Lesotho's democracy.

Although the struggle for dominance among Lesotho's political elites extends back to the country's independence in 1966, the military was never touched by these politics until the BNP administration indoctrinated it into politics during the 1970 general elections. Because of the politicisation of the military, politicians still determine and influence military recruitment and promotions. With the country's transition to democratic rule in 1993, the civilian government was confronted with a dilemma that was not of its creation. It had to contend with a heavily equipped military that was profoundly divided along political lines. As a result, the civilian authority was unable to regulate and modify the institution to conform to the ideal of neutrality of the military in a democratic dispensation. As a result, Lesotho and its democratic governments have never reaped the benefits of 30 years of civilian governance (Moremoholo, 2005, p. 5).

Lesotho needs to seriously embark on far-reaching governance and security sector reforms. This will enable democratisation in which democratic institutions could be strengthened and militarisation reversed, thus allowing for cordial civilian-military relations.

Security sector reform (SSR) aims at improving safety by enhancing the effectiveness and accountability of security institutions controlled by civilians and operating according to human rights and the rule of law (United Nations, 2008). The concept of security sector reform, as complex and controversial as it is, encompasses issues of security, conflict prevention, peacebuilding, development, good governance, human rights, civil society, state building, and democracy among others (Ball, 2010, p. 30).

SSR focuses on the need to strengthen justice and security institutions. This is because these institutions, especially issues of justice and security, are accessible and responsive to the needs and rights of all individuals, and are instrumental in building trust and promoting social cohesion and economic prosperity (Ebo and Powell, 2010, p. 128).

As far as Lesotho is concerned, the debate on Security Sector Reform and its relevance for conflict prevention, peace-building and development is a watershed moment in its security landscape (van Eekelen, 2005, p. 126).

SSR is necessary and/or useful in the following areas of Lesotho. First, the democratization of a state appears unattainable without altering the institutions and mechanisms of their oversight and control so that they are unable to act partisan in domestic politics. Establishing good governance practices entails placing elected officials in charge of all armed forces and security agencies. These officials would be responsible to the public, operate transparently, be able to strike a balance between competing political and social interests, be free of corruption and organized crime, and provide all citizens with affordable security (Caparini, 2010, p. 247-252).

Second, preventing internal and regional conflict necessitates a security sector that supports the effective management of internal tensions and conflicts, ensures security and justice for all citizens and social groups, and acts as an institution of confidence-building with the neighbouring states by being transparent in its organization, doctrine, and arms procurement (Ball, 2010, p. 39-40). Last but not least, the professionalization of the armed and security forces, which includes defining their roles and functions clearly, structuring them in accordance with these roles, accepting the rule of law and the dominance of democratically elected authorities, and making these forces effective in their actions aimed at protecting the state and its citizens (Galletti and Wodzicki, 2010, p. 285).

Several local, regional, and global actors are involved in SSR. On a national level, this consists of the following: the executive (head of state, government, other decision-making bodies); ministry of defence and other ministries; armed forces and security agencies (police, gendarmerie, intelligence services, border guards, customs officials, private security contractors); legislature (parliament and relevant committees); judicial, law enforcement, and penal institutions; and civil society actors (media, think tanks, civil society organizations) (Philander, 2000, p. 4-5; DCAF, 2021).

Velaphe (2020) asserts that Lesotho is seemingly taking a serious initiative in comprehensive national reforms. This is witnessed in the National Reforms Authority (NRA), with its committee elected in February 2020 following the passing of the Lesotho National Reform Bill by the Senate (Velaphe, 2020). In August 2019, the Lesotho Senate as the Upper House passed the National Reforms Authority (NRA) Bill passed the National Reforms Authority Bill, which codifies reforms backed by the Southern African Development Community (SADC). The act created a National Reforms Authority (NRA), which is charged with implementing expansive governance reforms (Freedom House, 2020).

DIRECTIONS FOR FUTURE RESEARCH

With the ongoing SSR aimed at re-establishing a non-partisan army that is de-politicised and professional, literature about the nature and causes of the politicisation of the military and militarisation of politics in Lesotho is critical. The ongoing SSR seek to inculcate a new culture of professionalism and de-politicisation of the military in an attempt to enhance the country's democratisation process and internal discipline within the military. Lesotho's citizenry needs a better understanding of the politicisation of the military vis-à-vis militarisation of politics if they intend to address issues affecting and/or relating to SSR, development, democratisation, peace and stability.

Future research could, for instance, investigate how a non-partisan force that is educated and politically aware but not politically active can contribute to the development, democratisation, peace and stability of Lesotho. Moremoholo (2005, p. 61) asserts that soldiers who took an active part in political contests lacked both education and professionalism. As a result, they were ill-disciplined and hence rebellious to the standards guiding soldier behaviour in a democratic society. Against this backdrop, education for military personnel becomes critical. Such research could contribute to identifying specific strategies and patterns of use that relate to successfully de-politicising and professionalising the military. Subsequently, this will allow for the successful implementation of SSR because as it stands, one of the key challenges to the reform processes is for the security sector to be apolitical (Philander, 2000, p. 4).

Adopting a comprehensive security sector reform would be the most effective way of improving Lesotho's security condition. Ideally, this would imply the establishment of a democratically controlled security sector with sufficient size, resources, and composition to meet the needs of crisis prevention. This should apply not only to the military but also to other institutions that comprise the state security sector, such as law enforcement and the courts. The reason behind this argument is based on the fact that the security sector, notably the police and military, play a critical role in defining how political crises proceed. When political disagreements become violent, these organizations might have an impact on whether the situation progresses or is defused. As a result, their professionalism will be a critical requirement for the consolidation of peace in Lesotho. As previously stated, the military has frequently operated outside the norms of neutrality in Lesotho politics and has been used to advance the objectives of competing elite groups (Moremoholo, 2005, p. 61-2).

A politicised military is devoted to a single political party and/or regularly advocates and defends partisan political positions and fortunes. An apolitical, nonpartisan military is a tenet of democracy and a hallmark of military professionalism. The military must see nonpartisan service as a fundamental tenet of the military profession. The military upholds the Constitution by obeying democratically elected civilian leaders regardless of political party or partisanship. This concept further underpins the peaceful transfer of power from one Prime Ministerial administration to the other and assures that Basotho can make decisions about government without fear of force.

Knowing that partisanship does not influence professional military advice permits elected officials to put their trust in senior commanders' competence and recommendations. Furthermore, if the military took partisan positions or demonstrated partisan loyalty, people may fairly conclude that the opposing party would be unable to manage the military if elected. In other words, democratically elected representatives of the people would be unable to rely on the military to faithfully execute national security policy if the military explicitly preferred the opposing party. Such circumstances would erode public trust in either the disfavoured party or the military, undermining the government's ability to function (Friend, 2017).

Friend (2017) further argues that another important benefit of a nonpartisan force is that it protects the military. Because the military serves elected representatives from all political parties equally, there is no reason for those representatives to treat the military differently based on partisan affiliation.

CONCLUSION

The chapter acknowledges Lesotho's long history of detrimental political and security relations and the subsequent instability. It further illustrates how certain underlying political issues have destabilised the military and thus threaten peace and security in the country. The authors in this regard further acknowledge the evident, persistent and unchallenged politicisation of the security sector. Civil–military relations in Lesotho must be democratised (Matlosa, 2020, p. 6).

It is evident that at some point in Lesotho's post-colonial era, particularly in the 1970s, the politicisation of the military and the militarisation of politics emerged thus chiselling the contemporary political-military alliance with adversely deteriorating civil-military relations.

In conclusion, Lesotho's political and security situation will continue to deteriorate and casualties will rise quickly if the aforementioned political-military linkages are neglected and misinterpreted. Additionally, regional and institutionally driven civilian workshops and seminars like the 2000 Institute of Security Studies (ISS) civil-military relations dialogue, state-driven military training operations like the 1998 Operation Maluti training operation and the 2001 Indian Army Training Team (IATT) operation, and government policies like the 1995 Lesotho Ministry of Defence policy; and, Additionally, regional initiatives like the Southern African Development Community (SADC) preventive mission, which among other important goals seeks to stabilize the political environment and make the LDF into an apolitical and accountable defence force, will repeatedly fall short of achieving the desired political and security results (Neethling, 1999, p. 2; Neethling, 2000, p. 13; Pule, 2002b, p. 242-4; Pherudi, 2003a, p. 124; Likoti, 2007, p. 253; Fabricius, 2017; Pherudi, 2018, p. 119; TimesLive, 2018).

Moreover, militarisation is one of many underlying factors that pose challenges to Lesotho's initiatives towards deepening democratic governance (Matlosa, 2020, p. 2). Since 2012, Lesotho has been characterized by coalition systems of governance[4] (News24, 2017a). Given the political and security complexities associated with this form of governance, solutions to this phenomenon of politicisation of the military are highly and urgently needed.

The assassinations of these two army commanders, military and political officials within these periods respectively, represent the apex of the politicisation of Lesotho's military and the militarisation of Lesotho's politics.

Although there are critical historical (i.e. pre-independent Lesotho) roots of Lesotho's political instability, however, the causes of instability were predominantly external rather than internal. On the one hand, Lesotho's instability in the pre-independence era was characterised by external factors in the sense that the main issue of instability related to threats to the territorial integrity of Lesotho as a whole with one group intending to forcefully claim and/or seize a whole and/or portions of its territory. Whereas on the other hand, issues around instability in the last 55 years of post-independent Lesotho are largely internal factors that evolve around the politicisation of the military and/or the militarisation of politics. According to Thabane (2017a, p. 17), many instances and circumstances that resulted in instability during the pre-colonial and colonial periods had never changed even in post-colonial Lesotho.

REFERENCES

Aerni-Flessner, J. (2017). Op-Ed: Will political and security unrest deepen in Lesotho? *Daily Maverick*. https://www.dailymaverick.co.za/article/2017-10-25-op-ed-will-political-and-security-unrest-deepen-in-lesotho/. Accessed: 19-08-2019.

Allison, S. (2017). New Lesotho murders highlight need for military reform. *Mail and Guardian*. https://mg.co.za/article/2017-09-05-new-lesotho-murders-highlight-need-for-military-reform/.

Ball, N. (2010). The evolution of the security sector reform agenda. In M. Sedra (Ed.), *The future of security sector reform. The Centre for International Governance Innovation* (pp. 29–43). CIGI.

Basotho Wars. (2020). South African History Online. https://web.archive.org/web/20141011134523/http://www.sahistory.org.za/south-africa-1806-1899/basotho-wars-1858-1868.

Bujra, A. (2002). *African Conflicts: Their Causes and Their Political and Social Environment. Development Policy Management Forum (DPMF)* (Occasional Paper). United Nations Economic Commission for Africa (UNECA). Addis Ababa.

Caparini, M. (2010). Civil Society and the future of security sector reform. In M. Sedra (Ed.), *The future of security sector reform. The Centre for International Governance Innovation* (pp. 244–262). CIGI.

Coakley, G. J. (2002). *The Mineral Industries of Lesotho and Swaziland*. U.S. Geological Survey Minerals Information. http://minerals.er.usgs.gov/minerals/pubs/country/africa.html#ir,

Deleglise, D., & Sejanamane, M. (2017). To Reform or Disband? The Future of the Military in Lesotho. In G. Khadiagala & D. Deleglise (Eds.), *Southern African Security Review. Centre for Defence and Security Management* (pp. 123–141). University of Witwatersrand.

Ebo, A., & Powell, K. (2010). Why is SSR important? A United Nations perspective. In M. Sedra (Ed.), *The future of security sector reform. The Centre for International Governance Innovation* (pp. 45–58). CIGI.

Electoral Institute for Sustainable Democracy in Africa (EISA). (2007). Lesotho National Assembly Elections. *EISA election observer mission report No.26*.

Fabricius, P. (2017). Is SADC at last flexing its muscles in Lesotho? *ISS Today*. https://issafrica.org/iss-today/is-sadc-at-last-flexing-its-muscles-in-lesotho

Freedom House. (2020). *Lesotho*. Freedom House. https://freedomhouse.org/country/lesotho/freedom-world/2020.

Friend, A. H. (2017). *Military Politicisation*. Center for Strategic and International Studies. https://www.csis.org/analysis/military-politicisation.

Galletti, N., & Wodzicki, M. (2010). Securing human rights: Shifting the security sector reform paradigm. In M. Sedra (Ed.), *The future of security sector reform. The Centre for International Governance Innovation* (pp. 281–300). CIGI.

Global Security. (2017a). *Basotho Wars (1858-68).* Global Security. https://www.globalsecurity.org/military/world/war/basotho.htm.

Global Security. (2017b). *Lesotho Defence Force.* Global Security. https://www.globalsecurity.org/military/world/africa/ls-army.htm.

Heywood, A. (2013). *Politics* (4th ed.). Palgrave Macmillan. doi:10.1007/978-1-137-27244-7

Khadiagala, G. M., & Lyons, T. (2001). Foreign Policy Making in Africa: An Introduction. In G. M. Khadiagala & T. Lyons (Eds.), *African Foreign Policies: Power and Processes* (pp. 1–14). Lynne Rienner Publishers, Inc. doi:10.1515/9781685850210-002

Khaketla, B. M. (1971). *Lesotho 1970: An African Coup Under the Microscope.* C. Hurst and Co.

Lelimo, M. M. (1998). The reasons for the annexation of Lsotho 1868: a new perspective. Submitted in fulfilment of the requirements for the degree Magister Artium. Department of History. University of the Free State, Bloemfontein.

Lesotho Defence Force Act. 1996 (Act No.4 of 1996). https://lesotholii.org/ls/legislation/num-act/1996/4.

Likoti, F. J. (2007). The 1998 Military Intervention in Lesotho: SADC Peace Mission or Resource War? *International Peacekeeping, 14*(2).

Lundahl, M., McCarthy, C., & Petersson, L. (2003). *In the Shadow of South Africa: Lesotho's Economic Future.* Ahsgate.

Mahao, L. (2006). *The Power of Hegemonic Theory in Southern Africa: Why Lesotho Cannot Develop an Independent Foreign Policy.* [Thesis submitted in Partial Fulfilment of the Requirements for the Master of Arts Degree in International Relations, Rhodes University].

Mahlakeng, M. K. (2014). *Political Will Versus Political Entitlement: The Left-Right Political Spectrum of Lesotho.* Southern African Peace and Security (SACCPS). http://saccps.blogspot.com/search/label/M.%20K.%20Mahlakeng.

Mahlakeng, M. K. (2017). *Lesotho's Upcoming Elections: The Collapse of a Second Coalition Government.* Southern African Peace and Security (SACCPS). http://saccps.blogspot.com/search/label/M.%20K.%20Mahlakeng. Accessed: 06-02-2019.

Mahlakeng, M. K. (2018). *Lesotho's rule of law and judicial independence under threat: attempts to politicise the Judiciary.* Southern African Peace and Security (SACCPS) http://saccps.blogspot.com/search/label/M.%20K.%20Mahlakeng. Accessed: 06-02-2019.

Mahlakeng, M. K. (2018). *Understanding Lesotho's political-security discourse and its historical and contemporary relevance.* Southern African Peace and Security (SACCPS). http://saccps.blogspot.com/search/label/M.%20K.%20Mahlakeng. Accessed: 06-02-2019.

Matlosa, K. (2005). From a destabilising factor to a de-politicised and professional force: The military in Lesotho. In M. M. Rupiya (Ed.), *Evolutions & Revolutions: A Contemporary History of Militaries in Southern Africa.* Institute for Security Studies.

Matlosa, K. (2017). Understanding political crisis of Lesotho's Post-2015 Elections. In M. Thabane (Ed.), *Towards an Anatomy of Persistent Political Instability in Lesotho, 1966-2016*. Morija Printing Works.

Matlosa, K. (2020). Pondering the culture of violence in Lesotho: A case for Demilitarisation. *Journal of Contemporary African Studies*, *38*(3), 381–398. doi:10.1080/02589001.2020.1749246

Mattlin, M. (2011). *Politicized society: The long-shadow of Taiwan's one-party legacy. Nordic Institute of Asia Studies*. NIAS.

Maundeni, Z. (2010). Developmental States: Their Historical Absence and their Emergence in Post Conflict Southern Africa. *The Open Area Studies Journal*, *3*(1), 30–40. doi:10.2174/1874914301003010030

Monyane, C. (2009). *The Kingdom of Lesotho: An Assessment of Problems in Democratic Consolidation*. [Dissertation presented for the Degree of Doctor of Philosophy at Stellenbosch University].

Moremoholo, E. (2005). The role of the military in the political conflict in Lesotho: with special reference to the 1998 failed Coup d'etat. University of Kwazulu Natal, Durban.

Mothibe, T. (2002). State and Society, 1824-1833. In Pule, N and Thabane, M (Eds.). Essays on Aspects of the Political Economy of Lesotho 15000-2000. National University of Lesotho. Morija Printing Works.

Mothibe, T., & Ntabeni, M. (2002). The Role of the Missionaries, Boers and British in Social and Territorial Changes, 1833-1868. In Pule, N and Thabane, M (Eds.). Essays on Aspects of the Political Economy of Lesotho 15000-2000. National University of Lesotho. Morija Printing Works.

Motseki, M., Maluleke, W., & Dlamini, S. (2020). Military role in democratic transition and succession: Lessons from the Kingdom of Lesothos. *Cogent Social Sciences*, *6*(1), 1. doi:10.1080/23311886.2020.1847845

Neethling, T. (1999, May). Military Intervention in Lesotho: Perspective on Operation Boleas and Beyond. *The Online Journal of Peace and Conflict Resolution*, *2*(2), 1–12.

Neethling, T. (2000). Conditions for Successful Entry and Exit: An Assessment of SADC Allied Operations in Lesotho. *Monograph No 44: Boundaries of Peace Support Operations*.

News24. (2017a). Zuma slams 'senseless' killing of Lesotho's chief of defence force. *News24*. https://www.news24.com/news24/africa/news/zuma-slams-senseless-killing-of-lesothos-chief-of-defence-force-20170905. Accessed: 19-08-2019.

News24. (2017b). Lesotho's political strife to cost SADC millions. News24, 17th September. https://www.news24.com/news24/southafrica/news/lesothos-political-strife-to-cost-sadc-millions-20170916. Accessed: 19-08-2019.

'Nyane, H. (2016). Formation of a government in Lesotho in the case of a hung parliament. *Law, Democracy and Development, 20*. Cape Town.

Nyeko, B. (2002a). Resistance to the Colonial Rule and the Emergence of Anti-Colonial Movements. In Pule, N and Thabane, M (Eds.). Essays on Aspects of the Political Economy of Lesotho 15000-2000. National University of Lesotho. Morija Printing Works.

Nyeko, B. (2002b). The Independence Movement, 1952-1966. In Pule, N and Thabane, M (Eds.). Essays on Aspects of the Political Economy of Lesotho 15000-2000. National University of Lesotho. Morija Printing Works.

Pherudi, L. M. (2003a, June). Operation Boleas under microscope, 1998-1999. *Journal of Contemporary History*, *28*(1).

Pherudi, L. M. (2003b). Lesotho: Political Conflict, Peace and Reconciliation in the Mountain Kingdom. In Erik Doxtader and Villa-Vicencio (Eds.). Through Fire with Water: The Roots of Division and the Potential for Reconciliation in Africa. Trenton, NJ: Africa World Press.

Pherudi, M. (2018). The assassination of military commanders in lesotho: Triggers and reactions. *Journal of Contemporary History*, *3*(2).

Philander, D. (2000). Security sector reform in Lesotho: Observations from a three day dialogue series. ISS Occasional Paper No. 45. July.

Proctor, J. H. (1969). Building a Constitutional Monarchy in Lesotho. [Institut de Sociologie de l'Université de Bruxelles.]. *Civilisations*, *19*(1).

Pule, N. W. (2002a). Politics since Independence. In Pule, N and Thabane, M (Eds.). Essays on Aspects of the Political Economy of Lesotho 15000-2000. National University of Lesotho. Morija Printing Works.

Pule, N. W. (2002b). Lesotho in Southern Africa. In Pule, N and Thabane, M (Eds.). Essays on Aspects of the Political Economy of Lesotho 1500-2000. National University of Lesotho. Morija Printing Works.

Sejanamane, M. (2017). Struggle Against Impunity in Lesotho. Morija: Morija Printing Works. p. 60.

Shale V. (2005). The 2005 Lesotho local government elections: Implications for development and governance. *Journal of African Elections*,*4*(1).

Sohn, L. B., & Gustafson, K. J. (1984). *The Law of the Sea in a Nutshell, January*. West Publishing Company.

Southall, R. (2017). Why Lesotho is Such a Mess and What Can be Done About It. University of Witwatersrand. https://www.wits.ac.za>news>latest-news.

Southall, R., & Petlane, T. (1995). *Democratisation and Demilitarisation in Lesotho: The General Election of 1993 and its Aftermath*. Africa Institute of South Africa.

Thabane, M. (2002). Aspects of Colonial Economy and Society, 1868-1966. In Pule, N and Thabane, M (Eds.). Essays on Aspects of the Political Economy of Lesotho 15000-2000. National University of Lesotho. Morija Printing Works.

Thabane, M. (2017a). Towards an identification of historical roots of Lesotho's political instability. In M. Thabane (Ed.), *Towards an Anatomy of Persistent Instability in Lesotho, 1966–2016. Morija: Morija Printing Works. National University of Lesotho. Morija: Morija Printing Works.*

Thabane, M. (2017b). Political Instability, multiple citizenship and citizenship legislation in independent Lesotho. In M. Thabane (Ed.), *Towards an Anatomy of Persistent Instability in Lesotho, 1966–2016. Morija: Morija Printing Works. National University of Lesotho. Morija: Morija Printing Works.*

The Geneva Centre for Security Sector Governance (DCAF). (2021). *Security Sector Integrity*. Geneva Centre for Security Sector Governance. https://securitysectorintegrity.com/security-sector-governance/security-sector-reform/. Accessed: 25-08-2021.

The Geneva Centre for Security Sector Governance (DCAF). (2023). *What is security sector reform. African Security Sector Network*. African Security Network. https://www.africansecuritynetwork.org/assn/what-is-security-sector-reform/#:~:text=Security%20Sector%20Reform%20(SSR)%20refers,of%20accountability%20and%20democratic%20governance. Accessed: 22-08-2023.

The Geneva Centre for the Democratic Control of Armed Forces (DCAF). (2015). *The Security Sector: Roles and responsibilities in security provision, management and oversight. SSR Backgrounder Series*. https://www.files.ethz.ch/isn/195675/DCAF_BG_3_The%20Security%20Sector.11.15.pdf.

TimesLive. (2018). Basotho favour monarchy over feuding politicians. *Timeslive*. https://www.timeslive.co.za/news/africa/2018-04-26-basotho-favour-monarchy-over-feuding-politicians/

United Nations (UN). (2008). *Security Sector Reform (SSR)*. United Nations and the Rule of Law. https://www.un.org/ruleoflaw/thematic-areas/access-to-justice-and-rule-of-law-institutions/ssr/.

Uprety, K. (2006). *Transit regime for landlocked states: international law and development Perspectives*. The World Bank.

van Eekelen, W. (2005). The parliamentary dimension of security sector reform. Security and Peace, 23(3). doi:10.5771/0175-274x-2005-3-126

Velaphe, N. (2020). *National Reform Authority CEO appointed*. NRA. https://www.gov.ls/national-reform-authority-ceo-appointed/.

Weisfelder, F. (1974). *Defining National Purpose: The Roots of Factionalism in Lesotho*. [Unpublished doctoral dissertation, Harvard University].

Willet, S. (1998). Demilitarisation, Disarmament and Development in Southern Africa. *Review of African Political Economy*, *77*(77), 409–430. doi:10.1080/03056249808704323

World Map. 2023. Lesotho. https://www.mapsofindia.com/world-map/lesotho/. Accedde: 10-10-2023.

ADDITIONAL READINGS

Deleglise, D., & Sejanamane, M. (2017). To Reform or Disband? The Future of the Military in Lesotho. In G. Khadiagala & D. Deleglise (Eds.), *Southern African Security Review. Centre for Defence and Security Management*. University of Witwatersrand.

Matlosa, K. (2020). Pondering the culture of violence in Lesotho: A case for Demilitarisation. *Journal of Contemporary African Studies*, *38*(3), 381–398. doi:10.1080/02589001.2020.1749246

Pule, N., & Thabane, M. (2002). Essays on Aspects of the Political Economy of Lesotho 15000-2000. National University of Lesotho. Morija Printing Works. Matlosa, K. (2005). From a destabilising factor to a de-politicised and professional force: The military in Lesotho. In M. M. Rupiya (Ed.), *Evolutions & Revolutions: A Contemporary History of Militaries in Southern Africa*. Institute for Security Studies.

Sejanamane, M. (2017). *Struggle Against Impunity in Lesotho.* Morija: Morija Printing Works.

Thabane, M. (2017). *Towards an Anatomy of Persistent Instability in Lesotho, 1966–2016.* Morija: Morija Printing Works.

KEY TERMS AND DEFINITIONS

Militarisation: The militarisation of political life entails the prioritization of military goals and the military's influence over citizens (Heywood, 2007, pp. 401). According to Matlosa (2020, pp. 5; 2017b, pp. 142) it can refer to either one of the following, that is, (a) the use of force in politics (including the abuse of the military by political actors to gain an advantage over rivals); (b) the establishment of armed militias and vigilante groups by political parties, which primarily involve youth; and (c) the involvement of the security forces (especially the military) in politics along partisan lines in order to advance the military's corporate interests and/or in the interests of the state.

Politicisation: In general, politicisation refers to the involvement and preference of political and group reasons and interests in judgments and actions. In the sphere of governance, politicisation is defined as the failure to maintain impartiality in policy-making and decision-making, as well as the intrusion of political beliefs, proclivities, and prejudices in professional affairs, which can occur at various levels and patterns. Although politicisation is one of the most significant damages and inefficiencies in all domains of governance, it has far-reaching repercussions in national security governance. In such a circumstance, agents, political actors, and strategic and intelligence analysts interfere in their political preferences at various phases (Mattlin, 2011, pp. 7).

Security Sector: The structures, institutions, and people in charge of providing, managing, and supervising security on a local and national level make up the security sector. The security sector encompasses both individuals who use force and those tasked with managing and supervising the use of force (Geneva: DCAF, 2015).

Security Sector Reform: According to DCAF (2023) "*Security Sector Reform (SSR) refers to the process of transforming the 'security sector' – those institutions that safeguard a country and its citizens from security threats – to ensure the provision of effective security to both the state and its people within a framework of accountability and democratic governance*".

ENDNOTES

1 Khaketla, 1971; Southall and Petlane, 1995; Southall 2017; Sejanamane, 2017; Thabane, 2017; Deleglise and Sejanamane, 2017; Matlosa, 2020.

2 This role is afforded to the Prime Minister (Mahlakeng, 2017).

3 States that are surrounded by a territory of only one other State (Uprety, 2006, p. 405).

4 "a coalition government is a cabinet of a parliamentary government in which several parties cooperate, and a common reason for such an agreement is that no party on its own can achieve a majority in parliament" (Heywood, 2013:239).

Section 5

Questions and Critique of Some Democratic Practices

Chapter 19
Digital Transformation in Africa: Is Democracy Under Threat?

Maxwell Makhangala Maseko
https://orcid.org/0000-0002-0512-7145
Wits University, South Africa

ABSTRACT

Democracy in many African countries faces serious challenges linked to weak leadership, poor governance, malfunctioning state institutions, and slow or stagnant development. For these countries, the challenges can be attributed to an exploitative system rooted in colonialism, neo-colonialism, imperialism, and apartheid. Digital transformation and the global rise of digital technologies have created new opportunities to meet the challenges of democracy concerning citizen engagement, broadening public debate, increasing transparency and accountability, and improving service delivery. This chapter critically examines whether using digital technologies in political settings strengthens or weakens democracy on the continent. It highlights three main scholarly debates about using digital tools to address the declining quality of democracy. Data from various secondary sources was used to address the problem. The author found that digitalisation undoubtedly exposes democracy to new threats, but its benefits far outweigh the concerns.

INTRODUCTION

The future of democracy in the digital age is the subject of many scholarly, civic, and civil debates globally. According to the Council of Europe (2021), significant efforts have been made since the 1950s to modernise governance to meet some of the historical challenges linked to poorly functioning states. Tar (2010) argues that this is particularly true for many African countries often classified as conflict-prone societies characterised by continued civil wars and power struggles. These countries often share a traumatic past marked by long periods of exploitative colonialism, neo-colonialism, imperialism, and apartheid (Khapoya, 2012; Hodges, 1972). Furthermore, they argue that attempts to deal with the democratic development impasse in Africa have also suffered considerably due to a lack of political will,

DOI: 10.4018/979-8-3693-0477-8.ch019

a key ingredient needed for success. The result is often violent service delivery protests, widespread corruption, and a general crisis of political legitimacy especially at the local government level closest to the people (Millstein, 2010).

This chapter aims to answer the question of whether digital transformation strengthens or weakens democracy in Africa. The potential of digital tools such as social media and others to invigorate citizen engagement, promote transparency and accountability and enhance the provision of public services has been recognised by many scholars including Soriano (2013), Oreskovich (2011), Shirky (2008), and Diamond (2010). Others including Castells (2012) have adopted a more cautious approach specifically arguing that social media for instance, potentially enhances access to information, enables citizen interactions, and facilitates discussions and opinion formation only under certain conditions. Current literature also shows that the rise of digital technologies especially during the height of the COVID-19 pandemic created new opportunities to meet the challenges faced by democracy. Increased Internet connectivity in many African countries also means that people can now interact with politicians or public officials from the comfort of their own homes without fear of public judgment or ridicule (Rumbul, 2015) in liberal societies.

Despite these gains, there are general concerns about the wider lack of access to digital tools and platforms in many African countries, the lack of affordability of digital-based solutions, the lack of knowledge and skills to use digital tools, biases, and exclusions from technology based on gender and race on the African continent. Furthermore, Rumbul (2015) also cautions that there is little evidence by way of research to demonstrate the real-world impact of digital platforms. She argues that current research projects on the subject although robust, do not answer the key basic question of who uses digital technology and why. This also begs the question, *how safe is online data in the hands of private actors in democratic societies?* Private actors, in particular giant Internet companies and social media platforms, increasingly play a central role in the public sphere in Africa and abroad as providers of infrastructure, content creators, and distributors. This therefore means that big tech companies play a gatekeeping role, selecting and curating information that is shared on social platforms, targeting specific audiences, and potentially influencing public opinion, political debate, and ultimately electoral results (Council of Europe, 2021).

Globally, the Cambridge Analytica scandal, whereby data analytics were used to influence and manipulate the 2016 US election, is one well-recorded example of the influence of digital technology on democracies. The reposting of fake news was also widely reported in the media during the Brexit vote in Europe. In Africa, Kenya, Nigeria, and South Africa have a legacy of players seeking to influence public opinion to achieve a political or economic end. For instance, Cambridge Analytica was reportedly hired by a wealthy Nigerian national to support the 2015 re-election campaign of then-president Goodluck Jonathan (The Conversation, 2020). They argue that the firm worked with Israeli intelligence to acquire hacked medical and financial information about Jonathan's opponent Muhammadu Buhari. In Kenya, the same company reportedly mined data from voters to help President Uhuru Kenyatta win disputed elections in 2017 (Washington Post, 2018). In South Africa, Bell Pottinger, an international public relations firm, reportedly tried to stir up racial tensions by using fake Twitter accounts among others in a bid to keep then President Jacob Zuma and his party, the ANC, in power despite ongoing reports of state capture by the Gupta family (Allen, 2023). Following the Cambridge Analytica scandal, then Kenyan President Uhuru Kenyatta signed into law the Data Protection Bill in 2020. The new law places restrictions on the collection and use of digital data by governments and private corporations. Similarly, Nigeria also passed a new data protection regulation in 2020 (The Conversation, 2020).

The rest of the chapter is organised to include discussions on methodology and theoretical reflections used to answer the key research question, painting a general picture of the state of democracy in Africa, discussing the threats it faces in the digital age (*including the role and impact of the worsening digital divide*), examining the key emerging debates around the adoption of digital technologies and their bearing on democracy in Africa, exploring the key lessons to be learned from the continent using country-specific case studies, discussing the key findings on the phenomena under study and what the future use of digital technologies looks like for scholars, researchers, and practitioners, and ascertaining whether the main research problem has been answered.

BACKGROUND

Theoretical Reflections

This chapter critically explores theoretical concepts and leading scholarly debates around the use of digital technologies and their impact on democracy in Africa. A thorough literature review has been done to intellectually justify the contribution of this chapter and advance the reader's understanding of the phenomenon being examined. The selection criteria of the papers reviewed in this chapter borrowed ideas from the latest 27-point checklist of the Preferred Reporting Items for Systematic Reviews and Meta-analyses (PRISMA 2020) approach. The PRISMA 2020 approach is generally preferred as a methodology for conducting systematic literature reviews, ultimately allowing readers to assess the trustworthiness and applicability of the review findings (Page, 2021). While this chapter is not a systematic literature review, it will benefit from adopting some of PRISMA's guidelines for identifying, selecting, appraising, and synthesizing research studies. Specifically, selected papers were classified according to their aim and content relevant to the phenomena under study.

Various secondary sources such as the 2022 Democracy Index have also been used to analyse how some African governments fit into the three main cyber-debates under discussion. Regarding digitalisation, this chapter's theoretical framework is based on the technology acceptance model (TAM) which is an information systems theory that models how users come to accept and use technology. Marangunić and Granić (2015) argue that the fast pace of technological development means that a decision regarding its acceptance or rejection remains an open question. Chau (1996) posits that perceived usefulness and perceived ease of use of technology are key to determining whether that technology will be accepted by potential users.

On the issue of democracy, the theoretical framework is based on two theoretical frameworks of democracy - procedural democracy and substantive democracy. According to Gagnon and Chou (2013), procedural democracy examines the institutional arrangements for instance, the holdings of elections, public participation, rule of law, and the supremacy of the constitution, etc. It is associated with liberal democracy and separation of powers rather than popular control. The bulk of scholars of democracy focus on procedural democracy. Meanwhile, substantive democracy focuses on the socio-economic conditions of the people.

Overview of Democracy in Africa

The right to freedom of expression is a foundational element of any democratic society and is well protected under international and regional law. According to the International Institute for Democracy and Electoral Assistance (2021), there has been a gradual decline in democratic quality in Africa in the past ten years leading to 2011, with the number of countries designated as authoritarian now outweighing those deemed to be democratic. Campbell and Quinn (2021) also argue that there is a democratic decline accelerated by the COVID-19 pandemic and more Africans live under fully or partially authoritarian states today compared to the last two decades. They also paint a picture of an increasing number of African heads of state moving towards undermining their term limits in office or rigging elections to remain in power. The National Academies of Sciences, Engineering, and Medicine (1992) also warns that democracy in Africa is still very much tied to donor aid. It argues that Africa's continuing reliance on foreign aid has increased opportunities for bilateral and multilateral aid agencies to influence policymaking in many countries.

Taylor (2018) argues that Africa's first formalized liberal democracies came with various legislatures left behind by colonialists. However, soon after independence, many leaders enforced their imprints on the states, restructuring, even abolishing, the various institutions they controlled, suggesting them to be colonial burdens inappropriate for African conditions. He argues that despite changes to one-party systems of government, the quality of democracy in Africa is uneven. Furthermore, the entrenchment of democratic values remains shallow and compromised. Democratic citizenship is about the active involvement of citizens in governance (Sandel, 1996, cited by De Vries, 2018), but this is happening less often due to failures in traditional methods of participation known as invited spaces of participation (Masiko-Kambala et al (2012). Furthermore, Sandel also argues that for democracy to work well, citizens should not be seen just as voters or customers, but they must share authority and collaborate with administrators in a democratic society. Fombad (2021) also adds that the trend in the evolution of electoral democracy in Africa in the last three decades points to an authoritarian mobilisation and resurgence. He posits that while elections have become the norm, they are being increasingly used to disguise forms of undemocratic governance in many countries. Furthermore, Fombad (2021: 1) argues that,

.... there is no African country where democracy and constitutionalism can be thought of as firmly consolidated and secure. The number of countries which are declining due to failed or flawed electoral processes, or which show signs of stagnation, far exceed those that have improved to one degree or another. Current developments are not random ad hoc efforts to undermine the credibility of elections and democracy but rather, rational, and well-calculated responses by ruling African elites who seek to perpetuate their rule. What this points to is the need to rethink strategies for promoting genuinely competitive elections, democracy, and constitutionalism.

When analysing participation in some democratic societies, Masiko-Kambala et al (2012) also paint a picture of citizens who have lost confidence and trust in the governance system and view governance processes as being unresponsive and unaccountable to the issues of citizens. In the same breadth, Lues (2014) and Tshuma and Zvaita (2019) argue that democracy is facing challenges in Africa because the roles of government and citizens are not properly integrated to ensure accountability, transparency, and the effective provision of services. Furthermore, young people especially, feel disempowered by their political parties and other officials in leadership positions, hence they withdraw from participating in governance processes. In its 2021 briefing, the European Parliament also raised concern about the general democratic decline in many African countries characterised by restrictions on the freedom of expression both online and offline, the undermining of term limits, and efforts by governments to control the media and non-governmental organisations. The parliament also highlighted other issues linked to the widespread prevention of opposition candidates from participating in elections through intimidation and violence and the presence of weak electoral institutions that were independent but not impartial.

On the economic front, Joseph (1997) argues that the economic cultures of many African countries are still underdeveloped and unstable. He adds that they lack the necessary conditions to institute liberal democracy such as a strong and independent middle class, a competitive party system; constitutionalism and rule of law; a neutral bureaucracy, and strong market economies. High-level corruption and financial impropriety are likely to thrive in such conditions as previously witnessed in Nigeria, Gabon, and Senegal (Tar, 2010). Having highlighted the negative challenges faced by democracy in Africa, there are however glimmers of hope for the continent. Tar (2010) argues that there has been a steady expansion of liberal democracy following democratic reforms implemented in the 1990s across the continent. Prominent examples include the collapse of the apartheid system in South Africa in favour of multi-party democracy and the collapse of decades of single-party dictatorships and military rule in countries such as Algeria, the Democratic Republic of Congo (DRC), and Kenya among others.

Threats to Democracy in the Digital Age

To understand the impact of digital transformation on democracy it is necessary to start by defining the two main terms which are the focus of this chapter - democracy and digital transformation. *Firstly*, we need to understand what constitutes a democracy. There are many philosophical and sociological definitions of democracy, and there is no agreement on an international legally agreed definition (Council of Europe, 2021; Gagnon and Chou, 2013). Furthermore, Gagnon and Chou (2013) add that what one theorist, political leader, or nation sees as democracy, others may label it as something altogether different. The common thread however amongst many scholars appears to be rooted in democracy being viewed as a system of government by the people in which they have the power to choose their leaders either directly or through their elected representatives. Furthermore, in a democracy, people have the power to choose their leaders through free and fair elections. *Secondly,* digital transformation at its core in the public space refers to the introduction of digital technologies to promote new ways of citizen engagement and enhance the delivery of public services (Haug, Dan, and Mergel, 2023). Although many governments including those on the African continent have still not realised their goal of digitising all their public services and administrative processes, they are making progress toward changing public sector organizations (Enang, Asenova, and Bailey, 2020).

According to Dahlgren (2005), a general international consensus emerged in the early 1990s that democracy had hit hard times giving rise to the idea that online platforms including social media would somehow have a positive impact on rejuvenating democracy and fostering citizen participation. However, in recent years, internal threats to democracy have increased. Tenove (2017) and Goldschmidt (2013) posit that external forces have long tried to influence the outcome of elections more recently using the Internet. A well-documented example is the use of technologically designed bots designed to corrupt information systems, polling, and voting in the American presidential election in 2016. Tenove (2017) argues that foreign actors can use digital techniques to manipulate fair opportunities for citizen participation in elections such as interfering with the voting system, election databases, or contributing to public debates. They can also influence public deliberation, which enables citizens to share and understand each other's insights and perspectives and can also impact the work of electoral commissions, political parties, and other organisations, including the enforcement of electoral regulations.

In 2010, the Arab Spring was hailed as a game-changer for global politics leaving many people including scholars to believe that digital democracy was on the rise. Cyber-optimists, for instance, swear on the potential of digital platforms to enhance political debate, gather a wider diversity of opinions, and bring governance closer to communities. Fast forward a few years, due to increased polarisation, Internet shutdowns, and heightened censorship are slowly becoming the norm in many African democracies (Gopaldas, 2019). He also argues that the full impact of this development is not yet fully understood on the African continent.

The Digital Rights Landscape in SADC Report (2022) lists several factors that may threaten democracy in the digital age, and these include inadequate access to the Internet, the cost associated with Internet access which remains excessive, placing a serious barrier to access in poor communities, and the lack of decisive policy initiatives to address current challenges. New areas of concern have also emerged around worsening illiteracy, inherent biases in the technology industry, and social, cultural, and economic norms that reinforce harmful divisions (Digital Rights Landscape in SADC Report, 2022). Furthermore, concerns about data protection online remain a challenge, so too are the poor implementation of existing laws which infringe on citizens' rights to adequate data protection, and poor resourcing for data protection institutions is another obstacle to effective implementation. In countries such as South Africa, there is concern about the inability of the state-owned electricity supplier, Eskom, to meet demand by constantly implementing power cuts often referred to as load shedding.

In 2020, a non-scientific canvassing based on a non-random sample of several international digital experts by the US-based Pew Research Center nevertheless revealed interesting results about democracy in the digital age. About half of the respondents said people's uses of technology will mostly weaken core aspects of democracy and democratic representation, but even those who expressed optimism often voiced concerns. Answers ranged from concerns about the power of Internet companies and governments who do not serve democratic goals but their own, increased digitally networked surveillance, using digital spaces to exploit those that are digitally illiterate to using technology to target vulnerable populations and engineer elections, sowing confusion amongst the public, and weakening journalism which is critical for holding officials to account. There also seemed to be serious concern about the failure of governments to limit the power of tech corporations in developed countries with devastating consequences for democracies of the Global South and a worsening knowledge gap between data-rich countries and data-poor countries.

Cybersecurity, safeguarding personal information collected during electronic voter registration, spreading fake news, and gathering voter data through social media are all big features in discussions around digital elections. According to Goyayi (2021), balancing the advantages of e-voting systems against these concerns is a task that the South African IEC and policymakers will have to confront. Furthermore, she argues that the intersection of corruption, determination to win elections, and other widely reported concerns such as database hacking, media manipulation, and foreign technological interference are another deadly combination threatening the integrity of elections. In this way, technology is both a weapon and a crippling agent to the election. Goyayi's sentiments are also shared by Gopaldas (2019) who argues that despite several positive aspects of social media, there is now a risk of negative factors surpassing the benefits. For instance, the reposting of fake news was seen in both the Brexit vote in Europe and the Cambridge Analytica scandal, whereby data analytics were used to influence and manipulate the 2016 US election.

Impact of the Digital Divide

There is growing literature pointing to the severe limits, dangers, and problems of digital technologies on democracy such as social media. It is well-documented that the digital divide is also significant along class and economic lines in Africa (The Digital Rights Landscape in SADC Report, 2022). They argue that there are disproportionate levels of development between urban, peri-urban, and rural areas, and the extent of rural-urban digital divides in some countries remains relatively under-researched. Furthermore, the report says in cases where data is available, it paints a worrying picture. Digital inequalities can result from unequal access to hardware and resources including mobile phones and computers (Van Dijk and Hacker, 2003; Fuchs and Horak, 2008). They also argue that the failure to understand digital communication, the lack of Internet affordability, and the lack of meaningful usage opportunities are common in developing countries.

Bornman (2019) also argues that developing countries are generally among the least computerised regions in the world due to the lack of network infrastructure and basic communication infrastructure, leaving people unable to upskill themselves. In some instances, it has taken longer to repair faulty undersea cables linking the whole of sub-Saharan Africa to the rest of the world due lack of maintenance infrastructure. In August 2023, the 'only' underwater cable-laying ship authorised to tackle such repairs was believed to be working more than 8,000 kilometres away from the site where two cables providing Internet services in South Africa had snapped on the same day (News24, 2023). A digital expert is quoted in the report as having said that despite a slow Internet service, the number of cables around the African continent is increasing rapidly, meaning that more breaks in the cables can be expected. The expert cautioned that the lack of repair infrastructure and maintenance skills on the continent needed to be reconsidered going forward.

As information technology revolves globally, concern is also mounting about the role of authoritarian governments in using online platforms to control and shape the behaviour of their citizens through surveillance, repression, manipulation, censorship, and the provision of services to retain and expand political control (Millstein, 2010). She further argues that these governments conduct disinformation campaigns to manipulate citizens while penalizing and censoring dissenting speech on the Internet and elsewhere using strict laws. Many scholars warn that this form of control may also facilitate the widespread abuse of human rights in these countries. The situation can be explained in reverse in liberal democracies such as South Africa where there is a general mood of optimism in government about the potential of digital technologies to improve services, increase citizen participation in government, and mobilise young people to re-engage politically.

Additionally, the digital divide in Africa presents barriers to digital access for specific demographics in both urban and rural areas, including women and children, and people living with disabilities (The Digital Rights Landscape in SADC Report, 2022). They argue that from an educational standpoint in many countries, there is generally a lower enrolment rate for girls in modules that would enhance their digital and technological literacy skills. Specific reference is made to Science, Technology, Engineering, and Mathematics skills. Furthermore, some countries have limited data on gender disparities in Information and Communications Technology (ICT), making it hard to determine what the real needs of those countries are (The Digital Rights Landscape in SADC Report, 2022). Norris (2001) argues that exclusion from ICT also affects citizens' chances of obtaining better careers and greater personal advancement besides educational opportunities. Norris' argument is best supported by Blignaut (2009) who posits by sighting various sources that the digital divide is not only a matter of possessing a household personal computer or having access to the Internet. Rather, it is the use of specific technology that determines who is ahead, who is catching up, and who is left behind in the information society.

Mutsvairo and Ragnedda (2019) argue that Africa is a complex continent and not every government considers access to digital information as a right (La Rue, 2011). According to Mutsvairo and Ragnedda (2019), policymakers keen to see much of the continent digitally connected do not realise or are not willing to accept that Africa is not a country. Therefore, they argue that it is important for communities to see the value of digital participation if the whole process is to be sustainable. This is particularly true for communities fighting against perceived integration into the so-called modern and civilized world. Furthermore, Mutsvairo and Ragnedda (2019) argue that there is a need to fix the digital gaps in Africa, but policymakers need to ensure that their solutions are in line with the realities of the complexities on the ground. The Digital Rights Landscape in SADC Report, 2022) also cites that the digital divide in Africa is also significant along class and economic lines. This is largely due to disproportionate levels of development between urban, peri-urban, and rural areas. Moreover, the report warns that the rural-urban digital divide is relatively under-researched, but the available data paints a worrying picture of the future of digital transformation in the continent.

THE CYBER-DEBATES

Many African governments have been forced to review their stance on digitalisation in a bid to resolve several social conflicts and other issues affecting the state of democracy. Three key debates are emphasized in this quest to confront the challenges on the continent. *Firstly,* there is one side backed by *cyber-optimists* which sees digital transformation as promoting and strengthening democracy (Driss, Mellouli, and Trabelsi, 2019), and *secondly*, there is a side backed by *cyber-pessimists* that argues that the use of social media by governments might reinforce existing power dynamics and create new challenges for inclusion, accountability, and democracy (Feeney and Porumbescu, 2020). These scholars are also concerned about the increase in the use of Artificial Intelligence and automated decision-making in the public sector and their contribution to widening the digital divide in developing countries, and the spread of fake news and misinformation often considered a threat to democracy, especially in authoritarian regimes. *Thirdly*, scholars such as Morozov (2009 and 2011) and Miller and Vaccari (2020) argue for a third side to the debate backed by *cyber-realists* who have opted to remain neutral about the reality of what is happening in cyberspace. Each of the cyber-debates is discussed in detail below.

Cyber-Optimist Debate

To cyber-optimists, the Internet is one of the biggest tools for democratisation and political freedom. According to Shirky (2008) and Diamond (2010), digital platforms such as social media can be branded as *liberation technology* and *technology of freedom*. They argue that digital technology assists activist groupings in their quest to reinvigorate democratic processes. Liberation technology is defined as any form of information and communication technology that can expand political, social, and economic freedom (Diamond, 2010). He also argues that this type of technology enables citizens to report news, expose wrongdoing, express opinions, mobilize protest, monitor elections, scrutinize government, deepen participation, and expand the horizons of freedom.

Cyber-optimists argue that researchers, governments, and citizens alike have little choice but to embrace new technological changes and try and incorporate them into their programmes and policies in a fast-changing world. They do caution, however, that this does not mean that citizens should discard their old beliefs, values, and morals (Maseko, 2022). Instead, citizens are urged to accept new ways of doing things and must be able to adapt to an advanced technological world. The technology of freedom can be best explained using the ideas of Soriano (2013) and Oreskovich (2011). According to Soriano (2013: 334), the Internet is a form of technology with 'intrinsically democratic characteristics and enjoys widespread popular acceptance.' Meanwhile, Oreskovich (2011) argues that if you want to free a society, just give them the Internet because it is potentially free of hierarchy and, can allow for interaction, talking, and listening. While Oreskovich's stance on the Internet is correct, it is somewhat debatable as evidence has shown through various research that sometimes people may not engage with their followers on online platforms such as social media presenting challenges for citizen participation in democratic processes.

The growth and evolution of digital platforms such as social media have created a new space for global activism with the introduction of prominent movements such as #BlackLivesMatter, #MeToo, and others (Sturgess et al., 2018). They argue that conversations on these platforms were related to race, violence, and law enforcement. The evolution of Twitter particularly has changed how Americans view social media's impact on political and civic engagement. For example, the #BlackLivesMatter was first coined in 2013 following the acquittal of George Zimmerman in the shooting of unarmed black teenager Trayvon Martin. The US-based Pew Research Center found that the hashtag had over 17 0000 tweets a day as of May 2018. According to Mickoleit (2014), governments have also witnessed how individuals and interest groups are influencing political agendas and policy processes through social media by discussing important topics such as elections, political campaigns, disasters and emergencies, and political unrest on Twitter, Facebook, and WhatsApp.

Cyber-Pessimist Debate

Cyber-pessimists argue that the most common uses of the Internet are for casual social interaction, entertainment, information-searching, and email (Day, Janus, and Davis, 2005, Nie and Erbring, 2000). They argue that citizens have less time left to devote to civic activities or social activities. Many people rely on social media for social acceptance by measuring the number of '*likes* ' of their posts. Crucially, digital online platforms are all commercial entities designed to make a profit through targeted advertising (Sytaffel, n.d.). Later cyber-pessimists (Morozov, 2011; Gladwell, 2010; Lindgren, 2017) argue the Internet may also promote reactionary and degrading processes such as child pornography, human trafficking, religious intolerance, fascism, and racism. Cyber-pessimists such as Putnam (2000); and MacKenzie and Wacjcman (1999) argue that the rise of the Internet has led to a proliferation of right-wing propaganda which can result in the collapse of modern governments. Lindgren (2017) argues that the Internet has led the world to a stage where people are using search engines such as Google to look for answers to life's problems instead of asking a friend. Cyber-pessimists question the revolutionary, democratic potential, and general benefits of social media in bringing about political change for various reasons. For example, Gladwell (2010) argues that social media platforms are built around weak ties with "friends" that one will probably never meet in real life.

Cyber-pessimists also argue that the digital divide, especially in developing countries poses a new threat to democracy. According to Lee (2018), the world has witnessed repeated scares around the impact of factors such as fake news, cybersecurity, and technology addiction. Major social media platforms and governments are adapting their digitalisation policies to see how they can deal with the challenges of breaches in data privacy, management, access, and affordability, for example. Makwana et al. (2018) also argue that at an individual level, social media can also have devastating effects on body image, self-concept, and body dissatisfaction. They argue that it can also cause people to doubt themselves such that they may not want to participate in democratic processes. Furthermore, social media usage can also lead to cyberbullying, especially among the youth through sending aggressive and unpleasant emails and posting unflattering and manipulated photos (Petersen, 2019). Consolidating democracy involves making African leaders accountable to citizens and responsive to their needs and aspirations. Pessimistic scholars agree that both democracy and development may be strengthened by including citizens in decision-making processes, especially at the local level. In many cases, the results of research have been far from the ideal, often pointing to further problems of exclusion due to weak democratic institutions and traditional methods of participation.

Cyber-Realist Debate

Cyber-realists adopt a more cautious approach that transcends both the cyber-optimist and cyber-pessimist schools of thought. Morozov (2011) argues that technology is not a quick-fix solution to the crisis faced by democracy, especially in developing nations. He argues that in authoritarian regimes, social media is being used to track, suppress, and silence dissidents. According to Morozov, a revolution online is only possible in a regime where the state apparatus is completely ignorant of the Internet and has no virtual presence of its own. Furthermore, Campbell and Quinn (2021) also warn that as many African governments become more authoritarian, citizens will be increasingly alienated from those claiming to represent them posing new threats and challenges to democracy.

According to Craig and Valeriano (2018), cyber-realists are also particularly concerned about cybercrime, the theft of classified government data, or the targeting of critical infrastructure by hackers. They also argue that cyber security poses a significant challenge to the economic and national security of countries globally, more so in Africa. In fact, according to The Economist (2010), cyberspace is now considered the fifth domain of warfare after land, sea, air, and space. This means that many countries are strengthening their cyber defence, cyber intelligence, and offensive capabilities online.

Cyber-realists, like cyber-pessimists, argue that the rise of digital media can cause the mass surveillance of citizens, and spread disinformation, electoral interference, and partisan polarization. Furthermore, Miller and Vaccari (2020) raise concerns about increased toxicity online, coordinated hate, and intimidation which threaten democratic norms, institutions, and governance. They argue that the once-heralded tools of digital liberation have been repurposed and distributed in antidemocratic ways that were never imagined by theorists of digital politics a decade ago. To advance their understanding of some potential sources of digital threats to democracy and how citizens are affected, Miller and Vaccari sought perspectives from twenty-three countries covering four different continents in 2020. The insights ranged in a nutshell from scholars who expressed concern about covert foreign propaganda on social media threatening electoral integrity and democratic sovereignty to citizens overwhelmed by constant misinformation and disinformation in the digital age.

CASE STUDIES

The most recent 2022 Democracy Index compiled by the respected Economist Intelligence Unit (EIU) is used to analyse how some African governments fit into the three main cyber-debates discussed above. The annual report assesses the state of democracy in nearly 170 countries. Based on the score a country receives ranging from 0 to 10, it is either classified as a *full democracy, flawed democracy, hybrid regime*, or an *authoritarian regime*. The EIU index assesses countries based on electoral processes, political culture, participation, government functioning, and civil liberties, providing a comprehensive understanding of democratic performance. It is, however, worth noting that there are a few other democracy indexes that can be used for analysis. Country-specific case studies were drawn from South Africa, Kenya, the Democratic Republic of Congo, and Ethiopia for various reasons specified below. Many other examples from across the African continent can be used to illustrate the cyber-debate discussed in this chapter.

On the *optimistic* side, two countries (*South Africa and Kenya*) have been randomly selected from the Top 10 overall categories of those leading in the 2022 democracy index rankings. These countries were selected because they also enjoyed some of the highest Internet connections on the African continent with 41.19 million and 23.35 million Internet users respectively in January 2022 according to Oluwole (2022). This will make it simpler to analyse their digital performance about their democratic standing and prospects for the future. On the *pessimistic/realist* side, experiences are drawn from countries such as the Democratic Republic of the Congo and Ethiopia which were found to be amongst the most authoritarian regimes in Africa. Interestingly, these countries were also found to have some of the highest Internet users on the African continent with 16.50 million and 29.83 million Internet users respectively in January 2022 (Oluwole, 2022).

Lessons From South Africa

According to the Democracy Index (2022), South Africa is ranked 45th and is classified as having a '*flawed democracy*' meaning that elections are free and fair, and even if there are problems such as infringements on media freedom, basic civil liberties are respected (Economist Intelligence Unit, 2022). Furthermore, the EIU argues that in this category, there are still significant weaknesses in other aspects of democracy, including problems in governance, an underdeveloped political culture, and low levels of political participation.

South Africa became a democracy in 1994 after transitioning from the formal system of apartheid (Siddle and Koelble, 2016; Rossouw, 2019). Apart from being a victim of colonialism, systematic racism, apartheid, sexism, and oppressive legislation, the country has one of the most unequal societies in the world (World Bank, 2018). Hopes of a better life were high for children born after the first democratic election in 1994, but almost 30 years later since they have come of age, they are still impacted by a range of inequalities, especially race, class, and gender. Attempts by the ruling African National Congress to wipe away the legacy of apartheid and colonialism have failed to narrow the imbalance between the rich and the poor (Sguazzin, 2021). Inequality has also manifested itself in unequal access to other services such as education, health, and jobs. The youth unemployment rate increased to 62.1 % in the first quarter of 2023 in South Africa according to data published quarterly by the government (Statistics South Africa, 2023).

Despite the government's efforts aimed at inclusion, almost three decades later there are still some fundamental problems with the quality of South Africa's democracy (Masiko-Kambala et al, 2012; Koma, 2010). They generalise that the delivery of services and other developmental mandates is still weak, especially at the local government level which is the sphere of government closest to the people. The outlook for democracy is also not promising partly due to its dependence on opposition politics to ensure accountability (Schrire, 2001) and evidence of state capture emphasizing widespread corruption in government. The poor financial status of some local governments has led to deepening levels of distrust in government institutions Coughlan (2020).

The advent of new technologies has impacted democratic and political engagement in South Africa, creating new opportunities for participation in political and governance processes. This is not to say that there are no challenges, most notably issues of access to technology, lack of technological skills, privacy concerns online, high data costs, and the spread of fake news (*including misinformation and disinformation*). While digital platforms such as Twitter, Facebook, and WhatsApp have arguably provided new avenues for political engagement as argued by cyber-optimists, there are still issues of youth voter apathy evidenced by low voter turnouts and declining registration numbers in the 2021 local government election and other previous elections. A worsening digital divide has also cast doubt on existing and often formalised methods of citizen participation in political processes for the youth classified as those between the ages of 14 and 35 years old. Jensen (2001) argues that Internet access in South Africa has been largely confined to urban areas. Internet users were predominantly white, city-dwellers, relatively affluent, and well-educated (Jensen, 2001).

Despite its challenges, South Africa, with over 40 million active Internet users at the start of January 2022 (Statista, 2023), had some of the highest numbers of Internet users in Africa. Statistics also show that 28 million people or around 46% of the population use social media. All this evidence makes the country fertile ground for showcasing how digital transformation benefits or threatens democracy. Manual voting presented various challenges in the 2021 local government election given the outbreak of the COVID-19 pandemic. The Independent Electoral Commission (IEC), while ensuring adherence to national health regulations to protect the general population from the pandemic, embarked on a pilot project on the use of voter management devices (VMDs) to boost electoral management in the country. Over 30 000 of such devices were deployed countrywide and they were centrally connected through an access point network. According to Mzekandaba (2021), the VMDs enabled the strengthening of controls in the voting process, however, there were still some challenges (Mare, 2022). For instance, he argues that the details of over 60,000 voters were not uploaded into the electoral system and as a result, they could not vote. Cautiously though, Mare feels technology is not to blame for the exclusions but rather a shorter-than-usual time to organise the 2021 elections.

The IEC also wanted to test e-voting, but this proposal was rejected by the Parliamentary Portfolio Committee for Home Affairs, citing fears of hacking and insufficient budgets. In their study of youth political engagement in South Africa's 2014 general election, Mhlomi and Osunkunle (2022) also found evidence that social media played a significant role in political campaigns. This was especially true for participants of the study who had access to the Internet and were active users of social media platforms. Although small, their study, including this one, serves to indicate the possibilities of online engagement, especially when the effectiveness of traditional participation methods is being questioned.

Lessons From Kenya

The Republic of Kenya is considered a leader in digitalisation in Eastern Africa (Estonian Centre for International Development, 2022). They argue that Kenya has good Internet connectivity, a hugely successful mobile money service, and a wide range of electronic services available to the public. The country also launched the National Digital Master Plan for 2022–2032 covering various programmes aimed at promoting better Internet connectivity at the local level, digitisation of government records, and automation of all government systems. Kenya became a republic in 1964. According to the Democracy Index (2022), Kenya is ranked 94th and is classified as a *'hybrid regime'* meaning that elections have substantial irregularities that often prevent them from being both free and fair (Economist Intelligence Unit, 2022). Furthermore, the EIU argues that government pressure on opposition parties and candidates may be common in Kenya, and typically in hybrid regimes, corruption tends to be widespread, and the rule of law is weak. Civil society is also weak.

A study on Kenya's Digital Readiness shows that in 2021, the country had 21.75 million Internet users and an Internet penetration rate of 40%. Furthermore, the report shows that there were 59.6 million mobile connections in Kenya, out of which 33.1 million feature phones and 26.5 million smartphones. According to the Communications Authority of Kenya, at least 94% of the Kenyan population was covered by the 4G network at the end of 2021. These statistics are crucial for determining the level of Internet connectivity in the country and understanding how digital technology could be used to benefit democratic online participation. Despite the impressive connectivity statistics, the Digital Readiness Report cautions that the digital divide is still high in Kenya with 44% of the urban population having access to the Internet compared to only 17% in rural areas. The gaps in basic digital skills are said to reinforce this divide. The government has also been lauded for supporting digital technology through various initiatives including the recently launched Kenya National Digital Master Plan 2022-2032.

According to Nitsche (2019), e-citizenship services, super-fast Internet speeds, and homegrown digital innovations have also made Kenya a *digital-first society*. He also argues that Kenyans use social media platforms including Twitter, Facebook, and Instagram to voice their opinions about various issues affecting the country and citizens often rally around the popular hashtag #KOT or Kenyans on Twitter to debate political and societal matters. He also argues that local bloggers are increasingly gaining the recognition of mainstream journalists as reliable sources of information. However, Nitsche warns that the urban and well-educated elite seem to be benefitting more from Internet connections compared to people living in rural areas where digital participation is still relatively weak. He attributes the problem to high data and hardware costs and the lack of necessary digital skills. Kenya's 2017 general elections are reported to have exposed the very worst that technology in Kenya has to offer. Nitsche (2019) argues that rival political camps paid bloggers to spread propaganda on social media in their parties' interest.

Lessons From the Democratic Republic of Congo

According to the Democracy Index (2022), the Democratic Republic of Congo (DRC) is ranked 162nd and is classified as being run by an *authoritarian government*. Many countries in this category are outright dictatorships (Economist Intelligence Unit, 2022). Furthermore, some formal institutions of democracy may exist, but these have little substance. The EIU also argues that if elections do occur in authoritarian governments, they are not free and fair and there is a disregard for abuses and infringements of civil liberties.

Tungali (2017) argues that the first shutdown of digital communications in the DRC was in December 2011 and lasted for 25 days. He further argues that at the time, few people appreciated the magnitude of this state-initiated act or knew how to respond to it. There have been a few other shutdowns also leading to the chaotic presidential poll of December 2018 Gopaldas (2019). He argues that a total block on Internet connectivity and SMS services was imposed and there was very little news coming of the country, also making it increasingly difficult for civil society and protesters to mobilise themselves. Furthermore, independent electoral observers could also not communicate and share their findings. The government tried to justify its actions of shutting down the Internet in the name of protecting citizens in what became widely seen as the repression of digital liberties (Gopaldas, 2019). The Internet was also shut down in December 2019 in a likely attempt to dampen speculation about the presidential election results (Aljazeera, 2019). This time, a senior advisor to President Joseph Kabila said this was done to preserve public order after *fictitious results* began circulating on social media.

According to Gopaldas (2019), a pattern has emerged in authoritarian regimes where leaders simply learn new tricks to undermine and manipulate their electorates. He also argues that many such countries have limited mechanisms to combat such interference. Tungali (2017) argues that in a country of over 70 million people where only 4% of the inhabitants are connected to the Internet due to limited infrastructure and high access costs, Internet shutdowns by the government and surveillance and censorship practices, undermine the development of an inclusive Internet society.

Lessons From Ethiopia

According to the Democracy Index (2022), Ethiopia is ranked 122nd and is classified as being run by an *'authoritarian' government'* just like the DRC above. Ethiopia's digital drive and current policies to advance and implement digital transformation are inspired by China, particularly the role played by digital technologies in integrating small businesses (Tesfachew, 2022). He also makes an argument that Ethiopian policymakers have a poor understanding of the policy, regulatory measures, and scale of investment undertaken by China also ranked as an authoritarian government in the democracy index. According to Feldstein (2021), since the early 2000s, Ethiopia has displayed a dismal track record when it comes to digital freedom. Feldstein argues that this is evidenced by Internet shutdowns, rising disinformation, and traditions of online censorship and surveillance.

According to the Digital Ethiopia 2025 strategy, the government views digital technology as key to achieving an *inclusive, knowledge-based, and prosperous society.* The local Center for Advancement of Rights and Democracy (2023) also known as CARD argues despite the strategy, Internet access across the country remains unequal and expensive, with large portions of people completely excluded from accessing the Internet. Those who are excluded include people living in rural areas, older people, and the poor (CARD, 2023). Statistics show that most Ethiopians can access the Internet from their mobile phones. The disparity is explained by several infrastructure challenges, including poor electricity coverage (CARD, 2023). Various literature shows that other factors include low Internet penetration and poorly developed telecommunications infrastructure, lack of a proper legal and regulatory framework for e-government, and lack of leadership commitment and investment in the local Telecom sector.

Critiques say the Ethiopian government is also notorious for shutting down the Internet, not only damaging the trust of citizens in the government but also failing to uphold human rights. The Ethiopian government often uses excuses of national security concerns, public order, insecurity, and others as the main reasons for the Internet shutdown (CARD, 2023). They argue that the worst crisis is in the region of Tigray where the Internet and most other means of communication have been completely shut down since November 2020. According to Desta (2018), Ethiopia's increasing digital divide is worrisome and the government seems to allow the development of the sector in a highly controlled environment or a slower manner.

FINDINGS AND DISCUSSION

The debate around the adoption of digital tools to possibly solve some of the historical challenges faced by democracy in Africa continues. Even in countries with free and fair elections and good Internet connectivity such as South Africa and Kenya, there are still some concerns about the failures of digital technology to deliver on its promises. Take South Africa for example, the use of VMDs in the 2021 local government elections failed to address ongoing and well-documented issues of voter apathy, low voter turnouts, and trust in government. This means more work for researchers through potential collaborations with practitioners and other stakeholders to further investigate the root causes of the persistent challenges. The evidence presented in this chapter also shows that digitalisation undoubtedly exposes democracy to new threats across the continent, but its benefits cannot be understated. Authoritarian governments also recognise the power of digital tools such as the Internet to influence their electorates. Their ongoing attempts to intimidate, undermine, and manipulate their nationals using Internet shutdowns, especially around election time, is evidence of the power and influence of digital technologies. Based on the TAM theoretical framework, some government leaders in Africa remain sceptical about endorsing the use of digital technologies albeit for different reasons. Those that do, seem to be driven by selfish motives. The application of the principles of liberal democracy is therefore questionable under such leaders.

DIRECTIONS FOR THE FUTURE

The author hopes that the lessons drawn from this paper will assist scholars, researchers, and practitioners in their quest to better understand the complexities presented by digital technologies in cyberspace. It is hoped that they will be inspired to do more research in this field while keeping up with the demands of a global digital explosion and a worsening digital divide in the developing world. Collaborations between digital media companies who care about democracy and policymakers can help the world understand the threats posed by digital transformation to democracy in Africa. This is particularly important given the many benefits of democracy towards improving the lives of ordinary citizens on the continent.

CONCLUSION AND RECOMMENDATIONS

This chapter highlighted concerns from cyber-pessimists and others about the spread of fake news, the failure to safeguard personal information collected using digital tools such as VMDs during elections, and the processing and handling of voter data collected through social media. Collectively, these issues feature prominently in discussions around the impact of digital technologies on democracy in Africa. Therefore, to answer whether democracy is indeed under threat in Africa due to digital transformation, it can be concluded that without proper policies in place and the lack of political will (especially in authoritarian states), the future of democracy in these countries is bleak. On their own, digital technologies will not deepen citizen engagement and promote service delivery which are the expected outcomes in healthy democracies. Accountability and transparency in state institutions are also likely to fail if some citizens are excluded from accessing the technologies to participate in politics. What is required are new frameworks developed through processes such as rigorous research to keep up with the rapid adoption of digital technologies and their impacts on democratic processes.

REFERENCES

Aljazeera. (2019). *DR Congo internet restored after 20-day suspension over elections*. Aljazeera. https://www.aljazeera.com/news/2019/1/20/dr-congo-internet-restored-after-20-day-suspension-over-elections

Allen, K. (2023). *A key feature in Kenya was influencers trying to delegitimise the media by presenting them as partisan.* ISS Africa. https://issafrica.org/iss-today/risks-of-digital-influence-lessons-for-south-africas-2024-election

Blignaut, P. (2009). A bilateral perspective on the digital divide in South Africa. *Perspectives on Global Development and Technology*, *8*(4), 581–601. doi:10.1163/156915009X12583611836091

Bornman, E. (2019). *Information society and digital divide in South Africa: Results of Longitudinal Surveys*. Department of Communication Science. University of South Africa.

Campbell, J., & Quinn, N. (2021). What's happening to democracy in Africa? CFR. https://www.cfr.org/article/whats-happening-democracy-africa

Castells, M. (2012). *Networks of outrage and hope: Social movements in the internet age*. Polity Press.

Center for Advancement of Rights and Democracy. (2023). *Digital divide in Ethiopia*. CARDETH. https://www.cardeth.org/digital-divide

Chau, P. Y. K. (1996). An empirical assessment of a modified technology acceptance model. *Journal of Management Information Systems*, *13*(2), 185–204. doi:10.1080/07421222.1996.11518128

Coughlan, S. (2020). *Dissatisfaction with democracy 'At record high.'* BBC. https://www.bbc.com/news/education-51281722

Council of Europe. (2021). *Study of the impact of digital transformation on democracy and Good Governance*. European Committee on Democracy and Governance.

Craig, A., & Valeriano, B. (2018). *Realism and cyber conflict: Security in the digital age*. E-IR. https://www.e-ir.info/2018/02/03/realism-and-cyber-conflict-security-in-the-digital-age/

Dahlgren, P. (2005). *The internet, public spheres, and political communication: Dispersion and deliberation.* Taylor & Francis. https://www.tandfonline.com/doi/pdf/10.1080/10584600590933160

Day, J. C., Janus, A., & Davis, J. (2005). *Computer and internet use in the United States: 2003* (October 2015 ed.). US Department of Commerce. https://www.census.gov/prod/2005pubs/p23-208.pdf,

De Vries, S. (2018). *Enhancing participatory democracy in municipal affairs through the ward committee system: A participatory monitoring and evaluation approach.* [Master's Thesis, University of Western Cape].

Desta, T. (2018). Comments on the digitalization and digital divide in the Horn of Africa (HoA), Kenya and Ethiopia: The Media Perspective. *Global Media Journal.*

Diamond, L. (2010). Liberation technologies. *Journal of Democracy, 21*(3), 69–83. doi:10.1353/jod.0.0190

Digital Rights Landscape in SADC. (2022). *The digital rights landscape in Southern Africa.* CHR. https://www.chr.up.ac.za/images/researchunits/dgdr/documents/reports/Digital_Rights_Landscape_in_SADC_Report.pdf

Driss, O. B., Mellouli, S., & Trabelsi, Z. (2019). From citizens to government policymakers: Social media data analysis. *Government Information Quarterly, 36*(3), 560–570. doi:10.1016/j.giq.2019.05.002

E-Governance Academy. (2022). *Kenya digital readiness: A journey towards human-centred digitilisation.* e-Governance Academy.

Economist Intelligence Unit. (2022). *Frontline democracy and the battle for Ukraine.* EIU Report. EIU.

Enang, I., Asenova, D., & Bailey, S. J. (2022). Identifying influencing factors of sustainable public service transformation: A systematic literature review. *International Review of Administrative Sciences, 88*(1), 258–280. doi:10.1177/0020852319896399

Estonian Centre for International Development. (2022). *Team Europe launch digital readiness study for Kenya to support Kenya's digitalisation efforts as the Silicon Savannah.* ESTDEV. https://estdev.ee/estdev-en/1778/?lang=en

European Parliament. (2021). *State of democracy in Sub-Saharan Africa: Democratic progress at risk.* European Parliament. https://www.europarl.europa.eu/RegData/etudes/BRIE/2021/690647/EPRS_BRI(2021)690647_EN.pdf

Feeney, M. K., & Porumbescu, G. (2020). The limits of social media for public administration research & practice. *Public Administration Review, 81*(1), 792.

Feldstein, S. (2021). *Transformation and setbacks in Ethiopia, The rise of digital repression: How technology is reshaping power, politics, and resistance.*

Fombad, C. M. (2021). An overview of the state of electoral democracy in Africa. *African Journal of Legal Studies, 14*(2), 245–268. doi:10.1163/17087384-12340087

Fuchs, C., & Horak, E. (2008). Africa and the digital divide. *Telematics and Informatics,* 25(2), 0736-5853. doi:10.1016/j.tele.2006.06.004

Gagnon, J., & Chou, M. (2013). *The theories, concepts and practices of democracy.* Palgrave Macmillan.

Gladwell, M. (2010). Small change: Why the revolution will not be Tweeted. *The New Yorker.* Retrieved from https://www.newyorker.com/magazine/2010/10/04/small-changemalcolm-gladwell

Goldschmidt, R. (2013). *Cyber space and protection of critical infrastructures.* Knesset Centre for Research Information (Hebrew).

Gopaldas, R. (2019). *Digital dictatorship versus digital democracy in Africa.* South African Institute of International Affairs. https://www.jstor.org/stable/resrep25956

Haug, N., Dan, S., & Mergel, I. (2023). Digitally induced change in the public sector: A systematic review and research agenda. *Public Management Review*, 1–25. doi:10.1080/14719037.2023.2234917

Hodges, N. E. (1972). Neo-Colonialism: The new rape of Africa. *The Black Scholar, 3*(5), 5, 12–23. doi:10.1080/00064246.1972.11431211

Institute for Democracy and Electoral Assistance. (2021). *The state of democracy in Africa and the Middle East 2021: Resilient democratic aspirations and opportunities for consolidation.* IDEA. https://www.idea.int/democracytracker/sites/default/files/2022-11/state-of-democracy-in-africa-and-the-middle-east-2021.pdf (Accessed 10 August 2023).

Jensen, M. (2001) *The African internet - A 2001 status report.* Digital Divide. http://www.digitaldivide.net/articles/view.php?ArticleID=322

Joseph, R. (1997). Democratization in Africa after 1989: Comparative and theoretical perspectives. *Comparative Politics, 29*(3), 363–382. doi:10.2307/422126

Khapoya, V. B. (2012). Colonialism and the African experience. In *The African Experience* (4th ed.). Routledge.

Koma, S.B. (2010). The state of local government in South Africa: Issues, trends and options. *Journal of Public Administration.*

La Rue, F. (2011). *Report of the special rapporteur on the promotion and protection of the right to freedom of opinion and expression.* United Nations General Assembly.

Lee, B. (2018). *Social media is changing: These 3 things are the key to staying ahead of it.* INC. https://www.inc.com/ben-lee/heres-what-an-evolving-social-medialandscape-means-for-business-owners.html

Lim, M. (2013). Framing Bouazizi: White lies, hybrid network, and collective/connective action in the 2010–11 Tunisian uprising. *Journalism, 14*(7), 921–941. doi:10.1177/1464884913478359

Lindgren, S. (2017). Digital media and society. *Sage (Atlanta, Ga.).*

Lues, L. (2014). Citizen participation as a contributor to sustainable democracy in South Africa. *International Review of Administrative Sciences, 80*(4), 789–807. doi:10.1177/0020852314533450

Makwana, B., Lee, Y., Parkin, S., & Farmer, L. (2018). *Selfie-Esteem: The relationship between body dissatisfaction and social media in adolescent and young women.* The Inquisitive Mind.

Marangunić, N., & Granić, A. (2015). Technology acceptance model: A literature review from 1986 to 2013. *Universal Access in the Information Society, 14*(1), 81–95. doi:10.100710209-014-0348-1

Mare, A. (2021). WiFi 6 tech deployed for the first time in SA Elections. ITWeb. https://www.itweb.co.za/content/PmxVE7KlPQpMQY85

Maseko, M. M. (2022). *Social media, protest and citizen participation in local government: A comparison between the City of Cape Town and Johannesburg metropolitan municipalities: 2010 to 2017.* [PhD Thesis, University of the Western Cape].

Masiko-Kambala, P., Görgens, T., & van Donk, M. (2012). Advancing 'networked spaces': Making a case for communities of practice to deepen public participation. In *GGLN (Good governance learning network) Putting participation at the heart of development//Putting development at the heart of participation.* GGLN and Isandla Institute.

Mickoleit, A. (2014). Social media use by governments: A policy primer to discuss trends, identify policy opportunities and guide decision makers. *OECD Working Papers on Public Governance, No. 26.* OECD Publishing.

Miller, M. L., & Vaccari, C. (2020). Digital threats to democracy: Comparative lessons and possible remedies. *The International Journal of Press/Politics, 25*(3), 333–356. doi:10.1177/1940161220922323

Millstein, M. (2010). Limits to local democracy: The politics of urban governance transformations in Cape Town, Working Paper No. 2, *Swedish Centre for Local Democracy (ICLD): ICLD*, Visby.

Morozov, E. (2009). Iran: Downside to the "Twitter revolution". *Dissent, 56*(4), 10–14. doi:10.1353/dss.0.0092

Morozov, E. (2011). *The net delusion: The dark aide of internet freedom.*

Mutsvairo, B. and Ragnedda, M. (2019). *Comprehending the digital disparities in Africa.* Springer. . doi:10.1515/9789048538225-003

Mzekandaba, S. 2021. New tech 'catapulted' electoral management, says IEC. ITWeb. https://www.itweb.co.za/content/JN1gP7OYgWwqjL6m

National Academies of Sciences, Engineering, and Medicine. (1992). *Democratization in Africa: African Views, African Voices.* The National Academies Press. . doi:10.17226/2041

News24. (2023). *Only one cable-laying ship can fix snapped underwater cables and it's still on the other side of Africa.* News24. https://www.news24.com/news24/tech-and-trends/news/only-one-cable-laying-ship-can-fix-snapped-underwater-cables-and-its-still-on-the-other-side-of-africa-20230815

Nie, N. H., & Erbring, L. (2000). Internet and society: A preliminary report. *Stanford Institute for the Quantitative Study of Society., 3*, 14–19.

Nitsche, L. (2019). *A tale of two Kenyas: Digitalization has brought change but not always for the better.* Akademie. https://akademie.dw.com/en/a-tale-of-two-kenyas-digitalization-has-brought-change-but-not-always-for-the-better/a-47198710 (Accessed 7 August 2023).

Norris, P. (2001). *Digital divide: Civic engagement, information poverty, and the internet worldwide.* Cambridge University Press. doi:10.1017/CBO9781139164887

Oluwole, V. (2022). 10 African countries that have the most number of internet users in 2022. In *Business Insider Africa.* https://africa.businessinsider.com/local/markets/10-african-countries-that-have-the-most-number-of-internet-users-in-2022/cy3p01v

Oreskovich, A. (2011). *Egyptian activist creates image issue for Google*. Reuters. https://www.reuters.com/article/us-egypt-google-idUSTRE71B0L520110212

Page, M. (2021). *PRISMA 2020 explanation and elaboration: Updated guidance and exemplars for reporting systematic reviews*. BMJ. https://www.bmj.com/content/372/bmj.n160

Pew Research Center. (2020). *Many experts say digital disruption will hurt democracy*. Pew Research Center. https://www.pewresearch.org/internet/2020/02/21/concerns-about-democracy-in-the-digital-age/

Rossouw, M. (2019). *Public participation: An imperative for governance and human rights – lessons from South Africa*. Future Africa Forum. http://futureafricaforum.org/2019/03/04/publicparticipation-an-imperative-for-governance-and-human-rights-lessons-from-south-africa/

Rumbul, R. (2015). *Who benefits from civic technology? Demographic and public attitudes research into the users of civic technologies*. mySociety.

Schrire, R. (2001). The realities of opposition in South Africa: Legitimacies, strategies and consequences. *Democratization*, *8*. . doi:10.1080/714000189

Sguazzin, A. (2021). South Africa wealth gap unchanged since apartheid, says world inequality lab. *Time Magazine*. https://time.com/6087699/south-africa-wealth-gap-unchanged-since-apartheid/

Shirky, C. (2008). *Here comes everybody: The power of organizing without organisations*.

Siddle, A. & Koelble. (2016). Local government in South Africa: Can the objectives of the developmental state be achieved through the current model of decentralised governance? Swedish International Centre for Local Democracy. https://icld.se/app/uploads/files/forskningspublikationer/siddle-koelble-icld-report-7.pdf.

Soriano, M. R. T. (2013). Internet as a driver of political change: Cyber-pessimists and cyber-optimists. *Journal of the Spanish Institute of Strategic Studies*, *1*, 332–352.

Statista. (2023). *Digital population in South Africa as of January 2022*. Statista. https://www.statista.com/statistics/685134/south-africa-digital-population/

Statistics South Africa. (2023). *60,6 Million people in South Africa*. SSA. https://www.statssa.gov.za/?p=15601

Tar, U. A. (2010). The challenges of democracy and democratisation in Africa and Middle East. *Information, Society and Justice*, *3*(2), 81-94.

Taylor, I. (2018). *Democracy in Africa, African politics: A very short introduction, Very short introductions*. Academic. https://academic.oup.com/book/682/chapter-abstract/135365487?redirectedFrom=fulltext

Tenove, C. (2017). *Digital threats to democratic elections: How foreign actors use digital techniques to undermine democracy*. Centre for the Study of Democratic Institutions. The University of British Columbia. https://democracy2017.sites.olt.ubc.ca/files/2018/01/DigitalThreats_Report-FINAL.pdf

Tesfachew, T. (2022). Ethiopia's drive to advance digital transformation. UNCTAD. https://unctad.org/system/files/information-document/BRI-Project_policy-brief-02_en.pdf.

The Conversation. (2020). How the Nigerian and Kenyan media handled Cambridge Analytica. *The Conversation*. https://theconversation.com/how-the-nigerian-and-kenyan-media-handled-cambridge-analytica-128473 (Accessed 11 October 2023).

The Economist. (2010). War in the fifth domain. *The Economist.* https://www.economist.com/briefing/2010/07/01/war-in-the-fifth-domain

Tshuma, D., & Zvaita, G. T. (2019). *Political fatalism and youth apathy in South Africa: An analysis of the 2019 general elections*. Accord. https://www.accord.org.za/conflicttrends/political-fatalism-and-youth-apathy-in-south-africa/

Tungali, A. (2017). The evolution of internet shutdowns in DR Congo. CIPESA. https://cipesa.org/2017/03/the-evolution-of-internet-shutdowns-in-dr-congo/

Van Dijk, J., & Hacker, K. (2003). The digital divide as a complex, dynamic phenomenon. *The Information Society*, *19*(4), 315–326. doi:10.1080/01972240309487

Washington Post. (2020). How Cambridge Analytica poisoned Kenya's democracy. *Washington Post.* https://www.washingtonpost.com/news/global-opinions/wp/2018/03/20/how-cambridge-analytica-poisoned-kenyas-democracy/

ADDITIONAL READINGS

Hlomani, H., & Ncube, C. B. (2023). Data regulation in Africa: Free flow of data, open data regimes and cybersecurity. In B. Ndemo, N. Ndung'u, S. Odhiambo, & A. Shimeles (Eds.), *Data governance and policy in Africa. Information Technology and Global Governance*. Palgrave Macmillan. doi:10.1007/978-3-031-24498-8_5

Mathe, L. (2022). The adoption of digital technology for South Africa's 2021 Municipal Elections, and prospects for the future. *Digital Policy Studies Journal, 1*(1), 13–26. doi:10.36615/dps.v1i1.1252

Peters, B. L. (2002). *The Challenges of democracy and democratisation in Southern Africa*. SA Yearbook of International Affairs.

KEY TERMS AND DEFINITIONS

Africa: The world's second largest continent mostly classified as underdeveloped.

Citizen Engagement: A form of interaction between citizens and their governments that is at the core of democracy and a representative government.

Democracy: A system of government in which people have the power to choose their leaders through free and fair elections.

Digital Technologies: The use and development of technology to enable citizen engagement and increased participation in political processes and transforming democratic decision-making.

Digital Transformation: The use of computer-based technologies to strengthen democracy and good governance.

Governance: A system by which a country is governed and controlled, and its officials are held to account.

Technology: The application of computerised knowledge to improve the performance of governments and citizen engagement.

Chapter 20
Media, Advocacy, and the Public Interest: Reflections From Southern Africa

Clayton Peel
https://orcid.org/0000-0002-7004-7416
Namibia University of Science and Technology, Namibia

ABSTRACT

The roles played by advocacy groups and the media in engaging governments as long-term partners are at once important and problematic. While some governments are progressive and happy to include alternative views, others eschew consultations. This study of civil society and state disaccord in three country contexts of the southern African region interrogates the non-governmental partners' roles at critical junctures. Partnerships between state and non-state actors are buffeted by geo-political dynamics and economic reversals that have rattled the post-liberation project in three countries. This chapter explores how a multi-sectoral oversight of key policy initiatives might avert the possibility of political expediency impinging on the imperatives of good governance and economic stability. The chapter incorporates conversations that ensued during a two-day inclusive democracy for sustainable development conference in Windhoek, Namibia, attended by government and civil society actors. It also draws on desk research and personal observations.

INTRODUCTION

The roles played by advocacy groups and the media in engaging governments as long-term partners for maintaining stability in African post-colonial states are at once important and problematic, given the differing attitudes of governments towards non-governmental partners[1] who seek to influence policy. While some governments are progressive and are happy to include alternative views, or at least to listen to them, others assert their mandates to rule and to make policies based on having won elections, thus eschewing consultations with the wider body politic. A synopsis of recent areas of disagreement in three

DOI: 10.4018/979-8-3693-0477-8.ch020

country contexts of the southern African region – Namibia, South Africa, and Zimbabwe – is provided in this chapter to assess the value of non-governmental partners' participation in the region's economies in their current stages of political, social, and economic transformation. Avenues of partnership are explored between state and non-state actors in what historically have been free market economies but are now prone to statist prerogatives of labour and land rights interventions, company takeover actions, and equal opportunities legislation. Considering these geo-political dynamics, which have been accompanied by economic reversals that have rattled the post-liberation project in all three countries, this chapter was developed to advocate for a multi-sectoral oversight of key policy initiatives, to avert the possibility of populism impinging on the imperatives of good governance and economic stability. The author presented a draft of this chapter to the two-day Inclusive Democracy for Sustainable Development conference in Windhoek, Namibia which ended on November 28, 2018. Desk research and personal observations have informed the chapter's findings. Overall, the chapter set out to achieve the objectives outlined below.

- To study the role of non-governmental actors in the pursuit of public interest and good governance in three sub-Saharan African contexts: Namibia, South Africa, and Zimbabwe.
- To examine how these non-state actors are perceived as they seek to influence public policy and practice.
- To provide models of state-civil society engagement that have emerged in US and Asian contexts and assess their suitability for sub-Saharan Africa.

BACKGROUND

The developmental state, as described by Takagi, et al. (2022), advocates a close economic and social partnership between governments and non-governmental networks, including media and advocacy groups (Chuma, 2011; Nyabuga & Otieno, 2018; Peel, 2010). Government bureaucracies can benefit from the expertise of their non-governmental partners, especially those whose advocacy is driven by entrepreneurship, business acumen, and social license (Guy & McCandless, 2020). The benefit to governments of interactions with these partners is inclusive statecraft sensitive to what Takagi et al. describe as the necessity of

close and productive ties to the business communities to formulate and implement effective industrial and trade policies. Otherwise, the state would fall into the predatory state, whose political elites exploit natural resources without providing social welfare to the people in general...(Takagi, et al., 2022, p. 4)

Not only should there be a close relationship between the state and private players in ensuring economic stability, but they should also collaborate in other sectors like food production; energy and water provision; and health, education, and social welfare services (Kumar, 2021). Yet, when criticized for making unilateral and poorly conceived choices which have seriously undermined the efficiency of these key sectors, governments in some developing countries, having resisted prior advice from the outside, descend into furious finger-pointing tirades against their critics (Akbarzadeh, et al, 2021; Dempers, 2018; Masunungure, 2015). Civil society organisations are targeted in the rhetorical firestorm, as are "unpatriotic" academics, those from the degreed community who dare to question government policy, students, residents associations, and even faith communities (Melber, 2014). Those at the end of government opprobrium often share one single misfortune. They are a coalition of local and multinational interest groups, often well-meaning but barely tolerated (Onwuegbuchulam & Matambo, 2023), and operating in a void created by "suboptimal and dysfunctional" national governance systems (Rana & Sorensen, 2020, p. 270).

The coalition of local and international actors reflected in resident non-governmental institutions is a particular irritant to some developing world governments, who see it as foreign interference, particularly in the areas of governance and human rights (Makulilo & Ntaganda, 2016). Those in government would claim that they were elected to take charge of national affairs in roles of supremacy clearly defined. In their view, only the nuisance of rights-based advocacy that comes with (often Western world) patronage creates the noises demanding recognition of alternative views (Akbarzadeh, *et al.,* 2021). Yet not-for-profit voluntary and philanthropic agencies are not alone in this public advocacy role (Naguib, 2015; Swilling, et al., 2017). The socio-political and economic transitions underway in southern African countries have exercised the agencies of local businesses, trade unions, farmers' organisations, students, and academics in parallel and conflicting ways (Cedras & Kuye, 2013; Mwaradzika, 2015). Often with the best intentions, each agency seeks to apprise national governments of pitfalls and opportunities to be navigated in these transitions (Stroup & Wong, 2018).

The country contexts of the state-civil society engagements explored by this research have similar histories. Their governments are formed by former liberation movements whose armed resistance helped to dismantle colonial legacy governments. Having assumed power, the former liberation movements prefer alternative models of governance to those favoured by the so-called "Washington Consensus" of international financial institutions and governments (Sindzingre, 2021). As Sindzingre notes, approaches favoured by left-leaning sub-Saharan African governments include active state intervention to direct wealth distribution and influence shareholding in private companies, in contrast with the IFI framework of free enterprise, the opening of most sectors of the economy to private and even international ownership, and protections of private investments from compulsory state takeover or control share acquisition. The "Washington Consensus" gave "very limited importance" to the "active role of the state and public policies. Economic efficiency is viewed as firstly driven by market forces" (Sindzingre, 2021, p. 2). Later concessions under what was called the "Post-Washington Consensus" allowed governments "appropriate" discretion in "promoting" education and technology, "supporting" the financial sector and infrastructural investment, preventing environmental degradation, and "creating and maintaining a social safety net" (Sindzingre, 2021, p. 3). Even so, the "Post-Washington Consensus" maintained an overriding "disqualification of the intervention of the government in the economy" (Sindzingre, 2021, p. 3).

As will be discussed in each of the country case studies, the dichotomies between governments and non-governmental entities have even strained relationships between the state and some of its former allies. Labour and human rights advocacy groups who were at one time organically linked with, or sympathizers of, the pre-democracy liberation cause became critics of the governments formed by those liberation movements.

THE KEY ISSUES

Governments in many developing countries are inclined to be fickle partners, challenging or ignoring the already narrow spaces for constructive interaction in a way that disdains significant actors (Helliker & Murisa, 2020; International Institute for Democracy and Electoral Assistance, 2018; Mendelson, 2015).

For such governments, it is their privilege to operate as a minority of decision-makers, to legislate and implement policies on behalf of everyone, without consulting and taking advice from anyone outside of their decision-making circles (Koch, 2022). Theirs is the concept of "representative democracy" (Keane, 2015) where the electorate votes them into government once every four or five years (sometimes longer), and then submit to their rule as they make decisions on the populace's behalf (Qhobosheane, 2018). However, there are serious challenges to good governance rooted in a confrontational relationship between the state and other stakeholders. Government actions are often more politically motivated than research-based, and their consequences across sectors have created unstable economies, compromised service delivery, breached human rights, and degraded living standards (Helliker & Murisa, 2020; Matambo, et al., 2022; Peel, et al., 2022). By contrast, intra-European economic, humanitarian and development initiatives by non-government partners such as businesses, banks, Oxfam, Doctors Without Borders (*Medecins Sans Frontieres*- MSF) and Doctors of the World (*Medecins du Monde*-MDM) interact with governments across Europe at multiple levels, including with national political authorities as well as the European Union leadership in Brussels. This serves to inform policymakers of sector-specific concerns and mitigates risks to sustainable development (Salgado, 2017).

Namibia, South Africa, and Zimbabwe have elective parliamentary democracies, but the scope for negotiated policymaking is narrowed by the significant parliamentary majorities enjoyed by the former liberation movements that are now the governing parties (Mlambo & Kapingura, 2019). Views from non-state actors are shut out from the decision-making matrix, which has hurt governance, the economy, human rights, and living standards (Onwuegbuchulam & Matambo, 2023). Yet non-state actors can be accessories to good governance and accountability if their alternative voices are allowed and considered (Iroanya, et al., 2018). This study intends to show how the use of non-state actors as "smart partners" can inform policymakers of sector-specific concerns and mitigate risks to sustainable development (McGann, 2016; Naguib, 2015; Peel, et al., 2022).

METHODOLOGY

The research used a qualitative case study design. Data was electronically recorded and transcribed from the exchange of ideas by civil society representatives, government ministers, and academics from the three country cases. The discussions took place during six sessions of the Inclusive Democracy for Sustainable Development Conference hosted by the Government of the Republic of Namibia and the Nordic-based International Institute for Democracy and Electoral Assistance (International IDEA) in Windhoek, Namibia from 27-28 November 2018. The author was privileged to be a panellist on the sixth and final session on Media Advocacy and Civil Society and attended the other five sessions that made up the duration of the two-day event. Each session was followed by in-depth question-and-answer sessions in which academics, non-state activists and government officials interacted, debated, and at times reached a consensus on the difficulties of forging a mutually beneficial partnership for the sake of social progress. Participants were drawn from the three southern African countries that are the focus of this paper, plus attendees from NORDIC countries, from Canada, and the co-sponsoring International IDEA secretariat.

The research sought to analyse the status of CSOs in the three selected countries and draw out similarities and contrasts. This necessitated the extraction of insights from speeches, Question and Answer interactions, panel deliberations, audience responses, and library research. The insights were analysed according to the following multivariate themes (Rawat, 2021): the three country contexts as independent variables, and the dependent variables of government actions, civil society advocacy, points of divergence, and public interest in correcting inefficiencies (Posner, 1974). Content which was deemed irrelevant to these variables was excluded from the analysis.

THEORETICAL FRAMEWORK

Public Interest Theory

Governments and civil society actors claim to serve the public interest (Wang, *et al.,* 2023), yet their functions diverge into different regulation and advocacy roles (Upadhyay, 2023). Society represents our wants and needs, and governments "our wickedness…by restraining our vices", Upadhyay (2023, p.53) quoted the US founding father and co-author of the Declaration of Independence, Thomas Paine, as having written. Upadhyay implied that the public understood its needs better than the government did. Although governments had power, their use of it should be monitored by society to challenge predatory tendencies. Instead, governments should be persuaded towards accomplishments that achieve discernible public benefits (Upadhyay, 2023).

The Public Interest Theory therefore holds that regulation must respond to the demand of the public "for the correction of inefficient or inequitable practices" (Posner, 1974, p. 1). Regulation is assumed to benefit society (Koch, 2022); hence the government should regulate in the interests of society rather than the interests of the regulators (International Institute for Democracy and Electoral Assistance, 2018). The government can be assisted in navigating this role through the advocacy of non-state actors (Singh, 2023). This is because, whether elected or not, *governments do not always get key decisions right* (Mwaradzika, 2015; Qhobosheane, 2018; Swilling, et al., 2017). They wield administrative authority (Onwuegbuchulam & Matambo, 2023), but may alternatively exhibit what Upadhyay (2023, p. 379) called a "quality of politics and presence" without "strong moral mettle", thereby compromising the exercise of virtue across different spheres of governance.

This chapter cross-examines polarizing interests of elected governments and civil society actors in Namibia, South Africa, and Zimbabwe, and whether they have upheld public interest values (International Institute for Democracy and Electoral Assistance, 2018; Posner, 1974). Posner's Public Interest Theory provides a framework for interrogating evidence or lack of state coherence with non-state actors in these three contexts.

The Othering of Citizens

The shrinking spaces for non-state actors to advocate for legitimate public causes have been noted on a broader international scale. Mendelson (2015, p.1) warned of "the closing space" as a "global problem" often accompanied by governments' harassment of independent organisations. She added that "this wave of targeting has a 21st-century twist. Specifically, as citizens find new ways to organise, assemble, and express themselves through the use of affordable technology, governments have found new ways to restrict public political space, suppress information, and label anything that they do not like as 'foreign' ".

The othering of citizens and citizen groups is a sinister plot by some governments against their critics. Yet not all non-western polities disfavour collaboration. Former Malaysian Prime Minister, Mahatir

Mohamad, championed a smart partnership between his government and a range of interest groups in the 1990s (Naguib, 2015). For Mahatir, this was an efficient channel of ventilating discontent both ways on specific issues, and he sought to export the concept to governments of other developing countries by hosting an annual international dialogue between heads of government and business elites as well as not-for-profit agencies. Called the Langkawi Dialogue, the annual meetings would tap into the narratives emerging from non-government sectors to improve governance in developing countries, while setting out government objectives in the hope that other partners would recognise their merits and bring their expertise to bear on the planning and implementation of key initiatives (Naguib, 2015). These smart partnerships, Mahathir said,

...are about government, organisations, and people working together for long-term mutual gains to help bring about global harmony and cooperative prosperity. They require the following ingredients for success: a shared vision, common goals, a clear understanding of each partner's strengths and weaknesses, a willingness to compromise, and patience and tolerance. [Smart partnerships'] originality lies in the practice and not the principle (cited and quoted in Naguib, 2015, p. 134).

In Southern Africa, long-time president Robert Mugabe of Zimbabwe warmed to the cause, and his initial enthusiasm for the smart partnership dialogues saw him host a Malaysian-inspired international dialogue for southern African states in the Zimbabwean resort town of Victoria Falls in 1999 (Midlands State University, n.d.). Locally, a Zimbabwean National Economic Consultative Forum was formed with Mugabe's backing, sometimes even his presence and participation (Midlands State University, undated). Regional sub-structures of the NECF, each comprising state and non-state actors, sprouted across the country. Zimbabwe, it seemed, was first off the block among African countries in embracing Mahatir's model.

However, these initial positive signs fizzled out as the advice from the non-government partners increasingly diverged from the practical measures that Mugabe's government was taking on the ground. With a defeat in the constitutional reform referendum in the year 2000, and a tough re-election battle in 2002 (Khampepe & Moseneke, 2002), Mugabe's government became increasingly resistant to dialogue. Politicians began to grumble, in Stalinist terms, that the non-state actors were getting ahead of themselves in thinking that they could dictate to the government. It was soon time to drop the bonhomie, remind the non-state actors who were in charge, and threaten a wholesale review of existing laws so that greedy capitalists, meddling non-profits, and their "lackeys" in the media and other public forums could be regulated (Mwaradzika, 2015). Criticism of government intentions was taken as hostility towards the government's development goals, and the business, farming, and other non-state sectors were told they were going to be "transformed" (Helliker & Murisa, 2020).

By the year 2000, Mugabe was still travelling to every Langkawi Dialogue each year to talk about smart partnerships. But back home, his government was no longer listening to other partners and had created and funded a coterie of substitute business and civil society organisations to remodel the "partnership" around state-acquiescent groups (Masunungure, 2015; Mwaradzika, 2015). This sort of affray between government and non-government actors has been repeated in many contexts (see e.g. Assal, 2016 on the restriction and expulsions of development partners in Sudan; Mendelson, 2015, on the formation of countermovements to check non-governmental partners in Egypt, and Ethiopia, Venezuela and Russia; and the suppression and replacement of student, labour and intellectual activities by what Razzaghi, 2010 called Iran's "garrison-based state").

STATE AND CIVIL SOCIETY INTERACTIONS IN SOUTHERN AFRICA

The Case of Namibia

Who speaks for the public? Suggestions that civil society organisations (CSOs) have no mandate to criticize government actions and that the state was not obliged to heed advice from this sector, came under tough examination by the coordinator of the Namibian Non-Governmental Organisations Federation, Uhuru Dempers, in his presentation to the Inclusive IDEA Conference Round Table on the Role of Civil Society (Dempers, 2018). Addressing an audience which included senior government officials, Dempers said: "You make representations to the Government, and then you're told: 'We (the government) were elected; who elected you (the CSOs)?'" It was as if Namibian civil society was dealing with a government which found it hard to listen, said Dempers.

However, Namibia's Deputy Minister for International Relations and Corporation, Christina Hoebes, who was among government officials present, explained that the mood in the Namibian government was not one of indifference. The government knew that its partners in civil society were part of the social infrastructure, and that's why it took consultations seriously. So where was the problem? In a brutally frank confession, Deputy Minister//Hoebes said the government did not take criticism from its partners very well.

"We know that civil society was part of the struggle for the liberation of our country, especially the churches, labour, and the student movement. Uhuru Dempers was my senior when we were demonstrating as students in Katutura during the apartheid years. But when we became the government, we were surprised that our colleagues were criticizing us. We said, 'These are our comrades; why are our friends attacking us?' We found that difficult to accept" (Hoebes, 2018).

In a presentation at the same conference, the author of this chapter warned against civil society and the media being assimilated into political supporting roles. My fear that such assimilation would occur came from precisely that mindset advanced by Deputy Minister Hoebes; that governments are only comfortable working with uncritical supporters and are affronted by questions that governments should take responsibility for. It represented a profound misunderstanding of the government-civil society relationship. Civil society should "serve as a vital source of new ideas and critical thinking that provide 'just in time' information and analysis for the critical decisions that policymakers make daily" (McGann, 2016, pp. 1-2). Civil society partners should not be craven appendages of the ruling party and government, however closely they might have worked when the governing party was in opposition.

Deputy Minister Hoebes also accepted that when her government banned state departments and enterprises from advertising in *The Namibian* newspaper, an independent daily that had for years before independence resisted South African occupation and rule[2], it was with the same sense of disappointment that a medium which was viewed as supportive of the South West Africa People's Organisation (SWAPO) liberation movement in the apartheid era would become a critic once the movement was in government after independence. "But I am happy to report that we have reached out to Gwen Lister (the founder-proprietor of *The Namibian*); we are talking again, and government advertisements are appearing in *The Namibian*", said Ms Hoebes (Hoebes, 2018).

Gwen Lister and *The Namibian's* fallout with the SWAPO government was another painful example of how heroes of the struggle against apartheid in Namibia could come to be maligned by the post-independence SWAPO government (Melber, 2014). SWAPO's failure to recognize the role of an independent media and unfettered civil society caused the government to turn on its critics when their scrutiny became uncomfortable. It was a dilemma captured by the Namibian anti-apartheid academic and SWAPO member, Henning Melber, who lamented how, in the post-independence dynamics, reactions from political office bearers involved "insults …for publicly questioning and interrogating the claimed progress, combined with a refusal to accept these challenges as a necessary, integral part of a vibrant civil society and a contribution to social justice and equity…" (Melber, 2014, p. xvii). This tenuous position in which Namibian non-governmental actors are perceived as adversaries instead of partners is an example of the misaligned expectations of state and social actors in the pursuit of pro-development models of engagement (Marenga, 2020).

The Case of South Africa

In South Africa, observers like Fine (1992) saw the emergence of tensions between civil society and the political elites even before the African National Congress-South African Communist Party alliance swept to power in the landmark first democratic elections of 1994. Writing already in 1992, Fine had warned of emerging binaries between "the political leadership identified with the ANC-SACP leadership, returned home after many years of exile", and "the organisations which grew up within the country independently" during apartheid (Fine, 1992, p.20). Those binaries have been exacerbated over time. Groups like the Congress of South African Trade Unions (COSATU) and the National Union of Metalworkers of South Africa (NUMSA) which were aligned with the liberation movements in the pre-democracy era, now put daylight between themselves and the ANC-SACP alliance on matters as diverse as e-tolling (effectively an intended road tax), poor service delivery, and wage negotiations (Cedras & Kuye, 2013).

In the era of liberation, South African civil society has espoused a "dual track strategy…a combination of good government on one side, and dynamic community, trade union, and other associations on the other" (Fine, 1992, p.19). The idea of ideological and structural assimilation into the liberation movement-turned-government is viewed in terms of capture by the state, and even COSATU, which retains an alliance status with the ANC, is independent in its lobbying for workers and other non-governing constituencies in opposition to certain government policies and actions (Cedras & Kuye, 2013).

At the same time, much as had occurred in Namibia, the struggle era affinity between progressive media houses which had been persecuted under apartheid and the ANC-SACP alliance dissipated when the liberation movement took over government. Newspapers like the *Mail and Guardian*, successor to the *Weekly Mail,* found themselves resorting to the apartheid-era blacking-out of pages to indicate where threats from the ANC government had forced a story to be heavily edited (Lloyd, 2013). *Mail and Guardian* columnist, Verashni Pillay, drew parallels between blacking out sections of stories in a June 26, 1986 edition of the *Weekly Mail*, and following the same recourse in the *Mail and Guardian's* 2011 spat with the ANC government over content from an interview with the then Presidential spokesman, Mac Maharaj by South Africa's National Prosecution Authority.

As with the apartheid government in 1986, the publication of the content under dispute in 2011 displeased the ANC government (Lloyd, 2013). Whereas the apartheid government in 1986 used apartheid-era law and order legislation, the post-apartheid government in 2011 used a section of the National Prosecution Authority Act which punishes, with a 15-year jail term, the release of information from a confidential interview with state prosecutors. The *Mail and Guardian* had argued that the content was publishable in the public interest. Pillay observed that "25 years later, and it's the same story with a different cast: the party that fought for a free South Africa turned into a government using similar censorship tricks on its media" (Lloyd, 2013, p. 8).

There had been concerns during the Jacob Zuma presidency in South Africa (2009-2018) that the news reporting by some media houses, allegedly influenced by hostile interests, was too passionately aligned against the ANC (Prinsloo, 2014), influencing inflammatory media coverage of the ruling party and government (Desai, 2018). These criticisms were contested by Desai, who insisted the Zuma government was the author of its misfortunes,

[a]lready shoved off the cliff…dangling on the withered roots of battered constitutional institutions. It was only through the tightening grip of the press who the ANC so despised; the judges it derided and liberal Non-Governmental Organisations it accused of being CIA (the US Central Intelligence Agency), that South Africa was saved from the failed state rocks below (Desai, 2018, p. 508).

How do we reflect on these trust gaps between the state and non-state actors? Malmberg has implied that media advocacy should principally be guided by the public interest – the need to correct inefficiencies that could adversely affect people's lives. Media should not publish merely to satisfy their stakeholder biases. Instead, media advocacy should evaluate divergent opinions without "affective psychic mechanisms" that privilege the media's pet causes (Malmberg, 2023, p. 20). That way, the fourth estate can escape being labelled mouthpieces of vested interests. Indeed, the media's public interest values should address John Kingdon's three "streams": problems, policies, and politics.

- *Problems:* News media should convey to the authorities the inefficiencies that discomfort, or have the potential to discomfort citizens (Taylor, 2013). The degree of social consciousness of the issues, and whether the problems are solvable with clear alternatives, should also inform the media's coverage (Beauclerk, et al., 2011).
- *Policies:* An independent media, drawing on a range of credible sources, should ensure policymaking in a democracy is collaborative. By creating public understanding (Nyabuga & Otieno, 2018) and giving a platform to state and non-state actors, the media should provide a critique that examines whether government policies prevent and resolve inefficiencies (Posner, 1974). Resolutions do not come only from the government's "elected minds", hence, Nyabuga and Otieno aver that without consultative policymaking, democracy would not survive (Nyabuga & Otieno, 2018).
- *Politics:* Decisions, and criticisms of them, should be alive to the "swings in national mood" and interest group advocacy campaigns (Beland & Howlett, 2016, p. 221). All options should be carefully considered and incorporated into media coverage and public advocacy campaigns.

That civil society and the media exposed flaws in the Zuma administration long before the ANC had the guts to demand Zuma's resignation as the fourth President of the Republic on 14 February 2018 proves how a vibrant media and civil society's long-term vigilance can be effective, more so when their advocacy rises above sectarian bias (Swilling, et al., 2017). Zuma went on to blame white people for orchestrating his removal (Hans & Mtshali, 2018), yet he had survived no fewer than eight confidence votes in parliament, and a ninth motion against him was pending by the time the ANC, which had a parliamentary majority, withdrew its support for his presidency (Desai, 2018). The former President's racial slur against civil society and the media did not convince many commentators (Desai, 2018). They saw a multifaceted, well-informed coalition turn against Zuma, acting on home-grown investigative journalism and their cognizance. For instance, a submission to the Public Protector's Office by the historically ANC-aligned NUMSA in 2014 objected to the government's awarding of a R50 billion contract for the building of 1064 locomotives by the state-owned Transnet transport corporation. It split the contract between four major train builders – China South Rail, Bombardier, General Electric and China North Rail. NUMSA contended that the government's policy of localization and job creation had been abused by "the implementation of opaque and underhand business dealings to line the pockets of a selected minority business and political elite" (Swilling, et al., 2017, p. 27).

Academics were part of the evidence-gathering. Prof Mark Swilling and others not only worked with what independent journalists had dug up; they "joined the dots" to produce an account of how the "constitutional state" of South Africa was corrupted, transferring considerable power to a "shadow state" of influential brokers who had taken control of institutions and strategic enterprises (Swilling, et al., 2017, p. 27). The South Africans had a name for it: they called it "state capture". What the synergy between academics, the media, trade unionists and even religious denominations demonstrated in South Africa was that the pursuit of the public good is a shared concern. All citizens, from whatever sector or status, should be concerned about poor services, poor governance, stealing from the public purse, and surrendering public assets to individuals or cartels. These run contrary to the public good, and in fact, actively diminish it. State actors' dereliction of duty towards the public good must be challenged (Mbeki, et al, 2015).

McGann suggests that civil society is obliged to provide "discipline and rigour in public debate" and "compensation for inadequacies of government" (McGann, 2016, p. 1). In their varied and concerted actions against the documented excesses of the Zuma administration, civil society in South Africa certainly kept up a robust and informed debate, and refused to be deterred by insinuations that it was South African whites alone who wanted Zuma held accountable (Hans & Mtshali, 2018).

The Case of Zimbabwe

Mwaradzika's (2015) study of civil society in Zimbabwe shows it to have pre-existed liberation movements as a significant network of non-violent groups resisting colonial rule and its excesses. Non-partisans were active several decades before the emergence of political movements in the 1960s, and they included the Trade Unions Congress, the Christian Action Group, the Southern Rhodesia Legal Aid and Welfare Fund Committee, the Multi-Racial Association, and the Citizens Against the Colour Bar Association. These organisations were to induct nationalists like Joshua Nkomo, George Nyandoro, Masotsha Ndlovu, Nathan Shamuyarira, James Chikerema, and Stanlake Samkange into the liberation movements that later took shape (Mwaradzika, 2015; Ranger, 2013).

Yet years after Zimbabwe's independence, when the ruling ZANU-PF turned its attention to radical economic transformation measures, it became inconvenient to acknowledge the days when advocacy for social change was guided by commonsense and a coalition of actors of goodwill instead of partisan and destructive rhetoric. Even as late as 1997, when Mugabe's National Economic Consultative Forum included specific collaborative "task forces" on agrarian reform and industry and everyone had a seat at the discussion table (Midlands State University, undated), few could have foreseen the descent into economic chaos and political intolerance when Mugabe and his government gave up on round-table discussions with other stakeholders and embarked on unilateral legal and illegal measures to transform the economy.

The economic meltdown that followed Mugabe's possession of not just white-owned farmland, but also businesses (Ranchhod, 2016) ruined his country's stability. The government would not admit it, saying the economic hardships were inflicted by Western countries' "sanctions" designed to punish

Zimbabwe for its pro-transformation approach. African countries largely supported Mugabe's view (Helliker & Murisa, 2020). Yet the question for many non-state players and observers was not of the rectitude of postcolonial agrarian and other reforms, but the need for such reforms to follow an ordered, legal process (Ndakaripa, 2021). The results of such orderliness and competence would have created a win-win situation for all Zimbabweans.

Instead, non-state actors bemoaned a descent into lawlessness that furthered the ambitions of the ruling ZANU-PF and its supporters through assassinations, arson, assaults, and gross economic mismanagement (Matambo, et al., 2022). It was a far cry from the Mahatir model of smart partnerships (Naguib, 2015), and it created credibility gaps that considerably retarded Zimbabwe's image for decades. The Zimbabwe Congress of Trade Unions, a successor to the Trade Unions Congress of the 1950s and 60s, refused to support such violations (Masunungure, 2015; Sadomba, 2013). They were joined by church groups, development agencies, and the trade, commerce, and industry federations in condemning the madness. In time, the Government of Zimbabwe fostered its trade union, supportive religious groups, development agencies, media organisations, and pro-government business federations to challenge the narrative of the longer-serving CSOs. Of these government-bred and funded CSOs, Masunungure wrote:

Without exception, they are formed as rivals and counterweights to existing CSOs deemed to be anti-regime/pro-opposition. They thus play the role of spoiler, undermining the credibility and effectiveness of mainstream civics. A classic example – and one of the first such organisations – was the Zimbabwe Federation of Trade Unions. It was created in 1998 as a rival to the ZCTU, which the government accused of abandoning workers and having a political agenda ... (Masunungure, 2015, p. 11)

By the year 2000, the government and mainstream civil society seemed irreconcilable. Masunungure (2015) quotes Mair and Sithole as describing the confrontational relationship in 2002, where

The growing inability of the government to provide social services, the increasing corruption in the government coupled with rising repression, the failure and social costs of economic reform... forced the established interest groups into politics and confrontation with the government and made the trade unions the backbone of the newly formed opposition movement. The uniting and mobilizing issues for this heterogeneous coalition were constitutional reform and, later, the removal of Mugabe from power (Masunungure, 2015, p.9 citing Mair & Sithole, 2002, 11-12).

What governments like Mugabe's in Zimbabwe were inclined to do was to define the public interest in the state's terms, and then establish a clientelistic relationship with sub-structures supportive of the state. Puppet organisations which feed off the state's largesse cannot properly be described as NGOs, nor even civil society, and the deliberate attempts to shun and countermand the inputs of established non-state actors with the necessary qualifications and competencies would have denied opportunities for debate and exploring alternative options to the government's plans. The self-serving nature of the Zimbabwean state, barely reformed under Mugabe's successor, President Emmerson Mnangagwa (Matambo, et al., 2022), is laid bare in how it has treated its natural constituencies. Some surprising victims of the monopolising power of the state in Zimbabwe are the very footsoldiers of state action: veterans of the liberation war, and rural peasants who were galvanised into a critical mass for the land occupations and evictions of white farmers. Having thrown their lot in with the state and the governing party, ZANU-PF, throughout the social and economic upheavals of the last two decades, they have themselves subsequently suffered evictions from some resettled farms, to make way for elite politicians (Sadomba, 2013).

Sadomba, whose scholarship has tracked various dimensions of Zimbabwe's land reform history, described how "the alliance of nationalist elites (politicians) with revolutionaries (liberation war veterans and peasants) was just a marriage of convenience since the two had antagonistic class interests" (Sadomba, 2013, p. 109).

DIFFERENCES BY COUNTRY CONTEXT

The data has shown that a common characteristic in Namibia, South Africa and Zimbabwe's liberation was the alignment of political actors with other interest groups seeking social change. Evidence from the IDEA conference in Windhoek (//Hoebes, 2018; Dempers, 2018), corroborated by the literature (Cedras & Kuye, 2013; Masunungure, 2015; Melber, 2014), confirms that ties forged between civil society and the liberation movements were significant, even at times of acute repression by colonial and successor settler authorities (IFEX, 2018; Mwaradzika, 2015; Ranger, 2013). The measure of this cooperation was not how everyone followed the direction of the biggest liberation movement. Rather, the internal networks of labour and student movements together with progressive faith groups, media and lobby organisations drove their anti-settler initiatives of strikes, rent boycotts and mass rallies in townships like Katutura in Namibia, Soweto in South Africa, and Highfields in Zimbabwe (Melber & Saunders, 2001; Ranger, 2013). This parallel dimension of civil-led struggle within the countries no doubt helped keep the pressure on the authorities when the liberation movements were banned or restricted. But it also showed that there can be common ground between ascendant political entities and civilian coalitions in achieving social change objectives. This was certainly the case in the three country contexts, in the pre-independence freedom struggles. A key point of departure would come when dealing with the inefficiencies of policies and practices once the political partners in the former liberation movements became governments running those countries. As this chapter has shown, it has been a common thread in the experiences of the three countries that the political leaders were unhappy with independent-minded criticisms from their former allies, now acting as watchdogs and advocates for change in the post-apartheid dispensations.

The sentiments of Deputy Minister //Hoebes in her exchanges with Namibian civil society leaders are worth repeating in this regard. She said: "We know that civil society was part of the struggle for the liberation of our country, especially the churches, labour, and the student movement... But when we became the government, we were surprised that our colleagues were criticizing us. We said, 'These are our comrades; why are our friends attacking us?' We found that difficult to accept" (//Hoebes, 2018).

According to Melber and Saunders, the difficulties SWAPO encountered in making the transition from a liberation movement to a democratic government in Namibia were noted in South Africa, where the ANC under the first elected government of Nelson Mandela tried to accommodate a range of social actors – including members of the far-right Afrikaner resistance movements. In their variety, these social movements at first found a listening ear during the transitional negotiations, the landmark 1994 elections, and the drawing up of the 1996 South African constitution. Furthermore, the collaboration with civil society during Mandela's five-year term (1994-1999) and in the presidential terms of his successor, Thabo Mbeki (1999-2008) was generally regarded as having been smooth (African National Congress, 2012). As scholars noted (Cedras & Kuye, 2013), South African civil society was embedded in the socio-political transition, with each political party buttressed by aligned social movements, labour unions, and industry players. The ANC, having seen how the fissures developed in Namibia and other independent states, thought it prudent to maintain a good rapport with those actors. "The difficulties encountered by SWAPO, in transforming itself from a liberation movement to a political party, constrained by democratic politics, cannot have been lost on the African National Congress (ANC)" (Melber & Saunders, 2001, p. 8).

Yet as discussed in this chapter, the ANC's unease grew as its partners in civil society became more vocal in their advocacy, openly disagreeing with the government and expressing their alarm at spending, mismanagement of state assets, and suspicious awarding of contracts, particularly during the Zuma presidency (Desai, 2018; Swilling, et al., 2017). The party began to respond aggressively, publicly disagreeing with its allies like COSATU and NUMSA and threatening to legislate into existence a media tribunal to rein in the media (Thomas & Sookrajowa, 2017). Still, the South African government has hardly translated its frustrations into regulation. Like the SWAPO government in Namibia to some degree, the ANC government has sulked and scolded, sometimes even threatened. But both governments have withheld themselves from enacting laws that shrink the public space for debate to the extent that the Zimbabwe Government has been accused of (Masunungure, 2015). Neither Namibia nor South Africa have surrogate pro-government movements funded to countermand civil society organisations, as happened in Zimbabwe (Masunungure, 2015; Mwaradzika, 2015). This variation by country context may be attributed to the degrees of vibrancy and resilience of non-state agencies in each country. It may also indicate the degree to which totalitarian rule has become entrenched in Zimbabwe (Ndakaripa, 2021), to the extent that legislative action by the ZANU-PF government has been bold beyond any regulatory actions recorded against CSOs in Namibia and South Africa.

CONCLUSION

Insights into the public advocacy dynamics in the three country case studies were analysed according to multivariate themes (Rawat, 2021). Each country and its peculiarities were treated as independent variables that customised the variables of government action, public advocacy, disagreements, and public interest in the correction of inefficiencies (Posner, 1974). Social historians (e.g. Cedras & Kuye, 2013; Melber & Saunders, 2001) have noted that the present-day variations in the robustness of non-state actors derive from the strengths of their transitions from being internal resistance movements during the settler-colonial periods to stakeholders who are keen to shed or moderate their political ties to the former liberation movements that are now in government (Fine, 1992).

What should be the take-home from the reflections in this chapter? Certainly, Southern African governments need to accept a more broad-based, horizontal partnership with genuinely independent non-state actors instead of substituting these actors with state-friendly henchmen. To take the Zimbabwean option of generating a state-mobilised civil society is a dangerous short-circuiting of the requirements of ensuring public service, public welfare, and the public good. To continue unilaterally and ineffectively, as did the ANC government under Zuma in South Africa – the consequences of which are still being unravelled as we write – is a betrayal of the public good. To abandon old friends, who speak the truth to power, will be unhelpful to Namibia's socio-economic trajectory at a critical time in its history. In all three case studies, the public needs will, in the end, be subordinated to government priorities under this fortress model. It will not work for the common good.

REFERENCES

African National Congress. (2012). *The Second Transition? Building a national democratic society and the balance of forces in 2012.* ANC. https://www.anc1912.org.za/wp-content/uploads/2021/05/Discussion-Documents-2012-The-Second-Transition-Building-a-national-democratic-society-and-the-balance-of-forces.pdf

Assal, M. (2016). *Civil society and peace building in Sudan.* CHR Michelsen Institute. https://www.cmi.no/publications/file/5807-civil-society-and-peace-building-in-sudan.pdf

Beauclerk, J., Pratt, B., & Judge, R. (2011). *Civil society in action: Global case studies in a practice based framework.* Itrac.

Beland, D., & Howlett, M. (2016, July 18). The Role and Impact of the Multiple-Streams Approach in Compartivie Policy Analysis. *Journal of Comparative Policy Analysis, 18*(3), 221–227. doi:10.1080/13876988.2016.1174410

Canache, D. (2007). *Chavismo and Democracy in Venezuela. Prospects for Democracy in Latin America.* University of North-Texas.

Cedras, J., & Kuye, J. (2013). The impact of tripartite politics on the leadership function in public administration: Dialogue between the ANC, COSATU and the SACP in South Africa. *African Journal of Public Affairs, 6*(3). https://repository.up.ac.za/bitstream/handle/2263/41039/Cedras_Impact_2013.pdf?sequence=1&isAllowed=y

Cotterill, J. (2017, August 8). Jacob Zuma survives vote of no confidence. *Financial Times (SA).* https://www.ft.com/content/978055ec-7c4a-11e7-ab01-a13271d1ee9c

Dempers, U. (2018, November 28). The Role of Civil Society. *Inclusive Democracy for Sustainable Development Conference.* Windhoek, Namibia: International Institute for Democracy and Electoral Assistance.

Desai, A. (2018). The Zuma moment between tender-based capitalism and radical economic transformation. *Journal of Contemporary African Studies, 36*(4), 409–513. doi:10.1080/02589001.2018.1522424

Fernandes, S. (2007, April 12). *Hugo Chavez as an expression of urban popular movements.* Venezuela Analysis. http://venezuelanalysis.com/analysis/2334

Fine, R. (1992). Civil society theory and the politics of transition in South Africa. *Review of African Political Economy, 55*(55), 71–83. https://www.jstor.org/stable/4006073. doi:10.1080/03056249208703969

Hans, B., & Mtshali, S. (2018, March 9). Zuma blames whites for his removal. *Independent On Line.* https://www.iol.co.za/dailynews/zuma-blames-whites-for-his-removal-13672294

Helliker, K., & Murisa, T. (2020). Zimbabwe: Continuities and changes. *Journal of Contemporary African Studies, 38*(1), 5–17. doi:10.1080/02589001.2020.1746756

Hoebes, C. (2018, November 28). *Response by the Deputy Minister of International Relations and Corporation to the presentations of Round Table 5.* Inclusive Democracy for Sustainable Development Conference. Windhoek, Namibia.

Hoffman, J. (2004). *Citizenship beyon the state*. SAGE Publications. doi:10.4135/9781446216842

IFEX. (2018, March 6). *Gwen Lister: A Fearless Commitment to Speaking Truth to Power.* IFEX. https://www.ifex.org/namibia/2018/03/06/gwen-lister-profile/

International Institute for Democracy and Electoral Assistance. (2017). *The Global State of Democracy: Exploring Democracy's Resilience*. International IDEA.

International Institute for Democracy and Electoral Assistance. (2018). The Global State of Democracy: (2018 Reprint ed.). Stockholm: International IDEA. doi:978-91-7671-1293

International Institute for Democracy and Electoral Assistance. (2018). *The global state of democracy: Exploring democracy's resilience*. International IDEA.

Iroanya, R., Dzimiri, P., & Phaswana, E. (2018). Human rights-based service delivery: Assessing the role of national human rights institutions in democracy and development in Ghana and Uganda. *Regions & Cohesion : the Journal of the Consortium for Comparative Research on Regional Integration and Social Cohesion*, *8*(2), 1–26. doi:10.3167/reco.2018.080202

Keane, J. (2015, July 3). Why we should still be reading democracy in America. *The Conversation*. doi:https://theconversation.com/why-we-should-still-be-reading-democracy-in-america-44174

Khampepe, S., & Moseneke, D. (2002). *Report on the 2002 Presidential Elections in Zimbabwe*. Office of the President of South Africa. Pretoria: Judicial Observer Commission. http://zimbabwe-today.com/wp-content/uploads/2014/11/Report-on-the-2002-Presidential-Elections-of-Zimbabwe.pdf

Koch, M. (2022). State-civil society relations in Gramsci, Poulantzas and Bourdieu: Strategic implications for the degrowth movement. *Ecological Economics*, *193*, 107275–107300. doi:10.1016/j.ecolecon.2021.107275

Kumar, R. (2021). Bringing the developmental state back in: Explaining South Korea's successful management of COVID-19. *Third World Quarterly*, *42*(7), 1397–1416. doi:10.1080/01436597.2021.1903311

Lloyd, L. (2013). *South Africa's Media 20 years after Apartheid*. Centre for International Media Assistance.

Makulilo, B., & Ntaganda, E. (2016). *Election management bodies in East Africa*. African Minds. doi:10.47622/9781920677978

Malmberg, T. (2023). Media studies, Le Bon's psychology of crowds, and qualitative-normative research on propaganda, 1880-2020. *Nordic Journal of Media Studies*, *5*(1), 17–31. doi:10.2478/njms-2023-0002

Marenga, R. (2020). Analysing the performance of public enterprises in Namibia: A challenge for the practice of public administration? *Journal of Governance &Regulation*, *9*(3), 96–109. doi:10.22495/jgrv9i3art7

Masunungure, E. (2015). *The Changing Role of Civil Society in Zimbabwe's Democratic Processes: 2014 and Beyond*. Harare: Frederich Ebert Stiftung. https://library.fes.de/pdf-files/bueros/simbabwe/13718.pdf

Matambo, M., Moyo, G., Mukonza, R., & Lewis, E. (2022). Corporate governance and credibility gap: Four decades of struggling reform efforts in Zimbabwe. *African Renaissance*, *19*(4), 105–126. doi:10.31920/2516-5305/2022/19n4a5

Mbeki, T. (2015). *Illicit Financial Flows: Report on the High Level Panel on Illicit Financial Flows from Africa.* Addis Ababa: African Union Commission/United Nations Economic Commission for Africa. https://www.uneca.org/sites/default/files/PublicationFiles/iff_main_report_26feb_en.pdf

McGann, J. (2016). *The Fifth Estate: Think Tanks, Public Policy and Governance*. The Brooking Institution Press.

Melber, H. (2014). *Understanding Namibia: The trials of independence*. Ocford University Press., doi:10.1017/S0022278X15000543

Melber, H., & Saunders, C. (2001). *Transition in Southern Africa: Comparative Aspects.* Nordiska Afrikainstitutet. https://www.files.ethz.ch/isn/102626/10.pdf

Mendelson, S. (2015). Why governments target civil society, and what can be done in response: A new agenda. Centre for Strategic and International Studies. Midlands State University. *Social Dialogue.* www.msu.ac.zw/elearning/.../1173420720SOCIAL%20DIALOGUE%20NOTES.doc

Mlambo, C., & Kapingura, F. (2019). Factors influencing women political participation: The case of the SADC region. *Cogent Social Sciences*, *5*(1), 1681048. doi:10.1080/23311886.2019.1681048

Mwaradzika, M. (2015). *The role of civil society organisations in promoting democratic process in Zimbabwe, 1980-2013. Unpublished mini-thesis. Gweru.* Midlands State University.

Naguib, R. (2015). The behaviour of multi-national enterprises in developing countries: Having a sense of the "good" through smart partnerships in Malaysia. In R. Molz, C. Ratiu, & A. Taleb (Eds.), *Local versus Global Logic: The Multinational Enterprise in Developing Countries* (pp. 134–153). Routledge.

Ndakaripa, M. (2021). Zimbabwe's economic meltdown: Are sanctions really to blame? *The Washington Quarterly*, *44*(2), 95–120. doi:10.1080/0163660X.2021.1934997

Nyabuga, G., & Otieno, C. (2018). *Mediating Politics and Democracy: Making Sense of the Role of the Media in Kenya.* Nairobi: Media Focus on Africa Foundation. https://www.mediafocusonafrica.org/media-roundtables/result/mediatising-politics-and-democracy-making-sense-role-media-kenya

Onwuegbuchulam, S., & Matambo, E. (2023). Constraining space for civil society participation and contestation in Nigeria's politics. *African Renaissance*, 13-33. doi:10.31920/2516-5305/2023/20n2a1

Peel, C. (2010). Exile and the Internet: Ndebele and Mixed-Race Diaspora 'Homes' Online. In J. McGregor & R. Primorac (Eds.), *Zimbabwe's New Diaspora: Displacement and the Cultural Politics of Survival* (pp. 229–245). Berghahn Books. doi:10.1515/9781845458416-016

Peel, C., Hamalwa, A., & Kaisara, G. (2022). Public Procurement and Stakeholders: Assessing Namibia's Consultative Processes and and Challenges. In I. Tshabangu (Ed.), *Interdisciplinary Approaches to the Future of Africa and Policy Development* (pp. 137–149). IGI-Global. doi:10.4018/978-1-7998-8771-3.ch008

Posner, R. (1974). *Theories of Economic Regulation.* National Bureau of Economic Research. doi:10.3386/w0041

Prinsloo, J. (2014). Examining the relationship between the news nedia and the ANC: A case study of Nkandla coverage. *Equid Novi: African Journalism Studies*, *35*(2), 23–29. doi:10.1080/02560054.2014.919946

Qhobosheane, L. (2018). The Impact of Political Interference in State-owned Companies: A Case Study of the South African Broadcasting Corporation (SABC). [Unpublished LLM thesis, University of the Free State]. https://scholar.ufs.ac.za/handle/11660/9256

Rana, M., & Sorensen, O. (2020). Levels of legitimacy development in internationalisation: Multinational enterprise and civil society interplay in institutional void. *Global Strategy Journal, 269-270.* doi:10.1002/gsj.1371

Ranchhod, H. (2016). *Zimbabwe Indigenisation Law*. Hussein Ranchhod and Co. Legal Practitioners. https://www.huranco.com/2016/01/07/zimbabwe-indigenisation-law/

Ranger, T. (2013). *Writing Revolt: An Engagement with African Nationalism 1957-67*. Weaver Press.

Rawat, A. (2021, March 31). *An Overview of Descriptive Analysis*. Analytic Steps. https://www.analyticssteps.com/blogs/overview-descriptive-analysis

Razzaghi, S. (2010). *State of Civil Society in Iran: Challenges, Opportunities, and Strategies*. Universiteit van Amsterdam. https://www.arsehsevom.org/en/wp-content/uploads/2010/10/State-of-Civil-Society-Iran-by-Sohrab-Razz

Sadomba, Z. (2013). A Decade of Zimbabwe's Land Revolution: The Politics of the War Veteran. In S. Moyo & W. Chambati (Eds.), *Land and Agrian Reform in Zimbabwe: Beyond White Settler Capitalism* (pp. 79–121). University of Zimbabwe. doi:10.2307/j.ctvk3gnsn.9

Salgado, R. (2017). Europeanisation of Civil Society Organisations in times of crisis? Exploring the evolution grant-seeking strategies in the EU multi-level system. *European Politics and Society, 18*(4), 511-528. https://www.tandfonline.com/doi/full/10.1080/23745118.2017.1286283

Sindzingre, A. (2021). *Economic relationships between sub-Saharan Africa and China: an alternative theoretical and policy paradigm?* African Studies Association (ASA) 64th Annual Meeting. Virtual. https://shs.hal.science/halshs-03625159/document

Singh, R. (2023, July 31). India: Civil society organisations and governments need to work together to ensure overall progress of society. *Mena Report*. Proquest. https://www.proquest.com/wire-feeds/india-civil-society-organisations-amp-governments/docview/2843926296/se-2

Stroup, S., & Wong, W. (2018). *The Authority Trap: Strategic Choices of International NGOs*. Cornell University Press., doi:10.7591/9781501709777-003

Swilling, M., Bhorat, H., Buthelezi, M., Chipkin, I., Duma, S., Mondi, L., & Friedenstein, H. (2017). *Betrayal of the Promise: How South Africa is being stolen*. Johannesburg: State Capacity Research Project. https://pari.org.za/wp-content/uploads/2017/05/Betrayal-of-the-Promise-25052017.pdf

Takagi, Y., Kanchootat, V., & Sonobe, T. (2022). Introduction: The Nexus of Developmental Policy and State Building. In Y. Takagi, V. Kanchootat, & T. Sonobe (Eds.), *Developmental State Building: The Politics of Emerging Economies* (pp. 1–18). Springer Nature. doi:10.1007/978-981-13-2904-3_10

Taylor, J. (2013). Struggles agains systems that impoverish: South African civil society at the crossroads. *Development in Practice*, *23*(5/6), 617–630. https://www.jstor.org/stable/24565438. doi:10.1080/09614524.2013.800833

Thomas, M., & Sookrajowa, S. (2017). The Media Appeals Tribunal and the Protection of Information Bill as Challenges to Freedom of Expression and Good Governance in South Africa. *Afrika Focus*, 29-50.

Upadhyay, R. (2023). Ethics, Integrity and Aptitude in Governance (1st ed.). S. Chand Publications.

Wang, X., Zhao, X., & McNamara, N. (2023). *Environmental Public Interest Litigation in China*. SpringerNature., doi:10.1007/978-3-031-26526-6

ENDNOTES

1. The chapter uses a broader embrace of non-state actors than the conventional understanding of "NGOs" might permit, including for-profit entities whose partnership with the state in policy development and execution is, I argue, as vital as the social advocacy of the not-for-profit groups.
2. South African occupation of Namibia started in May 1915 when General Louis Botha, the first Prime Minister of the Union of South Africa, ordered 40,000 South African troops into the territory, ending 31 years of German rule. The South African occupation ended on the eve of Namibian independence in March 1990.

Chapter 21
The Economic Freedom Fighters and Politics of Populism:
Enhancing Political Participation, or a Threat to Democracy?

Kealeboga Aiseng
https://orcid.org/0000-0002-5684-9519
Rhodes University, South Africa

ABSTRACT

This study presents a novel approach to understanding the economic freedom fighters (EFF) role in South African politics. The party has been called populist, fascist, and a threat to South Africa's democracy. This study was conducted through virtual ethnography research on the role of the EFF in South Africa's politics and presents the research findings here to understand if the EFF is merely populist, a threat to democracy, or encouraging citizens' political participation. The study's findings indicate that the EFF uses populist stances to attract supporters and voters to the party. But unlike the views of some commentators and scholars, the study presents different findings regarding the EFF's populist attitudes in the country's democracy. While some see such populist stances as a threat to democracy, the study views it as the party's advantage, among others, to encourage citizen political participation.

INTRODUCTION

Discussions surrounding the effect of populism on democracy and viewing it as a form of democratic participation are rife. Existing literature is divided on this topic; some view populism as a threat to democracy (Mudde & Kalwasser, 2017), while others view it as a modification or a reform of democracy (Zaslove et al., and Akkerman, 2020). According to Taggart (2002), populism has an ambivalent relationship with representative politics. Urbinati (2014) states that the relationship between populism and democracy is parasitical. These arguments imply that populism is part of democracy, whether as a

DOI: 10.4018/979-8-3693-0477-8.ch021

threat or an opportunity. This study intends to investigate the Economic Freedom Fighters (EFF) role in South Africa's politics using the frameworks of populism, political participation, and democracy.

Populism denotes a political discourse that stands for a political position that engages in confrontational, anti-establishment politics to displace the ruling elites in representative liberal democracies (Muller, 2019). Populism is a stance against liberal democracy and not merely an anomaly – like a transitory ani-system protect vote intended to shake democracy (Muller, 2019). However, Barber (2019) cautions that there is a commonality among the critics of populism: policies and political styles they dislike are regarded as mere populism. These include examples such as Bretix, the rise of Donald Trump, and Russia's military invasion of Ukraine. These policies and political styles are treated as constitutionally and democratically flawed. These arguments are prevalent in this study, as they set the basis upon which this paper will approach the attachment between the EFF and populism in South Africa.

The EFF was formed on the 27th of July 2013. The party was formed by former African National Congress Youth League leader (ANCYL) Julius Malema and former ANCYL spokesperson Floyd Shivambu. Malema was suspended from the ANC for five years for sowing divisions within the ANC. Shivambu and the league's secretary-general were also suspended for three years. This suspension led the duo to leave the ANC and form the EFF to continue to fight for economic freedom, a policy position they believed the ANC had abandoned.

The party describes itself as

A radical and militant economic emancipation movement...to bring together revolutionary, militant activists, community-based organizations, as well as lobby groups under the umbrella of the political party pursuing the struggles of economic emancipation (EFF, 2020, p. 1).

The EFF's primary policy focuses on the previously oppressed and exploited blacks' total ownership of economic and natural resources. Marxism, Leninism, and Fanonism ideologies influence the party's radical, leftist, and anti-capitalist positions (EFF, 2020). The party states they are a socialist movement modelled after Latin American socialism led by leaders such as Che Guevara and Fidel Castro.

In its first electoral participation in 2014, the EFF gained 6% of the votes (31 members of Parliament). This was the beginning of the new political culture in South Africa. The arrival of the EFF in parliament injected vibrancy and dynamism into parliament. The EFF has forced parliament to engage communities on the possible amendment of Section 25 of the constitution to allow land expropriation without compensation. This is the first time since 1994 that parliament has embarked on this process. The EFF has also led the insourcing of workers into government employment; they have proposed the establishment of the state bank in parliament.

The EFF revived political participation in South Africa (Mbete, 2014). Young and older people in the country talk about the EFF, their left-wing, radical policies, their actions of disrupting local and national legislative settings, and their influence in governance even though they are the country's second most prominent opposition party. All these issues have made the EFF emerge as a "populist organization." Some political commentators have viewed the EFF as a populist organization threatening South Africa's democracy (Fogel, 2013; *Sunday Independent*, 2014; Mbete, 2014; Van Onselen, 2018; *Sowetan*, 2018). *Business Tech* (2017) stated that the EFF, with its radical attitudes, has disrupted the formal State of the Nation Address (SONA) on many occasions. Fisher (2014) states that the EFF leaders have often failed to appear in formal parliamentary hearings. Other criticisms against the EFF and its political stances are that the EFF reportedly participated in illegal protests alleging the H&M store displaced a racist advertisement on its website (*Times Live*, 2018). The radical political behaviour of the EFF has proven to be against the "normal" way of "doing things politically." The party has adopted methods and strategies that disrupt "normal politics." In as much as some deem the party's methods and strategies undemocratic and unconstitutional, a deeper evaluation of the party's role in South African politics is necessary.

The current study aims to investigate the role of the EFF in South Africa's politics and democracy. Using the overhead views that the EFF is a populist organization, the paper examines whether the EFF is reviving and enhancing political participation or is killing democracy in South Africa. Ultimately, the paper proposes that, with constant political transformations in the world, the EFF's populism cannot just be criticized as a threat to democracy; it must also be seen as a new form of democracy that attracts people to democratic and political participation. The study argues that political spaces are intense and competitive, and political parties are willing to go to the extreme to win votes and take over governments. Therefore, populism in this context is seen as one of the many techniques politicians use to harvest support for their parties and win governments. existing scholarship that debates this issue. This study takes the view of the local scholars and critics that classify the EFF as a populist political party, but with a different view that proposes that the said EFF's "populism" encourages active citizen political participation. The newness proposed by this study is that while local scholars and critics have called the EFF a populist organization that threatens the constitution and democracy of South Africa, the party uses social media platforms such as Twitter to make more people informed and participate in social, political, and economic matters. This paper opens a new window to look at the presence of populist political parties in social media.

BACKGROUND

Across the world, there is a growing culture of backlash toward mainstream politics (Inglehart & Norris, 2016). People in many parts of the world are tired of capitalism, neoliberalism, rising unemployment, food insecurity, climate change, and wealth inequalities. People are losing hope in their current and dominant political institutions. Consequently, left-wing organizations emerge as alternatives to care for the needs of those who feel their governments leave them behind. These organizations emerge as "messiahs" that will bring back power to the people, prioritize the needy and the poor, and encourage political participation.

Political participation is essential in every democratic regime. Fayomi and Adebayo (2017) state that political participation allows citizens to participate in political matters and to communicate with government officials about their concerns and preferences. However, Gale (cited in Fayomi and Adebayo, 2017) notes that more people discuss politics than vote, and some just vote without being interested in political matters. These arguments call for an examination of politicians in enhancing political participation. Answers are needed regarding how political parties evoke active citizen political participation. In this study, I demonstrate through existing examples how the EFF has used Twitter to enhance citizen political participation.

Political commentators in South Africa agree that the EFF is active on social media. du Preez (2018) states that the EFF members and its leadership are active on Twitter, always ready to attack, insult, curse, and threaten anyone who tries to criticize the EFF or one of its leaders. Haffajee (2019) argues that the EFF has the most digitally brutal cyber army, with members and the leadership always ready to attach journalists. According to Kanyane (2019), social media has helped the EFF mobilize and galvanize its messaging; the party members are using social media to create and sustain conversations on the political, social, and economic issues affecting South Africa. Social media is inevitably essential for the EFF to spark debates, make itself relevant, grow, attract new members, and spread its policies. All of these contribute to political participation; when more people see the EFF constantly talking about its policies, attacking the ruling party, and taking a firm position against racism, they will likely be interested in and participate in political affairs. As scholars allude to, social media is powerful in enhancing political participation (Kim & Chen, 2016).

Key to this study is also the issue of how populism can threaten democracy. Daly and Jones (2020) argue that the rise of authoritarian populist, illiberal, far-right, nativist, and extremist parties continues to threaten liberal democracy worldwide. The duo calls these movements parties with "questionable commitments" to liberal democracy. The coming into power of the following leaders: Doland Trump (United States of America), Boris Johnson (United Kingdom), and Rodrigo Duterte (Philippines) are usually used as examples of threats to liberal democracy.

With this background, this paper seeks to situate the EFF within these arguments and investigate whether alternative voices should always be dismissed or seen as threats to democracy, especially if they go against the establishment. The paper asks if democracy should always be viewed in one way (the liberal). The point here is that democracy is not static. With rapid political, economic, and social changes, democracy is subject to transformation, and many people will interpret it differently. Hence, political parties that challenge the traditional understanding of liberal democracy cannot be chastised for challenging liberal democracy. Because, after all, liberal democracy allows for the contestation of ideas.

This study focuses on 2020 and EFF's contribution to citizen political participation. When South Africa, like many other countries, was in a national lockdown due to the Coronavirus regulations, many political activities were halted. Political parties could not engage with their voters and supporters as they were used to. Political rallies and campaigns were halted, and gatherings were banned. However, the EFF continued to use Twitter to remain relevant by evoking political discussions. The study looks at three trending Twitter topics within which the EFF was at the centre and how the EFF used those issues to enhance political participation in South Africa. The three topics to be analysed are #SONA2020, #Senekal and #PutSouthAfricansFirst.

These themes/topics/hashtags were relevant to South Africa's political space in 2020. #SONA2020 was a trending topic during the SONA. During the SONA of 2020, the EFF disrupted proceedings and delayed the president's address in Parliament for more than an hour before they could leave Parliament. The EFF demanded that former president FW de Klerk should not have been invited to the SONA as he presided over the Apartheid government, which killed and oppressed black people. The EFF also demanded that the president fire the Minister of Public Enterprises (Pravin Gordan) for his role in failing State-Owned Enterprises and purging black executives in government entities.

The second theme involves racial tensions in the small town of Senekal in the Free State province, South Africa. After the murder of a young Afrikaner farmer in Senekal, two black men were arrested and appeared before the magistrate as suspects. During their court appearance, violence erupted with Afrikaner farmers demanding that the accused be handed to them. The farmers stomped into the courtrooms, and gunshots were fired. Police vehicles were also torched. The following week when the accused appeared in court for the second time, the EFF descended to Senekal to "defend" the state properties. The EFF went to Senekal to defend the country's democracy against Afrikaners who wanted to take the law into their own hands (*News24*, 2020).

The third theme also dominated the country's debates a lot in 2020. With many South Africans joining the #PutSouthAfricansFirst because of their frustrations against illegal immigrants in South Africa taking their jobs, committing crimes, and enjoying socio-political benefits more than South Africans, the EFF is in the middle of this conversation. The EFF's ideology is that Africa must be one, without borders, with one currency and one president. Hence, they welcome foreign nationals in South Africa despite their legal status. This topic has always put the EFF in contentious debates with South Africans who believe that South African borders and immigration policies should be tightened against the influx of illegal foreign nationals into South Africa.

EFF's Populism

Populist movements have used social media platforms to spread their messages and gain support. According to Brookings (2017), social media has allowed populist movements to bypass traditional media outlets and communicate directly with their supporters. For example, leaders such as Donald Trump, Marine Le Pen, and Matteo Salvini have used social media to reach out to their followers and spread their messages (Brookings, 2017).

El-Ibiary and Calfano (2022) further note that populists throughout the West were early adopters of social media, and these platforms quickly became favourite tools for political communication. It has also become evident that social media platforms have turned populists into stars in political cyberspace, far outshining their centrist opponents (El-Ibiary & Calfano, 2022).

Populism can also be seen across some African countries. Michael Sata, who served as Zambia's president from 2011 until he died in 2014, was known for his populist rhetoric and anti-establishment stance; Raila Odinga, a former Kenyan Prime Minister, has been described as a populist leader who appeals to the masses by promising to fight corruption and inequality; John Magufuli, who served as Tanzania's president from 2015 until he died in 2021, was also known for his populist policies and anti-corruption stance (Melber, 2021).

Various commentators and political analysts have labelled the EFF a violent organization, a fascist and populist movement (Fogel, 2013; *Sunday Independent*, 2014; Whelan, 2014). Friedman (2014) dismissed the EFF's prominence, labelling it a case of media hype over substance. Fakir (2014, p. 5) described the party as "a hodge-podge of different ideological and political strains melding the incendiary politics of 'radical blackness' with the seeming elements of socialism." Fakir went on (2014, p. 5) to argue that "it is (EFF) essentially an empty rhetoric captured in the politics of spectacle."

The party is also described by the so-called "bad manners." The party is accused of disregarding appropriate ways of acting in politics, especially in parliament. As Moffitt and Tormey (2014) put it, populist movements mark themselves as practitioners of low politics, the people's politics, instead of politics of the elites, high politics. These groups set themselves apart from the elites, identify as part of the people, and challenge how politics are conducted. This can be seen in the EFF's continuous disruption of parliamentary processes, using violent language and gestures to threaten members of parliament who do not agree with or support them. The party has demonstrated a disdain for parliamentary rules.

In the current study, I argue that the EFF relies on these strategies to build its support base and revitalize political participation, especially among those members of society that have given up or lost interest in politics. It is the EFF's left populism that provides a distinct language and strategy for political participation in the country.

Agustin (2020) argues that populism is often accused of threatening democracy, while mainstream politics are regarded as the pillars of the democratic system. Some view populism as a form of anti-elitism (Ernst et al., 2017). On the other hand, Muller (2017) argues that populism should not be seen primarily as a form of anti-elitism. Instead, it should also be seen as a form of democracy because it "claims" to represent the people (or what populists often refer to as "the real people"). In South Africa, the EFF refers to those it represents as "our people" or what they refer to as the silent majority. The party's focus is on achieving economic emancipation for this group.

Muller (2017) also states that populists reject the legitimacy of other political parties for power and often discredit all other contenders. Further than that, populists do not just disagree with their contenders on policy or even values. Instead, they personalize and moralize political conflict and insist everyone else is corrupt and crooked (Muller, 2017). They allege that everyone else is not working for "the people" but only for themselves.

These arguments capture the essence and the political style of the EFF. The party strongly appeals to the concept of "our people." African National Congress (ANC), the ruling party, also uses the concept. The EFF strongly believes that the actual holders of power in society are the people, as opposed to the elites, which they describe as exploitative or corrupt. The EFF views the elites, the political and the economic class, as the source of some societal crises (Mbete, 2015). The result is that the party has distanced itself from the elite or power block in several ways. They have adopted the popular language (they use a linguistic style that resonates with the masses, the majority of whom are the poor and the working class). They have also adopted gestures and fashion that appeal to the poor and working class. For example, when the EFF arrived in parliament, they refused to wear a formal dress code. The party opted for overalls, saying that this attire symbolizes those the EFF represents; domestic workers, mine workers, security guards, patrol attendants, and farm workers. The party said they want their voters to see themselves represented in parliament. The EFF has also adopted old military language from the days of the liberation struggle (Mbete, 2015). This is a strategy to make itself relevant as a "revolutionary movement" in the struggle for economic emancipation (as its founding manifesto states).

In the context of Africa's economic interactions, the EFF's influence is predominately felt in South Africa, the continent's most industrialized economy. The party's advocacy for a more interventionist state and economic nationalism can impact foreign investment and trade relationships. Potential investors may view the EFF's policies as risky, which could affect the inflow of foreign capital.

Globally, the EFF's populist stance may influence how South Africa is perceived in international markets. While some may see the party as championing economic justice, others may view its policies as threatening business interests and economic stability. This perception may impact South Africa's standing in global economic forums and negotiations.

LITERATURE REVIEW

Political participation

Research has proven that citizens have become increasingly disengaged from the traditional channels of political participation (Norris, 2001; 2010; Badaru & Adu, 2020). Citizens' disengagement from traditional political participation channels is evident in low voter turnout, rising anti-party sentiment, and the decay of civic organizations. Over the past years, scholars (Polat, 2005; Kam, 2012; Chen, 2012; Moeller et al., Hinnerich & Petterson-Lidbom, 2014; 2014; Yao & You, 2018; Li et al., 2022) have demonstrated interest in political participation. Ekman and Aman (2012, p. 283) argue that

There are declining levels of civic engagement, low electoral turnout, eroding public confidence in the institutions of representative democracy, and other signs of public weariness, scepticism, cynicism, and lack of trust in politicians and political parties.

Traditional forms of civic engagement, such as voting, have seen declining participation. Norris (2010) submits that this is due to several factors, such as generational change, socialization, and the changing nature of work. The *Mail and Guardian* (2023) also reports that the younger generation is less likely to participate in politics than their older counterparts. Also, the rise of individualism and the decline of traditional sources of reference, such as family, community, and social class, have contributed to political disengagement among young people (*Mail & Guardian*, 2023). This might also be attributed to changing patterns of political involvement, with people increasingly turning to alternative avenues like online activism or issue-specific advocacy rather than engaging with mainstream political processes. It is in the interest of this study to understand the role of the EFF in enhancing active citizen political participation in South Africa through populist activities.

Verba et al. (1978, p. 1) define political participation as "legal acts by private citizens that are more or less directly aimed at influencing the selection of governmental personnel and action they take." Similarly, Parry, Moyser, and Day (1992) add that political participation involves actions or activities in which people voluntarily participate in political issues that affect them. According to Brady (1999), political participation encompasses manifest and observable actions or activities in which people voluntarily participate. Political participation also includes deliberate attempts to influence people in power to make a difference (Ekman & Amna, 2012).

However, Brady (1999) notes that being interested in politics and societal issues or discussing politics frequently is insufficient. Political participation must include attempts to influence others – any powerful actors, groups, or business enterprises – and their decisions concerning societal issues (Ekman & Amna, 2012).

Political participation includes voting in elections, working on political campaigns, donating money to candidates or causes, contacting public officials, petitioning, protesting, and working with other people on issues. The health of a democratic nation's government is often measured by how actively its citizens participate in politics. Political participation and engagement are essential for democracy to function effectively (Pontes et al., 2018).

The voting system is one of the essential barometers of active citizen political participation. For a long time, voting was seen as the primary way for citizens to make their voices heard in the political system, and voting was described as the most commonly used measure of citizen participation (Ekman & Amna, 2012). However, electoral participation has dropped significantly over the years in South Africa. In the 2014 national elections, only 73% of the eligible population participated; this dropped by 8% to 66% in the 2019 national elections (Schulz-Herzenberg, 2020). The decline in voter participation indicates citizens' mistrust of the political institutions.

Furthermore, in certain instances, low electoral turnout and a lack of trust in democratic institutions and political parties affect people's interest in politics. However, Griffiths et al. (2018) argue that while political participation is slowly decreasing in some parts of the world, it is also being redefined in other parts of the world. The critical issue is that young people find interest in political issues and create alternative forms of political participation (Griffiths et al., 2018). Sairambay (2020) states that political participation has evolved to include online activities that attempt to affect the outcome of political institutions or their structures. Also, political participation now includes ordinary citizens who are not interested in gaining political power but are just interested in political changes (Sairambay, 2020). These discussions show that political understanding in theory and practice is not stagnant; it constantly evolves with context. This leads us to view activities that evoke political participation with a critical mindset.

Social media has become an increasingly vital platform for political participation. The advent of social media has led to renewed hopes that technological ease would ignite online and offline political engagement (Bruns, 2008; Holt et al., 2013). Holt et al. (2013) assert that using social media for political purposes exposes an individual to political information and suggests a certain motivation to process this content. Social media tools have also expanded our political activities with new modes of action, such as using protest hashtags or joining online groups involved in political issues (van Deth, 2014; Theocharis & van Deth, 2016). This demonstrates that a new log of political participation has emerged.

However, the role of social media in political participation and spreading populist ideas cannot be underestimated. Politicians have massive access to their supporters in a world where new media and old media are intertwined and complement each other (Chadwick, 2013; Kubler & Kriesi, 2017). Social media spaces provide politicians with free access to the public and allow the public to communicate with their leaders (Ernst et al., 2017). According to Gerbaudo (2018), the mass appeal of social media spaces makes it a suitable ground to spread populist ideas. Gerbaudo (2017, p. 746) further notes that "social media has favoured populists against established movements by providing the former a suitable channel to invoke the support of the ordinary people against the latter."

According to Griffiths et al. (2018), the conventional image dominating societies is that young people are less interested in politics than older generations. However, the presence of the EFF in South African politics has changed that perception; due to the party's activities on Twitter, and the party's incorporation of young and old generations in its parliamentary members, the party has created new forms of participation, which have caused people to divert from traditional forms of political participation to new methods. These include incorporating voting and protesting as forms of political participation to hold office bearers accountable.

South Africa is one of the countries where political participation is regarded as low. This is due to public dissatisfaction with the ability of governments to deliver socio-economic goods (Fintel & Ott, 2017). Such a political culture in South Africa is of concern in this study. Almond and Verba (1963, p. 13) define political culture as "the attitudes towards the political system and its various parts and the attitudes towards the role of the self in the system." This point highlights the role of individuals and public citizens as the underlying foundation behind the strength of the political culture of a given country (Fintel & Ott, 2017).

Democratic South Africa presents an exciting model for investigating the political culture because it is a country with a multi-party democracy, multiracial, multicultural, and diverse in many other aspects of society. The traditional model of political culture in South Africa has been expressed usually through protests and elections (Fintel & Ott, 2017). This has shown profound public discontent with socio-political issues in the country. The EFF, with its populist agenda, has added a new flavour to political participation in the country. Mbete (2015) argues that an examination of the EFF's politics is necessary to understand and understand how it affects the political culture in South Africa.

RESEARCH DATA AND METHODS

The research methods adopted for the current study are virtual ethnography and content analysis. The data was collected through virtual ethnography and analysed using content analysis. Content analysis was done on the tweets to find mentions of the word "EFF."

The paper analysed 600 Tweets, 200 belonging to each trending topic: #SONA2020, #Senekal, and #PutSouthAfricansFirst. The study analysed Tweets and retweets of the above topics to find out how the EFF is influencing political participation in the country. The focus was looking at how people on social media were engaging with the above topics and the EFF's position on those topics. However, some commentators have called the EFF's political activities and approach to populism a threat to democracy; when analysing these Tweets, the study also paid attention to this and examined whether the EFF is a threat to democracy.

The issue of "trend" became essential in this study as it proved to be driving the EFF's presence on Twitter. A trend is a name, phrase, or topic mentioned more than others. When a name or topic is mentioned more often than others, it is called a "trending topic" (Annamorandnejad & Habibi, 2019). Topics that are trending have a great potential to influence public opinion; they can promote events, create public discussions, lead to political debates, and raise awareness.

Virtual ethnography is a response to studying communities where electronic communications are routinely used (Hine, 1994). Virtual ethnography has also been described as exploring how people make sense of the life that the internet offers them (Hine, 2008). Bell (2001, p. 195) makes an interesting point about the relationship between the Internet and ethnography. This is an ethnographic work that attempts to mimic ethnographic fieldwork (Driscoll & Gregg, 2010). However, virtual ethnography is not a replacement for traditional ethnography; instead, it is a continuation through which electronic communications are used to study the way of life instead of fieldwork.

In this study, social media is approached as a culture, as a social domain. The virtual world consists of sophisticated social networks where people communicate and create some expressions. Drawing from Hine (2000), our rationale for choosing a virtual space to study public participation is that the internet is a natural field/site for studying what people do while they are online and free to express their views. Also, social media spaces such as Twitter have become spaces for engagement and participation more accessible. Social media have become virtual spaces where ideas, perspectives, and debates are exchanged on social matters (Mehta & Gretter, 2016). Furthermore, Rheingold (1993, p. 5) conceptualized virtual communities as "social aggregations that emerge from the Net when enough people carry on those public discussions long enough, with sufficient human feeling to form webs of personal relationships in cyberspace."

FINDINGS

During the 2020 SONA, topics such as #EFF, #Malema, #SONA2020, and #DeKlerkMustFall dominated Twitter in South Africa. Due to the EFF's radical actions in Parliament, people resonated with their stances and started talking about what the EFF was doing. The impact of the EFF on South Africa's Twitter users cannot be ignored. The party's presence on this platform is evident. The party leads Twitter users to participate in political matters.

One of the topics that caught the attention of Tweeps was the #DeKlerkMustFall. In the SONA of 2020, EFF called for former president FW de Klerk to be removed from Parliament, saying that it was a mistake for Parliament to invite a "murderer" to the SONA. This topic was debated by many people on Twitter, with some supporting the EFF and angry at the ANC for inviting de Klerk to Parliament. Some users argued that de Klerk is also a former president and deserved the benefits that other former presidents are getting.

#SONA2020

Example 1

@BeynonSammy: As it stands, the #EFF is leading the agenda of Parliament. Thinking back over the past & in honest reflection, it is the red berets who have shaped the national dialogue. #SONA2020

The user notes that EFF shapes the national dialogue in the above example. That is, it leads and determines conversations of national importance. In this tweet, the user has inevitably acknowledged the work EFF does in Parliament.

Example 2

@MightiJamie: Part of leadership – is setting the agenda of national dialogue. Hate it or love it. The @ EFFSouth Africa managed to do that using the President's platform of the #SONA2020. We are taking more of their issue #DeKlerkMustFall than the issues raised by the President.

In this example, the user is also in support of the user in example 1, and the ability of the EFF to set the national dialogue is also raised. Here we also see the user indicating that if it were not for the EFF, the #Deklerkmustfall would not be discussed. Due to the EFF raising the issue of the former Apartheid president's presence in parliament, people are focusing on De Klerk's presence in parliament rather than on the actual SONA by the president.

Example 3

@Sgoloza_Esmehlo: EFF is very important in South African politics as an opposition party coz they are the bravest, they don't buy a face, if you are upset abt their behaviour you deserve to be a graduate that is sitting at home romancing an ANC t-shirt. #SONA2020.

Here the user is raising an issue about the role of the EFF in raising pertinent issues in parliament. According to the user, the EFF's bravery comes from speaking the truth without hiding it. The user also notes that those who are upset about the behaviour of the EFF in parliament do not see the failures of the ruling party, the ANC.

Example 4

@Ferialhaffajee: Comment: That's 60 minutes! Whatever happens now, Julius Malema and the EFF have won. They are the story, not the #SONA2020 address. Brilliant politics. But not for the country.

Nevertheless, some users also find the behaviour of the EFF inappropriate. The user in this tweet complains that the EFF have wasted 60 minutes with their politics which does not benefit the country.

Example 5

@AshfafGarda: Battling to understand why and how they've won? This disruptive tactical campaign was brilliant in one year, but now, it's as boring and laborious as load-shedding. Citizens will switch on to #SONA one hour later, but more importantly, they will switch off the EFF.

Another criticism of the EFF's behaviour is brought forward. This Tweet explains that the politics of the EFF are outdated and no longer relevant. Moreover, this will cost the EFF their voters.

Example 6

@BigDaddyLiberty: The Fauxrage over De Klerk from the #EFF is meaningless to me, when these same asshats were praising the mass-murder, #Mugage! Their theatrics at #SONA2020 ring hallow. Malema is merely looking for any excuse to continue his campaign of hatred against SA's racial minorities.

In this Tweet, we see the work of the EFF as "meaningless"; the user argues that they are complaining against DeKlerk but praising Robbert Mugabe. This user states that the EFF's leader, Malema, continues his hatred against South Africa's racial minorities.

Many people on Twitter used the platform to support the work that the EFF has done in Parliament. However, some have voiced their disagreements with the EFF. Also, these debates on the role of EFF in South Africa's Parliament cross racial, ethnic, age, and gender boundaries.

These tweets are a demonstration of active citizen political participation. Different Twitter users are participating in a political discussion around the presence of the former head of state in parliament. The role of the EFF in this discussion cannot be ignored; the party started the issue in parliament just before the president could start with his SONA. This was a strategic move for the party to capture the attention of people expecting to see and hear the SONA. At this event, the EFF demonstrated its populist characteristic, "opportunists who, in practice, put themselves and their eternal hold on power above any democratic appeal that they may have in particular moments" (Scheppele, 2019). However, this behaviour spiked debates on Twitter, and the party, through its populist behaviour, achieved active citizen political participation.

However, the people on Twitter do not take the EFF for a religion or a dogma that cannot be questioned. People who disagree with the EFF express their stance and support them. On the #Senekal, some users felt that the EFF only fueled racial tensions instead of providing solutions. Other users argued that the EFF is doing an excellent job by confronting racism in the manner that it deserves.

The topic of #PutSouthAfricansFirst is also a contentious issue involving the EFF. The EFF opposes those that seek to chase away illegal foreigners in South Africa and argues that building one African country will benefit Africa and its people. The EFF feels that South Africa, already one of the most developed African countries, must lead the unification of Africans. However, some South Africans on Twitter oppose this view and feel that the government is not doing enough to protect South Africans from the challenges brought by foreign nations.

#PutSouthAfricansFirst

Example 7

@MbuyiseniNdlozi: The put South Africa first message is driven by idiocy, & outright fascism! And stop threatening us with losing our votes; we've been advocating for Pan-Africanism since 2013. We have never lost votes. Instead, we remain the ONLY significant party that increased its votes in 2019.

The Tweet, by the former spokesperson of the EFF, dismisses those that fight for the prioritization of South Africans in South Africa's economy against African foreign nationals. The EFF prides itself on advocating for Pan-Africanism.

Example 8

@Julius_S_Malema: Looking forward to receiving and being entertained by my brother @burnaboy here at his home called South Africa. No mascot can stop him from performing, he's one of our own and we will protect him. We must resolutely oppose regionalism led by political illiterates.

Julius Malema is challenging Tweets against a Nigerian musician, Burna Boy, performing in South Africa. Malema insists that the EFF opposes regionalism and refers to those that promote regionalism as "political illiterates"

Example 9

@nkeleakDK: Of course, protecting other nationalism than your own, is one of the reasons why EFF will lever lead this country.

Commenting on the Burna Boy saga, this Tweet is dissatisfied with the EFF protecting people from other countries over South Africans. This Tweet indicates that such stances will affect the EFF's electoral performance.

Example 10

@ayanda_yandiey: I voted for the EFF too but they can miss me in the next elections.

@MissB20_10: I swear EFF is being funded by one of the drug lords from Nigeria stru bob.

Here we are seeing two Tweets that are dismayed by the EFF's stances on those that seek to fight for the prioritization of South Africans in the country's economy. The first Tweep suggests they will not vote for the EFF in the next elections. The second one states that the EFF is protecting foreign nationals in South Africa because they must be funded by Nigerian drug lords.

Example 11

@Julius_S_Malema: I won't be intimidated or blackmailed by bed-wetting boys, welcome home @burnaboy. South Africa is a home for all Africans, kill me for defending an African brother, bloody Cowards.

Again, Malema is responding to comments about Burna Boy; he is not ready to compromise on the policy of the EFF when it comes to fighting for an "African brother" who is being chastised by South Africans.

Example 12

@Mswati93: The way #Malema sides with Nigerians over his people, one might begin to believe that the EFF is funded by Nigerian drug money.

This is another Tweet that believes that EFF protects foreign nationals in the country because of their dealings with Nigerian drug lords. This is another dissatisfaction with the EFF.

Twenty-nine years after South Africa became a democratic country, racial tensions are still rife. The EFF has positioned itself as a party that fights racism, which has led to some black people asking for assistance from the EFF when facing racial attitudes at their workplaces. The topic of #Senekal is among the highly debated on South African Twitter, and the EFF found itself at the centre of the discussions because of its actions. In the Tweets below, we see how the party managed to spark conversations and make itself a central topic in this issue even though initially it had nothing to do with the EFF.

The issue of illegal migrants in South Africa is one of the issues that the ANC has left unattended for a very long time. Some South Africans are frustrated by the government's will to deal with illegal immigration. The EFF has taken advantage of this situation and used it to spread its open-border policy, building one African continent. The party is eating from the ANC's lack of urgency to deal with this issue. Many people in South Africa, when they talk about #PutSouthAfricansFirst, mention the EFF. The two movements are almost inseparable. Whether the EFF's policy affects them in recruiting voters is beyond this study, but the party uses this hashtag to ignite socio-political debates in South Africa. With many other trending topics on illegal immigration, such as #PutSouthAfricansFirst, Operation Dudula, and Operation Fiela, the EFF finds itself at the centre of these discussions. The party is at loggerheads with South Africans that believe the EFF is protecting illegal foreigners in South Africa.

#Senekal

Example 13

@Happy36996506: Fighters our enemies are angry and hurting, they thought that we couldn't neutralize racism in #Senekal but we did it. Let us enjoy our victory throughout this beautiful weekend and to the attention seekers, let us see them on Monday. Aluta Continua.

The above Tweet seems to be coming from a supporter/member of the EFF. The Tweet is encouraging the EFF to continue its fight against racism and the fight against the struggle of black people.

Example 14

@MtwanaXabiso: I just received a call from a farm worker. This guy is working in PE. Kelkoot. They are very pleased about the recent EFF protest against white arrogance in #Senekal. He says he would be happy if @Julius_S_Malema could visit them so that they can talk to him face-to-face.

Here the work of the EFF is being commended for fighting against the conditions of farmworkers. The Tweet references a conversation with a farmworker who is happy about the EFF and wishes for Julius Malema to visit their farm.

Example 15

@10ousmaneSembene: Electorally, the EFF will deservedly cash-in on #Senekal, #Clicks, and now #brackenfellhigh programs. In the face of an indifferent, I-Don't-Care ANC, the EFF is successfully entrenching itself as the sole bodyguard of Afrikans against all manner of racist white violence onslaughts.

In this Tweet, the work of the EFF in three different programs involving racism is being raised. The Tweet engages how the EFF is at the forefront of fighting racism in South Africa, more than the ANC is doing.

Example 16

@MTshwaku: Proud member of the #EFF under the capable leader of CIC #Julius Malema. You are appreciated Mhlekazi. Your speeches always lift our defeated souls caused by colonisers. We are going to #Senekala and will face racists from toe to toe!

The Tweet appreciates the leadership of Julius Malema when it comes to lifting the souls of black people against white people. The work of Julius Malema is encouraging this Tweep to go to Senekal and fight against racism.

Example 17

@Monique_taute: #Afriforum is submitting charges at the Equity Court against @EFFSouthAfrica & @Julius_S_Malema after members @ their leaders sang "Kill the Boer, kill the farmer" on various occasions incl. outside the court in #Senekal whilst the #MurderCase of #BrendinHorner. #FarmMurders.

This Tweet focuses on those that do not agree with the politics of the EFF and Julius Malema. The Tweet comments that a civil rights group is taking the EFF to court for singing a song deemed hate speech in South Africa.

Example 18

@Jay_du_Plessis: So the #Terrorist organization EFF sings this song soon after #Senekal many farms are burning down. They sing #KilltheBoer and more #FarmMurders take place. #Farmattacks have increased. How can the rest of SA be so quiet? If you're silent, you're complicit! #EnoughisEnough.

Here the EFF is referred to as a terrorist organization that sings about burning properties, and the country does not say anything about that. The Tweet insists that those that are silent about the EFF's destruction of democracy are complicit in the crime.

The issue of racial tensions is another irksome one in South Africa. Again, from these tweets, the EFF has made itself the mediator and the battalion against racism against black people. Tweets are thrown around about the ANC's failure to deal with racism and how the EFF is the alternative for black people. The EFF channels people to fight against racism, it makes people aware of racial issues in the country, and the party makes people question the working conditions of the black farmworkers working for white farmers. By more actively engaging in these discussions, the EFF is growing and staying relevant in the country's political discourse.

DISCUSSION AND CONCLUSION

These results show that democracy is not stagnant; it is forever evolving, and many political parties resort to extra means to win the support of the people. Moreover, populism is one of the mechanisms politicians use to attract specific components of the voters to their parties. The EFF uses Twitter to spread its left-wing ideas and make itself a relevant political party in the country by initiating trending topics. Twitter is a powerful medium through which the EFF communicates its policies and political style. This leads to citizens of the country being informed of social and political matters that affect them. Anduiza, Guinjoan, and Rico (2018) state that the presence of populist ideas among citizens encourages their political participation.

With the EFF's populist stances, the party and the country's democracy benefit. The EFF can win itself, voters, and supporters, by focusing on and popularizing socio-political and economic issues that affect ordinary men and women in South Africa. However, these stances also encourage people to participate in political parties, which enhances democracy in the country. Democracy requires vibrancy and activeness to survive, and the EFF's populist stances are doing that. The party simplifies the country's extreme socio-political and economic matters to evoke people's frustrations, participation, and conversations on these issues.

In the Tweets above, the EFF inevitably relies on Twitter to encourage people to condemn the ruling elites (political and economic), develop a sense of belonging and identity, and criticize institutions of power such as the police and justice system. The EFF is using Twitter to reject the establishment. Anduiza et al. (2018) state that populist ideas can help correct some democratic deficiencies.

These findings also are an extension of the previous work that has been done on topics such as populism, a threat to democracy, political participation, and social media. Social media is paramount in activating citizens' political participation. Moreover, the EFF has mastered using this space to engage citizens. The internet represents a place, cyberspace. It is where culture is formed and reformed (Hine, 2000). Woolgar (1996) and Hine (2000) further argue that the Internet should also be viewed as a cultural artefact. The internet is a product of culture: a technology produced by people with situated goals and priorities (Hine, 2000). Speaking of the internet as a cultural artefact suggests its usage is context-based or context-situated; it is relevant to a particular people or culture.

Evidence suggests that social media facilitates political participation (Kim & Chen, 2015). The popularity of social media has influenced political parties such as the EFF to explore the role these spaces can play in growing their parties, spreading their policies, and attracting new members. With traditional media having institutional barriers for left-wing movements to grow, social media becomes an alternative option. As seen in the above Tweets, EFF leaders can tweet their messages without gatekeepers, people can criticize the EFF without fear, and EFF supporters can show support for their parties' political stances freely. This is one of the ways through which political participation is achieved.

From the findings above, inevitably, the EFF has drastically changed the South African political culture; it has opened more dialogue about political issues, raised policy issues that the "masses" can resonate with, and has made people more interested in parliamentary issues. The change in this political culture should be seen within the framework of how democracies have permanently changed with time. Democracies are not stagnant; they forever transform with the socio-political conditions of the time. Political culture does not exist in a vacuum; it develops against a backdrop of democracy. It is not deniable that the EFF has claimed the space in South African politics, and they resonate with people's needs and frustrations against socio-political and economic conditions. For example, the EFF's perpetual point-of-orders against the presidents when addressing the nation in the annual SONAS is against Western-style democracy. In other words, the EFF's populist stances and citizens' use of social media to participate in political issues are constitutive of post-Apartheid democracy and closely related.

The approach taken in this paper opens doors for more discussions and research on how liberal democracy is understood. This research implies that democracy should always be reconceptualized when the need arises. Therefore, when new forms of political activities arise, such as populism, democracy should also be revisited. As the field of political sciences evolves, ideas must also catch up. There needs to be a new understanding of how political parties and politicians aim to win votes and stay in power.

The paper has developed a platform for systematically identifying how politicians use social media to activate citizen political participation in South Africa. The EFF is inevitably making people talk on Twitter about socio-political issues. This cannot be ignored or dismissed because it is against the establishment or the party is challenging the status quo. With the data collected and analysed, the EFF is central in driving socio-political discussions among political parties in South Africa.

With #SONA2020, the EFF evoked many conversations and comments among South Africans on Twitter. Many South Africans resonated with the EFF's sentiments, while others rejected their manners of dealing with dissents. The topic on #Sekenal also made South Africans on Twitter talk about issues of racial tension in post-Apartheid South Africa. Some users questioned the role of the ANC in dealing with racism while it is the EFF at the forefront of every racial battle in the country. #PutSouthAfricans-First also finds the EFF battling issues of national and xenophobia on Twitter. While the EFF is against nationalism, South Africans who are for the #PutSouthAfricansFirst feel that the EFF is putting the interests of foreign nationals above those of South Africans. These issues demonstrate that the EFF is driving political conversations in South Africa, but mainly, the party is invoking political participation.

Online spaces such as social media are known to expose their users to populist ideas and lead to the users developing populist attitudes (Anduiza et al., 2018). With the EFF using Twitter effectively to spread its ideologies, policies, and political stances, the party is using its populist character to grow its support base. However, this makes more South Africans conscious of their politics.

REFERENCES

Agustin, O. G. (2020). *Left-Wing Populism: The Politics of the People*. Emerald Publishing Limited. doi:10.1108/9781839092039

Almond, G. A., & Verba, S. (1963). *The Civic Culture*. Princeton University Press. doi:10.1515/9781400874569

Anduiza, E., Guinjoan, M., & Rico, G. (2018). Populism, participation, and political equality. *European Political Science Review*, *11*(1), 109–124. doi:10.1017/S1755773918000243

Annamorandnejad, I., & Habibi, J. (2019). *A comprehensive analysis of Twitter trending topics*. 2019 5th International Conference on Web Research (ICWR), Tehran, Iran.

Badaru, K. A., & Adu, E. O. (2020). University students' media use and political participation in South Africa. *South African Journal of Higher Education*, *34*(1), 18–36. doi:10.20853/34-1-3382

Barber, N. W. (2019). Populist leaders and political parties. *German Law Journal*, *20*(2), 129–140. doi:10.1017/glj.2019.9

Brady, H. (1999). Political participation. In Robinson, J.P. Shaver, P.R. and Wrightsman, L.S (Eds.). Measures of Political Attitudes. Academic Press.

Brookings. (2017). *Why are populists winning online? Social media reinforces their anti-establishment message*. Brookings. https://www.brookings.edu/articles/why-are-populists-winning-online-social-media-reinforces-their-anti-establishment-message/>

Bruns, A. (2008). *Blogs, Wikipedia, Second Life, and Beyond: From Production to Produsage*. Peter Lang.

Chadwick, A. (2013). *The Hybrid Media System: Politics and Power*. Oxford. University Press. doi:10.1093/acprof:oso/9780199759477.001.0001

Chen, J. (2012). Voter participation and the effects of distributive spending on political participation. *American Journal of Political Science*, *57*(1), 200–217. doi:10.1111/j.1540-5907.2012.00613.x

Dalby, T. G., & Jones, B. C. (2020). Parties versus democracy: Addressing today's political party threats to democratic rule. *International Journal of Constitutional Law*, *18*(2), 509–538. doi:10.1093/icon/moaa025

Driscoll, C., & Melissa, G. (2010). My profile: The ethics of virtual ethnography. *Emotion, Space and Society*, *3*(1), 15–20. doi:10.1016/j.emospa.2010.01.012

du Preez, M. (2018). The use of social media by politicians and political parties. *News24*. https://www.news24.com/news24/columnists/maxdupreez/the-use-of-social-media-by-politicians-and-political-parties-20181227>

Economic Freedom Fighters. (2020). *Welcome to the Economic Freedom Fighters*. EFF. https://effonline.org

Ekman, J., & Amna, E. (2012). Political participation and civic engagement: Towards a new typology. *Human Affairs*, *22*(3), 283–300. doi:10.247813374-012-0024-1

El-Ibiary, R., & Calfano, B. (2022). Editorial: Media populism: How media populism and inflating fear empowers populist politicians. *Frontiers in Communication*, *7*, 996795. doi:10.3389/fcomm.2022.996795

Ernst, N., Engesser, S., & Esser, F. (2017). Bipolar populism? The use of anti-elitism and people-centrism by Swiss parties on social media. *Schweizerische Zeitschrift für Politikwissenschaft*, *23*(3), 253–261. doi:10.1111psr.12264

Fakir, E. (2014). *The loss of trust and confidence in political parties*. EISA. https://www.eisa.org.za/eu/2014eu4aeditorial.htm>

Fayomi, O., & Adebayo, G. T. (2017). (Eds.). Political participation and political citizenship. In Palgrave Handbook of African Politics, Government and Development. New York. Palgrave Macmillan.

Fintel, M., & Ott, G. (2017). Political culture and participation in South Africa: The role of socio-economic factors. *Taiwan Journal of Democracy*, *13*(1), 77–99.

Fisher, S. (2014). *EFF members a no-show at a parliamentary disciplinary hearing*. EFF. https://ewn.co.za/2014/10/08/EFF-members-refuse-to-show-up-at-disciplinary-hearing>

Fogel, B. (2013). *Julius Malema's EFF and South Africa's Left*. Africa's Country. https://africasacountry.com/2013/11/julius-malemas-economic-freedom-fighters-and-the-south-african-left>

Friedman, S. (2014). EFF frenzy a case of media hype over substance. *Business Live*. https://www.businesslive.co.za/bd/opinion/columnists/2014-03-05-eff-frenzy-a-case-of-media-hype-over-substance/>

Gerbaudo, P. (2017). Social media and populism: An elective affinity? *Media Culture & Society*, *40*(5), 745–753. doi:10.1177/0163443718772192

Haffajee, F. (2019). EFF leads the information war with its cyber army. *Daily Mavrick*. https://www.dailymaverick.co.za/article/2019-03-07-eff-leads-the-information-war-with-its-cyber-army/>

Hine, C. (1994). *Virtual Ethnography*. Paper presented at the 13th International Conference on Public Communication of Science and Technology (PCST), Montreal, Canada.

Hine, C. (2008). Virtual ethnography: modes, varieties, affordances. In Fielding, N. Lee, R.M. Blank, G (Eds.). The Sage Handbook on Online Research Methods. London. Sage Publications. doi:10.4135/9780857020055.n14

Hinnerich, B. T., & Petterson-Lidbom, P. (2014). Democracy, redistribution, and political participation: Evidence from Sweden 1919-1938. *Econometrica*, *82*(3), 961–993. doi:10.3982/ECTA9607

Holt, K., Shehata, A., Stromback, J., & Ljungberg, E. (2013, February). Age and the effects of news media attention and social media use on political interest and participation: Do social media function as leveller? *European Journal of Communication*, *28*(1), 19–34. doi:10.1177/0267323112465369

Inglehart, R., & Norris, P. (2016). Trump, Brexit, and the rise of populism: Economic have-nots and cultural backlash. *Harvard Kennedy School Faculty Research and Working Papers*, *16*(26), 1-52.

Kam, C. D. (2012). Risk attitudes and political participation. *American Journal of Political Science*, *56*(4), 817–836. doi:10.1111/j.1540-5907.2012.00605.x

Kanyane, C. (2019). EFF seizes the future through social media. *Times Live*. https://www.timeslive.co.za/sunday-times/opinion-and-analysis/2019-03-24-eff-seizes-the-future-through-social-media/>

Kim, Y., & Chen, H. T. (2016). Social media and online political participation: The mediating role of exposure to cross-cutting and like-minded perspectives. *Telematics and Informatics*, *33*(2), 320–330. doi:10.1016/j.tele.2015.08.008

Kubler, D., & Kriesi, H. (2017). How globalization and mediatization challenge our democracies: Results from the NCCR Democracy. *Schweizerische Zeitschrift für Politikwissenschaft*, *23*(3), 321–245. doi:10.1111psr.12265

Li, D., Wei, L. Q., Cao, Q., & Chen, D. (2022). Informal institutuions, entepreneurs' political participation, and venture internationalization. *Journal of International Business Studies*, *53*(6), 1062–1090. doi:10.105741267-021-00402-9

Mbete, S. (2014). The Economic Freedom Fighters: South Africa's turn towards populism? *Journal of African Elections*, *14*(1), 35–59.

Mehta, R., & Gretter, S. (2016. Hashtag activism and gender advocacy: A virtual ethnography of activism on Twitter. Conference paper: *Literacy Research Associated*. Nashville, TN.

Melber, H. (2021). Populism in southern Africa under liberation movements as governments: The cases of Namibia, South Africa, and Zimbabwe. In Oswald, M (Ed). The Palgrave Handbook of Populism. Cham. Palgrave Macmillan.

Moeller, J., Vreeese, D., Esser, F., & Ķunz, R. (2013). Pathway to political participation: The influence of online and offline news media on internal efficacy and turnout of first-time voters. *The American Behavioral Scientist*, *58*(5), 689–700. doi:10.1177/0002764213515220

Moffit, B., & Tormey, S. (2014). Rethinking populism: Politics, mediation and political style. *Political Studies*, *62*(2), 381–397. doi:10.1111/1467-9248.12032

Mudde, C. (2014). The populist Zeitgeist. *Government and Opposition, 39*(4), 541–563. doi:10.1111/j.1477-7053.2004.00135.x

Mudde, C., & Kaltwasser, C. R. (2017). *Populism: A very short Introduction*. Oxford University Press. doi:10.1093/actrade/9780190234874.001.0001

Muller, A. (2019). The meaning of populism. *Philosophy and Social Criticism, 45*(9-10), 1025–1057. doi:10.1177/0191453719872277

Muller, J. W. (2017). The rise of populism. In F. Gonzalez (Ed.), *The Age of Perplexity: Rethinking the World We Knew*. Penguin Random House.

News24. (2020). Senekala: Malema instructs EFF supporters to 'march into town'. News24. https://www.news24.com/news24/southafrica/news/senekal-malema-instructs-eff-supporters-to-march-into-town-20201016>

Norris, P. (2001). *Digital Divide: Civic Engagement, Information Poverty, and the Internet Worldwide*. Cambridge University Press. doi:10.1017/CBO9781139164887

Norris, P. (2010). *Democratic Phoenix: Reinventing Political Activism*. Cambridge University Press.

Parry, G., Moyser, G., & Day, N. (1992). *Political Participation and Democracy in Britain*. Cambridge University Press. doi:10.1017/CBO9780511558726

Polat, R. K. (2005). The Internet and political participation: Exploring the explanatory links. *European Journal of Communication, 20*(4), 435–459. doi:10.1177/0267323105058251

Pontes, A., Henn, M., & Griffiths, M. D. (2018). Towards a conceptualization of young people's political engagement: A qualitative focus group study. *Societies (Basel, Switzerland), 8*(17), 1–17. doi:10.3390oc8010017

Rheingold, H. (1993). *The Virtual Community: Homesteading on the Electronic Frontier*. Addison-Wesley.

Sairambay, Y. (2020). Reconceptualising political participation. *Human Affairs, 30*(1), 120–127. doi:10.1515/humaff-2020-0011

Scheppele, K. L. (2019). The opportunism of populists and the defence of constitutional liberalism. *German Law Journal, 20*(3), 314–331. doi:10.1017/glj.2019.25

Schulz-Herzenberg, C. (2020). The South African non-voter: An analysis. *The Midpoint Paper Series N 2/2020*. https://www.kas.de/documents/261596/10543300/The+South+African+non-voter+-+An+analysis.pdf/acc19fbd-bd6d-9190-f026-8d311078b670?version=1.0&t=1608>

Sowetan. (2018). *EFF's fascist agenda rapidly clarifies itself through Malema's racial outburst*. Sowetan Live. https://www.sowetanlive.co.za/opinion/columnists/2018-07-02-effs-fascist-agenda--rapidly-clarifies-itself-through-malemas-racial-outbursts/>

Taggart, P. (2001). Populism and the pathology of representative politics. In Y. Meny & Y. Surel (Eds.), *Democracies and the Populist Challenge* (pp. 62–80). Palgrave Macmillan.

Theocharis, Y., & van Deth, J. W. (2018). The continuous expansion of citizen participation: A new taxonomy. *European Political Science Review*, *10*(1), 139–163. doi:10.1017/S1755773916000230

Urbinati, N. (2014). *Democracy Disfigured*. Harvard University Press. doi:10.4159/harvard.9780674726383

van Deth, J. W. (2014). A conceptual map of political participation. *Acta Politica*, *49*(3), 349–367. doi:10.1057/ap.2014.6

van Onselen, G. (2018). Why the EFF is a fascist political party. *SA History*. https://www.sahistory.org.za/archive/why-eff-fascist-political-party-gareth-van-onselen-26-march-2018>

Versa, S. Nie, N.H. and Him, J.O. *Participation and Political Equality: A Seven-Nation Comparison*. Chicago. University of Chicago Press.

Yao, Y., & You, W. (2018). Women's political participation and gender gaps of education in China: 1950-1990. *World Development*, *106*, 220–237. doi:10.1016/j.worlddev.2018.01.004

Zaslove, A., Geurkink, B., Jacobs, K., & Akkerman, A. (2020). Power to the people? Populism, democracy, and political participation: A citizen's perspective. *West European Politics*, *44*(4), 727–751. doi: 10.1080/01402382.2020.1776490

Chapter 22
When Will Africa Bridge the Political and Economic Development Gap?

Opeyemi Idowu Aluko
Ajayi Crowther University, Oyo, Nigeria

ABSTRACT

There is a gap between development and underdevelopment. To cross from one level to the other requires a bridge. This is the developmental gap bridge that will enhance the crossover from the underdeveloped status to the developed status. This study focuses on Africa as largely on the underdeveloped or developing status and requires to use the bridge so as to cross over to the developed level. The research question pertinent to be answered is when will Africa bridge the development gap? The World Bank data using nine variables are analysed, the findings revealed that Africa is lagging behind in most sectors and must cross the bridge of development to the developed status. Political and economic solutions are proffered to correct this skirmish.

INTRODUCTION

There is no doubt that there is the persistent presence of a gap, fissure and or lacunae in global politics. The entire world countries and continents alike are differently endowed by Divine providence. The uniqueness in the difference among the country and continent comparatives is sufficient to make them develop at their own independent pace at a relatively equally developmental rate and mutually aligned (Aluko, 2020; Adedeji, 2023; Ajide & Dada, 2023). This implies that the natural endowment of each country can make it rich and developed to a substantial level when compared with other countries.

Africa is a continent with sixty-five (65) countries. Each country can be divided into five regions. These include; West Africa, East Africa, South Africa, Central Africa and North Africa. Each country and region has a great deal of both natural and human resources. These esteemed resources have the potential to transform every section of the governance and politics of the country. These include; the economic, social (religious and ethnic), political educational and psychological sectors. The geographi-

DOI: 10.4018/979-8-3693-0477-8.ch022

cal terrains are diverse and vary from region to region. It ranges from extreme hot in North Africa and Central Africa to extreme cold in South Africa and North Africa respectively.

However, almost all the countries in Africa had passed through a form of political, social and economic subjugation by external forces from Europe, America and or Arabia. These include either colonialism or apartheid rule. These experiences of either colonialism or apartheid rule had a transforming effect on each country. This can be divided into the good, the bad and the ugly effects. The proportion of the good, the bad and the ugly effects in each country and indeed in the continent varied. These variations eventually determine the future success or failure of the country (Aluko, 2017; Aluko & Oluwadele, 2023; Edo, Matthew & Ogunrinola, 2023).

This study is poised to reveal the level of development gap that is in Africa and the extent of work that is needed to be done in other to ensure that the gap is filled up within a systematic time frame. The methodology adopted uses the World Bank data since 2015 extrapolated to date. Nine (9) variables are randomly selected to express areas that need to be focused on for the development gap to be closed in Africa. These include access to finance, corruption, and social disorder as factors hindering development, firm ownership, infrastructure, technology innovation, trade, workforce and general performance.

BACKGROUND

Concept of Development, Underdevelopment and Development Gap

There are various perspectives on development and underdevelopment. Development in the light of the global north is the availability of all basic needs of life in a single location with little or no collaboration with others. It is the proof of the political correctness of a country in making timely decisions with calculated precisions and the economic viability of its worth among the comity of nations. Development is the absence of poverty and the ability of an individual to be able to cater his basic needs as a function of the national provisions.

Under development is the status of a country living below its development potential due to some unfavourable conditions restraining it from expressing its full potential. It is the situation where a state is living below her political sovereignty to determine her decisions and choice of interactions among the comity of states. It is the status of economic restrictions that a country is operating under that restrict it from exploring and exploiting more options for better living. It is the state of poverty that reflects on a state due to her inability to make full decisions on political, economic and social issues affecting her development.

There are different types of developments and underdevelopments. These include; political development, economic development, social development and psychological development or underdevelopment. Political development is the situation of political libration into full development without restrictions to exploiting options that will sustain the country and make it compete evenly among the comity of nations. Economic development is the scenario whereby a country has the full economic wherewithal to get its full needs without restrictions or limitations thereby becoming self-sufficient to a large extent. Social development is also a situation whereby the social life of a country is not restricted from getting its full potential of freedom and liberty from primordial or external restrictions from self-expression. Psychological development is the freedom from cynical expression restricting a country from participating in global or universal events and the unrestricted liberty of citizens to express themselves in all lawful activities.

The variations in underdevelopments on the other hand imply that political underdevelopment is the situation of political garrison preventing full political expression of a country leading to restrictions to exploiting options that will sustain the country and make it compete evenly among a community of nations. Economic underdevelopment is the scenario whereby a country has a poor economic wherewithal to get her full needs thereby experiencing restrictions or limitations and becoming largely insufficient to provide basic needs for her citizens to a large extent. Social underdevelopment is also a situation whereby the social life of a country is restricted from getting its full potential of freedom and liberty from primordial or external restrictions on self-expression. Psychological underdevelopment also is the poor or no freedom from cynical expression restricting a country from participating in global or universal events and the unrestricted liberty of citizens to express themselves in all lawful activities.

The development gap therefore is the difference between the two countries in terms of several items used in measurements. It is the variation in the level of doing things and the corresponding outcomes. It is the calculation of growth differences over some time between or among countries organizations or individuals. For development gaps to be measured there must be at least two groups of people or country. The measurement could be inter-group or intra-group calculations. Also, there must be some variables common to them that could be juxtaposed over some time. The developmental gap can be expressed in the form of political, economic development gap and social development gaps.

The political development gap is the measure of difference or variation of similarities in the political landscape between or among states using similar measures of variables. The economic development gap is the measure of difference or variation of similarities in the economic landscape between or among states using similar measures of variables. The social development gap also is the measure of difference or variation of similarities in the social landscape between or among states using similar measures of variables.

Intra Africa's Development Gap

The World Bank's (2015) data on the economy of Africa which includes the finance, firm ownership, infrastructure, technology innovation level, economic performance, trade and workforce are analysed to reveal the present level of Africa in the global political economy. This section analyses the World Bank Report on Africa's Development. The analysis includes access to finance, corruption, and social disorder as factors hindering development, firm ownership, infrastructure, technology innovation, trade, workforce and general performance.

Table 1. Access to Finance, Corruption and Social Disorder as Factors Hindering Development

	Percent of Firms Identifying Access to Finance as a Major Constraint	Percent of Firms Identifying Corruption as a Major Constraint	Percent of Firms Identifying Crime, Theft and Disorder as a Major Constraint
North Africa	35.7	53.2	26.4
Sub Sahara Africa	37.3	37	16.4

Sources: World Bank 2015 (updated, 2023)

Figure 1. Africa Finance Analysis

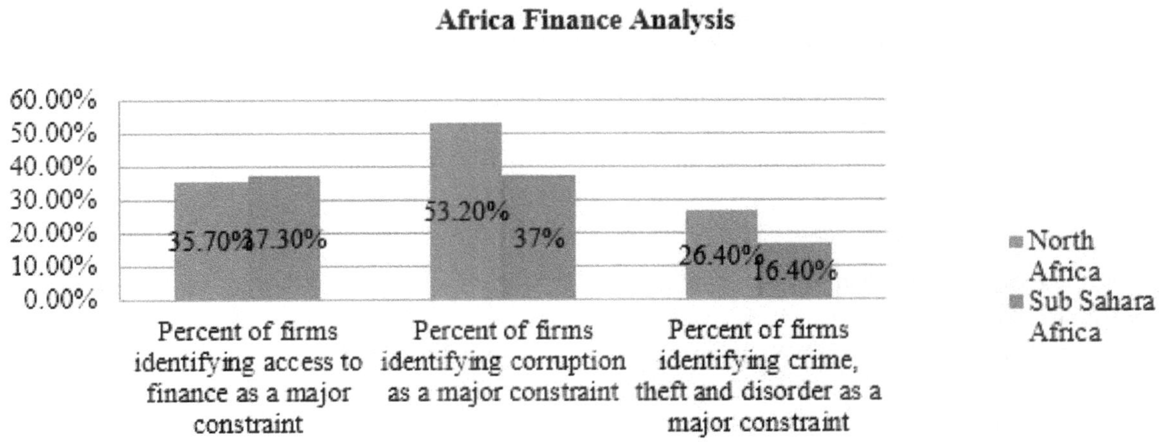

It is perceived in Table 1 that the percentage of firms that identify access to finance as a major constrain in North Africa is about thirty-six per cent (36%) a relatively high percentage, the percentage of firms that perceived corruption as a major constrain to development is fifty-three per cent (56%) a highly significant percentage whereas the percentage of firms identifying crime, theft and disorder as a major constrain to development is about twenty-six per cent (26%) relatively low.

This perception is not too far from the Sub-Saharan African perception of the development gap. The percentage of firms that identify access to finance as a major constraint is about thirty-seven per cent (37%) a relatively high percentage, the percentage of firms that perceived corruption as a major constraint to development is thirty-seven per cent (37%) a highly significant percentage. However, the percentage of firms identifying crime, theft and disorder as major constrain to development is about sixteen percent (16%) a relatively low percentage.

Figure 2. Firm ownership in Africa

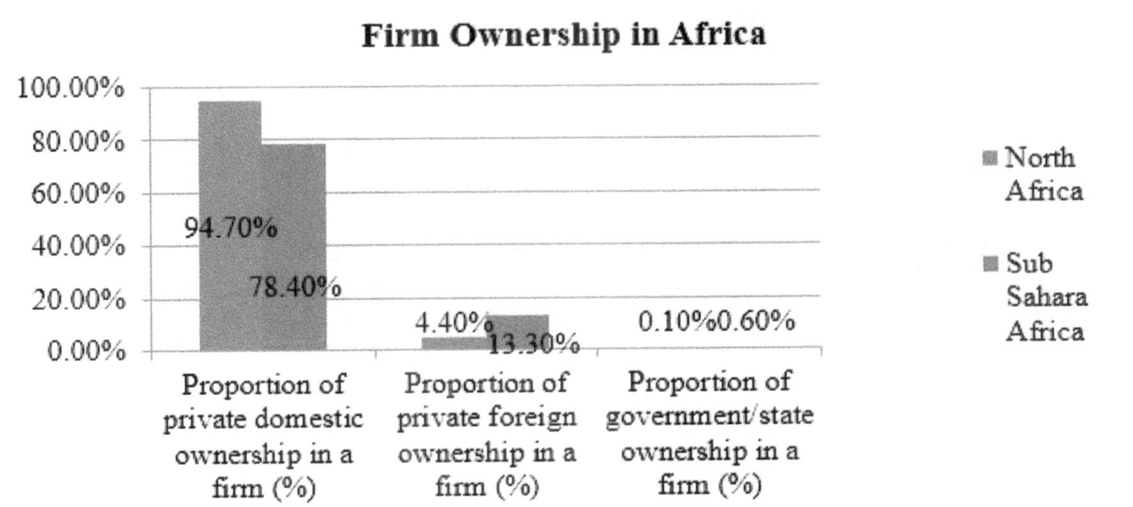

Table 2. Firm Ownership

	The proportion of Private Domestic Ownership in a Firm (%)	The proportion of Private Foreign Ownership in a Firm (%)	Proportion of Government/State Ownership in a Firm (%)
North Africa	94.7	4.4	0.1
Sub Sahara Africa	78.4	13.3	0.6

Sources: World Bank 2015(updated, 2023)

There is a highly significant improvement in the proportion of private domestic ownership of firms in both North Africa and Sub-Saharan Africa. This is about ninety-five per cent (95%) and seventy-eight (78%) of North African and Sub-Saharan African firms respectively. This indicates that the African economy is largely driven by private domestic ownership of firms. The proportion of private foreign ownership in firms is quite lower in North Africa while that of Sub-Saharan Africa is low having about four per cent (4%) and thirteen per cent (13%) respectively. This indicates that foreign ownership of firms as a form of neo-colonialism is low in Africa considering their numbers but not their impact on the economy. The Government or state ownership of firm proportion in Africa is much lower as both North and Sub-Sahara Africa have less than one per cent in the state control of the economic process of firm establishments. This is an indication of capitalism as a major order of the economy in Africa while the level of socialism as controlled by the government is very little (Aluko, 2015; Namahoro, Qiaosheng & Hui, 2023; Yimer, 2023). Invariably, there is a mixed economy which tilts more towards the capitalist than the socialist.

Figure 3. Infrastructure Development in Africa

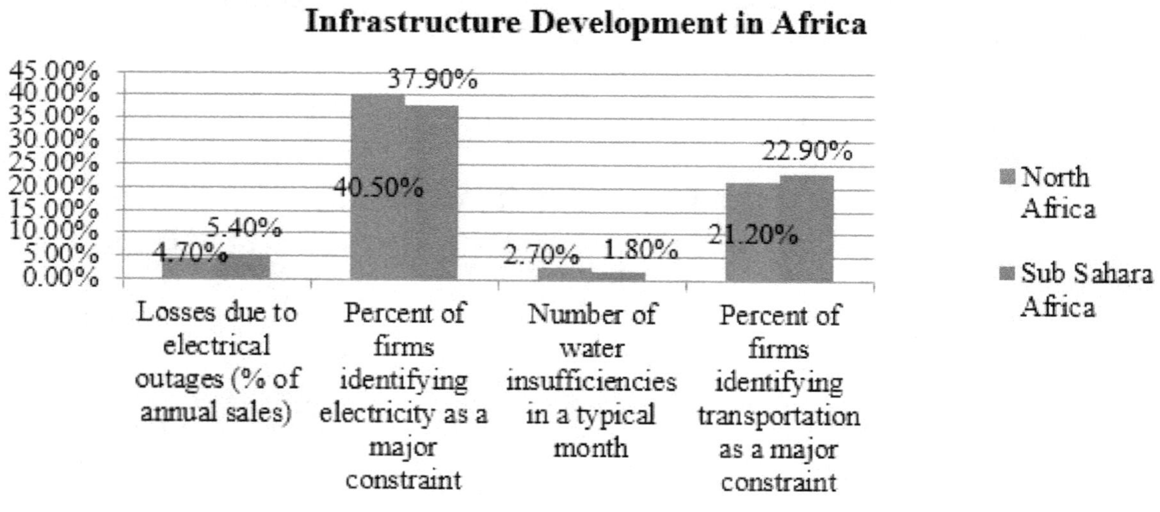

Table 3. Infrastructure

	Losses Due to Electrical Outages (% Of Annual Sales)	Percent of Firms Identifying Electricity as a Major Constraint to Development	Number of Water Insufficiencies in a Typical Month	Percent of Firms Identifying Transportation as a Major Constraint to Development
North Africa	4.7	40.5	2.7	21.2
Sub Sahara Africa	5.4	37.9	1.8	22.9

Sources: World Bank 2015(updated, 2023)

From Table 3 above, it is observed that the level of constraints encountered in the infrastructural development is quite enormous. The losses due to electrical power outages gulp about five per cent (5%) of the annual sales both in North Africa and Sub-Saharan Africa. The percentage of firms in North Africa and Sub-Saharan Africa that identify electricity infrastructure as a major constraint cumulates to about forty-one per cent (41%) and thirty-eight per cent (38%) respectively.

The number of water insufficiencies recorded in a typical month in North Africa and Sub-Saharan Africa is worrisome. This goes as high as about three per cent (3%) and two per cent (2%) per month for North Africa and Sub-Saharan Africa respectively. In extension to a typical year, it could go up to as high as about thirty-six per cent (36%) and twenty-four per cent (24%) for North Africa and Sub-Saharan Africa respectively.

The percentage of firms that identify transportation as a major constraint to Africa's development records a high level of dissatisfaction. North Africa and Sub-Saharan Africa record about twenty-one per cent (21%) and twenty-three per cent (23%) respectively. From the aforementioned analysis, all the major infrastructures such as the efficient and effective electricity supply, adequate potable water supply and efficient and effective transportation system which serves as the bedrock for a virile economy are all at unsatisfying levels in the continent (Namahoro, Qiaosheng & Hui, 2023; Mohamed, 2023).

Figure 4. Technology innovation level in Africa

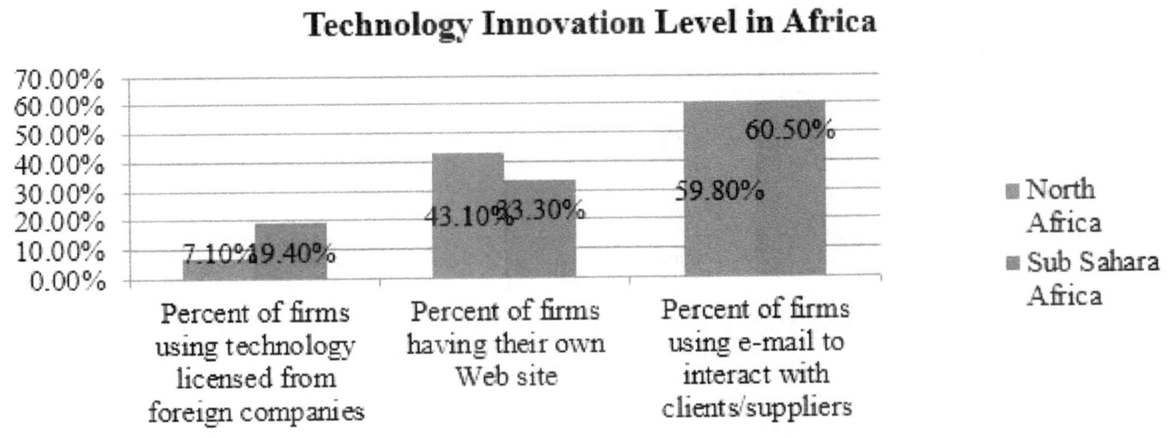

Table 4. Technology Innovation Level in Africa

	Percent of Firms Using Technology Licensed from Foreign Companies	Percent of Firms Having their Web Site	Percent of Firms Using E-Mail to Interact with Clients/Suppliers
North Africa	7.1	43.1	59.8
Sub Sahara Africa	19.4	33.3	60.5

Sources: World Bank 2015(updated, 2023)

Table 4 above depicts the situation of technological innovation in Africa. It is revealed that seven per cent (7%) of North African firms use technology licensed by foreign companies while the states in the Sub Sahara Africa at a record high of about twenty per cent (20%) use technology licensed by foreign companies. However, the percentage of firms in North Africa that have their website is about forty-three per cent (43%) while the percentage of firms in Sub-Saharan Africa that have their website is about thirty-three per cent (33%).

However, there is an increase in the percentage of firms in both North Africa and Sub-Saharan Africa that use the Internet and e-mail to interact with their clients or suppliers. There are about sixty per cent (60%) of North African states use the Internet and e-mail to interact with their clients or suppliers while a corresponding sixty-one per cent (61%) of Sub-Saharan African states use the Internet and e-mail to interact with their clients or suppliers. The above data analysis revealed that the level of technology usage in Africa is on the increase and it keeps appreciating daily (Awodumi, 2023; Appiah, Gyamfi, Adebayo & Bekun, 2023).

Table 5 and the corresponding figure 5 above analyse the proportion of Africa's domestic and foreign trades. In North Africa, the proportion of total domestic sales is eight-nine per cent (89%) while the proportion of total sales that are domestic in Sub Sahara Africa is about ninety-three per cent (93%). On the other hand, the proportion of total sales that are exported directly in both North Africa and Sub-Saharan Africa is relatively low. These are nine per cent (9%) and four per cent (4%) for North Africa and Sub-Saharan Africa respectively.

This shows that a very significant percentage of Africa's trade is predominantly domestic with little foreign exchange. A very low export will make the state's economy have a retarded and slow growth. Africa's economy is not export-oriented but import-oriented (Aluko, 2021; Chindengwike, 2023; Espoir, Sunge & Bannor, 2023). For growth to come, the export orientation of Africa must be boosted by producing export-oriented products.

Table 5. Trade

	The proportion of Total Sales that are Domestic Sales (%)	The proportion of Total Sales that are Exported Directly (%)
North Africa	89	8.5
Sub Sahara Africa	93.4	3.7

Sources: World Bank 2015, (updated, 2023)

Figure 5. Trade in Africa

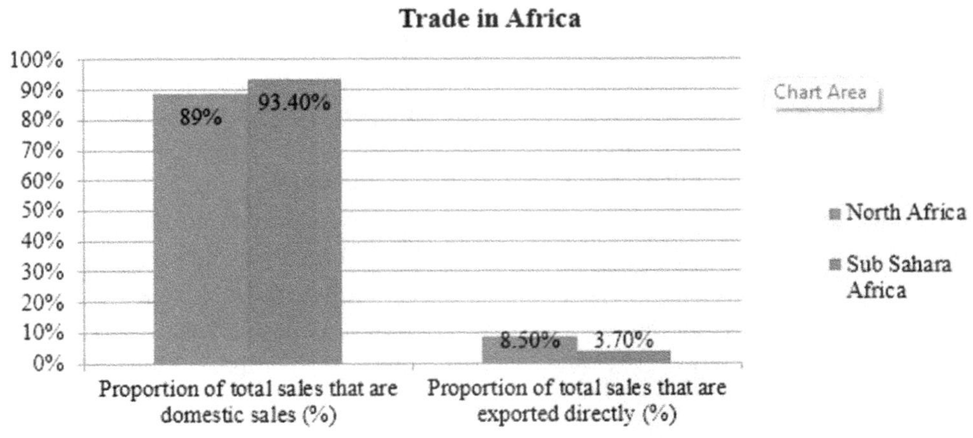

Table 6. Workforce

	Number of Permanent Production Workers	Number of Permanent Non-Production Workers	Number of Permanent Skilled Production Workers	Number of Permanent Unskilled Production Workers
North Africa	28.6	8.7	16.7	11
Sub Sahara Africa	39	10.9	23.6	14.1

Sources: World Bank 2015(updated, 2023)

Figure 6. Work force in Africa

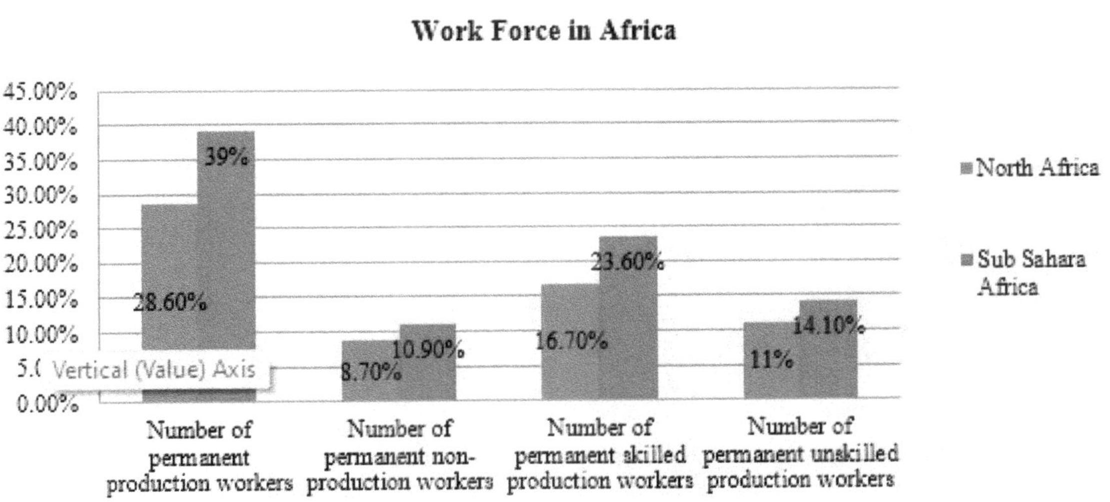

Table 6 and the corresponding figure 6 analyses the type of workforce in Africa's political economy. The number of permanent production workers in North Africa and Sub-Saharan Africa is less significant. North Africa has a total of about twenty-nine per cent (29%) of permanent production workers while Sub-Saharan Africa has about thirty-nine per cent (39%). However, the percentage of permanent non-production workers in the North Africa region is about nine per cent (9%) while this makes up eleven per cent (11%) in the Sahara Africa region.

The percentage of permanent skilled production workers in the North Africa region is about seventeen per cent (17%) while the Sub-Saharan Africa region has about twenty-four per cent (24%) of permanent skilled production workers. The percentage of permanent non-skilled production workers in the North Africa region is eleven per cent (11%) while the percentage in Sub-Saharan Africa is about fourteen per cent. The analysis above shows that the level of permanent production workers in Africa is as small as the number of skilled production workers (Aluko, 2018; Tete, Soro, Sidibé & Jones, 2023).

Table 7. Performance

	Capacity Utilization (%)	Annual Employment Growth (%)	Annual Labour Productivity Growth (%)
North Africa	64.1	3.1	-8.6
Sub Sahara Africa	70.2	6.3	-4.8

Sources: World Bank 2015(updated, 2023)

Figure 7. Performance of Africa economy

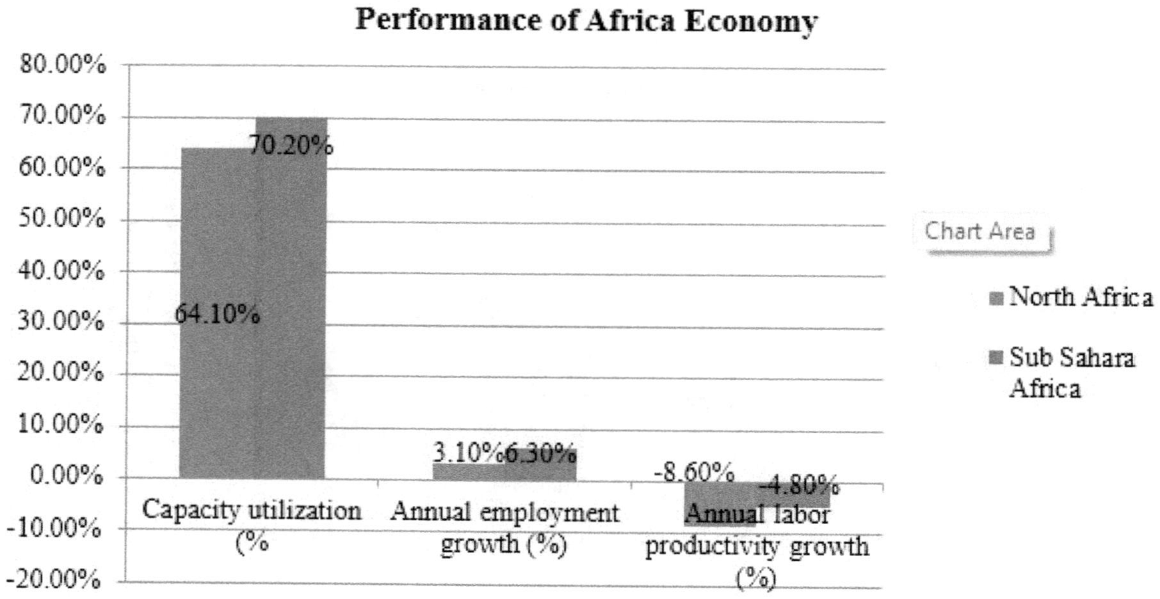

Table 7above shows the performance of the African economy. It revealed that the percentage of capacity utilization is of high significance. The North African states have a percentage of capacity utilization of about sixty-four per cent (64%) while the percentage of capacity utilization of Sub Sahara Africa is about seventy per cent (70%). This shows that Africa is using a highly significant percentage of its developmental capacity. However, this turns out to be a poor annual employment growth in both North Africa and Sub-Saharan Africa's political economy. These have three per cent (3%) and about six per cent (6%) in North Africa and Sub-Saharan Africa.

The annual productivity growth percentage is grossly poor and non-significant to the capacity of political economic utility in Africa. North Africa has a negative annual productivity growth rate of about minus nine per cent (-9%) while Sub-Saharan Africa has a negative annual productivity growth rate of about minus five per cent (-5%). This shows that the performance of the African economy over time did not help the giant model of development to be a reality (Ogundare, 2023; Aluko, 2023; Nguea, Noula & Noumba, 2023). The under-giant model is still much in vogue in Africa.

Effects of Development Gaps in Africa

There are several effects of the development gaps in Africa. These can be summarized into the good bad and ugly effects. These effects include the following,

a. Development gaps in Africa reveal that some African states have bad leaders that had failed to make use of political, economic and social levels of development to enhance their predicaments over some time.
b. Development gaps in Africa reveal that some African states have taken some self-deliberate actions to limit their rate of development by employing policies that make their economy less effective despite the abundance of resources in the country.
c. Development gaps in Africa also revealed that some external powers have limited the extent of speed the country could undertake due to some global restrictions and conditions attached to some international relations that could help the countries.
d. Development gaps in Africa show that some African countries are doing better which shows that gaps can be limited by determination in terms of psychological development.
e. Development gaps in Africa also revealed that so far the conditions are favourable; Africa can also make a better difference among the comity of states.
f. Development gaps in Africa, as compared, showed that development models in Africa can be utilized by other countries with the same conditions to enhance their conditions.
g. Development gaps in intra-Africa revealed that much of the natural and human resources are the most important assets that the continent must build on in other to be able to close the gap or help her citizens become respectable as global citizens.

CONCLUSION

Africa is indeed ready for development and to break the shackles of poverty off her citizens but the trend of events keeps the continent under perpetual underdevelopment. The availability of raw materials needed for the rapid development of hi-tech equipment such as uranium, gold, crude oil and gas among others placed Africa among the potential world movers and shakers. However, the nature of leadership and the citizens' response to leadership failure make the continent to be a perpetual backward region among the comity of continents.

The study revealed that North Africa and South Africa are making significant economic performance in terms of growth and development while Central Africa and West Africa are mostly hit with poverty and underdevelopment. A few selected countries in West Africa are making waves of development but not commensurate with the extent of need at hand. East Africa is in between the divide but more twisted towards poverty and poor development.

The intra-development gaps in Africa can therefore be narrowed by mitigating the rate of poverty. This can be reduced by increasing the employment rate in each country. The level of unemployment is directly proportional to the extent of poverty in the country. Both the skilled and the unskilled workforce should be adequately catered for to improve the entire sector. Technology development must be greatly improved and enhanced to promote the ease of doing business in the continents. Technology drives the economy and modern equipment will help in supplying in large quantity and quality for the entire population of a country and be able to export to others. This would improve the revenue generation of the country as well.

The bane of development in Africa is corruption. This must be institutionally and generally curbed in society. The law made by the government must be binding on both official and unofficial members. Strict laws must be made against corrupt practices such as money laundering, embezzlement of public funds and diversion of public utilities to the private realms. The line of separation between the private realm and the public realm must be conspicuous so that it will be difficult to cross it in pretence, it will be evidence to have crossed it and it will be conspicuous if it has not been crossed to effect the right measure of punishment on the offender.

REFERENCES

Adedeji, A. (Ed.). (2023). *Indigenization of African economies*. Taylor & Francis.

Ajide, F. M., & Dada, J. T. (2023). Poverty, entrepreneurship, and economic growth in Africa. *Poverty & Public Policy*, *15*(2), 199–226. doi:10.1002/pop4.368

Aluko, O. I. (2015). Political economy of crony capitalism: The prospect and the bane. *Journal of Economics Library*, *2*(3), 192–197.

Aluko, O. I. (2017). Political economy of crony inequality among nations: A study on capitalism and socialism. [Humanities and Social Sciences]. *Journal of Community Development Research*, *10*(2), 25–36.

Aluko, O. I. (2018). Entangled in the "New World Order": Africa's (In-) Security Quandaries and Prospects. *Rethinking Securities in an Emergent Technoscientific New World Order: Retracing the Contours for Africa's Hi-jacked Futures*, 171.

Aluko, O. I. (2020). Chapter Six Soft Power and the State of Nigeria's Economic Diplomacy. *Power Politics in Africa: Nigeria and South Africa in Comparative Perspective, 109.*

Aluko, O. I. (2021). Cycle of Poverty in Developing Countries. In *Handbook of Research on Institution Development for Sustainable and Inclusive Economic Growth in Africa* (pp. 126–139). IGI Global.

Aluko, O. I. (2023Aluko, O. I. (2023). Cycle of Violence, Transport Chain Theory, and Election Disputes in Developing Countries: A Case of Nigeria. In Insights and Explorations in Democracy, Political Unrest, and Propaganda in Elections (pp. 175-186). IGI Global.

Aluko, O. I., & Oluwadele, L. B. (Eds.). (2023). *Insights and Explorations in Democracy, Political Unrest, and Propaganda in Elections*. IGI Global. doi:10.4018/978-1-6684-8629-0

Appiah, M., Gyamfi, B. A., Adebayo, T. S., & Bekun, F. V. (2023). Do financial development, foreign direct investment, and economic growth enhance industrial development? Fresh evidence from Sub-Sahara African countries. *Portuguese Economic Journal*, *22*(2), 203–227. doi:10.100710258-022-00207-0

Awodumi, O. B. (2023). Does foreign direct investment matter for environmental innovation in African economies? *Economic Change and Restructuring*, *56*(1), 237–263. doi:10.100710644-022-09421-4

Chindengwike, J. (2023). The Nexus between Inflation and Economic Growth in Sub-Saharan Africa Countries.: An Empirical Study using VECM. *Journal of Global Economics*, *19*(2), 109–136. doi:10.1956/jge.v19i2.672

Edo, S., Matthew, O., & Ogunrinola, I. (2023). Bilateral and multilateral aid perspectives of economic growth in sub-Saharan Africa. *African Journal of Economic and Management Studies*, *14*(1), 1–17. doi:10.1108/AJEMS-02-2022-0047

Espoir, D. K., Sunge, R., & Bannor, F. (2023). Economic growth, renewable and nonrenewable electricity consumption: Fresh evidence from a panel sample of African countries. *Energy Nexus*, *9*, 100165. doi:10.1016/j.nexus.2022.100165

Mohamed Sghaier, I. (2023). Trade openness, financial development and economic growth in North African countries. *International Journal of Finance & Economics*, *28*(2), 1729–1740. doi:10.1002/ijfe.2503

Namahoro, J. P., Qiaosheng, W., & Hui, S. (2023). Economic growth, natural resource rents, and business openness nexus in regions and income levels of Africa: Evidence from recent panel estimators. *Mineral Economics*, *36*(4), 1–16. doi:10.100713563-022-00362-y

Nguea, S. M., Noula, A. G., & Noumba, I. (2023). Financial globalization and democracy: Implications for economic growth in African countries. *Journal of the Knowledge Economy*, 1–25. doi:10.100713132-023-01311-y

Ogundare, Y. D. (2023). Governance and Public Protest: Exercising Democratic Accountability in Lebanon. In Insights and Explorations in Democracy, Political Unrest, and Propaganda in Elections (pp. 69-81). IGI Global.

Tete, K. H., Soro, Y. M., Sidibé, S. S., & Jones, R. V. (2023). Assessing energy security within the electricity sector in the West African economic and monetary union: Inter-country performances and trends analysis with policy implications. *Energy Policy*, *173*, 113336. doi:10.1016/j.enpol.2022.113336

World Bank. (2015) *Africa Economy Performance*. Washington, DC: World Bank Data Base.https://www.worldbank.org/en/region/afr/overview

Yimer, A. (2023). The effects of FDI on economic growth in Africa. *The Journal of International Trade & Economic Development*, *32*(1), 2–36. doi:10.1080/09638199.2022.2079709

Compilation of References

AbdullahiS. I. (2018). *Nigerian economy: business, governance and investment in period of crisis*. doi:10.2139/ssrn.3310120

Abebe, R., Aruleba, K., Birhane, A., Kingsley, S., Obaido, G., Remy, S. L., & Sadagopan, S. (2021, March). Narratives and counternarratives on data sharing in Africa. In *Proceedings of the 2021 ACM conference on fairness, accountability, and transparency* (pp. 329-341). 10.1145/3442188.3445897

Abegunrin, O. (2009). *Africa in global politics in the twenty-first century: A Pan-African perspective*. Springer. doi:10.1057/9780230623903

Abiddin, N. Z., Ibrahim, I., & Abdul Aziz, S. A. (2022). Non-governmental organizations (NGOs) and their part towards sustainable community development. *Sustainability (Basel)*, *14*(8), 4386. doi:10.3390u14084386

Abima, B., Engotoit, B., Kituyi, G. M., Kyeyune, R., & Koyola, M. (2021). Relevant local content, social influence, digital literacy, and attitude toward the use of digital technologies by women in Uganda. *Gender, Technology and Development*, *25*(1), 87–111. doi:10.1080/09718524.2020.1830337

Ace Project. (2003). *Democracy: What the hell is that?* http: //www.aceproject.org/main/english/ve/vek05b01.htm

Achebe, C. (1983). *The Trouble with Nigeria*. Heinemann.

AcsZ. J.AudretschD. B.BraunerhjelmP.CarlssonB. (2004). The missing link: The knowledge filter and entrepreneurship in endogenous growth. *Available at* SSRN 667944.

Acs, Z. J., Audretsch, D. B., & Lehmann, E. E. (2013). The knowledge spillover theory of entrepreneurship. *Small Business Economics*, *41*(4), 757–774. doi:10.100711187-013-9505-9

Acs, Z. J., Stam, E., Audretsch, D. B., & O'Connor, A. (2017). The lineages of the entrepreneurial ecosystem approach. *Small Business Economics*, *49*(1), 1–10. doi:10.100711187-017-9864-8

Acs, Z. J., & Szerb, L. (2007). Entrepreneurship, economic growth and public policy. *Small Business Economics*, *28*(2-3), 109–122. doi:10.100711187-006-9012-3

Addae-Korankye, A. (2014). Causes of poverty in Africa: A review of literature. *American International Journal of Social Science*, *3*(7), 147–153.

Adebayo, K. O., & Njoku, E. T. (2023). Local and transnational identity, positionality and knowledge production in Africa and the African diaspora. *Field Methods*, *35*(1), 18–32. doi:10.1177/1525822X211051574

Adedeji, A. (Ed.). (2023). *Indigenization of African economies*. Taylor & Francis.

Adefisoye, T. O., & Adefisoye, I. (2019). Nigeria and the implementation of the United Nations Security Council Resolution 1325 on women, peace and security. *Journal of Public Administration and Development Alternatives*, *4*(1), 16–29.

Adekoya, R. (2019). Democracy has failed in Nigeria when voters no longer care who wins. https://www.theguardian.com/commentisfree/2019/mar/01/democracy-failed-nigeria-turnout presidential-election

Adelmann, M. (2004). Quiet diplomacy: The reasons behind Mbeki's Zimbabwe policy. *Africa Spectrum*, 249–276.

Adenekan, A. T., Sanni, G. K., & Itodo, A. I. (2019). Investigating the Impact of Exchange Rate Volatility on Naira Exchange Rate in Nigeria. *Central Bank of Nigeria Economic and Financial Review.*, *57*(3), 17–38.

Adenikinju, A. F. & Alabi, G. A. (1997). The impact of exchange rate instability on Nigerian non oil exports. *Journal of Social and Management Studies, 3-4*, 1-21.

Adeogun, T. J., & Muthuki, J. M. (2018). Feminist perspectives on peacebuilding: The case of women's organisations in South Sudan. *Agenda (Durban, South Africa)*, *32*(2), 83–92. doi:10.1080/10130950.2018.1450572

Adetoye, D., & Omilusi, M. (2016). Pains of Development and Electoral Politics in Nigeria's Democracy: Ekiti State in Perspective. *European Journal of Research in Social Sciences*, *4*(1), 27–33.

Adetula, V. A. O. (2011). *Measuring democracy and good governance in Africa: A critique of assumptions and methods.* HSRC Press.

Adewale, F. B., & Musa, Z. A. (2023), 'Voter Apathy and its Implication for Democratic Consolidation in Nigeria' Being text of a chapter presented at the third International Conference of the Department of Political Science and International Studies, Ahmadu Bello University, Zaria on "Beyond Sustainable Elections: Interrogating the Challenges of Leadership and Governance in Nigeria." July 9th – 12th, 2023.

Adjei, M. (2019). Women's participation in peace processes: A review of literature. *Journal of Peace Education*, *16*(2), 133–154. doi:10.1080/17400201.2019.1576515

Adner, R. (2017). Ecosystem as structure: An actionable construct for strategy. *Journal of management, 43*(1), 39-58. *Agricultural Sustainable Practice.*, *1*(2), 69–70.

Adogamhe, P. G. (2008). Pan-Africanism revisited: Vision and reality of African unity and development. *African Review of Integration*, *2*(2), 1–34.

Adong, M., Opio, M., & Mwesigwa, D. (2020). Consequence of Land Conflicts to Small-Holder Farmers in Masindi District, Mid-Western Uganda. *Journal of Agricultural and Rural Research*, *5*(1), 36–46.

Aeby, M. (2019). *SADC–the southern arrested development community?: Enduring challenges to peace and security in Southern Africa.* Nordiska Afrikainstitutet.

Aerni-Flessner, J. (2017). Op-Ed: Will political and security unrest deepen in Lesotho? *Daily Maverick.* https://www.dailymaverick.co.za/article/2017-10-25-op-ed-will-political-and-security-unrest-deepen-in-lesotho/. Accessed: 19-08-2019.

Afolaranmi, A. O. (2021). Conflict Resolution Strategies in Resolving Religious Conflict in Nigeria. *Academia Letters*, 2.

Africa Commission. (2009). *Realizing the Potential of Africa's Youth: Report of the Africa Commission.* Author.

African Development Bank. (2001). A Note on the Contribution of the African Development Bank to Economic Knowledge and Policy in Africa. *African Development Review*, *13*(1), 145–172. doi:10.1111/1467-8268.00034

African Development Bank. (2004). *Cameroon—Country Governance Profile.* https://www.afdb.org/en/documents/project-operations/country-governance-profiles

African Development Bank. (2015). *Uganda Rural Electricity Access Project 285-300.* Available afdb.org

African Development Bank. (2019). *Integrity in Development Projects: The African Development Bank and GE Power Reach Settlement on Legacy Alstom Misconduct.* Available: https://www.afdb.org/en/news-and-events/integrity-in-development-projects-the-african-development-bank-and-ge-power-reach-settlement-on-legacy-alstom-misconduct-19116

African Development Bank. (2022). *African Development Bank debars Entreprise de Commerce et de Construction Immobilière for nine months for fraudulent practices.* Available: https://www.afdb.org/en/news-and-events/press-releases/african-development-bank-debars-entreprise-de-commerce-et-de-construction-immobiliere-nine-months-fraudulent-practices-53730

African National Congress. (2012). *The Second Transition? Building a national democratic society and the balance of forces in 2012.* ANC. https://www.anc1912.org.za/wp-content/uploads/2021/05/Discussion-Documents-2012-The-Second-Transition-Building-a-national-democratic-society-and-the-balance-of-forces.pdf

Agbalajobi, D. T. (2010). The role of women in conflict resolution and peacebuilding. *Understanding Africa's contemporary conflicts*, 233.

Agbiboa, D. E. (2012). Saving the few, starving the many: How corruption underdeveloped Nigeria and how there is an alternative perspective to corruption cleanups. *Africa Today, 58*(40).

Agra, K. L. R. P. (2020). Epistemic Injustice, Epistemic Paralysis, and Epistemic Resistance: A (Feminist) Liberatory Approach to Epistemology. *Kritike: An Online Journal of Philosophy, 14*(1).

Agustin, O. G. (2020). *Left-Wing Populism: The Politics of the People*. Emerald Publishing Limited. doi:10.1108/9781839092039

Agwu, E. (2014). Foreign Direct Investments: A Review from The Nigerian Perspective. *Research Journal of Business & Management, 1*(3).

Ahenkan, A., & Osei-Kojo, A. (2014). Achieving sustainable development in Africa: Progress, challenges and prospects. *International Journal of Development and Sustainability, 3*(1), 162–176.

Ahmed, S. A. (2022). *The role of women in reconciliation and peace building process in Somalia= Somali'de uzlaşma ve barış inşa sürecinde kadınların rolü.* Sakarya Üniversitesi.

Ahwireng-Obeng, F., & McGowan, P. J. (1998). Partner or Hegemon? South Africa in Africa: Part one. *Journal of Contemporary African Studies, 16*(1), 5–38. doi:10.1080/02589009808729619

Aid and Political Reform. (1992). Briefing Paper, Overseas Development Institute.

Aidis, R. (2017). Do institutions matter for entrepreneurial development? IZA World of Labor, 334. Bonn: Institute for the Study of Labor (IZA). doi:10.15185/izawol.334

Aimola, B. F. (n.d.). *Citizenship Education for National Re-orientation: A Handbook for Nigerians.* Loyce Graphic Printer & Publishers.

Aisen, A., & Veiga, F. J. (2011). *How Does Political Instability Affect Economic Growth?* IMF Working Paper, WP/11/12.

Ajibola, I. O., Udoette, S. U., Muhammad, R. A., & Anigwe, J. O. (2020). Currency Substitution and Exchange Rate Volatility in Nigeria: An Autoregressive Distributed Lag Approach. *CBN Journal of Applied Statistics, 11*(2), 1–28.

Ajide, F. M., & Dada, J. T. (2023). Poverty, entrepreneurship, and economic growth in Africa. *Poverty & Public Policy, 15*(2), 199–226. doi:10.1002/pop4.368

Ajodo-Adebanjoko, A. (2021). Giving Voice to the Voiceless: The Challenges of Women Legislators in Nigeria's National Assembly. *Two Decades of Legislative Politics and Governance in Nigeria's National Assembly: Issues, Achievements, Challenges and Prospects*, 317-343.

Akampumuza, J. (2007). *The Management of Uganda's Privatisation Since 1982* [PhD thesis]. University of London.

Ake, C. (1996). *Democracy and development in Africa*. Brookings Institution.

Ake, C. (1996). *Theory of human life for citizenship and civil society*. http: //www.istr.org/conferences/toronto/abstracts/Isumonah.pdf

Ake, C. (1967). *A Theory of Political Integration*. The Dorsey Press, Inc.

Ake, C. (1990). *The case for democracy in The Carter Centre African governance in the 1990s: Objectives, Resources and Constraints*. The Carter Centre of Emory University.

Akindiyo, O., & Olawole, A. (2015). Devaluation of Nigerian Naira: Bane or Panacea? *Review of Public Administration and Management.*, *4*(8), 98–123.

Akinkunmi, K. (2021). An Analysis of "Encountering Development: The Making and Unmaking of the Third World" by Arturo Escobar. *Sustinere—The University of Toronto's Journal of Sustainable Development, 1*(1), 64-71.

Akinlo, A. E., & Yinusa, D. O. (2007). Exchange Rate versus Capital Account Liberalization in Nigeria: Some Important Issues. *CBN Economic and Financial Review.*, *45*(4), 69–89.

Akintunde, Y. W., Ebunoluwa, O. O., Jelilov, G., & Haruna, T. M. (2019). Determinants of Exchange Rate in Nigeria: A Comparison of the Official and Parallel Market Rates. *The Economics and Finance Letters*, *6*(2), 178–188. doi:10.18488/journal.29.2019.62.178.188

Akiyemi, S. (2019). *Voter apathy: a threat to democracy in Nigeria*. Retrieved from: http://democracyinafrica.org/voter-apathy-threat-democracy-nigeria/

Akokpari, J. (2016). The challenges of diplomatic practice in Africa. *Journal of Contemporary History*, *41*(1), 1–17.

Akoleowo, V. O. O. (2022). African feminism, activism and decolonisation: The case of Alimotu Pelewura. *African Identities*, 1–16. doi:10.1080/14725843.2022.2157246

Akpa-Inyang, F., & Chima, S. C. (2021). South African traditional values and beliefs regarding informed consent and limitations of the principle of respect for autonomy in African communities: A cross-cultural qualitative study. *BMC Medical Ethics*, *22*(1), 1–17. doi:10.118612910-021-00678-4 PMID:34391415

Akpan, E. O., & Atan, J. A. (2011). Effects of Exchange Rate Movements on Economic Growth in Nigeria. *CBN Journal of Applied Statistics*, *2*(2), 1–14.

Al Jazeera Investigative Unit. (2023). *Six Secrets Uncovered by Aljazeera's Gold Mafia investigation*. https://www.aljazeera.com

Alao, A. (2012). *Mugabe and the Politics of Security in Zimbabwe*. McGill-Queen's Press-MQUP. doi:10.1515/9780773587748

Alden, C., & Le Pere, G. (2009). South Africa in Africa: Bound to lead? *Politikon: South African Journal of Political Studies*, *36*(1), 145–169. doi:10.1080/02589340903155443

Alden, C., & Soko, M. (2005). South Africa's economic relations with Africa: Hegemony and its discontents. *The Journal of Modern African Studies*, *43*(3), 367–392. doi:10.1017/S0022278X05001011

Alden, C., & Vieira, M. A. (2005). The new diplomacy of the South: South Africa, Brazil, India, and trilateralism. *Third World Quarterly*, *26*(7), 1077–1095. doi:10.1080/01436590500235678

Aldrich, H., & Zimmer, C. (1986). Entrepreneurship through social networks. In H. Aldrich (Ed.), *Population Perspectives on Organizations* (pp. 13–28).

Alelaimat, M.S (2019). Factors affecting political participation (Jordanian universities students' voting: Field study 2017-2018). *Review of Economics and Political Science.* . doi:10.1108/REPS-05-2019-0072

Aligica, P. D. (2006). Institutional and stakeholder mapping: Frameworks for policy analysis and institutional change. *Public Organization Review*, *6*(1), 79–90. doi:10.100711115-006-6833-0

Aliyu, S. U. R. (2011). *Real Exchange Rate Misalignment: An Application of Behavioural Equilibrium Exchange Rate (BEER) to Nigeria.* Central Bank of Nigeria Occasional paper No. 41.

Aljazeera. (2019). *DR Congo internet restored after 20-day suspension over elections*. Aljazeera. https://www.aljazeera.com/news/2019/1/20/dr-congo-internet-restored-after-20-day-suspension-over-elections

Aljazeera. (2022). *Tunisia set for runoffs after low turnout parliamentary elections.* https://www.aljazeera.com/news/2022/12/19/runoffs-due-in-most-tunisian-districts-in-parliament-election

Alkire, S., & Foster, J. (2011). Counting and multidimensional poverty measurement. *Journal of Public Economics*, *95*(7–8), 476–487. doi:10.1016/j.jpubeco.2010.11.006

Allen, K. (2023). *A key feature in Kenya was influencers trying to delegitimise the media by presenting them as partisan.* ISS Africa. https://issafrica.org/iss-today/risks-of-digital-influence-lessons-for-south-africas-2024-election

Allison, S. (2017). New Lesotho murders highlight need for military reform. *Mail and Guardian*. https://mg.co.za/article/2017-09-05-new-lesotho-murders-highlight-need-for-military-reform/.

Almond, G. A., & Verba, S. (1963). *The Civic Culture*. Princeton University Press. doi:10.1515/9781400874569

Aloysius, I. S., Edeh, E. C., Emma, A. O., Onwe, O. S., & Ernest, E. N. (2019). Voting apathy among the Nigerian electorates in 2019 general elections: The role of INEC, issues and the way forward. *International Journal of Business and Management Invention*, *8*(12), 64–74.

Al-Saidi, M., & Hefny, A. (2018). Institutional arrangements for beneficial regional cooperation on water, energy and food priority issues in the Eastern Nile Basin. *Journal of Hydrology (Amsterdam)*, *562*, 821–831. doi:10.1016/j.jhydrol.2018.05.009

Altunbas, Y., Evans, L., & Molyneux, P. (2001). Bank Ownership and Efficiency. *Journal of Money, Credit and Banking*, *33*(4), 926. doi:10.2307/2673929

Aluko O.I. (2017). Political Economy of Crony Inequality Among Nations: A Study on Capitalism and Socialism. *Journal of Community Development Research (Humanities and Social Sciences), 10*(2).

Aluko, O. I. (2018). Entangled in the "New World Order": Africa's (In-) Security Quandaries and Prospects. *Rethinking Securities in an Emergent Technoscientific New World Order: Retracing the Contours for Africa's Hi-jacked Futures*, 171.

Aluko, O. I. (2020). Chapter Six Soft Power and the State of Nigeria's Economic Diplomacy. *Power Politics in Africa: Nigeria and South Africa in Comparative Perspective, 109.*

Aluko, O. I. (2023Aluko, O. I. (2023). Cycle of Violence, Transport Chain Theory, and Election Disputes in Developing Countries: A Case of Nigeria. In Insights and Explorations in Democracy, Political Unrest, and Propaganda in Elections (pp. 175-186). IGI Global.

Aluko, O. I., & Aderinola, G. (2019). E-Governance and Corruption Impasse In Nigeria: A Developmental Expedition Synopsis. In R. Abassi & A. Ben Chehida Douss (Eds.), Security Frameworks in Contemporary Electronic Government (pp. 129-149). Hershey, PA: IGI Global. doi:10.4018/978-1-5225-5984-9.ch006

Aluko, O. A., Opoku, E. E. O., Ibrahim, M., & Kufuor, N. K. (2023). Put on the light! Foreign direct investment, governance and access to electricity. *Energy Economics*, *119*, 106563. doi:10.1016/j.eneco.2023.106563

Aluko, O. I. (2015). Political economy of crony capitalism: The prospect and the bane. *Journal of Economics Library*, *2*(3), 192–197.

Aluko, O. I. (2017). Political economy of crony inequality among nations: A study on capitalism and socialism. [Humanities and Social Sciences]. *Journal of Community Development Research*, *10*(2), 25–36.

Aluko, O. I. (2021). Cycle of Poverty in Developing Countries. In *Handbook of Research on Institution Development for Sustainable and Inclusive Economic Growth in Africa* (pp. 126–139). IGI Global.

Aluko, O. I., & Oluwadele, L. B. (Eds.). (2023). *Insights and Explorations in Democracy, Political Unrest, and Propaganda in Elections*. IGI Global. doi:10.4018/978-1-6684-8629-0

Aluko, Y. A. (2015). Patriarchy and property rights among Yoruba women in Nigeria. *Feminist Economics*, *21*(3), 56–81. doi:10.1080/13545701.2015.1015591

Amanyie, N. S., Bariledum, K., & Lucky, N. B. (2015). Electoral violence and political apathy in Nigeria: Issues and challenges. *British Journal of Humanities and Social Sciences*, *13*(1), 155–173.

Amendolagine, V., Hansen, U. E., Lema, R., Rabellotti, R., & Ribaudo, D. (2023). Do green foreign direct investments increase the innovative capability of MNE subsidiaries? *World Development*, *170*, 106342. doi:10.1016/j.worlddev.2023.106342

Amin, M. (2010). *'Necessity vs opportunity entrepreneurs in the informal sector', Enterprise Analysis Unit*. World Bank.

Amos, S. (2010). The role of South Africa in SADC regional integration: The making or braking of the organization. *J. Int'l Com. L. & Tech.*, *5*, 124.

Amtaika, A. (2017). The particularistic and Universality of political Cultural Beliefs and Values: Western Liberalism, Islamic Fundamentalism and African Theoretical Perspectives. In A. Amtaika (Ed.), *Culture, Democracy and Development in Africa*. Pan-African University Press.

Andre, G. F. (1972). The Development of Underdevelopment. In J. D. Cockcroft, A. G. Frank, & D. Johnson (Eds.), *Dependence and Underdevelopment* (p. 3). Anchor Books.

Andriani, L., & Escudero Loaiza, M. M. (2021). Institutional trust and corruption: Evidence from Latin America. *Revista Debates*, *15*(1), 247–274. doi:10.22456/1982-5269.112643

Anduiza, E., Guinjoan, M., & Rico, G. (2018). Populism, participation, and political equality. *European Political Science Review*, *11*(1), 109–124. doi:10.1017/S1755773918000243

Aniche, E. T., & Ukaegbu, V. E. (2016). Structural dependence, vertical integration and regional economic cooperation in Africa: A study of Southern African Development Community. *African Review (Dar Es Salaam, Tanzania)*, *8*(2), 108–119. doi:10.1080/09744053.2016.1186866

Anifowose, R., & Enemuo, F. (2015). *Elements of Politics* (2nd ed.). Sam Iroanusi Publications.

Annamorandnejad, I., & Habibi, J. (2019). *A comprehensive analysis of Twitter trending topics*. 2019 5th International Conference on Web Research (ICWR), Tehran, Iran.

Annan, K. (1999). *Preventing War and Disaster.* Annual Report on the Work of the Organization.

Antin, D., (2013). The South African mining sector: An industry at a crossroads. *Economy Report South Africa*, (2013), 1-22.

Anyanwu, J. C. (2017). Foreign direct investment. Handbook of Globalisation and Development, 131.

Anyanwu, J. C., & Salami, A. O. (2021). The impact of COVID-19 on African economies: An introduction. *African Development Review*, *33*(1), S1. doi:10.1111/1467-8268.12531 PMID:34149237

Aoyama, Y. (2009). Entrepreneurship and regional culture: The case of Hamamtsu and Kyoto, Japan. *Regional Studies*, *43*(3), 495–512. doi:10.1080/00343400902777042

Appiah, M., Gyamfi, B. A., Adebayo, T. S., & Bekun, F. V. (2023). Do financial development, foreign direct investment, and economic growth enhance industrial development? Fresh evidence from Sub-Sahara African countries. *Portuguese Economic Journal*, *22*(2), 203–227. doi:10.100710258-022-00207-0

Arab Barometer. (2022). *Arab Barometer Wave VII – Arab Barometer.* https://www.arabbarometer.org/surveys/arab-barometer-wave-vii/

Aragonès, E., Postlewaite, A., & Palfrey, T. (2007). Political Reputations and Campaign Promises. *Journal of the European Economic Association*, *5*(4), 846–884. doi:10.1162/JEEA.2007.5.4.846

Arbab, F. (2006). Impact of Mugabe's policies on the prospects for democracy in Zimbabwe. *Strategic Studies*, *26*(1), 147–179.

Arenas, G., Engel, J., Kotschwar, B., & Maliszewska, M. (2018). *Supporting Lesotho's economic diversification and trade integration: structural transformation through greater export competitiveness.* World Bank. doi:10.1596/30178

Aristotle. *Politics*, Book III, section 1279b.

Aron, J., Elbadawi, I., & Kahn, B. (1997). *Determinants of Real Exchange Rate in South Africa.* CSAE Working Paper, WPS/ 97 – 16, CSAE.

Arrow, K. (1962). The Economic Implication of Learning by Doing. *The Review of Economic Studies*, *80*(3), 155–173. doi:10.2307/2295952

Arthur, P. (2017). Promoting security in Africa through regional economic communities (RECs) and the African union's African peace and security architecture (APSA). *Insight on Africa*, *9*(1), 1–21. doi:10.1177/0975087816674577

Ascoli, K., & Benzaken, T. (2009). *Public policy and the promotion of corporate social responsibility.* BSR. http://www.bsr. org/research/reports-bycategory. cfm

Asongu, S. A., & De Moor, L. (2017). Financial globalisation dynamic thresholds for financial development: Evidence from Africa. *European Journal of Development Research*, *29*(1), 192–212. doi:10.1057/ejdr.2016.10

Aspen Network of Development Entrepreneurs (ANDE). (2013). *Entrepreneurship ecosystem diagnostic kit.* https://www.aspeninstitute.org/publications/entrepreneurial

Assal, M. (2016). *Civil society and peace building in Sudan.* CHR Michelsen Institute. https://www.cmi.no/publications/file/5807-civil-society-and-peace-building-in-sudan.pdf

Asuelime, R. A., & Enaifoghe, A. O. (2018). Southern African Regional and Economic Integration: The free trade zone strategy for South Africa? *Journal of African Union Studies*, *7*(2), 85–107. doi:10.31920/2050-4306/2018/v7n2a5

Atoi, N. V., & Nwambeke, C. G. (2021). Money and Foreign Exchange Markets Dynamics in Nigeria: A Multivariate GARCH Approach. *CBN Journal of Applied Statistics*, *12*(1), 109–138. doi:10.33429/Cjas.12121.5/6

Atta-Krah, K., & Laryea, T. (2021). *Multilateral development banks and sanctions*. Presentation available https://www.orrick.com/en/Events/2021/08/Multilateral-Development-Bank-Sanctions-and-Investigationspresentation

Audretsch, D. B., & Thurik, R. (2001). What's new about the new economy? Sources of growth in the managed and entrepreneurial economies. *Industrial and Corporate Change, 10*(1), 267-315. . 1. 267 doi:10.1093/icc/10

Audretsch, D. B., Grilo, I., & Thurik, A. R. (2007). Explaining entrepreneurship and the role of policy: a framework. The handbook of research on entrepreneurship policy, 1-17.

Audretsch, D. B., & Keilback, M. (2007). The Localisation of Entrepreneurship Capital, Evidence from Germany. *Papers in Regional Science*, *863*(3), 351–365. doi:10.1111/j.1435-5957.2007.00131.x

Audretsch, D., Heger, D., & Veith, T. (2015). Infrastructure and entrepreneurship. *Small Business Economics*, *44*(2), 219–230. doi:10.100711187-014-9600-6

Avis, W. (2021). *Incorporating Gender Perspective in Peace Operations since 2018*. Academic Press.

Awodumi, O. B. (2023). Does foreign direct investment matter for environmental innovation in African economies? *Economic Change and Restructuring*, *56*(1), 237–263. doi:10.100710644-022-09421-4

Babatope, E. (1997). *The Struggle for Democracy in Nigeria*. Ebino Topsy.

Babu, A. M. (1981). *African socialism or socialist Africa?* Zimbabwe Publishing House.

Babu, M. M., Dey, B. L., Rahman, M., Roy, S. K., Alwi, S. F. S., & Kamal, M. M. (2020). Value co-creation through social innovation: A study of sustainable strategic alliance in telecommunication and financial services sectors in Bangladesh. *Industrial Marketing Management, 89*, 13-27. doi:10.1016/j.indmarman.2020.06.003

Badaru, K. A., & Adu, E. O. (2020). University students' media use and political participation in South Africa. *South African Journal of Higher Education*, *34*(1), 18–36. doi:10.20853/34-1-3382

Bailey, R. (Ed.). (2000). *Teaching Values and Citizenship Across the Curriculum*. Kogan Page.

Baird, F. E. (2010). Philosophic Classics, Volume I: Ancient Philosophy. Routledge.

Bakashaba, R. (2019). *Entrepreneurial income and barriers to firm growth: a study of rural small and medium enterprises in Uganda* [Doctoral dissertation]. University of Reading.

Bako, M. J., & Syed, J. (2018). Women's marginalization in Nigeria and the way forward. *Human Resource Development International*, *21*(5), 425–443. doi:10.1080/13678868.2018.1458567

Ball, N. (2010). The evolution of the security sector reform agenda. In M. Sedra (Ed.), *The future of security sector reform. The Centre for International Governance Innovation* (pp. 29–43). CIGI.

Bal, M., Bryde, D., Fearon, D., & Ochieng, E. (2013). Stakeholder engagement: Achieving sustainability in the construction sector. *Sustainability (Basel)*, *5*(2), 695–710. doi:10.3390u5020695

Baltoi, D. (2023). *A deeper look into the West African Coup Wave*. Foreign Policy Research Institute.

Bamidele, S. (2020). Ethnic conflict and the politics of spoils in Nigeria. *Social Change*, *50*(4), 569–583. doi:10.1177/0049085720964280

Bank of Namibia. (2019). *GDP by activity: Annual percentage changes*. Annual Report.

Barash, D. P. (2001). *Understanding Violence*. Allyn and Bacon.

Barber, J. (2005). The new South Africa's foreign policy: Principles and practice. *International Affairs*, *81*(5), 1079–1096. doi:10.1111/j.1468-2346.2005.00503.x

Barber, N. W. (2019). Populist leaders and political parties. *German Law Journal*, *20*(2), 129–140. doi:10.1017/glj.2019.9

Barker, E. (1979). *Greek political theory: Plato and his predecessors*. Methuen and Co.

Barnhart, J. (2016). Status competition and territorial aggression: Evidence from the scramble for Africa. *Security Studies*, *25*(3), 385–419. doi:10.1080/09636412.2016.1195620

Barquet, K., Segnestam, L., & Dickin, S. (2022). *MapStakes: a tool for mapping, involving and monitoring stakeholders in co-creation processes*. Stockholm Environment Institute. doi:10.51414ei2022.014

Barrow, E. G., Clarke, J., Grundy, I., Jones, K.R., & Tessema, Y. (2002). *Analysis of stakeholder power and responsibilities in community involvement in forest management in Eastern and Southern Africa* (No. 9). IUCN.

Barua, S. (2020). Financing sustainable development goals: A review of challenges and mitigation strategies. *Business Strategy & Development*, *3*(3), 277–293. doi:10.1002/bsd2.94

Basotho Wars. (2020). South African History Online. https://web.archive.org/web/20141011134523/http://www.sahistory.org.za/south-africa-1806-1899/basotho-wars-1858-1868.

Bassey, O.B. (2023). *Leadership and the Success of African Integration and Development Agenda: Juxtaposing the African continental free trade area-AfCFTA and Agenda 2063*. Academic Press.

Bates, R. H. (2010). Democracy in Africa: A Very Short History. *Social Research*, *77*(4), 1133–1148. doi:10.1353or.2010.0036

Batti, R. C. (2014). Challenges facing local NGOs in resource mobilization. *Humanities and Social Sciences*, *2*(3), 57–64. doi:10.11648/j.hss.20140203.12

Baum, J. R., Frese, M., Baron, R. A., & Katz, J. A. (2007). In J. R. Baum, M. Frese, & R. A. Baron (Eds.), *The Psychology of Entrepreneurship* (pp. 1–18). Lawrence Erlbaum.

Bayart, J. F. (1993). *The State in Africa: The Politics of the Belly*. Longman.

Beauclerk, J., Pratt, B., & Judge, R. (2011). *Civil society in action: Global case studies in a practice based framework*. Itrac.

Becattini, G. (1990). The Marshallian industrial district as a socio-economic notion. In F. Pyke, G. Becattini, & W. Sengenbeiger (Eds.), *Industrial districts and inter-firm co-operation in Italy*. International Institute for Labour Studies.

Beck, M., Cadwell, J., Kern, A., Wu, K., Dickerson, M., & Howard, M. (2022). Critical feminist analysis of STEM mentoring programs: A meta-synthesis of the existing literature. *Gender, Work and Organization*, *29*(1), 167–187. doi:10.1111/gwao.12729

Beegle, K., Christiansen, L., Dabalen, A., & Gaddis, I. (2016). *Poverty in a rising Africa: Overview*. World Bank. doi:10.1596/978-1-4648-0723-7

Behuria, P. (2023). The political economy of a tax haven: The case of Mauritius. *Review of International Political Economy*, *30*(2), 772–800. doi:10.1080/09692290.2022.2069144

Beland, D., & Howlett, M. (2016, July 18). The Role and Impact of the Multiple-Streams Approach in Compartivie Policy Analysis. *Journal of Comparative Policy Analysis*, *18*(3), 221–227. doi:10.1080/13876988.2016.1174410

Bellin, E. (2004). The Robustness of Authoritarianism in the Middle East: Exceptionalism in Comparative Perspective. *Comparative Politics*, *36*(2), 139–157. doi:10.2307/4150140

Bell, S., Morse, S., & Shah, R. A. (2012). Understanding stakeholder participation in research as part of sustainable development. *Journal of Environmental Management*, *101*, 13–22. doi:10.1016/j.jenvman.2012.02.004 PMID:22387326

Bennett, D. L. (2019). Infrastructure investments and entrepreneurial dynamism in the US. *Journal of Business Venturing*, *34*(5), 991–993. doi:10.1016/j.jbusvent.2018.10.005

Beny, L. N., & Snyder, M. (2012). Analysis of the Republic of South Sudan's Accession to the East African Community: Benefits, Detriments and Recommendations. *U of Michigan Public Law Research Paper*, (337).

Beregovskiy, A. (2019). *Effect of the two-party system on voter turnout in the United States of America* [Master of Arts Thesis]. The Johns Hopkins University.

Berenstain, N. (2016). *Epistemic exploitation.* Academic Press.

Bernecker, S. (2022). Knowledge from Falsehood and Truth-Closeness. *Philosophia*, *50*(4), 1623–1638. doi:10.100711406-022-00479-y

Besley, T. (2005). Political Selection. *The Journal of Economic Perspectives*, *19*(3), 43–60. doi:10.1257/089533005774357761

Bhagwati, J. (1995). New Thinking on Development. *Journal of Democracy, 6*(4), 59.

Bhagwati, J. (1966). *Economics of Underdeveloped Countries.* McGraw-Hill.

Bharti, M. S. (2022). The Development of China's Economic Cooperation in the Horn of Africa: Special Reference to the Belt and Road Initiative. *African Journal of Economics, Politics and Social Studies*, *1*(1), 17–30. doi:10.15804/ajepss.2022.1.12

Bharti, M. S. (2023). The Sustainable Development and Economic Impact of China's Belt and Road Initiative in Ethiopia. *East Asia (Piscataway, N.J.)*, *40*(1), 175–194. doi:10.100712140-023-09402-y PMID:37065271

Bharti, M. S., & Goswami, A. (2023). Geopolitical Perspective of the EU's Post-Pandemic Public Diplomacy Prospects and Challenges. In S. Kavoğlu & E. Köksoy (Eds.), *Global Perspectives on the Emerging Trends in Public Diplomacy* (pp. 24–49). IGI Global. doi:10.4018/978-1-6684-9161-4.ch002

Bhatia, R. (2021). *India–Africa Relations: Changing Horizons*. Taylor & Francis. doi:10.4324/9781003044550

Bhuiya, S., & Jahan, M. (2023). The justification of Democracy Peace Theory in the 21st century. *Social Science Review*, *39*(1), 211–229. doi:10.3329sr.v39i1.64921

Bilal, S. (2017). *SADC institutional capacity to deliver on its mandate*. Paper prepared for the SADC Strategic Ministerial Retreat - "The SADC We Want", 12-14 March 2017, Kingdom of Swaziland.

Birch, D. G. (1979). *The job generation process*. University of Illinois at Urbana-Champaign's Academy for Entrepreneurial Leadership Historical Research Reference in Entrepreneurship.

Birgul, C., & Sevcan, G. (2016). Marshall-Lerner Condition Analysis: Turkey Case. *Economics, Management, and Financial Markets*, *11*(1), 272–283.

Bislev, A. (2018). *Analysis of Anti-Corruption measures in Multilateral Development Banks. Masters Thesis*. University of Aalborg. Available https://projekter.aau.dk/projekter/files/290704827/Analysis_of_anti_corruption_measures_in_multilateral_development_banks.pdf

Blais. (2000). *To Vote or Not to Vote – The merits and limits of rational choice theory*. University of Pittsburgh Press.

Blakemore, K., & Cooksey, B. (2017). *A sociology of education for Africa* (Vol. 8). Routledge. doi:10.4324/9781315412733

Blignaut, P. (2009). A bilateral perspective on the digital divide in South Africa. *Perspectives on Global Development and Technology, 8*(4), 581–601. doi:10.1163/156915009X12583611836091

Block, J. H., Kohn, K., Miller, D., & Ullrich, K. (2015). Necessity entrepreneurship and competitive strategy. *Small Business Economics, 44*(1), 37–54. doi:10.100711187-014-9589-x

Bloomfield, B. P., & Vurdubakis, T. (1999). The outer limits: Monsters, actor networks and the writing of displacement. *Organization, 6*(4), 625–647. doi:10.1177/135050849964004

Bøås, M. (1998). Governance as Multilateral Development Bank Policy: The Cases of the African Development Bank and the Asian Development Bank. *European Journal of Development Research, 10*(2), 117–134. doi:10.1080/09578819808426720

Bodenheimer, S. (1971). Dependency and Imperialism: The Roots of Latin American Underdevelopment. In *Readings in U.S. Imperialism.* Boston: Porter Sargent.

Bonga, W. G., Chiminya, J., & Mudzungiri, C. (2021). An Explanatory Analysis of the Economic and Social Impact of Corruption in Zimbabwe. *IOSR Journal of Economics and Finance(IOSR-JEF), 6*(1), 11-20.

Bonilla, T. (2021). *The Importance of Campaign Promises.* Cambridge University Press.

Bornman, E. (2019). *Information society and digital divide in South Africa: Results of Longitudinal Surveys.* Department of Communication Science. University of South Africa.

Börzel, T. A. (2016). Theorizing regionalism. The Oxford handbook of comparative regionalism, 41-63.

Bose, T. K., Uddin, M. R., & Mondal, A. (2013). Impacts of electricity access to rural SMEs. *International Journal of Managing Value and Supply Chains, 4*(4), 17–28. doi:10.5121/ijmvsc.2013.4402

Bosworth, B.P., & Collins, S.M. (1999). Capital flows to developing economies: implications for saving and investment. *Brookings Papers on Economic Activity*, 1.

Bouris, D., & Schumacher, T. (2017). *The Revised European Neighbourhood Policy.* Palgrave Macmillan. doi:10.1057/978-1-137-47182-6

Bourque, S. C., & Warren, K. B. (2010). *Women of the Andes: patriarchy and social change in two Peruvian towns.* University of Michigan press.

Brady, H. (1999). Political participation. In Robinson, J.P. Shaver, P.R. and Wrightsman, L.S (Eds.). Measures of Political Attitudes. Academic Press.

Bratton, M. (2008). Vote buying and violence in Nigerian election campaigns. *Electoral Studies, 27*(4), 621–632. doi:10.1016/j.electstud.2008.04.013

Bratton, M., & Masunungure, E. (2007). Popular Reactions to State Repression: Operation Murambatsvina in Zimbabwe. *African Affairs, 106/422*(422), 21–45. doi:10.1093/afraf/adl024

Broch-Due, V. (2005). *Violence and belonging: the quest for identity in post-colonial Africa.* Routledge.

Brookings. (2017). *Why are populists winning online? Social media reinforces their anti-establishment message.* Brookings. https://www.brookings.edu/articles/why-are-populists-winning-online-social-media-reinforces-their-anti-establishment-message/>

Bruce, V., & Young, A. (1998). *In the eye of the beholder: The science of face perception.* Oxford university press.

Bruck, N. (2001). Development Banking Concept and Theory. In *Principles and practices of development banking.* ADFIAP-IDF.

Bruns, A. (2008). *Blogs, Wikipedia, Second Life, and Beyond: From Production to Produsage.* Peter Lang.

Bryson, J. M. (2003). *What to do when stakeholders matter: A guide to stakeholder identification and analysis techniques.* London School of Economics and Political Science.

Bryson, J. M. (2004). What to do when stakeholders matter: Stakeholder identification and analysis techniques. *Public Management Review*, *6*(1), 21–53. doi:10.1080/14719030410001675722

Buiter, W., & Fries, S. (2002). *What Should the Multilateral Development Banks do?* Working Paper, 74. European Bank for Reconstruction and Development.

Bujra, A. (2002). *African Conflicts: Their Causes and Their Political and Social Environment. Development Policy Management Forum (DPMF)* (Occasional Paper). United Nations Economic Commission for Africa (UNECA). Addis Ababa.

Bukae, N. M. (2017). South Africa: A Benign or Malign Regional Hegemon? The Case of the 1998 South Africa-Led Military Intervention in Lesotho. *Lonaka Journal of Learning and Teaching*, *8*(1), 112–141.

Bukusi, A. D. (2022). Why you must vote in an African democracy. *American Journal of Leadership and Governance*, *7*(1), 19–28. doi:10.47672/ajlg.942

Bunich, G. A., Rovenskiy, Y. A., Akhvlediani, J. T., & Yuriev, Y. (2019). Regional Development Banks: Theory And Practice. *Opcion, 35*(19), 2861-2871.

Burger, P. (2016). *Getting It Right: A New economy for South Africa. Santon.* Review Publishing.

Cabeza-García, L., Del Brio, E. B., & Oscanoa-Victorio, M. L. (2019). *Female financial inclusion and its impacts on inclusive economic development.* Women's Studies International Forum.10.1016/j.wsif.2019.102300

Calderon, C., & Serven, L. (2010). Infrastructure and economic development in Sub-Saharan Africa. *Journal of African Economies*, *19*(Suppl_1), i13–i87. doi:10.1093/jae/ejp022

Calfucura, E. (2018). Governance, land and distribution: A discussion on the political economy of community-based conservation. *Ecological Economics*, *145*, 18–26. doi:10.1016/j.ecolecon.2017.05.012

Camara, A. (2023). The effect of foreign direct investment on tax revenue. *Comparative Economic Studies*, *65*(1), 168–190. doi:10.105741294-022-00195-2

Cameron, W. (2004). Public Accountability: Effectiveness, equality and ethics: worlds apart. *Canadian Journal of Political Science*, *38*(4), 1003–1028.

Campbell, J., & Quinn, N. (2021). What's happening to democracy in Africa? CFR. https://www.cfr.org/article/whats-happening-democracy-africa

Campbell, I. (1994). Nigeria's Failed Transition: The 1993 Presidential Election. *Journal of Contemporary African Studies*, *12*(2), 179–199. doi:10.1080/02589009408729556

Campbell, J., & Quinn, N. (2021). What's happening to Democracy in Africa? Carreras, M and Irepoglu, Y (2013). Trust in elections, vote buying, and turnout in Latin America. *Electoral Studies*, *32*, 609–619.

Canache, D. (2007). *Chavismo and Democracy in Venezuela. Prospects for Democracy in Latin America.* University of North-Texas.

Caparini, M. (2010). Civil Society and the future of security sector reform. In M. Sedra (Ed.), *The future of security sector reform. The Centre for International Governance Innovation* (pp. 244–262). CIGI.

Caramani, D. (2008). Comparative Politics (2nd ed.). Academic Press.

Carrasco, Carrington, & Lee. (Eds.). (2009). Governance and Accountability: The Regional Development Banks. Boston University International Law Journal, 27(1), 58. doi:10.4324/9781315254098

Carreras, M., & Irepoglu, Y. (2013). Trust in elections, vote buying, and turnout in Latin America. *Electoral Studies, 32*, 609–619.

Carroll, T., & Jarvis, D. S. L. (2017). Disembedding Autonomy: Asia after the Developmental State. In T. Carroll & D. S. L. Jarvis (Eds.), *Asia after the Developmental State: Disembedding Autonomy* (pp. 3–48). Cambridge University Press. doi:10.1017/9781316480502.002

Carter, J. A. (2017). Epistemological Implications of Relativism. In J. J. Ichikawa (Ed.), *The Routledge Handbook of Epistemic Contextualism.* Routledge. doi:10.4324/9781315745275-24

Castells, M. (2012). *Networks of outrage and hope: Social movements in the internet age.* Polity Press.

Catley, A. (1999). *Methods on the move: A review of veterinary uses of participatory approaches and methods focusing on experiences in dryland Africa.* International Institute for Environment and Development.

Catt, H. (1999). *Democracy in practice.* Routledge. doi:10.4324/9780203270240

Cavatorta, F. (2018). The Middle East and North Africa. In Democratisation (pp 364-383). Oxford University Press.

Cavatorta, F. (2018). The Middle East and North Africa. In *Democratization* (pp. 364–383). Oxford University Press.

Cawthra, G. (2010). *The role of SADC in managing political crisis and conflict: The cases of Madagascar and Zimbabwe.* Friedrich-Ebert-Stiftung Mozambique.

Ceadel, M. (1980). *Pacifism in Britain, 1914-1945: the defining of a faith.* Clarendon Press.

Cedras, J., & Kuye, J. (2013). The impact of tripartite politics on the leadership function in public administration: Dialogue between the ANC, COSATU and the SACP in South Africa. *African Journal of Public Affairs, 6*(3). https://repository.up.ac.za/bitstream/handle/2263/41039/Cedras_Impact_2013.pdf?sequence=1&isAllowed=y

Center for Advancement of Rights and Democracy. (2023). *Digital divide in Ethiopia.* CARDETH. https://www.cardeth.org/digital-divide

Cevik, S. (2011). Myths and Realities on Islam and Democracy in the Middle East. *Estudios Politicos, 0*(38), 121–144. doi:10.17533/udea.espo.10057

Chadwick, A. (2013). *The Hybrid Media System: Politics and Power.* Oxford. University Press. doi:10.1093/acprof:oso/9780199759477.001.0001

Chamber, E. C. O. S. O. C. (2018). *Financing for SDGs: Breaking bottlenecks of investment from policy to impact.* The United Nations.

Chamberlin, R. (1989). *Free children and democratic schools: a philosophical study of liberty and education.* Falmer.

Chau, P. Y. K. (1996). An empirical assessment of a modified technology acceptance model. *Journal of Management Information Systems, 13*(2), 185–204. doi:10.1080/07421222.1996.11518128

Chen, J. (2012). Voter participation and the effects of distributive spending on political participation. *American Journal of Political Science*, *57*(1), 200–217. doi:10.1111/j.1540-5907.2012.00613.x

Chevallier, R., Gosling, A., & Chesterman, S. (2020). Structures, policies and stakeholder landscape relevant to climate change and agriculture in the SADC Region. SADC Futures: Developing Foresight Capacity for Climate Resilient Agricultural Development Knowledge Series. CCAFS Report. Wageningen, the Netherlands: CGIAR Research Program on Climate Change. *Agriculture & Food Security*.

Chibbonta, W., Mayondi, M., & Mulenga, R., A. (2022). *Reflection on Zambia's Development Strategies since Independence-1964 to 2021*. Academic Press.

Chigudu, D. (2021). Economic Integration in Southern Africa through SADC's Revised Priorities (2015-2020) for Sustainable Development: A Mirage? *J. Legal Ethical & Regul. Isses*, *24*, 1.

Chikerema, A.F. (2013). Citizen Participation and Local Democracy in Zimbabwean Local Government System. *Journal of Humanities and Social Science, 13*(2), 87-90.

Chikwanha-Dzenga, Masunugure, & Madzingira. (2001). *Democracy and national Governance in Zimbabwe: A country survey Report*. IDASA.

Chindengwike, J. (2023). The Nexus between Inflation and Economic Growth in Sub-Saharan Africa Countries.: An Empirical Study using VECM. *Journal of Global Economics*, *19*(2), 109–136. doi:10.1956/jge.v19i2.672

Chingono, T. T., & Mbohwa, C. (2023). Disasters in Selected Emerging Economies. In Supply Networks in Developing Countries: Sustainable and Humanitarian Logistics in Growing Consumer Markets (pp. 31-44). Emerald Publishing Limited. doi:10.1108/978-1-80117-194-620231003

Chinkin, C., & Yoshida, K. (2020). *40 years of the convention on the elimination of all forms of discrimination against women*. Academic Press.

Chitakira, M., Nhamo, L., Torquebiau, E., Magidi, J., Ferguson, W., Mpandeli, S., Mearns, K., & Mabhaudhi, T. (2022). Opportunities to improve eco-agriculture through transboundary governance in transfrontier conservation areas. *Diversity*, *14*(6), 461. doi:10.3390/d14060461

Chitando, E. (2010). Equipped and ready to serve? Transforming theology and religious studies in Africa. *Missionalia*, *38*(2), 197–210.

Chiweshe, M. K., & Mahiya, I. (2021). Corruption and the Morality of Everyday Life in Urban Harare, Zimbabwe. *Africa Today*, *68*(1), 72–92. doi:10.2979/africatoday.68.1.04

Chlouba, V., Smith, D. S., & Wagner, S. (2022). Early statehood and support for autocratic rule in Africa. *Comparative Political Studies*, *55*(4), 688–724. doi:10.1177/00104140211036031

Choi, S., & Richards, K. (2017). *Interdisciplinary discourse: Communicating across disciplines*. Springer. doi:10.1057/978-1-137-47040-9

Chopra, M., Singh, S. K., Gupta, A., Aggarwal, K., Gupta, B. B., & Colace, F. (2022). Analysis & prognosis of sustainable development goals using big data-based approach during COVID-19 pandemic. *Sustainable Technology and Entrepreneurship*, *1*(2), 100012. doi:10.1016/j.stae.2022.100012

Christensen, D., & Laitin, D. D. (2019). *African states since independence: Order, development, and democracy*. Yale University Press.

Chukwudi, C. E. (2022). Governance Factor and Effects of Political Apathy in Nigerian Political Culture: A Prognostic Analysis. *Socialscientia: Journal of Social Sciences and Humanities, 7*(4).

Cipolla, C. M. (1981). *Before the industrial Revolution: European Society and Economy, 1000–1700* (2nd ed.). Cambridge University Press.

Claassens, A., & Matlala, B. (2014). Platinum, poverty and princes in post-apartheid South Africa: new laws, old repertoires. In G. M. Khadiagala, P. Naidoo, D. Pillay, & R. Southhall (Eds.), *New South African Review* (Vol. 4). Wits University Press. doi:10.18772/22014047632.12

Claes, R., & Ruiz-Quintanilla, S. A. (1998). Influences of early career experiences, occupational group, and national culture on proactive career behavior. *Journal of Vocational Behavior, 52*(3), 357–378. doi:10.1006/jvbe.1997.1626

Clark, W. C., Van Kerkhoff, L., Lebel, L., & Gallopin, G. C. (2016). Crafting usable knowledge for sustainable development. *Proceedings of the National Academy of Sciences of the United States of America, 113*(17), 4570–4578. doi:10.1073/pnas.1601266113 PMID:27091979

Cloke, K., & Goldsmith, J. (2002). *The end of management and the rise of organisational democracy*. Jossey-Bass.

Coakley, G. J. (2002). *The Mineral Industries of Lesotho and Swaziland*. U.S. Geological Survey Minerals Information. http://minerals.er.usgs.gov/minerals/pubs/country/africa.html#ir,

Coetzee, C. (2004). *South Africa's foreign policy of quiet diplomacy towards Zimbabwe: constructivism as a framework to highlight the contradictory norms of human rights and African solidarity* [Doctoral dissertation]. Stellenbosch University.

Cole, M. J., & Broadhurst, J. L. (2022). Sustainable Development in Mining Communities: The Case of South Africa's West Wits Goldfield. *Frontiers in Sustainable Cities, 4*, 87. doi:10.3389/frsc.2022.895760

Commonwealth Secretariat. (2002). *The quality of democracy in the Pacific*. A Report for the 2002 Roundtable of Heads of Government [Denarau Island, Fiji Islands, 19-20 August 2002].

Constitution of the Republic of South Africa. (1996). Government Printers.

Cooke, P., Uranga, M. G., & Etxebarria, G. (1997). Regional innovation systems: Institutional and organisational dimensions. *Research Policy, 26*(4-5), 47. doi:10.1016/S0048-7333(97)00025-5

Cope, L. W. (2002). Madagascar mining—open for business. *Engineering and Mining Journal, 203*(4), 24.

Coppedge, M. (2012). *Democratization and Research Methods*. Cambridge University Press., doi:10.1017/CBO9781139016179

Corner, L. (1997). *Women's participation in decision-making and leadership: A global perspective*. A paper presented at a conference on Women in Decision-making in Cooperative held by the Asian Women in Cooperative Development Forum (ACWF) and the International Cooperative Alliance Regional Office for Asia and the Pacific (ICAROAP).

Cotterill, J. (2017, August 8). Jacob Zuma survives vote of no confidence. *Financial Times (SA)*. https://www.ft.com/content/978055ec-7c4a-11e7-ab01-a13271d1ee9c

Cottey, A. (2012). Regionalism and the EU's neighbourhood policy: The limits of the possible. *Southeast European and Black Sea Studies, 12*(3), 375–391. doi:10.1080/14683857.2012.711090

Coughlan, S. (2020). *Dissatisfaction with democracy 'At record high.'* BBC. https://www.bbc.com/news/education-51281722

Council of Europe. (2021). *Study of the impact of digital transformation on democracy and Good Governance*. European Committee on Democracy and Governance.

Craig, A., & Valeriano, B. (2018). *Realism and cyber conflict: Security in the digital age*. E-IR. https://www.e-ir.info/2018/02/03/realism-and-cyber-conflict-security-in-the-digital-age/

Crain, W. (1992). *Theories of Development*. Prentice Hall.

Crawford, G. (1998). Human Rights and Democracy in EU Development Co-operation: Towards Fair and Equal Treatment. In M. Lister (Ed.), *European Union Development Policy*. Palgrave Macmillan. doi:10.1007/978-1-349-26858-0_10

Crick, B. (2002). *Democracy: a very short introduction*. Oxford University Press.

Croese, S., & Duminy, J. (2023). Co-producing urban expertise for SDG localization: The history and practices of urban knowledge production in South Africa. *Urban Geography*, *44*(3), 538–557. doi:10.1080/02723638.2022.2079868

Cunliffe, A. L., & Scaratti, G. (2017). Embedding Impact in Engaged Research: Developing Socially Useful Knowledge through Dialogical Sensemaking. *British Journal of Management*, *28*(1), 29–44. doi:10.1111/1467-8551.12204

Dahlgren, P. (2005). *The internet, public spheres, and political communication: Dispersion and deliberation*. Taylor & Francis. https://www.tandfonline.com/doi/pdf/10.1080/10584600590933160

Dahl, R. (1995). *Modern Political Analysis*. Prentice Hall of India.

Dahl, R. A. (1961). *Who Governs?* Yale University Press.

Dahl, R. A. (1989). *Democracy and its Critics*. Yale University Press.

Dalby, T. G., & Jones, B. C. (2020). Parties versus democracy: Addressing today's political party threats to democratic rule. *International Journal of Constitutional Law*, *18*(2), 509–538. doi:10.1093/icon/moaa025

Damane, M., & Sekantsi, P. (2018). The Sources of Unemployment in Lesotho. *Modern Economy*, *9*(5), 937–965. doi:10.4236/me.2018.95060

Danakol, S. H., Estrin, S., Reynolds, P., & Weitzel, U. (2017). Foreign direct investment via M&A and domestic entrepreneurship: Blessing or curse? *Small Business Economics*, *48*(3), 599–612. doi:10.100711187-016-9792-z

Dandashly, A. (2015). The EU response to regime change in the wake of the Arab revolt: Differential implementation. *Journal of European Integration*, *37*(1), 37–56. doi:10.1080/07036337.2014.975988

Dandashly, A. (2018). EU democracy promotion and the dominance of the security–stability nexus. *Mediterranean Politics*, *23*(1), 62–82. doi:10.1080/13629395.2017.1358900

Day, J. C., Janus, A., & Davis, J. (2005). *Computer and internet use in the United States: 2003* (October 2015 ed.). US Department of Commerce. https://www.census.gov/prod/2005pubs/p23-208.pdf,

Ddumba, S., & Mugume, A. (2001). *The Privatization Process and its Impact on Society*. In Uganda National NGO Forum/Structural Adjustment Participatory Review Initiative, Kampala.

De Almeida, L. D. C. T. (2019). Diamond Export and Economic Growth in Angola. *International Journal of Academic Research in Business & Social Sciences*, *9*(9). Advance online publication. doi:10.6007/IJARBSS/v9-i9/6382

De Brauw, A., & Bulte, E. (2021). *African farmers, value chains and agricultural development*. Springer International Publishing. doi:10.1007/978-3-030-88693-6

De Carolis, D. M., & Saparito, P. (2006). Social capital, cognition, and entrepreneurial opportunities: Atheoretical framework. *Entrepreneurship Theory and Practice*, *30*(1), 41–56. doi:10.1111/j.1540-6520.2006.00109.x

De Coning, C. (2020). Adaptive peace operations: Navigating the complexity of influencing societal change without causing harm. *International Peacekeeping*, *27*(5), 836–858.

De Luna-Martínez, J., & Vicente, C. L. (2012). *Global Survey of Development Banks*. The World Bank. doi:10.1596/1813-9450-5969

De Vries, S. (2018). *Enhancing participatory democracy in municipal affairs through the ward committee system: A participatory monitoring and evaluation approach.* [Master's Thesis, University of Western Cape].

Debski, J., Jetter, M., Mösle, S., & Stadelmann, D. (2018). Gender and corruption: The neglected role of culture. *European Journal of Political Economy*, *55*, 526–537. doi:10.1016/j.ejpoleco.2018.05.002

Deleglise, D., & Sejanamane, M. (2017). To Reform or Disband? The Future of the Military in Lesotho. In G. Khadiagala & D. Deleglise (Eds.), *Southern African Security Review. Centre for Defence and Security Management* (pp. 123–141). University of Witwatersrand.

Deming, S. H. (2010). Anti-Corruption Policies: Eligibility and Debarment Practices at the World Bank and Regional Development Banks. *The International Lawyer*, *44*(2), 871–885.

Dempers, U. (2018, November 28). The Role of Civil Society. *Inclusive Democracy for Sustainable Development Conference*. Windhoek, Namibia: International Institute for Democracy and Electoral Assistance.

Dencker, J. C., Gruber, M., & Shah, S. K. (2009). Individual and opportunity factors influencing job creation in new firms. Academy of Management Journal, 52(6). doi:10.5465/amj.2009.47084648

Desai, A. (2018). The Zuma moment between tender-based capitalism and radical economic transformation. *Journal of Contemporary African Studies*, *36*(4), 409–513. doi:10.1080/02589001.2018.1522424

Desai, B. H., & Mandal, M. (2021). Role of climate change in exacerbating sexual and gender-based violence against women: A new challenge for international law. *Environmental Policy and Law*, *51*(3), 137–157. doi:10.3233/EPL-210055

Desbordes, R., & Wei, S. J. (2017). The effects of financial development on foreign direct investment. *Journal of Development Economics*, *127*, 153–168. doi:10.1016/j.jdeveco.2017.02.008

Desta, T. (2018). Comments on the digitalization and digital divide in the Horn of Africa (HoA), Kenya and Ethiopia: The Media Perspective. *Global Media Journal*.

Destradi, S. (2010). Regional powers and their strategies: Empire, hegemony, and leadership. *Review of International Studies*, *36*(4), 903–930. doi:10.1017/S0260210510001361

Detges, A. (2017). Droughts, state-citizen relations and support for political violence in Sub-Saharan Africa: A micro-level analysis. *Political Geography*, *61*, 88–98. doi:10.1016/j.polgeo.2017.07.005

Devereux, M. B. (1997). Real Exchange Rates and Macroeconomics: Evidence and Theory. *The Canadian Journal of Economics. Revue Canadienne d'Economique*, *30*(4), 773–808. doi:10.2307/136269

Devuyst, D. (2000). Linking impact assessment and sustainable development at the local level: The introduction of sustainability assessment systems. *Sustainable Development (Bradford)*, *8*(2), 67–78. doi:10.1002/(SICI)1099-1719(200005)8:2<67::AID-SD131>3.0.CO;2-X

Dharmapuri, S. (2012). Implementing UN security council resolution 1325: Putting the responsibility to protect into practice. *Global Responsibility to Protect*, *4*(2), 241–272. doi:10.1163/187598412X639728

Diaby, A., & Klingelschmitt, N. (2023). De Facto Sovereignty and Multilateral Sanctions for a Return to Constitutional Order in a Context of Regional Armed Conflict: The Case of Mali. In *War, State and Sovereignty: Interdisciplinary Challenges and Perspectives for the Social Sciences* (pp. 185–207). Springer Nature Switzerland. doi:10.1007/978-3-031-33661-4_9

Diamond, L. (1996). Is the Third Wave Over? *Journal of Democracy*, *7*(3), 20–37. doi:10.1353/jod.1996.0047

Diamond, L. (2010). Liberation technologies. *Journal of Democracy*, *21*(3), 69–83. doi:10.1353/jod.0.0190

Diamond, L. (2015). Facing up to the democratic recession. *Journal of Democracy*, *26*(1), 41–55. doi:10.1353/jod.2015.0009

Diamond, L., Linz, J. J., & Lipset, S. M. (1990). Introduction: Comparing experiences with democracy. In L. Diamond, J. J. Linz, & S. M. Lipset (Eds.), *Politics in developing countries: Comparing experiences with democracy* (pp. 1–38). doi:10.1515/9781685853150-002

Digital Rights Landscape in SADC. (2022). *The digital rights landscape in Southern Africa*. CHR. https://www.chr.up.ac.za/images/researchunits/dgdr/documents/reports/Digital_Rights_Landscape_in_SADC_Report.pdf

Dinc, I. (2005). Politicians and banks: Political influences on government-owned banks in emerging markets. *Journal of Financial Economics*, *77*(2), 453–479. doi:10.1016/j.jfineco.2004.06.011

Dlamini, L.N. (2019). *Determinants of commercial orientation and the level of market participation by women maize farmers in Eswatini*. Academic Press.

Dlamini, K. (2002). Is Quiet Diplomacy an Effective Conflict Resolution Strategy? *South African Yearbook of International Affairs*, *3*, 171–178.

Dlamini, T. S., Mlipha, S., Mohammed, M., & Sacolo, T. (2018). Path to economic recovery and sustainable growth in the Kingdom of Eswatini. *African Review of Economics and Finance*, *10*(2), 3–9.

Dobbs, K. L. (2021). Active on the street but apathetic at the ballot box? Explaining youth voter behavior in Tunisia's new democracy. *British Journal of Middle Eastern Studies*. Advance online publication. doi:10.1080/13530194.2021.1962243

Doğan, B., Rao, A., Ferraz, D., Sharma, G. D., & Shahzadi, I. (2023). What do we learn from Nexus between trade diversification and structural change: Informing the future about climate action and Sustainability. *Environmental Science and Pollution Research International*, 1–20. PMID:37486468

Dossani, S. (2012). Malawi: A development puzzle? *Global Majority E-Journal*, *3*(1), 20–32.

Downs, A. (1957). *An economic theory of democracy*. Harper and Row.

Dreher, A., Kotsogiannis, C., & McCorriston, S. (2009). How Do Institutions Affect Corruption and the Shadow Economy? *International Tax and Public Finance*, *16*(6), 773–796. doi:10.100710797-008-9089-5

Driscoll, C., & Melissa, G. (2010). My profile: The ethics of virtual ethnography. *Emotion, Space and Society*, *3*(1), 15–20. doi:10.1016/j.emospa.2010.01.012

Driss, O. B., Mellouli, S., & Trabelsi, Z. (2019). From citizens to government policymakers: Social media data analysis. *Government Information Quarterly*, *36*(3), 560–570. doi:10.1016/j.giq.2019.05.002

Du Bois, S. G. (1958). Du Bois Speaks to Africa. In *The life of W.E. B. Du Bois: Cheer the Lonesome Traveller*. The Dial Press.

du Preez, M. (2018). The use of social media by politicians and political parties. *News24*. https://www.news24.com/news24/columnists/maxdupreez/the-use-of-social-media-by-politicians-and-political-parties-20181227>

Dunning, J. (1993). *Multinational Enterprises and the Global Economy.* Addison-Wesley.

Dupuy, K., & Prakash, A. (2022). Why restrictive NGO foreign funding laws reduce voter turnout in Africa's national elections. *Nonprofit and Voluntary Sector Quarterly, 51*(1), 170–189. doi:10.1177/0899764019897848

Duri, J. (2020). *Overview of corruption and anti-corruption in sub-Saharan Africa.* Academic Press.

Dzimiri, P. (2017). African Multilateral responses to the crisis in Zimbabwe: A responsibility to protect perspective. *SRSA, 39*(2), 50–77.

Ebenezer, L. (2018). *Political accountability and voter turnout in Nigeria's elections (1999-2015)* [PhD thesis]. University of Port Harcourt.

Ebenezer, L. (2017). Political accountability and voter turnout in Nigeria's elections (1999-2016). *Quarterly Journal of Contemporary Research, 5*(2), 135–146.

Ebenezer, L. (2017). Trend analysis of voter turnout in Nigeria's elections (1999-2016) [Nigeria Edition]. *African Social and Educational Journal, 6*(2), 198–209.

Ebo, A., & Powell, K. (2010). Why is SSR important? A United Nations perspective. In M. Sedra (Ed.), *The future of security sector reform. The Centre for International Governance Innovation* (pp. 45–58). CIGI.

Economic Freedom Fighters. (2020). *Welcome to the Economic Freedom Fighters.* EFF. https://effonline.org

Economist Intelligence Unit. (2022). *Frontline democracy and the battle for Ukraine.* EIU Report. EIU.

Economist Intelligence Unit. (2023). *Democracy Index 2022: Frontline democracy and the battle for Ukraine.* https://pages.eiu.com/rs/753-RIQ-438/images/DI-final-ver sion-report.pdf

Economist. (2005). *India: Democracy vs. development: A false choice.* http: //www.economist.com

ECOSOC Chamber (2018). *Financing for SDGs: Breaking bottlenecks of investment from policy to impact.* The United Nations.

Edeh, S. C. (2020). *Pillars of Democracy: 7 Essential Pillars of a Democratic Government.* https://bscholarly.com/pillars-of-democracy/

Edelenbos, J., Van Buuren, A., & van Schie, N. (2011). Co-producing knowledge: Joint knowledge production between experts, bureaucrats and stakeholders in Dutch water management projects. *Environmental Science & Policy, 14*(6), 675–684. doi:10.1016/j.envsci.2011.04.004

Edo, S., Matthew, O., & Ogunrinola, I. (2023). Bilateral and multilateral aid perspectives of economic growth in sub-Saharan Africa. *African Journal of Economic and Management Studies, 14*(1), 1–17. doi:10.1108/AJEMS-02-2022-0047

Edwards, S. (1989). *Real Exchange Rates, Devaluation and Adjustment: Exchange Rate Policy in Developing Countries.* MIT Press.

Egbetokun, O. A. (2009). Provision of rural infrastructures in Oyo State of Nigeria. *Journal of Ekonomie, 11*(1), 26–32.

E-Governance Academy. (2022). *Kenya digital readiness: A journey towards human-centred digitilisation.* e-Governance Academy.

Eisner, E. W. (2017). *The enlightened eye: Qualitative inquiry and the enhancement of educational practice.* Teachers College Press.

Ekman, J., & Amna, E. (2012). Political participation and civic engagement: Towards a new typology. *Human Affairs, 22*(3), 283–300. doi:10.247813374-012-0024-1

Electoral Institute for Sustainable Democracy in Africa (EISA). (2007). Lesotho National Assembly Elections. *EISA election observer mission report No.26.*

El-Husseini, R. (2015). Is gender the barrier to democracy? Women, Islamism, and the "Arab spring.". *Contemporary Islam, 10*(1), 53–66. Advance online publication. doi:10.100711562-015-0324-4

Eliasson, G. E. (1995). *Economic Growth Through Competitive Selection.* Paper presented at 22nd Annual EARIE Conference 3–6 September 1995.

El-Ibiary, R., & Calfano, B. (2022). Editorial: Media populism: How media populism and inflating fear empowers populist politicians. *Frontiers in Communication, 7*, 996795. doi:10.3389/fcomm.2022.996795

El-Khawas, M. (2012). Tunisia's Jasmine Revolution: Causes and Impact. *Mediterranean Quarterly, 23*(4), 1–23. doi:10.1215/10474552-1895357

Emerson, R. W. (2015). Convenience sampling, random sampling, and snowball sampling: How does sampling affect the validity of research? *Journal of Visual Impairment & Blindness, 109*(2), 164–168. doi:10.1177/0145482X1510900215

Enang, I., Asenova, D., & Bailey, S. J. (2022). Identifying influencing factors of sustainable public service transformation: A systematic literature review. *International Review of Administrative Sciences, 88*(1), 258–280. doi:10.1177/0020852319896399

Eni, O., Nnam, M. U., & Udu, E. A. (2022). The Right to Participate in Political and Decision-Making Process under the Maputo Protocol: Normative Masculinity and Nigerian Women. *The Age of Human Rights Journal*, (18), 397–423. doi:10.17561/tahrj.v18.6633

Enqvist, J. P., & Ziervogel, G. (2019). Water governance and justice in Cape Town: An overview. *WIREs. Water, 6*(4), e1354. doi:10.1002/wat2.1354

Erasmus Khan, D., Lagrange, E., Oeter, S., & Walter, C. (Eds.). (28 Nov. 2022). Democracy and Sovereignty. Brill | Nijhoff. doi:10.1163/9789004508712

Erdmann, G. (2011). *Transition from Democracy.: Loss of Quality, Hybridisation and Breakdown of Democracy*. German Institute of Global and Area Studies (GIGA). https://www.jstor.org/stable/resrep07511

Erika, K.-M., & Mario, S. (2014). *UNESCO Science Report: Towards 2030.* UNESCO.

Ernst, N., Engesser, S., & Esser, F. (2017). Bipolar populism? The use of anti-elitism and people-centrism by Swiss parties on social media. *Schweizerische Zeitschrift für Politikwissenschaft, 23*(3), 253–261. doi:10.1111psr.12264

Espoir, D. K., Sunge, R., & Bannor, F. (2023). Economic growth, renewable and nonrenewable electricity consumption: Fresh evidence from a panel sample of African countries. *Energy Nexus, 9*, 100165. doi:10.1016/j.nexus.2022.100165

Estonian Centre for International Development. (2022). *Team Europe launch digital readiness study for Kenya to support Kenya's digitalisation efforts as the Silicon Savannah.* ESTDEV. https://estdev.ee/estdev-en/1778/?lang=en

Etzioni, A. (1996). *The New Golden Rule: Community and Morality in a Democratic Society*. Harper Collins.

European Commission. (2011). A New Response to a Changing Neighbourhood: A Review of European Neighbourhood Policy. *COM, 2011*(303), 25.

European Commission. (2011). Joint Communication to the European Council, the European Parliament, the Council, the European Economic and Social Committee and the Committee of the Regions. A Partnership for Democracy and Shared Prosperity with the Southern Mediterranean. COM(2011) 200 final (Brussels).

European Commission. (2016). *European Neighbourhood Policy and Enlargement Negotiations (Tunisia), last updated 23 June 2016.* Available at https://ec.europa. eu/enlargement/neighbourhood/countries/tunisia/index_en.htm

European Commission. (2016). *Tunisia Financial Assistance Fiche*. Author.

European External Action Service. (2017). *Second High-level Political Dialogue on 'Security and Counter-terrorism': European Union and Tunisia Renew their Cooperation (Brussels).* Available at https://eeas.europa.eu/headquarters/headquarters-homepage/19207/second-high-level-political-dialogue-security-and-counter-terrorism-europeanunion-and-tunisia_en

European Parliament. (2021). *State of democracy in Sub-Saharan Africa: Democratic progress at risk.* European Parliament. https://www.europarl.europa.eu/RegData/etudes/BRIE/2021/690647/EPRS_BRI(2021)690647_EN.pdf

Eweje, G., Sajjad, A., Nath, S. D., & Kobayashi, K. (2021). Multi-stakeholder partnerships: A catalyst to achieve sustainable development goals. *Marketing Intelligence & Planning, 39*(2), 186–212. doi:10.1108/MIP-04-2020-0135

Eyoh, D., & Sandbrook, R. (2003). Pragmatic neo-liberalism and just development in Africa. *States, markets, and just growth: Development in the twenty-first century*, 227-57.

Fabiyi, O. (2009). Apathy of Nigerian Voters Worrisome- Iwu. In Falade, D. A Political Participation in Nigerian Democracy: A Study of Some Selected Local Government Areas in Ondo State, Nigeria. *Global Journal of Human-Social Science: F. Political Science (Wellington, N.Z.), 14*(8), 16–23.

Fabricius, P. (2017). Is SADC at last flexing its muscles in Lesotho? *ISS Today*. https://issafrica.org/iss-today/is-sadc-at-last-flexing-its-muscles-in-lesotho

Fact Sheet. (2023). *Military Coup in Niger*. https://acleddata.com/2023/08/03/fact-sheet-military-coup-in-niger/

Fagunwa, T. (2015). *Voter apathy and Nigeria's electioneering process: a synopsis on 2015 general elections*. Academic Press.

Fakir, E. (2014). *The loss of trust and confidence in political parties*. EISA. https://www.eisa.org.za/eu/2014eu4aeditorial.htm>

Falade, D. A. (2014). Political participation in Nigerian democracy: A study of some selected local government areas in Ondo State, Nigeria. *Global Journal of Human & Social Science: f Political Science, 14*(8), 17–23.

Faller, J. K. (2015). The system matters: Corruption and vote choice in Uganda. *Commonwealth and Comparative Politics, 53*(4), 428–456. doi:10.1080/14662043.2015.1094891

Falola, T. (2022). *Decolonizing African Knowledge: Autoethnography and African Epistemologies*. Cambridge University Press. doi:10.1017/9781009049634

Falola, T., & Ezekwem, O. (2016). *Writing the Nigeria-Biafra War*. Boydell & Brewer. doi:10.1017/9781782047735

Fanon, F. (1965). *Wretched of the Earth*. Penguin.

Farahat, M. A. (2016). African Continental Free Trade Area: Policy and Negotiation Options for Trade in Goods. In *UN Conference on Trade and Development* (*Vol. 2*). Academic Press.

Faraj, H. F., Bouchoucha, N., & Maktouf, S. (2020). *Political stability and economic growth: the role ofexchange rate regime*. MPRA Paper No. 104586. https://mpra.ub.uni-muenchen.de/104586/

Fariello, F. A., & Daly, C. C. (2013). Coordinating the Fight Against Corruption among MDBS: The Past, Present and Future of Sanctions. *The George Washington International Law Review*, 45.

Farrell, M.J. (n.d.). The measurement of Productive Efficiency. *Journal of the Royal Statistical Society, 120*(3), 253-290.

Fauzel, S., Seetanah, B., & Sannassee, R. V. (2016). A dynamic investigation of foreign direct investment and poverty reduction in Mauritius. *Theoretical Economics Letters*, *6*(2), 289–303. doi:10.4236/tel.2016.62033

Fawole, O. I. (2018). The Role of Poverty and Income Inequality in Voter Apathy: Evidence from Sub-Saharan Africa. *Journal of African Elections*, *17*(1), 109–126.

Fayomi, O., & Adebayo, G. T. (2017). (Eds.). Political participation and political citizenship. In Palgrave Handbook of African Politics, Government and Development. New York. Palgrave Macmillan.

Feagin, J. (2013). *Systemic racism: A theory of oppression*. Routledge. doi:10.4324/9781315880938

Feddersen, T. J., & Pesendorfer, W. (1996). The Swing Voter's Curse. *The American Economic Review*, *86*(3), 408–424.

Feddersen, T. J., & Pesendorfer, W. (1999). Abstention in Elections with Asymmetric Information and Diverse Preferences. *The American Political Science Review*, *93*(2), 381–398. doi:10.2307/2585402

Feeney, M. K., & Porumbescu, G. (2020). The limits of social media for public administration research & practice. *Public Administration Review*, *81*(1), 792.

Feketha, V. (2019, Nov. 12). *Message to African Economies*. Mercury, p. 6.

Feldman, M., Francis, J., & Bercovitz, J. (2005). Creating a cluster while building a firm: Entrepreneurs and the formation of industrial clusters. *Regional Studies*, *39*(1), 129–141. doi:10.1080/0034340052000320888

Feldman, M., & Zoller, T. D. (2012). Dealmakers in place: Social capital connections in regional entrepreneurial economies. *Regional Studies*, *46*(1), 23–37. doi:10.1080/00343404.2011.607808

Feldstein, M. (2000). *Aspects of Global Economic Integration: Outlook for the Future*. National Bureau of Economic Research. NBER Working Paper No.7899.

Feldstein, S. (2021). *Transformation and setbacks in Ethiopia, The rise of digital repression: How technology is reshaping power, politics, and resistance*.

Ferejohn, J. (1986). Incumbent performance and electoral control. *Public Choice*, *50*(1), 5–25. doi:10.1007/BF00124924

Fernandes, S. (2007, April 12). *Hugo Chavez as an expression of urban popular movements*. Venezuela Analysis. http://venezuelanalysis.com/analysis/2334

Ferreira, V., Barreira, A. P., Loures, L., Antunes, D., & Panagopoulos, T. (2020). Stakeholders' engagement on nature-based solutions: A systematic literature review. *Sustainability (Basel)*, *12*(2), 640. doi:10.3390u12020640

Fiandrino, S., Scarpa, F., & Torelli, R. (2022). Fostering social impact through corporate implementation of the SDGs: Transformative mechanisms towards interconnectedness and inclusiveness. *Journal of Business Ethics*, *180*(4), 959–973. doi:10.100710551-022-05189-9

Fine, R. (1992). Civil society theory and the politics of transition in South Africa. *Review of African Political Economy*, *55*(55), 71–83. https://www.jstor.org/stable/4006073. doi:10.1080/03056249208703969

Fintel, M., & Ott, G. (2017). Political culture and participation in South Africa: The role of socio-economic factors. *Taiwan Journal of Democracy*, *13*(1), 77–99.

Fioramonti, L., & Mattheis, F. (2016). Is Africa really following Europe? An integrated framework for comparative regionalism. *Journal of Common Market Studies*, *54*(3), 674–690. doi:10.1111/jcms.12307

Fisher, S. (2014). *EFF members a no-show at a parliamentary disciplinary hearing*. EFF. https://ewn.co.za/2014/10/08/EFF-members-refuse-to-show-up-at-disciplinary-hearing>

Fisher, J. (2014). Framing Kony: Uganda's war, Obama's advisers and the nature of 'influence' in Western foreign policy making. *Third World Quarterly*, *35*(4), 686–704. doi:10.1080/01436597.2014.924068

Flahaux, M. L., & De Haas, H. (2016). African migration: Trends, patterns, drivers. *Comparative Migration Studies*, *4*(1), 1–25. doi:10.118640878-015-0015-6

Flekky, M. G. E., & Kaufman, N. H. (1997). *The Participation Rights of the Child: Rights and Responsibilities in Family and Society*. Jessica Kingsley Publishers.

Flemes, D. (2009). Regional power South Africa: Co-operative hegemony constrained by historical legacy. *Journal of Contemporary African Studies*, *27*(2), 135–157. doi:10.1080/02589000902867238

Flint, R. W. (2013). *Practice of Sustainable Community Development A Participatory Framework for Change*. Springer. doi:10.1007/978-1-4614-5100-6

Flores, K. M. G., & Kovács, J. K. (2018). Defining the entrepreneurship ecosystem. *SEA-Practical Application of Science*, (18), 299–306.

Foelster, S. (2000). Do entrepreneurs create jobs? *Small Business Economics*, *14*(2), 137–148. doi:10.1023/A:1008141516160

Fogel, B. (2013). *Julius Malema's EFF and South Africa's Left*. Africa's Country. https://africasacountry.com/2013/11/julius-malemas-economic-freedom-fighters-and-the-south-african-left>

Fombad, C. M. (2021). An overview of the state of electoral democracy in Africa. *African Journal of Legal Studies*, *14*(2), 245–268. doi:10.1163/17087384-12340087

Fontaine, T. (2005). *Currency Crises in Developed and Emerging Market Economies: A Comparative Empirical Treatment*. IMF Working Paper, WP/05/13, January.

Forster. (1993). *People and Education in the Third World*. Longman.

Fowler, A. G. (2013). *Five Studies on the Causes and Consequences of Voter Turnout* [Doctoral dissertation]. Harvard University.

Fox, H. M. (2017). A way of knowing in search of our true identity. *Self and Society*, *45*(1), 72–75. doi:10.1080/03060497.2017.1290453

Fox, S. (2014). The political economy of slums: Theory and evidence from Sub-Saharan Africa. *World Development*, *54*, 191–203. doi:10.1016/j.worlddev.2013.08.005

Freedom House. (2020). *Lesotho*. Freedom House. https://freedomhouse.org/country/lesotho/freedom-world/2020.

Freedom House. (2022). *Tunisia: Freedom in the World 2022 Country Report*. Freedom House. https://freedomhouse.org/country/tunisia/freedom-world/2022

Freeman, R. E. (1984). *Strategic management: A stakeholder approach*. Pitman.

Freeman, R. E., Kujala, J., & Sachs, S. (2017). *Stakeholder engagement: Clinical research cases.* Springer. doi:10.1007/978-3-319-62785-4

Freire, A. M. A., & Macedo, D. (Eds.). (1998). The Paulo Freire reader. Continuum.

Freire, P. (1970). *Pedagogy of the Oppressed.* Penguin.

Friedman, S. (2014). EFF frenzy a case of media hype over substance. *Business Live.* https://www.businesslive.co.za/bd/opinion/columnists/2014-03-05-eff-frenzy-a-case-of-media-hype-over-substance/>

Friedman, S. (2008). We met the and he is us: Domestic politics and South Africa's role in promoting democracy. *African Journal of International Affairs, 11*(2), 29–53. doi:10.4314/ajia.v11i2.57263

Friend, A. H. (2017). *Military Politicisation.* Center for Strategic and International Studies. https://www.csis.org/analysis/military-politicisation.

Frigerio, M., & Vandone, D. (2020). European development banks and the political cycle. *European Journal of Political Economy, 62*, 101852. doi:10.1016/j.ejpoleco.2019.101852

Fryer, D., & Payne, R. (1984). Proactive behaviour in unemployment: Findings and implications. *Leisure Studies, 3*(3), 273–295. doi:10.1080/02614368400390231

Fuchs, C., & Horak, E. (2008). Africa and the digital divide. *Telematics and Informatics*, 25(2), 0736-5853. doi:10.1016/j.tele.2006.06.004

Fukuyama, F. (1992). *The end of history and the last man.* Penguin.

Gagnon, J., & Chou, M. (2013). *The theories, concepts and practices of democracy.* Palgrave Macmillan.

Gallarotti, G. M. (2011). Soft power: What it is, why it's important, and the conditions for its effective use. *Journal of Political Power, 4*(1), 25–47. doi:10.1080/2158379X.2011.557886

Galletti, N., & Wodzicki, M. (2010). Securing human rights: Shifting the security sector reform paradigm. In M. Sedra (Ed.), *The future of security sector reform. The Centre for International Governance Innovation* (pp. 281–300). CIGI.

Galston, W. (2018). Populist challenge to liberal democracy. *Journal of Democracy, 29*(2), 5–19. doi:10.1353/jod.2018.0020

Garba, G. K. (2016). *Building women's capacity for peace building in Nigeria.* Academic Press.

Garner, R., Ferdinand, P., & Lawson, S. (2009). *Introduction to Politics.*

Garratt, D. (2003). Education for Citizenship. In D. Burton & S. Barlet (Eds.), *Education Studies: themes and issues.* Sage.

Gartner, W. B. (1988). "Who is an entrepreneur?" is the wrong question. *American Journal of Small Business, 12*(4), 11–32. doi:10.1177/104225878801200401

Garwe, E. C., & Gwati, L. (2018). The role of international and regional quality assurance bodies. *Higher Education Research, 3*(1), 15–22. doi:10.11648/j.her.20180301.14

Gause, F. G. (2011, July 1). Why Middle East Studies Missed the Arab Spring. *Foreign Affairs, 2011*(July/August). https://www.foreignaffairs.com/articles/middle-east/2011-07-01/why-middle-east-studies-missed-arab-spring

Gberevbie, D. E. (2004). Democracy, democratic Institutions and Good Governance in Nigeria. *Eastern Africa Social Science Research Review, 30*(1), 133–152. doi:10.1353/eas.2014.0005

George, A. L., & Bennett, A. (2005). *Case studies and theory development in the social sciences*. MIT Press. http://bvbr.bib-bvb.de:8991/F?func=service&doc_library=BVB01&doc_number=013153145&line_number=0001&func_code=DB_RECORDS&service_type=MEDIA

Gerbaudo, P. (2017). Social media and populism: An elective affinity? *Media Culture & Society*, *40*(5), 745–753. doi:10.1177/0163443718772192

Gersbach, H. (2020). Democratizing Tech Giants! A roadmap. *Economics of Governance*, *21*(4), 351–361. doi:10.100710101-020-00244-5

Geys, B. (2006). National theory of voter turnout: A review. *Political Studies Review*, *4*(1), 16–35. doi:10.1111/j.1478-9299.2006.00034.x

Ghaebi, M. R. (2017). The Role of South-South Cooperation in Realization of the Right to Development: The Way Forward. *Int'l Stud. J.*, *14*, 169.

Ghai, Y. P. (2014). State, ethnicity and economy in Africa. In Ethnic Diversity and Economic Instability in Africa. Cambridge University Press.

Ghisellini, P., Cialani, C., & Ulgiati, S. (2016). A review on circular economy: The expected transition to a balanced interplay of environmental and economic systems. *Journal of Cleaner Production*, *114*, 11–32. doi:10.1016/j.jclepro.2015.09.007

Ghosh, A. R., Jonathan, D. O., & Mahvash, S. Q. (2014). *Exchange Rate Management and Crisis Susceptibility: A Reassessment*. IMF Working Paper, WP/14/11, January.

Ghosh, S., Gregoriou, A., & Mitra, A. (2013). *On the Role of Democracy in the Ethnicity-Growth Relationship: Theory and Evidence*. Working Paper, Brunel University.

Gibbens, M., & Schoeman, C. (2020). Planning for sustainable livelihood development in the context of rural South Africa: A micro-level approach. *Town and Regional Planning*, *76*(1), 14–28. doi:10.18820/2415-0495/trp76i1.2

Gladwell, M. (2010). Small change: Why the revolution will not be Tweeted. *The New Yorker*. Retrieved from https://www.newyorker.com/magazine/2010/10/04/small-changemalcolm-gladwell

Glancey, K., McQuaid, R., & Campling, J. (2000). *Entrepreneurial economics*. Macmillan. doi:10.1057/9780333981245

Global Security. (2017a). *Basotho Wars (1858-68)*. Global Security. https://www.globalsecurity.org/military/world/war/basotho.htm.

Global Security. (2017b). *Lesotho Defence Force*. Global Security. https://www.globalsecurity.org/military/world/africa/ls-army.htm.

Global Strategy, E. U. (2016). *Shared Vision, Common Action: A Stronger Europe*. European External Action Service.

Goetz, A. M., & Jenkins, R. (2016). Agency and accountability: Promoting women's participation in peacebuilding. *Feminist Economics*, *22*(1), 211–236. doi:10.1080/13545701.2015.1086012

Goldschmidt, R. (2013). *Cyber space and protection of critical infrastructures*. Knesset Centre for Research Information (Hebrew).

Golub, S., & Varma, A. (2014). Fishing exports and economic development of least developed countries: Bangladesh, Cambodia, Comoros, Sierra Leone and Uganda. UNCTAD. Swarthmore College.

Gopaldas, R. (2019). *Digital dictatorship versus digital democracy in Africa*. South African Institute of International Affairs. https://www.jstor.org/stable/resrep25956

Gorokhovskaia, Y., Shahbaz, A., & Slipowitz, A. (2023). *Marking 50 Years in the Struggle for Democracy*. Freedom in the World. Freedom House.

Govender van-Wyk, S., & Wilson, D. (2009). Sustainable Tourism on Commonages: An Alternative to Traditional Agricultural-based Land Reform in Namaqualand, South Africa. In Sustainable tourism in Southern Africa: Local communities and natural resources in transition. Academic Press.

Goyol, Y. I. (2019). The role of women in peacebuilding: Liberia in perspective. *International Journal of Development and Management Review*, *14*(1), 123–135.

Gozzi, G.J. (2018). *Critical Perspectives on Euro-Mediterranean Relations after the "Arab Spring"*. Academic Press.

Graaf, G. D. (2007). Causes of Corruption: Towards a Contextual Theory of Corruption. *Public Administration Quarterly*, *32*(1), 39–86.

Gramsci, A. (2011). *Prison Notebooks, Volumes 1-3*. Academic Press.

Grant, R., Carmody, P., & Murphy, J. T. (2020). A green transition in South Africa? Sociotechnical experimentation in the Atlantis Special Economic Zone. *The Journal of Modern African Studies*, *58*(2), 189–211. doi:10.1017/S0022278X20000208

Gray, B. (1989). *Collaborating: Finding Common Ground for Multiparty Problems*. Jossey-Bass.

Gregory, A. J., Atkins, J. P., Midgley, G., & Hodgson, A. M. (2020). Stakeholder identification and engagement in problem structuring interventions. *European Journal of Operational Research*, *283*(1), 321–340. doi:10.1016/j.ejor.2019.10.044

Gressel, C. M., Rashed, T., Maciuika, L. A., Sheshadri, S., Coley, C., Kongeseri, S., & Bhavani, R. R. (2020). Vulnerability mapping: A conceptual framework towards a context-based approach to women's empowerment. *World Development Perspectives*, *20*, 100245. doi:10.1016/j.wdp.2020.100245 PMID:32835139

Griffith, R. (1998). *Educational Citizenship and Independent Learning*. Jessica Kingsley.

Groenendijk, N. (1997). A principal-agent model of corruption. *Crime. Crime, Law, and Social Change*, *27*(3/4), 207–229. doi:10.1023/A:1008267601329

Grugel, J. (2002). *Democratization: A Critical Introduction*. Palgrave Macmillan.

Gujadhur, T. (2001). *Joint Venture Options for Communities and Safari Operators in Botswana*, CBNRN Support Programme Occasional Paper No. 6. SNV/IUCN.

Gumede, V., & Oloruntoba, S. (2018). Regional Integration and African Renaissance: Moving Beyond the Rhetoric. In C. Landsberg (Ed.), *Africa Rising Up: Perspectives on African Renewal* (pp. 245–258). Real African Publishers.

Günay, C., & Sommavilla, F. (2019). Tunisia's democratization at risk. *Mediterranean Politics*, *25*(5), 1–9. doi:10.1080/13629395.2019.1631980

Gunda, M. R. (2018). At the Cross Roads: A call to Christians to act in faith for an alternative Zimbabwe. In *Bible in Africa Studies* (Vol. 21). University of Bamberg.

Guseh, J. S., & Oritsejafor, E. (2007). Government size, Political freedom and Economic growth in Nigeria, 1960-2000. *Journal of Third World Studies*, *24*(1), 139–165.

Gutierrez, E., Rudolph, H. P., Homa, T., & Beneit, E. B. (2011). Development Banks Role and Mechanisms to Increase their Efficiency. *World Bank Policy Research Working Paper*, *5729*(July), 1–37. doi:10.1596/1813-9450-5729

Guttal, S. (2021). Re-imagining the UN Committee on World Food Security. *Development*, *64*(3-4), 227–235. doi:10.105741301-021-00322-z PMID:34703165

Habib, A. (2009). South Africa's foreign policy: Hegemonic aspirations, neoliberal orientations, and global transformation. *South African Journal of International Affairs*, *16*(2), 143–159. doi:10.1080/10220460903265857

Habiyaremye, A. (2020). *Fast tracking the SADC integration agenda to unlock regional collaboration gains along growth corridors in Southern Africa* (No. 2020/95). WIDER Working Paper.

Haffajee, F. (2019). EFF leads the information war with its cyber army. *Daily Mavrick*. https://www.dailymaverick.co.za/article/2019-03-07-eff-leads-the-information-war-with-its-cyber-army/>

Haider, H. (2009). *Community-based approaches to peacebuilding in conflict-affected and fragile contexts*. Academic Press.

Hainz, C., & Kleimeier, S. (2012). Political risk, project finance, and the participation of development banks in syndicated lending. *Journal of Financial Intermediation*, *21*(2), 287–314. doi:10.1016/j.jfi.2011.10.002

Hamill, J., & Hoffman, J. (2009). 'Quiet diplomacy or appeasement? South African policy towards Zimbabwe. *The Round Table*, *98*(402), 373–384. doi:10.1080/00358530902895584

Hammar, A., McGregor, J., & Landau, L. (2010). Introduction. Displacing Zimbabwe: Crisis and construction in Southern Africa. *Journal of Southern African Studies*, *36*(2), 263–283. doi:10.1080/03057070.2010.485779

Hanachor, M., & Echezu, B. C. (2021). Contributions of faith-based organizations towards peace building for sustainable community development in Rivers State, Nigeria. *International Journal of Education, Learning and Development*, *9*(3), 11–18.

Hanke, S. H., & Kwok, A. K. (2009). On the measurement of Zimbabwe's hyperinflation. *The Cato Journal*, *29*, 364–353.

Hans, B., & Mtshali, S. (2018, March 9). Zuma blames whites for his removal. *Independent On Line*. https://www.iol.co.za/dailynews/zuma-blames-whites-for-his-removal-13672294

Hansen, L. P. (1982). Large Sample Properties of Generalized Method of Moments Estimators. *Econometrica*, *50*(4), 1029–1054. doi:10.2307/1912775

Harber, C. (1995). *Developing Democratic Education*. Education Now Books.

Harber, C. (1999). *Voices for Democracy: a North – South Dialogue on Education for Sustainable Democracy*. Education Now Books.

Hardi, P., & Zdan, T. (1997). *Assessing Sustainable Development: Principles in Practice*. International Institute for Sustainable Development.

Harms Smith, L. (2019). *Epistemic decoloniality as a pedagogical movement: A turn to anticolonial theorists such as Fanon, Biko and Freire*. Taylor & Francis.

Harvey, C., (1996). *Banking policy in Botswana: Orthodox but untypical*. Academic Press.

Haug, N., Dan, S., & Mergel, I. (2023). Digitally induced change in the public sector: A systematic review and research agenda. *Public Management Review*, 1–25. doi:10.1080/14719037.2023.2234917

Head. (2004). For Richer or Poorer—Assessing the Criticisms Directed at the Multilateral Development Banks. *U. Kan. L. Rev.*, *54*(241).

Heater, D. B. (1964). *Political ideas in the modern world.* George G. Harrap & Co. Ltd.

Hébert, R. F., & Link, A. N. (1982). *The Entrepreneur: Mainstream Views and Radical Critiques*. Praeger.

Heilman, M. E. (2001). Description and prescription: How gender stereotypes prevent women's ascent up the organizational ladder. *The Journal of Social Issues*, *57*(4), 657–674. doi:10.1111/0022-4537.00234

Helliker, K., & Murisa, T. (2020). Zimbabwe: Continuities and changes. *Journal of Contemporary African Studies*, *38*(1), 5–17. doi:10.1080/02589001.2020.1746756

Hendricks, C., & Majozi, N. (2021). South Africa's International Relations: A New Dawn. *Journal of Asian and African Studies*, *56*(1), 64–78. doi:10.1177/0021909620946851

Henrekson, M., Johansson, D., & Karlsson, J. (2021). *To be or not to be: The entrepreneur in endogenous growth theory.* IFN Working Paper No. 1385, 2021

Hester, J. P. (2020). The Subjective Import of Moral Knowledge. *Humanities Bulletin*, *3*(2), 140–156.

Heyns, E. (2022). *An analysis of effects of economic growth on the financial performance of Namibian listed companies* [Doctoral dissertation]. University of Namibia.

Heywood, A. (2002). *Politics* (2nd ed.). Palgrave.

Hickey, S. (2004). *Participation: From tyranny to transformation: Exploring new approaches to participation in development.* Zed books.

Hill, C. (2000). *International Business - Competing in the Global Marketplace.* Irwin McGraw-Hill.

Hill, D. (2009). *American Voter Turnout: An Institutional Perspective (Transforming American Politics).* Routledge: Westview Press.

Hine, C. (1994). *Virtual Ethnography.* Paper presented at the 13th International Conference on Public Communication of Science and Technology (PCST), Montreal, Canada.

Hine, C. (2008). Virtual ethnography: modes, varieties, affordances. In Fielding, N. Lee, R.M. Blank, G (Eds.). The Sage Handbook on Online Research Methods. London. Sage Publications. doi:10.4135/9780857020055.n14

Hinnerich, B. T., & Petterson-Lidbom, P. (2014). Democracy, redistribution, and political participation: Evidence from Sweden 1919-1938. *Econometrica*, *82*(3), 961–993. doi:10.3982/ECTA9607

Hirsch, A. (2021). 'The African Union's Free Movement of Persons Protocol: Why has it faltered and how can its objectives be achieved? *South African Journal of International Affairs*, *28*(4), 497–517. doi:10.1080/10220461.2021.2007788

Hlongwane, N. W., & Daw, O. D. (2023). Determinants of public debt in South Africa: A Regime-Switching Approach. *International Journal of Economics and Finance Studies*, *15*(1), 142–163.

Hodges, N. E. (1972). Neo-Colonialism: The new rape of Africa. *The Black Scholar*, *3*(5), 5, 12–23. doi:10.1080/00064246.1972.11431211

Hodzi, K. 2018. *The Prosecutor General's Speech (Guest of Honour) at the Occassion of the Mutare Anti-Corruption Commission Court.* https://jsc.org.zw/jscbackend/upload/Publications/prosecutor%20general%20speech.pdf

Hoebes, C. (2018, November 28). *Response by the Deputy Minister of International Relations and Corporation to the presentations of Round Table 5.* Inclusive Democracy for Sustainable Development Conference. Windhoek, Namibia.

Hoff, J. (1999). *Towards a Theory of Democracy for the Information Age.* Discussion paper democracy platform UK-Nordic Meeting Copenhagen. http: //virtualsociety.sbs.ox.ac.uk/nordic/democracyplatform.htm

Hoffman, J. (2004). *Citizenship beyon the state.* SAGE Publications. doi:10.4135/9781446216842

Hofstede, G. (1980). *Culture's Consequences: International Differences in Work-related Value*. Sage.

Hofstede, G., & Hofstede, G. J. (1995). *Allemaal andersdenkenden: Omgaan met cultuurverschillen* [Cultures and Organizations: Software of the Mind]. Contact.

Holt, K., Shehata, A., Stromback, J., & Ljungberg, E. (2013, February). Age and the effects of news media attention and social media use on political interest and participation: Do social media function as leveller? *European Journal of Communication*, *28*(1), 19–34. doi:10.1177/0267323112465369

Honey, M. (1999). *Ecotourism and Sustainable Development: Who Owns Paradise?* Island Press.

Honwana, A. (2013). The Time of Youth; Works, social Change and Politics in Africa. Kumarian Press.

Hope, K. R. Sr. (2005). Toward good governance and sustainable development: The African peer review mechanism. *Governance: An International Journal of Policy, Administration and Institutions*, *18*(2), 283–311. doi:10.1111/j.1468-0491.2005.00276.x

Hopkins, A. G. (2019). *An economic history of West Africa*. Routledge. doi:10.4324/9780429400582

Hopper, T., Lassou, P., & Soobaroyen, T. (2017). Globalisation, accounting and developing countries. *Critical Perspectives on Accounting*, *43*, 125–148. doi:10.1016/j.cpa.2016.06.003

Hora, E. A. (2014). Factors that affect women participation in leadership and decision making position. *Asian Journal of Humanity, Art and Literature, 1*(2).

Hornby, A. S. (2006). *Oxford Advanced Learner's Dictionary of Current English* (7th ed.). Oxford University Press.

Horn, J. (2020). Decolonising emotional well-being and mental health in development: African feminist innovations. *Gender and Development*, *28*(1), 85–98. doi:10.1080/13552074.2020.1717177

Hosea, P., & Khalema, E. (2020). Scoping the nexus between climate change and water-security realities in rural South Africa. *Town and Regional Planning*, *77*, 18–30.

Hossen, M. S. (2020). Patriarchy practice and women's subordination in the society of Bangladesh: An analytical review. *Electronic Research Journal of Social Sciences and Humanities*, *2*, 51–60.

Howard-Hassmann, R.E. (2010). Mugabe's Zimbabwe, 2000-2009: Massive Human rights violations and the failure to protect. *Hum.RTS.Q., 32,* 898.

Hu, B., Schclarek, A., Xu, J., & Yan, J. (2022). Long-term finance provision: National development banks vs commercial banks. *World Development*, *158*, 105973. Advance online publication. doi:10.1016/j.worlddev.2022.105973

Hudson, H. (2006). *Human security and peacebuilding through a gender lens: Challenges of implementation in Africa*. JSTOR.

Hüllen, V. V. (2012). Europeanisation through Cooperation? EU Democracy Promotion in Morocco and Tunisia. *West European Politics*, *35*(1), 117–134. doi:10.1080/01402382.2012.631317

Huntington, S. P. (1991). *The third wave: Democratization in the late twentieth century*. University of Oklahoma Press. https://opac.eui.eu/client/en_GB/default/search/detailnonmodal/ent:$002f$002fSD_ILS$002f0$002fSD_ILS:392477/one

Hurlbut, C. D. (2021). *Crit: A Mixed Methods Examination of Epistemic Cognition During Source Evaluations*. McGill University.

Hurt, S. R. (2003). Co-operation and coercion? The Cotonou Agreement between the European Union and acp states and the end of the Lome´ Convention. *Third World Quarterly*, *24*(1), 161–176. doi:10.1080/713701373

Hussein, Z. (2018). *Democratic Accountability*. Dawn.

Hyland, P. (2003). The Enlightenment: a sourcebook and reader. London: Routledge.

Ibrahim, S. G., Oranyeli, S. O., & Bibi, F. I. (2021). Challenges of Democratization in Africa, North Asia. *International Research Journal of Business Economics & Management*, *5*(9). Advance online publication. doi:10.6947/2277-1018.2021.00009.8

Idris, S., Shuaibu, M., & Aliyu, Y. (2023). *Voter Dissatisfaction, Leaders' Performance Evaluation, and Voters Turnout in Nigeria's Fourth Republic.* Paper presented at the third International Conference of the Department of Political Science and International Studies, Ahmadu Bello University, Zaria on "Beyond Sustainable Elections: Interrogating the Challenges of Leadership and Governance in Nigeria." July 9th – 12th, 2023.

Ifarajimi, G. D., & Onyejiuwa, D. C. (2017). Exchange Rate Fluctuation, Stock Market Performance And Economic Growth In Nigeria Under Democratic Dispensation. *International Journal of Innovative Research and Advanced Studies*, *4*(1), 270–277.

IFEX. (2018, March 6). *Gwen Lister: A Fearless Commitment to Speaking Truth to Power.* IFEX. https://www.ifex.org/namibia/2018/03/06/gwen-lister-profile/

Igwe, P. A., & Icha-Ituma, A. (2020). A review of ten years of African entrepreneurship research. *Research handbook on entrepreneurship in emerging economies.*

Indabawa. (1993). *Education, Autonomy and Democratic Citizenship- Philosophy in a changing world.* Routledge.

INEC & FES. (2011). *Voter apathy and the 2011 elections in Nigeria: a research report*. INEC & FES Publication.

INEC. (2023). *Voters Turnout in 2023 Presidential Election*. Retrieved June 23, 2023, from www.inec.org

Inglehart, R., & Norris, P. (2016). Trump, Brexit, and the rise of populism: Economic have-nots and cultural backlash. *Harvard Kennedy School Faculty Research and Working Papers*, *16*(26), 1-52.

Inkpin, A. (2021). Merleau-Ponty's 'sensible ideas' and embodied-embedded practice. *Phenomenology and the Cognitive Sciences*, 1–24.

Institute for Democracy and Electoral Assistance. (2021). *The state of democracy in Africa and the Middle East 2021: Resilient democratic aspirations and opportunities for consolidation.* IDEA. https://www.idea.int/democracytracker/sites/default/files/2022-11/state-of-democracy-in-africa-and-the-middle-east-2021.pdf (Accessed 10 August 2023).

International IDEA. (2016). *Voter Turnout Trends around the World*. International IDEA.

International IDEA. (2020). *Voter Turnout since 1990 in Africa: A Global Report*. International IDEA.

International IDEA. (2021). *The state of democracy in Africa and the Middle East. Resilient democratic aspirations and opportunities for consolidation*. https://www.idea.in7>files

International Institute for Democracy and Electoral Assistance. (2017). *The fundamentals of a constitution*. https://www.idea.int/sites/default/files/publications/the-fundamentals-of-a-constitution.pdf

International Institute for Democracy and Electoral Assistance. (2017). *The Global State of Democracy: Exploring Democracy's Resilience*. International IDEA.

International Institute for Democracy and Electoral Assistance. (2018). The Global State of Democracy: (2018 Reprint ed.). Stockholm: International IDEA. doi:978-91-7671-1293

International Institute for Democracy and Electoral Assistance. (2018). *The global state of democracy: Exploring democracy's resilience*. International IDEA.

International Monetary Fund. (2014). *Angola: Second Post-Program Monitoring*. IMF Country Report No. 14/81, March 2014.

Investopedia. (2017). *Foreign Direct Investment – FDI*. http://www.investopedia.com/terms/f/fdi.asp#ixzz4kYzUFivt

INVOLVE. (2005). *People and participation: how to put citizens at the heart of decision-making*. INVOLVE. https://www.involve.org.uk/resources/publications/practical-guidance/people-and-participation-how-put-citizens-heart-decision

Iriye, A., Goedde, P., & Hitchcock, W. I. (Eds.). (2012). *The human rights revolution: an international history* (Vol. 3). Oxford University Press.

Iroanya, R., Dzimiri, P., & Phaswana, E. (2018). Human rights-based service delivery: Assessing the role of national human rights institutions in democracy and development in Ghana and Uganda. *Regions & Cohesion : the Journal of the Consortium for Comparative Research on Regional Integration and Social Cohesion*, *8*(2), 1–26. doi:10.3167/reco.2018.080202

Isaac, S. K. (2013). Rethinking the New ENP: A Vision for an Enhanced European Role in the Arab Revolutions. *Democracy and Security*, *9*(1-2), 40–60. doi:10.1080/17419166.2012.736308

Island, S. (2013). Legal analysis on. *Violence Against Women*.

Israel, J. (2011). *A Revolution of the Mind: Radical Enlightenment and the Intellectual Origins of Modern Democracy*. Princeton University Press.

ISS. (2004). *Terrorism Legislation in Zimbabwe*. www.issafrica.org/cdct/mainpages/pdf/ Terrorism/Legislation/Zimbabwe/Zimbabwe%20Serious%20offences%20Confiscation%20of%20Profits%20Act%201990.pdf

Iteyo, C., & Mumbi, A. (2020). Challenges and opportunities of women's peace building activities in Nairobi county Kenya. *Journal of Public Policy and Administration*, *5*(1), 47–61.

Ittner, S. (2009). *Fighting corruption in Africa: A comparative study of Uganda and Botswana* [Doctoral dissertation]. Deutsche Universität für Verwaltungswissenschaften.

Jackson RJ & D, (1997), *A Comparative Introduction to Political Science*. Prentice Hall.

Jackson, I., Watson, D. L., White, C. D., & Gallo, M. (2022). Research as (re) vision: Laying claim to oral history as a just-us research methodology. *International Journal of Research & Method in Education*, *45*(4), 330–342. doi:10.1080/1743727X.2022.2076827

Jah, E. A., Kurmi, A. N., Paul, T. S., & Henry, L. H. (2022). Women and peace processes in Nigeria. *Wukari International Studies Journal*, *6*(1), 13–13.

Jamal, T., & Stronza, A. (2009). Collaboration theory and tourism practice in protected areas: Stakeholders, structuring and sustainability. *Journal of Sustainable Tourism*, *17*(2), 169–189. doi:10.1080/09669580802495741

Jani, V., De Wit, A. H., & Webb, N. L. (2022). Evaluating the relevance of the CAMPFIRE principles to wildlife utilization in northern Zimbabwe. *African Journal of Wildlife Research*, *52*(1), 56–71. doi:10.3957/056.052.0056

Jansen, L. J., & Kalas, P. P. (2020). Improving governance of tenure in policy and practice: A conceptual basis to analyze multi-stakeholder partnerships for multi-stakeholder transformative governance illustrated with an example from South Africa. *Sustainability (Basel)*, *12*(23), 9901. doi:10.3390u12239901

Jendia, C. (2020). Conspicuously absent: Womens role in conflict resolution and peace building in northern Uganda in the context of United Nations resolution 1325. *Journal of Law and Conflict Resolution, 11*(1), 1–14. doi:10.5897/JLCR2019.0285

Jenkins, C., & Thomas, L. (2002). *Foreign Direct Investment in Southern Africa: Determinants, Characteristics and Implications for Economic Growth and Poverty Alleviation, Globalization and Poverty Project*. University of Oxford.

Jensen, M. (2001) *The African internet - A 2001 status report*. Digital Divide. http://www.digitaldivide.net/articles/view.php?ArticleID=322

Jensen, P. S., & Justesen, M. K. (2014). Poverty and vote buying: Survey-based evidence from Africa. *Electoral Studies, 33*, 220–232. doi:10.1016/j.electstud.2013.07.020

Jewett, R. L., Mah, S. M., Howell, N., & Larsen, M. M. (2021). Social cohesion and community resilience during COVID-19 and pandemics: A rapid scoping review to inform the United Nations research roadmap for COVID-19 recovery. *International Journal of Health Services, 51*(3), 325–336. doi:10.1177/0020731421997092 PMID:33827308

Jiao, W., Yang, X., & Min, Q. (2022). A review of the Progress in globally important agricultural heritage systems (GIAHS) monitoring. *Sustainability (Basel), 14*(16), 9958. doi:10.3390u14169958

Jiménez, A. C., Galilei, G., Strathern, M., & Serres, M. (2017). How knowledge grows: an anthropological anamorphosis. *Cosmopolitics*, 227.

John, O. I., Messina, G. M., & Odumegwu, A. C. (2023). The Effects of Neocolonialism on Africa's Development. *PanAfrican Journal of Governance and Development, 4*(2), 3–35. doi:10.46404/panjogov.v4i2.4846

Johnson, S., Kaufmann, D., Shleifer, A., Goldman, M. I., & Weitzman, M. L. (1997). The unofficial economy in transition. *Brookings Papers on Economic Activity, 1997*(2), 159–239. doi:10.2307/2534688

Jones, M. G. (2023, August 4). *What the Niger coup means for Europe's relationship with the Sahel*. Euronews. https://www.euronews.com/my-europe/2023/08/04/what-does-the-niger-coup-mean-for-europes-relationship-with-the-sahel

Jones, D. (2016). *Magna Carta: The Birth of Liberty*. Penguin Books.

Joseph, R. (1997). Democratization in Africa after 1989: Comparative and theoretical perspectives. *Comparative Politics, 29*(3), 363–382. doi:10.2307/422126

Joshua, S., & Olanrewaju, F. (2017). The AU's Progress and Achievements in the Realm of Peace and Security. *India Quarterly, 73*(4), 454–471. doi:10.1177/0974928417731639

Joy, S., & Kolb, D. A. (2009). Are there cultural differences in learning style? *International Journal of Intercultural Relations, 33*(1), 69–85. doi:10.1016/j.ijintrel.2008.11.002

Kaatz, E., Root, D. S., Bowen, P. A., & Hill, R. C. (2006). Advancing key outcomes of sustainability building assessment. *Building Research and Information, 34*(4), 308–320. doi:10.1080/09613210600724608

Kagan, D. (1998). *Pericles Of Athens and The Birth of Democracy*. Free Press.

Kam, C. D. (2012). Risk attitudes and political participation. *American Journal of Political Science, 56*(4), 817–836. doi:10.1111/j.1540-5907.2012.00605.x

Kangalawe, R. Y., Noe, C., Tungaraza, F. S., Naimani, G., & Mlele, M. (2014). Understanding of traditional knowledge and indigenous institutions on sustainable land management in Kilimanjaro Region, Tanzania. *Open Journal of Social Sciences, 4*(13), 469.

Kanyane, C. (2019). EFF seizes the future through social media. *Times Live*. https://www.timeslive.co.za/sunday-times/opinion-and-analysis/2019-03-24-eff-seizes-the-future-through-social-media/>

Kanyenze, G., Chitambara, P., & Tyson, J. (2017). *The outlook for the Zimbabwean economy.Supporting Economic Transformation*. UkAid.

Kaplan, M., Sanchez, M., & Hoffman, J. (2017). Intergenerational Strategies for Establishing Sustainable Work Environments. In *Intergenerational Pathways to a Sustainable Society* (pp. 141–162). Springer International Publishing. doi:10.1007/978-3-319-47019-1_7

Kasemsap, K. (2017). Foreign Direct Investment. Handbook of Research on Economic, Financial, and Industrial Impacts on Infrastructure Development, 239.

Kassa, S. (2015). Challenges and opportunities of women political participation in Ethiopia. *Journal of Global Economics*, *3*(4), 1–7. doi:10.4172/2375-4389.1000162

Katono, I. W. (2020). *Cultural predictions of entrepreneurial orientation and the moderating role of entrepreneurial competencies on graduate entrepreneurial intentions: A cross-sectional survey of East Africa*. https://scholar.google.com/citations?user=HQE6PycAAAAJ&hl=en&oi=sra

Kautonen, T., & Palmroos, J. (2010). The impact of a necessity-based start-up on subsequent entrepreneurial satisfaction. *The International Entrepreneurship and Management Journal*, *6*(3), 285–300. doi:10.100711365-008-0104-1

Keane, J. (2015, July 3). Why we should still be reading democracy in America. *The Conversation*. doi:https://theconversation.com/why-we-should-still-be-reading-democracy-in-america-44174

Kennedy, P. (1988). *African Capitalism: The Struggle for Ascendancy*. Cambridge University Press.

Kestin, T., van den Belt, M., Denby, L., Ross, K., Thwaites, J., & Hawkes, M. (2017). *Getting started with the SDGs in universities: A guide for universities, higher education institutions, and the academic sector*. Academic Press.

Keukeleire, S., & Delreux, T. (2014). *The Foreign Policy of the European Union* (2nd ed.). doi:10.1007/978-1-137-02576-0

Khadiagala, G. (2013). Theories and concepts of regional integration in Africa. In D. Monyae & S. Nkala (Eds.), The Quality for Unity: An Appraisal of Regional Integration in Africa (pp. 21-41). Sunnyside: Jacana Media Ltd.

Khadiagala, G. M., & Lyons, T. (2001). Foreign Policy Making in Africa: An Introduction. In G. M. Khadiagala & T. Lyons (Eds.), *African Foreign Policies: Power and Processes* (pp. 1–14). Lynne Rienner Publishers, Inc. doi:10.1515/9781685850210-002

Khadiagala, L. S. (2001). The failure of popular justice in Uganda: Local councils and women's property rights. *Development and Change*, *32*(1), 55–76. doi:10.1111/1467-7660.00196

Khaketla, B. M. (1971). *Lesotho 1970: An African Coup Under the Microscope*. C. Hurst and Co.

Khampepe, S., & Moseneke, D. (2002). *Report on the 2002 Presidential Elections in Zimbabwe*. Office of the President of South Africa. Pretoria: Judicial Observer Commission. http://zimbabwe-today.com/wp-content/uploads/2014/11/Report-on-the-2002-Presidential-Elections-of-Zimbabwe.pdf

Khapoya, V. B. (2012). Colonialism and the African experience. In *The African Experience* (4th ed.). Routledge.

Khavul, S., Bruton, G. D., & Wood, E. (2009). Informal family business in Africa. *Entrepreneurship Theory and Practice*, *33*(6), 1219–1238. doi:10.1111/j.1540-6520.2009.00342.x

Kiamba, J. M. (2009). Women and leadership positions: Social and cultural barriers to success. *Wagadu Volume 6. Journal of International Women's Studies, 10*(1), 89.

Kibler, E., Kautonen, T., & Fink, M. (2017). Regional social legitimacy of entrepreneurship: Implications for entrepreneurial intention and start-up behaviour. In *Entrepreneurship in a Regional Context* (pp. 57–77). Routledge. doi:10.4324/9781315691985-4

Kidane, Y. (2014). Women's leadership role in post-conflict peacebuilding process. *Journal of African Union Studies, 3*(2-3), 87-101.

Kimani, E. N., & Kombo, D. K. (2010). Gender and poverty reduction: A Kenyan context. *Educational Research Review, 5*(1), 24.

Kimenyi, N. S. & Mbaku, J. K. (2011). Africa's war on corruption: foresight Africa: The continent's greatest challenges and opportunities. *The Brookings Institutions*, 30-32.

Kim, Y., & Chen, H. T. (2016). Social media and online political participation: The mediating role of exposure to cross-cutting and like-minded perspectives. *Telematics and Informatics, 33*(2), 320–330. doi:10.1016/j.tele.2015.08.008

Kinsella, E. A. (2010). Professional knowledge and the epistemology of reflective practice. *Nursing Philosophy, 11*(1), 3–14. doi:10.1111/j.1466-769X.2009.00428.x PMID:20017878

Kirchgassner, G. (2003). *Abstention because indifference and alienation and its consequences for party competition: a simple psychological model.* University of Gallen: Economics Discussion paper 12.

Kitchner, K. S. (1983). Cognition, metacognition, and epistemic cognition. *Human Development, 26*(4), 222–232. doi:10.1159/000272885

Klinke, H. (Ed.). (2014). *Art theory as visual epistemology.* Cambridge Scholars Publishing.

Klobucista, C., & Mariel Ferragamo, M. (2023). *Africa's 'Leaders for Life.* Council on Foreign Relations.

Knappe, H. (2017). Participatory and Deliberative Democracy: From Equality Norms to Argumentative Rationalities. In Doing Democracy Differently (pp. 45–76). Verlag Barbara Budrich. doi:10.2307/j.ctvbkk41f.8

Knight, F. (1921). *Risk, Uncertainty and Profit.* Houghton Mifflin.

Koch, M. (2022). State-civil society relations in Gramsci, Poulantzas and Bourdieu: Strategic implications for the degrowth movement. *Ecological Economics, 193*, 107275–107300. doi:10.1016/j.ecolecon.2021.107275

Koma, S.B. (2010). The state of local government in South Africa: Issues, trends and options. *Journal of Public Administration.*

Koohafkan, P., & Delacruz, M. (2011). Conservation and adaptive management of globally important agricultural heritage systems (GIAHS). *Journal of Resources and Ecology, 2*, 12–13.

Kovalchuk, S., & Rapoport, A. (2020). *Democratic Citizenship Education in Non-Western Contexts: Implications for Theory and Research.* Routledge. doi:10.4324/9780429293313

Koyame, M., & Clark, J. F. (2002). The economic impact of the Congo War. In *The African stakes of the Congo war* (pp. 201–223). Palgrave Macmillan US. doi:10.1057/9781403982445_12

Krapohl, S., Meissner, K. L., & Muntschick, J. (2014). Regional Powers as Leaders or R ambos? The Ambivalent Behaviour of Brazil and South Africa in Regional Economic Integration. *Journal of Common Market Studies, 52*(4), 879–895. doi:10.1111/jcms.12116

Krasner, S. D. (1981). Power structures and regional development banks. *International Organization, 35*(2), 303–328. doi:10.1017/S0020818300032458

Kreiser, P. M., Marino, L. D., Dickson, P., & Weaver, K. M. (2010). Cultural influences on entrepreneurial orientation: The impact of national culture on risk taking and proactiveness in SMEs. *Entrepreneurship Theory and Practice, 34*(5), 959–983. doi:10.1111/j.1540-6520.2010.00396.x

Kropotkin, P. (1897). *The State*. Freedom Press.

Krüger, L., & Ratka, E. (2014). *"A new response to a changing neighbourhood?": The Perception of European Policies in Tunisia after the Arab Spring*. Academic Press.

Kubler, D., & Kriesi, H. (2017). How globalization and mediatization challenge our democracies: Results from the NCCR Democracy. *Schweizerische Zeitschrift für Politikwissenschaft, 23*(3), 321–245. doi:10.1111psr.12265

Kujala, J., & Sachs, S. (2019). The practice of stakeholder engagement. In J. Harrison, J. Barney, & R. E. Freeman (Eds.), *The Cambridge handbook of stakeholder theory* (pp. 121–140). Cambridge University Press. doi:10.1017/9781108123495.014

Kumar, R. (2021). Bringing the developmental state back in: Explaining South Korea's successful management of COVID-19. *Third World Quarterly, 42*(7), 1397–1416. doi:10.1080/01436597.2021.1903311

Kurki, M. (2012). *How the EU can adopt a new type of democracy support.* Fundación para las Relaciones Internacionales y el Diálogo Exterior - FRIDE, Working paper No. 112, Madrid.

Kurtishi-Kastrati, S. (2013). The Effects Of Foreign Direct Investments For Host Country's Economy. *European Journal of Interdisciplinary Studies, 5*(1).

Kuumba, M. B. (2006). African women, resistance cultures and cultural resistances. *Agenda (Durban, South Africa), 20*(68), 112–121.

Kwakwa, P. A., Adzawla, W., Alhassan, H., & Oteng-Abayie, E. F. (2023). The effects of urbanization, ICT, fertilizer usage, and foreign direct investment on carbon dioxide emissions in Ghana. *Environmental Science and Pollution Research International, 30*(9), 23982–23996. doi:10.100711356-022-23765-4 PMID:36331739

Kwon, S.-W., Heflin, C., & Ruef, M. (2013). Community social capital and entrepreneurship. *American Sociological Review, 78*(6), 980–1008. doi:10.1177/0003122413506440

La Rue, F. (2011). *Report of the special rapporteur on the promotion and protection of the right to freedom of opinion and expression.* United Nations General Assembly.

Laeven, L., & Valencia, F. (2008). *Systemic Banking Crises: A New Database.* IMF Working Paper 08/224.

Lakoff, S. (1996). *Democracy: history, theory, practice.* Westview. Press.

Lall, S. (2005). FDI, AGOA and manufactured exports by a landlocked, least developed African economy: Lesotho. *The Journal of Development Studies, 41*(6), 998–1022. doi:10.1080/00220380500155254

Lall, S., & Streeten, P. (1977). *Foreign Investment, Transnationals and Developing Countries.* Macmillan. doi:10.1007/978-1-349-02290-8

Lamarche, C; Toysen, T; & Wishart, A (2019). *The country that cannot collapse: Fragility Analysis of Zimbabwe: Policy recommendations for USAID.* Academic Press.

Landes, D. S. (2000). Culture Makes Almost All the Difference. In Culture Matters: How Values Shape Human Progress. Basic Books.

Landsberg, C. (2005). Toward a Developmental Foreign Policy?: Challenges for South Africa's Diplomacy in the Second Decade of Liberation. *Social Research*, *72*(3), 723–756. doi:10.1353or.2005.0041

Landsberg, C. (2018). Introduction: Bolstering pan-African Agency: From Africa Rising to Africa rising up! In C. Landsberg (Ed.), *Africa Rising Up: Perspectives on African Renewal* (pp. 15–36). Real African Publishers.

Landsberg, C., & Graham, C. (2017). *Government and Politics in South Africa- Coming of age* (5th ed.). Pretoria Van Schaik Publishers.

Latour, B. (1986). Visualization and cognition. *Knowledge in Society*, *6*(6), 1–40.

Latour, B. (1999). *Pandora's hope: Essays on the reality of science studies.* Harvard university press.

Lawal, A. (2022). *Professor Matthew Statler Economic Inequality: Perspectives, Policies, and Practices I.* Introduction.

Lawton Smith, H., Chapman, D., Wood, P., Barnes, T., & Romeo, S. (2014). Entrepreneurial academics and regional innovation systems: The case of spin-offs from London's universities. *Environment & Planning*, *32*(2), 341–359.

Lazzarini, S. G., Musacchio, A., Bandeira-de-Mello, R., & Marcon, R. (2015a). What do state-owned development banks do? Evidence from BNDES, 2002-09. *World Development*, *66*, 237–253. doi:10.1016/j.worlddev.2014.08.016

Le Pere, G. L. (2014). Critical themes in South Africa's foreign policy. *Strategic Review of Southern Africa, 36*(2), 31.

Lee, B. (2018). *Social media is changing: These 3 things are the key to staying ahead of it.* INC. https://www.inc.com/ben-lee/heres-what-an-evolving-social-medialandscape-means-for-business-owners.html

Lekalake, R. (2017). *Beyond the Arab Spring: Will economic and security challenges further test Tunisia's democracy?* [Policy paper]. Afrobarometer Policy Paper. https://www.afrobarometer.org/publication/pp40-beyond-arab-spring-will-economic-and-security-challenges-further-test-tunisias/

Lelimo, M. M. (1998). The reasons for the annexation of Lsotho 1868: a new perspective. Submitted in fulfilment of the requirements for the degree Magister Artium. Department of History. University of the Free State, Bloemfontein.

Lesotho Defence Force Act. 1996 (Act No.4 of 1996). https://lesotholii.org/ls/legislation/num-act/1996/4.

Lessig, L. (2013). "Institutional Corruption" Defined. *The Journal of Law, Medicine & Ethics*, *41*(3), 553–555. doi:10.1111/jlme.12063 PMID:24088144

Lewis, D., & Jackson, J. (2005). Safari hunting and conservation on communal land in southern Africa. People and Wildlife, Conflict or Co-existence? 9, 239. doi:10.1017/CBO9780511614774.016

Lewis, C. (1991). *The Ethics Challenge in Public Service: A Problem-Solving Guide.* Jossey-Bass.

Lewis, J. (1970). *History of Philosophy*. The English Universities Press Ltd.

Li, D., Wei, L. Q., Cao, Q., & Chen, D. (2022). Informal institutuions, entepreneurs' political participation, and venture internationalization. *Journal of International Business Studies*, *53*(6), 1062–1090. doi:10.105741267-021-00402-9

Likoti, F. J. (2007). The 1998 Military Intervention in Lesotho: SADC Peace Mission or Resource War? *International Peacekeeping*, *14*(2).

Lim, M. (2013). Framing Bouazizi: White lies, hybrid network, and collective/connective action in the 2010–11 Tunisian uprising. *Journalism*, *14*(7), 921–941. doi:10.1177/1464884913478359

Liñán, F., & Chen, Y. W. (2009). Development and Cross-Cultural application of a specific instrument to measure entrepreneurial intentions. *Entrepreneurship Theory and Practice*, *33*(3), 593–617. doi:10.1111/j.1540-6520.2009.00318.x

Lindgren, S. (2017). Digital media and society. *Sage (Atlanta, Ga.)*.

Lindner, R. (2023). Green hydrogen partnerships with the G lobal South. Advancing an energy justice perspective on "tomorrow's oil". *Sustainable Development (Bradford), 31*(2), 1038–1053. doi:10.1002d.2439

Lin, N. (1999). Building a network theory of social capital. *Connections, 22*(1), 28–51.

Linz, J. J., & Stephan, A. (1996). Towards Democratic Consolidated Democracy. *Journal of Democracy, 7*(2), 45–57. doi:10.1353/jod.1996.0031

Lipsey, R., & Chrystal, A. (2005). *Economics*. Oxford University Press.

Lipton, M. (2009). Understanding South Africa's foreign policy: The perplexing case of Zimbabwe. *South African Journal of International Affairs, 16*(3), 331–346. doi:10.1080/10220460903495181

Lisakafu, J. (2017). The Southern African Development Community and the Challenges of Southern Africa Regional Security. *Huria: Journal of the Open University of Tanzania, 24*(1), 163–190.

List, F. (2022). *The National System of Political Economy*. Imperium Press.

Liu, H., Saleem, M. M., Al-Faryan, M. A. S., Khan, I., & Zafar, M. W. (2022). Impact of governance and globalization on natural resources volatility: The role of financial development in the Middle East North Africa countries. *Resources Policy, 78*, 102881. doi:10.1016/j.resourpol.2022.102881

Lloyd, L. (2013). *South Africa's Media 20 years after Apartheid*. Centre for International Media Assistance.

Locatelli, G., Mariani, G., Sainati, T., & Greco, M. (2017). Corruption in public projects and megaprojects: There is an elephant in the room! *International Journal of Project Management, 35*(3), 252–268. doi:10.1016/j.ijproman.2016.09.010

Lorenzini, S. (2014). Comecon and the South in the years of détente: a study on East–South economic relations. *European Review of History: Revue européenne d'histoire, 21*(2), 183-199.

Lucas, R. E. Jr. (1988). On the Mechanics of Economic Development. *Journal of Monetary Economics, 22*(1), 3–42. doi:10.1016/0304-3932(88)90168-7

Lues, L. (2014). Citizen participation as a contributor to sustainable democracy in South Africa. *International Review of Administrative Sciences, 80*(4), 789–807. doi:10.1177/0020852314533450

Lundahl, M. O., & Petersson, L. (2019). *The Dependent Economy: Lesotho and the Southern African Customs Union*. Routledge. doi:10.4324/9780429309984

Lundahl, M., McCarthy, C., & Petersson, L. (2003). *In the Shadow of South Africa: Lesotho's Economic Future*. Ahsgate.

Luo, Y. (2005). An Organizational Perspective of Corruption. *Management and Organization Review, 1*(01), 119–154. doi:10.1111/j.1740-8784.2004.00006.x

Lyatuu, E.T., Nie, F., & Fang, C. (2015). *The role of agriculture in the economic growth and poverty reduction in Tanzania*. Academic Press.

MacEwan, A. (1999). *Neo-liberalism or Democracy? Economic strategy, markets, and alternatives for the 21st century*. Zed Books.

MacGregor, S. (2010). *The Politics of Poverty: Elites, Citizens and States: Findings from ten years of DFID-funded research on Governance and Fragile States 2001–2010*. A Synthesis Paper.

Maclean, S. J. (2002). Mugabe at war: The political economy of conflict in Zimbabwe. *Third World Quarterly*, *23*(3), 513–528. doi:10.1080/01436590220138402

Madir, J. (2019). *What Process is Due – Sanctions Regimes of Multilateral Development Banks*. University of Westminster.

Madu, A. Y., & Abdulmalik, T. A. (2020). *An assessment of factors responsible for voter apathy in Africa: Empirical evidence from 2019 Nigerian presidential election*. The International Seminar on Regional Politics, Administration and Development 2020 (INSORPAD2020), STISIPOL Raja Haji, Riau, INDONESIA, 14-15.

Magi, L. M. (2007). To create or conserve, that is the question: The case of St. Lake Lucia. *Journal of Tourism & Hospitality (Los Angeles, Calif.)*, *4*(2), 1–12.

Mahadea, D. (2023). Economic Progress, Poverty. The Nexus between Poverty and Corruption: Quo Vadis? 322.

Mahao, L. (2006). *The Power of Hegemonic Theory in Southern Africa: Why Lesotho Cannot Develop an Independent Foreign Policy.* [Thesis submitted in Partial Fulfilment of the Requirements for the Master of Arts Degree in International Relations, Rhodes University].

Mahlakeng, M. K. (2014). *Political Will Versus Political Entitlement: The Left-Right Political Spectrum of Lesotho.* Southern African Peace and Security (SACCPS). http://saccps.blogspot.com/search/label/M.%20K.%20Mahlakeng.

Mahlakeng, M. K. (2017). *Lesotho's Upcoming Elections: The Collapse of a Second Coalition Government.* Southern African Peace and Security (SACCPS). http://saccps.blogspot.com/search/label/M.%20K.%20Mahlakeng. Accessed: 06-02-2019.

Mahlakeng, M. K. (2018). *Lesotho's rule of law and judicial independence under threat: attempts to politicise the Judiciary*. Southern African Peace and Security (SACCPS) http://saccps.blogspot.com/search/label/M.%20K.%20Mahlakeng. Accessed: 06-02-2019.

Mahlakeng, M. K. (2018). *Understanding Lesotho's political-security discourse and its historical and contemporary relevance.* Southern African Peace and Security (SACCPS). http://saccps.blogspot.com/search/label/M.%20K.%20 Mahlakeng. Accessed: 06-02-2019.

Maier, K. (2000). *This House has fallen: Nigeria in Crisis*. Westview.

Makgoba, M. W. (1997). Mokoko, the makgoba affair: A reflection on transformation. Florida Hills, South Africa: Vivlia.

Makulilo, B., & Ntaganda, E. (2016). *Election management bodies in East Africa*. African Minds. doi:10.47622/9781920677978

Makwana, B., Lee, Y., Parkin, S., & Farmer, L. (2018). *Selfie-Esteem: The relationship between body dissatisfaction and social media in adolescent and young women*. The Inquisitive Mind.

Malatji, T. L. (2021). Unemployment and regional human mobility; all roads lead to South Africa. *African Journal of Development Studies*, *11*(3), 169.

Malefane, M. R. (2021). Investigating the Core–Periphery Relationship in the Southern African Customs Union. *The Review of Black Political Economy*, *48*(2), 190–205. doi:10.1177/0034644620963040

Malefane, M. R., & Odhiambo, N. M. (2016). The Evolution of Trade Policy in Botswana. *Global Journal of Emerging Market Economies*, *8*(1), 22–34. doi:10.1177/0974910115613705

Malimela, L. P. (2010). *Analyzing Thabo Mbeki's policy of quiet diplomacy in the Zimbabwean crisis* [Master's thesis]. University of Cape Town.

Malindini, K., & Mackett, O. (2018). Trade liberalisation and female employment in Botswana and South Africa. *GLOBUS Research Paper, 14*.

Maliszewska, M., van der Mensbrugghe, D., Pereira, M., Osorio-Rodarte, I., & Ruta, M. (2020). *The African Continental Free Trade Area: Economic and Distributional Effects*. Academic Press.

Malmberg, T. (2023). Media studies, Le Bon's psychology of crowds, and qualitative-normative research on propaganda, 1880-2020. *Nordic Journal of Media Studies, 5*(1), 17–31. doi:10.2478/njms-2023-0002

Malone, A. (1990). Quotable quotes for quoters. *The Clarion (Guwahati)*.

Mamokhere, J., & Meyer, D. F. (2023). *Towards an Exploration of the Significance of Community Participation in the Integrated Development Planning Process in South Africa*. Academic Press.

Mandaza, I. (1991). *The one party state and democracy: The Zimbabwe debate*. Academic Press.

Manggat, I., Zain, R., & Jamaluddin, Z. (2018). The impact of infrastructure development on rural communities: A literature review. *International Journal of Academic Research in Business & Social Sciences, 8*(1), 637–648. doi:10.6007/IJARBSS/v8-i1/3837

Mangu, A. M. (2014). The African Union and the promotion of democracy and good political governance under the African Peer-Review Mechanism: 10 years on. *African Review (Dar Es Salaam, Tanzania), 6*(1), 59–72. doi:10.1080/09744053.2014.883757

Mankiw, N. G. (2007). *Macroeconomics*. Worth publishers.

Manoel, L., Costa, A. C., & Cabral, P. (2022). Voter turnout in Portugal: A geographical perspective. *Papers in Applied Geography, 8*(1), 88–111. doi:10.1080/23754931.2021.1958251

Mapfumo, L. (2019). *Public Participation and Collaborative Governance in Zimbabwe flea Markets: A case study of the City of Harare*. Academic Press.

Maphiri, M., Matasane, M. A., & Mudimu, G. (2021). Challenges to the effective implementation of SDG 8 in creating decent work and economic growth in the Southern African Hemisphere: Perspectives from South Africa, Lesotho and Zimbabwe. In *Global Challenges to CSR and Sustainable Development: Root Causes and Evidence from Case Studies* (pp. 39–63). Springer International Publishing. doi:10.1007/978-3-030-62501-6_3

Mapuva, J. W. M. (2014). The SADC regional bloc: What challenges and prospects for regional integration? *Law, Democracy & Development, 18*(1), 22–36. doi:10.4314/ldd.v18i1.2

Marango, T., Francis, J., & Adgibolosso, S. (2016). Realities of Communication and Social Inclussion in Zimbabwe Local Government: A Case of the Eastern Chimanimani District. *Review of Human Factor Studies, 22*(1), 104–128.

Marangunić, N., & Granić, A. (2015). Technology acceptance model: A literature review from 1986 to 2013. *Universal Access in the Information Society, 14*(1), 81–95. doi:10.100710209-014-0348-1

Maraswa, T., Mongale, I. P., & Mokgola, A. (2020). The ramifications of non-elite political instability on the Zimbabwean economy: Vecm analysis. *African Journal of Development Studies, 10*(3), 253–275. doi:10.31920/2634-3649/2020/10n3a13

Marazza, D., Campanale, L., Wur, G.V.V., & Balugani, P.E. (2021). *Integrated study and modelling of the factors affecting small-scale subsistence farming in eSwatini (southern Africa) through the use of causal diagrams and agent-based models*. Academic Press.

Mare, A. (2021). WiFi 6 tech deployed for the first time in SA Elections. ITWeb. https://www.itweb.co.za/content/PmxVE7KlPQpMQY85

Marenga, R. (2020). Analysing the performance of public enterprises in Namibia: A challenge for the practice of public administration? *Journal of Governance &Regulation*, *9*(3), 96–109. doi:10.22495/jgrv9i3art7

Markauskaite, L., & Goodyear, P. (2017). Professional Epistemic Games. In *Epistemic Fluency and Professional Education* (pp. 395–434). Springer Netherlands. doi:10.1007/978-94-007-4369-4_14

Marquette, H., & Pfeiffer, C. (2015). *Corruption and collective action.* The Developmental Leadership Program (DLP) and U4 Research Paper 32.

Marsteintredet, L., & Malamud, A. (2019). Coup with Adjectives: Conceptual stretching or Innovation in comparative research? *Political Studies*, 1–22. doi:10.1177/0032321719888857

Martinsson, J. (2021). Combatting institutional corruption: The policy-centered approach. *Crime, Law, and Social Change*, *75*(3), 267–280. doi:10.100710611-021-09934-5

Marumahoko, S., & Chigwata, T. C. (2020). The idea of a new Zimbabwe post-Mugabe. *The History and Political Transition of Zimbabwe: From Mugabe to Mnangagwa*, 299-329.

Marumo, P. O., & Chakale, M. (2018). Mbeki on African Renaissance: A vehicle for Africa development. *African Renaissance*, *15*(4), 179–191. doi:10.31920/2516-5305/2018/V15n4a9

Maseko, M. M. (2022). *Social media, protest and citizen participation in local government: A comparison between the City of Cape Town and Johannesburg metropolitan municipalities: 2010 to 2017.* [PhD Thesis, University of the Western Cape].

Mashimye, R. (2023). The ideological roots of regional integration in Africa. In D. Monye & S. Nkala (Eds.), The Quality for Unity: An Appraisal of Regional Integration in Africa (pp. 43-64). Sunnyside: Jacana Media Ltd.

Masiko-Kambala, P., Görgens, T., & van Donk, M. (2012). Advancing 'networked spaces': Making a case for communities of practice to deepen public participation. In *GGLN (Good governance learning network) Putting participation at the heart of development//Putting development at the heart of participation*. GGLN and Isandla Institute.

Masoud, T. (2015). Has the Door Closed on Arab Democracy? *Journal of Democracy*, *26*(1), 74–87. doi:10.1353/jod.2015.0013

Masoud, T. (2018). Review Chapter: Why Tunisia? *Journal of Democracy*, *29*(4), 166–175. doi:10.1353/jod.2018.0071

Masunungure, E. (2015). *The Changing Role of Civil Society in Zimbabwe's Democratic Processes: 2014 and Beyond.* Harare: Frederich Ebert Stiftung. https://library.fes.de/pdf-files/bueros/simbabwe/13718.pdf

Mataka, B., & Nkandu, M. O. (2020). The effects of voter apathy on the growth of electoral democracy in Zambia with a special focus on Kabwe central constituency. *Global Journal of Advanced Research*, *7*(3), 81–87.

Matambo, M., Moyo, G., Mukonza, R., & Lewis, E. (2022). Corporate governance and credibility gap: Four decades of struggling reform efforts in Zimbabwe. *African Renaissance*, *19*(4), 105–126. doi:10.31920/2516-5305/2022/19n4a5

Mathlouthi, N. (2019). *EU As a Normative Power in The Med Region: Democracy Promotion in Tunisia* [Thesis].

Matlosa, K. (2023). The free movement of persons and African integration. In D. Monye & S. Nkala (Eds.), The Quality for Unity: An Appraisal of Regional Integration in Africa (pp. 265-289). Sunnyside: Jacana Media Ltd.

Matlosa, K. (2005). From a destabilising factor to a de-politicised and professional force: The military in Lesotho. In M. M. Rupiya (Ed.), *Evolutions & Revolutions: A Contemporary History of Militaries in Southern Africa*. Institute for Security Studies.

Matlosa, K. (2017). Understanding political crisis of Lesotho's Post-2015 Elections. In M. Thabane (Ed.), *Towards an Anatomy of Persistent Political Instability in Lesotho, 1966-2016*. Morija Printing Works.

Matlosa, K. (2020). Pondering the culture of violence in Lesotho: A case for Demilitarisation. *Journal of Contemporary African Studies, 38*(3), 381–398. doi:10.1080/02589001.2020.1749246

Matos, A., Barraza, L., & Ruiz-Mallén, I. (2021). Linking conservation, community knowledge, and adaptation to extreme climatic events: A case study in Gorongosa National Park, Mozambique. *Sustainability (Basel), 13*(11), 6478. doi:10.3390u13116478

Mattlin, M. (2011). *Politicized society: The long-shadow of Taiwan's one-party legacy. Nordic Institute of Asia Studies*. NIAS.

Maundeni, Z. (2010). Developmental States: Their Historical Absence and their Emergence in Post Conflict Southern Africa. *The Open Area Studies Journal, 3*(1), 30–40. doi:10.2174/1874914301003010030

Maunganidze, F., Bonnin, D., & Ruggunan, S. (2021). Economic Crisis and professions: Chartered Accountants in Zimbabwe. *SAGE Open, 11*(1), 1–14. doi:10.1177/2158244021994802

Mazarura, J. (2016). Is Public Corruption the Main Cause of Low Foreign Direct Investment in Zimbabwe? *British Journal of Economic Finance and Management Sciences, 13*(1), 1–18.

Maziriri, E. T., Mapuranga, M., Maramura, T. C., & Nzewi, O. I. (2019). Navigating on the key drivers for a transition to a green economy: Evidence from women entrepreneurs in South Africa. *Entrepreneurship and Sustainability Issues, 7*(2), 1686–1703. doi:10.9770/jesi.2019.7.2(62)

Mbah, S., & Igariwey, I. E. (2001). *African Anarchism: The History of a Movement Tucson*. Sharp Press.

Mbaku, J. M. (2020). Threats to democracy in Africa: The rise of the Constitutional Coup. Brookings.

Mbeki, T. (2015). *Illicit Financial Flows: Report on the High Level Panel on Illicit Financial Flows from Africa*. Addis Ababa: African Union Commission/United Nations Economic Commission for Africa. https://www.uneca.org/sites/default/files/PublicationFiles/iff_main_report_26feb_en.pdf

Mbella, M. R. E., Yari, A. F., & Sama-Lang, R. B. (2018). Youths and Peacebuilding in Africa: Socio-Political & Economic Exclusion and the Role Youths Play in Peacebuilding in Africa. *Young African Leaders Journal of Development, 2*(1), 8. doi:10.32727/24.2018.33

Mbete, S. (2014). The Economic Freedom Fighters: South Africa's turn towards populism? *Journal of African Elections, 14*(1), 35–59.

Mbigi, L., & Maree, J. (1995). *Ubuntu: The spirit of African transformation and management*. Sigma Press.

Mbuende, K. M. (2014). Namibia and the southern African development community. Namibia's Foreign Relations: Historic Contexts, Current dimensions, and Perspectives for the 21st Century, 231-252.

McAdam, R., Hazlett, S., & Casey, C. (2005). Performance management in the UK public sector: Addressing multiple stakeholder complexity. *International Journal of Public Sector Management, 18*(3), 256–273. doi:10.1108/09513550510591542

McDowall, A. (2022, August 17). Tunisia constitution giving President wider powers comes into effect. *Reuters*. https://www.reuters.com/world/africa/tunisia-constitution-giving-president-wider-powers-comes-into-effect-2022-08-16/

McGann, J. (2016). *The Fifth Estate: Think Tanks, Public Policy and Governance*. The Brooking Institution Press.

McGregor, J., & Primorac, R. (Eds.). (2010). *Zimbabwe's new diaspora: Displacement and the cultural politics of survival* (Vol. 31). Berghahn Books.

McKay, S. (2004). Women, human security, and peacebuilding: A feminist analysis. *Conflict and human security: A search for new approaches of peacebuilding, 19*, 152-170.

Mdlovu, N. (2021). *Exchange rate pass-through to domestic prices under the common monetary area of Southern Africa: the case of Eswatini*. University of Johannesburg.

Mehta, R., & Gretter, S. (2016. Hashtag activism and gender advocacy: A virtual ethnography of activism on Twitter. Conference paper: *Literacy Research Associated*. Nashville, TN.

Melber, H. (2021). Populism in southern Africa under liberation movements as governments: The cases of Namibia, South Africa, and Zimbabwe. In Oswald, M (Ed). The Palgrave Handbook of Populism. Cham. Palgrave Macmillan.

Melber, H., & Saunders, C. (2001). *Transition in Southern Africa: Comparative Aspects*. Nordiska Afrikainstitutet. https://www.files.ethz.ch/isn/102626/10.pdf

Melber, H. (2014). *Understanding Namibia: The trials of independence*. Ocford University Press., doi:10.1017/S0022278X15000543

Mellor, K. (2022). Developing a decolonial gaze: Articulating research/er positionality and relationship to colonial power. *Access: Critical Explorations of Equity in Higher Education, 10*(1), 26-41.

Mendelson, S. (2015). Why governments target civil society, and what can be done in response: A new agenda. Centre for Strategic and International Studies. Midlands State University. *Social Dialogue*. www.msu.ac.zw/elearning/.../1173420720SOCIAL%20DIALOGUE%20NOTES.doc

Merdith, M. (2018). Mugabe misrule. And how it will hold Zimbabwe back. *Foreign Affairs, 97*(2), 129–138.

Meunier, S. (2017). Integration by stealth: How the European Union gained competence over foreign direct investment. *Journal of Common Market Studies, 55*(3), 593–610. doi:10.1111/jcms.12528

Mfundisi, A. (2006). Civic Participation and Voting Patterns in Botswana. *Journal of African Elections*.

Mhango, G. A. (2012). *Is Quiet Diplomacy in Consonance with Meaningful peace-making in SADC?* Lessons from Zimbabwe.

Micco, A., Yanez, M., & Panizza, U. (2007). Bank ownership and performance. Does politics matter? *Journal of Banking & Finance, 31*(1). doi:10.1016/S0305-750X(01)00073-0

Michau, L., Horn, J., Bank, A., Dutt, M., & Zimmerman, C. (2015). Prevention of violence against women and girls: Lessons from practice. *Lancet, 385*(9978), 1672–1684. doi:10.1016/S0140-6736(14)61797-9 PMID:25467577

Micheal, O. E. (2018). Politics and governance: A critique of the 2019 Nigeria presidential election. *International Journal of Academic Research in Public Policy and Governance, 5*(1), 50–70.

Mickoleit, A. (2014). Social media use by governments: A policy primer to discuss trends, identify policy opportunities and guide decision makers. *OECD Working Papers on Public Governance, No. 26*. OECD Publishing.

Milazzo, A., & Goldstein, M. (2019). Governance and women's economic and political participation: Power inequalities, formal constraints and norms. *The World Bank Research Observer, 34*(1), 34–64. doi:10.1093/wbro/lky006

Miller, L. E., Martini, J., Larrabee, F. S., Rabasa, A., Pezard, S., Taylor, J. E., & Mengistu, T. (2012). Democratization and Democracy Promotion: Trends, Theories, and Practices. In *Democratization in the Arab World* (pp. 9–34). RAND Corporation. https://www.jstor.org/stable/10.7249/mg1192rc.10

Miller, M. L., & Vaccari, C. (2020). Digital threats to democracy: Comparative lessons and possible remedies. *The International Journal of Press/Politics*, *25*(3), 333–356. doi:10.1177/1940161220922323

Millstein, M. (2010). Limits to local democracy: The politics of urban governance transformations in Cape Town, Working Paper No. 2, *Swedish Centre for Local Democracy (ICLD): ICLD*, Visby.

Mirembe, R., & Davis, L. (2001). Is schooling a risk? Gender, power relations and school culture in Uganda. *Gender and Education*, *13*(4), 401–416. doi:10.1080/09540250120081751

Miščević, N. (2017). Thought experiments in political philosophy. In *The Routledge companion to thought experiments* (pp. 153–170). Routledge. doi:10.4324/9781315175027-9

Mitchell, R. K., Agle, B. R., & Wood, D. J. (1997). Toward a theory of stakeholder identification and salience: Defining the principle of who and what really counts. *Academy of Management Review*, *22*(4), 853–886. doi:10.2307/259247

Miti, K. (2012). South Africa and conflict resolution in Africa: From Mandela to Zuma. *Southern African Peace and Security Studies*, *1*(1), 26–42.

Mkandawire, E., Mentz-Coetzee, M., Mangheni, M. N., & Barusi, E. (2021). Enhancing the Glopan Food Systems Framework by Integrating Gender: Relevance for Women in African Agriculture. *Sustainability (Basel)*, *13*(15), 8564. doi:10.3390u13158564

MKandirwe, T., & Soludo, C.C. (1999) Our Continent, Our Future: African Perspectives on Structural Adjustment. Trenton, NJ: Africa World Press.

Mkhize, M. C. (2008). *Assessing South Africa's" quiet diplomacy" towards Zimbabwe: strengths and weaknesses* [Doctoral dissertation].

Mlambo, D. N. (2017). *Regional supremacy or coalition? Evaluating South Africa's regional integration efforts within the Southern African Development Community (SADC)* [Doctoral dissertation]. University of Zululand.

Mlambo, D.N. (2015). *The role of the SADC as a tool for regional integration in Southern Africa*. Academic Press.

Mlambo, A. S. (2014). *A history of Zimbabwe*. Cambridge University Press. doi:10.1017/CBO9781139128919

Mlambo, A., & Raftopoulos, B. (2010, April). The regional dimensions of Zimbabwe's multi-layered crisis: An analysis. In *Election processes, Liberation movements and Democratic change in Africa Conference*. CMI and IESE.

Mlambo, C., & Kapingura, F. (2019). Factors influencing women political participation: The case of the SADC region. *Cogent Social Sciences*, *5*(1), 1681048. doi:10.1080/23311886.2019.1681048

Mlambo, D. N., & Adetiba, T. C. (2020). Post-1994 South Africa's peacekeeping and military intervention in Southern Africa, reference from the Democratic Republic of Congo (DRC) and Lesotho. *Journal of Public Affairs*, *20*(1), e1984. doi:10.1002/pa.1984

Mlambo, D. N., & Adetiba, T. C. (2020). South Africa and regional integration in Southern Africa post-1994: Realities, challenges, and prospects. *Journal of Nation-Building and Policy Studies*, *4*(1), 5–33. doi:10.31920/2516-3132/2020/v4n1a1

Mlambo, D. N., & Mlambo, V. H. (2021). To What Cost to its Continental Hegemonic Standpoint: Making Sense of South Africa's Xenophobia Conundrum Post Democratization. *Journal of Ethnic and Cultural Studies*, *8*(2), 347–361. doi:10.29333/ejecs/696

Mlambo, D. N., & Ogunnubi, O. (2018). South Africa's integration efforts within the Southern African Development Community: Regional supremacy or coalition? *Journal of Public Affairs*, *18*(4), e1856. doi:10.1002/pa.1856

Mlambo, S. (2013). Becoming Zimbabwe or Becoming Zimbabwean: Identity Nationalism, or State-Building. *Africa Spectrum*, *1*(1), 49–70. doi:10.1177/000203971304800103

Mlambo, V. H., Thusi, X., Zubane, S., & Mlambo, D. N. (2022). The African Continental Free Trade Area: Challenges and Possible Successes. *Latin American Journal of Trade Policy*, *5*(12), 75–106. doi:10.5354/0719-9368.2022.64897

Mmaduabuchi, G. S. (2015). Elections and voting behavior. In R. Anifowose & F. C. Enemuo (Eds.), *Element of Politics* (2nd ed., pp. 210–226). Sam Iroanusi Publications.

Mmereki, D., Baldwin, A., & Li, B. (2016). A comparative analysis of solid waste management in developed, developing and lesser developed countries. *Environmental Technology Reviews*, *5*(1), 120–141. doi:10.1080/21622515.2016.1259357

Mngomezulu, B. (2021). *Foreign Policy Posture in Post-Apartheid South Africa: Consistencies and Ambiguities*. Cambridge Scholars Publishing.

Mo Ibrahim Foundation. (2023). *2022 Ibrahim Index of African governance*. https://mo.ibrahim.foundation/iiag/downloads

Modi, I. (2015). Social exclusion and inequality: Challenges before a developing society. *Sociological Bulletin*, *64*(1), 3–14. doi:10.1177/0038022920150101

Moeller, J., Vreeese, D., Esser, F., & Kunz, R. (2013). Pathway to political participation: The influence of online and offline news media on internal efficacy and turnout of first-time voters. *The American Behavioral Scientist*, *58*(5), 689–700. doi:10.1177/0002764213515220

Moffit, B., & Tormey, S. (2014). Rethinking populism: Politics, mediation and political style. *Political Studies*, *62*(2), 381–397. doi:10.1111/1467-9248.12032

Mofya, T. N. (2022). Role of Women in Peace Building in Zambia: Case of Northern Province. *International Journal of Conflict Management*, *3*(1), 61–95. doi:10.47941/ijcm.1010

Mohamed Sghaier, I. (2023). Trade openness, financial development and economic growth in North African countries. *International Journal of Finance & Economics*, *28*(2), 1729–1740. doi:10.1002/ijfe.2503

Moliki, A. O., & Dauda, K. O. (2014). Political apathy, electoral process and Nigeria's democracy: A study of the 2014 Ekiti governorship election. TASUED. *Journal of Applied Education and Vocational Research*, *12*(1).

Montgomery, A. W., Dacin, P. A., & Dacin, M. T. (2012). Collective social entrepreneurship: Collaboratively shaping social good. *Journal of Business Ethics*, *111*(3), 375–388. doi:10.100710551-012-1501-5

Monyane, C. (2009). *The Kingdom of Lesotho: An Assessment of Problems in Democratic Consolidation*. [Dissertation presented for the Degree of Doctor of Philosophy at Stellenbosch University].

Moraghen, W., Seetanah, B., & Sookia, N. U. H. (2023). The impact of exchange rate and exchange rate volatility on Mauritius foreign direct investment: A sector-wise analysis. *International Journal of Finance & Economics*, *28*(1), 208–224. doi:10.1002/ijfe.2416

Moremoholo, E. (2005). The role of the military in the political conflict in Lesotho: with special reference to the 1998 failed Coup d'etat. University of Kwazulu Natal, Durban.

Morisset, J. (2000). Foreign Direct Investment in Africa: Policies Also Matter. *Transnational Corporations*, *9*(2).

Morozov, E. (2011). *The net delusion: The dark aide of internet freedom*.

Morozov, E. (2009). Iran: Downside to the "Twitter revolution". *Dissent, 56*(4), 10–14. doi:10.1353/dss.0.0092

Morrison, A. (2000). Initiating entrepreneurship. In *Enterprise and Small Business: Principles, Practice and Policy.* Prentice Hall.

Morrow, S. (2015*). Causes of low voter turnout of the Hispanic Population in South-West Texas* [Doctoral dissertation]. Walden University.

Mothibe, T. (2002). State and Society, 1824-1833. In Pule, N and Thabane, M (Eds.). Essays on Aspects of the Political Economy of Lesotho 15000-2000. National University of Lesotho. Morija Printing Works.

Mothibe, T., & Ntabeni, M. (2002). The Role of the Missionaries, Boers and British in Social and Territorial Changes, 1833-1868. In Pule, N and Thabane, M (Eds.). Essays on Aspects of the Political Economy of Lesotho 15000-2000. National University of Lesotho. Morija Printing Works.

Motoyama, Y., & Watkins, K. (2014). *Examining the connections within the start up ecosystem.* Kauffman Research Series on City, Metro, and Regional Entrepreneurship.

Motseki, M., Maluleke, W., & Dlamini, S. (2020). Military role in democratic transition and succession: Lessons from the Kingdom of Lesothos. *Cogent Social Sciences, 6*(1), 1. doi:10.1080/23311886.2020.1847845

MoyerJ. D.KabandulaA.BohlD.HannaT. (2021). Conditions for success in the implementation of the African continental free trade agreement. *Available at* SSRN 3941470. doi:10.2139/ssrn.3941470

Moyo, N & Besada, H (2008). Zimbabwe in Crisis: Mugabe's Policies and Failures. *The Centre for International Governance Innovation Technical Paper, 38*, 1-29.

Moyo, M., Simson, R., Jacob, A., & De Mevius, F. (2012). *Attaining middle income status-Tanzania: growth and structural transformation required to reach middle income status by 2025.* International Growth Centre, London School of Economics and Political Science.

Moyo, S. (2013). Regime survival stratergies in Zimbabwe in the 21st century. *AJPSIR, 7*(2), 67–78.

Moyo, S., & Yeros, P. (2007). The Radicalised State: Zimbabwe's Interrupted Revolution. *ROAPE, 34*(111), 103–121.

Mpofu, F. Y. (2022). Green Taxes in Africa: Opportunities and challenges for environmental protection, sustainability, and the attainment of sustainable development goals. *Sustainability (Basel), 14*(16), 10239. doi:10.3390u141610239

Mpuga, P. (2010). Constraints in access to and demand for rural credit: Evidence from Uganda. *African Development Review, 22*(1), 115–148. doi:10.1111/j.1467-8268.2009.00230.x

Mtiki, L. (2022). Mineral Resource Management and Economic Growth: What Zambia Should Learn from Chile. *Journal of Economics, Finance and Accounting Studies, 4*(2), 191–205.

Muboko, N. (2017). The role of transfrontier conservation areas and their institutional framework in natural resource-based conflict management: A review. *Journal of Sustainable Forestry, 36*(6), 583–603. doi:10.1080/10549811.2017.1320224

Mudde, C. (2014). The populist Zeitgeist. *Government and Opposition, 39*(4), 541–563. doi:10.1111/j.1477-7053.2004.00135.x

Mudde, C., & Kaltwasser, C. R. (2017). *Populism: A very short Introduction.* Oxford University Press. doi:10.1093/actrade/9780190234874.001.0001

Mude, T., & Chigora, P. (2013). Promoting good governance in crisis ridden country: The Zimbabwean dilemma in the 21st century. *JASPS, 1*(1), 27–33.

Mueller, S. L., & Thomas, A. S. (2001). Culture and entrepreneurial potential: A nine country study of locus of control and innovativeness. *Journal of Business Venturing*, *16*(1), 51–75. doi:10.1016/S0883-9026(99)00039-7

Mukumbang, F. C., Ambe, A. N., & Adebiyi, B. O. (2020). Unspoken inequality: How COVID-19 has exacerbated existing vulnerabilities of asylum-seekers, refugees, and undocumented migrants in South Africa. *International Journal for Equity in Health*, *19*(1), 141. doi:10.118612939-020-01259-4 PMID:32819364

Mulinge, M. M., & Lesetedi, G. N. (1998). Interrogating Our Past: Colonialism and Corruption in Sub-Saharan Africa. *Afri J Polit Sci*, *3*(2), 15–28.

Muller, A. (2019). The meaning of populism. *Philosophy and Social Criticism*, *45*(9-10), 1025–1057. doi:10.1177/0191453719872277

Muller, J. W. (2017). The rise of populism. In F. Gonzalez (Ed.), *The Age of Perplexity: Rethinking the World We Knew*. Penguin Random House.

Munene, J. C., Schwartz, S. S., & Smith, P. B. (2000). Development in Sub-Saharan Africa: Cultural influences and managers' decision behavior. *Public Administration and Development*, *20*(4), 339–351. doi:10.1002/1099-162X(200010)20:4<339::AID-PAD139>3.0.CO;2-#

Mungai, E. N., & Ogot, M. (2012). Gender, culture and entrepreneurship in Kenya. *International Business Research*, *5*(5), 175-183.

Mungwari, T. (2017). *Representation of political conflict in the Zimbabwean press: The case of the Herald, the Sunday Mail, Daily News and the Standard, 1999-2016* [Unpublished PhD Thesis]. University of South Africa, Pretoria.

Muqayi, S., & Chimwara, O. (2019). The Sustainability of Diamond Mining in Zimbabwe. *The Sustainability Ethic in the Management of the Physical, Infrastructural andNatural Resources of Zimbabwe*, 423.

Muriisa, R. (2005). *The Privatisation Experience in Uganda: Prospects and Challenges in its Implementation. In The potentiality of 'developmental states' in Africa: Botswana and Uganda compared*. CODESRIA.

Musa, A. A. (2014). Political parties and democratic consolidation in Nigeria. In *Democracy and Development in Nigeria*. Palgrave Macmillan.

Musendekwa, M. (2016). Colonisation as an obstacle to Civilisation: a critical evaluation of Albert Schweitzer's Experiences and Observations. In I.J.J. Spangenberg & C. Landman (Eds.), The legacies of Albert Schweitzer reconsidered. Cape Town: AOSIS.

Musendekwa, M. (2018). Messianic characterisation of Mugabe as rhetorical propaganda tolegitimise his authority in crisis situations. *Studia Historiae Ecclesiasticae*, *44*(3), 1–17. doi:10.25159/2412-4265/4059

Musingafi, M C, Chadamoyo, P., & Dumbu, E. (n.d.). Fighting corruption in post-conflict situations'. *International Journal of Innovative Research in Management*, *4*(1), 12-24.

Musingafi, M. C., Mupa, P., Dumbu, E. (2011). Post-conflict reconstruction: A

Mutambara, T. E. (2009). Regional transport challenges within the Southern African Development Community and their implications for economic integration and development. *Journal of Contemporary African Studies*, *27*(4), 501–525. doi:10.1080/02589000903399488

Mutanda, D. (2014). The Impact of the Zimbabwean Crisis on the Parastatals. *International Journal of Politics and Good Governance*, *5*(2), 1-14.

Mutsvairo, B. and Ragnedda, M. (2019). *Comprehending the digital disparities in Africa*. Springer. . doi:10.1515/9789048538225-003

Mutumwa, W. T., & Ufuwoma, A. (2022). *Critical Journalism and Media Convergence During the COVID-19 Pandemic: Representation of Corruption in Zimbabwean Online News. In health Crisis and Media Discourses in Sub-Saharan Africa*. Springer.

Muyambwa, D. F. (2018). *Corruption as a violation of Human and People's Rights: Implications for Youth in Zimbabwe*. Academic Press.

Muzurura, J. (2016). Is public corruption the main cause of low foreign direct investment in Zimbabwe. *British Journal of Economics. Finance and Management Sciences, 13*(1), 1–18.

Mwananyanda, M. (n.d.). *Obituary: Robert Mugabe- 1924-2019, a liberator turned an oppressor*. https://www.amnesty.org/

Mwaradzika, M. (2015). *The role of civil society organisations in promoting democratic process in Zimbabwe, 1980-2013. Unpublished mini-thesis. Gweru*. Midlands State University.

Mwatwara, W., Mujere, J., & Mkodzongi, G. (2022). Between violence and negotiation: Gold-rushes, gang violence, and negotiated access in artisanal gold mining along Zimbabwe's Great Dyke. *The Extractive Industries and Society, 11*(11), 101103. doi:10.1016/j.exis.2022.101103

Mwavu, E. N., Ariango, E., Ssegawa, P., Kalema, V. N., Bateganya, F., Waiswa, D., & Byakagaba, P. (2016). Agrobiodiversity of homegardens in a commercial sugarcane cultivation land matrix in Uganda. *The International Journal of Biodiversity Science, Ecosystem Services & Management, 12*(3), 191–201. doi:10.1080/21513732.2016.1177595

Mzekandaba, S. 2021. New tech 'catapulted' electoral management, says IEC. ITWeb. https://www.itweb.co.za/content/JN1gP7OYgWwqjL6m

Nagar, D., & Paterson, M. (2013). The History of Regionalism in Southern Africa: From SADCC to SADC. In *South Africa in Southern Africa* (pp. 9–12). Centre for Conflict Resolution. https://www.jstor.org/stable/resrep05170.6

Naguib, R. (2015). The behaviour of multi-national enterprises in developing countries: Having a sense of the "good" through smart partnerships in Malaysia. In R. Molz, C. Ratiu, & A. Taleb (Eds.), *Local versus Global Logic: The Multinational Enterprise in Developing Countries* (pp. 134–153). Routledge.

Namahoro, J. P., Qiaosheng, W., & Hui, S. (2023). Economic growth, natural resource rents, and business openness nexus in regions and income levels of Africa: Evidence from recent panel estimators. *Mineral Economics, 36*(4), 1–16. doi:10.100713563-022-00362-y

Nassif, H. B. (2022). Coup in Tunisia: Why the Military Abandoned Democracy. *Journal of Democracy, 33*(1), 27–39. doi:10.1353/jod.2022.0002

Nathan, L. (2005). Consistency and inconsistencies in South African foreign policy. *International Affairs, 81*(2), 361–372. doi:10.1111/j.1468-2346.2005.00455.x

National Academies of Sciences, Engineering, and Medicine. (1992). *Democratization in Africa: African Views, African Voices*. The National Academies Press. . doi:10.17226/2041

National Information Technology Authority Survey 2017/18 Report. (n.d.). https://www.nita.go.ug/sites/

National Open University. (2015). *Politics of Development and Underdevelopment*. The National Open University of Nigeria.

NCHE. (2018/19). State of higher education and Training in Uganda. A Report on Higher Education Delivery and Institutions, Kampala.

Ncube, N. (2011). *Zimbabwe 2011.* Global Integrity Report.

Ndaguba, E. A., & Hanyane, B. (2019). Stakeholder model for community economic development in alleviating poverty in municipalities in South Africa. *Journal of Public Affairs, 19*(1), e1858. doi:10.1002/pa.1858

Ndakaripa, M. (2021). Zimbabwe's economic meltdown: Are sanctions really to blame? *The Washington Quarterly, 44*(2), 95–120. doi:10.1080/0163660X.2021.1934997

Ndala, N. N., & Pelser, T. (2019). Examining the effectiveness of entrepreneurship policy implementation in Malawi. *Journal of Contemporary Management, 16*(2), 234–255. doi:10.35683/jcm19036.34

Ndlela, N (2017). The African paradigm: The Coverage of the Zimbabwean Crisis in the Norwegian media. *Strategic Review for Southern Africa, 39*(2), 71-90.

Ndlovu-Gatsheni, S. J., Ruhanya, P., Ndlovu-Gatsheni, S., & Ruhanya, P. (2020). Postscript: A tale of broken promises. In *The history and political transition of Zimbabwe: From Mugabe to Mnangagwa* (pp. 389-398). News24. https://www.news24.com

Ndofirepi, A. P., & Gwaravanda, E. T. (2019). Epistemic (in) justice in African universities: A perspective of the politics of knowledge. *Educational Review, 71*(5), 581–594. doi:10.1080/00131911.2018.1459477

Ndonga, D., Chihaka, S., & Fielder, A. (2021). Integration of gender practices and promotion of diversity in customs and trade: The case of East and Southern Africa. *World Customs Journal, 15*(1).

Ndonga, D., Laryea, E., & Chaponda, M. (2020). Assessing the potential impact of the African continental free trade area on least developed countries: A case study of Malawi. *Journal of Southern African Studies, 46*(4), 773–792. doi:10.1080/03057070.2020.1767888

Ndou, D. N. (2012). *An investigation into the reasons for failure of community-based projects at Folovhodwe, Limpopo* [Doctoral dissertation].

Nduwimana, F. (2006). *United Nations Security Council Resolution 1325 (2000) on Women, Peace and Security Understanding the Implications, Fulfilling the Obligations. Office of the Special Adviser on Gender Issues and Advancement of Women.* OSAGI.

Neethling, T. (2000). Conditions for Successful Entry and Exit: An Assessment of SADC Allied Operations in Lesotho. *Monograph No 44: Boundaries of Peace Support Operations.*

Neethling, T. (1999, May). Military Intervention in Lesotho: Perspective on Operation Boleas and Beyond. *The Online Journal of Peace and Conflict Resolution, 2*(2), 1–12.

Nelson, R. M. (n.d.). *Multilateral Development Banks: Overview and Issues for Congress.* Academic Press.

Nelson, R. R., & Winter, S. G. (1982). *An evolutionary theory of economic change.* Harvard University Press.

Neocosmos, M. (2010). *From Foreign Natives to Native Foreigners. Explaining Xenophobia in Post-apartheid South Africa: Explaining Xenophobia in Post-apartheid South Africa: Citizenship and Nationalism, Identity and Politics.* African Books Collective.

News24. (2017a). Zuma slams 'senseless' killing of Lesotho's chief of defence force. *News24.* https://www.news24.com/news24/africa/news/zuma-slams-senseless-killing-of-lesothos-chief-of-defence-force-20170905. Accessed: 19-08-2019.

News24. (2017b). Lesotho's political strife to cost SADC millions. News24, 17th September. https://www.news24.com/news24/southafrica/news/lesothos-political-strife-to-cost-sadc-millions-20170916. Accessed: 19-08-2019.

News24. (2020). Senekala: Malema instructs EFF supporters to 'march into town'. News24. https://www.news24.com/news24/southafrica/news/senekal-malema-instructs-eff-supporters-to-march-into-town-20201016>

News24. (2023). *Only one cable-laying ship can fix snapped underwater cables and it's still on the other side of Africa.* News24. https://www.news24.com/news24/tech-and-trends/news/only-one-cable-laying-ship-can-fix-snapped-underwater-cables-and-its-still-on-the-other-side-of-africa-20230815

Ngoma, M., Ntale, P. D., & Castro, M. (2021). Entrepreneurial activity in the Albertine Graben region of Uganda: The role of infrastructure development and entrepreneurial orientation. *World Journal of Entrepreneurship, Management and Sustainable Development, 17*(3), 601–615. doi:10.1108/WJEMSD-04-2020-0028

Nguea, S. M., Noula, A. G., & Noumba, I. (2023). Financial globalization and democracy: Implications for economic growth in African countries. *Journal of the Knowledge Economy*, 1–25. doi:10.100713132-023-01311-y

Ngugi, W. A. (1981). Decolonising the Mind: The Politics of Language in African Literature. Heinemann.

Ngumbela, X. G., Khalema, E. N., & Nzimakwe, T. I. (2020). Local worlds: Vulnerability and food insecurity in the Eastern Cape province of South Africa. *Jamba (Potchefstroom, South Africa), 12*(1), 1–10. doi:10.4102/jamba.v12i1.830 PMID:32832036

Nguyen, T. T., Grote, U., Neubacher, F., Do, M. H., & Paudel, G. P. (2023). Security risks from climate change and environmental degradation: Implications for sustainable land use transformation in the Global South. *Current Opinion in Environmental Sustainability, 63*, 101322. doi:10.1016/j.cosust.2023.101322

Ngwoke, P. N., & Ituma, E. A. (2020). Ethno-religious conflict and sustainable development in Nigeria. *Hervormde Teologiese Studies, 76*(4).

Nichter, S. (2014). Conceptualizing vote buying. *Electoral Studies, 35*, 315–327. doi:10.1016/j.electstud.2014.02.008

Nie, N. H., & Erbring, L. (2000). Internet and society: A preliminary report. *Stanford Institute for the Quantitative Study of Society., 3*, 14–19.

Nitsche, L. (2019). *A tale of two Kenyas: Digitalization has brought change but not always for the better.* Akademie. https://akademie.dw.com/en/a-tale-of-two-kenyas-digitalization-has-brought-change-but-not-always-for-the-better/a-47198710 (Accessed 7 August 2023).

Niyonkuru, F. (2016). Failure of foreign aid in developing countries: A quest for alternatives. *Business and Economics Journal, 7*(3), 1–9.

Nkala, S., & Monyae, D. (2023). Introduction: Regional integration in Africa's development. In D. Monye & S. Nkala (Eds.), The Quality for Unity: An Appraisal of Regional Integration in Africa (pp. 1-17). Sunnyside: Jacana Media Ltd.

Nkondo, M. (2023). African lingua francas and African knowledge systems; A framework for regional integration. In D. Monye & S. Nkala (Eds.), The Quality for Unity: An Appraisal of Regional Integration in Africa (pp. 65-85). Sunnyside: Jacana Media Ltd.

Norgaard, K. M. (2019). *Salmon and acorns feed our people: Colonialism, nature, and social action.* Rutgers University Press.

Norris, P. (2001). *Digital divide: Civic engagement, information poverty, and the internet worldwide.* Cambridge University Press. doi:10.1017/CBO9781139164887

Norris, P. (2010). *Democratic Phoenix: Reinventing Political Activism*. Cambridge University Press.

North, D. C., & Weingast, B. N. (1989). Constitution and Commitment: The Evolution of Institutional Governing Public Choice in Seventeenth Century England. *The Journal of Economic History*, *49*(4), 803–832. doi:10.1017/S0022050700009451

Noutcheva, G. (2015). Institutional governance of European Neighbourhood Policy in the wake of the Arab Spring. *Journal of European Integration*, *37*(1), 19–36. doi:10.1080/07036337.2014.975987

Nshimbi, C. C., Moyo, I., & Oloruntoba, S. O. (2018). Borders, informal cross-border economies and regional integration in Africa-an introduction. *Africa Insight*, *48*(1), 3–11.

Nthontho, A. N. (2017). Children as stakeholders in education: Does their voice matter? *South African Journal of Childhood Education*, *7*(1), 7. doi:10.4102ajce.v7i1.434

Nwaoba, P. I. (1999). Critical factors affecting Nigeria's foreign exchange flows. *CBN Economic & Financial Review*, *37*(3), 1-17.

Nwosu, P. O. (2009). Understanding Africans' conceptualizations of intercultural competence. The SAGE handbook of intercultural competence, 158-178.

Nxopo, Z. (2014). *The Role of Government in Empowering Female Entrepreneurs in the Western Cape, South Africa* [Master's dissertation]. Cape Peninsula University of Technology, Cape Town.

Nyabuga, G., & Otieno, C. (2018). *Mediating Politics and Democracy: Making Sense of the Role of the Media in Kenya*. Nairobi: Media Focus on Africa Foundation. https://www.mediafocusonafrica.org/media-roundtables/result/mediatising-politics-and-democracy-making-sense-role-media-kenya

Nyadera, I. N., Agwanda, B., Onder, M., & Mukhtar, I. A. (2022). Multilateralism, Developmental Regionalism, and the African Development Bank. *Politics and Governance*, *10*(2). Advance online publication. doi:10.17645/pag.v10i2.4871

'Nyane, H. (2016). Formation of a government in Lesotho in the case of a hung parliament. *Law, Democracy and Development, 20*. Cape Town.

Nyasimi, M., Okang'a, J., Mutuo, M., & Masira, J. (2009). Change from within: Engaging local communities in achieving the Millennium Development Goals in Sub–Sahara Africa. *Omertaa J. Appl. Anthropol*, 474-494.

Nye, J. S. (1990). Soft power. *Foreign Policy*, (80), 153–171. doi:10.2307/1148580

Nyeko, B. (2002a). Resistance to the Colonial Rule and the Emergence of Anti-Colonial Movements. In Pule, N and Thabane, M (Eds.). Essays on Aspects of the Political Economy of Lesotho 15000-2000. National University of Lesotho. Morija Printing Works.

Nyeko, B. (2002b). The Independence Movement, 1952-1966. In Pule, N and Thabane, M (Eds.). Essays on Aspects of the Political Economy of Lesotho 15000-2000. National University of Lesotho. Morija Printing Works.

Nzegwu, N. (2019). African Art in Deep Time: De-race-ing Aesthetics and De-racializing Visual Art: Nzegwu African Art in Deep Time. *The Journal of Aesthetics and Art Criticism*, *77*(4), 367–378. doi:10.1111/jaac.12674

O'Dwyer, M., & Gilmore, A. (2015). Value and alliance capability and the formation of strategic alliances in SMES: The impact of customer orientation and resource optimization. *Journal of Business Research*, *87*, 58–68. doi:10.1016/j.jbusres.2018.02.020

Obangome, G. W. (2023). *Gabon officers declare military coup, President Ali Bongo detained*. Reuters. https://www.reuters.com/world/africa/gabonese-military-officers-announce-they-have-seized-power-2023-08-30

Obeyori, F. (2009). Poverty and Underdevelopment: Threat to participatory democracy. *The Constitution: A Journal of Constitutional Development, 9*(3), 17-25.

Obiagu, U. C., Udeji-Okpalaku, C. O., & Udeh, C. O. (2021). The Undermining Consequences of Inconclusive Elections on Democratic Consolidation in Africa: Interrogating Nigerian Elections, 2011-2019. *African Journal of Democracy and Election Research, 1*(2), 7–40.

Obonyo, J. A. (2014). A gendered critique of women in peace and conflict situations in Africa. *Research on Humanities and Social Sciences, 4*(26), 87–96.

Odigbo, J., & Okafor, C. O. (2019). State militarization of election and management of electoral process in Nigeria's 2019 general elections. *Kwararafa Journal of Contemporary Research, 7*(1), 69–83.

OECD/African Development Bank. (2012). *Stocktaking of Business Integrity and Anti-Bribery Legislation, Policies and Practices in Twenty African Countries.* Available: https://www.oecd.org/daf/anti-bribery/stocktakingofbusinessintegrity-andanti-briberylegislationpoliciesandpracticesintwentyafricancountries

Ogege, S. O. (2009). Conflict resolution and peace building: the gender question in the Niger delta crisis in Nigeria. *African Research Review, 3*(5).

Ogudare, Y. D. (2023). *Governance and Public Protests.* IGI Global.

Ogundare, Y. D. (2023). Governance and Public Protest: Exercising Democratic Accountability in Lebanon. In Insights and Explorations in Democracy, Political Unrest, and Propaganda in Elections (pp. 69-81). IGI Global.

Ogundiya, I. S. (2020). Democracy and good governance: Nigeria's dilemma. *African Journal of Political Science and International Relation, 5*(6), 201–208.

Ogunnubi, O., & Isike, C. (2015). Regional hegemonic contention and the asymmetry of soft power: A comparative analysis of South Africa and Nigeria. *Strategic Review for Southern Africa, 37*(1), 152.

Ogunnubi, O., & Tella, O. (2017). Framing South Africa's soft power through non-state sources. *Strategic Analysis, 41*(5), 478–495. doi:10.1080/09700161.2017.1343228

Ojakorotu, V., & Adeleke, A. A. (2018). Nigeria and conflict resolution in the sub-regional West Africa: The quest for a regional hegemon. *Insight on Africa, 10*(1), 37–53. doi:10.1177/0975087817735386

Ojo, O. (2022). More than victims: The roles of women in conflict resolution and peacebuilding in Nigeria. *KIU Interdisciplinary Journal of Humanities and Social Sciences, 3*(2), 92–111.

Okafor, O. C., Odigbo, J., & Okeke, C. R. (2022). Two Decades of Electoral Democracy: Voter Apathy and Democratization Process in Nigeria. Social Sciences and Education Research Review, 9(1).

Okafor, H. O. (2018). Multilateralism, regionalism, and the effectiveness of trade policy in sub-Saharan African. In C. Landsberg (Ed.), *Africa Rising Up: Perspectives on African Renewal* (pp. 197–209). Real African Publishers.

Okafor, V. O. (2005). *A Roadmap for understanding African Politics: Leadership and Political Integration in Nigeria.* Routledge.

Okey, R. (1986). *Eastern Europe 1740-1985: feudalism to communism.* Hutchinson Education.

Okolie, A., Nnamani, K. E., Ezirim, G. E., Enyiazu, C., & Ozor, A. C. (2021). Does liberal democracy promote economic development? interrogating electoral cost and development trade-off in Nigeria's fourth republic. *Cogent Social Sciences, 7*(1), 1918370. doi:10.1080/23311886.2021.1918370

Okoronkwo-Chukwu, U. (2013). Female representation in Nigeria: The case of the 2011 general elections and the fallacy of 35% affirmative action. *Research on Humanities and Social Sciences, 3*(2), 39–46.

Okunloye, R. W. (2017). Monetization of Politics and Elections in Fourth Republican Nigeria: Implications for Sustainable Democratic Governance. *KIU Journal of Social Humanities, 2*(2A), 77–85.

Olagbaju, O. O., & Awosusi, O. E. (2019). Herders-farmers' communal conflict in Nigeria: An indigenised language as an alternative resolution mechanism. *International Journal of Multidisciplinary and Current Research, 7*.

Olaifa, O. (2017). Curbing violent extremism through peace building in Nigeria. *Journal of US-China Public Administration, 14*(4), 221–223.

Olaitan, Z. (2023). Feminist Rethinking of the Representation of African Women in Peacebuilding: A Theoretical Analysis. *African Journal of Gender Social Development, 12*(1), 185.

Olaitan, Z. M. (2018). *Women's Participation in Peace Processes in Nigeria*. Challenges and Prospects.

Olamide, A. O. (2018). Foreign Exchange Market Efficiency in Nigeria (The Past and Current Exchange Rate Returns). *Sumerianz Journal of Economics and Finance, 1*(1), 14–21.

Olander, S. (2007). Stakeholder impact analysis in construction project management. *Construction Management and Economics, 25*(3), 277–287. doi:10.1080/01446190600879125

Oloka-Onyango, J. (Ed.). (2001). *Constitutionalism in Africa: Creating opportunities, facing challenges*. Fountain Publishers.

Olonade, O. Y., Oyibode, B. O., Idowu, B. O., George, T. O., Iwelumor, O. S., Ozoya, M. I., Egharevba, M. E., & Adetunde, C. O. (2021). Understanding gender issues in Nigeria: The imperative for sustainable development. *Heliyon, 7*(7), e07622. doi:10.1016/j.heliyon.2021.e07622 PMID:34377858

Olonisakin, F., Barnes, K., & Ikpe, E. (2010). *Women, peace and security: translating policy into practice*. Routledge. doi:10.4324/9780203837085

Oloo, J. O., Makenzi, P. M. D., & Mwangi, J. G. P. (2013). Influence of traditions/customs and beliefs/norms on women in tree growing in Siaya County, Kenya. *Global Journal of Environmental Science and Technology, 1*(1), 1-6.

Oloruntoba, S. O. (2023). The state, Regional Integration, and Economic Development in Africa: Rethinking the Neo-Liberal Paradigm. In C. Landsberg (Ed.), *Africa Rising Up: Perspectives on African Renewal* (pp. 1211–1226). Real African Publishers.

Olsen, G. R. (1998). Europe and the Promotion of Democracy in Post-Cold War in Africa: How Serious is Europe and for What Reason? *African Affairs, 97*(388), 343–367. doi:10.1093/oxfordjournals.afraf.a007948

Olufade, A. O. (2013). Nigerian Women, Politics and the National Identity Question. *American Educational Research Journal, 1*(3), 161–170.

Olusanya, S. (2013). Impact of Foreign Direct Investment Inflow on Economic Growth in a Pre and Post Deregulated Nigeria Economy. A Granger Causality Test (1970-2010). *European Scientific Journal, 9*(25).

Olusola, O. R. (2013). *Hegemonic order and regional stability in Sub-Saharan Africa: a comparative study of Nigeria and South Africa* [Doctoral dissertation].

Oluwagbohunmi, M. F. (2020). Political Apathy: A Worrisome Impediment to Electoral Process in Nigeria. International Institute for Science, Technology and Education, 4(4).

Oluwole, V. (2022). 10 African countries that have the most number of internet users in 2022. In *Business Insider Africa*. https://africa.businessinsider.com/local/markets/10-african-countries-that-have-the-most-number-of-internet-users-in-2022/cy3p01v

Oluwole, V. (2023). African countries leading in democracy index rankings. *Business Insider, Africa.*

Oluwole, V. (2023). *African nations leading in democracy index rankings*. Business Insider Africa.

Omagor, C., & Mubiru, P. (2014). Courage, Purpose and Entrepreneurship. *International Journal of Business and Social Science*, *5*(6), 239–246.

Omitola, B., Akinrinde, O. O., & Omitola, A. (2021). Traditional Institutions and Socio-economic Development in Nigeria: A Critical Analysis. *Journal of Law and Legal Reform*, *2*(4), 539–552. doi:10.15294/jllr.v2i4.48587

Omotola, J. S. (2010). Political liberalization and democratization in Africa: Theoretical perspectives and methodological approaches. In *The Democratization Project in Africa*, Accomplishments, Challenges, and Prospects. Palgrave Macmillan.

Omotola, J. S. (2014). Governance and corruption in Nigeria: The way forward. In *Good Governance and Development in Nigeria*. Palgrave Macmillan.

Onebunne, J. I., & Okechukwu, S. (2021). African Ecological Crisis and Education. *Journal of African Studies and Sustainable Development.*

Onoge, O. (1997). *The democratic imperative in Africa. Claude Ake Memorial lecture series no. 1*. African Centre for Democratic Governance.

Onuoha, F., & Ojo, J. (2018). *Practice and Perils of Vote Buying in Nigeria's Recent Election Pretoria*. African Center for the Constructive Resolution of Dispute.

Onwe, P. S. (2021). An examination of good governance and the state of security in Nigeria. In A. S. Ihuah & P. A. Idachaba (Eds.), *Philosophy and national security: Interrogations in a distressed nation* (Vol. 1, pp. 25–64). Eagle Prints.

Onwuegbuchulam, S., & Matambo, E. (2023). Constraining space for civil society participation and contestation in Nigeria's politics. *African Renaissance*, 13-33. doi:10.31920/2516-5305/2023/20n2a1

Onyebukwa, C. F. (2021). The Dilemma of natural resources and upsurge of conflicts in Africa: A cursory look at the Marikana management approaches in South Africa. Political economy of resource, human security and environmental conflicts in Africa, 277-296.

O'Reilly, M., Súilleabháin, A. Ó., & Paffenholz, T. (2015). *Reimagining peacemaking: Women's roles in peace processes*. Academic Press.

Oreskovich, A. (2011). *Egyptian activist creates image issue for Google*. Reuters. https://www.reuters.com/article/us-egypt-google-idUSTRE71B0L520110212

Osaghae, E. (1988). *Political Analysis (POS 211)*. UI External Studies Programme.

Osei, M. J., & Kim, J. (2023). *Financial development and the growth effect of foreign direct investment: Does one size fit all?* International Economics.

Osler, A., & Starkey, H. (2005). *Changing Citizenship – Democracy and Inclusion in Education*. Open University Press.

Osoba, S. O. (1996). Corruption in Nigeria: Historical Perspectives. *Review of African Political Economy*, *69*(69), 371–386. doi:10.1080/03056249608704203

Ossome, L. (2020). African feminism. In *Routledge Handbook of Pan-Africanism* (pp. 159–170). Routledge. doi:10.4324/9780429020193-11

Ostrovsky, A. (2015). *The Invention of Russia: The Journey from Gorbachev's Freedom to Putin's War*. Atlantic Books.

Osvaldo, S. (1969). National Development Policy and External Dependence in Latin America. *The Journal of Development Studies*, *6*(1).

Oteh, A., (2010). *Making capital markets work for SMEs in Africa*. A paper presented as the key note address of the 2010 Kikonyogo Capital Markets Award on 6th May 2010.

Owen-Smith, J., & Powell, W. (2004). Knowledge networks as channels and conduits: The effects of spillovers in the Boston biotechnology community. *Organization Science*, *15*(1), 5–21. doi:10.1287/orsc.1030.0054

Oyelaran-Oyeyinka, O., & Lal, K. (2016). Structural transformation in developing countries: cross regional analysis. *United Nations Human Settlements Program (UN-Habitat), 1*.

Özçelik, A. (2018). *A Litmus Test for Europe: EU Mediterranean Politics After the Arab Spring*. The World Community and the Arab Spring.

Ozekhome, H. O. (2021). Determinants of Real Exchange Rate in Nigeria: An Empirical Investigation. *Asian Journal of Economic and Finance*, *3*(4), 487505.

Paciello, M. C. (2011). *Tunisia: Changes and Challenges of Political Transition*. Istituto Affari Internazionali (IAI). https://www.jstor.org/stable/resrep09864.7

Paffenholz, T. (2018). Women in peace negotiations. *Gendering diplomacy and international negotiation*, 169-191.

Page, J. M. (2016). *Industry in Tanzania: Performance, prospects, and public policy* (No. 2016/5). WIDER Working paper.

Page, M. (2021). *PRISMA 2020 explanation and elaboration: Updated guidance and exemplars for reporting systematic reviews*. BMJ. https://www.bmj.com/content/372/bmj.n160

Page, M. J., McKenzie, J. E., Bossuyt, P. M., Boutron, I., Hoffmann, T. C., Mulrow, C. D., Shamseer, L., Tetzlaff, J. M., Akl, E. A., Brennan, S. E., Chou, R., Glanville, J., Grimshaw, J. M., Hróbjartsson, A., Lalu, M. M., Li, T., Loder, E. W., Mayo-Wilson, E., McDonald, S., ... Moher, D. (2021). The PRISMA 2020 statement: An updated guideline for reporting systematic reviews. *International Journal of Surgery*, *88*, 105906. doi:10.1016/j.ijsu.2021.105906 PMID:33789826

Pakenham, T. (1991). *The Scramble for Africa: 1876-1912*. Jonathan Ball Publishers.

Pandey, R. (2013). Trade Elasticities and the Marshal Lerner Condition for India. *Global Journal of Management and Business Studies,* 423-428.

Pandey, N., de Coninck, H., & Sagar, A. D. (2022). Beyond technology transfer: Innovation cooperation to advance sustainable development in developing countries. *Wiley Interdisciplinary Reviews. Energy and Environment*, *11*(2), e422. doi:10.1002/wene.422

Panse, G., Fyall, A., & Alvarez, S. (2021). Stakeholder views on sustainability in an urban destination context: An inclusive path to destination competitiveness. *International Journal of Tourism Cities*, *7*(4), 895–915. doi:10.1108/IJTC-10-2020-0225

Park, S. (2023). The African Development Bank and the Accountability Policy Norm: Endogenous Change, Norm Conformance, and the Development Finance Regime Complex. *Global Governance: A Review of Multilateralism and International Organizations, 29*(1), 61–84. doi:10.1163/19426720-02901003

Park, C. L. (2017). Distinctions to promote an integrated perspective on meaning: Global meaning and meaning-making processes. *Journal of Constructivist Psychology, 30*(1), 14–19. doi:10.1080/10720537.2015.1119082

Parlevliet, M. (2010). Rethinking conflict transformation from a human rights perspective. *Human rights and conflict transformation: The challenges of just peace*, 15-46.

Parreñas, R. S. (2009). Transnational mothering: A source of gender conflicts in the family. *North Carolina Law Review, 88*, 1825.

Parry, G., Moyser, G., & Day, N. (1992). *Political Participation and Democracy in Britain*. Cambridge University Press. doi:10.1017/CBO9780511558726

Pasara, M. T., & Diko, N. (2020). The effects of AfCFTA on food security sustainability: An analysis of the cereals trade in the SADC region. *Sustainability (Basel), 12*(4), 14–19. doi:10.3390u12041419

Patience, J.J., & Nel, D. (2022). *Governance, Democracy and Accountability from a Network Governance Perspective within the City of Ekurhuleni*. Academic Press.

Patrick, H. O. (2020). Winning hearts and minds; fostering inclusiveness through community development tactics in South Africa. In P. Kariuki, M. Goyayi, & S. Mhlongo (Eds.), *Social Cohesion in the Last Decade: Taking Stock to Inform the New Decade* (pp. 119–161). Democracy Development Program. Atlas Printers.

Patrick, H. O., Ugwanyi, J. I., Akuche, A. B., & Mba, C. C. (2022). Federalism and the Politics of Restructuring in Nigeria (Vol. 19).. African Renaissance. https://journals.co.za/doi/abs/10.31920/2516-5305/2022/19n3a12

Pawar, M. (2017). The need for enhanced community participation. *Future Directions in Social Development*, 79-98.

Peel, C. (2010). Exile and the Internet: Ndebele and Mixed-Race Diaspora 'Homes' Online. In J. McGregor & R. Primorac (Eds.), *Zimbabwe's New Diaspora: Displacement and the Cultural Politics of Survival* (pp. 229–245). Berghahn Books. doi:10.1515/9781845458416-016

Peel, C., Hamalwa, A., & Kaisara, G. (2022). Public Procurement and Stakeholders: Assessing Namibia's Consultative Processes and and Challenges. In I. Tshabangu (Ed.), *Interdisciplinary Approaches to the Future of Africa and Policy Development* (pp. 137–149). IGI-Global. doi:10.4018/978-1-7998-8771-3.ch008

Pereira, J.C. (2009). *The impact of democracy in Mozambique: Assessing political, social and economic developments since the dawn of democracy*. Academic Press.

Pereira, C. (2005). Domesticating women? Gender, religion and the state in Nigeria under colonial and military rule. *African Identities, 3*(1), 69–94. doi:10.1080/14725840500065937

Perkins, K. (2004). *A History of Modern Tunisia*. Cambridge University Press.

Perold, H. (2006, November). Volunteering as a strategy to foster civic participation among youth in southern Africa. In *Presentation made to XIX IAVE World Volunteer Conference on Volunteering for Peace in Multicultural Societies, Delhi* (pp. 10-13). Academic Press.

Perry, T. (2022, July 25). Factbox: What's in Tunisia's new Constitution? *Reuters*. https://www.reuters.com/world/africa/whats-tunisias-new-constitution-2022-07-25/

Persson, A., Rothstein, B., & Teorell, J. (2013). Why Anticorruption Reforms Fail-Systemic Corruption as a Collective Action Problem: Why Anticorruption Reforms Fail. *Governance: An International Journal of Policy, Administration and Institutions, 26*(3), 449–471. doi:10.1111/j.1468-0491.2012.01604.x

Pew Research Center. (2020). *Many experts say digital disruption will hurt democracy.* Pew Research Center. https://www.pewresearch.org/internet/2020/02/21/concerns-about-democracy-in-the-digital-age/

Phale, K., Li, F., Adjei Mensah, I., Omari-Sasu, A. Y., & Musah, M. (2021). Knowledge-based economy capacity building for developing countries: A panel analysis in Southern African Development Community. *Sustainability (Basel), 13*(5), 2890. doi:10.3390u13052890

Pherudi, L. M. (2003b). Lesotho: Political Conflict, Peace and Reconciliation in the Mountain Kingdom. In Erik Doxtader and Villa-Vicencio (Eds.). Through Fire with Water: The Roots of Division and the Potential for Reconciliation in Africa. Trenton, NJ: Africa World Press.

Pherudi, L. M. (2003a, June). Operation Boleas under microscope, 1998-1999. *Journal of Contemporary History, 28*(1).

Pherudi, M. (2018). The assassination of military commanders in lesotho: Triggers and reactions. *Journal of Contemporary History, 3*(2).

Philander, D. (2000). Security sector reform in Lesotho: Observations from a three day dialogue series. ISS Occasional Paper No. 45. July.

PIAC (Office of Integrity and Anti-Corruption) African Development Bank Group. (2022). *Annual Report.* Available: https://www.afdb.org/en/documents/integrity-and-anti-corruption-department-annual-report-2022

Pillay, I. (2021). The impact of inequality and COVID-19 on education and career planning for South African children of rural and low-socioeconomic backgrounds. *African Journal of Career Development, 3*(1), 7. doi:10.4102/ajcd.v3i1.36

Piore, M., & Sable, C. (1984). *The Second Industrial Divide: Possibilities for Prosperity.* Basic Books.

Plaatjies, D. (2013). *Protecting the inheritance: Governance and Public Accountability in Democratic South Africa.* Academic Press.

Ploeg, M., Knoben, J., & Vermeulen, P. (2022). We are in it together: Communitarianism and the performance- Innovation relationships. Research Polity, 51(5).

Pogodda, S., Richmond, O. P., & Visoka, G. (2023). Counter-peace: From isolated blockages in peace processes to systemic patterns. *Review of International Studies, 49*(3), 491–512. doi:10.1017/S0260210522000377

Polat, R. K. (2005). The Internet and political participation: Exploring the explanatory links. *European Journal of Communication, 20*(4), 435–459. doi:10.1177/0267323105058251

Political Parties Finance Act. (1992).

Political Party Funding Act (2018). Act No 6 of 2018.

Pollner, M. (1975). 'The very coinage of your brain': The anatomy of reality disjunctures. *Philosophy of the Social Sciences, 5*(3), 411–430. doi:10.1177/004839317500500304

Polyarchy Organisation. (2003). *Polyarchy: A paradigm.* http: //www.polyarchy.org/paradigm/english/democracy.html

Pomper, M. G. (1968). *Elections in America.* Dodd, Mead & Company, Inc.

Pontes, A., Henn, M., & Griffiths, M. D. (2018). Towards a conceptualization of young people's political engagement: A qualitative focus group study. *Societies (Basel, Switzerland), 8*(17), 1–17. doi:10.3390oc8010017

Popper. (1945). *Teaching Values and Citizenship.* Sage.

Popper, K. R. (1972). *Objective Knowledge: An Evolutionary Approach.* University Press.

Porter, E., & Every, D. (2009). Peacebuilding: Women peaceworkers. In Mediation in the Asia-Pacific Region (pp. 47-65). Routledge.

Porter, M. (1990). *The Comparative Advantage of Nations*. Free Press. doi:10.1007/978-1-349-11336-1

Porter, M. E. (1998). Clusters and the new economics of competition. *Harvard Business Review*, (November-December), 77–90. PMID:10187248

Porter, M. E. (1998). *On competition*. Harvard Businesss School Press.

Posner, R. (1974). *Theories of Economic Regulation*. National Bureau of Economic Research. doi:10.3386/w0041

Potter, D. (2004). *Democratization, Good Governance and Development*. Allen Publishers.

Potter, D., Goldplatt, D., Kiloh, M., & Lewis, P. (1997). *Democracy: From Classical times to the present*. Polity Press.

Powell, J. M., & Thyne, C. L. (2011). Global Instances of Coups from 1950 to 2010: A New Dataset. *Journal of Peace Research*, *48*(2), 249–259. doi:10.1177/0022343310397436

Prauscello, L. (2014). *Performing Citizenship in Plato's Laws (Cambridge Classical Studies)*. Cambridge University Press. doi:10.1017/CBO9781139680882

Pretorius, M., & Van Vuuren, J. (2002). *The Contribution of Support and Incentive Programs to Entrepreneurial Orientation and Start up Culture in South Africa. Presented At South African Entrepreneurship and Small Business Association Conference*, Sun City.

Prince, R. J., & Marsland, R. (Eds.). (2013). *Making and Unmaking Public Health in Africa: ethnographic and historical perspectives*. Ohio University Press.

Prinsloo, J. (2014). Examining the relationship between the news nedia and the ANC: A case study of Nkandla coverage. *Equid Novi: African Journalism Studies*, *35*(2), 23–29. doi:10.1080/02560054.2014.919946

Proctor, J. H. (1969). Building a Constitutional Monarchy in Lesotho. [Institut de Sociologie de l'Université de Bruxelles.]. *Civilisations*, *19*(1).

Prys, M. (2007, September). Regions, power, and hegemony: South Africa's role in Southern Africa. In *Sixth Pan-European International Relations Conference* (*Vol. 12*, p. 15). Academic Press.

Przeworski, A., Alvarez, M. E., Cheibub, J. A., & Limongi, F. (2012). Democracy and Development: Political Institutions and Well-Being in the World, 1950–1990. Cambridge University Press.

Public Protector Act. Act 23 of 1994.

Pule, N. W. (2002a). Politics since Independence. In Pule, N and Thabane, M (Eds.). Essays on Aspects of the Political Economy of Lesotho 15000-2000. National University of Lesotho. Morija Printing Works.

Pule, N. W. (2002b). Lesotho in Southern Africa. In Pule, N and Thabane, M (Eds.). Essays on Aspects of the Political Economy of Lesotho 1500-2000. National University of Lesotho. Morija Printing Works.

Qhobosheane, L. (2018). The Impact of Political Interference in State-owned Companies: A Case Study of the South African Broadcasting Corporation (SABC). [Unpublished LLM thesis, University of the Free State]. https://scholar.ufs.ac.za/handle/11660/9256

Qi, X., Zhu, Y., Wang, Y., He, Q., Hee, J., Chen, W., Takesue, R., & Tang, K. (2022). Socio-economic inequalities in children's nutritional status in Democratic Republic of the Congo in 2017–2018: An analysis of data from a nationally representative survey. *Public Health Nutrition*, *25*(2), 257–268. PMID:34615568

Qobo, M., & Nyathi, N. (2016). Ubuntu, public policy ethics and tensions in South Africa's foreign policy. *South African Journal of International Affairs*, *23*(4), 421–436. doi:10.1080/10220461.2017.1298052

Quixina, Y., & Almeida, A. (2014). *Financial development and economic growth in a natural resource based economy: Evidence from Angola. FEP-UP*. School of Economics and Management, University of Porto.

Raftopoulos, B. (2003). *Education and the Crisis in Zimbabwe, Cannon Collins Memorial Lecture 2003*. Canon Collins Educational Trust.

Raimundo, A. (2020). *From the Treaty of Rome to Cotonou*. The Routledge Handbook of EU-Africa Relations. doi:10.4324/9781315170916-8

Rakner, L. (2021). Don't Touch My Constitution! Civil Society Resistance to Democratic Backsliding in Africa´ s Pluralist Regimes. *Global Policy*, *12*(S5), 95–105. doi:10.1111/1758-5899.12991

Rakotondramaro, H., & Andriamasy, L. (2016). Multivariate Granger Causality among tourism, poverty and growth in Madagascar. *Tourism Management Perspectives*, *20*, 109–111. doi:10.1016/j.tmp.2016.08.005

Rana, M., & Sorensen, O. (2020). Levels of legitimacy development in internationalisation: Multinational enterprise and civil society interplay in institutional void. *Global Strategy Journal*, *269-270*. doi:10.1002/gsj.1371

Ranchhod, H. (2016). *Zimbabwe Indigenisation Law*. Hussein Ranchhod and Co. Legal Practitioners. https://www.huranco.com/2016/01/07/zimbabwe-indigenisation-law/

Rand, A. (1990). *Introduction to Objectivist Epistemology: Expanded* (2nd ed.). Penguin.

Ranger, T. (2013). *Writing Revolt: An Engagement with African Nationalism 1957-67*. Weaver Press.

Ranger, T. O. (2007). City versus state in Zimbabwe: Colonial antecedents of the crisis. *Journal of Eastern African Studies : the Journal of the British Institute in Eastern Africa*, *1*(2), 161–192. doi:10.1080/17531050701452390

Rankopo, M.J., & Diraditsile, K. (2018). Perspectives on pro-poor policies in Botswana: Issues, challenges and prospects for Social Work. *Human needs in the 21st century: Perspectives from Botswana and Germany*.

Ranney, A. (1974). *The Governing of Men* (4th ed.). The Dryden Press.

Rautenbach, I. M., & Malherbe, E. F. (2004). *Constitutional law*. LexisNexus Butherworth.

Rawat, A. (2021, March 31). *An Overview of Descriptive Analysis*. Analytic Steps. https://www.analyticssteps.com/blogs/overview-descriptive-analysis

Razzaghi, S. (2010). *State of Civil Society in Iran: Challenges, Opportunities, and Strategies*. Universiteit van Amsterdam. https://www.arsehsevom.org/en/wp-content/uploads/2010/10/State-of-Civil-Society-Iran-by-Sohrab-Razz

Reddy, P.S. (1999). *Local government and democratisation: A review of the Southern African Region*. Juta & Co.

Reed, M. S., Graves, A., Dandy, N., Posthumus, H., Hubacek, K., Morris, J., Prell, C., Quinn, C. H., & Stringer, L. C. (2009). Who's in and why? A typology of stakeholder analysis methods for natural resource management. *Journal of Environmental Management, 90*(I5), 1933-1949. doi:10.1016/j.jenvman.2009.01.001

Reed, D. (1996). *Structural adjustment, the environment, and sustainable development*. Earthscan publications.

Reed, M., & Curzon, R. (2015). Stakeholder mapping for the governance of biosecurity: A literature review. *Journal of Integrative Environmental Sciences*, *12*(1), 15–38. doi:10.1080/1943815X.2014.975723

Rekiso, Z. S. (2017). Rethinking regional economic integration in Africa as if industrialization mattered. *Structural Change and Economic Dynamics, 43*, 87–98. doi:10.1016/j.strueco.2017.10.001

Republic of Zambia. (2013). Zambia Review (14th ed.). Ministry of Commerce, Trade and Industry.

Resurrección, B. P., Bee, B. A., Dankelman, I., Park, C. M. Y., Haldar, M., & McMullen, C. P. (2019). *Gender-transformative climate change adaptation: advancing social equity.* GCA.

Revenue Mobilizations Allocation and Fiscal Package. (2023). *Salary of Nigerian Governors, Deputy, Ministers, Senators.* https://nigerian.com/salary-nigerian-governors/

Reynolds, Bygrave, Autio, Cox, & Hay. (2002). *Global Entrepreneurship Monitor, 2002 Executive Report.* Babson College, London Business School and Kauffman Foundation.

Rheingold, H. (1993). *The Virtual Community: Homesteading on the Electronic Frontier.* Addison-Wesley.

Ridley, J., & Jones, L. (2002). *User and public involvement in health services: a literature review.* Partners in Change.

Rijal, S. (2023). The Importance of Community Involvement in Public Management Planning and Decision-Making Processes. *Journal of Contemporary Administration and Management, 1*(2), 84–92. doi:10.61100/adman.v1i2.27

Rivera-Batiz, F. L. (1999). *Democracy, governance and economic growth: Theory and evidence.* Columbia University.

Rivera-Escartin, A. (2022). Tunisia's democratisation process: When 'consensus democracy' undermines democratic consolidation. *Third World Quarterly, 43*(2), 414–431. doi:10.1080/01436597.2021.2015315

Robbins, K. (1976). *The Abolition of War: the Peace Movement in Britain, 1914–1919.* The University of Wales Press.

Rodney, W. (1981). *How Europe Underdeveloped Africa.* Howard University Press.

Rodney, W. (2018). *How europe underdeveloped africa.* Verso Books.

Romer, P. (1986). Increasing Returns and Economic Growth. *The American Economic Review, 94*, 1002–1037.

Romer, P. M. (1990). Endogenous Technical Change. *Journal of Political Economy, 98*(5, Part 2), 71–102. doi:10.1086/261725

Rosenberg, J., Strauss, I., & Isaacs, G. (2021). COVID-19 impact on SADC labour markets: Evidence from high-frequency data and other sources. *African Development Review, 33*(S1), S177–S193. doi:10.1111/1467-8268.12528 PMID:34149243

Rosen, J., & Painter, G. (2019). From citizen control to co-production: Moving beyond a linear conception of citizen participation. *Journal of the American Planning Association, 85*(3), 335–347. doi:10.1080/01944363.2019.1618727

Roskin, M., Cord, R. L., Medeiros, J. A., & Jones, W. S. (1997). *Political Science: An introduction.* Prentice -Hall, International.

Rossouw, M. (2019). *Public participation: An imperative for governance and human rights – lessons from South Africa.* Future Africa Forum. http://futureafricaforum.org/2019/03/04/publicparticipation-an-imperative-for-governance-and-human-rights-lessons-from-south-africa/

Rothstein, B. (2018). Fighting Systemic Corruption: The Indirect Strategy. *Daedalus, 147*(3), 35–49. doi:10.1162/daed_a_00501

Rowe, R., & Shepherd, M. (2002). Public participation in the new NHS: No closer to Citizen Control? *Social Policy and Administration, 36*(3), 275–290. doi:10.1111/1467-9515.00251

Roy, I. (2002). 2AHIFA? JELAI. *Economic and Political Weekly*, 3591.

Rudebeck, L. (2016). Democracy and Development – A Disputed Pair. *Africa Development. Afrique et Developpement, 41*(1), 1–22. https://www.jstor.org/stable/90001832

Rugwiji, T. (2017). Land, farming and socio-economic crisis development in Yehud: A quest for sustainable development towards poverty reduction in Zimbabwe. *Scriptrura: Journal for Contextual Hermeneutics in Southern Africa, 116*(1), 1–34.

Rumbul, R. (2015). *Who benefits from civic technology? Demographic and public attitudes research into the users of civic technologies*. mySociety.

Rupasingha, A., & Stephan, J. G. (2013). Self-Employment and Local Economic Performance: Evidence from US Counties. *Papers in Regional Science, 92*(1), 141–161. doi:10.1111/j.1435-5957.2011.00396.x

Russell, T., & Martin, A. K. (2017). Reflective practice: Epistemological perspectives on learning from experience in teacher education. *Reflective theory and practice in teacher education*, 27-47.

Rwodzi, A. (2017). *Democracy Governance and Legitimacy in Zimbabwe since the November 2017 Military Coup*. Academic Press.

Sachikonye, L. M. (2002). Whither Zimbabwe? Crisis & Democratisation: The Challenge of Transition Process in Zimbabwe. *ROAPE, 29*(91), 13–20.

Sadomba, Z. (2013). A Decade of Zimbabwe's Land Revolution: The Politics of the War Veteran. In S. Moyo & W. Chambati (Eds.), *Land and Agrian Reform in Zimbabwe: Beyond White Settler Capitalism* (pp. 79–121). University of Zimbabwe. doi:10.2307/j.ctvk3gnsn.9

Saha, M., Varghese, D., Bartindale, T., Thilsted, S. H., Ahmed, S. I., & Olivier, P. (2022). Towards Sustainable ICTD in Bangladesh: Understanding the Program and Policy Landscape and Its Implications for CSCW and HCI. *Proceedings of the ACM on Human-Computer Interaction, 6*(CSCW1), 1-31. 10.1145/3512973

Sahoo, K. C., Sahay, M. R., Dubey, S., Nayak, S., Negi, S., Mahapatra, P., Bhattacharya, D., Del Barrio, M. O., & Pati, S. (2023). Community engagement and involvement in managing the COVID-19 pandemic among urban poor in low-and middle-income countries: a systematic scoping review and stakeholders mapping, *Global Health Action, 16*(1), 2133723.

Said, J., & Singini, K. (2014). *The political economy determinants of economic growth in Malawi*. Academic Press.

Saidin, M. I. S. (2018). Rethinking the 'Arab Spring': The Root Causes of the Tunisian Jasmine Revolution and Egyptian January 25 Revolution. *International Journal of Islamic Thought, 13*(1). Advance online publication. doi:10.24035/ijit.06.2018.007

Sairambay, Y. (2020). Reconceptualising political participation. *Human Affairs, 30*(1), 120–127. doi:10.1515/humaff-2020-0011

Salaudeen, A., & Gombi, D. D. (2019). Gender Mainstreaming in Peace Building and Conflict Resolution in Nigeria: North East in Focus. *KIU Journal of Social Sciences, 5*(1), 139–146.

Salem, M. B., & Brumberg, D. (2020). Tunisia's Endless Transition? *Journal of Democracy, 31*(2), 110–124. doi:10.1353/jod.2020.0025

Salgado, R. (2017). Europeanisation of Civil Society Organisations in times of crisis? Exploring the evolution grant-seeking strategies in the EU multi-level system. *European Politics and Society, 18*(4), 511-528. https://www.tandfonline.com/doi/full/10.1080/23745118.2017.1286283

Salih, M. M. A. (2001). *African Democracies and African Politics*. Pluto Press.

Salisu, A. A. (2011). Modelling and Forecasting Exchange Rate Volatility in Nigeria: Does One Model Fit All? *Central Bank of Nigeria Economic and Financial Review*, *49*(3), 1–30.

Sanches, E. R. (2020). *Democracy and human rights promotion*. The Routledge Handbook of EU-Africa Relations. doi:10.4324/9781315170916-16

Sánchez, J. C., & Licciardello, O. (2012). Gender differences and attitudes in entrepreneurial intentions: The role of career choice. *JWEE*, (1-2), 7–27.

Sandel, M. J. (2022). *Democracy's Discontent: A New Edition for Our Perilous Times*. Harvard University Press.

Sapienza, P. (2004). The effects of government ownership on bank lending. *Journal of Financial Economics*, *72*(2), 357–384. doi:10.1016/j.jfineco.2002.10.002

Sari, A. R. (2023). The Impact of Good Governance on the Quality of Public Management Decision Making. *Journal of Contemporary Administration and Management*, *1*(2), 39–46. doi:10.61100/adman.v1i2.21

Sarrasin, B. (2006). The mining industry and the regulatory framework in Madagascar: Some developmental and environmental issues. *Journal of Cleaner Production*, *14*(3-4), 388–396. doi:10.1016/j.jclepro.2004.03.004

Saurombe, A. (2011). *Regionalisation through economic integration in the Southern African Development Community SADC (SADC)* [Doctoral dissertation].

Saurombe, A. (2010). The role of South Africa in SADC regional integration: The making or braking of the organization. *Journal of International Commercial Law and Technology*, *5*(3), 124–131.

Schaffer, F. C., & Schedler, A. (2000). *What is Vote Buying? The Limits of the Market Model*. Lynne Rienner Publishers.

Schenoni, L. L. (2017). Subsystemic unipolarities? Power distribution and state behaviour in South America and Southern Africa. *Strategic Analysis*, *41*(1), 74–86. doi:10.1080/09700161.2016.1249179

Scheppele, K. L. (2019). The opportunism of populists and the defence of constitutional liberalism. *German Law Journal*, *20*(3), 314–331. doi:10.1017/glj.2019.25

Schmidt, E. (2013). Foreign intervention in Africa: From the Cold War to the war on terror (No. 7). Cambridge University Press.

Schraeder, P. J. (1995). *Understanding the "Third Wave" of Democratization in Africa*. Academic Press.

Schrire, R. (2001). The realities of opposition in South Africa: Legitimacies, strategies and consequences. *Democratization, 8*. . doi:10.1080/714000189

Schultes, I. (2022). *Western Africa's recent coups highlight the risk of trading off development for security, the rule of law, and rights*. Mo Ibrahim Foundation.

Schulz-Herzenberg, C. (2020). The South African non-voter: An analysis. *The Midpoint Paper Series N 2/2020*. https://www.kas.de/documents/261596/10543300/The+South+African+non-voter+-+An+analysis.pdf/acc19fbd-bd6d-9190-f026-8d311078b670?version=1.0&t=1608>

Schumpeter, J. A. (1950). *Capitalism, Socialism, and Democracy*. Harpers and Row.

Schutter, M. S., & Hicks, C. C. (2019). Networking the Blue Economy in Seychelles: Pioneers, resistance, and the power of influence. *Journal of Political Ecology*, *26*(1), 425–447.

Schwella, E. (Ed.). (2017). *South African Governance*. Oxford University Press.

Seanego, M. J., & Mogoboya, M. J. (2019). *Factors contributing to the decline of votes in South Africa: A case study of Mankweng community*. The 4th Annual International Conference on Public Administration and Development Alternatives 03 -05 July 2019.

Secure in Comfort. (2013/14). *Report no 25 of 2013/14*. Tamayaoc, M.J, Law Politics and Philosophy. http://tamayaosbc.wordpress.com

Seiler, N., & Madir, J. (2012). Fight Against Corruption: Sanctions Regimes of Multilateral Development Banks. *Journal of International Economic Law*, *15*(1), 5–28. doi:10.1093/jiel/jgr037

Sejanamane, M. (2017). Struggle Against Impunity in Lesotho. Morija: Morija Printing Works. p. 60.

Sen, A. (1999). *Development as Freedom*. Anchor Books.

Senaratne, M., Zimbroff, A., & Stevens, J. T. (2021). An instrument to assess Blue Economy entrepreneurship ecosystems: A case study from the Seychelles. *Journal of the Indian Ocean Region*, *17*(2), 205–223. doi:10.1080/19480881.2021.1969516

Sguazzin, A. (2021). South Africa wealth gap unchanged since apartheid, says world inequality lab. *Time Magazine*. https://time.com/6087699/south-africa-wealth-gap-unchanged-since-apartheid/

Shaaban, I. A., Ramzy, Y. H., & Sharabassy, A. A. (2013). Tourism as a tool for economic development in poor countries: The case of Comoro Islands. *African Journal of Business and Economic Research*, *8*(1), 127–145.

Shackelton, S., & Campbell, B. (2000). *Empowering communities to manage natural resources: case studies from Southern Africa*. Division of Water, Environment and Forestry Technology.

Shakespeare, H., & Petra, C. (2015). *Unpacking the Complexities of Mediation in Africa: Some Lessons from the SADC's Mediation Role in Zimbabwe between 2008 and 2013*. https://www.up.ac.za/media/shared/237/PDFs/International%20conference%202015/2.-s-hamauswa-paper-on-mediation.zp58697.pdf

Shale V. (2005). The 2005 Lesotho local government elections: Implications for development and governance. *Journal of African Elections,4*(1).

Sharifi, A., Simangan, D., Kaneko, S., & Virji, H. (2021). The sustainability–peace nexus: Why is it important? *Sustainability Science*, *16*(4), 1073–1077. doi:10.100711625-021-00986-z PMID:34149938

Sharma, G. (2017). Pros and cons of different sampling techniques. *International Journal of Applied Research*, *3*(7), 749–752.

Sheidu, C. F., & Patrick, H. O. (2023). Climate Change and Open Grazing impact on Agricultural production in Benue State, Nigeria. *African Journal of Public Administration and Environmental Studies*, *2*(1), 29–52.

Shepherd, A., & Bowler, C. (1997). Beyond the requirements: Improving public participation in EIA. *Journal of Environmental Planning and Management*, *40*(6), 725–738. doi:10.1080/09640569711877

Sheriff, M., & Muffatto, M. (2015). The present state of entrepreneurship ecosystems in selected countries in Africa. *African Journal of Economic and Management Studies*, *6*(1), 17–54. doi:10.1108/AJEMS-10-2012-0064

Shindler, B., & Cheek, K. A. (1999). Integrating citizens in adaptive management: A propositional analysis. *Conservation Ecology*, *3*(1), 9. doi:10.5751/ES-00112-030109

Shinnar, R. S., Giacomin, O., & Janssen, F. (2012). Entrepreneurial perceptions and intentions: The role of gender and culture. *Entrepreneurship Theory and Practice*, *36*(3), 465–493. doi:10.1111/j.1540-6520.2012.00509.x

Shirky, C. (2008). *Here comes everybody: The power of organizing without organisations.*

Shuaibu, M., Adamu, M. B., Abdullahi, S. I., Shehu, K. K., & Buba, S. I. (2022). International Trade and Export Dynamics in Nigeria: An ARDL Vector Error Correction Analysis. *Journal of Humanities. Arts and Social Science, 6*(1), 50–61. doi:10.26855/jhass.2022.01.005

Siakwah, P., Musavengane, R., & Leonard, L. (2020). Tourism governance and attainment of the sustainable development goals in Africa. *Tourism Planning & Development, 17*(4), 355–383. doi:10.1080/21568316.2019.1600160

Sibanda, P. (2015). Citizenship Education and its relevance to Zimbabwe. *Scientific Journal of Pure and Applied Sciences, 4*(10), 180–184. doi:10.14196jpas.v4.101908

Siddle, A. & Koelble. (2016). Local government in South Africa: Can the objectives of the developmental state be achieved through the current model of decentralised governance? Swedish International Centre for Local Democracy. https://icld.se/app/uploads/files/forskningspublikationer/siddle-koelble-icld-report-7.pdf.

Sidiropoulos, E. (2008). South African foreign policy in the post-Mbeki period. *South African Journal of International Affairs, 15*(2), 107–120. doi:10.1080/10220460802636158

Sidiropoulos, E. (2014). South Africa's emerging soft power. *Current History (New York, N.Y.), 113*(763), 197–202. doi:10.1525/curh.2014.113.763.197

Signe, L. (2019). *African Development, African Transformation: How Institutions Shape Development Strategy.* Cambridge university Press.

Simba, P., & Davids, N. (2020). Cultivating Third Space thinking in ('African') feminism through the works of Nandipha Mntambo. *Agenda (Durban, South Africa), 34*(3), 87–99. doi:10.1080/10130950.2020.1790302

Simkins, C. (2021). *The Southern African Development Community II – Economy: Levels, Growth, Structure, Income Distribution And Happiness.* Helen Suzman Foundation.

Simkova, E. (2008). *The sustainable development of rural areas and the role of tourism.* Academic Press.

Simo, R. Y. (2020). Trade in services in the African Continental Free Trade Area: Prospects, challenges and WTO compatibility. *Journal of International Economic Law, 23*(1), 65–95. doi:10.1093/jiel/jgz031

Sindzingre, A. (2021). *Economic relationships between sub-Saharan Africa and China: an alternative theoretical and policy paradigm?* African Studies Association (ASA) 64th Annual Meeting. Virtual. https://shs.hal.science/halshs-03625159/document

Singh, R. (2023, July 31). India: Civil society organisations and governments need to work together to ensure overall progress of society. *Mena Report.* Proquest. https://www.proquest.com/wire-feeds/india-civil-society-organisations-amp-governments/docview/2843926296/se-2

Siphambe, H.K. (2004). Botswana's economy and labour market: are there any lessons for SADC regional integration? *Development Southern Africa, 21*(2), 353-364.

Slim, H. C. (2020). Electoral process in Africa: The impact of COVID-19 and challenges for the EU. *European View, 19*(2), 212–221. doi:10.1177/1781685820971223

Snyder, R. E. (2011). The impact of age, education, political knowledge and political context on voter turnout. *UNLV Theses, Dissertations, Professional Papers, and Capstones.* https://digitalscholarship.unlv.edu/thesesdissertations/1400

Söderbaum, F. (2012). Theories of regionalism. Routledge handbook of Asian regionalism, 11-21.

Söderbaum, F. (2004). *The political economy of regionalism: the case of Southern Africa*. Springer. doi:10.1057/9780230513716

Sohn, L. B., & Gustafson, K. J. (1984). *The Law of the Sea in a Nutshell, January*. West Publishing Company.

Somerville, K. (2017). *Africa's long road since independence: the many histories of a continent*.

Sonn, I. K., Plessis, M. D., Vuuren, C. D. J. V., Marais, J. E., Wagener, E., & Roman, N. V. (2021, December 7). *Achievements and Challenges for Higher Education during the COVID-19 Pandemic: A Rapid Review of Media in Africa*. Academic Press.

Sørensen, B. B., Estmann, C., Sarmento, E. F., & Rand, J. (2020). *Economic complexity and structural transformation: the case of Mozambique* (No. 2020/141). WIDER Working Paper.

Soriano, M. R. T. (2013). Internet as a driver of political change: Cyber-pessimists and cyber-optimists. *Journal of the Spanish Institute of Strategic Studies*, *1*, 332–352.

Sour, L. (2017). Rethinking The Euro Med Policy: A Cooperative Approach in An Increasingly Transforming Region. *Romanian Review of Political Sciences & International Relations*, *14*(1).

Southall, R. (2017). Why Lesotho is Such a Mess and What Can be Done About It. University of Witwatersrand. https://www.wits.ac.za>news>latest-news.

Southall, R. (2010). Scramble for Africa? Continuities and Discontinuities with Formal Imperialism. In R. Southall & H. Melber (Eds.), *A New Scramble for Africa? Imperialism, Investment and Development. Scottsville*. University of KwaZulu-Natal Press.

Southall, R., & Petlane, T. (1995). *Democratisation and Demilitarisation in Lesotho: The General Election of 1993 and its Aftermath*. Africa Institute of South Africa.

Sowetan. (2018). *EFF's fascist agenda rapidly clarifies itself through Malema's racial outburst*. Sowetan Live. https://www.sowetanlive.co.za/opinion/columnists/2018-07-02-effs-fascist-agenda--rapidly-clarifies-itself-through-malemas-racial-outbursts/>

Spiegel, T. J. (2017). 2 Naturalism, Quietism. *On What It Is: Perspectives on Metaphilosophy*, 47.

Spigel, B. (2017). The relational organization of entrepreneurial ecosystems. *Entrepreneurship Theory and Practice*, *41*(1), 49–72. doi:10.1111/etap.12167

Spigel, B., & Harrison, R. (2018). Toward a process theory of entrepreneurial ecosystems. *Strategic Entrepreneurship Journal*, *12*(1), 151–168. doi:10.1002ej.1268

Stam, F. C., & Spigel, B. (2016). Entrepreneurial ecosystems. *USE Discussion Paper Series*, *16*(13).

Stam, E., & Spigel, B. (2017). Entrepreneurial ecosystems. In R. Blackburn, D. De Clercq, J. Heinonen, & Z. Wang (Eds.), *The SAGE Handbook of Small Business and Entrepreneurship*. SAGE.

Stapel, S., Panke, D., & Söderbaum, F. (2023). Regional international organizations in Africa as recipients of foreign aid: Why are some more attractive to donors than others? *Cooperation and Conflict*, *58*(4), 00108367221147791. doi:10.1177/00108367221147791

Statista. (2023). *Digital population in South Africa as of January 2022*. Statista. https://www.statista.com/statistics/685134/south-africa-digital-population/

Statistics South Africa. (2023). *60,6 Million people in South Africa*. SSA. https://www.statssa.gov.za/?p=15601

Steiner, A. (2019). Climate change, environment, and sustainable development in Africa. In *African Economic Development* (pp. 93–110). Emerald Publishing Limited.

Stephens, H. M., & Mark, D. P. (2011). Do Entrepreneurs Enhance Economic Growth in Lagging Regions? *Growth and Change*, *42*(4), 431–465. doi:10.1111/j.1468-2257.2011.00563.x

Stephens, H. M., Partridge, M. D., & Faggian, A. (2013). Innovation, entrepreneurship and economic growth in lagging regions. *Journal of Regional Science*, *53*(5), 778–812. doi:10.1111/jors.12019

Stiglitz, J. E. (2000). Whither Reform. In *Annual World Bank Conference on Development Economics,* 1999. Washington DC: World Bank.

Strong, C. F. (1963). *Modern Political Constitutions*. Academic Press.

Stroup, S., & Wong, W. (2018). *The Authority Trap: Strategic Choices of International NGOs*. Cornell University Press., doi:10.7591/9781501709777-003

Stubbs, R. (2017). The Origins of East Asian's Developmental States and the Pressures for Change. In *Asia after the Developmental State: Disembedding Autonomy* (pp. 51-71). Cambridge: Cambridge University Press. Retrieved October 13, 2023, from https://hsf.org.za/publications/hsf-briefs/the-southern-african-development-community-ii-economy-levels-growth-structure-income-distribution-and-happiness

Stupples, P. (2017). Beyond the predicted: Expanding our understanding of creative agency in international development through practice and policy. *International Journal of Cultural Policy*, *23*(1), 52–67. doi:10.1080/10286632.2015.1035264

Suberu, R. T. (2009). *Federalism and ethnic conflict in Nigeria*. United States Institute of Peace Press.

Sullivan, A., & Sheffrin, M. S. (2003). *Economics: Principles in action*. Pearson Prentice Hall.

Sultana, A. (2010). Patriarchy and women s subordination: a theoretical analysis. *Arts Faculty Journal*, 1-18.

Sutter, C., Bruton, G. D., & Chen, J. (2019). Entrepreneurship as a solution to extreme poverty: A review and future research directions. *Journal of Business Venturing*, *34*(1), 197–214. doi:10.1016/j.jbusvent.2018.06.003

Swedish International Development Cooperation Agency (SIDA). (2002). Good Governance. Division for Democratic Governance. Art.no:2845en, Sweden.

Swilling, M., Bhorat, H., Buthelezi, M., Chipkin, I., Duma, S., Mondi, L., & Friedenstein, H. (2017). *Betrayal of the Promise: How South Africa is being stolen*. Johannesburg: State Capacity Research Project. https://pari.org.za/wp-content/uploads/2017/05/Betrayal-of-the-Promise-25052017.pdf

Taggart, P. (2001). Populism and the pathology of representative politics. In Y. Meny & Y. Surel (Eds.), *Democracies and the Populist Challenge* (pp. 62–80). Palgrave Macmillan.

Takagi, Y., Kanchootat, V., & Sonobe, T. (2022). Introduction: The Nexus of Developmental Policy and State Building. In Y. Takagi, V. Kanchootat, & T. Sonobe (Eds.), *Developmental State Building: The Politics of Emerging Economies* (pp. 1–18). Springer Nature. doi:10.1007/978-981-13-2904-3_10

Takawira, T. (2017). Corruption and Bad Policies Repel Foreign Capital and Cause Domestic Capital to Flee: Is Jovanovic Right? *International Journal of Economics and Financial Issues*, *7*(5), 204–215.

Tam, H. (1998). Communitarianism. New York University Press.

Tamale, S. (2004). Gender trauma in Africa: Enhancing women's links to resources. *Journal of African Law*, *48*(1), 50–61. doi:10.1017/S0021855304481030

Tamayaoc, M.J, Law Politics and Philosophy. http://tamayaosbc.wordpress.com.

Tanyanyiwa, V. I., & Hakuna, C. (2014). Challenges and opportunities for regional integration in Africa: The case of SADC. *IOSR Journal of Humanities and Social Science*, *19*(12), 103–115. doi:10.9790/0837-19124103115

Tar, U. A. (2010). The challenges of democracy and democratisation in Africa and Middle East. *Information, Society and Justice*, *3*(2), 81-94.

Taruvinga, G. R. (2023). The Resurgence of Military Coups in Africa: The Case of West Africa and the Sahel. In *Contemporary Issues on Governance, Conflict and Security in Africa* (pp. 147–157). Springer Nature Switzerland. doi:10.1007/978-3-031-29635-2_9

Tavares, R. (2009). *Regional security: The capacity of international organizations*. Routledge. doi:10.4324/9780203874059

Tavares, R., & Tang, V. (2011). Regional economic integration in Africa: Impediments to progress? *South African Journal of International Affairs*, *18*(2), 217–233. doi:10.1080/10220461.2011.588826

Taylor, I. (2018). *Democracy in Africa, African politics: A very short introduction, Very short introductions*. Academic. https://academic.oup.com/book/682/chapter-abstract/135365487?redirectedFrom=fulltext

Taylor, I. (2018). *African politics: A very short introduction*. Oxford University Press. doi:10.1093/actrade/9780198806578.001.0001

Taylor, J. (2013). Struggles agains systems that impoverish: South African civil society at the crossroads. *Development in Practice*, *23*(5/6), 617–630. https://www.jstor.org/stable/24565438. doi:10.1080/09614524.2013.800833

Tebajjukira, M. (2009), *60,000 evicted in the last two year.* New Vision.

Tejedo-Romero, F., Araujo, J. F. F. E., Tejada, Á., & Ramírez, Y. (2022). E-government mechanisms to enhance the participation of citizens and society: Exploratory analysis through the dimension of municipalities. *Technology in Society*, *70*, 101978. doi:10.1016/j.techsoc.2022.101978

Tella, O. (2021). *Africa's Soft Power: Philosophies, Political Values, Foreign Policies and Cultural Exports*. Taylor & Francis. doi:10.4324/9781003176022

Tenove, C. (2017). *Digital threats to democratic elections: How foreign actors use digital techniques to undermine democracy*. Centre for the Study of Democratic Institutions. The University of British Columbia. https://democracy2017.sites.olt.ubc.ca/files/2018/01/DigitalThreats_Report-FINAL.pdf

ter Vrugte, J., & de Jong, T. (2017). Self-Explanations in Game-Based Learning: From Tacit to Transferable Knowledge. In Instructional Techniques to Facilitate Learning and Motivation of Serious Games (pp. 141-159). Springer International Publishing.

Tesfachew, T. (2022). Ethiopia's drive to advance digital transformation. UNCTAD. https://unctad.org/system/files/information-document/BRI-Project_policy-brief-02_en.pdf.

Teshome-Bahiru, W. (2008). Democracy and elections in Africa: Critical Analysis. *International Journal of Human Sciences*, *5*(2). https://ssrn.com/abstract=1164829

Tete, K. H., Soro, Y. M., Sidibé, S. S., & Jones, R. V. (2023). Assessing energy security within the electricity sector in the West African economic and monetary union: Inter-country performances and trends analysis with policy implications. *Energy Policy*, *173*, 113336. doi:10.1016/j.enpol.2022.113336

Teti, A., Thompson, D. A., & Noble, C. (2013). EU Democracy Assistance Discourse in Its New Response to a Changing Neighbourhood. *Democracy and Security*, *9*(1-2), 61–79. doi:10.1080/17419166.2012.736311

Thabane, M. (2002). Aspects of Colonial Economy and Society, 1868-1966. In Pule, N and Thabane, M (Eds.). Essays on Aspects of the Political Economy of Lesotho 15000-2000. National University of Lesotho. Morija Printing Works.

Thabane, M. (2017a). Towards an identification of historical roots of Lesotho's political instability. In M. Thabane (Ed.), *Towards an Anatomy of Persistent Instability in Lesotho, 1966–2016. Morija: Morija Printing Works. National University of Lesotho. Morija: Morija Printing Works.*

Thabane, M. (2017b). Political Instability, multiple citizenship and citizenship legislation in independent Lesotho. In M. Thabane (Ed.), *Towards an Anatomy of Persistent Instability in Lesotho, 1966–2016. Morija: Morija Printing Works. National University of Lesotho. Morija: Morija Printing Works.*

The Conversation. (2020). How the Nigerian and Kenyan media handled Cambridge Analytica. *The Conversation.* https://theconversation.com/how-the-nigerian-and-kenyan-media-handled-cambridge-analytica-128473 (Accessed 11 October 2023).

The Economist. (2010). War in the fifth domain. *The Economist.* https://www.economist.com/briefing/2010/07/01/war-in-the-fifth-domain

The Geneva Centre for Security Sector Governance (DCAF). (2021). *Security Sector Integrity.* Geneva Centre for Security Sector Governance. https://securitysectorintegrity.com/security-sector-governance/security-sector-reform/. Accessed: 25-08-2021.

The Geneva Centre for Security Sector Governance (DCAF). (2023). *What is security sector reform. African Security Sector Network.* African Security Network. https://www.africansecuritynetwork.org/assn/what-is-security-sector-reform/#:~:text=Security%20Sector%20Reform%20(SSR)%20refers,of%20accountability%20and%20democratic%20governance. Accessed: 22-08-2023.

The Geneva Centre for the Democratic Control of Armed Forces (DCAF). (2015). *The Security Sector: Roles and responsibilities in security provision, management and oversight. SSR Backgrounder Series.* https://www.files.ethz.ch/isn/195675/DCAF_BG_3_The%20Security%20Sector.11.15.pdf.

The World Commission on Environment and Development-WCED. (1987). *Our Common Future.* Oxford University Press.

Theocharis, Y., & van Deth, J. W. (2018). The continuous expansion of citizen participation: A new taxonomy. *European Political Science Review, 10*(1), 139–163. doi:10.1017/S1755773916000230

Theotonio, D. (1971). The Structure of Dependence. In *Readings in U.S. Imperialism.* Boston: Porter Sargent.

Therborn, G. (2019). South African inequalities in a global perspective. In C. Soudien, V. Reddy, & I. Woolard (Eds.), *Poverty & Inequality: Diagnosis, Prognosis Responses* (pp. 31–41). HSRC Press.

Thomas, M., & Sookrajowa, S. (2017). The Media Appeals Tribunal and the Protection of Information Bill as Challenges to Freedom of Expression and Good Governance in South Africa. *Afrika Focus*, 29-50.

Thomas, A. S., & Muller, S. C. (2000). A case for comparative entrepreneurship: Assessing the relevance of culture. *Journal of International Business Studies, 31*(2), 387–301. doi:10.1057/palgrave.jibs.8490906

Thompson, B. S. (2023). Impact investing in biodiversity conservation with bonds: An analysis of financial and environmental risk. *Business Strategy and the Environment, 32*(1), 353–368. doi:10.1002/bse.3135

Thompson, D. F. (2018). Theories of Institutional Corruption. *Annual Review of Political Science, 21*(1), 495–513. doi:10.1146/annurev-polisci-120117-110316

Thomson, A. (2010). *Introduction to African Politics* (3rd ed.). Routledge. doi:10.4324/9780203857946

Thomson, A. (2022). *An introduction to African politics*. Taylor & Francis. doi:10.4324/9781003031840

Thondhlana, G., Mubaya, C. P., McClure, A., Amaka-Otchere, A. B. K., & Ruwanza, S. (2021). Facilitating urban sustainability through transdisciplinary (TD) research: Lessons from Ghana, South Africa, and Zimbabwe. *Sustainability (Basel), 13*(11), 6205. doi:10.3390u13116205

Thorne, J., & du Toit, C. (2009). A macro-framework for successful development banks. *Development Southern Africa, 26*(5), 677–694. doi:10.1080/03768350903303183

Thorton, P. (1999). The Sociology of Entrepreneurship. *Annual Review of Sociology, 25*(1), 19–46. doi:10.1146/annurev.soc.25.1.19

Thurik, A. R. (2009). Entreprenomics: Entrepreneurship, economic growth and policy. *Entrepreneurship, Growth and Public Policy, 10*(6), 219-249.

Tikly, L. (2019). *Education for sustainable development in the postcolonial world: Towards a transformative agenda for Africa*. Routledge. doi:10.4324/9781315211343

TimesLive. (2018). Basotho favour monarchy over feuding politicians. *Timeslive*. https://www.timeslive.co.za/news/africa/2018-04-26-basotho-favour-monarchy-over-feuding-politicians/

Tobi, A. T. (2020). Towards a plausible account of epistemic decolonisation. *Philosophical Papers, 49*(2), 253–278. doi:10.1080/05568641.2020.1779602

Todd, M., & Stewart, P. (2006). After Mugabe: Applying post-conflict recovery lessons to Zimbabwe. *Africa Policy Journal, 1*, 21–36.

Tolbert, C. J., & Mcneal, R. S. (2016). Unraveling the effects of the Internet on political participation. *Political Research Quarterly, 56*(2), 175–185. doi:10.1177/106591290305600206

TolstoyL. N. (1894). *On Patriotism*. http: //www.panarchy.org/tolstoy/189

Tonello, S. (2020). *Resolving the democratic dilemma- Contestation, anti-power and democracy* [Thesis]. University of Wellington.

Tosun, C. (2006). Expected nature of community participation in tourism development. *Tourism Management, 27*(3), 493–504. doi:10.1016/j.tourman.2004.12.004

Transparency International. (2004). *Corruption Perceptions Index 2010*. Transparency International Press. www.unescap.org/pdd

Transperancy International Zimbabwe. (n.d.). *Aljazeera Gold Mafia Documentary Demonstrates Urgent Need to Combat Corruption in Zimbabwe*. Academic Press.

Trisnaningtyas, J. P. N. (2022). Forecasting Tunisia's Future: A Lesson Learned from the Past. *Ijd-Demos, 4*(1), 1. Advance online publication. doi:10.37950/ijd.v4i1.208

Trisnaningtyas, J. P. N. (2022). Forecasting Tunisia's future: A lesson learnt from the past. Ijd. *Demos (Mexico City, Mexico), 4*(1), 1. Advance online publication. doi:10.37950/iijd.v4:1.208

Tshabangu, T., & Salawu, A. (2021). An Evaluation of Constructive Journalism in Zimbabwe: A Case Study of the Herald's Coverage of the Coronavirus Pandemic. *Journal of African Media Studies, 13*(3), 477–490. doi:10.1386/jams_00060_1

Tshishonga, N. (2022). Afrophobic-Induced Violence on African Immigrants in South Africa. In Fighting for Empowerment in an Age of Violence (pp. 87-104). IGI Publisher. doi:10.4018/978-1-6684-4964-6.ch005

Tshishonga, N. (2022). The Impact of South Africa's Immigration Policies on Intra-African Trade and Development. In I. Tshabangu (Ed.), *Interdisciplinary Approaches to the Future of Africa and Policy Development* (pp. 119–136). IGI Publisher. doi:10.4018/978-1-7998-8771-3.ch007

Tshuma, D., & Zvaita, G. T. (2019). *Political fatalism and youth apathy in South Africa: An analysis of the 2019 general elections*. Accord. https://www.accord.org.za/conflicttrends/political-fatalism-and-youth-apathy-in-south-africa/

Tsoeu-Ntokoane, S., Kali, M., & Lemaire, X. (2022). Energy democracy in Lesotho: Prioritising the participation of rural citizens. *Cogent Social Sciences*, *8*(1), 2012973. doi:10.1080/23311886.2021.2012973

Tungali, A. (2017). The evolution of internet shutdowns in DR Congo. CIPESA. https://cipesa.org/2017/03/the-evolution-of-internet-shutdowns-in-dr-congo/

Turner, B. S. (Eds.). (1993). Citizenship and Social Theory. Sage.

Turyahikayo, E. (2015). Challenges faced by small and medium enterprises in raising finance in Uganda. *International Journal of Public Administration and Management Research*, *3*(2), 21–33.

Twine, F. (1994). *Citizenship and Social Rights*. Sage.

Tyrell, P., & Jurgens, B. (1983). *African Heritage*. Macmillan Press.

UBOS. (2022). *Multi-dimensional Poverty Index*. Multidimensional Poverty Index Report 2022 – Uganda | OPHI.

Uganda Bureau of Statistics UBOS. (2022). *Statistical Abstract*. UBOS.

Uganda Bureau of Statistics. (2017). *Uganda National House Survey UNHS 2017*. Author.

Ummatovich, K. M., Erkinjonovich, O. S., & Rahimovna, S. F. (2019). The Role Of Small Business And Private Entrepreneurship In Civil Society. *Frontiers in Finance & Economics*, *16*(2).

Umoru, D. (2012) Empirical investigation of the determinats and dynamic adjustment of the real exchange rate in Nigeria. In Studies in the state of the Nigerian economy. Department of economics, Umar Musa Yar'adua University, Katsina.

Umoru, D. (2013). Monetary models and exchange rate determination: The Nigerian Evidence. *International Journal of Development and Management Review*, *8*(1), 172–197.

UNCTAD. (2012). *World Investment Reports. United Nations Conference on Trade and Development.*

UNCTAD. (2014). *Foreign direct investments in Africa*. United Nations.

UNDP. (2010). *Fighting corruption in post-conflict and recovery situations: Learning from the past*. UNDP.

United Nations (UN). (2008). *Security Sector Reform (SSR).* United Nations and the Rule of Law. https://www.un.org/ruleoflaw/thematic-areas/access-to-justice-and-rule-of-law-institutions/ssr/.

United Nations Conference on Environment and Development. (1992). *Earth Summit Agenda 21*. The United Nations Programme of Action from Rio. UN. Available from: http://www.un.org/esa/ dsd/agenda21/index.shtml

Upadhyay, R. (2023). Ethics, Integrity and Aptitude in Governance (1st ed.). S. Chand Publications.

Uprety, K. (2006). *Transit regime for landlocked states: international law and development Perspectives*. The World Bank.

Urbinati, N. (2014). *Democracy Disfigured*. Harvard University Press. doi:10.4159/harvard.9780674726383

Usman, H. (2023). *The Nexus between Democracy and Conflict in Nigeria's Fourth Republic*. Paper presented at the third International Conference of the Department of Political Science and International Studies, Ahmadu Bello University, Zaria on "Beyond Sustainable Elections: Interrogating the Challenges of Leadership and Governance in Nigeria." July 9th – 12th, 2023.

Usman, H., & Patrick, H. O. (2020). Democracy, Good Governance, And Development in Nigeria: Familiar but Strange Bedfellows. In *Reinvigorating Nigerian Universities for Sustainable Development* (pp. 470–499). Ajayi Crowder University Press.

van Deth, J. W. (2014). A conceptual map of political participation. *Acta Politica*, *49*(3), 349–367. doi:10.1057/ap.2014.6

Van Dijk, J., & Hacker, K. (2003). The digital divide as a complex, dynamic phenomenon. *The Information Society*, *19*(4), 315–326. doi:10.1080/01972240309487

van Eekelen, W. (2005). The parliamentary dimension of security sector reform. Security and Peace, 23(3). doi:10.5771/0175-274x-2005-3-126

Van Eerdewijk, A., Wong, F., Vaast, C., Newton, J., Tyszler, M., & Pennington, A. (2017). *White paper: A conceptual model on women and girls' empowerment*. Academic Press.

van Onselen, G. (2018). Why the EFF is a fascist political party. *SA History*. https://www.sahistory.org.za/archive/why-eff-fascist-political-party-gareth-van-onselen-26-march-2018>

Van Veeren, E. (2019). Layered wanderings: Epistemic justice through the art of Wangechi Mutu and Njideka Akunyili Crosby. *International Feminist Journal of Politics*, *21*(3), 488–498. doi:10.1080/14616742.2019.1619468

Vaole, O. O. (2017). *The democratic Coup dëtat*. Oxford University Press.

Varela Pérez, P., Greiner, B. E., & von Cossel, M. (2022). Socio-Economic and Environmental Implications of Bioenergy Crop Cultivation on Marginal African Drylands and Key Principles for a Sustainable Development. *Earth (Basel, Switzerland)*, *3*(2), 652–682. doi:10.3390/earth3020038

Vatthauer, J.-P., & Irene, W.-F. (2017). *Economic and social challenges in Tunisia: Continuity in times of political change*. Peace Research Institute Frankfurt. https://www.jstor.org/stable/resrep14477.5

Vatuva, A., Filippelli, G., Gujar, A. R., Iyer, S. D., & Udayaganesan, P. (2022). Coastal and Nearshore Minerals: Blue Economy Potential and Prospects. In *Blue Economy: An Ocean Science Perspective* (pp. 221–249). Springer Nature Singapore. doi:10.1007/978-981-19-5065-0_8

Velaphe, N. (2020). *National Reform Authority CEO appointed.* NRA. https://www.gov.ls/national-reform-authority-ceo-appointed/.

Velluti, S. (2020). *The Role of the EU in the Promotion of Human Rights and International Labour Standards in Its External Trade Relations*. Academic Press.

Venter, A., & Landsberg, C. (2010). *Government and Politics in South Africa.* Van Schaik.

Verba, S., Schlozman, K. L., Brady, H. E., & Nie, N. H. (1995). Citizen activity: Who participates? What do they say? *The American Political Science Review*, *89*(3), 271–294.

Versa, S. Nie, N.H. and Him, J.O. *Participation and Political Equality: A Seven-Nation Comparison*. Chicago. University of Chicago Press.

Volk, C. (2018). On a radical democratic theory of political protest: Potentials and shortcomings. *Critical Review of International Social and Political Philosophy*, *24*(4), 437–459. doi:10.1080/13698230.2018.1555684

Volkmann, E. (2022). *Why are Tunisia's parliamentary elections so controversial?* https://www.aljazeera.com/news/2022/12/17/why-tunisia-elections-controversial-explainer

Vos, R., McDermott, J., & Swinnen, J. (2022). COVID-19 and global poverty and food security. *Annual Review of Resource Economics, 14*(1), 151–168. doi:10.1146/annurev-resource-111920-013613

Vyas-Doorgapersad, S. (2020). Gender equality in the sport sector: The case of selected Southern African countries. *International Journal of Social Sciences and Humanity Studies, 12*(1), 207–221.

Walton, G., & Jones, A. (2017). The Geographies of Collective Action, Principal-Agent Theory and Potential Corruption in Papua New Guinea. SSRN *Electronic Journal*. doi:10.2139/ssrn.2993709

Walton, H., & Smith, R. C. (2000). *American Politics and the African American quest for Universal Freedom*. Longman.

Wandera, D., & Nabukenya, N. (2023). *Nabakooba cautions Luweero RDC over contested land, halts boundary opening*. Monitor Publications. Available at https://www.monitor.co.ug/uganda/news/national/nabakooba-cautions-luweero-rdc-over-contested-land-halts-boundary-opening

Wang, H. (2017). New Multilateral Development Banks: Opportunities and Challenges for Global Governance. *Global Policy, 8*(1), 113–118. doi:10.1111/1758-5899.12396

Wang, Q., & Huang, R. (2021). The impact of COVID-19 pandemic on sustainable development goals–a survey. *Environmental Research, 202*, 111637. doi:10.1016/j.envres.2021.111637 PMID:34233155

Wang, X., Zhao, X., & McNamara, N. (2023). *Environmental Public Interest Litigation in China*. SpringerNature., doi:10.1007/978-3-031-26526-6

Washington Post. (2020). How Cambridge Analytica poisoned Kenya's democracy. *Washington Post*. https://www.washingtonpost.com/news/global-opinions/wp/2018/03/20/how-cambridge-analytica-poisoned-kenyas-democracy/

Wawrosz, P. (2022). How Corruption Is and Should Be Investigated by Economic Theory. *Economies, 10*(12), 326. doi:10.3390/economies10120326

Webb, J. A., Miller, K. A., Stewardson, M. J., de Little, S. C., Nichols, S. J., & Wealands, S. R. (2015). An online database and desktop assessment software to simplify systematic reviews in environmental science. *Environmental Modelling & Software, 64*, 72–79. doi:10.1016/j.envsoft.2014.11.011

Weisfelder, F. (1974). *Defining National Purpose: The Roots of Factionalism in Lesotho*. [Unpublished doctoral dissertation, Harvard University].

Welsh, D. (1994). *South Africa's Democratic Transition*. https://www.jstor.org/stable/24595472#metadata_info_tab_contents

Wengraf, L. (2018). *Extracting profit: Imperialism, neoliberalism and the new scramble for Africa*. Haymarket Books.

Wennekers, S., & Thurik, R. (1999). Linking entrepreneurship to economic growth. *Small Business Economics, 13*(1), 27–55. doi:10.1023/A:1008063200484

Wheare, K. c. (1966). *Modern Constitutions*. OUP.

White, D. D., Jones, J. L., Maciejewski, R., Aggarwal, R., & Mascaro, G. (2017). Stakeholder analysis for the food-energy-water nexus in Phoenix, Arizona: Implications for nexus governance. *Sustainability (Basel), 9*(12), 2204. doi:10.3390u9122204

Whittle, A., & Spicer, A. (2008). Is actor network theory critique? *Organization Studies*, *29*(4), 611–629. doi:10.1177/0170840607082223

Wielenga, C. (2022). African Feminisms and Justice on the Ground. *African Feminisms and Women in the Context of Justice in Southern Africa*, 19-39.

Wiklund, J., Patzelt, H., & Shepherd, D. A. (2009). Building an integrative model of small business growth. *Small Business Economics*, *32*(4), 351–374. doi:10.100711187-007-9084-8

Willet, S. (1998). Demilitarisation, Disarmament and Development in Southern Africa. *Review of African Political Economy*, *77*(77), 409–430. doi:10.1080/03056249808704323

Willett, S. (2010). Introduction: Security Council Resolution 1325: assessing the impact on women, peace and security. *International Peacekeeping*, *17*(2), 142–158. doi:10.1080/13533311003625043

Williams, J. J. (2006). Community Participation. *Policy Studies*, *27*(3), 197–217. doi:10.1080/01442870600885982

Williamson, P., & De Meyer, A. (2012). Ecosystem advantage. *California Management Review*, *55*(1), 24–46. doi:10.1525/cmr.2012.55.1.24

Williamson, T. (2003). *Targets and results in public sector management: Uganda case study*. Overseas Development Institute.

Wolfifinger, R. E., & Rosenstone, J. S. (1980). *Who Votes?* Yale University Press.

World Bank Group. (2018a). *Democratic Republic of Congo Systematic Country Diagnostic: Policy Priorities for Poverty Reduction and Shared Prosperity in a Post-Conflict Country and Fragile State*. World Bank.

World Bank Group. (2018b). *An Incomplete Transition Overcoming the Legacy of Exclusion in South Africa*. UCT Press.

World Bank Open Data. (2022). *Tunisia*. https://data.worldbank.org/country/tunisia

World Bank. (1992). *Government and development*. International Bank for Reconstruction and Development.

World Bank. (1994). *Governance*. The World Bank's Experience.

World Bank. (2008). *More people living below poverty line*. Author.

World Bank. (2015) *Africa Economy Performance*. Washington, DC: World Bank Data Base.https://www.worldbank.org/en/region/afr/overview

World Bank. (2017). *Foreign direct investment, net inflows (BoP, current US$) International Monetary Fund, Balance of Payments database, supplemented by data from the United Nations Conference on Trade and Development and official national sources*. www.worldbankdata.org

World Bank. (2021). *Tunisia Economic Monitor: Economic reforms to navigate out of the crisis*. https://documents1.worldbank.org/curated/en/454631642741750737/pdf/Executive- Summary.pdf

World Bank. (2022). *Tunisia Economic Monitor: Navigating the crisis during uncertain times*. https://documents1.worldbank.org/curated/en/099515309022233400/pdf/IDU0f8cf 9a5703e950485f0b2d0025e156f8091d.pdf

World Health Organization. (2018a). A vision for primary health care in the 21st century: towards universal health coverage and the Sustainable Development Goals (No. WHO/HIS/SDS/2018.15). World Health Organization.

World Health Organization. (2018b). WHO water, sanitation and hygiene strategy 2018-2025 (No. WHO/CED/PHE/WSH/18.03). World Health Organization.

World Map. 2023. Lesotho. https://www.mapsofindia.com/world-map/lesotho/. Accedde: 10-10-2023.

Wright, N. (2017). *One Race, The Human Race, Now! Crest-Gauteng*. Wright Publishing.

Wurth, B., Stam, E., & Spigel, B. (2022). Toward an entrepreneurial ecosystem research program. *Entrepreneurship Theory and Practice*, *46*(3), 729–778. doi:10.1177/1042258721998948

Xu, J., Marodon, R., Ru, X., Ren, X., & Wu, X. (2021). What are public development banks and development financing institutions? Qualification criteria, stylized facts, and development trends. *China Economic Quarterly International*, *1*(4), 271–294. doi:10.1016/j.ceqi.2021.10.001

Yagboyaju, D. A., & Akinola, A. O. (2019). Nigerian State and the Crisis of Governance: A critical Exposition. *SAGE Open*, *9*(3), 1–10. doi:10.1177/2158244019865810

Yakubu, M. U., Sani, Z., Obiezue, T. O., & Aliyu, V. O. (2019). Empirical Investigation on Exchange Rate Volatility and Trade Flows in Nigeria. *CBN Economic and Financial Review*, *57*(1), 23–46.

Yakubu, Y. A. (2012). Democracy and Political Apathy in Nigeria (1999-2011). *European Scientific Journal*, *8*(20), 38–48.

Yao, Y., & You, W. (2018). Women's political participation and gender gaps of education in China: 1950-1990. *World Development*, *106*, 220–237. doi:10.1016/j.worlddev.2018.01.004

Yardimci Geyikci, S., & Tür, Ö. (2018). Rethinking the Tunisian miracle: A party politics view. *Democratization*, *25*(5), 1–17. doi:10.1080/13510347.2017.1422120

Yeboah-Assiamah, E. (n.d.). *Low Voter Turnout and Poor Participation in District Level Elections in Ghana: Towards a new Explanation*. https://www.academia.edu/8922082/Low_Voter_Turnout_and_Poor_Partictipation_in_District_Level_Elections_in_Ghana_Towards_a_new _Explanation

Yildirim, Z., & Ivrendi, M. (2016). Exchange Rate Fluctuations and Macroeconomic Performance: Evidence from four Fast-Growing Emerging Economies. *Journal of Economic Studies (Glasgow, Scotland)*, *43*(5), 678–698. doi:10.1108/JES-01-2015-0010

Yilmaz, S. (2010). State, power, and hegemony. *International Journal of Business and Social Science*, *1*(3).

Yimer, A. (2023). The effects of FDI on economic growth in Africa. *The Journal of International Trade & Economic Development*, *32*(1), 2–36. doi:10.1080/09638199.2022.2079709

Youngs, R. (2015). *The Puzzle of non-western democracy*. Brookings Institution Press.

Yusheng, K., Atuahene Agyapong, S., Bentum-Micah, G., & Konadu Aboagye, A. (2019). Impact of foreign direct investment inflows on economic growth in small island developing states (Seychelles). *Scholars Bulletin*, *5*(5), 273–277.

Zafar, A. (2011). Mauritius: An economic success story. Yes Africa can: Success stories from a dynamic continent, 91-106.

Zahorik, J. (2018). Ethiopia and the colonial discourse. In Colonialism on the Margins of Africa. Routledge.

Zaloumis, A. (2007). A name for a miracle. *Isimangaliso News*, *1*(1), 1-10.

Zamfir, I. (2017). *EU support to democracy and good governance in Africa* [Briefing]. European Parliamentary Research Service.

Zaslove, A., Geurkink, B., Jacobs, K., & Akkerman, A. (2020). Power to the people? Populism, democracy, and political participation: A citizen's perspective. *West European Politics*, *44*(4), 727–751. doi:10.1080/01402382.2020.1776490

Zikiti, B. (2016). *How can Zimbabwe leverage its mineral resources for economic recovery and sustainable growth* [Doctoral dissertation].

Zimelis, A. (2011). *Conditionality and the EU–ACP Partnership: A Misguided Approach*. Academic Press.

Zinyama, M. T. (2013). Efficiency and effectiveness in public sector auditing: An evaluation of the comptroller and auditor general's performance in Zimbabwe from 1999 to 2012. *International Journal of Humanities and Social Science*, *3*(7), 267–282.

Zondi, S. (2012). *South Africa in Southern Africa: A perspective*. https://library.fes.de/pdf-files/bueros/mosambik/09403-no-8.pdf Accessed 17 June 2022

Zondi, S. (2023). The Southern African Development Community's pursuit of regional integration. In D. Monye & S. Nkala (Eds.), The Quality for Unity: An Appraisal of Regional Integration in Africa (pp. 89-108). Sunnyside: Jacana Media Ltd.

Zreik, M. (2021). China and Europe in Africa: Competition or Cooperation?. *MJIR| Malaysian Journal of International Relations, 9*(1), 51-67.

Zreik, M. (2022). Contemporary geopolitics of Eurasia and the Belt and Road Initiative. *Eurasian Research Journal*, *4*(1), 7–26. doi:10.53277/2519-2442-2022.1-01

Zreik, M. (2023). Harnessing the Power of Blockchain Technology in Modern China: A Comprehensive Exploration. In L. Ferreira, M. Cruz, E. Cruz, H. Quintela, & M. Cunha (Eds.), *Supporting Technologies and the Impact of Blockchain on Organizations and Society* (pp. 94–112). IGI Global. doi:10.4018/978-1-6684-5747-4.ch007

About the Contributors

Ndwakhulu Tshishonga (PhD) is a Pan-Africanist academic and a research fellow within the School of Built Environment & Development Studies at the University of KwaZulu-Natal. He specialises in Community Development, local economic development, local governance and citizenship, and African Politics. Over the past two decades, more than 50 scholarly papers and book chapters were contributed to local and international journals and edited books. His academic citizenship includes presenting at both national and international conferences as well engaging government departments in policy issues relating governance, democracy and professionalising community development in South Africa. He is also a Lead for Global Citizenship and Children's Rights Network (GLOCCRIN) and a Political Analysist on African and international Political Affairs.

Icarbord Tshabangu (PhD), is an Associate Professor at the Institute of Childhood and Education, Leeds Trinity University, UK. He has previously worked as a Senior Lecturer and Coordinator of Educational Foundations and Management programmes, teaching postgraduate and undergraduate courses at the University of Arusha, Tanzania and at the University of Namibia, Namibia. He was also associated with the University of Liverpool Online as Honorary Senior Lecturer in doctoral studies. He has served as an internal and external examiner at both undergraduate and postgraduate levels and continues to be a research supervisor. His teaching and research interests are largely on children's rights, democratic citizenship, Education policy and qualitative methodologies. He is also a coordinator for Global Citizenship and Children's Rights Network (GLOCCRIN) and former Non-Executive Director for Community Development and Services Alliances (CODESA), UK.

* * *

Shafiu Ibrahim Abdullahi is an academic researcher with specialization in Consumption, Development economics, Islamic economics and finance, International finance, Monetary economics, Marketing & Advertising, Econometrics applications, Field surveys, Mathematical modelling, Statistics. He has peer reviewed for journals/books published by IGI, Wiley and Emerald. His academic works have been published by SCOPUS Indexed journals. He has published two books on Islamic finance and Nigerian economy. He has over 17 years work experience in academic, banking and media.

Kealeboga Aiseng holds a PhD in African Languages and Linguistics from the University of the Witwatersrand. He is a journalism and media studies lecturer at Rhodes University, Makhanda. Aiseng's research interests are sociolinguistics, language policy, African popular culture, new media, and film studies. He has published articles in local and international journals. He also serves on numerous journal editorial boards.

Oluwole Aluko is a seasoned administrator, Human resources specialist. Has BSc Sociology, MSc Sociology and Masters in Business Administration.

Opeyemi Aluko is a scholar par excellence. Co-editor Insights and Explorations in Democracy, Political Unrest, and Propaganda in Elections. IGI Global. (2023). Has over 100 publications in reputable outlets across the world. Has a BSc, MSc and PhD in Political Science and specialist in Comparative Politics with research focus on Security studies, developmental studies, third World studies, food security studies among others.

Salisu Ameh Amodu is currently a lecturer in the Department of Philosophy at Kogi State University, Anyiba, Nigeria. He is a PhD candidate at the University of Nigeria, Nsukka. His area of interest lies in African Philosophy. He has authored and co-authored academic papers in peer-reviewed journals.

Akash Bag has completed his bachelor's degree from the prestigious Ravenshaw University, followed by his LLB from Utkal University and LLM from KIIT University, Bhubaneswar. He was affiliated with Kalinga University, where he taught for three years. He left his job in 2021 to pursue his Ph.D. He is currently associated with Amity University from where he is pursuing his Ph.D. in Digital Forensics and Cyber Security. He is well-versed in subjects such as the IPC, Jurisprudence, and Constitutional Law. He works as a freelancer now, where he helps fellow scholars with research and writing. He has published papers in prestigious journals and conferences such as IEEE, Springer, IGI Global, and AIP, and is currently working on a few projects on an international collaborative basis.

Mukesh Shankar Bharti is a research scholar with a research background in foreign policy analysis and social science research. The author holds a PhD degree in International Relations with a specialization in East and Central Europe. His research area includes democracy, political institutions, European Union and South Asia.

José Alberto Daniel Chemane is a passionate Applied Ethnomusicologist, accomplished drummer, percussionist, and dedicated educator hailing from Maputo, Mozambique. His lifelong fascination with Mozambican indigenous music and dance led him to become an active performer and advocate in the field. With a rich background, he has showcased his talents and shared his expertise through extensive performances and workshops both in Mozambique and abroad. Since 2011, he has served as a part-time lecturer specializing in African Music and Dance at the University of KwaZulu-Natal. In 2015, José played a pivotal role as a member of the Local Arrangement Committee for the 2015 ICTM-First International African Music Symposium hosted at UKZN. In 2018, he furthered his contributions by conducting a workshop presentation and performing with Ikusasa lethu at the PASMAE International Conference held in Seychelles. José's dedication to his craft and scholarly pursuits culminated in him presenting a paper at the ICTM's 47th World Conference in Legon, Ghana, in August of this year. He holds a Master of Arts Degree in Applied Ethnomusicology and is currently pursuing a Ph.D. in Music at the University of KwaZulu-Natal.

Maximino Costumado is a Ph.D. candidate in Community Development at the School of Built Environment & Development Studies (SOBEDS) at the University of KwaZulu-Natal, South Africa, and he holds a master's in population studies. He has more than ten years of experience in the academia and research industry, community development, volunteer and non-governmental organization sectors in Canada, Mozambique, and South Africa. He is currently a community Development lecturer and researcher at the School of Built Environment and Development Studies at the University of KwaZulu-Natal. He teaches in the bachelor and honors programs. His interest in research deals with thematic areas such as good governance and public transparency, Community mapping and GIS, Demographics and population; Environment and coastal management; Community and economic development; Human rights and development; Sustainable Development, Climate Change and Urbanization; Food security and safety; Youth empowerment, Responsible citizenship, and public participation in governance processes; Sexual health and reproductive rights; Public health; and Migration issues in the Sub-Saharan Africa region. He is skilled in designing qualitative and quantitative research instruments, using software analysis and production of research data, preparing technical reports, monitoring and evaluation, and writing articles.

Basil Osayin Daudu is a lecturer in the Department of Philosophy at Kogi State University, Anyigba, Nigeria. He obtained his PhD in Social and Political Philosophy from Nnamdi Azikiwe University, Nigeria. He specializes in African Studies (Society, Culture, and Politics). He is a certified teacher and a trained Microsoft Innovative Educator. He has published in several philosophical journals.

Arindam Goswami is a research scholar completing post-graduation in International Relations from Amity Institute of International Studies, Amity University, Noida, India. His areas of interest include defense and strategic studies, Chinese studies, African affairs, and European studies. Arindam recently won the Best Paper Award in an internal e-conference, and his paper is currently being published.

Catherine Hayes is Professor of Health Professions Pedagogy and Scholarship at the University of Sunderland, UK. She is a UK National Teaching Fellow and Principal Fellow of the UK Higher Education Academy. As a graduate of Podiatric Medicine in 1992, Catherine was a Founding Fellow of the Faculty of Podiatric Medicine at the Royal College of Physicians and Surgeons (Glasgow) in 2012 and was awarded Fellowship of the Royal College of Podiatry (London) in 2010. She is currently Programme Leader of the University of Sunderland's Professional Doctorate pathways for the DBA, EdD, DPM and DProf.

Mansur Idris is Professor of Economics at the Department of Economics Bayero University Kano, Kano state Nigeria.

Lucky Diliza Madikiza is based at the University of South Africa's Research, Postgraduate Studies, Innovation and Commercialisation Portfolio. His research interests, among others, are in Sustainability, Public Affairs and Development Finance. He has done consulting work involving quality assurance of South African national budget documents and conducted training programmes for parliamentarians across the SADC region. He holds postgraduate degrees in International Business, Public Policy and Communication Studies.

Mahlakeng Khosi Mahlakeng is a Lecturer at the National University of Lesotho (NUL) in the Department of Political and Administrative Studies and a research fellow at the University of the Free State (UFS) in the Department of Political Studies and Governance in South Africa. He is the author of "Water Scarcity and Conflict in African River Basins: The Hydropolitical Landscape".

Maxwell M. Maseko holds a PhD in Public Administration from the University of the Western Cape in Cape Town, South Africa. He also has 26 years of experience working as a journalist in various news media organisations in South Africa. Currently, he is a postdoc fellow at the Tayarisha Centre in the Wits School of Governance in Johannesburg. His research interests lie in the fields of media and governance, particularly in areas of democracy, digitalisation in the public sector, protests, and citizen participation.

Menard Musendekwa is a PhD holder in Theology (Old Testament). He doubles up as the Vice Principal of Murray Theological College and Chair of Theology at the Reformed Church University. He is a budding interdisciplinary scholar and has published in Old Testament, Church History, Gender Studies and Political Science.

Daniel Nkosinathi Mlambo (Ph.D.) holds a Postgraduate Diploma in Teacher Education from the Haaga-Helia University of Applied Sciences School of Vocational Teacher Education (Finland), a Ph.D. and Master's degree in Public Administration, an honours in International Relations, and a junior degree in Development Studies all from the University of Zululand. His research focuses on African Political Economy, Regional Integration, Governance and Democracy, Migration, and Security Studies.

Goddy Uwa Osimen is currently an independent consultant in peace and security matters. He is the Director/Co-ordinator of Third-Party Initiative Resolution. He is a member of the Society for Peace Studies and Practice (SPSP) and also a member of Amnesty International. He holds a PhD degree in Strategic Studies at Ambrose Alli University, Expoma, Edo State, Nigeria where he obtained his first Degree in Political Science and master's degree in international relations respectively. He had a Diploma Certificate in International Studies and Diplomacy and holds a second master's Degree in Peace and Conflict Resolution from the University of Ibadan. He has taught in various institutions of higher learning at different times and has authored many scholarly books. He is the editor and primary contributing author for the Journal of International Peace and Security which is a quarterly security and peace awareness multimedia publication by Intermediates Shield Publishers. He is a Senior lecturer and an Associate Research Fellow in the Department of Political Science and International Relations at Covenant University, Ota, Nigeria.

Shreesh K. Pathak is senior Assistant Professor at Amity Institute of International Studies in Amity University Noida.

Hosea Patrick holds a PhD in Political Science from the University of KwaZulu-Natal, South Africa. He is a transdisciplinary research scholar with an interest in environmental politics, restorative justice, sociotechnology, and social behavioural research.

Clayton Peel has research interests in the areas of communication and governance; innovative technologies as teaching tools; investigating the sociology of technology adoption among university educators and the influence of the environment on their digital practice; media regulation in emerging democracies; diaspora, media and ethnicity; and media and politics.

Souvik Roy is currently spearheading the Law School at Adamas University as the Associate Dean. He has a track record of successfully helping students achieve greater heights for more than a decade now and counting. Dr Roy completed his Ph.D. in the area of substantive criminal law from KIIT – D.U. not before completing his B.A. LL.B. from University of Calcutta. Subsequently, he pursued LL.M from Queen Mary, University of London (U.K) with Merit including Distinction in two disciplines. He was the recipient of the University of Calcutta Endowment Scholarship (final year) where he secured a First Class. Prior to his current stint here, Professor Souvik helmed the Law School of Dayananda Sagar University (DSU), Bengaluru and was also looking into admissions outreach programs beyond regular academics and administration. Dr Roy, is an educationist in the legal domain with earlier experiences of working as an Associate Professor with Department of Law-UEM Kolkata not before his prior stints with KIIT D.U., Bhubaneswar and National Law University Odisha (NLUO). Professor Roy also possesses industry experience in the corporate and litigation sector as a lawyer and subsequently as a foreign education counsellor and CLAT mentor, working in places like Mumbai, Bhubaneswar and Kolkata.

Comfort Fatimoh Sheidu is an esteemed professional renowned for her extensive expertise in the fields of Peace and Conflict Studies, Research and Development, Policy Analysis, and International Relations. She is the holder of a Bachelor's degree and a Master's degree in Political Science from Ahmadu Bello University, Zaria, Nigeria, in addition to a PhD in Policy Analysis from the University of Abuja, Nigeria. Her dedicated pursuits centre on the advancement of peace, cross-cultural comprehension, and the conduct of scholarly investigations aimed at enhancing our global landscape. With a substantial portfolio of publications to her credit, she is presently engrossed in the composition of several forthcoming academic papers.

Hezekiah Usman is a PhD candidate in the Department of Political Science and International Studies, Ahmadu Bello University, Zaria, Kaduna State, Nigeria. Usman's research interest covers democracy, governance, globalization, development studies, conflict and security studies.

Mohamad Zreik, a Postdoctoral Fellow at Sun Yat-sen University, is a recognized scholar in International Relations, specializing in China's Arab-region foreign policy. His recent work in soft power diplomacy compares China's methods in the Middle East and East Asia. His extensive knowledge spans Middle Eastern Studies, China-Arab relations, East Asian and Asian Affairs, Eurasian geopolitics, and Political Economy, providing him a unique viewpoint in his field. Dr. Zreik is a proud recipient of a PhD from Central China Normal University (Wuhan). He's written numerous acclaimed papers, many focusing on China's Belt and Road Initiative and its Arab-region impact. His groundbreaking research has established him as a leading expert in his field. Presently, he furthers his research on China's soft power diplomacy tactics at Sun Yat-sen University. His significant contributions make him a crucial figure in understanding contemporary international relations.

Index

E

F

G

H

I

J

L

M

www.ingramcontent.com/pod-product-compliance
Lightning Source LLC
LaVergne TN
LVHW062104300926
849161LV00010B/2372